Icon	Control Panel Applet	Applet Function	Setting
	Multimedia	Configures multimedia devices including audio, video, and CD	System
	Network	Configures the network adapter, protocols, and services	System
	PC Card (PCMCIA)	Examines and configures PCMCIA cards	System
	Ports	Specifies the communications parameters for serial ports	System
	Printers	Installs and configures local and remote printers	System
	Regional Settings	Sets up local language settings (language, keyboard, currency, and so on)	User/System
	SCSI Adapters	Installs and configures SCSI adapters and IDE CD-ROMs	System
	Server	Reviews and manages the properties of the Server service	System
	Services	Controls NT system services	System
	Sounds	Associates sounds with events	User
	System	Reviews and manages system settings	System
	Tape Devices	Installs and configures tape backup devices	System
	Telephony	Controls and configures telephony functions	System
	UPS	Configures the Uninterruptible Power Supply	

Windows NT® Workstation 4

Second Edition

Paul Cassel, Mike Sheehy, and Sean Mathias

SAMS
PUBLISHING

201 West 103rd Street
Indianapolis, IN 46290

UNLEASHED

I dedicate this book to the Tirilee who got it all together on St. Patrick's day. May she continue onward with her customary courage and spotless integrity. — Paul Cassel

To Rit petite the scouse jewel. — Mike Sheehy

Copyright © 1997 by Sams Publishing

SECOND EDITION

International Standard Book Number: 0-672-31081-3

Library of Congress Catalog Card Number: 97-65460

2000   99   98   97   4   3   2   1

Interpretation of the printing code: the rightmost double-digit number is the year of the book's printing; the rightmost single-digit, the number of the book's printing. For example, a printing code of 97-1 shows that the first printing of the book occurred in 1997.

Composed in AGaramond and MCPdigital by Macmillan Computer Publishing

Printed in the United States of America

President, Sams Publishing	*Richard K. Swadley*
Publishing Manager	*Dean Miller*
Indexing Manager	*Johnna L. VanHoose*
Director of Marketing	*Kelli S. Spencer*
Product Marketing Managers	*Wendy Gilbride, Kim Margolius*
Associate Product Marketing Manager	*Jennifer Pock*
Marketing Coordinator	*Linda Beckwith*

Acquisitions Editor
Grace M. Buechlein

Development Editor
Brian-Kent Proffitt

Software Development Specialist
Patty Brooks

Production Editor
Nancy Albright

Copy Editors
Charles A. Hutchinson
Bart Reed

Indexer
Christine Nelsen

Technical Reviewer
Toby Tapp

Editorial Coordinators
Mandie Rowell
Katie Wise

Technical Edit Coordinator
Lynette Quinn

Resource Coordinator
Jodi Jensen

Editorial Assistants
Carol Ackerman
Andi Richter
Rhonda Tinch-Mize

Cover Designer
Jason Grisham

Book Designer
Gary Adair

Copy Writer
David Reichwein

Production Team Supervisors
Brad Chinn
Charlotte Clapp

Production
Jeanne Clark
Cyndi Davis-Hubler
Gene Redding
Janet Seib

Contents

Acknowledgments

Without the help of Scotty, my uphill neighbor's St. Bernard dog, who stopped his barking long enough for me to write this book, it would never have gotten done. I acknowledge his personal sacrifice, yet don't welcome the resumption of the noise riot.

—Paul Cassel

I would like to thank the underrated Dublin NT Networking team (Hugh Marron, Howard Shortt, and Sean Stanford) for all their help along the way. Thanks also to my boss Martin Coughlan for his support and encouragement. Finally to Grace Buechlein, Brian Proffitt, and everyone behind the scenes at Sams—thanks, it's been a pleasure working with you.

—Mike Sheehy

About the Authors

Paul Cassel recently became interested in geneology and traced his ancestors all the way back to Roswell, New Mexico, summer of 1947. Further inquiries haven't as yet been fruitful. He got stuck to the tarbaby of electronics at 9 years old when he built his first computer, a battery logic binary math calculator. The project ended in failure when his fourth grade teacher refused to accept long division answers in binary notation and even denied that such notation was a number. Cast into the cruel sea of having to make a living at a very tender mental age, he clung to the liferaft of computers as a way to avoid the necessity indefinitely. Microsoft pulled him into the Windows NT project in pre-alpha days, probably due to a clerical error or the influence of another Roswellian. He's still levitating around New Mexico where he wins the occasional MVP award or other earthly honors for recognition of his work with Microsoft operating systems and database products.

Mike Sheehy was educated in Ireland and began working in the area of development and education before settling into what he calls "the most challenging and rewarding role of MIS." He has worked in Europe and in the United States with the Open Environment Corporation and was involved in the startup of Onewave, Inc. Mike is currently working for World Merchandise Exchange as an NT systems administrator. He is responsible for World Merchandise Exchange's NT WAN for Europe and the Middle East. You can reach Mike by sending e-mail to sheehy@womex.com.

Sean Mathias is a Microsoft Certified Systems Engineer living in Seattle, Washington. Primarily, his focus is designing and integrating fault-tolerant and secure network architectures using Windows NT, Microsoft BackOffice, and SUN Solaris. Currently, he is the Director of Network Services for Online Interactive/atOnce Software (www.atonce.com), and the Vice President of Technology for the BackOffice Professionals Association (www.bopa.org).

Contributing Authors

Joshua Allen is a senior consultant for Sirco Associates in Troy, Michigan, and a partner in Guild Communications Corporation, a Detroit-based Internet consulting company. He holds MCSE, MCSD, and MCPS Internet Systems certifications from Microsoft.

Thomas Lee is a computer consultant and educator living in the UK, and has been working with Windows NT since 1993. Educated at Carnegie Mellon University in the U.S., he worked on two successful operating systems projects (Comshare's Commander II and ICL's VME) before joining Andersen Consulting in 1981. Thomas founded PS Partnership, a Microsoft Solutions Provider, in 1987 and is today a partner. He is a Fellow of the British Computer Society, as well as an MCSE, MCT, and MVP. You can contact Thomas at tfl@psp.co.uk.

Jefferson M. Mousseau (jeffm@io.org) was educated at the University of Toronto's Trinity College. Currently, he lives in Toronto, Canada where he works for Clearnet Inc., a wireless PCS telecommunications company. There he takes care of network security, which includes firewalls, Cisco routers, and SecurID access servers. He is also in charge of Internet connectivity and enterprise messaging. He spends his spare time with his wife Orie, his son A.J., his daughter Sloane, and close friends A.L., C.M., and L.B.

Eric D. Osborne is the president of Micro Efficiencies, a Columbus, Ohio based consulting firm. Eric has an extensive background in UNIX, TCP/IP networking, telephony, and computer and network security. He was one of the primary architects of the NT/UNIX integration project recently completed by the CIS department at Ohio State. He has been involved in the design and administration of large distributed computing sites since 1984. He currently lives in Columbus with his two children.

Howard M. Swope III (http://www.voicenet.com/~hswope) wrote his first computer program at the age of ten. Since that time, the study of computers has been a pursuit of love and fascination. Howard studied computers and information technologies throughout his school years. He has been working commercially for the last nine years, doing everything from running mainframe cable, to programming, to network administration. Presently, he spends most of his time as a Programmer and Technical Advisor for the Wellness Web (http://www.wellweb.com), an award-winning patient care site on the Internet, and as a Consultant for Actium (http://www.actium.com), a consulting firm based in Conshohocken, Pennsylvania. Howard has been an advocate and student of Windows NT since its release.

Thomas Wölfer was born some years ago. Not much has happened since, but he currently plans to get a life. If possible, this would not include software development for civil engineers, which is what some people think is his current job. Thomas can be contacted at woelfer@muc.de.

Tell Us What You Think!

As a reader, you are the most important critic and commentator of our books. We value your opinion and want to know what we're doing right, what we could do better, what areas you'd like to see us publish in, and any other words of wisdom you're willing to pass our way. You can help us make strong books that meet your needs and give you the computer guidance you require.

Do you have access to the World Wide Web? Then check out our site at http://www.mcp.com.

> **NOTE**
>
> If you have a technical question about this book, call the technical support line at 317-581-3833 or send e-mail to support@mcp.com.

As the team leader of the group that created this book, I welcome your comments. You can fax, e-mail, or write me directly to let me know what you did or didn't like about this book—as well as what we can do to make our books stronger. Here's the information:

Fax: 317-581-4669

E-mail: opsys_mgr@sams.mcp.com

Mail: Dean Miller
         Comments Department
         Sams Publishing
         201 W. 103rd Street
         Indianapolis, IN 46290

Introduction

Windows, Windows everywhere! Unless you are new to this planet, you have probably heard of the Microsoft operating environment, *Windows*. Windows was a revolutionary improvement in the way PC users interacted with their computer systems. Historically, there was MS-DOS (and still is, much more than you might realize), which was implemented as a command-line interface. Using MS-DOS, you could give your computer instructions by typing them in one at time. This could be very archaic and time-consuming, and most potential computer users were reluctant to use this operating system due to its complexity.

The initial solution (or at least an attempt at a solution) was a new product called Microsoft Windows. It was supposed to change the lives of computer users and bring about an end to computing complexities, making computers more usable for the novice and the inexperienced.

To some degree, Windows' goal of easing the use of computers and shielding users from the DOS command prompt was achieved. However, through the succession of Windows versions, many problems associated with DOS remained, in addition to some problems that were entirely new to Windows. Keep in mind that Windows 3.*x* was only an operating environment that ran as an application on top of MS-DOS; it was not an operating system in itself. Although this was a vast improvement over DOS, the problems of memory usage and multitasking associated with DOS remained. MS-DOS is a single-tasking operating system, despite what you might have heard, which means that no more than one program can actually be running at a given time. If you are running Windows, that is the one program you can run. Within Windows it seems to be possible to run multiple programs at once, but looks can be deceiving. The reality is that at any given time, a single program is using the computer's resources and executing. You will notice that performance degrades significantly and proportionally to the number of programs you run (or try to run).

Another problem with MS-DOS was the use of memory. MS-DOS could not effectively address more than 16MB of RAM. When it was developed, this was not an issue because most systems did not have a hard drive that big! Over time, as computer hardware improved, this limitation became quite an obstacle, and it remained through MS-DOS 6.22.

Along with these problems, a more subtle problem arose. As the new Windows operating environment eased the use of computers, users began to see the potential for an even better and more robust system. Soon the users complained about the shortcomings of Windows and demanded more. In a relatively short time, Windows 3.1 was pushed beyond its limits with software applications that required a good portion of system resources and weren't always written to get along well with the other applications. Then came the introduction of the *General Protection Fault* and countless hours of lost work and productivity. Even the best of the best could not provide a consistent solution or explanation for these errors and system crashes.

As a result of all of these problems, after two years of shouting users and media hype, the fateful day came: August 24, 1995. This was the second coming of Windows—in the form of *Windows 95*, the solution to all of our problems. We were told again that this product would revolutionize how we use computers and that all of the problems would be a thing of the past. (Oh, and it would also bring peace to the world!)

Well, the second coming of Windows came and went, and the Earth did not open and reveal herself to us. But things did get somewhat better. No matter how you look at it, Windows 95 is considerably better than Windows 3.*x*. Yet, it still was not the answer we were looking for. Many of the historical problems with Windows 3.*x* were gone or masked, but limitations still existed. Despite what the media has said, Windows 95 is not a multitasking operating system; in fact, it is debatable whether it is an operating system at all. Underneath all of the bells and whistles lies MS-DOS 7.0. That aside, Windows 95 has greatly improved support for multimedia, networking, and a new thing called the Internet, along with a host of other features.

Now we must back up a little. During the course of Windows 3.1, another operating system was developed and released: Windows New Technology (NT) 3.1. It was delivered with far less fanfare than other Windows versions for some reason. Windows NT would be the foundation for the true answer users were looking for—robustness, stability, multitasking, excellent network support, and open systems architecture. Although the architecture was relatively sound and this was a good foundation, the problem with this new *operating system* (which uses no underlying DOS) was in its hardware requirements and speed. Consequently, Windows NT received little support or fanfare. So it was back to the drawing board.

Then, in the fall of 1994, Windows NT 3.5 was released. This was a remarkable improvement over version 3.1. The hardware requirements were basically the same, but this version was markedly faster and much more stable, and it looked to be a viable solution in the business computing environment. Approximately six months later, Windows NT 3.51 was released, which provided support for the PowerPC (NT already supported Intel, Alpha, and MIPS architectures) and a few other enhancements such as file compression.

Now let's return to the time when Windows 95 was released, in the fall of 1995, touting a new and more usable interface. Users were intrigued by this new environment, but too many shortcomings still existed to keep most businesses from being comfortable. The question of the hour was, "Should we use Windows 95 or Windows NT Workstation?" Windows NT had been building quite a name for itself over the course of 1995, and people were considering it as a viable option in the business world. Then, with the option of Windows 95 or Windows NT Workstation on the desktop, people had to stop and consider the dilemma of which one to use. The hardware requirements for Windows NT were only marginally greater than those of Windows 95, so why not go all the way and get the real deal? However, the new interface of Windows 95 was appealing to users, as were the new wizards and the relative ease with which the system could be configured.

Now users are closer than ever before to having their needs met. Microsoft has heard the cries of the masses. This is the dawn of Windows NT Workstation 4 targeting a corporate desktop near you. The new version of Windows NT incorporates the Windows 95 interface for ease of use, as well as many of the multimedia and networking features. The two operating systems look and feel so similar now that you might have to look at the Start menu to differentiate the two! Additionally, in the wake of Windows 95 comes a plethora of 32-bit applications that run on Windows NT as well. This opens the field to many new choices.

It is my opinion, based on extensive experience with Windows NT and countless users (and their problems), that Windows NT Workstation 4 is the right choice and the right solution for business computing. I further believe that many people out there feel the same way and are ready to deploy Windows NT Workstation 4 in their business environment, but they lack the knowledge and expertise to effectively deploy and support this new technology themselves. That is why this book has been written. Many small companies, or departments within large companies, do not have the luxury or the budget to have one or several full-time Windows NT engineers on staff to service and support the client population.

This book is intended to serve as a concise and comprehensive desktop resource and reference for power users and systems administrators alike. In this volume, we explore almost every aspect of Windows NT Workstation, we differentiate it from Windows 95, and we relate it to previous versions of Windows NT Workstation. I believe that this book is an indispensable resource for Windows NT users everywhere. Enjoy!

IN THIS PART

Start Windows NT

I

PART

What Is Windows NT Workstation?

by Paul Cassel and Sean Mathias

CHAPTER 1

IN THIS CHAPTER

Windows NT is designed to be a standalone operating system created from scratch without any serious architecture compromises. Unlike its Microsoft predecessors, MS-DOS and Windows, Windows NT has capabilities and security comparable to enterprise operating systems such as UNIX and VMS. In fact, the chief architect of Windows NT, Dave Cutler, was also the chief architect of VMS.

One of the philosophical differences between Windows NT and its enterprise competitors is NT's stress on being much easier to use and administer than anything else in its class. This, as well as many popularly priced applications, makes Windows NT Workstation a good, perhaps the best, choice not only for heavy-duty workstation type uses, but for general business computing as well.

Other equivalent operating systems, such as UNIX, lack Windows NT's wide array of applications or are very difficult to administer or both. Easy-to-administer operating systems, such as Windows 95 and its successors, lack Windows NT's robustness, multitasking abilities, and scaleability.

What today has evolved into Windows NT Workstation got off to a slow start in the market. Its hardware requirements, especially RAM, required a serious commitment in money, and the benefits, due mostly to a lack of native applications, were few. However, after its release, Microsoft began a developer relations campaign to create the applications that would make the use of Windows NT more attractive to both workstation types and to general business. With the introduction of Windows 95, this campaign intensified and developers responded. At roughly the same time, system component costs, especially RAM and hard disk costs, dropped dramatically.

The combination of low-cost Windows NT hardware and the burgeoning crop of interesting software for NT sparked quite a bit of interest in the adoption of Windows NT, not only for workstations, but for an everyday operating system to replace MS-DOS, Windows, or OS/2. The introduction of Windows NT 4 in 1996 saw that spark change to a conflagration.

Here at last was an operating system with an interface any user could love, an uncompromising architecture, and a huge selection of popularly priced applications. To top the cake, due to lower hardware prices, it ran on popularly priced computers. In many ways, Windows NT 4 is the apogee of operating systems. It fulfills the technical promise unmet by lesser operating systems, such as MS-DOS, Windows, and OS/2, while also meeting the user needs unmet by its technical equivalents, especially UNIX.

The Architecture of Windows NT

The processors capable of running Windows NT Workstation are also capable of running processes in various levels of privilege. A level of privilege gives certain power and also affords certain protection. For example, Intel processors use four privilege levels, or *Rings* in Intel terminology. Ring 0, the most privileged ring, pretty much allows any processes running there to do anything; Ring 3, the least privileged, affords the greatest protection while allowing little in the way of power.

Windows NT runs part of itself in Ring 0 and part of itself in Ring 3. NT's terminology for this split is *User mode* and *Kernel mode*. User mode is the part of NT running in Ring 3. It interacts with the user and the user applications. Kernel mode runs in Ring 0 and communicates with the hardware. Figure 1.1 illustrates the two modes of Windows NT. Note that there is no way for applications to communicate with the hardware except through Windows NT.

FIGURE 1.1.
The architecture of Windows NT blocks any direct interaction between the computer hardware and applications. NT itself runs in two modes, User and Kernel. In Intel processors, this is the equivalent of running in Ring 0 and Ring 3.

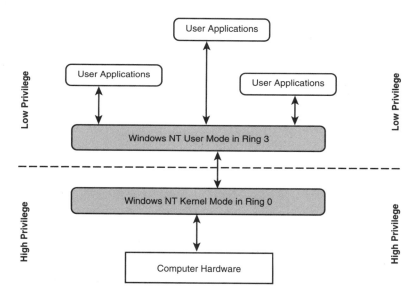

The reason for splitting NT this way is to prevent system anomalies, or, to put it bluntly, crashes. If an application can get to the most privileged areas of a computer, it can do anything it pleases. This way, an entire computer session is at the mercy of any application programmer's abilities and intentions.

The all-too-common lockups and crashes with MS-DOS and Windows are, for the most part, due to applications doing something wrong in an area of high privilege. Although NT can't do anything about bad programming, it can protect itself and the session from the consequences.

Why the Split?

Windows NT could have had only one mode, Kernel, affording the same protection as it does now—if it ran only native applications. Microsoft made the decision that Windows NT would be as much a universal operating system as feasible. That decision led to the splitting of Windows NT.

The User mode part of Windows NT is multifaceted. It can run not only Windows NT and other Windows programs, but some applications native to OS/2 and an emerging IEEE standard called POSIX. This decision was and remains controversial. There's no doubt that some enterprises, especially the governmental ones, could more readily adopt Windows NT if it ran a great array of existing applications; but this ability loads up Windows NT with capabilities rarely needed by the general public.

Although the splitting of NT into two modes doesn't compromise its security in any way, it does increase (if marginally) the size of any Windows NT installation. Some hope that future versions of Windows NT will drop OS/2 and POSIX support, but it's very unlikely that Windows NT will ever coalesce into a one-mode operating system. There's no functional reason for doing this; it would be a lot of work and quite disruptive to the Windows NT community.

With version 4 of Windows NT, Microsoft moved the GDI, or Graphics Device Interface (the display part of NT), to the Kernel. Previous versions of Windows NT had these services in User mode. This means that NT 4 is much faster in displaying graphics, but it also exposes the entire session to vagaries of display device drivers.

> **NOTE**
>
> Due to the move of GDI from User to Kernel, display drivers for NT made for previous versions of Windows NT won't work with version 4. You will need new drivers when upgrading from older versions of Windows NT.

This was another controversial move on Microsoft's part. Many pundits said that the company has sacrificed Windows NT's reliability on the altar of speed. However, in practice, Windows NT 4 has been at least as reliable as previous versions that had the GDI in User mode, so these fears have been proved unfounded.

At least part of the reason the fears about the consequences of GDI's move to Kernel have been unrealized is Microsoft's testing and certification of drivers. Unlike just about any service or program running under Windows NT, hardware and graphics drivers address the hardware directly, bypassing Kernel and even HAL (see later in this chapter for a short discussion on HAL). Thus, poorly made drivers of any type can destroy an NT session and even the entire installation.

Recognizing this, Microsoft has instituted a certification process for drivers that address the hardware. As each driver/hardware combination passes certification, Microsoft adds it to a Hardware Compatibility List (HCL). This is a constantly updated list available for downloading at various sites, including Microsoft at www.microsoft.com. If you use only those drivers appearing on the HCL, you can rest assured that your Windows NT installation will be as robust as possible.

> **NOTE**
>
> Windows NT will run only OS/2 version 1, or text mode applications. It will not run the later OS/2 graphical mode applications.

The OS/2 subsystem will fully work only under Intel versions of Windows NT. The RISC versions of Windows NT will run so-called "bound" OS/2 applications, those that will run under MS-DOS or OS/2 if support for MS-DOS is included in the installation of those RISC setups.

> **NOTE**
>
> Windows NT version 4 and later will not support OS/2's HPFS. This support was last supported under Windows NT version 3.51.

Part of POSIX compliance is the need for a file system supporting certain specifications that are part of POSIX. These specifications include certain security measures as well as case-sensitive filenames.

Although Windows NT 4 will support FAT16 and FAT32 volumes, these older style file systems don't have the capacity to meet POSIX's requirements; thus, you can't install, nor should you save, POSIX files to any volume other than NTFS. In some instances, you can save POSIX application files to a FAT volume without any warning from NT, but doing so will cause lost data.

DOS and Older Windows Applications

The User mode handles three types of applications: Win32 (or native Windows NT), POSIX, and OS/2. In addition, Windows NT's User side has the capacity to run DOS and Win16 applications. Together, these form the fourth facet of Windows NT. Due to its origins as a one-application/one machine-at-a-time operating system, Windows NT handles DOS applications differently from the others.

> **NOTE**
>
> POSIX and OS/2 facets of Windows NT communicate with the Kernel part through the Win32 subsystem for mouse, keyboard, and screen services. NT directs all other services for these facets directly to the Kernel. The Win32 facet uses the Win32 subsystem for all services.

Each DOS application gets its own virtual machine, courtesy of the NT Virtual Device Machine (NTVDM), an aspect of User mode. To a DOS application, Windows NT seems like its own *x*86 machine complete with I/O, a memory stack, and just about any other service it expects to find running under DOS. In this way, Windows NT runs DOS applications quite robustly. For many years, people hoped for a robust way to run multiple DOS applications on the same machine. OS/2 was first with this capacity, but Windows NT is going furthest with it.

The difference between running under Windows NT and DOS isn't apparent to most DOS applications. Windows NT "wraps" the DOS session in a protective layer, preventing the session from directly addressing the hardware, as is common with many DOS programs. When the DOS program makes a direct hardware call, Windows NT will trap that call, translate it into an acceptable set of instructions, and then reply to the call in a way that mimics the return from hardware the application expects. If Windows NT can't translate a call or a return, it politely shuts down the DOS application rather than risk corrupting the session.

Win16, or older Windows applications, have always been troublesome for the newer operating systems. These tend to be transition programs, not quite like DOS "cowboys," yet a far cry from modern Win32 applications. Windows NT 4, through the NTVDM, has two ways to run these applications: in a shared virtual machine and in a separate virtual (or memory space) machine.

Take a look at Figure 1.2. This shows the Windows NT Workstation Task Manager with a Win16 application launched.

FIGURE 1.2.

Launching a Win16 program in Windows NT Workstation starts the NTVDM. The Win16 program runs under this manager.

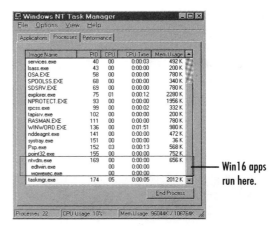

Win16 apps run here.

Note the three entries enclosed in the box. The first is the NTVDM, the second is the application itself, and the third is the WOW executive. WOW stands for Windows On Windows, the service NT uses to run older Windows applications.

Launching a DOS program, in this case PKZIP.EXE, launches its own NTVDM and runs in its own memory space, as you can see in Figure 1.3.

FIGURE 1.3.

Launching a DOS program launches another instance of the NTVDM. This runs it in its own virtual machine, or own address space.

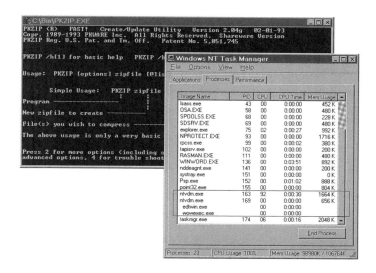

Closing the DOS program (for the sake of clarity) and opening another Win16 program, this time Fractal Design's Painter, shows that both Win16 programs, Edtwin.exe and Painter.exe, are running in the same virtual machine, as seen in Figure 1.4.

FIGURE 1.4.

Launching another Win16 program shows that, by default, Windows NT Workstation will run all such programs in the same address space.

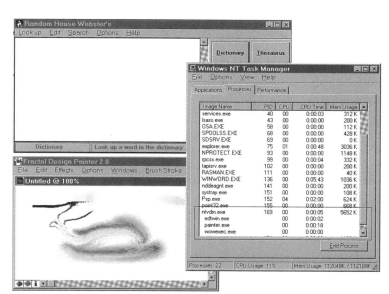

Windows NT Workstation has "wrapped" both Win16 programs in the same virtual machine where they cooperatively multitask with each other just as they would under Windows 3.*x*. They also, like Windows 3.*x*, share the same address space and therefore can interfere with each other. The NTVDM, while running Win16 programs, is susceptible to similar problems that plagued us under Windows 3.*x*. One misbehaved program can bring down all other programs. Figure 1.5 is a simplified schematic of how Win32, the 16-bit emulation of NT, and WOW work together.

FIGURE 1.5.

A simplified schematic of the 16-bit subsystem of Windows NT, WOW, and Win32 show their relationship to each other. The entire structure is the Windows NTVDM for Win16 applications.

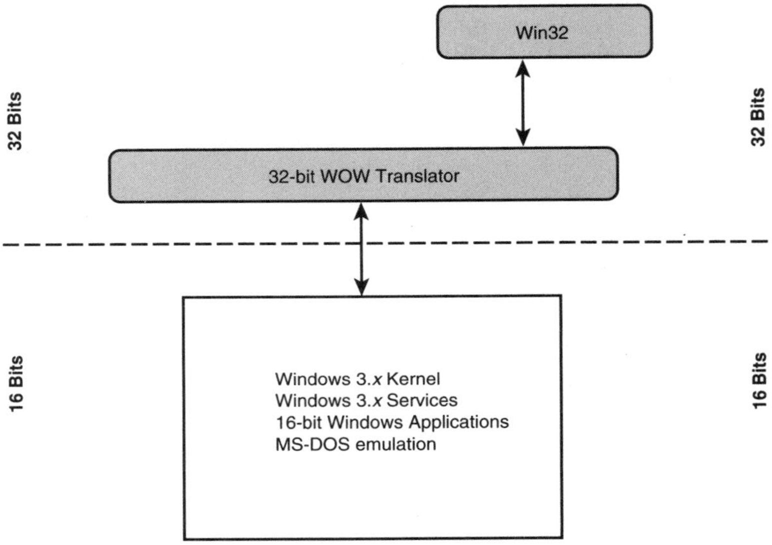

However, because Windows NT itself is controlling the NTVDM, Win16 programs can't bring down the entire computer session as they could under Windows 3.*x* and, to a lesser degree, under Windows 95.

You can optionally run Win16 programs in their own virtual machine. This topic and other hints for tuning legacy programs are covered in Chapter 8, "Tuning Windows NT Performance."

Portability

Windows NT's design includes a Hardware Abstraction Layer (HAL), a small executive that handles all communications with hardware. This allows Microsoft to port Windows NT to different hardware platforms by doing nothing more than rewriting the HAL.

Initially, Microsoft saw Windows NT as a universal operating system. The system would, for the most part, remain the same while each platform had its own HAL. This was a similar plan to Digital's with VMS.

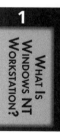

The four processors supported during the early part of NT's history were three RISC ones: Digital's Alpha, the MIPS, and Motorola's PowerPC. The single CISC processor supported was the Intel *x*86 series, such as the 80386, the 80486, the Pentium, or the Pentium Pro.

However, success on a platform requires more than just a good running HAL. It also requires native applications. Although Windows NT for a RISC processor will run common Intel CISC applications, it will run them slowly. The lack of native applications, and the prospect for native applications, along with the growing skepticism about RISC processors' advantages, has doomed two of these platforms—MIPS and the PowerPC—to NT history. Today, Microsoft supports only Intel CISC and Digital's Alpha RISC processors under Windows NT.

Although this situation might change to include more current processors, it's unlikely to. RISC's inroad into mainstream businesses hasn't occurred to any extent. Rather, Intel CISC processors now threaten traditional RISC territory, such as graphics workstations. Meanwhile, chip design teams from Intel and others are looking beyond both RISC and CISC architectures to new designs that will outperform both. In all likelihood, Windows NT will remain solely on the Alpha and Intel platforms until they're both succeeded by the newer designs, which will be supported by the then current versions of NT.

Multiprocessor Support

Windows NT will run on systems sporting more than one CPU, or processor. Very roughly speaking, each doubling of processor count increases performance of processor intensive operations 80 percent. Thus, a mainboard with two Pentium Pro processors will run *approximately* at 180 percent of the speed of a single processor mainboard, all other things being equal.

This speedup occurs only for computationally intensive operations (such as floating-point math) and not for the entire system. Some manufacturers are issuing proprietary systems having as much as eight Pentium Pro class processors for use with Windows NT and similar operating systems. Although aimed squarely at the server market, these systems will work with Windows NT Workstation, making, if equipped with a strong graphics subsystem, a great graphics workstation.

DirectX

Games sell computers. The big gripe about Windows from gamers is that it's slower to display graphics than MS-DOS when programmers aiming games for MS-DOS write routines to directly manipulate hardware. In addition, Microsoft conceptualized Windows NT as a graphics workstation operating system. Both games and graphics require fast displays.

Although Microsoft initially decided on a nongame type of accelerated graphic routines (such as OpenGL), it has recently had a rethink and has added DirectX support to all current versions of Windows, including NT. DirectX is a series of routines to make Windows as responsive as MS-DOS in graphics displays. Although DirectX isn't really the equivalent in speed to hardware-optimized direct addressing under MS-DOS yet, it's much faster than standard

Windows GDI. The video portion of DirectX is Direct Draw. In addition, DirectX adds services for sounds (Direct Sound) and intercomputer communications (Direct Play) for the purposes of multiple computer gaming.

The entire DirectX structure is quite complex. In short, Direct Draw resides between the application and the GDI. The Direct Sound resides between the application and the I/O manager in Kernel. Finally, Direct Play resides between the application and either TAPI (Telephony Application Programming Interface) and the TCP/IP socket, Winsock, or both. Microsoft hasn't included TAPI support in Windows NT version 4 before, but promises such an addition in a subsequent version or a service pack release.

Windows NT Workstation Security

Computer security spans two issues: data integrity and access control. Windows NT greatly exceeds any previous version of a Microsoft operating system in both aspects.

Windows NT Workstation requires a logon, and that logon governs most security issues. You can establish user accounts for yourself or others who might have access to your computer. There is no limit to the amount of accounts you establish. You can also group these accounts according to common permissions. That is, you can establish classes of users and assign rights to those classes; then when you establish a person as part of a class, that person is given the class rights. Windows NT refers to these classes as *user groups.*

The security model for Windows NT Workstation has four components:

- *Logon* establishes a user's identity. Logons can be either interactive, such as when you boot up Windows NT, or automatic, when a user logs on through RAS.
- *Security Account Manager (SAM)* is a database containing information about users, user groups, and their permissions. SAM contains validation routines used by the Local Security Authority.
- *Local Security Authority (LSA)* is the core process of NT security, which enforces those policies and permissions for users that are contained in the SAM.
- *Security Reference Monitor* "watches" a user's actions to make sure he or she has rights to perform attempted actions. This is the component that generates audit messages of attempted security violations when appropriate.

In simplified terms, the security process of Windows NT Workstation works like this:

1. A user logs on with a username and password.
2. The LSA checks in the SAM to see whether the combination of username and password is valid.
3. If the logon isn't valid, Windows NT Workstation deletes the attempted logon.
4. If the logon is valid, the user is assigned a security ID, and that ID is passed to the LSA. That ID contains data relating to a user's rights and permissions.

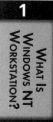

5. The validated logon calls the Win32 subsystem, launching a process with a "token" attached.

6. The Win32 system starts the user interface (UI) or desktop. The Security Reference Monitor keeps an eye on the user's actions, preventing and reporting on unauthorized access attempts for as long as the session persists.

This has been a very short overview of Windows NT Workstation security. Chapter 10, "Fine-Tuning NT Security," and Chapter 28, "Users and Groups on NT," both delve into this topic in detail as it relates to access control. Chapter 12, "Working with the NT File System," covers data integrity and some file-oriented aspects of data access.

Multitasking

Windows NT is a true 32-bit multitasking operating system. To again oversimplify, on a single-processor system only one instruction can be completed at a time, which might strike you as nullifying any advantage multitasking might offer. However, given today's Pentium-based systems, which process upwards of 200 million instructions per second (MIPS), and RISC chips such as the R10000, which have demonstrated speeds of up to 1700 MIPS, this concern is no less relevant. Multitasking in Windows NT refers primarily to the method in which the operating system handles multiple processes running concurrently.

First, it is helpful to understand a little bit about how Windows applications work. Windows applications at the system level are not event-driven applications; they are message-driven. Windows applications generate messages and respond to messages. To facilitate this, the operating system maintains what is called a *message queue.* This is a stream of messages waiting for system resources and processing cycles, a response from another application, or the operating system. First, let's look at how Windows 3.*x* handled multitasking, then at Windows 95, and finally at Windows NT. This will help demonstrate the progress Windows has made and will show how Windows NT surpasses the others in this area.

Windows 3.*x* is absolutely not a multitasking environment, despite opinions to the contrary. Because Windows 3.*x* is really just a shell sitting on top of DOS, and DOS is a single-tasking (non-reentrant) environment, it stands to reason that Windows cannot very well be multitasking. Although it is possible to have multiple applications open at once and even assign a priority to background applications, it is still a single-tasking environment. Anyone who has ever spooled a print job in the background has noticed significant performance degradation. The print job dominates the message queue while processing, rendering, spooling, and finally printing the job. Windows 3.*x* uses a single message queue and one shared memory pool. Because of this, if one application hangs or crashes, usually the rest of the system follows shortly thereafter. If the application is hung, it basically jams the message queue and no other applications can process their messages, usually resulting in the user having to violently reboot the system with the three-fingered salute, Ctrl+Alt+Del.

The other aspect is the shared memory pool. Because all applications share the same memory space, it is possible for one application to write to memory that is already allocated to another application or even the operating system, generally resulting in a General Protection Fault (GPF). Sometimes these are recoverable, but most often the system is unstable after this and needs to be rebooted.

Windows 95 has done a lot to alleviate the majority of these problems, but still suffers some of the same shortcomings. Windows 95 has mostly overcome the heap limits of Windows 3.*x.* Thus, it is uncommon to receive Out of Memory errors. Although it is still possible to receive these errors, it is usually due to a problem with the application and not Windows 95. Windows 95 falls between Windows 3.*x* and Windows NT in the way it multitasks.

Although not a true 32-bit multitasking environment, Windows 95 is a move in the right direction. Windows 95 handles Win32 and Win16 programs quite differently. It, too, has the ability to spawn VDMs similar to NT's. In it, Win32 applications each has its own message queue, but Win16 applications still share a common message queue. This means that the Win32 applications preemptively multitask among themselves while the VDMs preemptively multitask with the Win32 applications. The Win16 applications cooperatively multitask among themselves, with all Win16 applications sharing a common queue.

Suppose there are three Win32 applications, two Win16 applications, and two VDMs running. In a conceptually clockwise fashion (see Figure 1.6), each Win32 application and VDM has the opportunity to process a message, and one Win16 application has the opportunity to process a message (whichever application is next in the queue).

FIGURE 1.6.

An illustration of the Windows NT multitasking model.

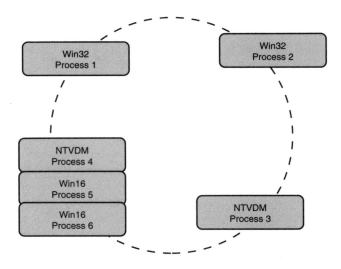

Referring to Figure 1.6, the message processing sequence would be as follows: 1, 2, 3, 4, 5, 1, 2, 3, 4, 6. This is how it works when everything is running smoothly and each process is running with the same priority. If needed, the system can increase or decrease a process's priority and allocate more processing time to another process, preempting the others (thus the name). In the event that a Win16 application will not release control of the Win16 queue, two scenarios are probable. Either that application will continue to process every time the Win16 queue has the opportunity for system resources, or the queue will hang, potentially crashing the Win16 applications. If a Win32 application hangs, the remaining applications continue to function properly, because each has its own queue, as do the VDMs. The benefit here is that if a single application hangs or misbehaves, it should not affect the rest of the system too drastically. Windows 95 also provides a feature of Windows NT, the Task Manager. By pressing the Ctrl+Alt+Del key sequence, a task list is brought up that enables you to terminate an application no longer responding to the system.

> **NOTE**
>
> Each Win16 application has one thread, each VDM has two threads, and each Win32 application has at least one thread (and possibly more, depending on the application).

In Windows 95, as with NT, each process can address up to 4GB of virtual memory, thus alleviating the Out of Memory errors for the most part. Of this 4GB of virtual memory, 2GB is system-addressable memory and 2GB is application-addressable memory. Obviously, most systems do not have this much memory. This is the theoretical limit that each process can map to. The Virtual Memory Manager (VMM) in Windows 95 uses demand paging to page memory to and from disk as needed, optimizing system performance.

As with Windows 95, Windows NT provides each application process with a 4GB virtual-memory address space and utilizes demand paging in the same fashion (demand paging was adopted from Windows NT into Windows 95). Being a true 32-bit environment, Windows NT uses a single Virtual Machine (VM) to run Win16 applications, just as it runs an emulator for OS/2 and POSIX applications. If you recall, the Win32 subsystem is at the core of the User mode environment. The Win16 subsystem is coordinated and scheduled by the Win32 subsystem. As with Windows 95, Windows NT preemptively multitasks Win32 applications. The key difference is in how it handles Win16 applications.

Win16 applications are multitasked in the same fashion as in Windows 95, all being queued in a single VM and cooperatively multitasking among themselves. However, remember, Windows NT offers an option of running a Win16 application in a separate memory space. This allows Win16 applications to have their own virtual address space, eliminating the possibility of one application violating another application's address space and corrupting it. The primary reason for the limitation on Win16 applications and multitasking is to have backward compatibility. This will be less of an issue in the future, because most popular applications now have

32-bit versions available. As with Windows 95, applications can be forcibly terminated, if necessary, by using the task list. The task list in NT 4 is brought up either by right-clicking the Taskbar and choosing Task Manager or by using the Ctrl+Alt+Del key sequence and selecting Task Manager. You can then select the application and choose End Task.

In theory, Windows 3.*x* will also allow shutting down of out-of-control tasks; but in practice, once a process or application runs wild, you usually cannot. Ironically, the reason is Windows 3.*x*'s lack of true multitasking. Processes can grab the entire operating system and prevent the events (keyboard or mouse) from breaking its cycle.

Windows 95 usually will allow you to break in on a runaway process, but not always. Early on, Windows 95 users ruefully learned that endless loops in Windows 95 could be as fatal as endless loops in older Windows. This is true in Win32 applications as well as Win16, although not as much of a problem as in Windows 3.*x*.

The serious problem remaining with Windows 95 is its lack of memory protection. Crashes in Windows 95 all too often wreak havoc with the operating system's stability, forcing a reboot. The good side is that these instabilities generally don't cause a system crash enabling an orderly shutdown/startup without data loss. Still, it's an inconvenience at the least. It can be a real time waster if the system that needs to be rebooted has shared resources, because the boot will disrupt any connected users.

Windows NT Workstation's chief contributions to the desktop are its multitasking abilities and its memory protection.

Improvements and Changes from Windows NT 3.5x

Windows 95 and Windows NT Workstation 4 share many common characteristics. Some of the concepts and technologies for Windows 95 were borrowed directly from Windows NT 3.5*x*; likewise, some of the aspects of Windows 95 have been incorporated into Windows NT 4. The following section describes the similarities between the two—and, more importantly, what differentiates them.

The User Interface

At first glance, Windows NT 4 looks identical to Windows 95. Looks can be deceiving. Beyond the interface and some navigational similarities, these two operating systems are worlds apart.

First, the similarities. The obvious likeness is the desktop itself. As you can see in Figure 1.7, Windows NT 4 has taken on the Windows 95 user interface. The initial layout is identical: My Computer, Network Neighborhood, Inbox, Recycle Bin, and the Briefcase, along with the

Taskbar and the familiar Start button. Architecturally, there are many more similarities, due mostly to the fact that much of the Windows 95 core architecture was borrowed and adapted from Windows NT 3.5*x* and Cairo (the next major release of Windows NT). Windows NT Workstation 4 has also included some other useful features of Windows 95, namely Wordpad (an enhanced version of Write), Internet Explorer 4.0, Autorun (automatically plays autorun-enabled CD-ROMs when inserted into the drive), 3-D Pinball, and the capability of dynamically changing screen resolution without restarting the system.

FIGURE 1.7.

The user interface (UI) in Windows NT Workstation 4 bears more than a little similarity to Windows 95.

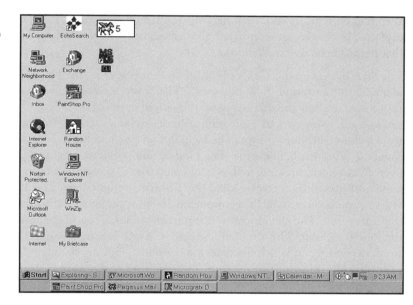

The User Interface of Windows NT Workstation

As with the Windows 95 desktop, My Computer is the container of storage devices, printers, and access to the Control Panel.

Network Neighborhood provides graphical browsing of your network (Microsoft, Banyan, TCP/IP and others) and the capability of using shared resources located on the network. The Inbox is the Microsoft Exchange e-mail client. This provides an inbox for various electronic-mail systems, including MS Mail, MS Exchange, and Internet (SMTP) Mail. Third-party MAPI drivers can be added for other services, such as CompuServe, as they are made available.

The Recycle Bin is a welcome addition to Windows NT. This can provide some degree of safety against accidentally deleted files. If you have ever mistakenly deleted important files, you will appreciate this.

> **NOTE**
>
> Many administrators choose to disable the use of the Recycle Bin due to disk space or security issues.

Another welcome feature of Windows NT 4 is My Briefcase. This optional component affords a simple form of data replication between computers. Although most people use this facility to keep files current between their desktop and laptop computers, it has capabilities that can be exploited by the entire enterprise. This is an example of a well-received feature of Windows 95 that has made its way to Windows NT 4.

The Start button on the Taskbar is just that—the place to start. This produces a pop-up menu identical to that found in Windows 95. The Shut Down option is used to initiate a system shutdown, to allow the user to log off the system or to log on differently. The Run command allows a GUI way to start a program. Alternatively, a user can launch from the Explorer or from a command-line prompt. The Help option provides access to system help files using the standard Windows help engine. The Find option provides searching capabilities (locally and over the network) for files, folders, and computers. The Settings entry provides access to the Control Panel, printer settings, and the Taskbar configuration. The Taskbar option also enables customization of the Programs menu and the option of clearing the Documents list from the Start menu. The Documents folder provides quick access to the most recently used files for the logged-on user. This can be files such as Word documents, Excel files, or Internet locations, depending on which file types are registered with the system.

Selecting the Programs choice from the Start menu will bring up many familiar items. Here, by default, you find at least three more folders: Accessories, Administrative Tools, and the Startup folder. There is also an item for Windows NT Books Online, a good old-fashioned DOS prompt for the Command Line Interface (CLI), and the Windows NT Explorer.

> **NOTE**
>
> What is the Explorer? That is a good question if you are not familiar with Windows 95. The Explorer, in the most fundamental explanation, is a replacement for File Manager. This can get confusing, because you can still use the old File Manager. And, whereas in Windows 3.x your operating shell was Program Manager (progman.exe), in Windows NT 4 and Windows 95 the default operating shell is Explorer (explorer.exe). However, both Windows NT Workstation 4 and Windows 95 include a version of Progman.exe for their operating systems. That will give a Windows 3.x or Windows NT 3.x look to those who, for whatever reason, prefer it to the new Explorer desktop. Although many requested the option of running Progman.exe instead of Explorer, the superiority of the Explorer UI makes its use quite rare.

Choosing the Accessories option produces more subfolders and programs. There is the familiar productivity killer, the Games folder, which has the ever-present Solitaire and Minesweeper, and a game called Freecell (a much more addicting variation of Solitaire). New to Windows NT 4 is the Multimedia folder. This is another feature found in Windows 95 and brought over by popular demand. Here, you will find a built-in CD Player, Media Player, and Sound Recorder, as well as a Volume Control—certainly nothing critical or earth-shattering, but useful nonetheless. Down the list, you find many familiar items:

Calculator

Character Map

Chat (From WfW 3.11)

Clipbook Viewer (From WfW 3.11)

Clock

Notepad

Object Packager

Paint

Print Manager

Write

Several items were excluded from the preceding list because they merit further explanation. Included from Windows 95 is HyperTerminal, a limited version of the commercial HyperTerminal product. This is a long overdue and welcome inclusion for those suffering with the older Terminal. It adds support for the more popular transfer protocols (such as Zmodem). There is also a Phone Dialer, one of the first telephony applications. This is basically a speed-dial program that enables you to dial out using your modem. It's not particularly useful or practical for most people unless combined with an application that can communicate with it. Also, if your computer has TCP/IP installed, there is a Telnet item. This is a terminal emulation program for use over TCP/IP networks such as the Internet. It is a bare-bones version that is limited to the most basic functionality, but in the absence of another version it does the job.

Other chapters cover various aspects of the Administrative Tools folder and further discuss its applications. This folder contains the system maintenance and administration applications. Here, you can do system backups, configure disk drives, manage users on the system, get specific information about the system, monitor performance, and view error logs. These applications are largely unchanged from previous versions but, as with Windows NT 3.5x, are often underutilized and not exploited to their full potential. These can be invaluable utilities to systems administrators and should not be discounted.

The Startup folder is identical to the group by the same name in previous versions of Windows. Anything placed in this folder will be run when a user logs on. Note that due to NT security, items put in the Startup folder do not start when the system starts, but when a user logs on. If the user does not have sufficient rights to execute the application, it will fail to launch. If you would like a program to start when the system starts, you must install it as a service and configure it appropriately.

Most setups will also include a Books Online entry, used for browsing through the Windows NT 4 documentation on CD. You can copy these files to the hard drive (network or local) for faster access, but they do soak up a lot of real estate if you do so. The Command Prompt item launches an NTVDM (NT's Virtual DOS Machine), which provides access to a DOS-style command prompt. Make no mistake—unlike other previous Windows versions, DOS doesn't lie beneath the surface of Windows NT. A NTVDM is a 32-bit emulation of the DOS environment, provided by the Win32 subsystem, which is user-configurable as desired. This can be extremely useful in many situations, specifically for troubleshooting network problems. Finally, there is the Windows NT Explorer, as mentioned previously.

The Control Panel

The Windows NT Workstation 4 Control Panel is very similar to that of Windows 95, as you can see in Figure 1.8. They do, in fact, share many common elements. Windows NT, however, has some applets that are absent in Windows 95. The following is a listing of the various Control Panel applets, each with a brief description of function:

FIGURE 1.8.

The Windows NT 4 Control Panel bears a great deal of similarity to the Windows 95 one.

- *Accessibility Options* provides usability features and enhancements for people with disabilities. Support has greatly improved over version 3.5*x*. This entry is optional and not installed in the Windows NT Workstation setup shown in Figure 1.8.

- *Add/Remove Programs* provides the ability to uninstall applications cleanly and completely, provided the application vendor included an uninstall script with the application. This applet also provides access to Windows NT Setup (not the same as the setup to change mouse/keyboard as described previously). Here you can add, remove, and reconfigure components of Windows NT.

- *Console* is used to customize the look, feel, and behavior of the Windows NT DOS-style command prompt.

- *Date/Time* is the standard applet to set the system date and time. A notable feature of NT available since version 3.5*x* is the capability to have the system automatically adjust for daylight savings time, if applicable to your locale.

- *Devices* lists all available and installed device drivers, their current status, and startup options. Devices can be stopped and started from here. Also, device startup options and hardware profiles can be configured here.

- *Dial-Up Monitor* monitors and displays statistics about any Dial Up networking session. You must have installed Dial Up networking to see this icon.

- *Display* is used to customize the desktop: color, wallpaper, pattern, screen saver, and font. It also has options to customize icon display and change the default system icons and specify, configure, and change video display options, such as resolution, color depth, and display adapter. This option is also available by right-clicking the desktop and selecting Properties.

- *Fonts* enables you to view currently installed fonts and add or remove fonts.

- *Internet* enables the system to be configured to access the Internet through a proxy server, configure Internet Explorer, configure mail and news (Usenet) clients, and set various options useful for Internet surfing and security.

- *Keyboard* enables configuration of repeat key delay and rate and cursor-blink rate. Additional locales may be added here also.

- *Mail and Fax* is installed as part of Office 97. It allows configuration of Outlook 97 services.

- *Modems* provides a modem wizard to assist in the installation and configuration of modems.

- *Mouse* enables configuration of double-click speed, swapping buttons, mouse speed, and animated cursors. If Intellimouse has been installed, it allows further options, such as wheel activation, cursor scrolling, wheel click and more.

- *Multimedia* enables all audio and video configuration. This is discussed further in Chapter 19, " Configuring Multimedia Devices."

- *Network* enables network installation and configuration. This option is also available by right-clicking the Network Neighborhood icon and selecting Properties.

- *ODBC* is a common way (a middleware) to connect to various data sources. If installed, this icon allows you to add, remove, and configure various data sources.

- *PC Card* is used to add, remove, and configure many different PC cards for use in laptops, as well as to configure the PC card controller.

- *Ports* is an applet to configure communications ports.

- *Printers* is an applet that greatly simplifies the installation and configuration of printers. Included is an Add New Printer wizard to assist in the installation of both local and network printers.

- *Regional Settings* enables localization of Windows NT Workstation 4. This allows options of local time zone, currency, date format, and other international settings.

- *SCSI Adapters* is a utility that has been moved from Windows NT Setup in version 3.5*x* to its own applet in version 4. This lists all installed SCSI adapters as well as ATAPI (IDE) CD-ROM devices and their respective drivers.

- *Server* is used to view currently connected users, shares available on the system, and files in use. Shares can be created or removed, users disconnected from resources, and administrative alerts configured here, as well as directory replication service configuration.

- *Services* is a GUI method to monitor the status of, start, and stop various services. The CLI offers the same options, but in a less user-friendly manner.

- *Sounds* is an applet for associating sounds with system and application events.

- *System* allows monitoring and configuration of systemwide options, such as performance tuning, startup options in BOOT.INI, environment, and hardware profiling.

- *Tape Devices* allows the adding or removing of any tape backup devices installed on the system.

- *Telephony* is an applet from Windows 95, ported to NT. Microsoft is adamant about promoting the use of telephony. Here you configure the properties for your location and phone system and add or remove telephony drivers.

- *UPS* provides native support for uninterruptible power supply devices, an integral piece of Windows NT's fault tolerance. This provides basic communication between the operating system and the UPS device, which facilitates sending alerts to appropriate individuals in the event of a power failure and shutting down the system cleanly prior to the battery failing. This requires a compliant UPS.

Most of these applets are directly adopted from either Windows 3.*x* or 95. The majority act identically or very closely to their counterparts, but Windows NT has an ever-growing list of Control Panel applets that are specific to it.

Quite a list, isn't it? This goes to show just how extensive and well thought out this operating system is. Microsoft has designed Windows NT to meet the most critical and demanding needs of computing today and leave room for future growth. This is the operating system for the next generation of computing.

Windows NT Networking

A major feature of Windows NT is its native networking support. Being one of the original design goals, network support is built into the operating system itself, providing a high degree of integration.

Natively, Windows NT Workstation supports many protocols and services for seamless network integration, even in heterogeneous environments. The following are the standard supported protocols:

- AppleTalk
- DLC
- NetBEUI
- NWLink IPX/SPX (Novell)
- TCP/IP

Additionally, Windows NT Workstation 4 provides a host of different network services:

- Client Service for NetWare (NDS aware)
- FTP server
- Microsoft TCP/IP printing support
- Network monitor agent
- Remote access service (RAS)
- RPC configuration (and RPC support for Banyan)
- SAP agent
- SNMP service
- PPTP client (point-to-point tunneling protocol)
- Peer Web Services

Clearly, Windows NT Workstation is capable of being integrated into almost any existing network.

> **NOTE**
>
> The client service for NetWare provides file and print support for NetWare 3.x and 4.x servers, and it allows for security authentication by NetWare servers and the execution of logon scripts. It does not, however, support NetAdmin or NWAdmin at the time of this writing.

The Network Monitor agent allows a remote server computer running Microsoft's Network Monitor to attach to the system running the agent and monitor another portion of the network. The RPC support has been improved to provide support for RPC on Banyan networks, in addition to TCP/IP-based networks. The SAP agent is for use with NetWare networks to broadcast available services and resources, and the SNMP service is for use on TCP/IP networks with monitoring applications that can respond to or monitor SNMP traps.

Windows NT Workstation 4 supports up to 10 inbound network connections and unlimited outbound connections (up to the limitations of the physical hardware of the network). The Remote Access component in NT Workstation 4 supports a single inbound dial-up connection, which can be useful for attaching to the network from a remote site. The RAS component can also be configured to dial out and serves very well as a dial-up PPP connector to an Internet service provider.

Windows NT Workstation 4 can operate in either a domain or workgroup environment. If it is on a network with Windows NT Server computers, it can be configured to participate in a domain to use centralized security accounts. It can also operate in a workgroup capacity for peer-to-peer networking, although this becomes fairly complicated if there are several NT Workstation computers—each will have its own set of user accounts and security database. Windows NT Workstation 4 can also use a NetWare server for centralized security and validation.

Fault Tolerance

Windows NT Workstation 4 supports the creation of volume sets, the combination of multiple partitions into a single logical volume, stripe sets without parity for improved disk access, and mirrored partitions.

Volume sets and stripe sets without parity must be formatted using NTFS. Existing volume sets can be extended as needed to include up to 32 separate partitions. Stripe sets can also include up to 32 partitions. Advanced disk features will be revisited in Chapter 12.

Windows NT Workstation 4 also provides features to support system backups and UPS subsystems that can perform a clean system shutdown in the event of a power failure.

Capacity

At this point, Windows NT Workstation will support up to two processors, but Microsoft's desire to market Windows NT to the graphic workstation market makes it a good bet that this will soon expand. Windows NT will recognize up to 2TB of storage memory and 4GB of physical RAM or VRAM.

File Systems

As implied earlier, Windows NT Workstation will natively recognize FAT16, FAT32, and NT File System (NTFS) volumes. Performance and security depend upon which file system NT is addressing. There's nothing NT can do to give the older FAT file systems added fault tolerance. Unless your volumes are quite small or need to be recognized by non-NT Windows or DOS, NTFS is the way to go. Chapter 12 explores this topic in detail.

Summary

Windows NT Workstation is the clear choice of operating systems for demanding users and critical environments, with the capacity to meet computing needs today and tomorrow. With features such as integrated networking and dial-up support, an intuitive user interface, an advanced file system and architecture, and fault-tolerant options, this truly is the operating system for the next generation of computing.

Preinstallation and System Analysis

by Paul Cassel

IN THIS CHAPTER

CHAPTER 2

Setting up Windows NT Workstation, like so many things in life, can be made much simpler and easier by adequate planning. The last thing you need is to be making critical decisions—or worse, buying and installing hardware—during the setup process. Given proper planning, setting up Windows NT Workstation on one computer or corporate-wide should go smoothly, with very little, if any, interaction on the part of the administrator (or user).

Speaking in the broadest terms, setup of Windows NT Workstation has three phases:

- Inventory hardware to assure the setup team, or yourself, that your target computers have adequate resources to run and are compatible with Windows NT Workstation
- Deciding on installation options
- Deciding on a setup strategy

That sounds simple, and in overview it is. However, the overview glosses over a lot of detail work that you need to get right to succeed in having a glitch-free setup experience. Take all the time you need to make sure your setup plan is complete and save yourself a lot of frantic worry during the actual setup process.

Inventory

Windows NT Workstation has a modest list of required hardware. Sticking to the minimums or even staying close to them isn't a good idea. There is a vast difference in how well Windows NT will run on a minimum machine as opposed to a truly proper one. Table 2.1 shows the minimum requirements and comment about those minimums.

Table 2.1. Minimum NT requirements.

Category	Minimum	Comment
RAM	12MB	Windows NT Workstation runs abysmally with less than 32MB RAM. It really starts to fly at 64MB.
Disk space for host		
volume	95MB	Unlike some Windows, Windows NT Workstation stores much data within its own directory. Like all Windows, its home directory expands as you install applications. The minimum practical disk requirement for Windows NT Workstation is closer to four times the minimum recommended by Microsoft. Even that's not generous. Practically speaking, the host volume for Windows NT Workstation should have at least 1.5GB of space. Alpha machines have slightly higher disk requirements than Intel.

Category	Minimum	Comment
Display	VGA	Windows NT Workstation and most of its applications don't look right in standard VGA resolution. The true minimum is a 15/16-bit display depth at 800×600 resolution. That will yield roughly 32,000 or 64,000 colors. Most people can't see a difference between 16-bit color depth and 24-bit depth capable of roughly 17,000,000 colors.
Mouse	Any compatible	The new wheel-equipped mice work with many Windows NT Workstation services and applications.
Removable drive		Disk for Intel, CD for other.
		CD for any workstation that will host the setup process.
Network Interface		Optional. Use self-configuring cards/mainboards if possible to decrease headaches significantly. A 32-bit adapter will pay off in increased network speed.

Hardware Compatibility

Making sure you have the iron to run Windows NT Workstation is only part of the battle. Windows NT has always been quite selective about what hardware it will support. In past versions of NT, Microsoft attempted to placate users of older hardware by making NT quite compatible with legacy components. This did not win NT many converts, nor did it show NT in the best light.

Rather than trying to make Windows NT 4 support even more existing hardware, Microsoft took the rather bold stance of tightening up NT's hardware support scope. To put it in a nutshell, Windows NT Workstation will run on today's and tomorrow's systems, but in many cases, not yesterday's. This will force some upgrading in many instances. Upgraders will have as a consolation the knowledge that they are getting a better system for their bother and expense.

Why the Lost Legacy?

Keep in mind that Windows NT 4 has moved the Graphics Device Interface (GDI) from User to Kernel. This requires a new driver specific to Windows NT 4 for every display adapter. In many cases, manufacturers weren't interested in updating the drivers for their older products, resulting in an orphaning of those products under NT 4. Microsoft will make homegrown drivers only for products it believes to be in wide use, not every product in existence.

Microsoft maintains a list of all hardware that it has tested and found to work properly with Windows NT 4. Getting a current version of this list to check on your equipment's NT compatibility is vital unless you are absolutely sure your hardware is NT-ready.

This list is the Hardware Compatibility List (HCL). There's a copy on the Windows NT distribution CD in the form of a standard Windows help file. This file is named for the month and year of its creation plus HCL and has the .hlp extension. Look in the root directory for it.

However, due to production lag, the list on any CD is out of date. Microsoft maintains a current version of this list on its Web site at http://www.microsoft.com/hwtest. It is also available at other Web and FTP distribution points.

> **NOTE**
>
> If you have cause to call Microsoft technical support for Windows NT Workstation, the staff will be very reluctant to troubleshoot problems that involve hardware not listed on the HCL.

Similarly, if you have an OEM version of Windows NT Workstation, the OEM will be very reluctant to help you if you have added legacy equipment to the hardware sold with the copy of NT. This is true even if the legacy hardware is from the same OEM.

The architecture of Windows NT is the reason behind all of the fuss involved with hardware support. Unlike previous versions of DOS and Windows, Windows NT does not allow User mode processes direct access to the hardware components. The reason for this design is portability and modularity, which is consistent with the rest of the Windows NT philosophy.

By implementing a Hardware Abstraction Layer (HAL), the underlying hardware is masked to the operating system. This allows a single device driver to be portable across all hardware platforms.

All non-I/O hardware requests (accessing a network resource, for example) are passed from the appropriate subsystem to the Win32 subsystem, which then sends the request through security validation, to the Executive Services, and then to the Kernel, which passes the request to the HAL. The HAL "virtualizes" this request, interprets it, and makes the appropriate hardware call (sending a data stream over the network interface).

This is a somewhat involved process; the preceding explanation is greatly simplified to illustrate the process involved. The end result is that the operating system is not restricted to a specific hardware architecture. This enables Microsoft to port Windows NT to other hardware platforms much more easily than it could rewrite all the hardware system calls. This also enables developers to write a single device driver for a specific piece of hardware.

Due to this hardware abstraction architecture, most communications programs (such as fax and modem software) do not function properly under Windows NT. These programs require direct access to the hardware components. Initially, this was a problem, but there are now a host of such applications for Windows NT—and support is growing.

Keep in mind that time is money. That includes your time as well as support's, either at Microsoft or an OEM. Most non-supported hardware problems can be resolved easily or shouldn't be attempted at all. After all, what gain is there in spending a full day getting a display adapter to work when you can buy a compatible one for under $100?

The safest path is to attempt an installation only on machines that have all their components on the HCL. It's not the only safe path, though. Microsoft can't test everything instantly, and there might be perfectly good hardware that for some reason or another hasn't made it to the HCL yet—or might never at all. If you have a trusted vendor who says his hardware is Windows NT 4–compatible, you should feel safe with that hardware even if it doesn't appear on the HCL. If you have a problem, you'll have to call the vendor, because Microsoft will, in all likelihood, say something like, "We told you so."

The Case for Windows 95

It's just ducky to say that all hardware should appear on the HCL, and if it doesn't, then go out and buy some that does before setting up. In reality, corporate policies often make such buying impossible even if it doesn't mean much expense.

Windows 95 is as supportive of out-of-date and weird hardware as Microsoft could make it. It's a good fallback position for client machines containing seriously incompatible hardware until they can be replaced or brought up to date. The workers using those client machines might not be thrilled at being passed over for Windows NT Workstation, but it's better than starting a battle against legacy hardware that you can't win.

The Checklist

Any enterprise-wide upgrade to Windows NT Workstation for network client machines should have a checklist to organize the operation. Here is a sample checklist—yours will no doubt vary, because no two installations are identical in all particulars:

1. Is the upgrade team assembled and identified? Have they received the proper training for the upgrade operation? Have they been selected not only for technical expertise, but for their "people abilities"?

2. Will you do a pilot rollout or try to install the upgrade over the entire enterprise at one time? Will you install by user class or by department? If you choose to do a department-by-department rollout, have you notified all affected departments of the rollout schedule to eliminate "NT envy"?

   If you choose a pilot program of one department or a group of users, have they received the needed training in advance of the program?

3. Have you tested all existing software with Windows NT Workstation for the target installation group?

4. Is all the hardware for the target group on the HCL? If not, are you sure you have the necessary drivers and have tested the unapproved hardware with Windows NT Workstation?

5. Have you decided whether to do a clean installation of Windows NT Workstation or install as a true upgrade over an existing operating system? Clean installations have a much greater chance of perfect-appearing setups, but require the users or the upgrade group to set up their applications software again. In some cases, you might decide to use centralized clean upgrade on both Windows NT Workstation and applications. This is particularly attractive if your upgrade to Windows NT Workstation is scheduled to occur at roughly the same time as your applications upgrade. In any case, a clean install of Windows NT Workstation will require a restoration of local (client-based) data files.

6. Have you assigned new passwords (if necessary) to the target group?

7. Have you performed the pre-setup steps of virus checking, disk defragmenting, and redundant backups?

8. Will you install locally or through a server using a tool like Systems Management Server (SMS)? If the latter, have you tried a pilot push installation prior to attempting installations on production machines?

9. When will you perform the upgrade to Windows NT Workstation? Will you try during normal work times to enlist the help of users or during off-hours to avoid disrupting the normal workflow?

10. Have you notified department managers of target upgrade groups what to expect during the upgrade process?

Although there's no technical reason to schedule a pilot upgrade program to a group that's similar in all but size to your enterprise, there's no better way to uncover faults in your assumptions and your checklist than doing this.

When choosing a pilot group for the upgrade test, make sure it includes a fair profile of your enterprise. Choosing a department full of power users with the latest equipment isn't a fair test if your enterprise includes many users with less motivation, older equipment, or both. You don't want to see surprises during the full installation effort that you've avoided during the pilot due to careful selection of a pilot group. Give it and your team a fair test.

Possible Trouble Spots

Some hardware means heartbreak for the administrator installing Windows NT Workstation. Here are some problematic items and areas.

■ *Oddball Hardware.* The computer industry is quite creative. Over the years, people and companies have brought out some interesting pieces of hardware. Unfortunately for the inventors and adopters, many of those items now reside in the bit bucket of the computer industry. In some cases, the hardware is quite useful, but also quite rare. Some examples of this hardware are robotic vision interfaces (video), robotic control hardware, and interfaces for controlling a security system.

If the manufacturer is still in business and interested in writing drivers for its older hardware, you might have a chance at getting some of this stuff to run under Windows NT 4. However, in too many cases, the manufacturer is gone or uninterested in putting in the effort to support older equipment. Sometimes the manufacturer will have new and improved stuff intended for use with Windows NT. If so, you can solve your problem by throwing money at it. If not, you're likely out of luck.

- *Older Disk Controllers.* Computer history has seen the wreck of many disk controller interface schemes that are little known today. Just a few years ago, SCSI was rare and unreliable in PCs, and IDE and EIDE were unknown. Disk interfaces were MFM, RLL, ESDI, and even the (then) hot ARLL.

  It's unlikely that you'll encounter those controllers today in a potential NT installation, because the capacities of those disks were tiny compared to today's disks. However, you might. If you do, and even if they work with Windows NT Workstation, consider ditching them in favor of EIDE or SCSI.

  Windows NT depends upon virtual RAM—RAM emulated in a paging, or swap, file. The speed of Windows NT depends upon the speed of this VRAM, which means that a potential bottleneck with NT is disk speed.

  ESDI, ARLL, MFM, and RLL disk/controller combinations operate at speeds that seem glacial today. In many cases, they'll fail to work under NT. In almost all cases, they should be replaced by their more modern counterparts.

- *Video Cards.* If there's a single place that's the heartbreak hill of NT setup, the lost world of orphaned video cards is it. Some cards even give Windows 95 a hassle.

  The world of video cards is one that changes faster than any other aspect of computer peripherals. There is constant intense competition between manufacturers to have the latest cards sporting the best speed, the newest interface, or the most features. The prize for having such a card is a top rating for that card in a national magazine, which will lead to millions of dollars in sales and a dominant position in the market. Once a manufacturer achieves dominance, it can set its own standards, thus cementing its position for quite a while.

  Manufacturers have all they can do to bring out new models intended to trump other manufacturers who are trying to do the same to them. They have little (if any) interest and no motive to support already sold cards with newer drivers.

- *Stealthy Peripherals.* These are hardware items that fool setup. In some cases, manufacturers intentionally make their hardware seem like something else for compatibility. Some IBM-brand hardware was "wired" to run only in IBM-brand computers. These approved computers had the trademark *IBM* in firmware (BIOS). Some cloners got around this move by putting a phrase like *not IBM* or *IBM-compatible* in their firmware. A search routine for the string *IBM* would find *IBM* without violating Blue's trademark. These strategies fool proprietary hardware and software. They can also fool setup programs.

In other cases, manufacturers modify their hardware during a model run. Most video cards and modems undergo firmware modifications during their model runs. These modifications can foil setup by seeming to run with a particular driver when they can't.

Unless your hardware is incredibly uniform, you are incredibly lucky, or your installation target is quite small, you will hit one or more hardware problems during setup. Careful inventory taking will eliminate or anticipate these trouble spots, but very rarely can eliminate them entirely.

The Inventory Process

If you're installing on a single machine or only a few, your inventory chores are rather easy. You can just make a list of what's in them and do an eyeball comparison to the HCL.

However, in a corporate setting having hundreds or even thousands of computers, you can't do an eyeball inventory. You should have a complete inventory already, but few do. Even those who try to maintain running inventories find that they are out of date. Users add stuff to their machines and swap parts around, departments go out and buy equipment to meet their particular needs, and other events conspire to make even the most well-kept list inaccurate.

Although you can walk around your organization taking a manual inventory similar to a retail item count, if you have more than a few computers, you should look into software that helps you manage networks including the inventory. One such program is Microsoft's Systems Management Server (SMS). Such a program has more uses than just inventory. For example, using SMS, you can arrange for a hands-off "push" setup of Windows NT.

After the Installation

The time to plan for after the Windows NT Workstation upgrade is before it's attempted. If your standard enterprise application suite is straightforward, such as a current version of Microsoft Office with a few Access or Excel custom applications, you shouldn't have any compatibility issues.

That's a dream situation. Most individuals and virtually all enterprises have at least a few oddball applications that departments either can't or choose not to upgrade to current technology. In addition, some users not familiar with the new user interface (UI) will be confused upon encountering it. To address these problems, you need to develop two programs prior to any pilot programs. The pilot installations, if you choose to perform them, will let you fine-tune your programs.

Supporting Users

If you have an existing support desk or system, you'll need to train its staff for anticipated problems users might hit when first using Windows NT Workstation. This is a Catch-22, because you can't know what problems your help desk people should anticipate until you do the rollout. This is an excellent reason to try a pilot program first.

Because you'll have to expand your support staff at least temporarily for the Windows NT Workstation rollout, you can afford to post a few of them at a time within the department or with users selected to be the pilot group. Rotate this close support staff regularly to give all your support people real experience with new NT users.

As your close support staff gains experience with the pilot users, enter their encountered problems and proven solutions in your support database. This will give all your support staff individuals the benefit of the entire support group's experiences. If you don't have a support desk database, consider creating one. Even a simple database—one that an experienced Access developer can put together in a day or so—will be very worthwhile in preventing your staff from solving already solved situations.

Training Users

It's simple. The way to reduce support costs is training. The way to increase user satisfaction with Windows NT Workstation is training. The way to increase enterprise productivity is training. The way to increase employee satisfaction on the job is training.

Nobody will dispute those claims, yet few enterprises take the steps to adequately train their users. Even those that plan to often fail to follow through on those plans. Here's an opportunity to be different, and in being so be better: train your users. This will make your life simpler and more peaceful.

The training specifics for your users depend on two things:

- Their level of expertise
- Their previous experience

Here are some topics to cover for a typical group of users migrating from Windows 3.*x*, the Macintosh, or a later version of OS/2. Users coming from MS-DOS or a text-based UNIX will need training in a GUI.

- The Windows NT Workstation desktop
- The organization and use of the Start button
- Using the Explorer on the local machine
- The meaning of shortcuts, creating shortcuts
- Sharing resources
- Locating shared resources through the Network Neighborhood, connecting to those resources

- Setting up a local printer, sharing that printer
- Getting help for Windows NT Workstation
- Using the context-sensitive right mouse button
- Installing local applications, saving data locally and to shared resources
- Using OLE in applications
- Creating and using scraps on the desktop
- Locating files, directories, and computers using the Find resource in Explorer and in Start
- Customizing settings, such as display colors, screen resolution, and color depth
- Assigning sounds to events
- A tour of the Control Panel
- The Command Line Interface (CLI)

In all likelihood, that entire list will have items you don't want to teach your users, and it makes some assumptions about your users' abilities that may not be true.

Any training program is better than no training program. A formal training program, even a very abbreviated one, is vastly superior to on-the-fly, trial-and-error experimenting. If your organization doesn't have the facilities for such training, consider leasing a facility that does.

Who Trains?

Try to have the same people responsible for user support do the training. Outside trainers will surely have their own agendas and their own slants. Also, they have no concern about what happens after the training session, because they'll have long moved on.

Consider running a pilot program with pilot training done by your support staff. Then have the same people support the users participating in the pilot program. They will gain experience with real users in the real situations in your real enterprise. This experience will point out not only checklist deficiencies, but also holes in the pilot training program.

Then have the now-experienced support staff train the rest of the staff, because by this iteration they have evolved into trainers who know what training your users need. They also have a great deal of self-interest in seeing the users get good training. Otherwise, the users might end up overwhelming the support staff, thereby making them look bad. There's nothing like self-interest to motivate a teacher.

Decide on Setup Options

For the most part, Windows NT Workstation will configure itself according to the client machine on which it finds itself. There's not that much you can do, or should even want to do, to change this.

However, there are several installation options over which you do have control. You'll find setup process in the next chapter, but before you actually run setup, or if you're planning a centralized setup, you need to make certain choices.

These choices come down to two broad categories: NT applet options and network protocols.

NT Applet Options

Windows NT, like Windows 95 and its predecessors, has many installation options. Microsoft chooses those options if you select the Typical or Compact setup choices. If you decide to do a "push" setup using a tool such as SMS or you decide to do a Custom setup at each console, you will face a wide choice of applet combinations.

In some cases, the applets you choose will depend upon company policy, but you should also, if possible, give weight to the following:

- User satisfaction
- User requirements
- Disk space

For a great many users, the more custom their workstation (client machine), the happier they are. This is the reason for the hearty sales of such non-productivity programs as the After Dark screen saver. Similarly, users like to install and play games, both those that come with Windows and those available *a la carte*.

> **NOTE**
>
> The term *applets* applies both to the little programs in Control Panel and to minor applications, such as the Calculator, distributed with Windows NT Workstation.

Although it's true that many users will spend company time using applets (especially games), in some ways, this time isn't wasted if it increases employee morale and therefore increases productivity. Employees have figured out how to really waste company time and assets well before the invention of the personal computer.

In very rare instances is disk space a consideration when it comes to installing applets. At worst, these will eat up a few megabytes of disk. When disks were 20MB total, this was a serious consideration. With today's typical business computer's disk space ranging above 2.5GB, it isn't.

Although the final decision as to what applets and games (if any) become part of an installation usually isn't part of a user's decision matrix, it's a prudent idea to give users' feelings consideration when deciding these things.

Network Options

Windows NT has been designed to work with a wide variety of standard networking protocols and services. The most common ones come standard with the distribution disk. In some rare cases, you'll need to contact the vendor for client drivers. Here is a list of the standard network clients bundled with Windows NT Workstation:

- *NetBEUI.* This is an extension of the older NetBIOS. It's a fast, small, limited protocol useful for small-to-medium-sized LANs of up to about 150 clients and servers.

  NetBEUI's great advantage is its simplicity. It self-configures at installation time, both as to addresses and binding to the client NIC (Network Interface Card). Its chief drawback is its inability to work with routers, therefore limiting its network size.

- *IPX/SPX or NWLink.* IPX/SPX is the protocol of the older Novell NetWare connectivity solution. Many enterprises have an installed NetWare as a legacy protocol. Some of these companies choose to upgrade to Windows NT piecemeal rather than all at once. This leaves islands of the older NetWare in an otherwise modern Windows NT networking installation.

  For those companies, Microsoft has included a NetWare client for Windows NT Workstation. This is NWLink, an enhanced version of Novell's NetBIOS. Both Microsoft's and Novell's protocols can simultaneously exist bound to the same NIC.

- *TCP/IP.* This is the standard networking of the Internet and UNIX. Due to its flexibility, it's finding wide support outside of its traditional bastions.

TCP/IP probably provides the best interoperability of all protocols. It's evolved into the *lingua franca* of computers. The *stack,* or TCP/IP layer, included with Windows NT Workstation is 32 bits and includes both SLIP and PPP services.

You can't go wrong by choosing this protocol, and in many cases, you'll have to opt for it either exclusively or in addition to another choice such as NetBEUI. Many networks run NetBEUI over TCP/IP.

If you choose this as your networking protocol, you'll need to assign IP numbers to each client on your network. If you choose Windows NT Server as your server operating system, you can assign a block of numbers to DHCP (Dynamic Host Control Protocol) for easier (after it's set up) client management. DHCP dynamically assigns an IP to a client upon logon.

If you run NetBEUI, you should also consider configuring a Windows Internet Naming Service (WINS) server. This handles name resolution between the TCP/IP and NetBEUI protocols.

Once you've set up a TCP/IP layer and configured all the needed services, you can connect to any other TCP/IP network or device:

- *AppleTalk.* This is a limited, but common (in the Macintosh world), protocol originally designed as a very simple connectivity solution for Apple brand computers.

This requires a server on the network to have installed Windows NT Services for the Macintosh. When all the pieces are in place, it allows Windows NT computers to talk to Macintosh ones. Although this protocol has some uses in a heterogeneous network, developers working on both Windows NT and Macintosh projects most often use it.

- *Data Link Control.* This is one part of a routine usually aimed at connecting to an IBM mainframe or a printer on the LAN without a computer host. DLC is only one part of what's necessary for the mainframe connection. You'll also need a 3270 terminal emulator for mainframes, 5250 emulator for AS/400s, or something like Microsoft SNA Server to complete the picture if either is on a token ring network.

  If you have a few MS-DOS computers left in your enterprise, you can use DLC to connect them to the network.

- *VINES.* This often praised but little used network protocol can work with Windows NT, but you need to contact the vendor, Banyan, for the drivers.

Remote Access Service

Remote Access Service (RAS) is a highly flexible service allowing client connection to a remote (not on the LAN or WAN) server. For the most part, people use RAS for the following:

- To access the company server or LAN from mobile (laptop) computers
- To allow telecommuting employees to participate, through dial-up lines, in a workgroup
- To allow connectivity to the Internet via dial-up for individual computer or those on a LAN/WAN without a gateway

Windows NT includes support for both the older SLIP and PPP standards. If your server supports both, use PPP, which has stronger authorization.

Peer-to-Peer Sharing

Peer-to-Peer sharing is an optional service for Windows NT Workstation installations, allowing resource sharing of any or all resources "owned" by the computer. These resources are usually drives (or volumes), directory structures, or printers. How and what is shared depends upon your company's security work policies. You can turn this capacity on or off using the User Rights Policy Editor.

The security for peer sharing is user-level based on the accounts established on the server. If you don't have server-based account validation, you can use share-level security for each resource. This works identically in Windows NT as it did in Windows 95 and Windows 3.11.

Summary

Windows NT has many hardware restrictions that most DOS and Windows users will be unaccustomed to and probably consider unnecessarily cumbersome. It is not without cause. This provides easy portability to other hardware platforms.

Just think. If there were some major technological breakthrough and suddenly systems were 2,500 percent faster for the price of today's desktop system, it wouldn't be too difficult or take too long for Windows NT to be ported to that platform!

Whenever possible, use hardware that is on the HCL. Remember that if it is not on the HCL, it might not work; or you might have to wait for driver support and, most likely, Microsoft technical support will not provide support for it.

Before buying any hardware not listed on the HCL, find out whether there are drivers available for Windows NT. Although this is a new concept, it does serve a good purpose. Save yourself headaches and buy supported hardware.

As with so many things, success with any Windows NT setup depends upon careful planning. Part of planning should include pilot setup testing, anticipation of after-installation user support needs, and user training. The more effort you put in planning the installation, the less effort you'll spend putting out fires.

Installing Windows NT Workstation

by Sean Mathias

CHAPTER 3

IN THIS CHAPTER

Installing Windows NT Workstation is very different from installing DOS or previous versions of Windows. Remember that Windows NT is a true operating system in itself. Additionally, there are several methods for installing Windows NT Workstation depending on your system type (Intel *x*86 or RISC), current system configuration, and media type. The supported installation media are CD-ROM or network installation. Floppy-disk installation is no longer supported and disks are not provided, nor is there a utility to make installation disks.

Setup: Step by Step

Setup for Intel- and RISC-based systems differs slightly and therefore will be discussed separately where appropriate. Also note that if you are installing Windows NT on a portable system using PC Card devices that you want to configure during setup, the devices must be inserted prior to starting setup.

The following are the supported installation methods for Windows NT Workstation 4:

- Using the three setup disks and CD-ROM drive (Intel)
- Booting from CD-ROM (RISC systems and supported Intel systems)
- Installing from a network share

NOTE

If you do not have the Windows NT Workstation setup disks or you need to re-create them, you can run the `winnt` or `winnt32` utility found on the Windows NT Workstation CD-ROM. From a DOS prompt or within Windows 3.x, run `winnt /o`; from Windows 95 or another version of Windows NT, run `winnt32 /o`. Another useful switch is the `/b` option. This option can be used from MS-DOS (`winnt /b`) or from an existing Windows NT installation (`winnt32 /b`). When you use this option, the install program copies all of the files necessary for setup to a directory on your local hard drive, eliminating the need for boot floppies and expediting the install process by using files from a hard disk rather than a CD-ROM.

To begin setup from the setup disks or CD-ROM, perform the following steps:

1. Turn off your computer.
2. Insert the disk labeled Windows NT Setup Boot Disk or, if your system BIOS supports bootable CD-ROMs, insert the Windows NT CD into the drive.
3. Turn on your computer.

For RISC-based systems, also perform these steps:

4. At the ARC screen, choose Run a Program from the menu.
5. At the command prompt, type `cd:\`*platform*`\setupldr` and press Enter.

To begin setup from a network share, perform the following steps:

1. Connect to the network share where the Windows NT Workstation 4 setup files are located.

2. If you are using a previous version of Windows NT, change to the appropriate directory for your hardware platform and run the `winnt32.exe` program; otherwise, run the `winnt.exe` program.

3. When the setup dialog shown in Figure 3.1 appears, choose Continue.

FIGURE 3.1.

The Windows NT Workstation 4 setup dialog.

The setup program copies the necessary files to your local machine. Then, when the copying is finished, it prompts you to restart your computer and continue setting up Windows NT Workstation 4.

> **NOTE**
>
> Previous versions of DOS, Windows 3.x, and OS/2 can be upgraded to Windows NT Workstation 4 or configured to dual-boot. Windows 95, however, cannot be upgraded. Windows NT Workstation 4 must be installed to a separate directory and configured to dual-boot.

Character Mode Setup

After you have finished copying files and restarted your computer, or you have begun setup from floppy disk or bootable CD-ROM, you are in the beginning phase of the character mode portion of Windows NT setup.

At this point, setup consists of a character-based blue screen similar to the old MS-DOS setup. In the bottom border of the screen is any pertinent information related to the current setup procedure—the current file being copied or loaded, for example, or various options that might be available at a given time.

The character-mode blue screen with Windows NT setup in the top-left corner appears and initial system files are loaded, as shown in the status filed in the bottom border of the screen.

If this is the first time you have run Windows NT Workstation setup on this machine, press Enter to continue setup. If you have a another version of Windows NT or have had a failed installation attempt, you will see an option to repair a damaged Windows NT installation.

At any point in setup, you can press F1 for help on the current item, or you can press F3 to exit the setup program. If you exit setup, you need to rerun setup later to install Windows NT Workstation 4. Typically, you do not want to end setup after it has begun unless there is a problem. If you do end setup, you probably can still boot to your previous OS, depending on how far the setup process went and how you chose to configure setup. Unless you reached the point of specifying where to install Windows NT and elected to upgrade your previous OS, you will be able to boot to your previous system when you restart the computer. If you chose to upgrade your current OS, the results will be unpredictable and you will probably have to successfully complete the installation of Windows NT or reinstall your previous OS.

Mass Storage Device Detection

After the initial process of loading the necessary device drivers and files needed for setup and making selections about your system type, Windows NT setup runs a mass storage device detection process to locate hard drives, CD-ROM drives, and SCSI or RAID controllers in your system. If you are using a controller or CD-ROM that is not on the Hardware Compatibility List (HCL), you need to have a driver disk for it available at this time. If you do not have the necessary drivers for your storage devices, Windows NT might not be able to find an appropriate location to install to.

First is the detection and specification of mass storage devices. CD-ROM drives (IDE and SCSI), hard disk drives, and SCSI and RAID controllers are detected here. Additional device controllers and storage devices can be explicitly specified here, as well as hardware for which you have an OEM-supplied driver disk. To specify additional drives, adapters, or controllers, press S. You are presented with a list of possible devices and given an option of Other (Requires disk provided by a hardware manufacturer).

If you have installed a device that is supported but is not detected, you can try to manually specify it, but you probably have a configuration problem that prevented Windows NT setup from detecting it.

To install support for a device for which you have a driver disk, select the Other option and provide the OEM-supplied disk when prompted. When a dialog is presented with the various devices supported by the supplied driver, select the appropriate device and press Enter. Windows NT setup will need to copy a few files from the disk at a later point in setup, so keep the disk available. It is also a good idea to keep all such device disks with your Windows NT setup boot disks and an emergency repair disk (discussed later in this chapter) in the event that you must reinstall Windows NT at a later time.

When you have finished specifying mass storage devices or all mass storage devices have been detected, press Enter to continue setup.

System Settings and Installation Location

Windows NT setup now examines all hard disks that have been found for content and available disk space, and then determines which file system is installed on the drive. If another version of Windows NT is found on any drive, you are prompted to decide whether to upgrade the existing installation or install a fresh copy of Windows NT Workstation. To upgrade the existing installation, press Enter; to install a fresh copy, press N.

Setup displays a list of hardware and software components of the current system as detected. This lists the computer type, display, keyboard and keyboard layout, and the pointing device. If you would like to change any items on the list, use the arrow keys to select the appropriate item, press Enter, and select the correct setting. When the settings are correct, press Enter.

You are now presented with a list of detected hard disks and partitions. Select the partition to which you want to install Windows NT Workstation 4 and press Enter. To create a partition on a drive with free space, use the arrow keys to select the partition, press C, specify the partition size, and press Enter.

To delete an existing partition, use the arrow keys to select the partition and press D. You are presented with a screen asking you to confirm that you want to delete the selected partition and warning you that all information contained will be lost. To delete the partition, press L. To go back and not delete the partition, press Esc.

When you are satisfied with the partition configuration and have selected a partition to install Windows NT Workstation to, press Enter.

Windows NT setup lists the partition to which you have chosen to install Windows NT Workstation 4; its file system type, partition size, and space free; and disk ID. Select the file system that you want to use for this partition—NTFS or FAT—and press Enter. If security is an issue or you intend to use drives larger than 2GB, I recommend NTFS as the file system for its advanced security capabilities and its ability to efficiently manage large drive volumes. In a standalone configuration or on dual-boot systems, FAT would be the appropriate choice.

Provide the directory name to install Windows NT Workstation 4 to. Make your naming selection carefully, because you will be unable to change this name later without reinstalling.

You are now prompted to indicate whether you would like Windows NT setup to perform an exhaustive secondary examination of your hard disks. To allow the examination, press Enter (and go to lunch). To skip the exhaustive examination, press Esc. Basically, the exhaustive secondary examination is similar to a surface scan by the old ScanDisk program in DOS. It thoroughly checks your drive for errors, but it is time-consuming. If this is a new drive or you believe it might be deteriorating in performance, you might want to use this option. However, if this drive has worked flawlessly in a previous OS, you can probably choose to skip this step.

Windows NT setup now builds a list of files that need to be copied and begins the copy process. The current file being copied is displayed in the bottom-right corner of the screen with a progress indicator in the center of the screen.

When the file copying is complete, Windows NT setup initializes your default configuration, and you are prompted to restart your computer to continue setup. Press Enter to restart your computer and continue.

Windows Portion of Setup

When your computer restarts, you are presented with the Windows NT boot menu. The installation reinitializes itself by default; do not choose another selection or you might have to begin setup all over again.

When Windows NT starts its Windows mode, setup continues and you are presented with a Software License Agreement (SLA). If, after reading this, you do not agree to the terms and choose No, setup closes. If you agree to the terms, select Yes.

Setup now reinitializes and continues copying files needed to complete setup. The rest of the setup process takes place using a setup wizard similar to that found in Windows 95. The initial screen advises you that the Wizard will guide you through the rest of the setup process. The next three steps in the setup process are as follows:

- Gathering information about your computer
- Installing Windows NT Networking
- Finishing setup

Gathering Information About Your Computer

When you are ready to continue, select Next. Setup now prepares your directory for Windows NT, displaying the progress in a progress bar. If at any time you want to go back and change a selection you have made, select the Back button.

You are now provided with a list of setup options, listed here:

- Typical (recommended)
- Portable (includes mobile computing support)
- Compact (if there is little available disk space)
- Custom (to select components individually)

The Typical option installs Windows NT with a standard set of options for things such as wallpapers and migrating programs from a previous version of Windows, and it automatically begins network and printer installation. The Portable option is ideal for installing on laptop computers because it automatically adds support for mobile computing and minimizes the optional files installed to conserve disk space. Compact is similar to Portable, except it does not install mobile computing support; it installs only the minimum files necessary to run Windows NT. Lastly, Custom allows the user to make all selections about what components are installed. This is my preferred method because it provides much better control over the install process.

Make your selection and choose Next. Regardless of which selection you make, you can go back after installation is complete and use the Add/Remove programs applet in Control Panel to install additional Windows NT components.

You are now prompted to enter your name and organization for registration. After you have provided this information, select Next. You now need to provide a name for the computer. This name can be up to 15 characters and should not contain any spaces. If you are on a network, consult your system administrator; there might be a standard naming convention that you must follow. Also, it is advisable to use only letters and numbers (no additional characters such as asterisks or underscores).

You are then prompted to provide the password for the administrator account for this computer. Again, you might want to consult your system administrator if on a network because a standard administrator password might be in use. When you have entered your password and confirmed it, select Next.

> **NOTE**
>
> Be sure to use a password you will not forget or record and store it in a safe place, because you might need this in the future if you encounter problems or need to reconfigure your system. If you forget the administrator password and have no other administrator accounts, you need to reinstall Windows NT Workstation to re-create the administrator account and specify a new password.
>
> Also note that passwords in Windows NT are case-sensitive. This means that Password, password, and PASSWORD are not the same. You must enter your password exactly as you entered it when you created the account.

Next, you are prompted to decide whether you want to create an emergency repair disk. It is recommended that you do create one in the event that your installation becomes corrupted and you need to repair it. If your installation becomes corrupted and you do not have an emergency repair disk, you might have to reinstall from scratch. Note that having an emergency repair disk is still not a guarantee that a corrupted system can be recovered, but you stand a better chance. Various system and registry files are placed on this repair disk. In the event that the system becomes corrupted, you use the emergency repair process and provide this disk to give Windows NT a good starting point to recover from any corruption or misconfiguration.

If you selected the Custom Setup option earlier, you are now prompted to select the Windows NT components that you want to install. The component categories are listed as follows:

- **Accessibility Options**. Options to change keyboard, sound display, and mouse behavior for people with physical impairments.
- **Accessories**. Optional applications such as calculator, Internet Jumpstart kit, and Imaging. These are some optional applets that are certainly not critical but are useful in many day-to-day functions.
- **Communication**. Communications utilities for online services.
- **Games**. The ever-present productivity killers.
- **Microsoft Exchange**. Electronic mail and messaging utilities.
- **Multimedia**. Programs for playing sound, video, and animation on multimedia-enabled systems.

To select an entire category, click on the corresponding check box. To select individual components of a category, highlight the category and select Details; check or clear the box next to each component as appropriate. When you are satisfied with the selections, select OK. The Reset button sets all categories back to their default selections. Information about the amount of space needed to install the components and available disk space is listed in the bottom-left corner. When you have completed your selections, click Next.

Installing Windows NT Networking

After you make your selections for Windows NT components, you are presented with an informational dialog that shows Installing Windows NT Networking as the next phase of setup. Click Next to begin installing the networking components of Windows NT Workstation.

You are given the option to not install Windows NT Networking at this time or to participate in a network. If you choose to not install networking support now, you can install it at any time after setup has completed by running the Network applet in Control Panel.

If you choose to install Windows NT Networking support, you have the option of choosing how you are to be connected to the network—either physically wired to it using some form of network adapter and communications medium, or remotely connected through the use of a modem.

If you choose not to install Windows NT Networking at this time, you are presented with an informational dialog stating that the last step is Finishing Setup. Click Next to finish the setup process and skip to the next section.

To configure Windows NT Networking, use the following procedure:

1. Select Wired to the Network or Remote Access to the Network as appropriate, and then click Next.
2. Click the Start Search or Select from List button to install a network adapter.

3. When all network adapters have been installed, choose Next.

4. Select the network protocols you will use. The default protocol is TCP/IP or IPX/ SPX, depending on any previous network software you might have had on your system. NetBEUI is also listed as an option, but it is no longer the default protocol for Microsoft networking. If the protocol you need is not listed, choose the Select from List button, which lists all available protocols. The only other communications protocol available is AppleTalk. Typically, most users will use one or more of the three defaults listed.

5. A default list of network services to be installed is displayed. If you require additional services, choose the Select from List button.

6. When all desired network services have been selected, choose Next.

7. You are informed that Windows NT is now ready to install the selected network components. Click Next to install Windows NT Networking or Back to make changes.

8. Depending on the adapters, protocols, and services selected, you are prompted for configuration information. If you are unsure of the correct configurations, consult your system administrator.

9. After all adapters, protocols, and services have been installed and configured, you are given a bindings configuration dialog where you can enable or disable specific bindings. If this is necessary, consult your systems administrator.

10. A dialog informs you that Windows NT is ready to start the network. Click Next to continue.

11. If the network fails to start, go back and change your configuration settings where necessary. Usually this will be due to an improperly configured network adapter. At times, it might be necessary to exit setup and run the configuration disk for the network adapter to obtain the correct settings. If this is the case, I recommend completing setup without installing network support, because this step can be completed after setup is complete. This saves you from having to repeat the entire setup process again. To install Windows NT with no networking support, you need to click the Back button until you reach the screen described in step 1, and then deselect any network options.

12. Decide whether this computer will be a member of a workgroup or participate in a domain environment. If it is to participate in a domain environment, an account for the computer must be created in that domain. The system administrator can do this on a domain controller or can provide a username and password to use to create the account.

13. Provide the name of the workgroup or domain to which this computer will belong. If using a domain, check the Create Computer Account in the Domain box if necessary.

14. If needed, you are prompted for a username and password with the right to create computer accounts on the domain. Provide this information and click OK.

3

INSTALLING
WINDOWS NT
WORKSTATION

Provided everything goes smoothly, the networking components are now installed and configured properly. If you experience extensive problems, continue setup without installing Windows NT Networking and finish setup of Windows NT. After setup is complete, you can install Windows NT Networking by choosing the Network applet in Control Panel and following the same process as just described.

Finishing Setup

Several dialog boxes are displayed as Windows NT configures your computer and creates menus and groups. You are then prompted to specify date and time properties for this system. On the Time Zone tab, select the time zone appropriate for your locale. If applicable, select Automatically adjust clock for daylight savings changes. Now select the Date & Time tab and adjust the date and time as needed. When this is complete, choose Close.

Windows NT setup now attempts to detect your display adapter. The screen will blink black and come back with a dialog stating which display adapter the setup program has found. Select OK and begin configuring your display settings.

Provided the display adapter was detected properly, configure the adapter with the resolution, color depth, and refresh rate as desired (within the recommended settings of the manufacturer). When you have selected the desired settings, choose the Test button. You are informed that the new mode will be tested. Select OK. When the mode is tested, a bitmap of colors and patterns showing the screen size is displayed. After a few seconds, you are returned to the setup program. If the bitmap appeared correctly, select Yes and then choose OK. If it did not appear correctly, choose No and reconfigure your settings.

If the display adapter was incorrectly detected, accept the default setting for now. You can reconfigure it or specify another display adapter after setup completes by using the Display applet in Control Panel.

At this point, Windows NT setup completes copying the necessary files to their permanent directory structure; updates all shortcuts, groups, and menus; removes temporary files; sets security information on files; and saves your configuration.

The process of saving the configuration consists of writing all configuration information to backup files located in `systemroot\repair`. Before completion of saving the configuration information, you are prompted to provide a high-density, formatted disk to create the emergency repair disk if you opted to create one earlier in setup. When this is complete, you are prompted to restart your computer. When you restart your computer, Windows NT will be installed and configured and you can begin using it or making modifications as necessary.

Summary

Now you can unclench your fists and stop gritting your teeth. It really is not too difficult to install Windows NT Workstation. If you are able to install Windows 95 in three days or less, this should pose no problem to you at all.

This chapter has touched on almost every aspect of installing Windows NT and should be able to help you make your choices during installation. You should now be able to resolve any potential problems that you might encounter during the course of installation.

3

INSTALLING
WINDOWS NT
WORKSTATION

Troubleshooting Setup

*by Paul Cassel and
Jefferson M. Mousseau*

IN THIS CHAPTER

CHAPTER 4

In a perfect world, setups would work perfectly every time. In an almost perfect world, Windows NT could diagnose and resolve any problems stemming from its own installation. However, we don't live in either such worlds.

The reality is that many Windows NT Workstation setups will be problematic to do and require after-the-act tuning. For the most part, the standard Microsoft documentation won't be able to help you when you run into those little glitches, because, by definition, if Microsoft had anticipated the specific problems, it would have fixed them.

The problem with all installations—Windows NT Workstation as well as any other operating system—is that there is no way the setup program or the vendor can anticipate all the combinations and permutations of hardware and existing software that exist in the field. Even in the most homogeneous corporate settings, differences in hardware crop up, because computer manufacturers usually make their products to a nominal specification.

For example, computer manufacturer Such-and-Such will catalog a machine for six months. Over that period, the machine might have several video cards. So even if a company orders the same machine for itself, it might find that it gets different video cards depending upon when it buys during the production run.

There is nothing wrong or unethical about this practice. When you buy a car, you don't know the manufacturer of the pistons. For all you know, you and your neighbor buying seemingly identical cars might, due to production differences, have engines with different pistons. There is no way this will affect the operation of your respective cars.

Unfortunately, this isn't true in computers. A manufacturer can't anticipate what software vendors will do or how you will use your computers. Thus, they might use components during a production run that won't operate satisfactorily with some combination of application and operating system or the future releases of either one. So it's all too easy for a manufacturer to make a computer that won't work or won't work easily with some future software release.

As the computer industry settles down, these hardware problems are growing more rare—but they still do occur. Chapter 5, "Not-Ready-for-Plug-and-Play Hardware," addresses hardware problems. The following sections go over software-based problems and some solutions.

The Trouble-Free Setup

The right setup is the one that goes smoothly and doesn't need any troubleshooting. Although nothing can absolutely assure that this will occur, you can increase your chances of success by taking a few precautions. In some cases, these precautions aren't practical—but if they are, heed them.

The first software problem area stems from setting up Windows NT Workstation over an existing Windows. Microsoft openly encourages this, but it's the most common software-based cause of failed setups or erratic Windows NT operations.

The problems from an upgrade setup come from the pre-NT installation. Most Windows installations contain bits and pieces of detritus from installed, then removed, applications, utilities, parts of Windows itself, and drivers. The most troublesome aspect of this detritus are those obsolete drivers, which come from removed or upgraded hardware, as well as newer versions of the drivers themselves.

When you install a new Windows, NT or another Windows version, over an existing installation, your new setup inherits all the problems of the existing Windows and generally stirs up some new ones of its own. A properly installed Windows NT Workstation is an amazingly robust operating system. An improperly installed Windows NT Workstation is only as stable as the basic system minus the sum of its inherited errors.

An Ideal Standalone Example

A typical Windows NT Workstation installation might have the following characteristics: a disk partitioned into a FAT16 and an NTFS volume, with the FAT16 volume being the boot volume. The boot volume hosts MS-DOS and the boot loader part of NT. The nonloader part of NT exists on an NTFS volume.

The following is an ideal NT setup example, which will result in an installation having those characteristics. If you want your setup to result in a different outcome, vary the following steps as needed:

1. Create an MS-DOS boot disk with real-time (DOS) drivers for any hardware not inherently supported by the MS-DOS operating system. Typically, this requires only drivers for your CD-ROM drive. Also include the two DOS utilities FDISK and FORMAT on this disk.

2. Boot from the floppy disk. Make sure all peripherals work as expected.

3. Run FDISK to partition your disk into two volumes. The primary partition (drive C:) will host the FAT16 volume. The extended partition will host the NTFS volume. Size the partitions accordingly.

4. Leave the extended FAT16 volume as one large partition. That is, don't create any additional logical drives.

5. Format both partitions as FAT16.

6. Install the MS-DOS operating system on drive C:. This will make drive C: bootable.

7. Boot the computer from the floppy disk you made in step 1. This will make your peripherals available. Configure your drive C: MS-DOS setup to meet your hardware needs.

8. Run the Windows NT Workstation setup program. When prompted, convert the extended partition to NTFS, but leave the primary partition as FAT16. This will result in a dual boot setup, allowing you the bootup options of Windows NT, Windows NT in VGA mode, and MS-DOS.

9. Install your applications.

The preceding steps will, if run on compatible hardware, almost always result in a good solid installation of Windows NT Workstation.

Few field situations permit this ideal setup. This chapter covers some time-saving tips about installing Microsoft Windows Workstation 4, coupled with some traps that readers should be aware of and some solutions to common setup woes.

Installation Switches

A number of extremely useful options are available to users when installing Windows NT Workstation 4. For instance, the /U switch, when used with the optional /S switch, enables users to install Windows NT 4 unattended. So if you are in charge of installing NT Workstation on a number of computers, you might want to consider using this option, because it can potentially save a lot of time.

By default, NT Workstation creates three installation disks when installing from the CD-ROM or from a network. This is when knowing about the /B switch can be very useful. This switch allows users to bypass the creation of the three Windows NT Workstation install disks. This is useful if you are installing NT from a CD-ROM or network connection and do not require the disks to initiate an install. On the other hand, if you need to create these disks without installing NT, typing winnt /o at the command prompt enables you to make three Windows NT Workstation 4 installation disks.

The following is a complete list of the switches available to you. You can also view this list by typing winnt /? ¦ more at the command prompt if you are installing from DOS, or typing winnt32 /? ¦ more if you are installing from DOS or upgrading from a previous version of NT:

```
WINNT [/S[:]sourcepath] [/T[:]tempdrive] [/I[:]inffile] [/O[X]] [/X ¦ [/F]
 [/C]] [/B] [/U[:scriptfile]] [/R[X]:directory]

/S[:]sourcepath This is a rarely if ever needed switch. See /B
Specifies the source location of Windows NT files.
Must be a full path of the form x:\[path] or
\\server\share[\path].
The default is the current directory.
/T[:]tempdrive
Specifies a drive to contain temporary setup files.
If not specified, Setup will attempt to locate a drive for you.
/I[:]inffile
Specifies the filename (no path) of the setup information file.
The default is DOSNET.INF.
/O      Create boot floppies only.
/OX     Create boot floppies for CD-ROM or floppy-based installation.
/X      Do not create the Setup boot floppies.
/F      Do not verify files as they are copied to the Setup boot floppies.
/C      Skip free-space check on the Setup boot floppies you provide.
/B      Floppyless operation
/U      Unattended operation and optional script file (requires /s).
/R      Specifies optional directory to be installed.
/RX     Specifies optional directory to be copied.
```

Although NT Workstation can be installed on computers with different types of processors, users installing it from DOS or the command (not shell) prompt of Windows 95 can speed up the installation process. At the DOS command prompt, start SMARTDRIVE. On a computer with an Intel system with 64MB of RAM, type `smartdrv 16000` at the command prompt. When the installation of NT begins and files are being copied to the temporary directory on the hard drive of the computer, DOS will have more cache to store the information, and users should notice an increase in the speed at which the NT installation occurs.

> **NOTE**
>
> If your setup seems to be running very slowly while copying setup files from the CD-ROM to the hard disk, the likeliest cause is the lack of a disk cache.
>
> You can either wait out the copying process, which can take several hours, or reboot, delete the partly installed temporary directory, then start MS-DOS's SMARTDRIVE from the command line.
>
> After launching the disk cache, rerun setup.

Setup Failures

Usually, setup will run to conclusion, and only then you'll discover any problems. In some cases, setup won't run. Luckily, those instances are rare. Here are a few examples of what can occur and the solutions:

Setup fails to make floppy disk set.

This seems to occur in some systems with embedded but disabled IDE controllers.

Solutions:

1. Run setup bypassing floppy disk creation.
2. Use floppies made during a Windows NT Workstation setup where the target directories and volumes are identical to the current machine.

During a network setup, Windows NT 4 hangs or crashes in Win32k.sys.

Solution:

Get the Service Pack 3 or higher from Microsoft.

4

TROUBLESHOOTING
SETUP

When using an upgrade version of Windows NT Workstation, setup refuses to recognize the distribution media of the upgraded system as valid.

Setup might demand a previous version of Windows NT's CD-ROM.

Solution:

Each upgrade version of Windows NT Workstation is keyed to a particular product or set of products. Make sure your Windows NT upgrade is intended to upgrade the operating system you currently own. If not, exchange your distribution disk for the proper one.

After an interrupted setup, the new setup has multiple identical options during bootup.

Solution:

This is a problem caused by having spurious entries in BOOT.INI. To solve:

1. Boot to DOS using a floppy disk if you don't have a dual boot setup. You can also launch an DOS session under NT.

2. Enter the command

   ```
   attrib -r -s c:\boot.ini
   ```

   to allow you to edit the file. To be safe, copy this file to another name, such as BOOT.BAK. This will allow you to restore your setup in case of an editing error.

3. Launch an editor, such as DOS's EDIT. Figure 4.1 shows a BOOT.INI file with some spurious entries loaded into Notepad.

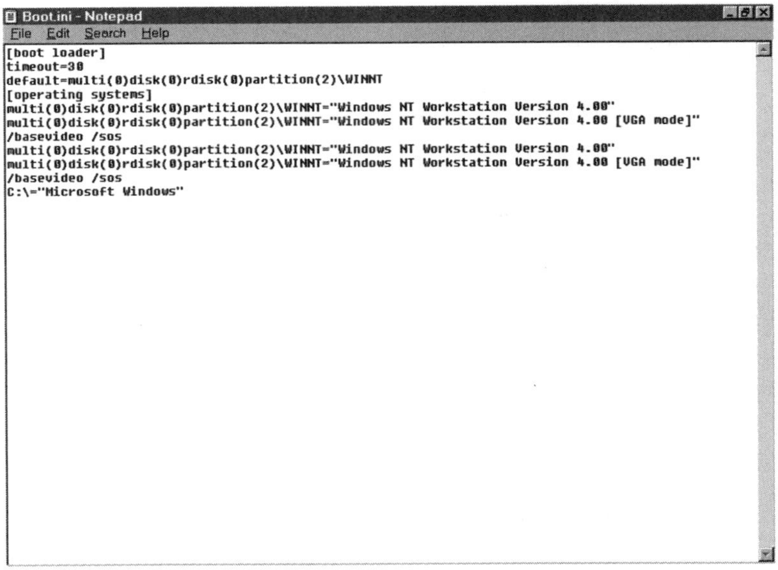

FIGURE 4.1.

An interrupted Windows NT Workstation setup can result in double vision.

```
Boot.ini - Notepad
File  Edit  Search  Help
[boot loader]
timeout=30
default=multi(0)disk(0)rdisk(0)partition(2)\WINNT
[operating systems]
multi(0)disk(0)rdisk(0)partition(2)\WINNT="Windows NT Workstation Version 4.00"
multi(0)disk(0)rdisk(0)partition(2)\WINNT="Windows NT Workstation Version 4.00 [VGA mode]"
/basevideo /sos
multi(0)disk(0)rdisk(0)partition(2)\WINNT="Windows NT Workstation Version 4.00"
multi(0)disk(0)rdisk(0)partition(2)\WINNT="Windows NT Workstation Version 4.00 [VGA mode]"
/basevideo /sos
C:\="Microsoft Windows"
```

4. Edit out the spurious entries.

5. Save the file.

When you reboot, you'll be rid of those extra entries.

Windows NT won't install on large EIDE drives.

Solution:

Windows NT 4 will run only on certain IDE extension schemes. These schemes extend IDE to beyond a half a gigabyte. The supported schemes are

- Logical Block Addressing (LBA)
- ONTrack Disk Manager
- EZDrive
- Extended Cylinder Head Sector (ECHS)

You need to switch to one of these schemes before using Windows NT Workstation as your operating system.

You're unsure of your hardware, or setup fails and you suspect a hardware conflict.

Given the wide variety of hardware, lack of standardization—even within a hardware vendor—and users' proclivity to fiddle with upgrades, this is more prevalent than most people think.

Solution:

Microsoft has included a utility, HQTOOL, to address this problem. To use HQTOOL:

1. Load the distribution CD-ROM in your drive.
2. Insert a formatted floppy in a floppy drive, usually drive A:.
3. Navigate to the \support\hqtool directory.
4. Run the batch file from the GUI by clicking on it. If you are at the command line interface, enter

   `makedisk`

   Figure 4.2 shows the `makedisk` utility running in a DOS session under Windows NT Workstation 4.

5. Restart the computer with the floppy drive made in steps 1 through 4 left in the drive.
6. After a bit of preparation, you will see a DOS graphics display allowing you to view various aspects of the local hardware. You can change what aspects you view by clicking on the buttons at the bottom of the display. To save the results of the hardware detection, click on the Save button.

FIGURE 4.2.

The makedisk *utility is the first step in hardware detection for mysterious computer installations.*

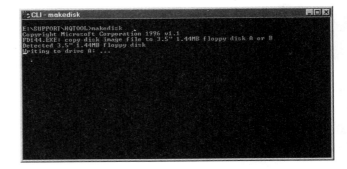

The Save button will create a DOS text file, NTHQ.TXT, containing the results of the detection. The information isn't particularly user-friendly, but it can help sort out mysterious problems. A file, README.TXT, will help you use the contents of NTHQ.TXT if the format isn't familiar to you. Figure 4.3 shows part of an NTHQ.TXT file.

FIGURE 4.3.

The NTHQ.TXT file contains the results of the hardware detection routine.

```
Nthq.txt - Notepad
File  Edit  Search  Help
Hard Disk Boot Sector Protection: OFF.
No problem to write to MBR

ISA Plug and Play Add-in cards detection Summary Report

Number of ISA PnP cards detected: 1


Summary for ISA PnP card number 1
-------------------------------------------------
Vendor ID: CTL0044
Serial Number: 000EB82E
Reported Checksum: 0xF5
PNP Version:   1.0
Vendor Ver.:   10
Device Description: Creative SB32 PnP
Device ID: CTL0031
Doesn't Support I/O Range Checking
Vendor Defined Logical Device Control Registers:
None

Device Description: Audio

Dependant Function 0
===========================
Best Possible Configuration

IRQ lines supported:
0x5
DMA Channels supported:
1

DMA Channel Characteristics:
8 bit only
Logical device is not a bus master
DMA may execute in count by byte mode
```

NOTE

On some distribution disks, the NTHQ.TXT file reports that the utility is still in beta testing. This is apparently something overlooked at Microsoft Central. It doesn't adversely affect the operation of the utility.

The distribution disk has a similar utility for detection of SCSI hardware. This utility, SCSITOOL, is located in the following directory:

```
\support\scsitool
```

To run this utility, navigate to the directory and run MAKEDISK.BAT with a formatted floppy in a drive, then reboot. You interpret the results similarly to the HQTOOL utility.

Setup or Windows NT Workstation runs erratically or freezes with a blue screen on startup.

Solution:

These symptoms stem from a huge array of issues, but you can eradicate many of them by taking these steps:

1. Run the HQTOOL utility described previously. Check very carefully to make sure no devices are trying to use the same base addresses, address ranges, IRQ, or other system resources.

2. Disable L2 cache in BIOS setup.

3. Disable any BIOS or video shadowing in BIOS setup.

4. Make sure there aren't any startup errors unrelated to NT's installation. Can you boot into MS-DOS using a floppy?

5. If all else fails, remove all optional hardware from your computer. If NT runs normally after this removal, add the hardware back one piece at a time until NT returns to its unsteady state. This should give you your culprit.

6. Disable any high-end features in nonoptional hardware. Windows NT Workstation 4 doesn't support the following features:

   - 32-bit I/O BIOS switch
   - Enhanced Drive Access
   - Multiple Block Addressing
   - Write Back Cache
   - Advanced Power Management features

Although these features shouldn't interfere with Windows NT Workstation, they don't do any good under it and might cause a problem; so if you can, disable them.

Choosing Alternative Setups

Unless you have a strong reason not to, run setup from the CD-ROM using no switches. If you've lost the distribution disks, then run with the /OX or the /B switches. If you choose to copy the contents of the CD to a hard disk and then run setup from there, keep in mind that the contents of an NT distribution directory can be quite large. The files for an Intel setup of Windows NT Workstation will eat up about 250MB of disk.

If you run setup from Windows and have setup hang or otherwise fail, you can use the un-documented /W switch. This will bypass many setup safety features, such as drive locking. Consider this option only in desperation and don't ask Microsoft for support if it fails. In most instances, you'll be better off doing a clean install rather than using the /W switch.

Failures After Setup Completes

This section describes some problems and their solutions for instances where setup ran to an apparent successful conclusion. These problems can crop up right after setup or years later.

The computer fails to do boot after a successful POST (Power On Self-Test).

These problems stem from major system errors. The following are some of the reasons:

- Corrupted Master Boot Record (MBR)
- Lost or incorrect CMOS information
- Corrupt partition information
- The boot loader, NTLDR, has become corrupted
- A peripheral card has lost contact with the mainboard
- A peripheral, such as a tape drive, has been left in an uncertain state
- And so forth

Solution:

To isolate the problem, see if you can boot into DOS using a floppy disk. If so, you may need to rerun setup using the Emergency Repair Disk (ERD). If not, you'll need to diagnose your system to clear up the hardware error. In some cases where hardware has entered an uncertain state, Windows NT Workstation will not soft-boot, but will boot all right after a complete power-down and startup, because this resets most hardware, thus clearing most uncertain states.

If your problems seem to be related to the partition table or the MBR, you can run FDISK again to clear the problem, but with data loss. Some third-party utilities claim to be able to restore lost partition tables or MBRs, too. The Resource Kit for Windows NT Workstation 4 has a utility, Diskprobe, that will allow you to examine and, to a limited extent, fix both the table and the MBR.

Most errors of this type result in your having to run FDISK to restore the partition and then setup Windows NT Workstation from scratch.

> **NOTE**
>
> Each fixed or hard disk in a computer has its own MBR. Windows NT Workstation 4 uses the MBR only on the first disk during startup.

NT startup fails after the boot loader initiates.

If your NT install hangs during the blue screen with the message

```
NTDETECT V1.X Checking Hardware
```

you probably have developed a hardware, driver, or hardware detection problem.

Solutions:

1. Try booting into VGA (fail-safe) mode if this is an option in BOOT.INI.

2. If you don't have a VGA mode option, edit BOOT.INI to add the /BASEVIDEO option. This will force VGA mode upon NT's startup and will eliminate video driver-based problems. Refer to Figure 4.1.

3. Add the /SOS switch to BOOT.INI to see a screen echo of the drivers as they are loaded. This will reveal the driver causing the problem. Refer to Figure 4.1.

4. If you suspect memory errors, add the /MAXMEM:*n* switch to BOOT.INI where :*n* is the RAM used, in megabytes. This will limit NT to a fixed amount of RAM. If your problem RAM exists above this ceiling, the /MAXMEM switch will reveal this fact. Windows NT Workstation will run in 8MB of RAM (a bit slowly to be sure), so the most extreme use of this switch is /MAXMEM:8.

You get a Stop 0x0000007B error.

This error comes from an inaccessible or corrupt Partition Boot Sector.

Solutions:

1. You have a virus. Boot into DOS and run a virus scan/cleaner.

2. You have activated LBA after partitioning the disk. Deactivate it. If you want to run LBA, you need to repartition the disk with LBA active and then set up Windows NT Workstation again.

3. You have a mechanical problem that has corrupted your Partition Boot Sector. You need to fix or replace the bad hardware, then see whether there is anything you can salvage from the existing setup. Usually, there isn't much, if anything, salvageable, and you need to run setup again.

4. Your experimenting with system programming has gone awry (this is the author's usual problem). Learn to program better with more skill or be less adventurous.

4

TROUBLESHOOTING SETUP

INSTALLING NT WITHOUT A CD-ROM DRIVE

If you don't have a CD-ROM drive and do have network access, you can install Windows NT Workstation from a remote computer's CD-ROM drive. You need the network drivers located on the NT Server distribution CD.

continues

continued

First make your hard disk bootable from DOS. Copy the network drivers from the \clients directory to a directory on your local hard disk. Start the network by entering the command

`Net use f:\\name\`*sharedname*

Substituting an available drive letter for the `f:`, the name of the computer having the shared CD-ROM drive for name, and the shared name of the CD-ROM device for *sharedname*.

Log on to the newly made drive (`f:` in this example), switch to the i386 directory, and then run setup as usual.

The Boot Process

As with other releases of Microsoft Windows NT Workstation, the boot process is often the area where the majority of troubleshooting occurs. Whether you are repairing corrupted boot files, such as the BOOT.INI or NTLDR, or tracking down conflicting IRQs, getting your hardware and NT to cooperate can sometimes be a time-consuming process. Ultimately, though, understanding NT's boot process helps increase your fundamental knowledge of the operating system and provides a good building block toward understanding its more complex functions and capabilities.

BOOT.INI

During some installations of Windows NT 4, it is possible for NT to incorrectly identify on what partition it has been placed. This information is contained in the BOOT.INI file, a hidden file located on the root of the boot or C:\> drive. You can use DOS's `attrib` command to change the attributes of this file in order to access it. If you've installed Windows NT 4 on an extended partition, your BOOT.INI file should look like this:

```
[boot loader]
timeout=30
default=multi(0)disk(0)rdisk(0)partition(2)\WINNT
[operating systems]
multi(0)disk(0)rdisk(0)partition(2)\WINNT="Windows NT Workstation Version 4.00"
multi(0)disk(0)rdisk(0)partition(2)\WINNT="Windows NT Workstation Version 4.00
[VGA mode]" /BASEVIDEO /SOS
C:\="MS Windows"
```

Terms of Reference

The terms of ARC or arcname reference for BOOT.INI are as follows:

- `multi` or `SCSI` refers to which bus—whether it is an AT-bus or a SCSI-bus—the system uses to access the NT 4 partition. SCSI can use the `multi` or `SCSI` arcnames, depending on the enabling of its BIOS. IDE uses `multi` only. For example, the first controller in IDE is `multi(0)`, the second, `multi(1)`.

- ■ `rdisk`, `disk` specifies the disk on which NT Workstation 4 was installed. `rdisk` is an element of `disk` allowing more than one LUN in a SCSI disk (rare). It also identifies the master and slave disks on a single IDE controller.

- ■ `disk` specifies the disk controller with which NT Workstation 4 can be accessed. In the previous example, NT Workstation was installed to be accessed with the first disk controller and as a result has a value of `0`.

- ■ `partition` specifies the partition of the disk on which NT Workstation 4 has been installed . In the previous example, NT is installed on an extended partition, and the value is `2`. Partitions are numbered starting from 1. Unused but allocated partitions aren't included in the count.

If you can't boot Windows NT Workstation 4 after installing it, check to see that all the entries in the BOOT.INI have been set to the correct value. This is another reason why you should install NT on an extended partition. If you have trouble accessing NT, you can boot to the DOS partition and then access the Windows NT 4 BOOT.INI file. Even if you specify to format the NT partition with NTFS, the system must reboot and run the convert utility to automatically convert the partition from FAT to NTFS for you. As a result, if you were unable to reboot, the partition should still be in FAT so that you can access it and check the partition.

If you have decided to install without a DOS partition and you were able to boot previously and make changes to the BOOT.INI, don't despair. There is help.

From the Internet, you can download a utility called NTFS File System Redirector for DOS/ Windows V1.1, written by Mark Russinovich and Bryce Cogswell. This utility enables you to read files on an NTFS partition from DOS by booting the workstation with a DOS boot disk. Then from a floppy containing NTFS File System Redirector and DOS's COPY.EXE, type `ntfsdos`. You can now access the NTFS partition and copy the BOOT.INI to a floppy disk, where you can make changes to it and then copy it back to the NTFS partition.

Troubleshooting Boot Errors

Like Windows NT Workstation 3.51, NT 4 uses the same type of boot process. So if you are familiar with troubleshooting NT boot problems, you will not have to jump through any hoops to feel comfortable here. Before restoring any of the following files, you should check the BOOT.INI file and make sure the values contained in it are set properly.

Boot NTLDR not found

If you receive the message `Boot NTLDR not found`, the NT's boot loader was either corrupted or deleted. You can restore the NTLDR.EXE file from the installation disks or the CD, and you should be able to boot your system.

4

TROUBLESHOOTING SETUP

NTDETECT failed

On Intel-based computers, NT 4 uses NTDETECT.COM to locate what type of hardware is installed on your system. If you receive the error `NTDETECT.COM failed`, you can restore from the installation disks or the CD, or you can copy from the install CD if NT was installed on a FAT partition.

File Format

Previous versions of Windows NT Workstation offered support for three file formats: FAT (File Allocation Table), NTFS (Microsoft's NT File System), and HPFS (OS/2's High Performance File System). Windows NT Workstation version 4 offers support for only two file formats: FAT and NTFS.

If security is not an issue when installing NT, choosing FAT might be a viable choice. However, if enhanced security is required, you should format the partition or drive using NTFS. If you format a drive in FAT and later decide that you need the enhanced security features of NTFS, this section shows you how the partition or drive can be converted from FAT to NTFS without losing any data.

Getting Help for Other Problems

No assemblage of setup errors and their solutions can possibly be complete, because new problems arise every day. By far the best resources for setup and other Windows NT Workstation woes is Microsoft's Knowledge Base. This is a database Microsoft maintains for all its products. It contains the collective experience of users, Solution Providers, field representatives, and support staff (AnswerPoint).

You can download the entire database from the FTP site:

`ftp.microsoft.com`

or search it from the Microsoft Web site:

`www.microsoft.com`

Some private sites such as that maintained by Windows NT Magazine:

`www.winntmag.com`

have their own versions of a Knowledge Base. These often contain information different from Microsoft's, but none of them are as large or comprehensive overall.

The Usenet is a hotbed of Windows NT Workstation interaction. Groups such as

`comp.os.ms-windows.nt.admin.misc`

are good places to exchange information and tips about Windows NT Workstation and related issues.

Online services, especially CompuServe, maintain forums dedicated to Windows NT Workstation support. In many cases, these forums are manned by users for peer-type support only, but the quality of the information is often as high as anywhere.

Finally, Microsoft maintains a support staff for non-OEM versions of Windows NT Workstation. The good support costs, but is often worth it. If you got your version of NT from a vendor such as Compaq, your first line of support is that vendor. The quality of this support varies enormously as you might suspect. If you're unhappy with your vendor's support of NT, you can always purchase the good stuff directly from Microsoft.

Summary

The topics covered in this chapter have provided you with the necessities to navigate through the sometimes less-than-perfect aspect of Windows NT Workstation's setup. Often, devices won't install as easily as they do on Windows 95. This should not cause users looking for a stable and secure operating environment to turn away from Windows NT Workstation 4.

Many corporations are deciding to pass on the opportunity to upgrade to Windows 95 and are migrating instead to Windows NT Workstation 4. They are making this decision based not just on the decreased licensing cost of upgrading from one operating system instead of two, but also based on the people hours involved in making two upgrades. In addition, commercial software and custom applications of a corporation, which ran predictably under Windows 3.*x* or Windows for Workgroups 3.11, need to be thoroughly tested and integrated. For many companies, such a move can't be taken lightly.

Windows NT Workstation 4 is improved over earlier releases, especially in the area of installation and detection. With these enhancements, users should find that troubleshooting, although not eradicated, is greatly reduced.

Not-Ready-for-Plug-and-Play Hardware

by Paul Cassel

CHAPTER 5

IN THIS CHAPTER

Windows NT Workstation version 4 uses hardware detection during its setup. This is a modest form of Microsoft's Plug and Play (PnP) initiative. During the process of installation, the setup program queries hardware using a database of known hardware profiles and adds known hardware to a list. This list, plus any additional hardware you tell setup about, tells setup which drivers to install.

Hardware and the Boot Process

When Windows NT Workstation starts, it executes a program, Ntdetect.com, right after NTLDR. This detects a few basic hardware components on Intel systems. They are

- Mouse
- Printer (parallel) ports
- Keyboard type
- Bus type
- Video card or subsystem
- Floppy disk drives
- Serial or other communication ports
- Computer ID (network)

> **NOTE**
>
> The architecture of RISC systems differs significantly from Intel systems. On these systems, Windows NT Workstation uses a program, Osloader.exe, to detect hardware. Rather than going to the hardware itself, Osloader.exe queries the firmware for hardware configuration.

When Ntdetect.com launches, it echoes

```
NTDECTECT V1.0 Checking Hardware..
```

to the screen. After it finds the basic hardware from the list, Windows NT Workstation's startup routine echoes

```
OS Loader V4.0
Press spacebar now to invoke Hardware Profile/Last Known Good menu
```

to the screen. This is the start of a bootup routine that will allow you to select a hardware profile. After allowing a short time to let you press the spacebar, Windows NT will allow you to choose from a menu of hardware profiles:

```
This menu allows you to select a hardware profile
to be used when Windows NT is started.
If your system is not starting correctly, then you may switch to a
```

```
previous system configuration, which may overcome startup problems.
IMPORTANT: System configuration changes made since the last successful
 startup will be discarded.

A New Configuration
Original Configuration

Use the up and down arrow keys to move the highlight
to the selection you want. Then press ENTER.
To switch to the Last Known Good Configuration, press 'L'.
To Exit this menu and restart your computer, press F3.

Seconds until the highlighted choice will be started automatically: 1
```

> **NOTE**
>
> You must have more than one hardware profile defined to see the screen described. To create a new hardware profile, see the section of that title just after this discussion.

At the next stage Windows NT Workstation loads.

Windows NT Workstation will highlight the first profile on the list; the one called A New Profile in the previous example. After you choose a profile, or let the selection time expire (thus letting NT make the choice for you), the boot process will load both the kernel and the Hardware Abstraction Layer. Then bootup will create the information in the Registry key, HKEY_LOCAL_MACHINE\SYSTEM from the file

```
[systemroot]\system32\config\system
```

Based on your choice in the hardware profile selection screen, Windows NT Workstation will choose a control set to use as the current control set. Figure 5.1 shows a Registry with two control sets, ControlSet001 and ControlSet002. In this case, ControlSet001 has been copied to the CurrentControlSet, which contains the profile for this Windows NT session.

Intel systems use the firmware (BIOS) INT13 to load this information into memory. RISC systems again call on Osloader to query firmware to locate and load into memory information about low-level hardware.

After creating the CurrentControlSet and initializing low-level hardware, the last stage of the primitive bootup starts with the following message:

```
Microsoft (R) Windows NT (TM) Version 4.0 (Build 1381)
1 System Processor (96 MB Memory)
```

This screen will also show any installed service packs. If you see this screen, it means that the kernel is initialized and it now has control of the computer.

The kernel then initializes the lowest-level devices, those having a Start value of 0 (see Figure 5.2). After having successfully started these, it moves to initializing device drivers identified by having a Start value of 1.

FIGURE 5.1.

The CurrentControlSet *is set during bootup, depending upon the information in the System file and the choice of hardware profile. This computer has two hardware profiles defined,* ControlSet001 *and* ControlSet002.

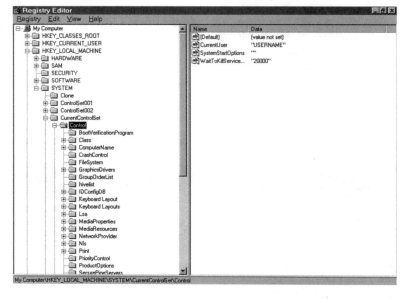

FIGURE 5.2.

The Start *value of* 0 *in this entry identifies this device as a low-level one.*

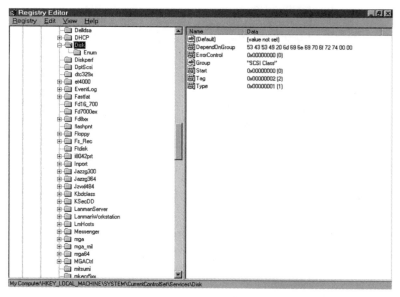

Each entry under Services for every ControlSet has a Start value. This value tells Windows NT Workstation when and if to load it. These values are

■ 0

Boot or lowest-level device drivers loaded by NTLDR in Intel systems and Osloader in RISC systems. These services are loaded before the kernel. Disk drives are in this category.

■ 1

Loaded and initialized concurrently with the kernel. These are low-level system drivers for such hardware as the floppy drives.

■ 2

Loaded by the Service Control Manager (SCM) for all sessions. These are the auto-loaded drivers such as the one for the Browser (see Figures 5.3 and 5.4).

FIGURE 5.3.

The Start *value of 2 identifies a service as being auto-loaded for every session. This entry is for the* Browser.

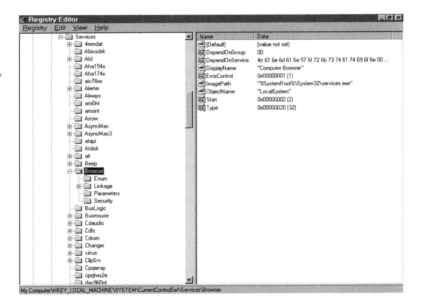

FIGURE 5.4.

The Service Control Manager (SCM) reflects the Start *value of 2 in the Registry. Note the second and third columns, labeled Status and Startup, respectively. The entry shown corresponds with the Registry entry shown in Figure 5.3.*

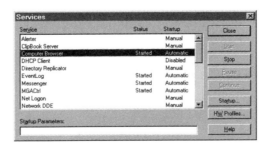

■ 3

These are the services loaded by the SCM on demand, as opposed to automatically for all sessions such as those with the Start value of 2.

■ 4

These are those services that are not to be loaded. Typically, these services are for hardware that NT knows about, but which isn't installed in the workstation. The exception to this is the file systems. These have a Start value of 4 but aren't disabled.

After loading services, the hardware part of the bootup process is completed. Each of the services also has an ErrorControl value telling the system what to do in case of an error starting the service. For example, the service Browser shown in Figure 5.3 has an ErrorControl value of 1. This causes NT to display a warning message, but continue to load other services and proceed with the bootup.

The ErrorControl values are

■ 0

Ignore errors in startup, continue with boot process, and show no warning message.

■ 1

Display a warning message. After displaying warning, continue with bootup.

■ 2

Automatically switch to LastKnownGood hardware profile and reinitialize the startup routine. If the LastKnownGood profile is in use, ignore error and proceed with startup.

■ 3

Same as 2, but fail to proceed if LastKnownGood hardware profile is in use and display failure message to screen.

Creating a New Hardware Profile

You need to be logged on with Administrator rights to create a new hardware profile. No lesser user rights will do for this system-level maintenance. The following are the steps to create a new profile:

1. Open the Control Panel.
2. Start the System applet.
3. Click the Hardware Profiles tab. Figure 5.5 shows the Hardware Profiles tab of the System applet.
4. Copy a current configuration to a new name.
5. Edit as desired.

FIGURE 5.5.

The Hardware Profiles tab of the System applet lists the current hardware profile for the local workstation.

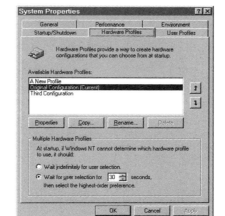

The Hardware Profiles tab also allows you to edit certain global settings for the hardware profile menu selection during the startup process, such as whether to automatically launch the highlighted choice and how long to await user input.

Figure 5.6 shows copying a profile to a new name. To do this, highlight the profile you wish to copy, click on the Copy button, then edit the popped-up dialog box with the new name for the copy. Two profiles can't share a name on the same computer.

FIGURE 5.6.

Creating a new profile starts by copying a current one.

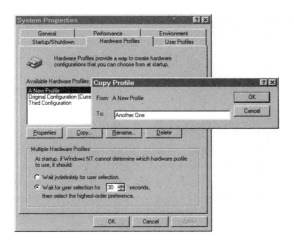

To edit the hardware profile after copying a profile to a new name, highlight the profile you want to edit, then click the Properties button. A dialog similar to the one in Figure 5.7 will appear. To delete a profile, click the Delete button with the target profile highlighted. You can't delete the configurations, so there are none.

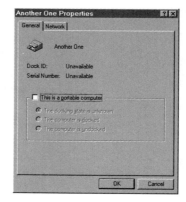

For example, to create a hardware profile that is the same as your Original Profile, but for a docked portable computer, do this:

1. Launch Control Panel.
2. Start the System applet.
3. Click the Hardware Profiles tab.
4. Click the Copy button to make a copy of the Original Configuration profile. Give it a new name, such as New Profile.
5. If necessary, highlight the new profile. Click the Properties button.
6. Click the General tab.
7. Check the box indicating this is a portable computer.
8. Select the appropriate docked state from the option box list.

You'll see additions and deletions to the Hardware Profile at the next bootup.

Adding Hardware

Unlike Windows 95, Windows NT Workstation is not true PnP, although some entries in the Registry imply PnP abilities. You cannot insert a sound card and have NT automatically detect it, prompt you for the driver disk, and automatically assign it an IRQ. This is true because NT does not allow hardware to directly access the hardware components of your system. As a result, with Windows NT 4, you will still find yourself manually configuring IRQs (interrupt requests) and addresses.

Windows NT Workstation does a good job of detecting existing hardware, so installing additional cards or peripherals isn't that much of a chore.

Existing Hardware

Before installing new hardware, you need to learn what you already have so you can make sure you don't install the new hardware in such a way that it conflicts with what's already installed. The way to do this in a running Windows NT Workstation installation is through the Windows NT Diagnostics program.

The Diagnostics program is a menu choice under Programs | Administrative Tools. Figure 5.8 shows this program after launching.

FIGURE 5.8.

The Windows NT Diagnostics program is a good way to learn the resources used by the current installation of Windows NT Workstation.

The most useful tab in Diagnostics for those installing new hardware or exploring problems with existing hardware is Resources. This tab has five different views:

- IRQ
- I/O Port
- DMA
- Memory
- Devices

The most problematic of these resources is IRQ. Figure 5.9 shows the IRQ display for the workstation shown in Figure 5.8.

Here's what the display in Figure 5.9 means:

- IRQ 0 (not shown here, but you can see it if you click on the Include HAL resources box) for the system timer.
- IRQ 1 is for the keyboard controller (chip 8042). You never want to set a peripheral for IRQ 1, or you'll risk interfering with the keyboard.

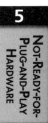

FIGURE 5.9.

*The IRQ screen of
Diagnostics is the single
most useful display for
determining what
resources are in use
or conflict.*

- IRQ 2 (not shown here, but you can see it if you click on the Include HAL resources box) is the cascaded port for the secondary programmable interrupt controller (PIC). This allows a total of 16 IRQs (each PIC can handle only 8).

- IRQ 3 is taken by a serial port with a Microsoft (MS) serial mouse.

- IRQ 4 is used by two serial ports. This could cause problems. In this machine, one port (COM3) is the modem, and COM1 is unused. If a user attaches a serial device, such as a tablet, to COM1, it can't be used at the same time as the modem without risking a device conflict.

- IRQ 5 is used by a sound card. In this setup, the user would have been better off configuring the sound card for another IRQ and the modem for IRQ 5 to avoid conflicts in serial devices.

- IRQ 6 is for the floppy drive. This is the standard IRQ for these types of devices.

- IRQ 12 is for the network interface card (NIC). This card is NE2000-compatible.

- IRQ 15 is for the SCSI controller.

Although IRQ conflicts cause the most device problems, don't ignore the other resource demands. Today, few devices use DMA channels, but those that do, such as sound cards and some tape backup devices, will not share those channels at all. The installation instructions for devices will mention whether they need DMA resources.

Devices require an address. In computer lingo, this is the I/O Port. Each port has a starting (base) address and a range. Figure 5.10 shows the I/O Port button display of Windows NT Diagnostics.

Figure 5.10 has the information for the parallel port highlighted. This shows that the port uses a base address of 0378 with a range of 3 to 037A. This is standard for the first parallel port, LPT1. The values in the I/O Port display are given in the hexadecimal (Base16) number system. If you subtract 378 from 37A, you end up with 3 in hexadecimal.

FIGURE 5.10.

The I/O Port display shows the base address and range for each device.

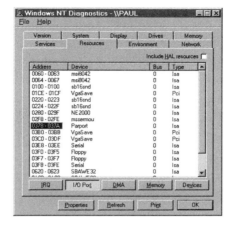

In rare cases, you'll end up with a memory address conflict. In DOS days, users stuffed as much as they could in "high DOS" to free up as much low DOS for their programs. This often caused conflicts between devices so stuffed. This isn't an issue with Windows NT, because the segmented 1MB maximum memory model of DOS (segment:offset) has been replaced with a flat memory model of enormously greater capacity. The DOS issues of "low" and "high" memory and their tiny capacities aren't relevant to Windows NT. Figure 5.11 shows the Memory display for a workstation.

FIGURE 5.11.

The Memory display for a workstation. This section has few conflicts under Windows NT, but was a real problem under DOS.

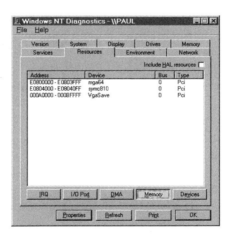

The only devices using this resource are the display adapter (first and third in the list), which has two distinct memory blocks, and the SCSI adapter, which has one.

Now for the New Hardware

Once you've determined what resources your computer still has free, you need to do only three more steps to complete the installation:

1. Physical installation
2. Setting component resources
3. Installing drivers

If the hardware uses manual settings for resources such as DIP switches or jumpers, set the new component before physical installation. If the hardware uses a setup program, as many now do, physically install the component, then run the setup program to configure the hardware to the resources available.

Adding drivers to Windows NT Workstation 4 isn't as straightforward as Windows 95. Whereas Windows 95 uses the Add Hardware applet and even detects all new hardware upon boot (or tries to), Windows NT remains mostly a manual procedure. This isn't necessarily a bad thing, because it gives you more control over the process, and very rarely, if ever, does NT insist it has found a nonexistent (or phantom) device as can occur with PnP.

The downside to not having a centralized place to install hardware is that you need to hunt through different applets in Control Panel to find the right place to do the installation. The following example uses a Sound Blaster 32 AWE as an example of installing new hardware. Here are the steps:

1. Make sure you have the proper drivers for your new device. Remember that Windows NT requires different drivers than previous versions of Windows or any version of MS-DOS. Most manufacturers have the new NT drivers available either at their FTP or Web sites or both.

2. Open the Control Panel and locate the Multimedia applet's icon. Double-click on this icon to launch the configuration and installation program. Figure 5.12 shows this dialog.

3. Click the Devices tab (the rightmost tab) to start to install a new device. Click the Add button to add a device. It doesn't make any difference what you have highlighted when you click the Add button. The .INF file included with the drivers will tell Windows NT what's available. If you see your device listed in the next screen, double-click on it. You will be given the option of installing the driver from your NT distribution disk or adding new drivers. Make your choice. If you choose an existing driver, skip to step 4. If not, tell NT where the new driver is. This can be your disk, a directory on the network, a floppy disk, or a CD. If your device isn't listed, double-click on the top entry:

   `Unlisted or Updated Driver`

   and tell NT where the driver is. You also have the option of browsing to find the driver. Figure 5.13 shows the installation process after locating the drivers.

FIGURE 5.12.

The Multimedia applet in Control Panel is the place to install drivers for a new multimedia device.

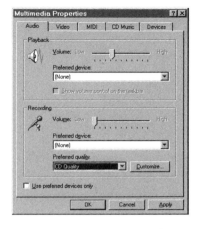

FIGURE 5.13.

Once you locate the driver and accompanying files, the .INF file will tell you what installable drivers you have available to you. The top window shows the .INF file in Notepad, the bottom, the Multimedia applet's reading of that file.

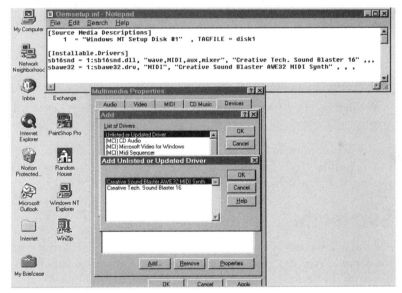

4. Choose the device you want to install by highlighting it. Click OK and the applet will do the work for you. In the case of an installable driver that must be loaded at bootup, NT will have to restart to activate the changes. For example, a new sound card or a card with a new driver will require an NT bootup before recognizing that new driver.

> **NOTE**
>
> Pay careful attention to any installation notes that come with your drivers. In many cases, you need to install drivers in a particular order for them to work properly or at all. In the previous example, the driver for the Sound Blaster 16 (second on the list) needs to be installed, but not necessarily initialized, before the Creative Sound Blaster AWE32 MIDI Synth can be.

Here are the major applets that control the installation and configuration of hardware devices, along with some of the types of devices they control:

- Multimedia: sound, video, music, compression services for video and music
- Network: adapters (NICs), protocols, services and bindings between them
- Modems: modems
- Display: video adapters and their settings
- Keyboard: new keyboards and their drivers, such as IntelliType
- Mouse: new mice and their special drivers, such as IntelliPoint
- Telephony: lower-level drivers for telephony services such as TAPI
- Mail and Fax: Outlook services if you have Outlook 97 installed
- Printers: printers and their drivers

You may have more or fewer applets in your Control Panel, depending upon what your workstation profile is like. The above list isn't comprehensive, but should give you an idea of which applets control which types of devices.

Summary

Although Windows NT Workstation 4 isn't fully PnP-enabled, it can run most, if not all, of the devices Windows 95 and its successors can. The critical item is the presence of the proper driver for the devices, because Windows NT, unlike Windows 95, can't use drivers created for older versions of Windows. Due to architectural changes, Windows NT 4 can't even use drivers from previous versions of Windows NT.

Once you have the proper drivers for your device, you need to determine what computer resources it's to use. One way to do this is to use the Windows NT Diagnostics program.

After determining what resources are free, you need to install the new hardware, configure it for the free resources, and then install the drivers. Unlike Windows 95, Windows NT doesn't have a centralized hardware installation routine. Instead, you install devices using their respective applet in Control Panel.

Touring the New GUI

by Howard M. Swope III

IN THIS CHAPTER

CHAPTER 6

A Summary of the New Features

The previous release of Windows NT Workstation, 3.51, had few new features. It was, after all, an interim release stepping up from the 3.5 to the 3.51 designation. A utility was provided for the detection and fixing of the Intel Pentium floating-point error. Intel's late detection of an error in its Pentium processors was the hottest issue in the computing world at the time, and it was of the utmost importance to the end user. Support for the Windows 95 common controls was added to NT. This eased the burden of software designers developing software for both the NT and 95 platforms. File compression for NTFS, the native NT file system, was now available. Increased support for certain PCMCIA cards was also added.

Windows NT Workstation 4 is a major revision upgrade jumping from 3.51 all the way to the 4.0 designation. Although it is termed the Shell Update Release, release 4 brings with it a slew of new features in its user interface, underlying architecture, application programming inter-faces, and provided applications. Many of the new features are included to bring the usability of Windows 95 to NT. Other features address key operating system architecture and program-ming issues. Several features expected to be released with NT 4 will be released just following the operating system release, and others will be held over until the next NT release (code-named Cairo) slated for 1997. The following is a list, by category, of new and deferred features with a brief summary of each. The remaining sections of this chapter focus on several of the key new features in NT Workstation 4.

Interface Features

- Windows 95 User Interface

  Windows NT Workstation now has the 95-era user interface. New interface features follow an object-oriented approach stressing efficiency of motion. See the next section, "The Explorer User Interface," for a detailed discussion of the new interface.

- Plus! Companion for Windows 95 Features

  Many of the features from the Microsoft Plus! Pack for Windows 95 come standard with NT Workstation. Plus! provides visual, sound, and font enhancements as well as Internet automation.

- Hardware Profile Support

  Hardware profiling allows a user to choose a specific hardware profile at boot up. A hardware profile can designate different services, devices, and settings.

System Architecture and Operation Features

- Kernel-Mode User and GDI

  NT 4 now has the User and GDI components moved from the Win32 subsystem to the NT Kernel. This is transparent to the end user but increases performance in the area of graphics display. See the section "Kernel-Mode User and GDI" for a more detailed description of the move and its ramifications.

- Network OLE

  Network OLE and Distributed COM (component object model) allow software components to work with each other across a network. See the section "Network OLE: Distributed COM" for a more detailed description of OLE and the added network support.

- Enhanced Metafile (EMF) Spooling

  This feature increases network printing speeds by redistributing the work load of EMF rendering.

- 486 Emulator for RISC Platforms

  The 486 emulator for RISC platforms allows 386 enhanced mode, 16-bit applications to run on RISC machines.

- Wins/DNS Integration

  Wins/DNS integration allows for the resolving of naming differences between Windows NT domains and the Internet. This allows NT workstations to access NT servers over the Internet.

- CDFS Enhancements

  This new feature provides enhancements for CD-ROMs. It incorporates the autoplay feature and the CD-XA format.

- NetWare 4 Client and Login Script Support

  File/print capabilities and login script support have been added to the NDS client for NT Workstation. VLM support has been deferred until the 1997 release of NT.

- Additional drivers

  Many additional drivers have been added in the NT 4 release.

Provided Applications

- Peer Web Services

  Peer Web Services is a light version of the Internet Information Server provided with the NT 4 Server product. Peer Web services provide basic Internet functionality for use in a peer environment.

- Internet Explorer

  The Internet Explorer, Microsoft's offering in the Web browser market, accompanies NT Workstation 4. The latest release of Internet Explorer brings with it many avenues for interactivity and secure transactions over the Internet.

- Microsoft Exchange Universal Inbox

  The Universal Inbox is an application that lets the user do all of his or her correspondence from a single location. You can send and receive faxes and send or receive e-mail to or from several different types of networks—all from a single application.

■ Windows 95 Compatible System Policies

An administration tool providing for the management of NT 4 workstations.

■ Windows 95 Nexus

A set of administration tools to aid in the administration of NT Servers.

■ Additional Applets

Several other small applications are provided with NT 4. These applications include WordPad, a text editor; HyperTerminal, a small communications terminal; and Phone Dialer, a small application that dials your telephone.

API Features

■ Direct Draw and Direct Sound Support

Direct Draw and Direct Sound provide the ability to develop and run Windows 95 games and other applications that require direct access to sound and video hardware. It is implemented in a way that does not sacrifice NT's security.

■ Telephony API (TAPI) and Unimodem

TAPI provides the ability to develop and run applications that take advantage of certain telephony technologies such as fax and the exchange client.

■ Cryptography API (CAPI)

CAPI provides the ability to develop and run applications that require security in nonsecure environments such as the Internet.

Deferred Features

■ FAX (will be delivered separately, following the release of Windows NT Workstation 4)

FAX refers to client software that facilitates the tasks encountered when sending faxes and cover pages, fax viewing, printing to fax, and so on. FAX utilizes exchange extensions allowing the fax client to coexist with other communications applications.

■ MSN (will be delivered separately, following the release of Windows NT Workstation 4)

Support for The Microsoft Network.

■ Plug and Play and Power Management (will be delivered in the 1997 release of Windows NT Workstation)

Plug and Play facilitates dynamic configuration of hardware devices. This does away with the need to set jumpers and settings manually for devices compliant with Plug and Play. Power management aids the user in managing and conserving machine power. This is of key importance to mobile computer users.

The Explorer User Interface

The most visible of the new features in Windows NT Workstation 4 is the user interface. So much importance was placed on the new shell that release 4 of NT has been termed the Shell Update Release (sometimes called SUR). Figure 6.1 shows the appearance of the Explorer interface.

FIGURE 6.1.

The appearance of the Explorer interface.

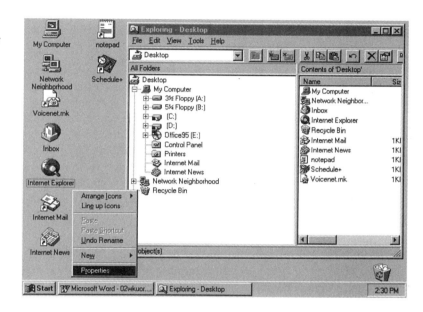

> **NOTE**
>
> The Program Manager shell is still available in Windows NT 4. However, its appearance and functionality have been altered. To change the shell of a particular machine, change the shell value in the registry under the following key:
>
> ```
> HKEY_LOCAL_MACHINE
> \Software
> \Microsoft
> \Windows NT
> \CurrentVersion
> \Winlogon
> ```
>
> The value should reflect the shell that you want to use—explorer.exe for the explorer shell, or progman.exe for the Program Manager shell. (Theoretically, you could use any shell that meets NT's shell specifications.) See Chapter 11, "The NT Registry," for information on the Registry.

The shell is called through `explorer.exe` and is therefore more properly referred to by the Explorer name. However, the interface connotes more than just the shell. It connotes a general appearance and style of use. This is why you hear the term *Windows 95 interface*. The *Windows 95* in this case doesn't refer to Microsoft's Windows 95 operating system, which premiered the interface; it refers to the 95-era windowing products from Microsoft.

The Explorer interface follows an object-oriented approach that stresses efficiency of motion and sight. It is much more user-oriented than its predecessor, the Program Manager. Despite its more elaborate and ornate appearance, the Explorer interface still has elegance and simplicity that make it very functional.

Object orientation is a concept that, like many of its uses, is abstract and has several levels of use. In the aforementioned instance, it is used in its most general form, meaning "of or relating to an object." Objects are defined as objects because they encompass several related issues of usefulness, which can be grouped under the idea of a single object and, therefore, are easier to work with. It is akin to words in a sentence. Individual words are not very useful except as explanatory entities, but words grouped together in a single sentence take on a complexity that is useful to the reader. The Explorer interface puts the focus on the object, whether it be a window, an icon, a file, a task, or any definable object. You can go to an object's representation on the screen and perform actions or retrieve properties for that specific object.

Efficiency of motion is a major factor in the new interface. Many actions that took several steps to perform under the old interface now take fewer steps or a single step. For example, you can close a window with a single click instead of a double click. This might seem like a minor factor, but when you consider the sheer number of times that this action and similar repetitive actions are performed, the importance of efficiency of motion is revealed.

Related to efficiency of motion is efficiency of sight. Efficiency of sight is also stressed in the Explorer interface. Icons, buttons, and menus have been shrunken, and much more can be seen in one glance at the screen than ever before. Because of this, you can open and close fewer windows, which saves time and movement. With more in sight at one time, you can see the bigger picture by viewing more objects and the way that they relate on the screen. All of this contributes to enabling you to deal with more complex tasks in one instance, which is why people invest so much money in these silly machines, after all.

Good software design dictates that a system should reflect to the user the real-world issues that it addresses, rather than the underlying computer science that allows the system to function. For example, assume that you are creating software to add two numbers inputted by a user. The two numbers that the user inputs will be stored in memory address A and memory address B until it is time for them to be added. This software should ask the user for two numbers to add, as opposed to asking for a value for memory addresses A and B.

The Program Manager interface dictates that only application windows or iconic application windows be open on the desktop window. If an application was running, it was running in an open window. If you wanted to run an application, you opened the Program Manager window. This was very simple and elegant if you were a computer (or someone who thought like one). However, most people work with items arranged on the desktop so that frequently used items can be reached quickly. Most people also tend to think more abstractly than the 1 or 0 mentality at the heart of the computer.

The Explorer interface follows a logic that is more complex and more intuitive to the user. The machine still receives the information and breaks it down to a few simple instructions for processing. The machine doesn't care how the information gets there; it only knows that it receives input, performs some action on the input, and returns a result. The user, however, works better if he or she can provide the information and get the information back in a meaningful way.

Personally, I have seen this in action. I was teaching a gentleman who was in his late forties to use a computer for the first time. He was not a computer professional and was not raised with computers. His relative lack of familiarity with computer logic makes him a perfect example. For the first month or so, he was using the Program Manager interface. Certain concepts just did not sink in. I told him that in order to accomplish task x, you must perform actions x, y, and z. No matter how many times we would go over performing a task, it just wouldn't sink in.

We eventually moved to the Explorer interface, and it was as if a light went on. Suddenly he was communicating with his machine in ways that were more natural to him. It made sense that in order to close a window he should press the X in the upper-right corner instead of choosing Exit from the File menu. To him a file was information residing in a drawer in a cabinet and had nothing to do with closing a window on a computer screen. The letter X is always associated with negation, and he could see it on the window's title bar. He almost intuitively clicked on the X.

The improved communication between user and machine is best illustrated by a look at the main interface implementations. The next several sections of this chapter cover these items in a general sense.

Right Mouse Activation

The Explorer interface activates the right mouse button. Once impotent or used only rarely in specific applications, the right mouse button comes alive in the Explorer interface of Windows NT Workstation 4.

NOTE

Usually, a left click on an item in Windows selects or activates that object. A right click usually provides further options for the object that was clicked. The additional options come in the form of a shortcut menu—a small popup menu with items specific to the object for which it was called. Figure 6.2 shows an example of a shortcut menu.

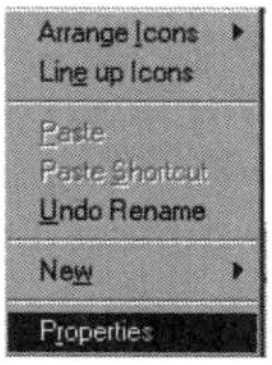

FIGURE 6.2.

A shortcut menu.

Right mouse activation is utilized in the object-oriented approach of the Explorer interface by tailoring the actions of the mouse click to the object on which it was clicked. Because you never have to leave the object in question, motion is conserved. The resulting shortcut menus are small and disappear after use, lending themselves to efficiency of sight. This approach is also intuitive because you expect options for a particular object to be available from that object, rather than from an obscure menu choice on a menu bar.

The Desktop

The desktop is considered the first open window of the system. Previously, in the Program Manager shell, only open application windows and iconic application windows resided within the desktop window. Under the Explorer interface, the desktop acts more like a folder. It can house files as well as two new additions: shortcuts and system folders. Figure 6.3 shows the new desktop.

Shortcuts such as the notepad shortcut in Figure 6.3 are program icons with advanced properties controlling program activation. The same properties and parameters can be set regardless of the executable that is activated by the shortcut.

System folders, such as the My Computer system folder in Figure 6.3, are also represented by program icons, but the actions that the system folders can initiate and the properties that they can have are dependent on the object they represent. The properties that are available for the My Computer system folder are properties relevant to my computer. If I were to view properties for Network Neighborhood, they would reflect network settings.

FIGURE 6.3.
The new desktop.

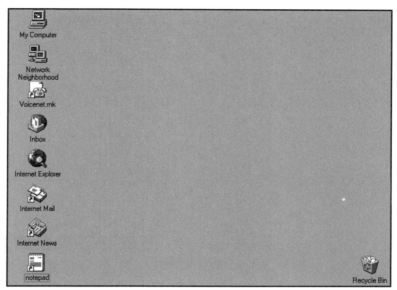

With files, shortcuts, and system folders residing on the desktop, it looks a bit more like an individual's desk. Items that are used frequently can be placed on the desktop for easy access. You can have a calculator, scheduler, and notepad out on the desktop. You can also place works in progress right on the desktop and then move them to a folder when they are finished. This method of organization is more akin to the way people are used to working. It is more complex and more intuitive than the old Program Manager interface.

The Taskbar

The Taskbar is a task management utility with running tasks appearing as buttons (see Figure 6.4). When you want to switch to a different task, you just click on the button representing the task and it is moved to the foreground. Under this system of task management, there is no more opening, closing, sizing, or hunting to find a particular window. If a task requires the constant switching of windows, the windows are only a single click away.

The Taskbar follows the principal of efficiency of motion. Task switching is done with only a single click, as opposed to the many actions that could be necessary under the Program Manager shell. The Taskbar also follows the efficiency of sight principle. It can be placed on any side of the screen, resized, and set to hide itself when not in use.

FIGURE 6.4.

The Taskbar.

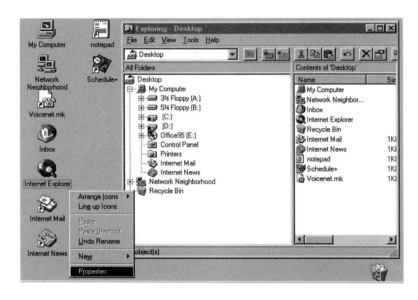

The Start Menu

The Start menu has received a lot of hype in the media. It has been a focal point for a lot of advertising and is the subject of a popular Rolling Stones song. No. That can't be right. The Stones wrote that tune before the Start menu was in existence. Despite the hype, the Start menu, shown in Figure 6.5, typifies the user focus of the Explorer GUI.

FIGURE 6.5.

The Start menu.

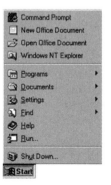

The Start menu itself is a popup menu and is out of sight when not in use. When open, the Start menu is a jumping off point for any activity. A user can activate a program, call up a document recently edited in any application, have access to all system settings, run a detailed search, or get help.

Never before in any interface has that kind of organization been brought to the end user. For those of us who are used to working with file managers, Program Managers, system utilities, and so on, this isn't that big a deal. We already know how to find these things. Imagine first-time users trying to initiate an action. Their first thought is not, "Hmmmmm, maybe I should double-click on a program item." A first-time user's first thought is probably more along the lines of, "How do I start this thing?"

The Explorer

The Explorer (not to be confused with the Explorer interface) is an application that provides management tools for an entire system. The Explorer uses a two-pane view, shown in Figure 6.6. In the left pane are icons representing your desktop, drives, system folders, and networked computers; in the right pane are the individual items contained within the selected object of the left pane.

FIGURE 6.6.

The Explorer.

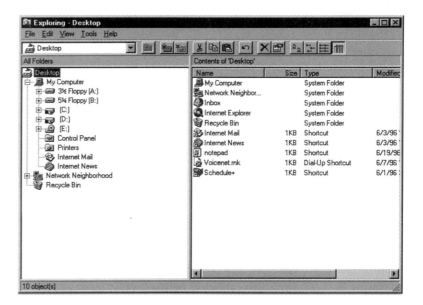

The two-pane view is quite popular and lends itself to efficiency of sight. The left pane holds a higher order of organization to give you the big picture; the right pane shows the lower order, or individual unit view. Applications such as the Explorer, which utilize this way of looking at things, are very efficient.

I have found that when working on a project, I need to listen to two voices within myself: the organizer and the doer. The organizer has to pay attention to the big picture and not focus on little details. Focusing on little details hurts the overall organization. The doer must focus on the task at hand and pay attention to detail. If the doer constantly focuses on organization, a job never gets done. The two-pane view within an application allows me to exploit both of those voices.

The Explorer has efficiency of motion, allowing you to navigate through the various objects of your system with a single click. A major advantage to this is being able to access a lower order of organization without leaving the selected object. For example, if you want to copy a file from the current directory into another directory that is not visible, you could navigate the Explorer to find the new directory in the left pane without losing sight of the file to be copied in the right pane.

The Explorer, like its namesake interface, follows an object-oriented approach. All available tools act on the object, selected with a left click. Properties are available for objects by right clicking.

> **TIP**
>
> Further options are available when moving objects if you right-click and drag the objects, as opposed to the traditional left mouse button drag.

Similar to the Start menu, the Explorer provides an organization to the end user. The end user gets a view of his or her entire system. The big picture is available to show how an object fits in with the rest of the system. At the same time, the individual, low-order object can be manipulated—and all from one location.

Kernel-Mode User and GDI

A major architectural change has been implemented in NT 4. The user and GDI components of the operating system have been moved from user-mode to kernel-mode. Except for noticeable performance gains, the change is transparent to the end user, systems administrator, and programmer alike. However, because of the magnitude of the change, the move warrants discussion.

As you see in Figure 6.7, the structure of NT can be divided into two sections: user-mode and kernel-mode. User-mode is made up of protected subsystems that run in separate processes, each with its own memory space. The protected subsystems provide the kernel-mode NT executive with user interfaces, programming interfaces, and execution environments. The executive provides lower-level operating system functionality. The two sections of the operating system communicate with each other through a uniform, complex message-passing schema.

FIGURE 6.7.

An NT component diagram from previous versions of NT.

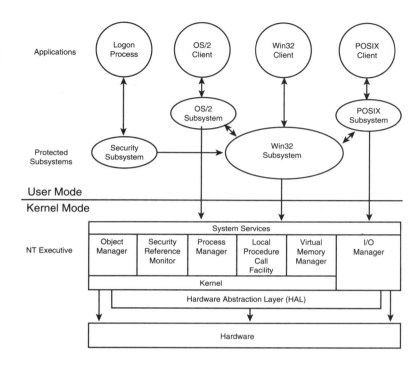

The exact nature of the communication system between the kernel and user modes isn't important for this discussion because it is of a fairly general nature. It is important to know that the communication, represented by the arrows in Figure 6.7, is implemented uniformly, and system resources are used in the implementation of the communications. The executive isn't concerned with which subsystem is sending a message as long it is using the proper protocol.

The idea of uniform communication is a constant theme throughout NT's internal communications. It provides for a high degree of security and modularity. Because processes can only communicate with the executive in a predefined fashion, the executive isn't subject to unexpected input or alteration, and it is therefore more secure. Also, because the communication is structured, the actual internal workings of the various components are not interdependent. One component could easily be switched with another as long as it follows the proper communication guidelines.

Although NT's internal messaging schema makes it easily changeable and secure, the level of abstraction that facilitates the messaging causes system overhead. An engine and data structures must exist to carry messages back and forth to the various NT subsystems. These structures take up memory and CPU time to perform their needed functions. Although they were highly optimized, the heavy traffic and shared nature of the user and GDI components under the old system made them ripe for performance degradation.

The user and GDI components of the operating system provide a large portion of NT's graphical capabilities. In previous versions of NT, these components were located in the Win32 subsystem, shown in Figure 6.8. Originally, the designers of NT planned to have the Win32 subsystem self-contained; but in order to reuse code and streamline performance, portions of the Win32 subsystem were used by other protected, user-mode subsystems. Refer to the arrows in Figure 6.7 for areas of communication with the Win32 subsystem. You can see that the heavy reliance on the Win32 subsystem, the increasing graphic intensity of modern applications, and the added overhead of a graphically intensive new shell can cause a great deal of traffic to this area to occur and is likely to eat up system resources.

FIGURE 6.8.

The Win32 subsystem in previous versions of NT.

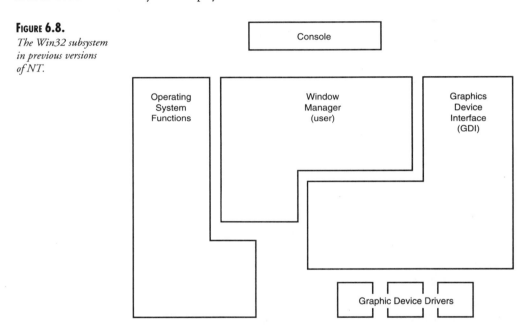

With the aforementioned concerns in mind, the NT design team moved the user, GDI, and related drivers to the NT executive. The result is improved graphics performance, smaller memory requirements, and a simplified Win32 subsystem. The new layout is shown in Figure 6.9.

Under the new design the user, GDI, and related drivers reside in the executive. The remaining portion of the Win32 subsystem is housed in the client/server subsystem. With the removal of the user and GDI, the client/server subsystem is much less complex, making it more efficient and closer to the intent of NT's original designers. The user and GDI—now in the kernel mode—do not create the vast system overhead that they would have if they used the complex message-passing schema required to maintain security in user mode.

Figure 6.9.

The NT component diagram from release 4.

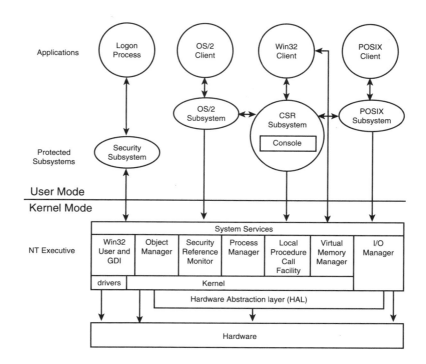

Network OLE: Distributed COM

Another major enhancement in NT 4 is the addition of Network OLE. OLE is a standard for communication between binary software components. OLE has not received the press that it deserves, but OLE has been evolving right along with the Windows operating systems. It is the technology at the heart of the evolution of windows into object-based operating systems. It allows for the integration of premade objects—regardless of creator, computer language, or version—into software and into end-user documents. Now, with the addition of network OLE, these integrated objects can reside on and be distributed across networks, including the Internet.

Originally, OLE (pronounced *O-L-E*) stood for object linking and embedding, which was the technology involved in making software that used compound documents. As the technology evolved to provide a set of interfaces and services through which components communicated, OLE began to be pronounced *o-lay*. Now it is common to hear OLE used interchangeably with COM (pronounced *kahm*), which stands for Component Object Model. COM encompasses the underlying technologies that allow OLE to function. With the recent addition of the technology allowing components to reside on and communicate over networks, you will often hear the terms Network OLE and Distributed COM.

OLE is a standard for communication between binary software components, which means that OLE provides a means for premade software components to interact. Neither of the communicating components is required to know the inner workings of the other. One component simply needs to have an interface to the other component so that it can request services or information from the other component. This interface is OLE.

OLE is likened to the technology that allows stereo components to work together. The turntable can be created by any manufacturer, and it can work any way that it wants. It outputs the appropriate signals to the receiver that, in turn, amplifies and sends the signal to the speakers. The speakers, too, could be made by any manufacturer and work in any fashion, as long as they receive the standard signal input and produce sound. Because of this, you can shop around and find the best sound system for your tastes. In a similar fashion, you can piece together a software solution that meets your needs.

Another scenario is to parallel OLE with current computer hardware standards. The hardware industry has many standards: for example, PCI bussing technology or VGA video technology. Because these standards are adhered to by manufacturers, you can use a VGA monitor made by any manufacturer with any video card that supports the VGA standard. If that particular VGA card applies PCI bussing technology, it can be placed in any machine that accepts PCI cards.

Similarly, if you are creating a hypothetical software solution to present company data on a series of global maps, you are unlikely to have the resources available to go out and map the world. You could easily purchase a map component that maps generic types of information. Because both the creator of the fictitious data mapping software and the creator of the map component adhered to the OLE standard, the map component could be used in the creation of the company data map software.

The learning curve, in this case, is relatively small because the software designers are familiar with the OLE standard and only the OLE specifics of the map component need to be learned. If you purchase a custom component (a component not adhering to a component standard), a unique interface must be learned. As the number of custom components increases, the learning curve increases over the life of the project.

The fictitious software could be written in any computer language that meets the needs of the project. The map component, because it is an OLE component, also could be written in the language best suited to the project of making an OLE map component. Because OLE facilitates communication on the binary level, the data map software and map component could work together even if one was written in C++, for example, and the other in Visual Basic.

Suppose that the developer of the map component came out with version 2 of its OLE map component software. The new version could be plugged into the existing version of the data mapping software without change. OLE requires backward compatibility. So now the existing software could have better, more colorful maps without any extra work. Then when version 2 of the data mapping software came out, the mapping software could take advantage of any new features added in version 2 of the map component.

The same power that OLE brings to the software designer can be wielded by the power user as well. A user can embed and edit from within an OLE application an object created by another OLE-enabled application. This object can, but is not required to be, linked to the original file housing the object.

For example, imagine that you are preparing a monthly financial synopsis. After typing a summary of the month's financial earnings in an OLE-enabled word processor, you can embed an OLE-capable spreadsheet containing the exact figures into the document. The spreadsheet can optionally be linked to the file housing the spreadsheet. If the spreadsheet object in the document is linked to the file housing the spreadsheet, any changes made to the figures in the spreadsheet are automatically updated in the document. Conversely, if you need to make last minute changes to the spreadsheet object, the object can activate its native application from within the document and make the necessary edits.

NT 4 adds Network OLE or Distributed COM. OLE has many such implementations, and with version 4 of NT comes the addition of Network OLE or Distributed COM. Network OLE brings with it the aforementioned characteristics of OLE, but now objects can be located anywhere on a network, including the Internet.

Suppose a software designer wants to create an application that uses up-to-the-minute stock data. The creator of this application could purchase an OLE component from an Internet stock service and use this component in the application. Whenever the application needs current stock information for whatever purpose, it navigates the OLE interface to retrieve the information necessary from wherever the stock service is located on the Internet. Figure 6.10 illustrates the layout of this fictitious system.

FIGURE 6.10.

The layout of a fictitious stock application.

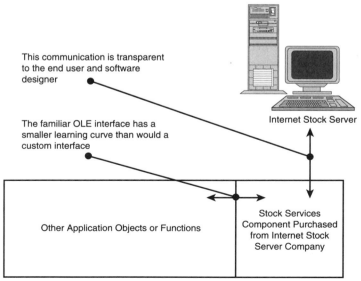

This communication is transparent to the end user and software designer

The familiar OLE interface has a smaller learning curve than would a custom interface

Internet Stock Server

Other Application Objects or Functions

Stock Services Component Purchased from Internet Stock Server Company

Stock Application Requiring Dated Stock Information

Similarly, OLE can be used by the power user. Imagine that you work in a financial institution that sends a lot of correspondence requiring up-to-the-minute stock information. You could create a document that embeds an object from software created by the aforementioned software designer. Each time the document is opened, a link to the stock software's object is updated, calling into the stock service to retrieve the timely data and updating the object in the document. Figure 6.11 illustrates the stock document scenario.

Figure 6.11.

A document requiring current stock information.

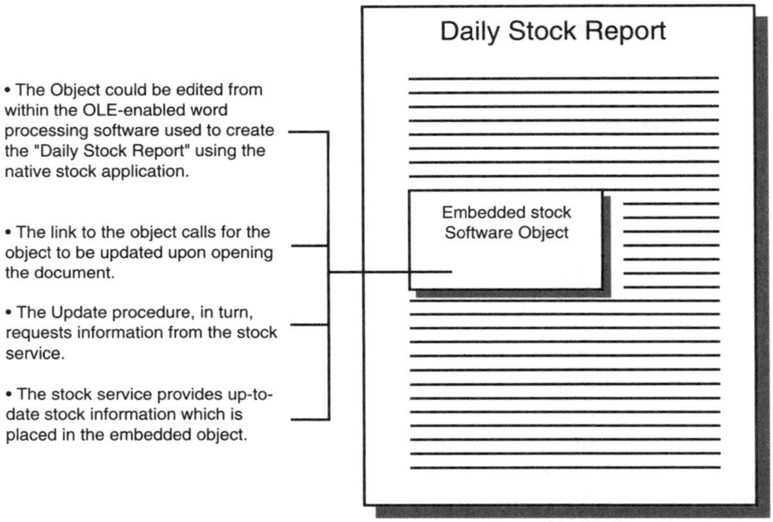

• The Object could be edited from within the OLE-enabled word processing software used to create the "Daily Stock Report" using the native stock application.

• The link to the object calls for the object to be updated upon opening the document.

• The Update procedure, in turn, requests information from the stock service.

• The stock service provides up-to-date stock information which is placed in the embedded object.

Daily Stock Report

Embedded stock
Software Object

The ramifications of OLE are many. This technology and technologies of this kind will be vital to take the next step in computing. Applications are becoming too complex to build from scratch. Too many resources are located in too many different places to manage. An object technology of this nature allows the multitude of resources to be codified and managed. OLE can provide for increasingly rapid development of increasingly complex applications, distributing their processes where needed. At the same time, the end user will be able to harness the power of complex applications in production-oriented tasks through compound documents and compound views.

Support for Mobile Computing

Release 4 of Windows NT Workstation adds increased support for mobile computing. Mobile computing is any computing that isn't done at a stationary workstation, or computing done on a portable computer. Mobile computing encompasses a wide range of implementations. Some users like to have a desktop at the office and bring work home on a notebook. People who spend a great deal of time traveling, such as people in sales, often have a notebook as their primary computer, and they rely on it for connectivity to the office when on the road. Other people use portable computers as data collection machines while visiting different locations, or they use them in the lab while working on various experiments. Often, users who use a notebook as their primary machine plug it into a docking station when at their primary location. Whatever the use, NT 4 has some handy features to help out the mobile user.

Dialup Networking

Dialup networking allows one computer to network with another computer remotely. The distinction between dialup networking and traditional remote computing is significant. In traditional remote computing, the end user often looks at a split screen, viewing remote and host data, respectively. Under dialup networking, communications between the host and remote computers are made as transparent as possible. Behind the scenes, various communications protocols handle the dialup-specific communications issues, while the remote user has the feeling that he or she is working in a traditional network environment.

Dialup networking can be used to connect to various types of machines and networks—for example, your office network or the Internet. The approach that dialup networking takes to remote computing is at the heart of the connectivity that has folks so excited about the Internet in recent times. The emphasis now rests with the information being communicated, as opposed to the engines or equipment that facilitate the communication.

Under the dialup networking scenario, remote connections to different types of networks are handled from a central location and handled in a uniform way. You could connect to the Internet or the office network over a phone line. The link can be initiated from one location or through the use of a shortcut. Figure 6.12 shows the methods for initiating a dialup networking session.

Different location profiles are available under dialup networking. You can set up different location profiles to use when dialing from different locations. You can specify the area code of a particular location and any dialing suffixes or prefixes. Dialup networking adds area code, suffix, or prefix to the number it dials, depending on the location from which the user is dialing.

Suppose a member of the sales team is on a tour of several countries to try to drum up business. The salesperson could dial in from a hotel to the office and conduct computing as if she were at the office. Obviously, the rate at which information is transferred is restricted by the medium on which that communication is taking place. At present, networking over a phone line is significantly slower than a standard network connection. Nevertheless, the salesperson could have access to her networked resources from anywhere with a phone.

To facilitate communications, the salesperson could set up different location profiles for each stop on her trip to reduce the overhead of changing calling numbers each time she arrived at a new location. If the salesperson is conducting business through electronic communications, she could connect to the Internet with dialup networking and send e-mail to her contacts at the other offices, informing them of timetables and related arrival times. At the same time, the salesperson could confirm travel plans or get information on the next location via the World Wide Web.

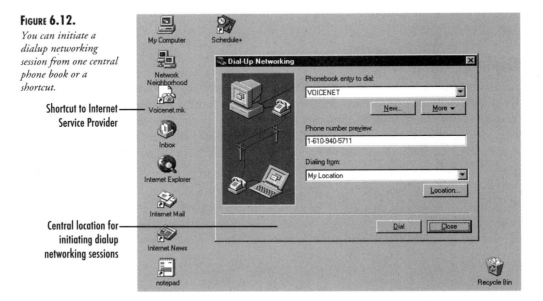

Briefcase

Briefcase coordinates the use of the same file on two machines. This is ideal for someone wanting to use both a notebook and a desktop machine. You can work on a file from your main desktop location, taking advantage of the niceties of the desktop such as a large monitor, keyboard, mouse, CD-ROM, and so on. Then, when the need arises to take that file on the road, you can drag it into the briefcase of a notebook computer for easy portability to different locations.

The briefcase requires that the two computers be connected via network or a cable to transfer the files. When connected, you can drag files from any location on the desktop computer to the briefcase on the portable computer. The notebook can then be detached and used on the road. The files in the briefcase will be altered with use. Upon returning to the desktop machine, the notebook computer needs to be reattached via network or cable. When it is connected, the original files on the desktop machine are updated with a click of the update files menu option. Figure 6.13 shows the process.

If you have to work overtime at home on a project from the office, you can drag the project-related files from the project folder on the desktop machine into the Briefcase on your notebook computer. Upon returning to work the next day, the original files from the project folder can be updated with the touch of a button. If you are collecting data on the road, you can drag your scheduler or contact management data files from any directory on the desktop machine

6

TOURING THE
NEW GUI

into the Briefcase of the notebook to keep track of appointments or contacts on the road. Any alterations to these files will easily be updated upon your return. The data files from the data collection software, set up beforehand on the desktop machine, are dragged into the briefcase. The data is then collected and the data files are updated on the desktop computer for data collation.

FIGURE 6.13.

Briefcase facilitates the use of the same file when stationary and on the road.

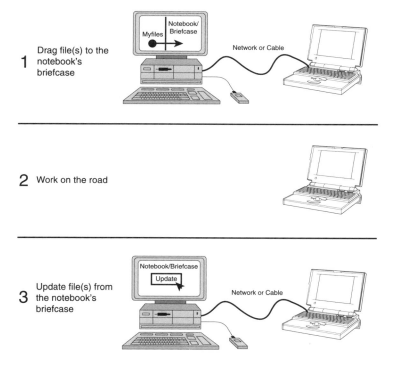

1   Drag file(s) to the notebook's briefcase

2   Work on the road

3   Update file(s) from the notebook's briefcase

With Briefcase, no copying or traditional file management is required. There is no need to find many files in many different directories in order to do updates, and the advantages of the desktop and notebook computers can be leveraged.

NOTE

The aforementioned file synchronization can also be accomplished by copying files to a local briefcase and copying the briefcase to a floppy disk for transport. However, in this scenario, briefcase size is limited by the size of the portable media.

Also, other cellular networking options are available that allow direct networked access to the files. These technologies are just beginning to be explored and are expensive. Cellular transmissions are presently not reliable and cellular modems are prohibited during commercial air travel.

Hardware Profiles and Docking Detection

NT 4 has the capability to set up different hardware profiles. Hardware profiles reflect installed devices and settings. Users can select a particular hardware profile at boot time, depending on what hardware is being used during the current session. NT 4 also has the capability to detect whether a notebook computer is docked and, if docking is detected, to select the appropriate hardware settings. Figures 6.14 and 6.15 show the dialog boxes used to facilitate hardware profiling and docking detection.

FIGURE 6.14.

The Hardware Profiles tab on the System Properties dialog is used to facilitate hardware profiling.

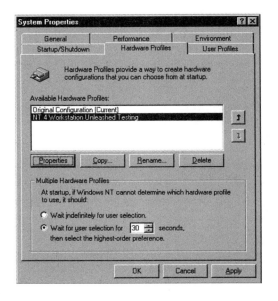

FIGURE 6.15.

Properties can be set for individual hardware profiles to facilitate docking detection and its appropriate hardware selection.

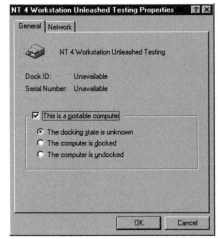

Suppose that you do a lot of work at the office and at home. Instead of using one of the briefcase scenarios from the "Briefcase" section of this chapter, you could use a notebook computer and docking station. At the office the notebook is plugged into the docking station. Attached to the docking station is a full-sized monitor, keyboard, mouse, and CD-ROM. NT 4 detects that the notebook is docked and chooses the appropriate settings to use the full-sized hardware components. Now the user has all the comforts of a desktop computer, but it's portable. When you leave for the evening, you detach the notebook from the docking station and easily transport the computer home. When the machine is used at home, NT detects an undocked state and chooses the appropriate hardware settings to use the notebook in the stand-alone state.

Another scenario in which you can take advantage of hardware profiling is when you use different hardware under different conditions. Perhaps you use a portable CD-ROM that plugs into a PCMCIA slot for various uses, but when not in use the PCMCIA slot is used for a modem. Under these circumstances, you could set up a hardware profile for both cases and select the appropriate one when needed.

The same example applies for lab-specific hardware. You might use a particular hardware device for chemical analysis but use a different type of hardware for monitoring temperature. You would set up a hardware profile for both cases. When chemical analysis was being done, you would select "my hardware profile—chemical," and when temperature-related experiments were being done, you would select "my hardware profile—temperature." There are as many scenarios as there are hardware devices and as many uses as there is imagination.

Internet Support Features

At present, society is in the middle of an Internet boom. Everywhere you turn (except perhaps the middle of a forest) you hear or see something about the Internet. But even the forests are affected by the Internet with its many animal rights and conservation areas. However, I doubt the creatures of the earth, except humans, care too much about the Internet. Nonetheless, if you are human and you watch TV, listen to the radio, read the newspaper, go to the movies, or read any computer literature, you will undoubtedly come into contact with the Internet.

Microsoft, sensing the growing importance of the Internet, has stopped on a dime and wholly embraced and extended the Internet. Microsoft has implemented plans to Internet-enable all its applications and operating systems. NT Workstation 4 is no exception. In the version 4 release of NT Workstation, several Internet support features are geared toward the workstation environment.

The growing Internet mania is bringing with it many new users and many new questions about the Internet, its use, and its ramifications. To dispel some confusion and provide further clarification, the next section of the chapter discusses the Internet in general, followed by an outline of the related features in NT Workstation 4.

A Clarification of Networking Logic

Because of the sudden Internet boom, people are rushing to get onto the Net. They feel that if they are not connected, they are somehow being left behind. To a certain degree this is true. More and more services and information are being provided via the Internet, and there are no signs of this trend being halted. As folks are rushing onto the Internet, they are desiring instant knowledge and gratification. Because they want to know how to do something right away, their focus is task-oriented and they lose sight of what the Internet is at its root—a network of computers.

When more than one computer is connected and sharing information, the computers are networked. This concept is basic and sometimes overlooked; however, it is important not to lose sight of this fact. In order for two computers to be connected, a hardware connection must be established. In order for two computers to share information, a communications protocol must be in place to facilitate the passing of information over the hardware connection. After a connection and a protocol for passing information is established between two machines, work can be done.

At this point, the two computers have met each other and have decided on a medium for communication. Now the communication must move to the next level of complexity by deciding what subject the connected computers want to discuss and what language will be used to discuss this subject. Ideally, the subject discussed and the work done through the communication will fulfill some type of need, and the language used to discuss the subject will be appropriate to the subject at hand.

To facilitate performing some useful task with the now connected computers, a client/server model is common and is used on the Internet. In its simplest form, the client requests information and the server responds by returning the requested information. Suppose that I said to you, "Please give me a dollar." You then hand me a dollar. We both know the English language, and the dollar is a form of currency in many English-speaking countries; therefore, it is appropriate that we speak English. The need being fulfilled would be financial transactions. I would be the client requesting a dollar, and you would be the server fulfilling my request by handing me that dollar.

> **NOTE**
>
> More often than not, machines are dedicated for performing server tasks, while other machines are used as clients. This better distributes the workload involved in performing tasks. If you are performing many types of client tasks, you don't want to have your machine bogged down by servicing the requests of many other machines. Therefore, it is common to have unmanned computers dedicated to performing server tasks. This is why it is common to refer to a particular computer as a *server* or *the* server. Although many dedicated server machines are put together with hardware better suited for server tasks, it is a common misconception that the term *server* is somehow a hardware designation.

Now you have more than one computer connected, an established means of communication, an established language and engine to perform a useful task, and an efficient distribution of workload. Figure 6.16 illustrates this logic. Take this model and apply it on a global scale, and you have the Internet.

FIGURE 6.16.

The basic networking logic behind the Internet.

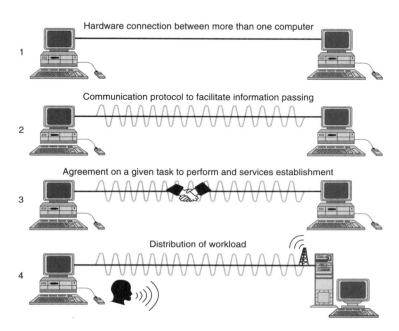

1 — Hardware connection between more than one computer

2 — Communication protocol to facilitate information passing

3 — Agreement on a given task to perform and services establishment

4 — Distribution of workload

The Features

NT 4 provides support for all steps of the networking logic model described in the previous section. The hardware connection to the Internet is made through NT's network adapter and modem support. NT includes Transmission Control Protocol/Internet Protocol (TCP/IP) to facilitate the passing of information over the communications medium. New to NT Workstation in version 4 are Internet Explorer and peer Web services, which provide Internet task-related services on both the client and server sides.

NT 4 supports, and previous versions of NT supported, a variety of network adapters and modems. You can add these devices through the control panel network and modem selections, respectively. Communications protocols can also be added through the control panel network option. The TCP/IP protocol used for Internet communications is included with NT 4.

The Internet Explorer is Microsoft's offering in the Web browser market. A Web browser and server use the http Internet protocol for implementing tasks related to the use of Web pages. The Web page gets its functionality through the use of Hypertext Markup Language (HTML)

files. These files, requested by the Web browser, present themselves as Web pages to the viewer. Web pages consist of text, graphics, sound bytes, and increasingly, multimedia implementations. One of the more versatile features of the Web page are hyperlinks, which provide jumping points to other pages on the Web. For example, if you are viewing information on cancer research, you might find a link to information specific to the prostate and have access to that information with a single click of the mouse. Figure 6.17 shows the Internet Explorer.

Figure 6.17.

The Internet Explorer is Microsoft's offering in the Web browser market.

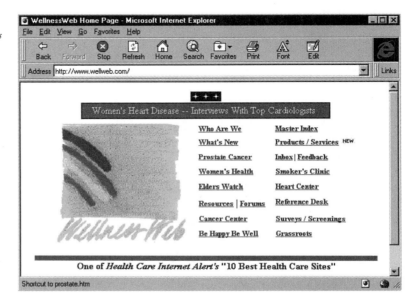

The latest version of the Internet Explorer, version 3, is a substantial improvement over previous versions. There is a new appearance, customization capabilities, speed enhancements, and a wide range of plug-in support applications and controls. This version brings with it ActiveX functionality. ActiveX is the name that is being used for some of the new technologies evolving at Microsoft for making the Internet more dynamic and interactive.

On the server side of Internet task-related applications, Windows NT Workstation 4 comes with Peer Web Services. Peer Web Services are a light version of the Internet Information Server provided with the NT Server product, and they provide server services for the three main Internet protocols: http, ftp, and gopher. These protocols facilitate Web page use, file transfers, and information search tasks, respectively. Figure 6.18 shows the Peer Web Services management utility.

Although Peer Web Services provide full Internet service functionality, they are geared toward working in the peer and intranet environment. Intranets are networks that are not connected to the Internet but implement services associated with the Internet. Because of some of the drawbacks to the Internet, such as poor bandwidth and security issues, many people are taking stock in intranets. The production, collaborative, and information-providing benefits of the Internet are being harnessed on company networks, which can provide better performance and improved security. Peer Web Services provide intranet capabilities on a workstation and workgroup level.

FIGURE 6.18.

The Internet Service Manager provides management features for the Peer Web Services provided with NT Workstation 4.

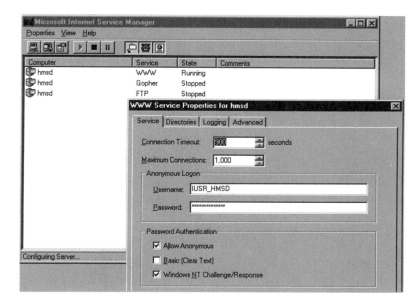

Summary

In this chapter, you got a quick glance at the new features in NT Workstation 4, followed by a general discussion of the more important features and their underlying technologies. The later chapters of the book will provide detailed discussion on usage. Because this is a book geared toward a particular release, I tried to focus on issues and technologies that are important in general but also important as they relate to the present state of computing.

Release 4 is a significant upgrade. The new interface brought with it increased ease of use and an improved graphical model, an expected feature of Windows. NT's strong, adaptable core, seen in the relative ease with which the user and GDI move was made, heals the instability that was the major rallying cry of Windows detractors. Release 4 also brings with it an amazing amount of connectivity features that hold much promise.

OLE and Distributed COM give you impetus to take the next step in computing. In order to move forward, applications must be highly complex and connected, but created in a reasonable amount of time. As the divisions that communications boundaries hold break down and applications become more integrated, the strength of components will become increasingly important.

Similarly, we will have to strengthen the infrastructure on which communication takes place as we extend it. The embrace and extend strategy that Microsoft espouses is evident in the many Internet and intranet features provided in release 4.

NT is an operating system that puts design on an equal level of importance with feature count and cosmetic appearance. This is the reason for its elegance and stability. However, there is something to be said for a rich feature set and visually pleasing appearance. This release brought with it enhancements in core underlying technologies, which are the cornerstone of NT's strength, as well as beautification and functionality enhancements.

CHAPTER 7

Customizing Windows NT Workstation

by Paul Cassel

IN THIS CHAPTER

You might feel that customizing a serious operating system such as Windows NT trivializes it. Nothing could be further from the truth. Your computer is a tool—perhaps your most valuable one—to enhance your productivity. The more your computer works for you and in the way you prefer, the better off you'll be. Customizing the way Windows NT Workstation looks and acts increases your efficiency and makes the time you spend at your console more enjoyable.

Microsoft received a lot of criticism for the Windows 3.*x* interface—the face Windows NT originally sported. Although user interface experts and adherents of competing operating systems such as the Macintosh and UNIX workstations jeered at this interface, users seemed to like it well enough. Still, it left a lot to be desired.

Microsoft spent a lot of time evaluating new metaphors for its next graphical user interface (GUI). The result of this evaluation was the GUI first seen in Windows 95. It proved to be so popular that the contemporaneous Windows NT interface, which was mostly a copy of the Windows 3.*x* GUI, appeared dingy by comparison. Microsoft went to work on NT's GUI to make it appear as modern as its lighter weight companion did. The GUI for Windows NT isn't identical in all respects to the one in Windows 95, due partly to incomplete implementation, but mostly due to functional differences between the two operating systems. If you're familiar with the Windows 95 GUI, you have a good idea of the Windows NT Workstation 4 one.

Security and Customization

Windows NT Workstation requires a logon sequence that not only sets your privilege level, but the face Windows NT shows you. In addition, applications installed in Windows NT can and often will have different configurations depending upon the logged on user. Figure 7.1 shows the desktop of a user logged on normally.

FIGURE 7.1.

The appearance of Windows NT Workstation can depend upon the logged on user.

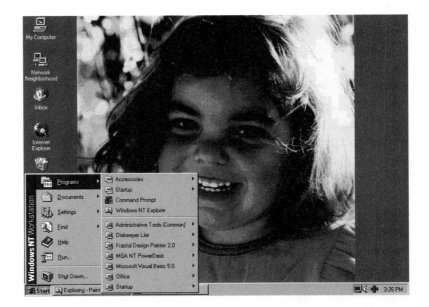

Figure 7.2 shows the same computer console with a different user logged on. The differences in the available programs, as well as the desktop, are all due to the stored profile of the two users.

FIGURE 7.2.

A different user logged on to the console shown in Figure 7.1 sees an entirely different user interface. Not only has this user configured his desktop differently, but he also has installed a different set of programs.

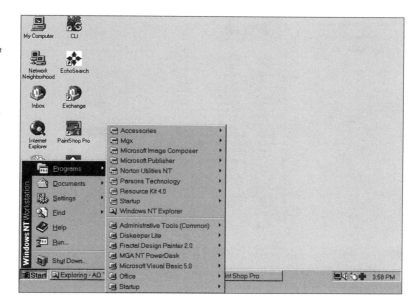

Even the configurations of the commonly installed programs differ between users. For example, the user logged on in Figure 7.1 will have a different profile set for Microsoft Office 97 Professional applications than the user in Figure 7.2. Office 97, as well as other programs, can tell who's logged on and set his or her options accordingly.

For a full discussion of security and users under Windows NT Workstation, see Chapter 10, "Fine-Tuning NT Security."

The Desktop

The Windows NT Workstation 4 desktop is infinity-configurable. That sounds like a brash statement, but it's true. There is no limit—other than your imagination and good taste—to what you can do.

Display Properties

The global display settings are likely the most used options in Windows. Windows NT is no different in this respect. To see the current settings and change them, click on an empty place on the desktop with your secondary mouse button (usually the right button) and hold. You'll see a context menu of the type familiar to those who've used Windows 95. Figure 7.3 shows this menu.

FIGURE 7.3.

Right-clicking on an empty place of the desktop produces a context menu with a Properties entry that leads to the display settings dialog box.

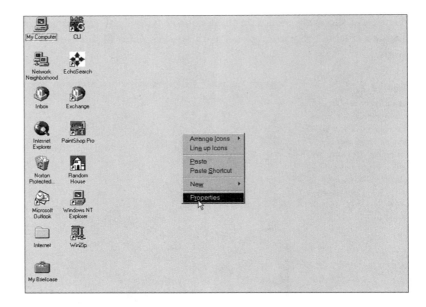

Choose the Properties entry, and you'll launch the Display Properties dialog box. You can also launch this dialog box by double-clicking on the Display applet in the Control Panel. The appearance of this dialog box will differ depending upon the installed video adapter and the logged-on profile. Figure 7.4 shows the Display Properties dialog box for a computer with a Matrox Millenium display adapter. Other display adapters will have different characteristics and so have different details in the respective dialog boxes. However, some choices will remain the same from display to display.

FIGURE 7.4.

The Display Properties dialog box will differ in details, depending on the installed display adapter, but all will have certain options in common.

To alter the display characteristics of your console, click on the appropriate tab, then set to your heart's desire. The Appearance tab sets colors, fonts, and font sizes for the desktop and applications. To set one of these options, click on the Appearance tab, then click on the item you want to change in the window display area. You can also make your setting choice by pulling down the Item combo box.

Figure 7.5 shows the Item combo box expanded with the Menu choice highlighted. This Item will set the characteristics or properties for all the menus in Windows NT.

FIGURE 7.5.

One Item in the Appearance section of the Display Properties dialog box sets the characteristics of all menus in Windows NT.

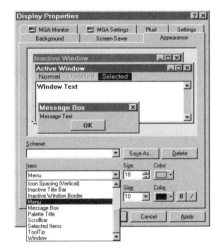

Changing the options for the Menu item from the defaults to a Menu size of 26 points and yellow color with a font size of 14 points with a color of gray, as shown in Figure 7.6, results in the rather bizarre menu appearance shown in Figure 7.7.

FIGURE 7.6.

Windows NT will go along with your appearance choices no matter how inadvisable they are.

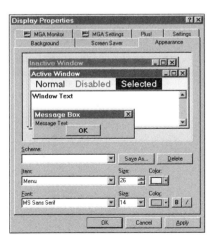

The properties set for the menu in Figure 7.6 are now global for this user in all applications running under Windows NT.

FIGURE 7.7.

The new global settings for the revised menu appearance show up as soon as you click the Apply button.

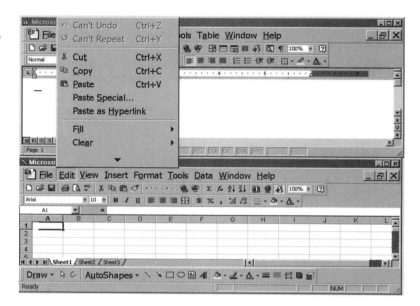

If you develop a desktop scheme you enjoy and want to return to, you can save it in the Appearance tab by clicking in the Scheme text box and entering a name. Windows NT comes with an interesting selection of appropriately named predefined Schemes.

The Settings tab of the Display Properties dialog box controls the color depth (called Color Palette in NT jargon), the general font size (large or small), and the resolution, and is also the place to change your display adapter. Figure 7.8 shows the Settings tab for a typical workstation.

FIGURE 7.8.

The Settings tab controls essential options for the display adapter. The options available depend on the type and capacity of the installed display adapter.

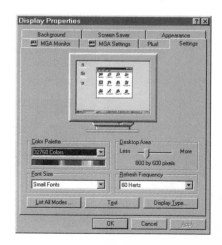

To change resolution, slide the Desktop Area slider control to the left or right. Click the Test button, and NT will try to resize your screen to the new resolution. After a few seconds' test, you'll return to the original resolution and be given an option to accept or reject the tested resolution.

Changing color depth is more complex for NT, because it needs, among other things, to rebuild the desktop to the new color set resource. To change color depth, pull down the combo box labeled Color Palette and then click OK or Apply. Windows NT Workstation will advise you that you must reboot to apply the new color depth.

If you change your display adapter, or just want to view its settings, click on the Display Type button. Figure 7.9 shows the results of clicking on this button.

FIGURE 7.9.

The Display Type button holds information about the display adapter and gives you the option of changing it to your new hardware profile.

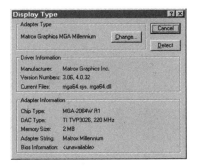

To change your display adapter, click the Change button shown in the dialog box in Figure 7.9. If you want NT to detect your installed adapter, click the Detect button. Windows NT Workstation is pretty good at detecting commonly used display adapters, especially later production ones.

The Background tab allows you to set the Wallpaper and Background for the desktop. You can edit the patterns for the Background by clicking on the Edit button in the Background section. You can also browse for new Wallpaper bitmaps by clicking on the Browse button in that section.

Figure 7.10 shows a graphic made in Micrografx's Designer program. Exporting this to a bitmap format and then using the Browse button to specify it as a Wallpaper results in the desktop shown in Figure 7.11.

FIGURE 7.10.

Creating a custom Wallpaper starts with making or otherwise acquiring the image you wish to use for your desktop. This example uses Micrografx's Designer program to make a network schema, which will be exported to a Windows bitmaps format for use as Wallpaper.

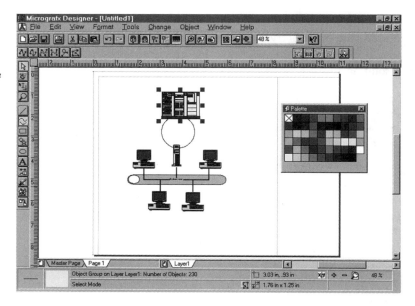

FIGURE 7.11.

Changing to a different Wallpaper by browsing for the desired bitmap can result in an unusual desktop look. This is why they're called personal computers—you can personalize them to your tastes.

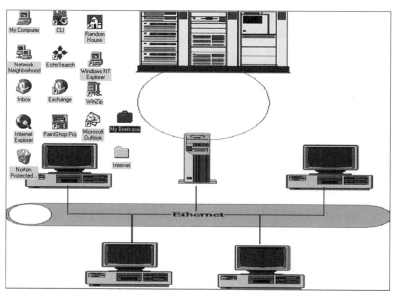

The Plus! tab in the Display Properties dialog box controls various options originally issued in the Plus Pack for Windows 95. Some options of the Plus Pack made their way into Windows NT Workstation 4:

- *Use large icons.* Resizes the icons on the desktop to roughly four times their default size. Good for the visually impaired user, but the larger icons suffer from the usual problems of resizing a bitmap. They get a case of the jaggies when made larger.

- *Show window contents while dragging.* Normally, Windows will blank out the contents of a window while you're dragging it. This option will prevent the blanking of the window, but will slow your machine if you don't have a fairly perky display adapter.

- *Smooth edges of screen fonts.* As fonts grow larger, they tend to grow jagged on their diagonal components. This option uses an anti-alias technique to make the larger screen fonts look smoother.

- *Show icons using all possible colors.* This prevents near color substitution for icons. Most people can't see any difference between the desktop with this option set or unset.

- *Stretch wallpaper to fit the screen.* Will deform, if necessary, the bitmap you choose for the wallpaper to fit your current screen resolution.

You can also use the Plus! settings to change the default icons for such desktop items as the Recycle Bin, Network Neighborhood, and My Computer. Microsoft added this option when many users complained about the lack of configuration options for these icons in Windows 95. Figure 7.12 shows the Network Neighborhood icon being altered from the default.

FIGURE 7.12.

The Plus! tab of the Display Properties dialog box allows you to change the icons for default desktop applets. The File Name text box allows you to change the file containing the selection of icon resources.

The final general tab for the Display Properties dialog box allows you to set the screen saver. Although modern monitors don't burn in like the older monochrome ones, screen savers have become somewhat of a tradition in personal computers. The screen saver in Windows NT Workstation has the utilitarian purpose of being optionally password-protected, allowing you to leave your workstation without fearing that unauthorized people can see your screen. Figure 7.13 shows the Screen Saver tab of the Display Properties dialog box. The options and settings you have will depend upon the particular screen saver you choose.

FIGURE 7.13.

The Screen Saver tab allows you to change the screen saver type and also configure its properties.

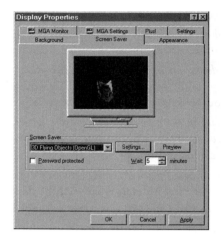

The Desktop Itself

The look of the desktop has practical as well as aesthetic value. Many people like to have often-used applications directly on their desktops—or there, but within folders. Also, some people like to have their desktop icons scattered willy-nilly around, and others enjoy them in some order.

To arrange your desktop icons, right-click on the desktop. Choose Arrange Icons from the context menu. Then choose from the offered sort orders. You can also choose Auto Arrange to have Windows NT Workstation arrange your icons while you work.

Figure 7.14 shows a desktop badly disordered, and Figure 7.15 shows the same desktop after the Arrange Icons by Name context menu choices.

The Line up Icons option on the context menu aligns the desktop icons to a grid, but doesn't change their positions any more than to square them up. In other words, it doesn't bunch or sort them like the Arrange Icons option does.

It's simple to add a shortcut to an application onto the desktop. Here's one way. From the Windows NT Explorer, find the application you want to add to the desktop. This can be either another shortcut or the application itself. Right-click on the file, then drag it to the desktop. Release the right mouse button and Windows NT Workstation will give you the option to

- Move it
- Copy it
- Create Shortcut(s) Here
- Cancel

Customizing Windows NT Workstation

Chapter 7

121

7

CUSTOMIZING
WINDOWS NT
WORKSTATION

Figure 7.14.

Right-clicking on the desktop opens a context menu offering a variety of ways to sort your icons.

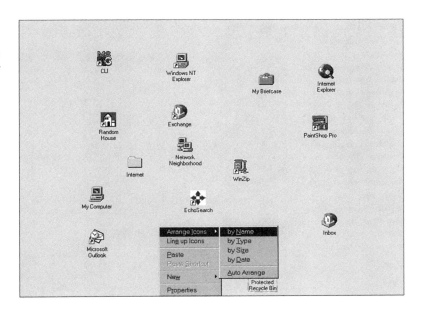

Figure 7.15.

The Arrange Icons options make for a neater desktop. Here is the result of applying the by Name option to the desktop shown in Figure 7.14.

Choosing the third option will create a shortcut on the desktop pointing to either the application itself or another shortcut, which eventually points to the application. Be careful about moving applications to the desktop, because this physically moves files from their folders to the Desktop folder. This will cause malfunctions in most Windows and Windows NT programs. Figure 7.16 shows the creation of a desktop shortcut.

FIGURE 7.16.

To create a shortcut on the desktop, locate the application you want to have a shortcut to, right-click on it, drag it to the desktop, release the mouse button, then choose the Create Shortcut(s) Here option from the offered menu. This creates a shortcut in your Desktop folder. If you have any difficulty doing this, you might need to examine your permissions settings.

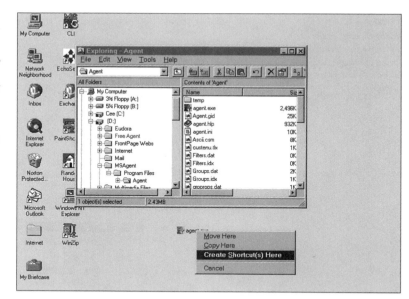

To create a New folder on the desktop or any registered application, right-click on the desktop, choose New from the context menu, then make the appropriate choice. Figure 7.17 shows the New context menu choices from one computer. Your New options will differ depending upon your registered programs and the logged on user.

FIGURE 7.17.

The New option from the right-click context menu for the desktop allows different choices, depending upon the installed programs and the logged on user.

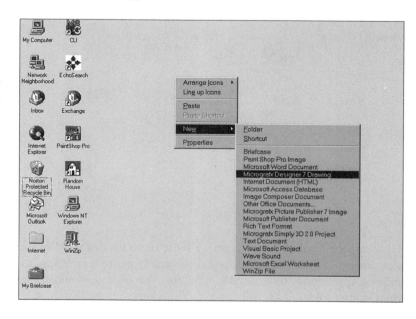

Like Windows 95, Windows NT Workstation 4 will allow folders within folders. This vastly simplifies organizing a desktop over versions of Windows that didn't allow this. Figure 7.18 shows the folder Microsoft Private in the Internet folder that's on (actually in) the desktop. Technically speaking, the desktop itself is a folder as well, so the Microsoft Private folder is really three-deep.

FIGURE 7.18.

Windows NT Workstation 4 will allow folders within folders. This facilitates desktop organization.

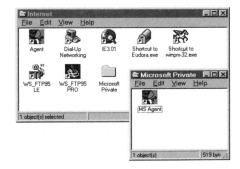

Right-clicking on a desktop icon will bring up a context menu that will differ slightly depending upon your installation. The Properties choice will bring up a dialog box, allowing you to change the General properties of the folder, including Sharing and Security. The Sharing options are covered in Chapter 12, "Working with the NT File System," and the Security options in Chapter 10. Figure 7.19 shows the desktop icon context menu for one computer, and Figure 7.20 shows the General tab of the Properties option of the context menu in Figure 7.19.

FIGURE 7.19.

This is the context menu for a desktop folder. The choices will vary, depending on the logged on user and the installed applications. For example, the Add to Zip option on this context menu appears only because an application, WinZip, is a registered program.

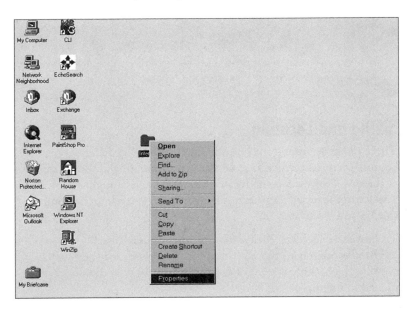

FIGURE 7.20.

The General tab from the Properties choice shown in Figure 7.19.

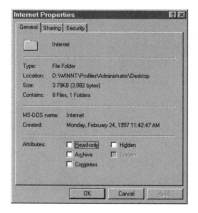

The context menu for a desktop folder is the same as the context menu for a folder in Windows NT Explorer. Similarly, the options for a desktop shortcut and applications are the same as for Explorer shortcuts and applications, respectively.

The Taskbar

The Taskbar is an elegant and simple addition to the Windows NT Workstation 4 interface. It's a convenient navigation tool to switch between programs, to keep minimized various utilities, and to keep track of what's running in your computer. It also is an alternative way to bring up the Task Manager, a valuable Windows NT tool.

> **NOTE**
>
> To switch between a few programs serially, you can use the cool switch, Alt+Tab. This is usually more convenient than using the Taskbar.

Sizing and Locating

The Taskbar appears at the bottom of your screen by default. This works well for most people, because there are fewer things occurring or appearing at the bottom of their applications than at the top. However, some users, especially those brought up on the Macintosh, prefer their Taskbar at the top of the screen. There is also a good use for locating the Taskbar at your screen's side, as you'll see later on.

To move the Taskbar, click on it with the primary (usually the left) mouse button, then drag the mouse pointer to the new location. Unlike some other objects, the Taskbar won't float, but must be anchored at one of the four corners of your desktop. Figure 7.21 shows the Taskbar moved to the top of a desktop.

FIGURE 7.21.

You can move the Taskbar to any border of your desktop, but unlike some other objects, it can't float in the middle of your screen. Here, the Taskbar resides at the top of the desktop—a place comfortable for some users, especially those used to the Macintosh.

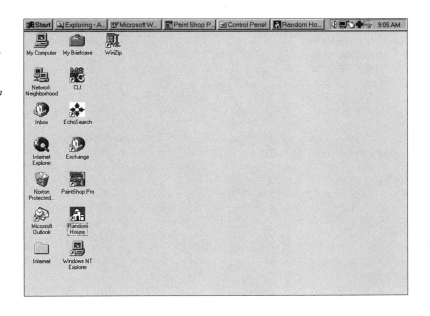

7

CUSTOMIZING
WINDOWS NT
WORKSTATION

Sizing

The Taskbar is expandable, allowing it to show more information about running applications and utilities than its default size. If you look at Figure 7.21, you have a pretty good idea of what applications are running, even though the Taskbar abbreviates them somewhat. They are from left to right:

- The Windows NT Explorer
- Microsoft Word
- Paint Shop Pro
- Control Panel
- The Random House dictionary

In addition, the utilities in the Tray (on the far right of the Taskbar) are, from left to right:

- The Volume applet
- MGA Quickdesk (specific to a particular video adapter)
- IntelliPoint
- Net.Medic
- Dial-up Networking
- The Windows NT clock/calendar

Take a look at Figure 7.22, which is the same Taskbar but with more applications launched.

FIGURE 7.22.

*Launching more than a
few applications makes
the Taskbar excessively
cryptic.*

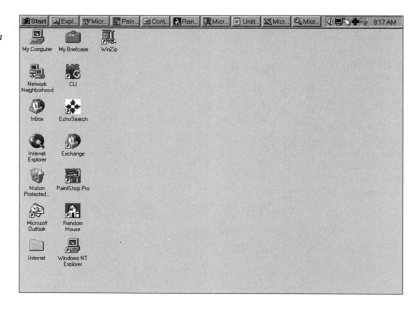

If you're familiar with the Microsoft icons, you might recognize the addition of Excel and Access, but note that the partial word `Micr` appears in three places. Two of them refer to Microsoft, Access and Excel, but the one on the left is short for Micrografx. Note also that Paint Shop Pro's placeholder has been shortened to `Pain`.

Obviously, the Taskbar needs some more real estate for its display. To widen the Taskbar, move your mouse pointer to the edge furthest away from the screen border. The cursor will change to a double arrow. Click and drag away from the border to size the Taskbar to your needs. Figure 7.23 shows the Taskbar expanded to twice its previous width and relocated to the bottom of the screen.

Taskbar Properties

The desktop shown in Figure 7.23 again has the icons for running applications in the Taskbar large enough to be understandable again, but eats up a significant amount of territory. One way around this is to set a property for the Taskbar to have it pop up only as needed. To get to the properties sheet for the Taskbar, click on the menu selections Start | Settings | Taskbar or right-click (the secondary mouse button click) on the Taskbar and choose Properties from the context menu. Figure 7.24 shows the Taskbar Properties dialog box.

FIGURE 7.23.

Expanding the Taskbar allows it to show more of the running applications, but also grabs a lot of territory.

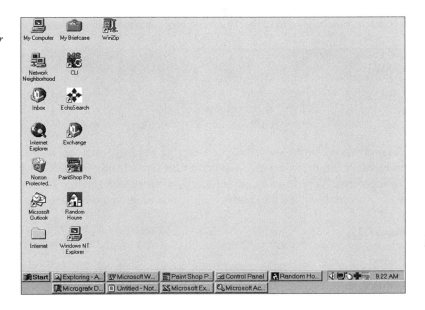

FIGURE 7.24.

The Taskbar Properties dialog box allows you to set certain Taskbar and Start menu properties.

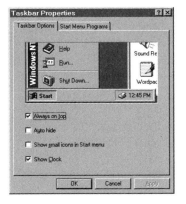

These properties are the following:

- *Always on top* allows the Taskbar to float over running applications. An on-top Taskbar will shove applications up or down to make room for itself without blocking other bars, such as status bars or title bars.

- *Auto hide* hides the Taskbar unless the mouse cursor moves over a hot area calling it back up.

- *Show small icons in Start menu* replaces the larger icons with smaller ones in the Start button menu. It makes the Start menu slightly more compact.

- *Show Clock* indicates whether to show the clock/calendar at the far right of the Taskbar.

Click on Auto hide to have the Taskbar out of the way when you're working within applications.

NOTE

If you have Always on Top deselected, you might lose the Taskbar. To pop it and the Start menu up, press Ctrl+Esc.

A good way to have a very lucid Taskbar that's not too intrusive is to set the Taskbar to Auto hide, make it quite wide, then move it to the left side of your desktop. Figure 7.25 shows this arrangement. Note how obvious the names of the running applications are. Because the Taskbar is set to Auto hide, it isn't intrusive when you're in an application.

FIGURE 7.25.

Combining a wide Taskbar with Auto hide on the left of a desktop makes for a non-intrusive, yet informative, Taskbar. Do not locate such a Taskbar on the right of your screen or you'll have problems using the vertical scroll bars within applications. Some displays, notably laptops, use drivers and hardware that can result in significantly different-looking displays than shown here. The screens here are typical of the majority of Windows NT displays, but individual screens will vary.

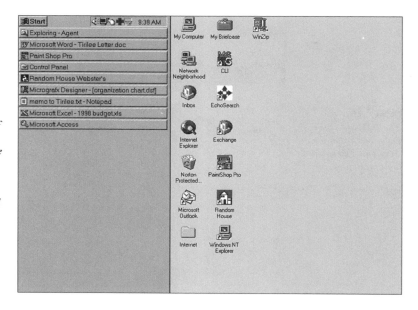

NOTE

Even if you don't have much of an application's button showing in the Taskbar, you can see the entire text of the application and, if enabled, its document, by allowing your mouse cursor to linger over the application's button. This will bring up the whole text in a way similar to a Tooltip.

Taskbar Control of Applications

The Taskbar can control how running applications appear on the desktop. Right-click on the Taskbar to pop up its context menu. Note the three top entries:

- *Cascade Windows* stacks the nonminimized applications like cards in a Solitaire game.
- *Tile Windows Horizontally* tiles (places side by side) windows for nonminimized applications across the screen so they each touch the left and right sides of the screen.
- *Tile Windows Vertically* tiles (places side by side) windows for nonminimized applications across the screen so they each touch the top and bottom of the screen.

Figure 7.26 shows several applications tiled vertically.

FIGURE 7.26.

Tiling windows vertically isn't terribly practical with many nonminimized applications.

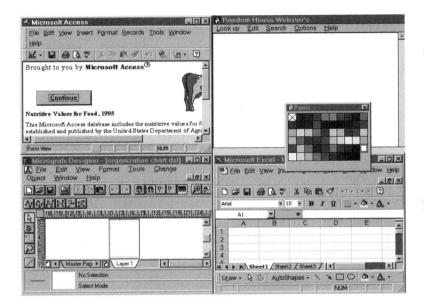

The second section of the context menu of the Taskbar has one entry to start, Minimize All Windows. This will give you fast access to your desktop by shrinking all applications down to their Taskbar icons. If you have your applications tiled or All Minimized, this section has an Undo entry allowing you to restore your applications to their state previous to your having tiled or minimized them. The Undo Minimize isn't active if you've minimized the applications one by one. It's only there if you've used the Minimize All Windows command from the Taskbar.

The final entry on the Taskbar context menu brings up the Task Manager. The use of the Task Manager is covered in Chapter 34, "Task Manager."

The Start Menu

You can customize the Start menu just about to your heart's content. One approach is to launch the Taskbar Properties dialog box by right-clicking on the Taskbar, then choosing Properties from the context menu or by choosing the menu choices Start | Settings | Taskbar.

> **NOTE**
>
> The Start menu is part of the Taskbar. This is why its properties appear in the Taskbar Properties dialog box.

Click on the Start Menu Programs tab. This will bring up a section of the dialog box shown in Figure 7.27.

FIGURE 7.27.

The Start Menu Programs tab is one place to configure the Start menu entries.

The Start Menu Programs tab has four buttons:

- *Add* brings up a simple wizard, allowing you to specify or browse for an application or document to add to the menu.
- *Remove* shows a hierarchical listing of the applications currently part of the Start menu, allowing you to delete any or all of them.
- *Advanced* brings up an Explorer view of the Programs group, allowing adding, deleting, or renaming of Start menu entries.
- *Clear* clears the Documents entries in the Start menu. This is good for cleaning out old business, as well as hiding evidence of what documents you've been accessing.

Drag and Drop to Start

You can also drag and drop applications from anywhere, including the Explorer, to the Start menu as a way to include them in this menu. To do this, just right-click and drag, dropping the application or shortcut on the Start button. Figure 7.28 shows a shortcut being dragged from a desktop folder to the Start button.

FIGURE 7.28.

You can drag and drop an application or shortcut from anywhere to have it appear on the Start menu. Here, a shortcut to the Pegasus e-mail program is being dragged to the Start button.

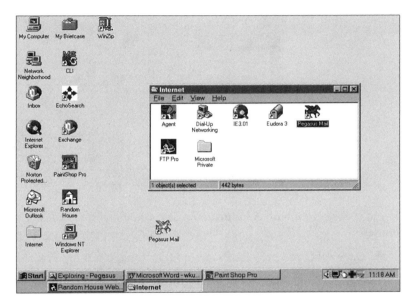

Figure 7.29 shows the results of dropping this shortcut on the Start button.

The same technique as shown in Figures 7.28 and 7.29 will work with folders, as well as applications and shortcuts.

Direct Manipulation of Start

Few, if any, people remain content with the organization of their Start menu. Windows NT Workstation has an easy method, allowing complete customization of this important section of the user interface (UI).

Right-click on the Start button itself. If you're logged on with Administrator rights, you'll see a two-section context menu appear. The top section (the only one if you're logged on without Administrator rights) has these entries:

- *Open* opens the Programs folder in icon view.
- *Explore* opens the Programs folder in the Explorer view.
- *Find* opens up the Find dialog box. This is the same dialog box available through the Explorer.

FIGURE 7.29.

Adding an application or document to the Start menu by dragging and dropping adds it to the uppermost section of the Start menu.

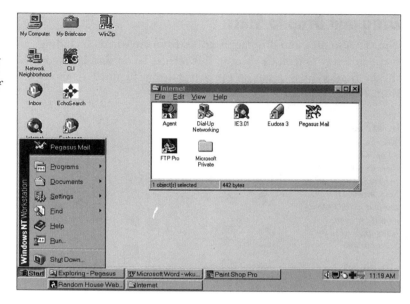

If you're logged on with Administrator rights, you'll also see a lower section with these two entries:

- *Open All Users* opens the Program folder for applications available to all users.
- *Explore All Users* opens the Program folder for applications available to all users in Explorer view.

Due to Windows NT Workstation's security, all users won't see all applications. In the same vein, users won't be able to configure the Start menu for applications unavailable to them. If you're logged on with Administrator rights, you will be able to configure any part of the Start menu.

The Open and Explore entries will give access to those Start menu entries that are above the divider line in Start | Programs. Figure 7.30 shows a Start | Programs menu for a workstation.

The applications from the MGX group to the Resource Kit 4.0 are exclusive to the logged-on user. The applications below the divider line, from Administrator Tools to Startup, are available to all users if they have the requisite permissions. For example, a user logged on as part of the default User group cannot create a new user group. This topic is covered in depth in Chapter 10.

While logged on with full rights, you can configure the entries in the Start menu three ways:

1. Choose the Open or Open All Users entry from the context menu of the Start button to see the menu laid out in icon view, similar to the Windows NT 3.51 interface.

2. Choose the Explore or Explore All Users entry from the context menu of the Start button to see the menu laid out in the Explorer view.

3. Use the Windows NT Explorer to locate the user you wish to configure under the [%windowsNT%]\Profiles directory.

7

CUSTOMIZING
WINDOWS NT
WORKSTATION

FIGURE 7.30.

The Start | Programs menu has two sections. The upper section applies to the logged on user; the lower one is for all users.

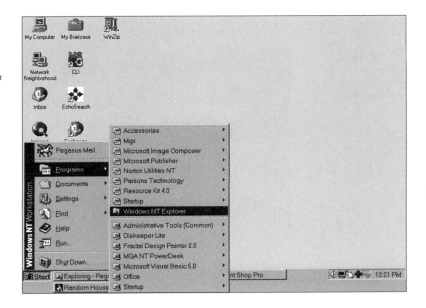

Figure 7.31 shows what happens when you choose the Open entry from the context menu for the Start menu.

FIGURE 7.31.

The Open choice from the Start context menu opens the Programs group in icon view, similar to older versions of Windows and Windows NT.

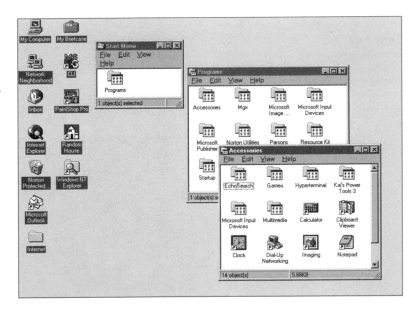

Figure 7.31 has the Accessories group open. Accessories is part of the Programs group. From this view, you can add, move, or delete any group or entries within the group. You can use the Explorer to locate and add (usually by dragging) any item or shortcut to any group or any part of the menu. Figure 7.32 shows the Resource Kit 4.0 group dragged into the Accessories group.

FIGURE 7.32.

Adding an entry to a group is as simple as dragging it there.

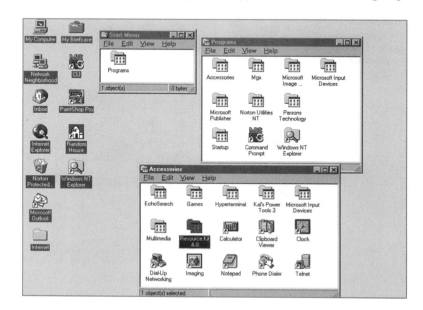

Figure 7.33 shows the results of that move in the Start menu.

FIGURE 7.33.

After deleting or adding an entry to the Start menu group, it appears as part of the Start menu.

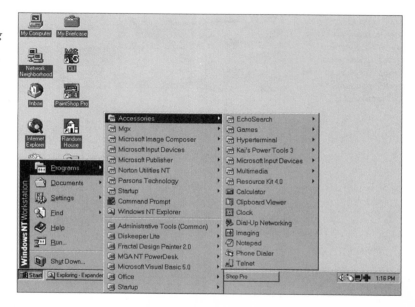

Figure 7.34 shows the Windows NT Explorer with the Administrator group under the Profiles directory. This is where the information for the user logged on as Administrator (user name, not user rights) is stored. There is an entry under Profiles for each user name.

FIGURE 7.34.

The Explorer reveals the location of user-specific profiles for the Start menu.

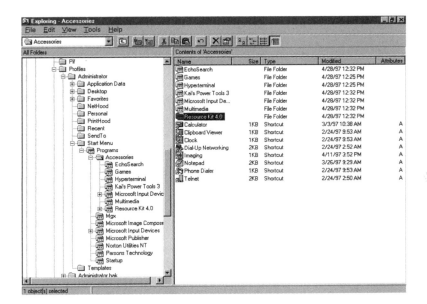

7

Note that the Resource Kit 4.0 is under the Accessories entry. This reflects the change made in Figure 7.32.

You can even make unconventional entries in the Start menu if you choose to. Figure 7.35 shows the results of dragging a shortcut to an Access database to the Norton Utilities NT program group. Doing so doesn't make much sense in an organizational sense, but it gives you an idea of how much flexibility you have.

You can add Control Panel items to the desktop or the Start menu using the same techniques as demonstrated with the previous examples. For example, to add the Sounds applet to the desktop, open the Control Panel, locate the Sounds applet, right-click on it, then drag and drop it on the desktop. Choose the Create Shortcut(s) Here option. Figure 7.36 shows the results of this operation.

Using the same technique as in Figure 7.36, you can add shortcuts to these applets to the Start menu.

FIGURE 7.35.

Although few people will want to do it, you can drag any object into a program group. Here, a Microsoft Access database shortcut has been added to the Norton Utilities NT program group.

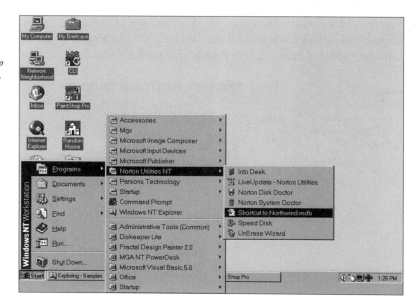

FIGURE 7.36.

You can drag and drop anywhere in the Start menu, program groups, or the Windows NT Explorer. Here, a Control Panel applet's shortcut has been added to the desktop.

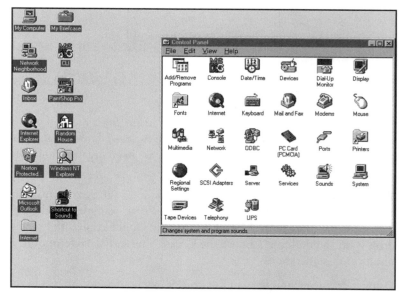

The Mouse and Other Pointing Devices

The configuration of your mouse depends upon your mouse brand and model. Even if you have a generic mouse with only two buttons and no supplied software, Windows NT Workstation will allow you to do basic operations, such as changing which button is primary (usually left) and which is secondary.

However, most mice and other pointing devices today come with some sort of enhancement software to add value to themselves over the $10.00 generic mice you can get at most discount stores. Figure 7.37 shows the mouse configuration software bundled with the Microsoft Mouse with a wheel.

FIGURE 7.37.

The customization options you'll see in Windows NT Workstation will depend upon your mouse's brand and model. Here is the dialog box for a Microsoft IntelliMouse with a wheel.

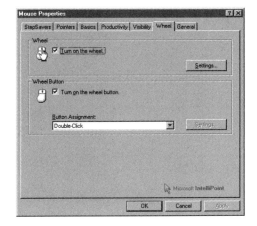

This dialog box is an example of the IntelliPoint software. Many of the options in this complex dialog box apply to nonwheel mice, too. Here is a list of the tabs and the options on those tabs:

- *Step Savers* has the pointer jump to the default button, slow over clickable objects, single-click where you usually double-click, and select a window by pointing to its title bar.

- *Pointers* allows selection of pointers (cursors) for various applications and the choice of cursor collections (schemes).

- *Basics* determines mouse speed, double-click speed, and choice of primary and secondary buttons.

- *Productivity* turns on the odometer, turns on single-click-to-drag, and changes mouse orientation (horizontal and vertical).

- *Visibility* shows "radar" waves around the cursor on pressing of the Ctrl key and hides the key during typing.

- *Wheel* turns on the wheel for scrolling and assigns a key sequence or click sequence to the wheel button.

- *General* supplies your device's make and model.

Customizing the Keyboard

Just as with pointing devices, the customizations available for your workstation's keyboard will depend upon the keyboard and its supplied software, if any. However, even if you have no software and a generic keyboard, Windows NT Workstation offers a surprisingly wide variety of options within the Keyboard applet in Control Panel.

Figure 7.38 shows the Keyboard applet running.

FIGURE 7.38.

*The Keyboard applet
within Control Panel
has three tabs holding a
wealth of customization
options.*

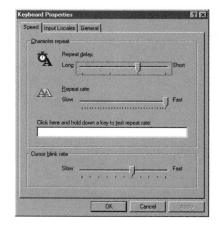

Here are the tabs, with a short explanation of the options available on each:

- *Speed* controls the rate for various elements associated with the keyboard, such as cursor blink rate, repeat rate, repeat delay.
- *Input Locales* allows switching to different International layouts and options within some of those layouts.
- *General* enables you enter the make and model of your keyboard.

The most interesting and complex tab is the middle one, Input Locale. Microsoft intended Windows NT Workstation 4 to be an international operating system capable of different character sets and layouts. One persistent mapping for different cultures is using different monetary symbols, but that's just scratching the surface.

To see the different keyboard drivers, open the Keyboard applet in Control Panel, click on the middle tab Input Locales, then click on the Add button. Figure 7.39 shows the results of doing that.

FIGURE 7.39.

*The Input Locales tab
has options for a
bewildering amount of
keyboard layouts if you
count variations to
those layouts.*

The list goes from Afrikaans to Ukrainian. There are roughly a dozen English types, from US English to Jamaican English and beyond. Figure 7.40 shows the results of switching to a Greek keyboard layout in Word and typing an English sentence. Note also the added icon directly to the left of the clock on the Taskbar. This announces what keyboard mapping is in use. The EN stands for US English. GK is Greek, AK is Afrikaans, and so forth.

FIGURE 7.40.

Windows NT Workstation has the capability of adding various keyboard layouts and switching between them with an icon in the Taskbar tray.

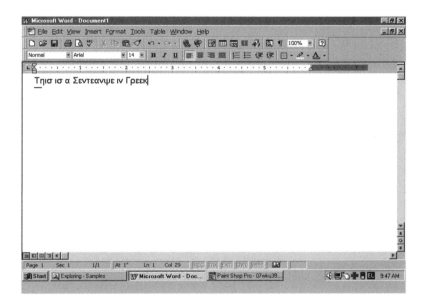

7

CUSTOMIZING
WINDOWS NT
WORKSTATION

You also have options within some international keyboard layouts. Some US English users are sold on the Dvorak keyboard, although the tests showing this layout might not have been carried out with as much scientific precision as its promoters claim. No matter, Windows NT Workstation gives you this option. To see what options are available for any keyboard, click on the Properties button with the target keyboard selected. Figure 7.41 shows the options for the US English keyboard.

FIGURE 7.41.

Windows NT Workstation not only allows you to use the rare Dvorak keyboard type, but variations within it.

Summary

Working efficiently means working the way you want to, not necessarily the way Microsoft believes most people enjoy. To that end, Windows NT Workstation offers you a wide array of customization options for the screen, desktop, Taskbar, pointing device, and keyboard.

Many of these options will depend upon your installed hardware. However, even the most generic hardware will allow some adjustment of screen resolution, screen color depth, pointing device options, and keyboard maps.

A little ingenuity and a dab of experimentation will get you a Windows NT Workstation console just as you like it.

Tuning Windows NT Performance

by Paul Cassel

IN THIS CHAPTER

CHAPTER 8

Everybody wants a fast computer. In fact, just about the only hard-and-fast rule that exists among all users is that they can never get enough speed. Most out-of-the-box Windows NT Workstation setups will show decent, if not optimum, performance. However, after a while, especially after a few months or years of driver installs and deinstalls (also called *uninstalls*) and application installs and deinstalls, performance of that setup will deteriorate. This chapter will help you identify the areas of slowdown (bottlenecks) and what you can do to speed up those areas.

Underlying Factors

The speed of a machine depends on several underlying factors. These factors determine the maximum performance level after tuning. Think of these factors using a car analogy. A perfectly tuned Neon won't be as fast as a slightly out-of-tune Viper, due to the underlying factor of power to weight ratio, as well as other related factors. If you want to go fast, the way to go is to get a Viper, not tune your Neon. This section covers the major factors that separate the Neons from the Vipers in the world of Windows NT Workstation.

Hard Disk Speed

There is nothing other than lack of RAM that will slow a Windows NT Workstation setup down like a pokey hard disk. Windows NT uses a sophisticated algorithm to start hard disk virtual memory (VRAM, or the paging file) well before physical RAM is exhausted. The reason is so that the step to VRAM isn't sudden, as it would be if NT waited until all physical RAM was used and then suddenly switched to a large unit of disk RAM. Because of this, the paging file comes into use even on very heavy workstations with greater than 64MB RAM. Actually, you'd be surprised at how fast today's applications eat RAM. Figure 8.1 shows the Performance Monitor with the Page File Use counter opened. This shows a 96MB computer running Microsoft Word and Excel for 97 and Paint Shop Pro. Each program has a small document loaded. Even so, the system has gone to the paging file for additional RAM.

Figure 8.2 shows the Performance tab of the Task Manager. This figure was captured at the same time as Figure 8.1. You can see that less than half of the total physical memory has been used by the few applications loaded, yet the system is still rather heavily using the paging file.

The paging file use is only part of the reason for getting a fast hard disk. Windows NT Workstation applications are large, as are their data files. Applications include dynamic libraries, which are loaded as your use demands. Opening, closing, and accessing data is dependent on your hard disk speed. Windows NT Workstation uses a disk cache to speed up apparent operations and repeat accesses, but your entire computer speed is largely governed by its hard disk throughput.

FIGURE 8.1.

Windows NT Workstation creates and uses a paging file (VRAM) with surprisingly few applications loaded.

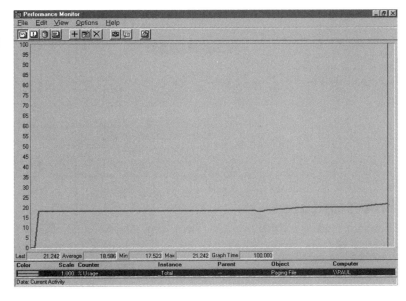

FIGURE 8.2.

Even with more than half of physical RAM remaining, Windows NT Workstation uses the paging file. A slow hard disk will drastically slow down operations even if much free physical RAM remains.

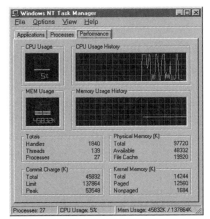

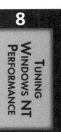

If you have even the slightest doubt remaining about the size of today's current application data files, take a look at Figure 8.3. This is a Microsoft Word 97 file containing one byte (the letter *k*) of data. It's almost 20KB large.

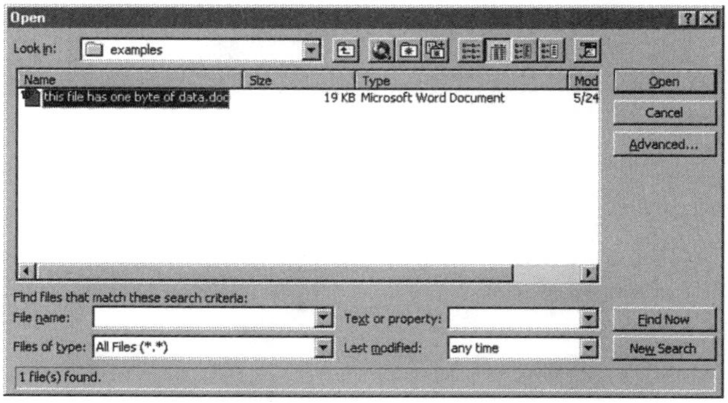

Figure 8.3.
Today's applications require file sizes of rather large granularity, due to the non-data information they store.

Processor Speed

Processor speed is a rather overrated element in total system performance. Surely in otherwise identical systems, the one with the fastest clock will be the fastest computer; however, for most uses, the processor speed isn't the single greatest bottleneck.

If all things are otherwise equal and you can afford the freight, by all means get a faster clock speed processor. But put the budget for this behind other, more important items, such as a speedy hard disk, the right processor type, RAM, and L2 cache.

Processor Type

If you're over in the Digital Alpha world, your choices are fairly straightforward. Faster Alphas cost a bit more and give a bit more in a manner a reasonable person can understand by reading DEC's catalogs. However, the world of Intel is the world of the marketer, and it seethes with confusion and traps. Each processor in Intel and Intel-clone land has its advantages and disadvantages. Choosing the optimum processor for your budget is more of a fine balancing act than a rational decision. Here is a short overview of the decision matrix for a few of the currently available processors.

When Windows NT Workstation 4 was new, most workstation buyers' only choice was a Pentium (now the Pentium I) in various clock speeds (from about 90 MHz to 150 MHz). They also had L2 (level 2, or fast cache running at system speed) from 0 to 512KB.

> **NOTE**
>
> Generally speaking, you should match your L2 cache to the total system RAM with nobody using 0 L2, those with 32MB RAM or less (running Windows NT Workstation?) with 256KB, and those with more than 32MB, 512KB. Those were simple times. After a while, the Pentium speeded up to 200MHz, where it topped out.

Soon the Pentium Pro, Pentium's next generation, dropped in price enough for people to consider this processor for workstations rather than servers (for which it was originally intended). Although there were a few slower Pros, most that were bought were either 180 or 200MHz models having an L2 going from 256 to 512KB.

The Pentium Pro was tuned specifically for 32-bit operating systems and for applications such as Windows NT Workstation. A 200MHz Pentium Pro with appropriate caches ran away from the same speed Pentium. Here is an example where clock speed doesn't dominate. A 180MHz Pentium Pro running Windows NT Workstation is much faster than the equivalent 200MHz Pentium. It's not even close.

Apparently dissatisfied with the lack of confusion in the marketplace, Intel introduced in quick succession the Pentium MMX and the Pentium II. The Pentium MMX is the regular Pentium I with certain matrix speeding instructions added. If you run MMX-enabled programs, it's faster (or can be faster) than the equivalent Pro, even running Windows NT. If you don't run MMX programs, it's slower than the Pro but faster than the Pentium, due to a larger on-board cache.

The Pentium II then came into the fray. This is the first Intel processor using the packaging (edge connections) that Intel says will power their future processors. Introduced in a 233MHz and a 266MHz model, with a 300MHz model hot on their heels, the Pentium II was originally a Pro with MMX extensions and a new package.

However, some things were lost along the way. The Pro runs its cache at full system speed, can natively scale to four processors, and is optimized for 32-bit operating systems and applications. The Pentium II runs its cache at half system speed (133MHz on the 266MHz processor), scales to only two processors, and has design compromises in order to run 16-bit operating systems and applications well. This 16-bit optimization came at the sacrifice of how well it runs 32-bit systems and applications.

With the Pentium II, the clock speed tends to overpower the optimization of the Pro. Therefore, a 266MHz II will run faster than a 200MHz Pro for workstation use. This edge tends to dissipate as you add processes, because as this occurs, the optimization of the Pro gives it an edge. This edge evaporates if you run MMX-enabled applications, where the Pentium II runs away from anything currently available in the Intel world.

However, if you run four (or more in a proprietary system) Pros in non-MMX applications sensitive to scaling, the Pro once again shines as the winner. This discussion doesn't even consider the offerings from Intel competitors Cyrix and AMD. The decision matrix for processors is more confusing and fraught with peril today than ever before. However, in this confusion is opportunity.

Something new showed up with the Pentium II. Previous to this chip's generation, Intel competitors had, at best, clone chips slower and of a generation behind Intel's offerings.

8

TUNING
WINDOWS NT
PERFORMANCE

However, the Pentium II has competition technically equal or superior to itself, with chips from Cyrix/IBM and AMD. These chips are roughly the equivalent of the Pentium Pro with MMX extensions and run at speeds similar to Intel's chips. Each competitor chip has a few points favoring it over Intel's, too.

Although the compatibility of these chips seems fine for at least mainstream business use, their widespread acceptance isn't assured yet. Intel has done a good job of cementing itself into a position where OEMs need to curry its favor. The general coalescing of the industry around a few huge OEMs tends to work against Intel's competition. Although each of the current OEMs is large enough to worry Intel (and risk retaliation), if it starts cranking out a lot of the competition's computers, none is large enough to face Intel down.

This leaves the Intel chip competition in the odd position of having competed well technically, but now having to fight the war of marketing and mindshare. The consumers will win if they prevail. If not, this will become a cold, grim world, where the only thing inside will be what Intel deigns to give us, sold at whatever Intel's price happens to be.

Way back when you could only choose a certain Intel processor with options such as speed and cache, you couldn't go too far wrong—but you couldn't optimize your purchase either. Today, you must consider not only what speed and cache to choose but also what operating systems and applications you'll use.

Physical RAM

This is simple: the more the better. If you have too little, you're wasting your time and money running Windows NT Workstation. Microsoft has some incredible minimum requirement of 12MB for Windows NT Workstation. This puts you heavily into paging before the system is even partially loaded. You should run a 12MB RAM system only if you are in training to be a saint. By the time you spend a few days with your system, nothing will try your patience ever again.

Realistically, the system RAM for Windows NT Workstation picks up where Windows 95 and its successors poop out. These systems perk up as you feed them RAM to about 32MB. That's also the realistic minimum level of physical RAM for Windows NT Workstation. Actually, 64MB is closer to the truth, with 96 or 128MB being a comfortable level if you run many processes or manipulate large files.

Figure 8.4 shows Micrografx Picture Publisher 7 with a large bitmap loaded. The same screen shows the Performance tab of the Task Manager. Note the use of memory is up to about 85MB on this 96MB system. Take a careful look at the other memory-eating statistics, such as threads, handles, and processes.

FIGURE 8.4.

Even efficient applications need to use a lot of RAM if you load them up with large data files.

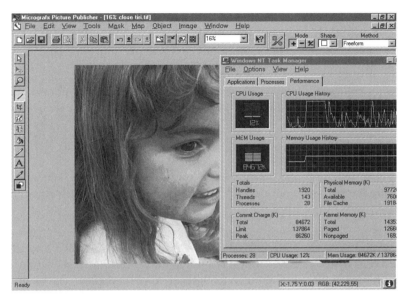

Figure 8.5 shows the same session as Figure 8.4, but the large bitmap has been closed and a smaller one opened in its stead. Note that the physical RAM released by Windows NT Workstation for this one change is roughly 30MB. Also note that the figures for threads, handles, and processes are almost identical to Figure 8.4. This shows that the only difference in whether the system uses roughly 85MB or 52MB RAM is the loaded image.

FIGURE 8.5.

Change the loaded file and this system uses a full 30MB less of RAM.

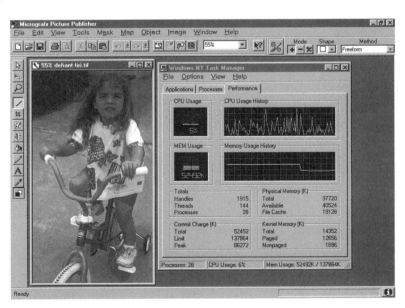

8

TUNING
WINDOWS NT
PERFORMANCE

The moral of this example is that you should know what you're doing. If you're sure you'll use, say, only Word or WordPerfect for simple documents, you don't need much RAM. As soon as you start running many applications concurrently or loading large files, you need to up your RAM.

This applies to any data. The example used a bitmap and a bitmap editor, but it could have just as easily shown the same phenomenon using a database such as Microsoft Access and a large file of that type.

The Buss

The system buss, often misspelled as *bus,* can drastically affect system speed. Luckily for most, the adverse choices once available aren't being marketed much anymore.

Although it has had some criticism from electrical engineers (EEs), the now almost universal PCI buss works decently enough for most uses. People will argue that the older MCI and EISA busses were superior, and maybe they were. However, the MCI buss died from being proprietary to IBM brand systems (or requiring brutal licensing fees), and the EISA buss today exists only on mainboards directed to the specialized server market. The somewhat fragmented VESA (or VL) buss has gone the way of the dodo.

You should make sure your critical system peripherals use the PCI buss instead of the ISA ones that usually accompany these systems. There's no harm in plugging a modem or sound card in an ISA slot, but an ISA video card has a distinct disadvantage compared to a PCI one.

Similarly, a 32-bit PCI NIC (Network Interface Card) is the way to go for speedy Net connections, rather than the slightly cheaper ISA ones. Although technically the NIC isn't a part of the local system, if you need much in the way of Net resources, a slow NIC can slow down the entire show.

Video Card

The speed of a system's video adapter greatly affects how fast a system seems to be. There's nothing like snappy screen refreshes to give the feeling of a snappy system.

Today, few video adapters run so slowly that they actually decrease the real-time use of a system. This implies that scrimping here won't make much, if any, difference in overall system performance. This is partly right and wholly wrong.

The two interfaces between users and the computer are the keyboard and the screen. Some would add the sound and video camera system, but these are outside the scope of a performance discussion. Just as a lousy keyboard will slow down even the most adept typist, a slow screen will give the user an impression of a slow system.

Perceptions count as much as reality does here. A barely adequate adapter will save $150 over an excellent general-purpose one. This savings can ruin the entire user interface, so in the end it's poor economy.

If you're exploring the high end of the graphical world, such as 3-D rendering, and have applications that support them, you should consider the specialized graphics adapters formerly available only for heavy workstations such as those manufactured by Silicon Graphics (SGI).

Similarly, today's buyer should consider not only traditional video adapters, but newer initiatives such as Intel's new AGP, the accompanying technology to some new chipsets and the next generation of Intel standards after the PCI.

A very fast video card can't make a slow system fast, but a mediocre card can make a fast system seem slow.

General Tuning by Option

Many people run a well-tuned system slower than its optimum speed because they unintentionally lard it up with baggage. This isn't necessarily the fault of users; it often occurs as installation programs add undetected services set to start up with the system.

There's nothing wrong with these services and programs, but they do rob your system of its speed as they eat RAM and launch processes.

PROCESSES AND THREADS

NT gains a process upon the launch of an application. A *process* is an executable program with at least one thread (naturally) and some memory addresses.

A *thread* is a part of a process running the program's instruction set. A program can launch many threads (multithreading), thereby concurrently executing several instruction sets at the same time.

For example, when Windows NT Workstation runs both Microsoft Word and Excel, it's running two processes. However, each process can launch more than one thread. If Word paginates at the same time that it is running a spell check, it's multithreading.

Here are some tips to reduce system load:

- Reduce color depth. A 24/32-bit display takes more processing power than a 15/16-bit one. Very few people can tell the difference between color depths of 16 and 24 bits. There is no advantage in the higher depth for business applications such as Lotus 1-2-3 or Microsoft Word.

- Dump your wallpaper. The wallpaper eats some system resources all the time, not just when you have the desktop on display. Because most people use their computers with all the desktop occupied by applications, wallpaper doesn't even provide a lot of amusement value.

■ Be aware of the resource cost of your add-ins. Many programs install themselves on your machine and then on your desktop and Start menu; also, they launch a part of themselves automatically at each startup. Figure 8.6 shows the Processes tab for a simple system.

FIGURE 8.6.

Programs often stealthily add themselves to your startup process. The Processes tab of the Task Manager is a good tool to detect such skullduggery.

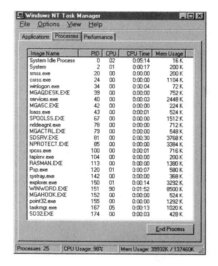

■ The entries nddeagnt.exe, SDSRV.EXE, and NPROTECT.EXE are all part of the Norton Utilities. These processes automatically launch themselves with each startup, even when the programs from the menus aren't started. There is nothing in the setup or the release notes for this program to indicate that this is the case.

They are necessary because without them the vital parts of the Norton suite, such as Norton Protection (unerase) and Speed Disk, can't work. However, these processes take in the aggregate almost as much RAM as the large application, WINWORD .EXE, which as you can see is also launched.

■ If you add the Norton Utilities to a marginal system, say one with 24MB of RAM, the system effectively loses 8MB of RAM, thus becoming a submarginal system.

■ The entries starting with MGA are part of the driver set that comes with the Matrox Millenium card that this system uses. Although they don't take up much RAM, they do eat resources by being processes.

■ Even the point32.exe process takes up 1.3MB RAM. This is the IntelliPoint software that comes with the Microsoft IntelliPoint Mouse (the wheel one). It wasn't that long ago that a heavy system came with one-half the total RAM this system uses to run the optional part of the mouse driver!

> **NOTE**
>
> The point isn't to eliminate these processes, but to be aware of them and the price that they exact on your system. Most people don't begrudge their systems the RAM for the Norton Utilities, because they figure the added safety worth the cost. Similarly, most people like the added features of the IntelliPoint mouse and gladly pay the cost in resources. However, if your system is marginal, the place to start investigating why it's fallen to submarginal is here.

- Detect and eliminate, if possible, defective programs having the Pac Man syndrome. Some programs won't release RAM as they close threads. The more you run these programs, the more resources they eat, until a modest program, running for days or doing a lot of opening and shutting of files, can grow to overwhelm your system.

- In a perfect world, programmers would test their programs using readily available tools from vendors such as Nu-Mega, but they don't. The only way to detect these programs with limitless appetites is to check their memory load using the Processes tab of the Task Manager or the Performance Monitor. Figure 8.7 shows the Performance Monitor tracking a few counters for processes.

FIGURE 8.7.

Defective processes can eat your system up like Pac Man run wild. Here, the Performance Monitor is tracking certain process counters.

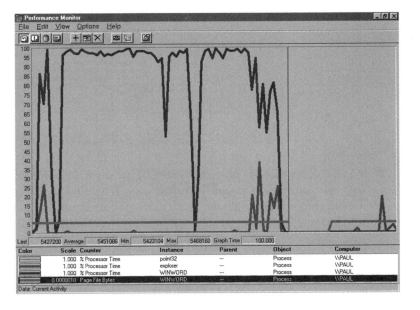

8

TUNING
WINDOWS NT
PERFORMANCE

■ Rid your system of orphaned shared resources. Windows NT Workstation does a good job of tracking shared resources and eliminating them when they come to the end of their usefulness. This happens when their entry in SharedDlls decrements itself to its final decrement (becomes zero). Figure 8.8 shows a typical SharedDlls section. However, no system is perfect, and older installs of Windows NT have a few old drivers or shared resources loading when they shouldn't. This is more prevalent if you use many older 16-bit applications. If you're hunting through the Registry manually, keep in mind that Windows NT Workstation uses two SharedDlls keys. One is HKEY_LOCAL_MACHINE\SOFTWARE\Microsoft\Windows\CurrentVersion\SharedDlls, and the other is under the Multimedia key.

FIGURE 8.8.

The entries for shared DLLs appear under the SharedDlls *key in the Registry.*

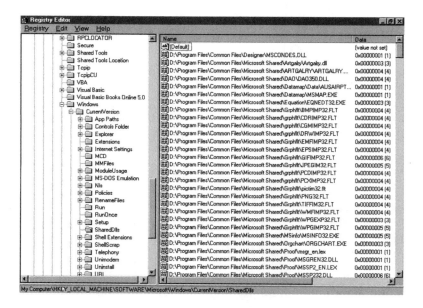

■ To clean your Registry of spurious entries, use the RegClean utility available for free from Microsoft. Also, manually inspect your System.ini and Win.ini files for un-needed entries. Finally, if you have a particular suspicion about an errant program, search through your Registry for it. Naturally, you should eliminate those keys only after taking the appropriate backup precautions.

■ Eschew icon madness. Every icon you see eats some resources. This is a big problem under Windows 3.11, but much less so under Windows NT or Windows 95 and its successors. However, this is a factor to keep in mind.

■ Use NTFS if at all possible. NTFS is much more efficient and safer, and it has features never dreamed of in any FAT or VFAT system. Unless you need your volumes accessible to non-NTFS systems, use this better system.

■ Locate your page file on a fast drive. If you have several disks in your system, use the fastest for the paging file. Remember, your system constantly accesses your paging file while you access even the most-used applications only occasionally. Figure 8.9 shows the dialog boxes where you can change the location and size of paging files.

FIGURE 8.9.

Windows NT Workstation allows you to change the size of a swapfile (paging file) and its location. You can have your paging file over more than one disk, too. The important thing to keep in mind is to keep the file on your fastest disk.

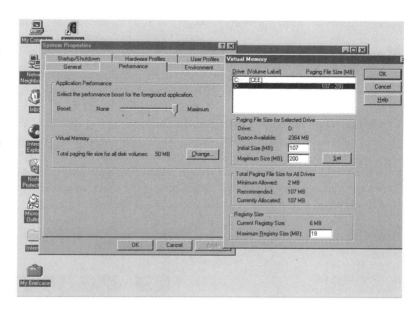

OPTIMIZING AND THE PAGING FILE

To get the best performance possible from your paging file, it needs to be optimized. Here is the best way to do this.

Relocate your paging file from your fastest disk/volume combination to any other place temporarily. Run a disk optimizer such as Diskeeper or Speed Disk on the volume that is the permanent home of the paging file. Then set your paging file back to this now optimized volume. This effectively defrags your paging file.

■ Optimize your disk regularly. There is a persistent myth that NTFS volumes never fragment. This is false. Just as optimizing (squeezing or defragmenting) is important on FAT volumes, it's equally important on NTFS ones.

■ Get an optimizer and run it often. Most come with schedulers, so this operation doesn't have to, and shouldn't, affect your interaction with the computer. Both Diskeeper and Speed Disk can run in the background, but this will slow the system down. Also, file accessing can slow a system down to the point where background running, especially on a badly fragmented disk, isn't such a hot idea.

Diagnosing Bottlenecks

Once you've got your system running efficiently by choosing the right hardware and eliminating unneeded resource eaters, it's time to roll up your sleeves and start tuning in earnest. The Performance Monitor is the primary tool for detecting performance problems. Chapter 33, "Performance Monitor," tells you how to use and understand this tool.

Memory

The simplest measure of how much your system is slowed by memory issues is to see how much memory is in use at any one time. The Performance tab of the Task Manager gives a summary of memory uses, whereas the Processes and Applications tabs give some detail information. Obviously, if you're running many applications or running applications that eat a lot of RAM, you're going to be seeing more of your memory accesses from the paging file. This is dramatically slower than from physical RAM. Therefore, if you see your used memory rising close to your total available memory, your system is suffering from lack of physical RAM. Figure 8.10 shows the Performance tab of the Task Manager for a system where the committed memory is just about equal to the total physical memory.

FIGURE 8.10.

This system has memory use just about at the limit of physical RAM. The Commit Charge figure for memory use is the total RAM, both physical and virtual, "committed" to use. In this case, there still remains physical RAM available, but the system is well into using the disk for RAM, thereby slowing performance slightly.

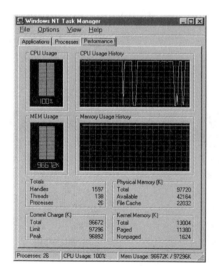

The more important performance statistic is the Hard Page Faults counter from the Performance Monitor. This measures when the system must access memory other than the physical memory allocated to it. The word *fault* in *hard page fault* doesn't indicate defect, but rather a less than ideal condition.

There are two kinds of page faults: hard faults and soft faults. A fault means that the system can't locate requested data from the working set or the memory currently available to an application. Hard faults mean the system must go to disk to resolve the information request. Soft faults mean the system can access the data from RAM. Naturally, a soft fault won't affect your system in any way you can detect, whereas a hard fault will.

Run the Performance Monitor and open the Page Faults counter from the Memory object. Figure 8.11 shows this counter running on the system shown in Figure 8.10.

FIGURE 8.11.

The Page Faults counter of the Memory object is a good indicator of memory performance problems.

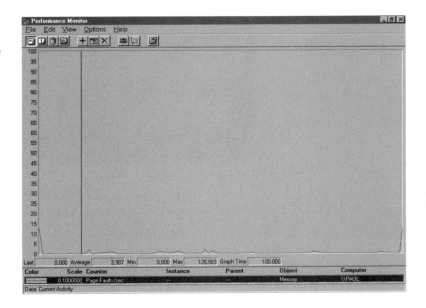

Here's how to interpret this counter:

< 4 faults/second average	This indicates no memory problems.
=4 < 7 faults/second average	This indicates a problem that bears monitoring. A system in this range isn't performing at top levels.
>7 faults/second average	This is a system seriously suffering from RAM starvation.

To get an idea of where your system's performance lies, log the Page Faults per second for the Memory and Process objects. You'd also do well to monitor other counters, such as the Page File Bytes from the Process object and Available Bytes from Memory. Run the log for several days of normal operation, logging at an interval of at the most a minute and the least five minutes.

You need to study the log carefully to see events in combination that might degrade performance. A combination of page faults and disk accesses is a big tip-off that your system is dragging.

A useful tool available with the purchase of the Windows NT Workstation Resource Kit is the Page Fault Monitor, which generates a continually updated list of page faults and their generating applications. Figure 8.12 shows the end of a short run for this resource against Microsoft Word 97.

FIGURE 8.12.

The pfmon utility is a relentless tracker of page faults, hard and soft.

In this run, you can see that the application generated about 1,600 faults, of which slightly under 500 were hard ones. You can also direct pfmon to create a log file using different formats.

Figure 8.13 shows the output of pfmon, pfmon.log, opened in Notepad. The .log file is readable by Notepad and able to be translated into programs such as Microsoft Access and Microsoft Excel for analysis. Usually, you'd be interested in the hard faults only when analyzing performance. Viewing the file in Notepad allows the leisurely examination of a pfmon run.

FIGURE 8.13.

The log file from pfmon allows careful examination of a run's results. This log captured both User and Kernel mode page faults for Winword.exe.

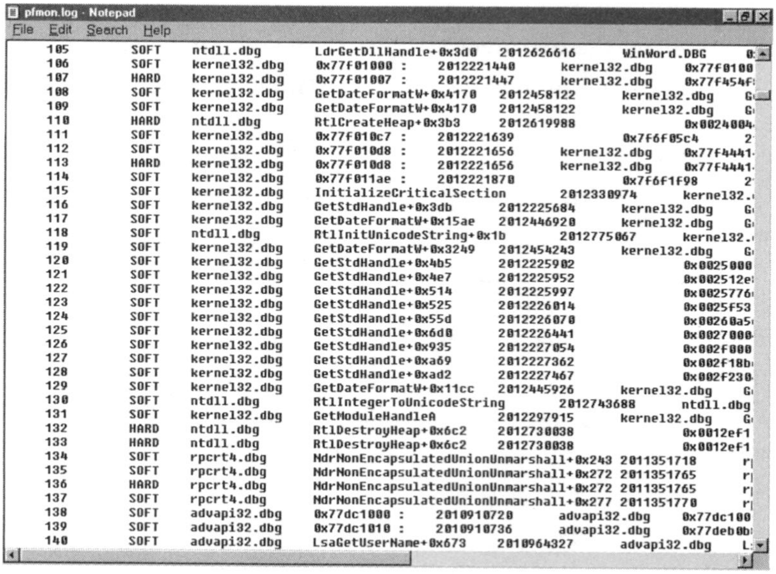

Although the Performance Monitor counter Page Faults/sec will report all page faults, the more important counter is hard page faults. Although there is no specific entry bearing that name as a Performance Monitor counter, the Page Reads/sec counter effectively reports this information.

When a hard page fault occurs, the system must read from disk rather than from either the working set or cached memory. These reads are page reads, and there is a counter called Page Reads/sec. For each hard page fault, you'll see a page read. Therefore, the page read, although not the same as a page fault, indirectly reports those hard faults.

The accompanying counter, Pages Output/sec, records how many pages need to be written to disk to clear the working set. Because either reading or writing to the disk eats up performance, monitor both.

In summary, to detect or monitor performance attributable to memory, log the counters for Page Faults/sec, Page Output/sec, and Page Reads/sec, at the very least. Log them at an interval of roughly 60 to 300 seconds for several days of typical use. Generally speaking, you don't need to do much analysis of the log. If either of the disk activity counters exceeds six or seven occurrences per second, you need more RAM or you need to load fewer processes on the computer. Figure 8.14 shows the charting of the counters needed for a memory analysis plus the counter for the Working Set. This machine has 96MB RAM and only a few programs loaded. The Working Set is roughly 45MB, leaving plenty of room for expansion. As you'd expect, there are few Page Faults or disk reads/writes. The spike of disk reads toward the right of the chart was caused by opening a program triggered by the AT command.

8

TUNING
WINDOWS NT
PERFORMANCE

FIGURE 8.14.

The chart in Performance Monitor tracking memory performance limiters plus a Working Set counter.

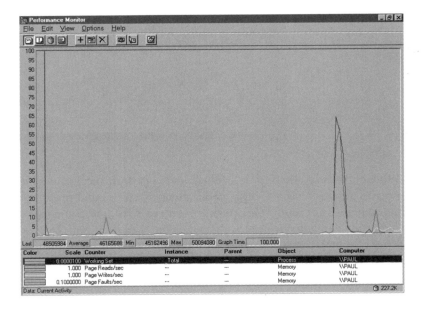

The other indication of a computer choking on too little RAM is the size of the paging file. Remember, this file is used by Windows NT Workstation starting well before the committed and reserved physical RAM grows to its end in order to make for an easy transition onto VRAM. The greater the percentage of total memory that is disk-based, the lesser the performance. To put it another way, disk RAM percentage is inversely proportional to total computer performance.

The object Process has a counter Page File Bytes:_Total and a counter for individual processes. The Total counter is of the most interest in determining the performance hit from the paging file. Figure 8.15 shows the chart from Figure 8.14 with the total page file counter added. This system has a paging file of about 20MB, even with a working set of only 45MB and a total RAM of 96MB. This graphically shows how early Windows NT Workstation goes to the paging file even in the presence of a good deal of physical RAM.

FIGURE 8.15.

The _Total instance of the Page File Bytes counter of the Process object in Performance Monitor is a good indicator of how much your system is depending on the paging file.

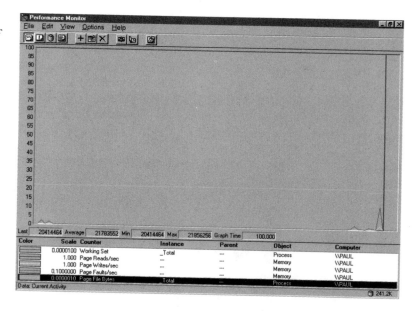

Although you can also track individual process performance, there's little you can do about it other than refusing to use piggy applications. Keep in mind the characteristics of individual applications while monitoring them (see Figure 8.16). For example, Microsoft Access will go to disk while transaction processing more often than Microsoft Word will while writing. That doesn't mean Access is a piggy application, but rather that it is inherently different by design.

The Working Set counter is useful when evaluating how much memory an application eats, but there's little you can do other than not use the application if you don't like what you find out.

FIGURE 8.16.

You can monitor individual processes, but you must take into account inherent differences between processes when interpreting the results.

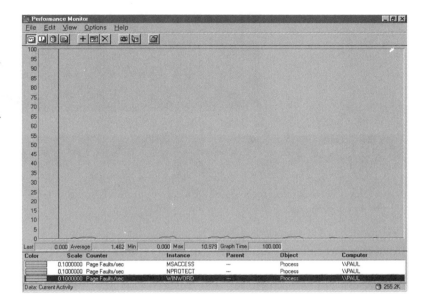

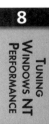

Disk Problems

You can use the Performance Monitor to determine various disk activity statistics using such counters as %Disk Write Time and Avg. Disk sec/Transfer. However, before these counters will work, you must activate the utility diskperf. To activate diskperf from the command line, start a CLI session and then enter diskperf -y or diskperf -ye if the Ftdisk (fault-tolerant) service is running. The -y switch says to start monitoring at next startup. The -ye (all case-insensitive) switch says to start monitoring at the next startup on machines with disk striping.

Check the Devices applet in Control Panel if you are unsure about Ftdisk. Next, reboot and launch Performance Monitor. You can start diskperf for a remote computer by specifying its name on the command line. For example, the following:

```
diskperf -y \\Tirilee
```

will start the diskperf utility on the computer \\Tirilee the next time that computer is booted. Figure 8.17 shows the initialization of disk monitoring.

Once you've started the diskperf utility, your Performance Monitor can swing into action.

FIGURE 8.17.

You need to start the diskperf *utility. This is part of the standard Windows NT Workstation distribution.*

UNCERTAINTY

Remember your Physics 101. When logging any disk performance objects, be sure to write your log to a disk other than the one being monitored. If you don't, the act of logging will affect your statistics.

If your Performance Monitor shows all zeros for disk counters, you need to start diskperf. Figure 8.18 shows the chart for a computer with diskperf running. As you can see, the counters provide a wealth of information.

FIGURE 8.18.

The chart in Performance Monitor can track various counters for the instances of logical and physical disks.

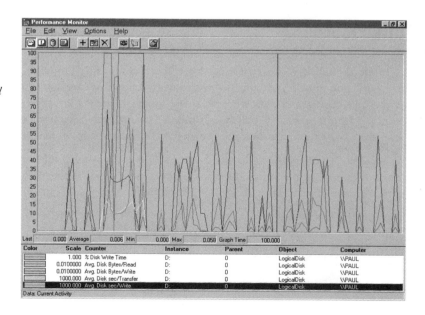

As colorful as the chart in Performance Monitor is, it's a little tough interpreting the display. To make some sense of the Performance Monitor's output, either log or view the output in the report form. Figure 8.19 shows the Report view of Performance Monitor during the same period as the chart shown in Figure 8.18.

FIGURE 8.19.

The Report view of the Performance Monitor is easier to interpret than the Chart view for some objects and their counters.

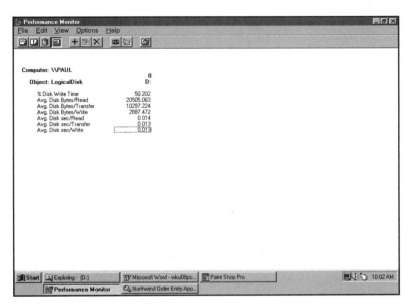

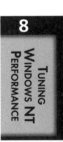

Here are some disk object counters to keep an eye on:

- *Disk Time:* The more disk thrashing, the less the performance. Make sure you're doing an apples-to-apples comparison here before coming to a conclusion.

- *Avg. Disk Queue Length:* This is the backlog of disk read/write requests. A long queue indicates the disk can't keep up with system requests.

- *Disk Bytes/sec:* How fast is throughput? This is a good measure for comparisons between physical disks, and even different computers.

Processor

It's rare to find a computer that's severely bound by a processor, but they're out there. The System object is the way to detect such performance eaters. In fact, if you had to pick one object from which to infer the performance of a machine, the System object is the best. However, there's no reason to limit yourself to one object because Performance Monitor allows you to mix and match objects, instances, and their counters.

Figure 8.20 shows a Performance Monitor chart showing processor counters. Applying a Gaussian Blur in Picture Publisher to a large bitmap caused the spikes in processor time and processor queue that start on the right of the chart and continue to the left.

FIGURE 8.20.

Most processors that are part of business-oriented computers loaf along, but they have their jobs cut out for them when doing chores such as Gaussian Blurs. Note the spike in Processor Queue Length, showing the processor here had developed a request backlog.

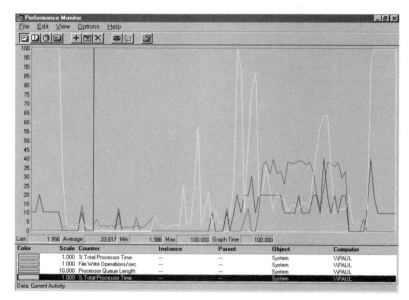

Here are some of the most relevant objects and their counters. Keep in mind that momentary readings of a chart aren't indicative of your system. To get a better idea of performance, log your computer over several days under a load you think is typical.

Processor Object:

- ■ *%User Time and %Privileged Time:* The time the processor spends executing user mode and privileged operations.
- ■ *%Processor Time:* How much of total time was the processor doing something? An idle processor is one with excess work capacity. Conversely, a processor that's busy chugging away constantly is working hard for its money.

Process Object:

- ■ *%Processor Time:* Use the _Total instance to measure the total of all tasks that take up processor power. You can also use each process' instance, but the _Total instance is the most critical measure for system information. This counter should remain about 100% because it's the total minus interrupts.
- ■ *%User Time and %Privileged Time:* The time the processor spends executing user mode and privileged operations.

System Object:

- *Processor Queue Length:* How many threads are stacked up awaiting attention by the processor? This is the processor backlog.

- *% Total Processor Time:* Shows percentage of clock time for a given interval that saw the processor(s) busy.

Thread Object:

- *Thread State:* The processor status of a particular thread. This will vary from state 1 (ready) to state 5 (waiting).

- *Priority Current:* The priority of a particular thread (instance).

Unless you're doing processor-intensive chores, the least likely place you'll find your performance improvement possibilities is in the objects of this section. If, however, you do a lot of computational-intensive operations, such as raster graphics, matrix math, or similar operations, you'll have to look elsewhere to speed up your computer. Surprisingly for many, even applications that you might think of as processor intensive, such as Microsoft Excel, generally don't exact too much of a toll on the processor as they do incremental calculations. If you want to see your processor-related instances soar, load a large spreadsheet and then force a recalculation. Other than rather artificial examples like that, most modern systems seem to be able to keep up with their processor requests.

Fixing It

Once you've found your performance problem areas, you can do two things: live with them, or fix them. Fixing disk and memory problems is fairly straightforward. You replace pokey disks with fast ones. Similarly, you just add physical RAM. The latter is more important because it affects the former. Adding RAM can effectively speed up a disk by increasing the room for a process' working set, thereby reducing the occurrence of page faults. More physical RAM also means more disk cache (dynamically created by Windows NT Workstation), which also effectively (if not actually) increases the disk speed. There is no such thing as a disk fast enough (other than RAM disks) to make up for the lack of physical memory.

The moral of this performance tale is to add RAM whenever in doubt. The only instance where more general RAM won't increase performance at least somewhat is when your computer is utterly processor-bound. Even then, an increase of L2 cache (usually static RAM) can give a goose to a computer slowed by its processor.

If that doesn't help, or if it's impossible, the only solution is a processor upgrade. This usually entails a mainboard (motherboard) switch, although the new Intel package found on the Pentium II and later Intel processors (SEC or Single Edge Connector) is supposed to offer processor upgrades with a current mainboard. This idea isn't new. In the past it hasn't worked, because when you want to change the processor, you usually want to change other mainboard items such as a support chipset.

The new Intel scheme is supposed to solve all these problems. The world now wonders if it will.

Summary

The best way to eliminate the need to tune performance is to create a system that comes tuned for the task at hand. A system should be designed for the applications it will run. This isn't usually the case at large shops, where all is sacrificed on the altar of uniformity.

The large shop's slouch toward mediocrity means those using common applications usually do all right. Grab any computer system off the shelf and it will run Microsoft Office 97 or WordPerfect 8 just ducky. The ones that suffer under the uniformity lash from generic systems are those running out-of-the-ordinary applications, such as Adobe PhotoShop, Micrografx Picture Publisher, video editors, CD creation, and other multimedia or 3-D applications.

Traditionally, those oddball application people required oddball machines such as the moribund Apple Macintosh. However, a little forethought combined with the type of system analysis possible when using the Performance Monitor can create and then tune a standard Intel or Alpha system to rival most specialized iron.

II
PART

Fine-Tuning Windows NT Workstation

Advanced Control Panel Tools

by Mike Sheehy and Thomas Lee

IN THIS CHAPTER

CHAPTER 9

The Control Panel comprises a number of applications, called *applets,* that allow users to configure NT Workstation. A Control Panel applet is a Windows NT dynamic link library (DLL) stored with the extension .CPL. Users can use applets to define preferences that govern the look and feel of the User Interface and also determine how NT Workstation interacts with its devices and the environment around it. Through these applets, you can configure different aspects of the system to suit your needs. These applets range from the simple, such as configuring your mouse, to the advanced, such as configuring the system for Uninterruptible power supply (UPS). Control Panel applets are found in the %SYSTEMROOT%\System32 directory. If you remove one or more of the applet files from the System32 directory, you will not see the applet's icon in the Control Panel the next time you invoke it. Likewise, you can add Control Panel applets simply by placing their files into the System32 directory.

In this chapter, you will take a closer look at the more advanced applets within the Control Panel and see how you can take advantage of what they offer. The Control Panel is accessed either by the My Computer program group or from the Start menu (click Start, select Settings, and then Control Panel), as shown in Figure 9.1.

FIGURE 9.1.

Accessing the Control Panel through My Computer or the Start menu.

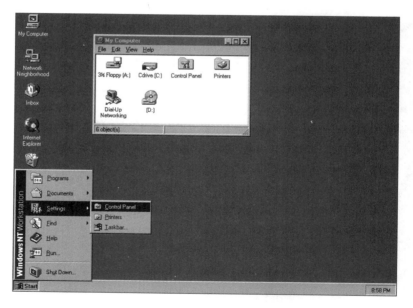

Client Service for NetWare (CSNW)

The first of these advanced tools we will look at is Client Service for NetWare (CSNW). Windows NT Workstation provides full client support for Novell NetWare 2.*x*, 3.*x*, and 4.*x* as standard. This client support is provided by loading the CSNW in the Network applet. With CSNW loaded, NT Workstation can access file and printer resources running on a NetWare server.

To configure the NT workstation to support CSNW, you must first load the CSNW service. The following procedure outlines the steps you must take to load the service:

1. Log on to the workstation as Administrator.

2. Open the Control Panel and double-click on the Network applet (see Figure 9.2).

TIP

You can also access the Network applet by right-clicking on the Network Neighborhood and selecting Properties from its menu.

FIGURE 9.2.

Accessing the Network applet in the Control Panel.

3. Select the Services tab and click on the Add button (see Figure 9.3).

FIGURE 9.3.

Adding Client Service for NetWare.

NOTE

You will be prompted for the path of the distribution files. If you have a CD-ROM, load it and enter the correct path before clicking OK.

4. Select Client Service for NetWare from the drop-down list and click OK (see Figure 9.4).

   At the end of the file copy, you should see the Client Service for NetWare entry added to the list of Network services within the Services tab.

FIGURE 9.4.

Select the Client Service for NetWare from the list of services.

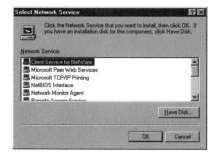

5. Click Close to exit the network settings. The setup program binds the new configuration and prompts you to reboot the workstation.

When the workstation reboots, you are prompted to configure the CSNW after you log on. You can do so at this point or at a later date by accessing the CSNW applet that has been added to the Control Panel.

The CSNW dialog, shown in Figure 9.5, is divided into four frames. Before you start configuring any settings, you must be aware of whether your NetWare network is running NDS. NDS is a global database containing user account and other configuration information. The default tree and context frame allow you to specify a default tree and context if your network uses NDS in a NetWare 4 environment. At login, your default tree and context define your NDS name and the position of the username you will use. This enables you to use all the resources without having to be prompted for further passwords.

Alternatively, you can specify a preferred server if you are in a non-NDS network. The Preferred Server frame allows you to specify a NetWare server to log onto initially. You can select one from the combo box, which contains all bindery-based NetWare servers that were discovered on the network. You also have the option of selecting <None>, in which case no login is attempted until you try to access a NetWare server. This applies primarily to NetWare 3.*x* or 2.*x* environments or 4.*x* with Binary Emulation.

FIGURE 9.5.

The Client Service for NetWare dialog box.

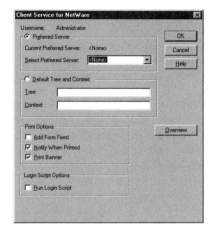

The Print Options frame allows you to set the following printer options:

- *Add Form Feed* causes the NetWare printer to add a form feed to the end of each document sent for printing.
- *Notify When Printed* provides notification messages when your documents have been printed.
- *Print Banner* generates a printer banner page for each document sent for printing.

The final frame on the dialog is the Login Script Options. By checking the Run Login Script check box, you enable the user's login script to run whenever a user logs onto a NetWare server or NDS tree.

All these settings are user-specific but are stored in the Registry in `HKEY_LOCAL_MACHINE\ SYSTEM\CurrentControlSet\Services\NWCWorkstation\Parameters\Options`. If you look at this key, you see a subkey per user (identified by the Windows NT SID), below which are the CSNW options. This means that these parameters are not transportable via roving profiles.

PCMCIA

PCMCIA devices, or PC cards as they are now referred to, are thin credit-card—sized devices for portable computers. The Personal Computer Memory Card International Association is the standards body for PCMCIA devices. With NT Workstation, there is no Plug and Play support, so your workstation will not automatically detect, install, or configure a PC card for you. Neither does NT Workstation support "hot swapping" of PC cards, so you have to shut down the workstation before you remove a PC card. Without the support of these two features, you must do all the work to get your PC cards installed and running. To add a PC card, such as a modem or a network card, you must go through the Control Panel and select the Modem or Network applet as appropriate. With each of the installations, you will be taken

9

ADVANCED
CONTROL PANEL
TOOLS

through the installation process by a Setup Wizard routine. The next section will use the installation of a network PC card to detail the steps of installing a PC card and ensuring that is running properly after installation.

Installing a PC Card

The following example takes you through the installation process for installing a PC card on a laptop running NT Workstation 4. Before I begin the installation process, take a look at the PC Card (PCMCIA) Devices dialog prior to the installation of any PC card devices. Figure 9.6 shows the PC Card (PCMCIA) Devices dialog with the Socket Status tab selected. As you can see, both sockets are empty. Now, to install a network PC card onto the workstation, use these steps:

FIGURE 9.6.

The PC Card Socket Status tab.

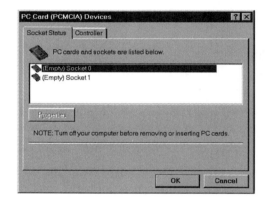

1. Click on the Network applet from the Control Panel.

2. If this is the first time that you have installed a network PC card, you will be presented with the Network Configuration dialog that informs you that Windows NT networking is not installed. You are prompted as to whether you want to install this software module. Click on Yes to install Windows NT Networking (see Chapter 26, "Windows NT Networking Protocols," on installing Networking software). If you have installed the network PC card or adapter previously, the Network software module will still be present, even if the adapter or PC card has been removed. To reinstall a PC card, select the Adapters tab from within the Network dialog and select the Add button (see Figure 9.7).

3. From the Select Network Adapter dialog (see Figure 9.8), scroll down through the Network Adapter list and select your chosen PC card from the list. Click OK to continue.

FIGURE 9.7.

The Network Adapters dialog box.

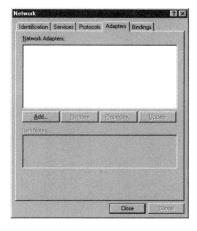

FIGURE 9.8.

The Select Network Adapter dialog box.

4. A new dialog opens, allowing you to configure the IRQ Level, Memory Base Address, and I/O Port Address. The default settings should be fine (see Figure 9.9). Click OK to continue.

FIGURE 9.9.

The IBM Ethernet PCMCIA and Compatible Adapter Card dialog box.

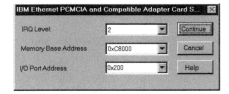

5. The next dialog requires you to enter the bus type bus number. Choose PCMCIA for the Type and the default Number (see Figure 9.10).

6. Now the setup routine needs to know the location of your setup files. Enter the path to the setup files and click OK.

FIGURE 9.10.

The PC Card Bus Type.

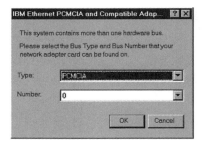

7. After the filecopy, you can see the added adapter to the list of loaded adapters. Selecting the Properties button will review the IRQ, memory, and I/O port addresses, as previously seen in Figure 9.9.

8. Click Close at the base of the Network dialog to be prompted to restart.

Confirming the Installation

When the workstation comes back online, you can confirm whether the PC card is working correctly by selecting the Network applet.

There are two tabs on the PC Card (PCMCIA) Devices dialog; they allow you to configure installed PC cards. The first, Socket Status, shows you the installed PC cards (see Figure 9.11). Highlight the newly installed PC card and press the Properties button.

FIGURE 9.11.

The PC Card Devices dialog.

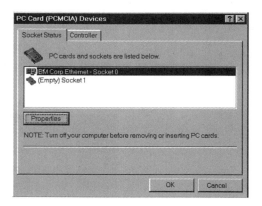

You are now presented with the PC Card Properties dialog (see Figure 9.12). The CardInfo tab gives you the current status of the card.

The second tab, Driver, allows you to add, remove, and configure the driver (see Figure 9.13). When you choose to configure the driver, you are presented with the same dialog as in Figure 9.9.

FIGURE 9.12.
*The PC Card
Properties dialog.*

FIGURE 9.13.
*The PC Card
Driver dialog.*

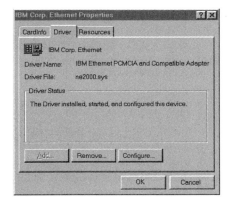

The last tab, Resources, confirms the IRQ, I/O, and memory ranges set during configuration (see Figure 9.14).

FIGURE 9.14.
*The PC Card
Resources dialog.*

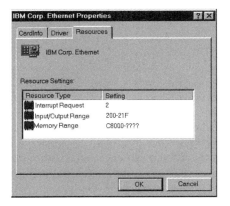

9
ADVANCED
CONTROL PANEL
TOOLS

Back in the main PC card dialog, there is a second tab next to Socket Status, called Controller. Selecting this tab reveals the current resources being used by the PC Card controller (see Figure 9.15).

FIGURE 9.15.

The PC Card Controller dialog.

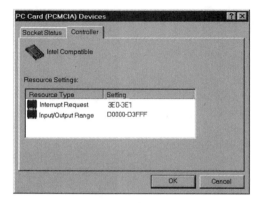

Ports

Personal computers connect with the outside world through ports. A *port* is simply a connection between the system and the external device. There are two types of ports that usually come as standard with PCs. The first type, called *serial or communication ports,* are ports where data is transferred to and from the device and the system serially, or one bit at a time. The other type, *parallel ports,* are ports that transfer data to and from the connected device eight bits at a time. Most PCs usually have two types of serial or communications ports that use either 9- or 25-pin serial connectors. You can connect a number of things to these serial I/O ports, such as a modem, a mouse, or a printer. Historically, all modem communication happens via the serial port. Parallel ports are usually used for connecting printers or external tape drives. Ports are configured through the Ports applet from the Control Panel.

> **NOTE**
>
> Although the applet is called Ports and the dialog boxes are titled the same, you can configure only serial ports with the Ports applet. You can't configure parallel (printer) parts with this applet.

Windows NT Workstation supports up to 256 serial ports, although some substantial hardware, such as a serial card, is required if you want to support all 256! One reason for extra serial ports, for example, might be the need to connect a large number of modems to your workstation, which is also acting as your RAS server.

Basic COM Port Settings

Once you select the Ports applet, you are presented with the Ports dialog, as in Figure 9.16. All the existing ports are listed in the Ports pane on the left side of the dialog. The specific settings required are usually defined either by the software connected to the serial port (for example, the modem, the printer, and so on) or by the software you use, so be sure to read the relevant manual. Figure 9.17 shows an example Settings dialog.

FIGURE 9.16.

The Ports dialog box.

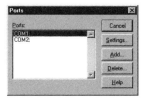

FIGURE 9.17.

The Settings dialog box.

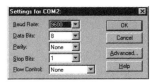

Use the Baud Rate box to set the speed for your port. If you are using a modem that supports data compression, you probably want to set the port to a speed that is higher than the line speed of the modem. If you have a modem that uses V.42 BIS at 28.8Kbps, for instance, you should set the port to 57,600 baud.

You can set the number of data bits sent in each character. For most practical purposes, this is set to 8. Some older systems might require 7 bits with a parity setting.

Because most modern modems use error-correcting techniques such as the MNP5 standard, parity bits are rarely required, so you usually set the parity to None. If necessary, you can set the parity to even, odd, mark, or space. A Stop Bits setting of 1 is almost always acceptable.

> **NOTE**
>
> The settings for parity, stop bits, and number of data bits must be consistent between your computer and the device on the other end of a connection. Check with your Internet service provider or the system manager of any remote systems to make sure that you have the correct settings for these communications parameters.

The Flow Control box allows you to choose None, Xon/Xoff, or Hardware. Choosing Hardware selects the CTS/RTS signal handshaking, described previously. This is the recommended setting for high-speed modems or other high-speed devices. Note that the use of hardware handshaking requires a cable containing modem control signals. You might want to use Xon/Xoff if you have a three-wire cable, if the device that you are connecting to doesn't support hardware handshaking, or if you are remotely connecting to a modem that doesn't support error correction. If all else fails, try setting Flow Control to None, but you should be aware that a setting of None will probably cause your system to drop characters at higher baud rates.

You can set more advanced options for the port by clicking the Advanced button. The dialog in Figure 9.18 shows the Advanced Settings options for COM ports.

FIGURE 9.18.

Advanced COM port settings.

The COM Port Number box allows you to choose which of the COM ports on your system you want to configure. The Base I/O Port Address box sets the hexadecimal port address at which the COM port is located. You usually accept the default for this setting, but if you have more than two COM ports, you might need to reconfigure it. The Interrupt Request Line setting specifies the IRQ number for the port. Again, the defaults are usually best, and whatever you select for the IRQ and port address, it must match your hardware. Remember that although you can configure two ports on a single IRQ, it usually won't work well.

Some COM ports, especially in newer systems, have an on-board buffer called a FIFO. If your system has FIFO-capable COM ports, enabling this option improves performance of the COM port at higher speeds. Your system might lose input characters at high baud rates if your port doesn't have a FIFO or if the FIFO Enabled check box is cleared. Clicking the check box turns FIFO buffering on or off.

Adding/Removing Ports

To add another serial port to the PC, simply click on the Add button within the Ports dialog (refer to Figure 9.16). You will be presented with the Advanced Settings for New Port dialog (see Figure 9.19).

FIGURE 9.19.

The Advanced Settings for New Port dialog box.

Within this dialog, you can select the port number from a drop-down list marked COM Port Number. You also have the ability to select a base I/O port address and interrupt level. Usually, selecting the defaults is safe enough. Once you have added the new port, you will be prompted to restart the workstation. Once restarted, the Ports dialog will have a complete list of all added ports, and you may now configure the settings of the newly added port.

To remove a port, simply highlight a port from the Ports dialog and click on Delete.

SCSI Adapters

SCSI, the Small Computer System Interconnect, is a means of attaching disks, tape drives, CD-ROM drives, and other types of devices to a system. There are several types of SCSI interfaces. The most common variant of SCSI is called SCSI-2. SCSI-2 devices have a maximum transfer rate of 10MB/s. SCSI-2 uses a parallel data bus, performing I/O transactions in 8-bit bytes. Wide SCSI uses a 16-bit data path. SCSI adapters and devices are available in both single-ended and differential versions. Single-ended SCSI uses cheaper cables, but the cables can't exceed about six meters of total length, including the length of the adapter and any cabling internal to system or drive enclosures. Differential SCSI can use longer cable lengths.

SCSI devices are intelligent. The analog read/write electronics of SCSI disks are embedded into the drives themselves. Data is transferred to the host using a completely digital format, so you can move SCSI disks between hosts without worrying about adapter incompatibility—at least between adapters of the same brand and model.

I/O requests are made to SCSI devices in a very high-level form. A command of the form "Send me three blocks of data starting at block 245" is issued. Commands are encoded as 6- or 10-byte packets. After a drive has received a command, it can disconnect from the SCSI bus until it has data available. At that point, it notifies the host that the data is available. This disconnection feature allows multiple parallel I/O seeks to occur on several drives connected to the same adapter.

Each SCSI device connected to an adapter has a unique ID. A single bit of the data path identifies each device during bus arbitration, so 8-bit SCSI can have a total of 8 devices, and wide SCSI can have 16 on a single bus. Because the host itself occupies one address, that means that an 8-bit SCSI-2 adapter can really connect up to 7 disks, tapes, or CD-ROMs. A wide SCSI bus can connect up to 15 devices, assuming that all the connected devices are capable of performing wide SCSI addressing and bus arbitration.

SCSI devices can be quite fast. The speed and flexibility of wide SCSI, combined with the high number of devices that can be supported, make it the interface of choice for most server-class systems. Increasing numbers of high-end workstations have SCSI adapters built into the motherboard.

Each SCSI bus must be terminated at both ends. You can usually configure your adapter board to terminate one end of the bus and then terminate the last device connected to the adapter. Note that if your adapter is connected to both internal and external devices, the adapter itself is probably *not* terminated. This means that both the last internal and the last external device must be terminated.

Make sure when adding SCSI devices that you don't configure the new device at an occupied target device address. Very unpredictable things can occur.

You can add SCSI adapters to your system by invoking the SCSI applet in the Control Panel. Invoking the SCSI applet produces a display similar to Figure 9.20.

FIGURE 9.20.

The Control Panel SCSI applet.

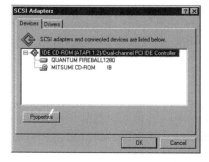

Any SCSI adapters that are currently configured into your system appear in the list box. Double-clicking an adapter shows all the devices that are known to be connected to the selected adapter. The adapter shown in Figure 9.20 is connected to a hard disk and a CD-ROM drive.

You can get information about any connected device by highlighting the device name and clicking the Properties button. In Figure 9.21, you see the Settings tab, which gives information about the manufacturer of the device, the firmware revision number, and the SCSI target ID and LUN numbers. The General tab includes the device status, from which you can determine whether the device is running correctly or not.

FIGURE 9.21.

The Settings tab.

SCSI devices connected to configured SCSI adapters generally require little or no configuration and are usually automatically detected at boot time.

You can add a SCSI adapter by clicking the Drivers tab, shown in Figure 9.22, and then clicking the Add button. You see a list of SCSI adapters that are known to Windows NT. If your adapter is listed, select it. If you have a driver disk from the SCSI manufacturer, you can select the Have Disk button to install it. Also in Figure 9.22, you can see the existing SCSI adapter driver that is already loaded.

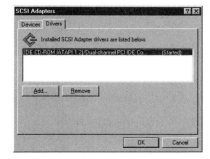

Because changing SCSI controllers and drivers is considered a relatively secure event, you must be a member of the Administrators local group on your machine before you can use the Device properties.

Tape Devices

For many users, tape backup is the main method of backup. With CDR drives becoming affordable and new devices such as Iomega's ZIP and JAZ drives becoming very popular, the primacy of tape is, if not threatened, at least under review for the Windows NT Workstation user. With disk prices falling by the week, why bother backing up?

The Windows NT operating system comes with its own built-in backup utility, NTBACKUP. The important thing about this program is that it can back up, and later restore, your Registry.

NT Backup supports only a small number of tape devices, including QIC 40 and QIC 80 IDE-based devices and a wide range of 4mm DAT drives. For full details of the devices supported, you should refer to the hardware compatibility list.

To install, you must first start the Tape Devices applet in the Control Panel, as shown in Figure 9.23. This simple applet lets you detect and install a tape drive and load and unload tape device drivers.

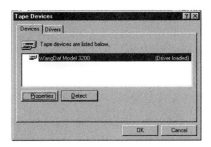

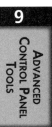

9

ADVANCED
CONTROL PANEL
TOOLS

As you can see, there is a tape device already installed, a WangDAT Model 3200 drive. Figure 9.24 shows you the tape driver that is loaded.

FIGURE 9.24.

The Tape Devices Drivers tab.

Choosing the Properties button on the Devices tab reveals the Properties dialog (see Figure 9.25), which contains two tabs. The first, General, shows some manufacturer information plus the status of the device. The second tab, Settings (see Figure 9.26), shows you additional device information.

FIGURE 9.25.

The Tape Devices Properties General tab.

FIGURE 9.26.

The Tape Devices Properties Settings tab.

UPS

Uninterruptible power supplies (UPSs) are basically batteries connected to a very fast switch and a charger. A PC is usually powered from the mains through a UPS. When system power fails, the UPS maintains power to your system for some fixed period of time. This gives your system time to shut down services in an orderly fashion and allows users to save any work that they might have open. A UPS is most useful when you have some sort of real-time transaction processing or database functionality on your system, but it can also be a lifesaver if you work in an area with unstable electrical power. UPSs, are becoming a more common sight, and with the cheap price for desktop UPSs, they are no longer considered a luxury.

The UPS Control Panel applet is shown in Figure 9.27. The typical UPS is equipped with an RS-232C control and communications interface that can be connected to your system via one of your COM ports. In the example shown in Figure 9.27, the UPS is connected to COM2.

FIGURE 9.27.
The UPS applet.

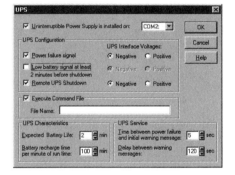

Configuring a UPS

The UPS toggles a signal when the power has failed. This signal should be connected to the CTS signal of the selected COM port. You have to indicate whether your UPS makes the signal go high-to-low or low-to-high on power failure by selecting either the Positive or Negative radio button. Select the Power failure signal button if your UPS supports this feature.

If your UPS has a low battery output signal, it should be connected to the DCD line of your COM port. As with the Power failure signal, you have to select the Positive or Negative button to indicate the polarity of the signal when the battery is low. Select the Low battery signal box if your UPS can send a low battery signal at least two minutes before your system must shut down.

The Remote UPS Shutdown indicates that your UPS can be turned off by the Windows NT UPS service. Connect the DTR line of your COM port to the remote shutdown signal of your UPS and then set the signal polarity to Positive or Negative as required.

The Execute Command File box specifies a command file that is run just before the system is shut down. You can put commands into the file that execute tasks such as logging messages, shutting down databases, or performing other orderly shutdown procedures.

The UPS characteristics and UPS service areas at the bottom of the UPS applet tell NT about your UPS and how you want NT to behave during a power failure. The Expected Battery Life indicates how many minutes the batteries in your UPS last after the power fails. The Battery recharge time box tells NT how long it takes to recharge the battery for each minute of battery time that is used. This allows NT to estimate how much charge is left in the UPS batteries if more than one power failure occurs.

The first of the two settings on the right tells NT how long to wait after a power failure before warning users. The second setting tells NT how long to wait between messages. Note that although the battery lifetime values are expressed in minutes, the warning message values are rated in seconds.

> **NOTE**
>
> NT 4 provides good basic UPS handling mechanisms, but if you have more sophisticated needs, you might want to investigate third-party software. PowerChute from APC is probably the best of the third-party power management software. You can get more information on PowerChute on the World Wide Web at http://www.apcc.com.

Services

Background processes of this type are called *services* in Windows NT. UNIX users might view services as equivalent to UNIX *daemon* processes. In both cases, the process runs in the background and requires no interactive control on the part of a user. Many services are actually incapable of interacting with the user in any direct sense. Most of the services described in Chapter 27, "Windows NT Network Services," fall into this category. Services can be configured to allow desktop interaction when required. See the "Service Startup Options" section of this chapter for information on configuring services for desktop interaction.

Understanding System Services

Microsoft Windows NT Workstation 4 incorporates a number of built-in services. The installation process configures many services to start automatically at system boot time. Other services must be started manually or configured for automatic startup by the user. Even if a process has been started automatically, it can still be stopped or paused by an authorized user. In general, it is possible to start, stop, or pause any service at any time. A user must usually have administrator privileges to stop system services, but most services can be started by ordinary users.

TIP

Services are special programs. It is usually not possible to use ordinary programs as services. If you need to use an ordinary program as a service, investigate the srvany.exe program supplied as part of the Microsoft Windows NT Resource Kit. The srvany.exe program allows you to run any program as a service. Another Resource Kit program, instsrv.exe, is used to actually install your service.

Services are installed, controlled, or examined by using the Services applet in the Control Panel. Figure 9.28 shows the resulting Services dialog box.

FIGURE 9.28.

The Services dialog box.

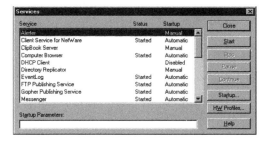

Although most services do not interact with the desktop, a few services do require human interaction. The Messenger service, which notifies selected users of critical system events, is one of the exceptions. Because the Messenger service sends messages to users, it has to be able to interact with the user's desktop.

Services must log onto the system before they are allowed to run. Each service is installed under an account that is used to log in the service. In general, the account specified is a special system account designated for use by services. It is possible, however, to install services to use nonsystem accounts.

The Windows NT installation process configures most important services to start automatically when your computer is booted. There are occasions when you must manually control a service. This can be necessary under any of the following circumstances:

- The service was installed to require manual startup.
- The service started automatically but terminated due to an error or some other condition.
- You want to temporarily disable a service for diagnostic reasons or for any other purpose.
- The service has become "confused."

9

ADVANCED CONTROL PANEL TOOLS

> **TIP**
>
> The Spooler is an example of a service that sometimes terminates for a variety of reasons. This can have unexpected side effects. If the Print Manager is unable to add a new printer definition, for instance, it might be because the Spooler service has terminated.

The state of the system's services can be seen in the Status column of Figure 9.28. Running services will have the word Started or Paused in this column. The column is blank if the service is not running at all. Select the service that you want to control, and click the Start, Stop, Pause, or Continue button, as appropriate.

Please note that when starting a service manually, it is possible to specify optional startup parameters in the Startup Parameters box shown at the bottom of Figure 9.28.

> **WARNING**
>
> Be extremely careful when starting and stopping services. Stopping the Server service, for instance, causes any remote user to be immediately disconnected from your system. Make sure to give remote users time to properly save work before stopping any service that could impact a remote user.

Service Startup Options

To configure the startup options for a service, start up the Services applet, shown in Figure 9.28. Select the service that you want to configure and click the Startup button. The dialog shown in Figure 9.29 appears. Select one of three Startup Type buttons. If the Automatic button is selected, the service is started by the system when your computer is booted.

FIGURE 9.29.

Setting Service startup options.

Note the selections at the bottom of the dialog under the Log On As heading. Most services, including the defaults, will operate under the special System Account. Select the This Account button only if your service *must* run under a specific, nonsystem account. This is required in certain situations. One thing to remember is that the system account is a strictly local account, and it does not have access to the network. Because of this, automatic network backup programs often must be run from an account that is a member of the Backup Operators group. In order to have such a program run automatically by the At command, the Schedule service would also have to log in using an account that was a member of the Backup Operators group.

> **WARNING**
>
> Services, like users, must issue a password to the system when logging on. Any account that is used by a service should have the Password Never Expires box checked in the User Manager. If the password on an account used by a service changes, the service will fail to start. In some cases, it is necessary to reinstall the service to correct the problem.

Selecting the Allow Service to Interact with Desktop box gives the service permission to display messages or receive input from the keyboard or mouse. Most services do not require such permission.

Select OK to record the desired settings for the service. You return to the dialog shown in Figure 9.28.

Services and Hardware Profiles

Versions of Windows NT prior to 4 had a significant failing. Unlike DOS, which had the capability of booting under multiple configurations through the use of special commands in the config.sys and autoexec.bat files, NT always assumed the same hardware configuration. This meant that it was very difficult to address the issue of portable systems or systems that might not always be connected to a given network.

Microsoft has addressed this issue in Windows NT 4 with the addition of hardware profiles. These profiles allow the user to run with networking either enabled or disabled. Hardware profiles can also be used to indicate the presence of a docking bay on portable computers.

It is possible to set individual services to be enabled or disabled, depending upon the hardware profile selected at boot time. This is done by selecting the desired service and then clicking the HW Profiles button shown in Figure 9.28. Clicking this button opens a dialog that can be used to associate service states with specific hardware profiles. This dialog is shown in Figure 9.30.

Click on the desired profile name in the selection box shown in Figure 9.30 and then select either Disable or Enable. Click OK to return to the Services configuration applet.

Figure 9.30.

Setting Service hardware profiles.

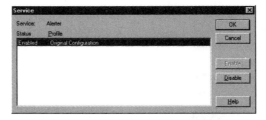

Managing Services

This section gives you descriptions of Windows NT's default services. (See Table 9.1.) Additional information on the control and management of the Alerter and Directory Replicator services is also included.

NOTE

Network-specific services are described in Chapter 27. Although the client/server nature of Windows NT often makes it difficult to distinguish network from non-network services, most of the services described in this section are either useful or required, even on standalone systems. Services described in Chapter 27 are generally useful only in networked environments.

Table 9.1. Windows NT's default services.

Service	Description
Clipbook Server	Provides pages to the Clipbook Viewer. Because it is a client/server application, the Clipbook Server is capable of providing pages to Clipbooks on remote systems.
Computer Browser	Maintains a list of computers on your network. Applications such as the Network Neighborhood selection in the Explorer use this list to display known computers.
Event Log	Accepts event notifications from system processes or from user programs and records them in the system event logs.
Messenger	This service is the delivery agent for messages sent by the Alerter service described later in this chapter. It is also used to send and receive messages sent by Administrators.
Net Logon	The Net Logon service is used for user authentication when a workstation is part of a domain. The workstation uses the Net Logon service to verify user account and password information against a domain controller. On server systems, the Net Logon service performs the actual authentication.

Service	Description
	It also synchronizes local authentication information with the domain controller's authentication database.
Network DDE	Provides Dynamic Data Exchange services to the network. This service acts as a network transport and security controller.
Network DDE DSDM	This service manages DDE conversations taking place across Network DDE.
NT LM Security Support	Many of the client/server facilities in Windows NT make use of distributed service requests called Remote Procedure Calls. Windows NT is capable of using several different transports to support these requests. Most use named pipes, but some must use a network transport such as TCP/IP. The NT LM Security Support Manager service provides security to RPC-based applications running across the various network transports.
RPC Locator	The list of available Remote Procedure Calls is dynamic. New RPC server applications can add new procedure calls to the list by registering their names with the RPC Locator service. Client applications can then query the RPC Locator service to find the desired RPC provider.
RPC Service	The RPC Service provides a number of miscellaneous control functions for the Windows NT RPC subsystem. One important task is *endpoint mapping,* which associates communications channels with new RPC requests. These endpoints can take the form of named pipes. In the case of TCP/IP connections, the endpoints are mapped to IP port numbers.
Schedule	Schedule services are the activation and completion agents for the AT command. The AT command is used to schedule events to run at some predetermined time and date. The commands scheduled with AT will never run if the Schedule service is not active.
Server	Provides additional RPC support, file, print, and other resource-sharing services. Note that users cannot attach to the resources of your system if the Server service is inactive. Stopping the Server service disconnects all attached users. Pausing it prevents new connections but maintains existing connections.

continues

9

ADVANCED CONTROL PANEL TOOLS

Table 9.1. continued

Service	*Description*
Spooler	Provides print spooling and print job notification.
UPS	The UPS service controls a connected Uninterruptible Power Supply. Responds to power failures with an orderly shutdown of the system.
Workstation	Provides the network and communications support required to connect an interactive user.

Default Services Requiring Additional Setup

Some of Windows NT's default services must be configured for your environment before they are actually useful. The setup of several such services is described in this section.

Alerter

The Alerter service allows your system to automatically send administrative messages to administrative accounts on your workstation or to other computers if you are connected to a network. The Alerter requires that the Messenger service be running in order to transmit its messages. Alerter receives messages from the Server service, among others.

After the Alerter service is running, it must be configured. This is done from the Server applet of the Control Panel, shown in Figure 9.31.

FIGURE 9.31.

The Server applet's dialog box.

Click the Alerts button to produce the dialog shown in Figure 9.32. Any user or computer listed in the Send Administrative Alerts To box will receive system-generated alert messages. To add a name to the list, type it in the New Computer or Username box and click the Add button. To remove a name, select the name and click the Remove button.

FIGURE 9.32.
Specifying alert recipients.

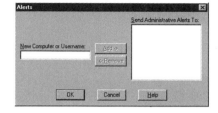

Directory Replicator

The Directory Replicator service, as its name implies, is used to copy directories and the files they contain from one place to another. The process is performed automatically at predetermined intervals. Windows NT 4 Advanced Server can both *export* (transmit) and *import* (receive) directories. Windows NT 4 Workstation can only import replicated directories.

Directory Replication is extremely useful for maintaining version control over pseudostatic information. Directory Replication is not suitable for highly volatile data for the following reasons:

- It does not update all copies of the data in real time.
- It copies at the file level. This means that if a single byte of a file changes, Directory Replicator will copy the entire file to the replication target.

Directory Replication is normally used in networked environments to distribute configuration information, logon scripts, and other types of nonvolatile data. A systems administrator needs to update only one copy of the data, and it will propagate to other systems on the network automatically.

The Server applet of the Control Panel is used to control Directory Replication. Invoke the Server applet as shown in Figure 9.31. Then click the Replication button to produce the dialog shown in Figure 9.33.

FIGURE 9.33.
Setting up directory replication.

Perform the following steps to allow remotely exported directories to be received and replicated by your workstation:

1. Enter the name of the domains or computers from which you want to import directories and files. Click on the Add button to display the dialog shown in Figure 9.34. Note that the captions on the entry fields in Figure 9.34 are somewhat deceptive. The box labeled Domain actually allows the entry of a domain or computer name. Computer names should be entered with a leading \\. You can get a list of the computers in a domain by double-clicking on the domain name in the Select Domain list. Click OK to return to the dialog shown in Figure 9.33.

FIGURE 9.34.

Selecting a replication source domain or computer.

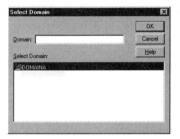

2. Specify the To Path. The replicated directories are copied to a point underneath the specified path. By default, this is %windir%\System32\Repl\Import. If you change the default, make sure to change the logon script path as well.

3. Click the Manage button to further control your import settings. This produces the dialog shown in Figure 9.35. The most important controls in Figure 9.35 are the Add Lock and Remove Lock buttons. Setting a lock on any subdirectory effectively prevents that directory from receiving updates from the replication export server. You can use this to restrict updates that you don't want to receive.

FIGURE 9.35.

Managing imported directories.

NOTE

The Add and Remove buttons shown in Figure 9.33 are of questionable utility, because any manual changes you make to the Sub-Directory list will be overridden by automatic updates from the Replication Export servers that you selected.

System

The System Control Panel applet is shown in Figure 9.36. This applet shows general information about the system and allows you to configure a number of system-level settings. You can also invoke the dialog by right-clicking on the My Computer icon on the desktop and choosing Properties from the menu. This applet has six tabs, each of which is described in the following sections in more detail.

FIGURE 9.36.

The System applet.

General

The General tab, which is shown in Figure 9.36, provides some basic information about the system, including the following:

- *System* shows which version of NT is installed on your system, along with the internal build number.
- *Registered to* shows the registered owner and organization. Usually, this is the information that was entered at the time Windows NT Workstation was installed, but you can change it (see the Tip after this list).
- *Computer* gives a summary of the type of computer and how much physical memory NT detected in your system.

You might need this information if you make any support calls to Microsoft.

9

ADVANCED
CONTROL PANEL
TOOLS

> **TIP**
>
> If you inadvertently enter the incorrect registered owner or organization when you install Windows NT Workstation, you can change it using the Registry Editor. Go to the `HKEY_LOCAL_MACHINE\SOFTWARE\Microsoft\WindowsNT\CurrentVersion` key where there are two value entries, `RegisteredOrganization` and `RegisteredOwner`. You can change both of these by clicking the value name and entering the new value.

Performance

The Performance dialog, shown in Figure 9.37, enables you to view and modify how much of a performance boost applications in the foreground get and the details of where Windows NT should place its paging files.

Figure 9.37.

The Performance tab.

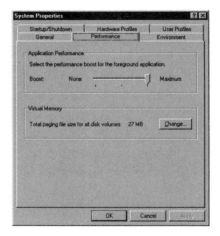

By default, applications running in the foreground get a scheduling boost over applications running in the background. For most Windows NT Workstation users, this is the correct behavior, but in certain circumstances, it might not be appropriate. If you are running a large FTP download or sending a large mail message, you want your FTP or mail application to get good performance, but you probably won't want to leave it in the foreground.

The application slider has three settings. Setting the boost to Maximum gives the foreground application the best response time. If you set the boost in the middle, the foreground application gets a "better" response time, whereas setting the boost to None means the foreground application never gets a priority boost. A boost of None is probably the correct setting if you use communications programs or have multiple CPU-intensive applications running concurrently.

NT achieves this better performance by increasing the internal priority of all threads belonging to the foreground application. As a result, with appropriate settings of Application Priority, the foreground applications usually get priority over the background.

The other function of the Performance dialog is to configure your virtual memory settings. Windows NT Workstation uses virtual memory extensively to enable it to swap information between the hard disk and physical memory. These settings can have a significant impact on performance. The current amount of virtual memory is defined as shown in the dialog box (see Figure 9.37). Clicking the Change button invokes the Virtual Memory dialog, shown in Figure 9.38, which enables you to make changes to your virtual memory allocation.

FIGURE 9.38.

The Virtual Memory dialog box.

The Virtual Memory dialog allows you to modify how much virtual memory is allocated on each disk partition in your system. You also use this dialog to change the maximum size of the Registry, which can be important if you load a large number of applications and other goodies onto your system. Only a member of the Administrators local group can manage page file settings.

The Virtual Memory page file is called PAGEFILE.SYS, and by using the Virtual Memory dialog, you can place a paging file on each partition of your system. You cannot put a paging file on a floppy or on the network.

The Virtual Memory dialog shows at the top of each partition in your system and shows how big a pagefile you have currently allocated on that drive. In the Paging File Size for Selected Drive, you can review and modify how big your paging file is for each partition.

After making any changes to your Virtual Memory settings, you must click the Set button for your changes to be registered. Additionally, you need to reboot before these new settings can take effect.

Total Paging File Size for All Drives shows how much total paging file space was allocated. This section also gives a recommendation on the minimum amount of paging file space that you should allocate.

The Virtual Memory dialog also allows you to change the maximum size of your system's Registry. Most users do not need to change this. However, if you load a large number of applications, you might need to increase this size.

As noted previously, if you make any changes to the virtual memory settings, including the size to the Registry, you need to reboot the system in order for the changes to take effect.

Unlike most of the Control Panel applets, the Virtual Memory dialog has a Help button and some good help information. If you're not a virtual memory whiz kid, you might find this information useful.

TIP

In general, it is best to have one paging file per volume. Having multiple files might enable you to fit more information on a particular partition, but it can result in more paging. If you have more than one physical disk on your system, you should try to put the paging file on the fastest disk.

Environment

Since the very early days of MS-DOS application, programs have used variables defined in the environment for extra control information. Although environment variables have been largely been superseded by INI files and the Registry for holding key configuration information, Windows NT still uses environment variables for holding extra information.

NT makes heavy use of a few important environment variables. The variable SYSTEMROOT holds the full path of where Windows NT Workstation is installed, and USERPROFILE contains the path to the currently logged-in user's profile. You can see all the variables currently available to you by typing SET from the command prompt (CMD.EXE). You can also use these variables at the command prompt and in batch files, although you must surround the variables with %. At the command prompt, you can issue the command DIR %SYSTEMROOT% /s to get a directory listing of all the files in the Windows NT installation directory. Windows NT Workstation has two types of environment variables: system and user. System environment variables are set system-wide, usually during the installation of an application or the operating system itself. User environment variables are set on a per-user basis. Both sets of variables are stored in the Registry. System environment variables are stored under the HKEY_LOCAL_MACHINE\SYSTEM\ CurrentControlSet\Control\Session Manager\Environment key. User environment variables are stored in the HKEY_CURRENT_USER\Environment key. Selecting the Environment tab brings up the Environment dialog, shown in Figure 9.39. This dialog shows all the currently set user and system environment variables.

FIGURE 9.39.

The Environment tab.

To set or enter a user environment variable, just enter the variable name and the value and click the Set button at the base of the Environment tab. To remove any variable, just click it and then click on the Delete button.

You can also set environment variables at the command prompt using the SET command (for example, SET MYFILE=c:\myfile.dat). However, any environment variables set this way are lost when you exit the command prompt.

> **TIP**
>
> The DIR command in the command prompt uses the internal directory order by default when displaying files. To get a nicely formatted listing, you can use the /o switch (for example, /ogne to get a listing with directories grouped at the top and sorted by name and extension). To make this a permanent setting, create the variable DIRCMD and set it to /ogne. I've set this as a system environment variable so that every user automatically gets nicely sorted directories.

Startup/Shutdown

With Windows NT Workstation startup, the NT system loader scans the file BOOT.INI, located in the root directory of your system disk, to build the boot selection menu. The BOOT.INI file contains a list of versions and where to load them from. This file is initially given the file attributes system and read-only, which makes it more difficult to accidentally erase.

My BOOT.INI file looks like the following:

```
[boot loader]
timeout=30
default=multi(0)disk(0)rdisk(0)partition(1)\WINNT
[operating systems]
multi(0)disk(0)rdisk(0)partition(1)\WINNT="Windows NT Workstation Version 4.00"
multi(0)disk(0)rdisk(0)partition(1)\WINNT="Windows NT Workstation Version 4.00 [VGA
➥mode]" /basevideo /sos
C:\="Microsoft Windows"
```

As you can see, the BOOT.INI file has two sections:

- Boot Loader tells the loader how long to wait for the user to make a selection before taking the default, which is also specified.

- Operating Systems contains all the various copies of Windows NT and Windows 95.

In both sections, each version of NT is shown using the ARC (Advanced RISC Computing) naming convention. This is followed by a string in quotes used to build the boot menu and some system startup options (for example, /sos to display the details of drivers loaded during the boot process). After parsing the BOOT.INI file, the NT Loader displays a screen that is derived from the BOOT.INI file. Based in the BOOT.INI shown previously, it might resemble the following segment:

```
OS Loader V4.00
Please Select the Operating System to Start:
Windows NT Workstation Version 4.00
Windows NT Workstation Version 4.00
Microsoft Windows

Use ↑ and ↓ to move the highlight to your choice
Press Enter to Choose

Seconds until highlighted choice will be started automatically:30
```

In this boot menu, the default, the first version of Windows NT Workstation 4, will be highlighted. You can then use the up and down arrows to choose one of the other operating systems and select it by pressing the Enter key. Alternatively, you can wait the configured amount of time for the default to start. If you move the up and down arrows, the last line of the menu disappears, and for any system to get loaded, you must select the system and press the Enter key.

NOTE

At first sight, the ARC names used in the BOOT.INI look a little odd. Why couldn't Microsoft use the convention c: or d:? To Windows NT, the name C: is just an alias that you can change to point to any partition you like, including the CD-ROM. Until Windows NT is loaded, it is not possible to work out that meaning of C:. Using ARC names gets around this because ARC names are related to the hardware.

The ARC convention is pretty simple when you get used to it. Basically, you see one of two formats for names:

- multi(a)disk(b)rdisk(c)partition(d) is used with IDE or EIDE disks or with SCSI disks when using the SCSI boot BIOS.
- Scsi(a)disk(b)rdisk(c)partition(d) is used for SCSI disks not using the controller's boot BIOS.

The value of *a* in these cases is the ordinal number of the hardware adapter/controller card, starting at 0 (that is, the first controller card is 0, the second is 1, and so on). If the disk is a SCSI disk, *b* is the hardware unit number of the disk (or LUN, if the controller supports logical units), and *c* is always 0. If the disk is IDE, *b* is always 0, and *c* is the ordinal number of the disk.

Finally, *d* is always the partition number on the chosen disk—confusingly, this starts at 1. Think of it this way: The ARC name tells you which physical controller, which disk on that controller, and which partition of that disk to use. ARC names are just super disk labels.

Although these ARC names can be useful for Windows NT Workstation users, they are very important when implementing NT Server on large servers with multiple disks.

With this introduction to ARC names and the boot up process out of the way, the Startup/ Shutdown dialog is shown in Figure 9.40.

FIGURE 9.40.

The Startup/Shutdown tab.

With the System Startup options, you can easily configure the [default] section of the BOOT.INI file, which is possibly the safest way for a beginner. Select the default operating system to load by choosing one from the Startup list. Determine, in seconds, how long the list appears before the default operating system is loaded, by selecting a value for Show list for.

The next frame, Recovery, tells Windows NT what actions are taken in the unlikely event of a system crash. Such a crash, which should be very rare, is also called the Blue Screen of Death, because all you see is a blue screen containing details of the crash.

You have several options, and you can choose any or all (or none) of them:

■ *Write an event to the system log.* When NT crashes, this option writes an event to NT's event log. You can review this later and determine the cause of the crash.

■ *Send an administrative alert.* This option sends an alert to any user or system configured to get administrative alerts. This alert is identical to the entry sent to the event log.

■ *Write debugging information to.* This choice determines whether you generate a full memory dump when the system crashes and where to write the memory dump.

For most users, these options are probably not all that useful. The memory dump in particular is huge and tends to be useful only to highly trained technicians.

Hardware Profiles

Hardware profiles are a good way to create different configurations that you can choose from at system startup. You can disable almost any device or driver in a profile. This can be very useful for laptop users whenever they are not connected to a docking station.

By reducing services you reduce the startup time. You should disable services that you have no intention of using. A good example of this would be disabling the Alerter service when undocked.

The Hardware Profiles dialog, shown in Figure 9.41, enables you to create, delete, and rename profiles and view and modify the properties of profiles. You can use this dialog to configure how NT should behave at startup with respect to hardware profiles.

FIGURE 9.41.

The Hardware Profiles tab.

To create a new hardware profile, select an existing profile and click the Copy button. After a profile is created, you can rename it or delete it. The profile at the top of the Available Hardware Profiles list box is the default profile, and you can use the arrow button at the side of the dialog to adjust the order of the list.

When you define multiple hardware profiles, the section at the bottom of the Hardware Profiles tab instructs Windows NT about its behavior at boot time. NT will either wait indefinitely for you to choose a profile or wait some predefined period of time, (the default being 30 seconds), and then choose the default hardware profile. Note that this menu appears in addition to the menu generated by the BOOT.INI file. You see this only if you have more than one hardware profile.

User Profiles

In Windows NT, all desktops and user-related settings are contained in a user profile and stored locally. These settings are set in the HKEY_CURRENT_USER tree in your Registry. In addition, Windows NT creates a set of folders in the %SYSTEMROOT%\Profiles*userid* directory, where *userid* is the username you logged in with. This folder which is also known as %Userprofile% contains the contents of your desktop, your personal start program menus, your favorite places, and your Send To menu.

If you use Windows NT Workstation on a computer that is a member of an NT Server Domain, you can have a roaming profile. With roaming profiles, your profile is stored on a server and downloaded, if necessary, to your Workstation each time you log on. Any changes are uploaded to the server when you log off.

Windows NT caches your profile locally and downloads your profile from a server only when the locally cached profile is older than the version on the server or when you have no profile currently cached on the system. Roaming profiles are advantageous for users on the move, but they do have their disadvantages.

Any file or folder stored on your desktop is automatically saved to a hidden directory, %USERPROFILE%\Desktop. Dragging a couple of large files onto your desktop can greatly increase the size of your Desktop subdirectory and the time it takes to load it from the server.

Each user that logs onto a Windows NT4 system automatically gets a new set of profile directories created on that system. That desktop remains on any system you log into until it is deleted.

The User Profiles dialog, shown in Figure 9.42, shows the profiles defined on the system, who created it, and its current size. For users in an NT domain, the profile can be changed from a local profile to a roaming profile—if you are not in a domain, this option is greyed out.

You should keep an eye on the sizes of these profiles if they are roaming profiles and ask users to restructure their desktops if they start getting too big.

9

ADVANCED
CONTROL PANEL
TOOLS

Figure 9.42.

The User Profiles tab.

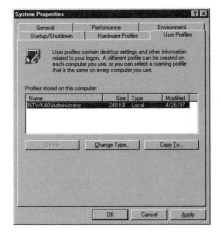

> **WARNING**
>
> If you delete a local profile, you could inadvertently lose data, programs, or both. A user could have created a lot of data on the desktop. By deleting the profile you delete all the data on that user's desktop. Ensure that a profile is not needed before deleting it.

Summary

This chapter covered the advanced applets in the Control Panel. These programs allow you to configure NT Workstation to suit your needs. You learned about the Client Service for NetWare, which enables you to configure clients using the Workstation who want to avail themselves of the benefits of a NetWare network. NT Workstation also supports PC cards when loaded on a laptop. Devices are connected to the workstation via ports, which are configurable through the Ports applet. This chapter also covered the configuration of these devices through the SCSI Adapters, Tape Devices, and UPS applets. Finally, you looked at the System applet, which allows you to configure system-level settings.

Fine-Tuning NT Security

by Mike Sheehy

IN THIS CHAPTER

CHAPTER 10

Security has always been a hotly debated subject in the computer industry. It is not a subject that should be taken lightly, and it requires constant review. A computer security plan relates to rules or implementations that govern the proper access to and utilization of computer systems. A good, vigorous security plan will always err on a denial of privilege. When you start your computer security plan, deny all rights and privileges and then loosen them as needed. The aim of a computer security plan is twofold:

- To allow only authorized personnel access to the system in a controlled manner
- To prevent damage to the system by unauthorized personnel

Like most operating systems, NT Workstation "straight out of the box" is not a highly secure operating system. Configuration is required to the operating system to tighten NT Workstation and to make its security features work for you. These configuration changes will not, on their own, wipe away all your anxieties unless they are part of an overall security policy implemented by you or your company. What good will it do you to execute all the changes I propose here if anybody can freely walk into your computer room and start wielding a sledge hammer? Your security policy should cover all aspects of security, ranging from broad issues such as who has access to the systems room to specifics such as who can change the system clock. This chapter will take you through the necessary steps required to tighten up NT Workstation.

NT Security Component

There are five components that make up the NT security model. You should be familiar with each of these components. The NT security model regulates access to the workstation and its objects as well as recording actions to these objects, directly and indirectly. The following are the five components within the security model:

- *Security Account Manager (SAM).* The Security Account Manager is responsible for maintaining a database of user and group account details.
- *Local Security Authority (LSA).* The Local Security Authority is at the core of the security architecture and is responsible for the following:

    The generation of access tokens for each successful user logon

    Maintaining the system security and audit policies

    Logging audit alerts

NOTE

An access token consists of a *security ID (SID)*, which uniquely identifies the user, SIDs of each group the user holds membership with, user rights that the user has been granted, the user's name, the groups the user holds membership with, and a default *access control list (ACL)* for that user object, which defines protections on the user object.

- *Security Reference Monitor (SRM).* The Security Reference Monitor (SRM) ensures that security rules are adhered to within the system. The SRM determines whether an object has the right to execute a particular action. The SRM responds with a successful flag if the action is allowed and returns a failure flag if not.
- *Objects.* Within NT Workstation, everything is identifiable as an object. By defining discrete objects, the security model can determine how these objects can be used and by whom. Objects, for example, include users, files, and printers.
- *Logon processes.* Logon processes enable users to log on to the NT Workstation either locally or remotely. It is through these logon processes that a user identifies and authenticates himself or herself with the LSA.

C2 Security

No discussion on security and computing is ever complete without reference being made to the term *C2*. The U.S. government has an agency called the National Computer Security Center (NCSC) that evaluates software according to a set of guidelines laid down in a publication called the Orange Book. The Orange Book is a part of a publication called the Rainbow Series, which is produced by the Department of Defense. Once software passes these criteria, it is given an accreditation level. The Orange Book, however, does not apply to networking components; it covers only a system in a standalone mode of operation. These networking components are detailed in the Red Book, another member of the Rainbow Series. Its requirements are no different from those in the Orange Book, but they describe how a system should operate in a networked environment. Again, there is a C2 accreditation associated with the Red Book. C2 accreditation is the benchmark by which each operating system is measured. Windows NT Workstation has been successfully accredited with C2 compliance under the Orange Book and is currently under evaluation for C2 compliance under the Red Book criteria.

User Manager

Your first port of call in securing your NT Workstation is to review users defined on the system. The User Manager is where you create, maintain, and remove users and groups. The User Manager is accessed from the Start menu. Select Start | Programs | Administrative Tools (Common) | User Manager.

Built-In Accounts

NT Workstation, upon installation, creates two accounts by default. These accounts are built-in accounts, and they serve a particular function within NT.

Guest Account

The Guest account is the first of two built-in accounts and deserves special attention. NT Workstation provides the Guest account to facilitate casual users, providing them with limited access. By default, on NT Workstation the Guest account is disabled. If enabled, anyone can log on and browse through your directory and connect to open file shares. You should ensure that the Guest account remains disabled.

To disable the Guest account, you must do the following:

1. Log on to the NT Workstation as Administrator.
2. Open the User Manager.
3. Highlight the Guest account and select properties from the file menu.
4. You are presented with the User Properties dialog box (see Figure 10.1). Check the Account Disabled check box to disable the account.

FIGURE 10.1.

Disabling the Guest account.

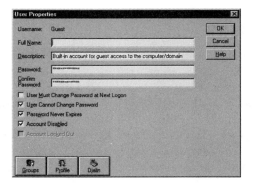

Unlike previous versions of NT Workstation, you are unable to delete the built-in Guest account under NT Workstation 4.0.

Administrator Account

The Administrator account is the second built-in account created by NT. Its significance should not be underestimated. The Administrator account is a powerful account, equivalent to the root account under UNIX. It is an account that has ultimate user authority and is primarily used to manage other users, groups, and resources on an NT system. It is for these reasons that hackers are attracted to the Administrator account, and why you must make this account as tight as possible. Again, as with the Guest account, the Administrator account cannot be removed. Also, the Administrator account can never be locked out by brute force password checking, nor can its administrative powers be removed. If your Administrator account ever does become the victim of a password attack, the Account Locked Out check box is checked to signify that a number of unsuccessful passwords have been entered. This does not, however, prevent you from logging in to the system as Administrator. This is illustrated by Figure 10.2.

To strengthen the Administrator account, Microsoft recommends that you rename the Administrator account. Even though the Administrator account can be renamed, it is not difficult for a hacker to pick up the new account name associated with the Administrator account. Nonetheless, you should rename the Administrator to deter the more inexperienced hackers.

FIGURE 10.2.

The Administrator account disabled.

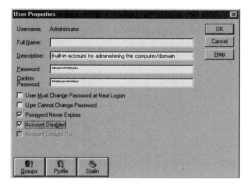

Rename the Administrator account with the following steps:

1. Log on to the NT Workstation as Administrator.
2. Open the User Manager.
3. Highlight the Administrator account and select Rename from the File menu.
4. You are presented with the Rename dialog box (see Figure 10.3). Enter the new account name in the Change To text field.

FIGURE 10.3.

Renaming the Administrator account.

The new account name you chose for the Administrator account can be totally arbitrary, but it should not be something that can easily be guessed. In addition to this, you should remove the commentary that describes this account as being the built-in account for administrating the system. Here's how to remove the commentary:

1. Highlight the Administrator account from the User Manager and select Properties from the File menu.
2. Delete the text from the Description text field as illustrated in Figure 10.4.

Once you have renamed the Administrator account, create a new account called Administrator and grant this account minimal privilege rights within your NT system.

To create this new account, you must take the following steps:

1. Log on to the NT Workstation as Administrator.
2. Open the User Manager.
3. Select New User from the User menu.

10

FINE-TUNING NT SECURITY

4. You are presented with the New User dialog box (see Figure 10.5). Enter Administrator in the Username text field.

5. Enter a description for the account along with a password and a confirmation password.

6. Disable the account.

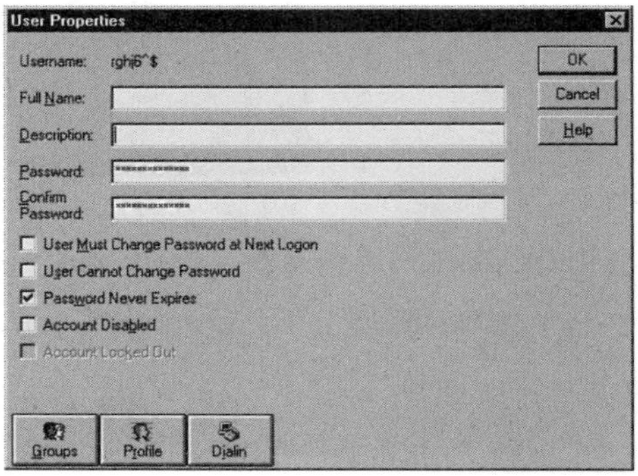

Figure 10.4.

Removing the descriptive text from the Administrator account.

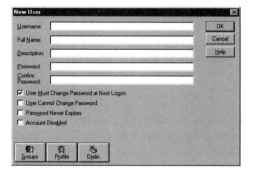

Figure 10.5.

Creating a bogus Administrator account.

You should monitor this bogus Administrator account by enabling auditing and watching for activity on this new account. I will elaborate more on auditing later in this chapter.

Groups

Groups are an important part of NT because their definition signifies users who have a common role or requirement. It is easier to define security measures at a group level than it is to do so at an individual level. The bottom pane of the User Manager dialog box lists the groups that are defined on the system. In Figure 10.6, you can see a list of defined groups and a description of each. The group description should clearly state the purpose of the group.

Figure 10.6.

The list of Groups within User Manager.

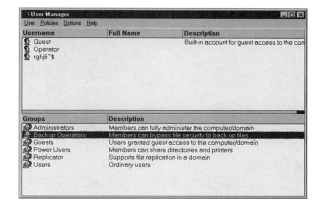

Reviewing Membership to Groups

To review membership to any group, simply double-click its entry in the lower pane or select Properties from the User menu when the entry is highlighted. Figure 10.7 shows you the properties of the Power Users group, which contains only one user: Operator. To remove any unsuitable user from a group, simply highlight the user entry within the Local Group Properties dialog box and click the Remove button. When you have finished reviewing the membership, click OK to return to the User Manager dialog box.

Figure 10.7.

Removing a user from a group.

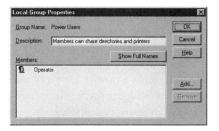

You should exercise this simple task regularly as part of your security policy, because any erroneous memberships can be easily rectified. Failure to discover such illegal members can lead to a user inheriting privileges beyond the account's entitlements. This can have detrimental effects on your workstation.

Membership to a group can also be reviewed on a user-by-user basis. You can see all the groups a user has membership to by clicking the Groups button from within the User Properties dialog box. The Group Memberships dialog box displays a list of groups the user is a member of (see Figure 10.8). To remove a user from a group, simply highlight the unwanted group and click the Remove button, located in the middle of the dialog box. Once you are satisfied that the user has correct group memberships, you can exit the Group Memberships dialog box by clicking the OK button. This returns you to the User Properties dialog box.

FIGURE 10.8.

The Group Member-
ships dialog box.

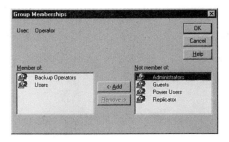

Everyone Group

The Everyone group is an NT built-in group that facilitates universal access to resources. You'll notice that you won't see any reference to the Everyone group within the User Manager. As a security risk, the Everyone group is a nightmare. Every user created on an NT Workstation gets added to the Everyone group. The Everyone group, as the name suggests, contains everyone regardless of whether he or she is defined on the Workstation or not. File shares, upon creation, grant full control to the Everyone group. If you're like I am and are uncomfortable with the openness of the Everyone group, I recommend that you consider creating a more controlled version. Create a new group and call it something like Everyuser. Include all existing users on your workstation in this new group. Replace the Everyone group with the Everyuser group for resource permissions and user rights (see the section on User Rights, later in the chapter). The only drawback with this procedure is that you have to manually add each new user to the Everyuser group as you create them.

Profiles

User profiles are another way of further controlling users within NT. NT Workstation automatically creates and maintains a profile for every user that has logged on. These profiles define the look and feel of the workstation that is presented to a user at logon. More importantly, profiles can be configured to restrict users while they are logged on. Administrators can configure profiles to disable the Run command and prevent users from changing certain program groups. Profiles are useful if multiple users are sharing the same workstation. To configure a user's profile, click the Profile button located at the base of the User Properties dialog box. The User Environment Profile dialog box appears (see Figure 10.9). Enter the path to and the name of the user's profile in the User Profile Path text box located within the User Profiles frame of the User Environment Profiles dialog box. For more on user profiles, see Chapter 9, "Advanced Control Panel Tools."

Dial-In

Remote access service (RAS) is the ability to enable remote users to connect to an NT workstation, server, or network. The Dial-In button located at the base of each User Properties dialog box allows an administrator to define security restrictions on a user's RAS rights. Because RAS is another access point to your workstation, it must also be reviewed from a security point of view. Only users who have been given permission to RAS should be configured to do so. In previous versions of NT Workstation, these restrictions were configured through the network applet in the Control Panel. Under Workstation 4.0, double-clicking the Dial-In button reveals the Dialin Information dialog box (see Figure 10.10).

FIGURE 10.9.
The User Environment Profile dialog box.

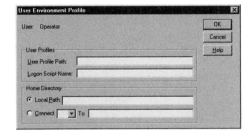

FIGURE 10.10.
The Dialin Information dialog box.

To enable a user to dial in and connect to a workstation via RAS, check the Grant dialin permission to user check box in the Dial Information dialog box. The Call Back frame contains a series of radio buttons defining constraints on call back options. Call back is when the RAS service calls the dial-in user back. The three options for call back are as follows:

- *No Call Back.* Call back is refused when this option is chosen.
- *Set By Caller.* The RAS service will call the user back at a number defined by the user on a call-by-call basis.
- *Preset To.* This option lets you fix a number at which the RAS service will call a user. This option is useful if you have remote users dialing in from a known and trusted location. The preset number will be associated with the location of the user, and it is only from there that this user can connect.

Logon Hours

If you add your NT Workstation to a domain and want to secure connections to it from domain users, you should load User Manager for Domains, which comes on the NT server CD-ROM. User Manager for Domains offers a couple of further configuration buttons, which appear at the base of each User Properties dialog box. The first of these extra buttons is the Logon Hours button, which allows you to restrict when a user can connect to the workstation. This configuration does not prevent a user from logging in to the workstation, but rather it disallows a user from making connections to a workstation over the network. Double-click the Hours button to reveal the Logon Hours dialog box (see Figure 10.11).

FIGURE 10.11.

The Logon Hours dialog box.

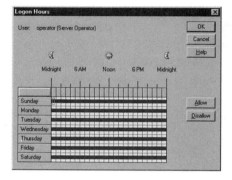

Within the Logon Hours dialog box, there is a table of days and hours. By default, a user is allowed to connect 24 hours a day, 7 days a week. A blue line through a cell signifies that the user can connect at the time represented by that cell. If, for example, you want to disallow the Operator account for the weekend, you must do the following:

1. Click on Sunday to the left of the grid. This highlights the entire day.
2. Click the Disallow button to disallow connection for Sunday. Once you click the Disallow button, the blue line is removed from those cells representing Sunday (see Figure 10.12).

FIGURE 10.12.

The operator is disallowed from connecting all day Sunday.

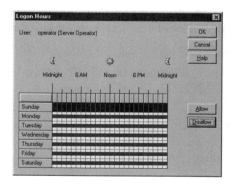

3. Repeat this for Saturday also.
4. Click OK to return to the User Properties dialog box.

If you want to disallow a number of hours, you can highlight the cell(s)in the grid representing the hour(s) you want to disallow. This is done by dragging the mouse over the cell(s) with the left button depressed. Once you have selected the desired hours, click the Disallow button.

Logon Hours is a useful option if you can identify users who work a fixed shift. You can disallow these users from connecting during off-shift hours. This helps to minimize the damage a hacker could do if a user account were to be hijacked during a period of exclusion. If the NT Workstation is added to a domain, you can forcibly log off a user during a disallowed period. This is done by checking the rather long-winded check box labeled Forcibly disconnect remote users from server when logon hours expire. This check box appears at the base of the Account Policy dialog box.

Logon To

The second button to appear in the User Properties dialog box, after membership to a domain is established, is the Logon To button. Click on the Logon To button to reveal the Logon Workstations dialog box (see Figure 10.13).

FIGURE 10.13.

The Logon Workstations dialog box.

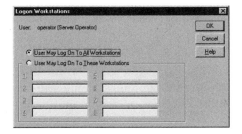

You have the choice of allowing a user to connect to all workstations in the domain by selecting the User May Log On to All Workstations radio button. If you want to restrict the number of workstations to which a user can connect, you can do so by selecting the User May Log On To These Workstations radio button and entering the names of those allowed workstations in each of the text boxes numbered 1 to 8. The workstation name you enter must be a NetBIOS name, and once you enter one workstation name, you immediately exclude access to all other workstations not entered on the list.

Account

The third and last button to appear in the User Properties dialog box, after domain membership is established, is the Account button. To bring up the Account Information dialog box, as illustrated by Figure 10.14, click the Account button.

The Account Information dialog box allows you to configure user accounts to expire on a particular date or remain valid indefinitely. These options are configurable by selecting either radio button within the Account Expires frame. By setting all accounts to expire at a particular time, it forces you to consciously review accounts when they become disabled upon expiration. All users who are logged in when their accounts expire will remain logged in but are unable to create any new network connections. Once logged off, a user will be unable to log on again until the account disabled status is changed.

FIGURE 10.14.

The Account Information dialog box.

Also in the Account Type frame, you can define an account to be either local or global by selecting either of the associated radio buttons. By default, all accounts are global, allowing full participation in a domain. A local account is an account that resides in a non-trusting/trusted domain and connects rather than logging in to the trusting account. With local accounts, you have to keep the passwords synchronized on the local workstation and on the domain.

Policies

Policies, as the name suggests, are a series of constraints administrators can implement on NT workstations. There are three constituent components to policies within NT Workstation. These are located under the Policies menu within the User Manager (see Figure 10.15).

FIGURE 10.15.

Policies within the User Manager.

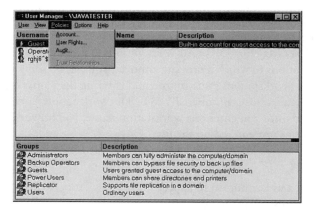

Account Policy

The first of these components is the Account Policy, which in essence defines a policy governing passwords and accounts. In Figure 10.16, you can see that the upper half of the Account Policies dialog box is devoted to defining criteria for acceptable account passwords. All NT passwords are not stored in plain text, but rather are encrypted using a hash algorithm. This hashing algorithm, however, does not offer invincibility to user accounts. You do need to further define constraints on user passwords to strengthen them against malicious attack. Tools are available today that can attack an account using a username coupled with repeated passwords attempts taken from a dictionary. Given enough time, and with an accurate and large enough dictionary, simple passwords can be hacked, leaving an account and its privileges open to misuse. Apart from the constraints you can define through Account Policy, you should tutor your users on how to choose passwords. The following are a couple of hints you might want to consider:

■ Passwords should not contain their own associated username.

■ Passwords should not be a common word found in a dictionary or in slang.

■ Passwords should contain a mixture of uppercase letters, lowercase letters, numerals, and special characters.

Figure 10.16 shows the Password Restrictions frame within the Account Policies dialog box. This frame allows an administrator to define such criteria as the following:

■ *Maximum Password Age.* By default, NT passwords never expire, but with Maximum Password Age, you can decide whether a password is valid indefinitely or will become obsolete after a certain number of days. It is advisable that you choose an expiration period in the range of 1 to 999 days (45 days is the advised period).

■ *Minimum Password Age.* Minimum Password Age allows you to define whether a user can change a password immediately or has to wait until the current password is 1 to 999 days old. Again, you should not allow a user's password to be changed immediately. The Minimum Password Age works in tandem with Password Uniqueness, detailed next.

■ *Password Uniqueness.* Password Uniqueness is an option to prevent users from using the same password over and over. An administrator can configure NT Workstation to remember the last 1 to 24 passwords a user defined and force the user to create a unique password not remembered by NT. If you check Do Not Keep Password History, all users can simply reuse the same password each time it expires, thus defeating any password aging constraints. You should set NT to remember at least the last three passwords.

■ *Minimum Password Length.* The shorter the password, the easier it is to crack. Minimum Password Length allows you to configure user passwords to be either zero-length passwords or to force users to create passwords between 1 to 14 characters long. Microsoft recommends that you set the length of passwords to six characters, but you should specify a password length greater than six because hackers will always try a dictionary comprising of six-character words in the hopes that you have followed Microsoft's recommendations.

FIGURE 10.16.

The Account Policy
dialog box.

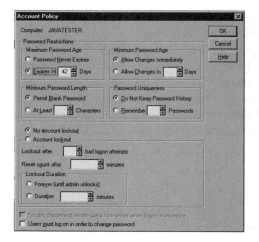

Administrators also have the ability to enforce account lockout. When you enable the Account lockout option within the Account Policy dialog box, you can define criteria that will force an account to become locked. This is an invaluable option, because it protects your passwords against hackers using a password-guessing program.

The following are configurable options within Account lockout:

■ *Lockout after.* You can define how many incorrect passwords a user can enter before an account is locked. This value can range between 1 and 999. I recommend a value greater than 3 to allow a user grace if a password was typed incorrectly.

■ *Reset count after.* You can define a period of time in minutes that must pass between any two login attempts to prevent the account from being locked. This period of time can be anything from 1 to 99999 minutes.

■ *Lockout Duration.* The duration a locked account remains locked can be defined within a range of 1 to 99999 minutes. Alternatively, you can choose that the account remain locked until the administrator unlocks it.

There is one final check box located at the base of the Account Policy dialog box that, when checked, forces a user to be logged on in order to change an existing password. Once you have given careful consideration to the options in this list and have chosen settings that best suit your environment, click OK to return to the User Manager dialog box.

User Rights

The second component of policies is user rights. With each user right, there is an associated action a user or group can execute on the system. The user rights are accessed by selecting User Rights in the Policies menu within User Manager. You are presented with the User Rights Policy dialog box, as illustrated in Figure 10.17. There are a number of user rights you should be aware of and should audit.

FIGURE 10.17.

*The User Rights Policy
dialog box.*

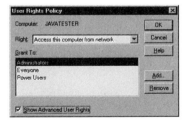

There are 27 rights, 17 of which are advanced rights. To view the advanced rights, check the Show Advanced User Rights check box located at the base of the User Rights Policy dialog box. You can select any user right from the Right drop-down list. The Grant To box lists the groups and users who have been granted the user right that is currently highlighted in the Right box.

To grant rights to or revoke rights from users and groups, you should use the Add and Remove buttons. To grant a right to a user or group, you need to take the following steps:

1. Highlight the right you want to grant.
2. Click Add to be presented with the Add Users and Groups dialog box (see Figure 10.18).

FIGURE 10.18.

*Granting a user right to
users or groups.*

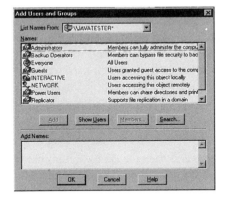

3. To grant a right to a group, simply select that group from the Names list within the Add Users and Groups dialog box and click the Add button. You'll see the selected group appear in the Add Names list at the bottom of the dialog box.
4. To add a user, click the Show Users button to view existing users.
5. Highlight the user to which you wish to grant the right and then click Add. Again, you can see the user added to the Add Names list.

10

**FINE-TUNING
NT SECURITY**

6. Click OK to finalize the addition and return to the User Rights Policy dialog box. The additional group or user now appears in the Grant To list (see Figure 10.19).

FIGURE 10.19.

Adding a group to a user right.

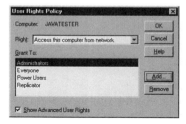

To revoke a right from a user or group, you must execute the following steps:

1. Ensure that the user right you are revoking is selected in the Right list.
2. Highlight the user or group you want to remove and then click the Remove button.

There are a few rights that require attention as a matter of great importance. These rights are important because if they are improperly configured, they can cause problems. Here are the user rights that require careful attention:

■ *Log on Locally.* The Log on Locally user right determines which users and groups can log on physically at the workstation console. By default, the Administrator, Backup Operator, Everyone, Guest, Power User, and User accounts are granted this right. I recommend that you grant Log on Locally only to those users and groups who can justify a need to log on at the workstation. Also, I recommend that you revoke this right from Guest and Everyone for starters.

■ *Shut down the system.* This is another important right that requires careful consideration. By default, the Administrator, Backup Operator, Everyone, Power User, and User accounts are granted this right. Again, a good starting point would be to remove Everyone and User.

■ *Access this computer from the network.* This user right, when granted, allows users to connect to the NT workstation over the network. You can filter what users can avail of the workstation's resources. By revoking this right from everyone and granting it to a smaller controlled group, you can greatly tighten security to the workstation over the network.

The remaining rights you should review on a case-by-case basis and tailor them to suit your environment. The following is a list of the remaining user rights, their significance, and who they are granted to by default:

■ *Act as part of the operating system.* This advanced right enables a user to act as a trusted part of the operating system. This right, by default, is not granted to any user or group.

■ *Add workstation to domain.* This right allows a user to add a workstation to a domain. This allows a workstation to recognize a domain's users and global groups. This is currently not implemented.

■ *Backup files and directories.* This right allows a user to back up files and directories. The Backup files and directories right overrules file system permissions and is granted to administrators and backup operators by default.

■ *Bypass traverse checking.* This advanced right allows a user to change to a directory and access files and subdirectories even though access to the parent directory is denied. This right, by default, is not granted to any user or group.

■ *Change the system time.* This right allows a user to change the system clock. This right, by default, is granted to administrators and power users.

■ *Create a page file.* This advanced right allows a user to create a page file. This is currently not implemented.

■ *Create a token object.* This advanced right allows a user to create access tokens. Only the Local Security Authority can have this privilege. This right, by default, is not granted to any user or group.

■ *Create a permanent shared object.* This advanced right allows a user to create permanent special objects within NT, such as \\device. This right, by default, is not granted to any user or group.

■ *Debug programs.* This advanced right allows users to debug applications. This right, by default, is granted to administrators.

■ *Force shutdown from a remote machine.* This right allows users to remotely shut down NT Workstation. This is currently not implemented.

■ *Generate security audits.* This advanced right allows a user to generate security audit entries. This right, by default, is not granted to any user or group.

■ *Increase quotas.* This advanced right allows a user to increase object quotas. Every NT object has a quota associated with it. This right is currently not implemented.

■ *Increase scheduling priority.* This advanced right allows a user to increase the priority level associated with a process. This right, by default, is granted to administrators and power users.

■ *Load & unload device drivers.* This right allows a user to load and remove device drivers. This right, by default, is granted to administrators.

■ *Lock pages in memory.* This advanced right allows a user to prevent pages in memory from being swapped out. This right, by default, is not granted to any user or group.

■ *Log on as a batch job.* This advanced right allows a user to log on to the system as a batch job. This is currently not implemented.

■ *Log on as a service.* This advanced right allows a user to log on to the system as a service. This right, by default, is not granted to any user or group.

■ *Manage auditing & security.* This right allows a user to manage auditing of system objects. This right, by default, is granted to administrators.

■ *Modify firmware environment values.* This advanced right allows a user to change system environment variables. This right, by default, is granted to administrators.

■ *Profile single process.* This advanced right allows a user to observe a process's performance. This right, by default, is granted to administrators and power users.

■ *Profile system performance.* This advanced right allows a user to observe the system performance. This right, by default, is granted to administrators.

■ *Replace a process level token.* This advanced right allows a user to modify a process's security access token. This right, by default, is not granted to any user or group.

■ *Restore files & directories.* This right allows a user to restore files and directories. The Restore files & directories right overrules file system permissions and, by default, is granted to administrators and backup operators.

■ *Take ownership of files or other objects.* This right allows a user to take ownership of an NT Workstation resource and overrules the existing resource permissions.

If you are not happy with granting a user right to the Everyone group, consider replacing it with the newly created Everyuser group mentioned earlier.

Auditing

Auditing is the third and final component of policies. It allows you to monitor and record various events on the system. Also, auditing is useful for identifying security breaches and, more importantly, recording these breaches. There is a minimal performance hit incurred when you enable auditing, but the benefits far outweigh this small overhead. To configure auditing to a level that best suits your needs, select Audit from the Policies menu within User Manager. Enable auditing by selecting the Audit These Events radio button from the Audit Policy dialog box (see Figure 10.20).

FIGURE 10.20.

Enabling auditing.

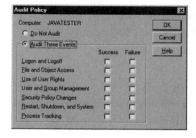

Within the Audit These Events frame, you can monitor the success or failure of the following events:

■ Logon and Logoff

- File and Object Access
- Use of User Rights
- User and Group Management
- Security Policy Changes
- Restart, Shutdown, and System
- Process Tracking

If you are using the backup and restore user rights, you might want to add the following key to the Registry to enable auditing of these rights:

Key: HKEY_LOCAL_MACHINE\SYSTEM\CurrentControlSet\Control\Lsa

Name: FullPrivilegeAuditing

Type: REG_BINARY

Value: 1

> **NOTE**
>
> To add keys to the Registry, refer to the "Registry" section (later in the chapter) or to Chapter 11, "The NT Registry." Great care should be taken when editing the Registry.

Auditing the Registry

It is also possible to turn on auditing for keys within the Registry. To enable auditing of Registry keys, you must execute the following steps:

1. Run the Registry editor, regedt32, from the Run text box.
2. Highlight the key you want to audit and select Audit from the Security menu.
3. The Registry Key Auditing dialog box appears, as shown in Figure 10.21. Check Audit Permission on Existing Subkeys if you want to audit the selected key's subkeys.
4. To audit a group's or user's actions on the key, click the Add button.
5. Scroll down the Names list box and highlight your chosen group.
6. Click Add; the group appears in the Add Names pane.
7. To add a user to the Names list box, click the Show Users button.
8. Once you have completed adding a user or group, click the OK button. You are returned to the Registry Key Auditing dialog box with the new user or group added to the Name pane.
9. Within the Events to Audit frame, you have a series of events whose success or failure can be audited once the appropriate check box is checked. The events to audit include the following:

- The Query Value entry audits system activity that attempts to open the selected key with Query Value access.
- The Set Value entry audits system activity that sets value entries in a Registry key.
- The Create Subkey entry audits the creation of subkeys on a selected Registry key.
- The Enumerate Subkeys entry audits events that attempt to identify the subkeys of a Registry key.
- The Notify entry audits notification events from a key in the Registry.
- The Create Link entry audits events that create a symbolic link in a particular key.
- The Delete entry audits attempts to delete a Registry object.
- The Write DAC entry audits the attempt of a user to gain access to a key for the purpose of writing a discretionary ACL (security permission) to the key.
- The Read Control entry audits the attempts of users to access the discretionary ACL (security permission) on a key.

FIGURE 10.21.

The Registry Key Auditing dialog box.

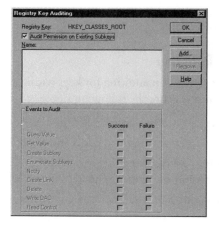

Services

NT services run under a privilege level associated with a User account. By default, services run under the System account. Go to the Control Panel and open the Services applet, highlight a service, and then click the Startup button to see such an example. Open the Startup dialog box to view the account settings of a service. Figure 10.22 shows the startup options of the EventLog service. As you can see from the Log On As frame, the service uses the System account to run.

FIGURE 10.22.

The EventLog service runs under the System account.

Not all services need to run under the System account. You should create new accounts whose sole purpose is to act as a privilege level for a service. These service accounts should have only enough privileges to serve their associated services.

Here are some services that do not need to run under the System account:

- Scheduler
- Third-party application services
- Replicator

If you are not using services such as Scheduler, you might want to disable them by selecting Manual from the Startup Type within the particular service's dialog box.

Registry

NT Workstation has a database, called the Registry, that stores all the system configuration information. Applications that are installed on the workstation register with or make changes to the Registry. In addition, the SAM database, which contains information on user and group accounts, is also stored within the Registry. Have no doubt that the Registry is an important component of NT Workstation; you need to take every possible measure to ensure that it is well protected. The Registry is vulnerable to attack from users logged on at the workstation and also from users with the ability to connect to it over the network.

Under NT Workstation 4, only the Administrator group can connect to the Registry over the network. Some services such as replication, however, need to connect remotely to the Registry. As mentioned earlier, you should run these services against a User account created specifically for that service and give the User account permission to connect remotely. These User accounts can be given remote access to the Registry as follows:

1. To kick off the Registry editor, type `regedt32` in the Run text box on the Start menu (see Figure 10.23).

10

FINE-TUNING
NT SECURITY

FIGURE 10.23.

Starting the Registry editor.

> **WARNING**
>
> Great care should be taken when editing the Registry. Incorrect entries can render your workstation unusable.

2. Select the HKEY_LOCAL_MACHINE window (see Figure 10.24) and traverse the hive tree to HKEY_LOCAL_MACHINE\SYSTEM\CurrentControlSet\Control.

FIGURE 10.24.

The HKEY_LOCAL_MACHINE *Registry hive.*

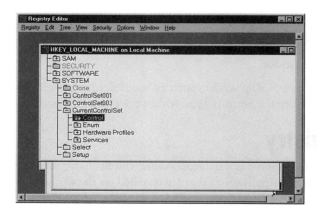

3. With this subkey highlighted, select Add Key from the Edit menu. The Add Key dialog box will appear (see Figure 10.25).

FIGURE 10.25.

The Add Key dialog box.

4. Enter SecurePipeServers in the Key Name text field and REG_SZ in the Class text field.
5. Highlight the newly created subkey and again click Add Key from the Edit menu.

6. Enter `winreg` in the Key Name text field and `REG_SZ` in the Class text field.

7. Highlight the newly created `winreg` key and click Add Value from the Edit menu.

8. Enter `Description` in the Value Name text field and select REG_SZ from the drop-down box. Enter a description in the String text box that appears in the String Editor dialog box afterward.

9. Highlight the `winreg` key again and select Permissions from the Security menu. The Registry Key Permissions dialog box appears (see Figure 10.26).

FIGURE 10.26.

The Registry Key Permissions dialog box.

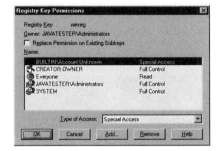

10. Click the Add button to view the Add Users and Groups dialog box (see Figure 10.27).

11. To add a user, click the Show Users button to include users in the Names list box.

12. Scroll down the Names list box and highlight your chosen user.

13. Click Add; the group appears in the Add Names pane.

14. Once you have completed adding users, click the OK button. You are returned to the Registry Key Permissions dialog box with the new users added to the Name pane.

FIGURE 10.27.

The Add Users and Groups dialog box.

You have now configured these users to connect to the Registry remotely. You must now secure the Registry from within. By default, permissions on the Registry are not that strong and only ensure access rather than consciously restrict access. For example, the Everyone group is given read access to areas of the Registry, such as the HKEY_LOCAL_MACHINE\HARDWARE, that it really does not need. Access to this key enables members of the Everyone group to access the complete hardware makeup of the workstation. To restrict permissions within the Registry is a delicate operation—one wrong configuration change can lead to disastrous results. A practical hint is to replace the Everyone group permissions on the following keys with Query Value, Read Control, Enumerate Subkeys, and Notify access:

```
HKEY_LOCAL_MACHINE\Software\Microsoft\RPC
HKEY_LOCAL_MACHINE\Software\Microsoft\WindowsNT\CurrentVersion
HKEY_LOCAL_MACHINE\Software\Windows 3.1 Migration Status
HKEY_CLASSES_ROOT
```

> ## WARNING
>
> You might also want to consider using your secure Everyuser account instead of the Everyone group. Great care should be taken when editing the Registry. Be careful not to propagate conflicting permissions to subkeys.

To change existing permissions for a user, double-click a user within the Registry Key Permissions dialog box to be presented with the Special Access dialog box. The Special Access dialog box allows you to set full control on a key by selecting the Full Control radio button (see Figure 10.28).

FIGURE 10.28.

The Special Access dialog box.

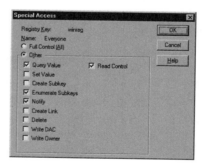

Alternatively, and more wisely, you can set the following access on the selected key from within the Other frame:

- *Query Value.* Assigns the right to read a value entry from a Registry key.
- *Set Value.* Assigns the right to set value entries in a Registry key.
- *Create Subkey.* Assigns the right to create subkeys on a selected Registry key.

- *Enumerate Subkeys.* Assigns the right to identify the subkeys of a Registry key.
- *Create Link.* Assigns the right to create a symbolic link in a particular key.
- *Delete.* Assigns the right to delete the selected key.
- *Write DAC.* Assigns the right to gain access to a key for the purpose of writing to the key a discretionary ACL.
- *Write Owner.* Assigns the right to gain access to a key for the purpose of taking ownership of it.
- *Read Control.* Assigns the right to gain access to the security information on the selected key.

C2 Settings

As part of the Resource Kit for NT Workstation, Microsoft has included a tool to enable your NT Workstation to be a C2-compliant system. The C2 Configuration Manager is a tool that helps you make your workstation C2-compliant. Don't panic if you don't have the Resource Kit installed, because most of the changes made by the C2 Configuration Manager can be executed by changes in the Registry. In Figure 10.29, you can see a list of configuration changes recommended by the C2 Configuration Manager. To access the C2 Configuration Manager, click Start and then select Programs | Resource Kit 4 and Configuration | C2 Configuration.

FIGURE 10.29.

The C2 Configuration Manager dialog box.

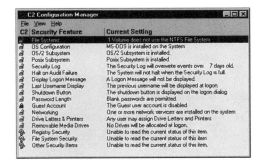

The blue open lock icons to the left of each entry signify that the associated security measure has not been executed. Once you secure an entry, this icon will change to a red closed lock. Double-clicking any entry will bring up a dialog box for that entry. To execute the change, click the C2 or Secure button. The following is a list of C2 and additional changes you can execute:

- *File Systems.* To comply with C2-level security, the file system has to be NTFS, which supports access control. If you don't have NTFS, clicking the C2 button within the C2 Configuration - File System dialog box will convert any selected non-NTFS volumes to NTFS.

- *OS Configuration.* C2-level security requires that NT be the only operating system loaded and that the boot.ini timeout section is set to zero seconds. Complying with C2 for this entry will set your initial boot window to zero seconds and will remove all other operating systems, namely MS-DOS. You can manually edit the boot.ini file and set the timeout variable to zero. The boot.ini is located off the root of the system partition.

- *OS/2 Subsystem.* OS/2 is not C2-compliant and will have to be removed to meet C2-level security.

- *Posix Subsystem.* Posix is not C2-compliant and will have to be removed to meet C2-level security.

- *Security Log.* C2 security requires that security logs cannot be overwritten. This option can be set from within the log settings of the event viewer also.

- *Halt on Audit Failure.* Setting this option halts the system whenever the security log fills as an added, but drastic, security measure. This prevents unaudited security violations. This is not a C2 requirement.

- *Display Logon Message.* Some countries legally require that you display a logon banner informing the user that sensitive information is contained on the system and that only authorized users are allowed on the system. This banner is displayed prior to logon. This change can be manually executed by adding the following changes to the Registry:

  Hive: `HKEY_LOCAL_MACHINE\SOFTWARE`

  Key: `\Microsoft\Windows NT\Current Version\Winlogon`

  Name: `LegalNoticeCaption`

  Type: `REG_SZ`

  Value: `Company ABC Ltd.`

  Hive: `HKEY_LOCAL_MACHINE\SOFTWARE`

  Key: `\Microsoft\Windows NT\Current Version\Winlogon`

  Name: `LegalNoticeText`

  Type: `REG_SZ`

  Value: Unauthorized Access Denied

WARNING

Remember to exercise extreme caution whenever you edit the Registry. Misconfigurations within the Registry can leave your workstation unusable.

■ *Last Username Display.* NT Workstation can hide the name of the last user to log on as an added security precaution. This change can be manually executed by adding the following changes to the Registry:

> Hive: `HKEY_LOCAL_MACHINE\SOFTWARE`
>
> Key: `\Microsoft\Windows NT\Current Version\Winlogon`
>
> Name: `DontDisplayLastUserName`
>
> Type: `REG_SZ`
>
> Value: `1`

■ *Shutdown Button.* NT Workstation can remove the Shutdown button from the logon display dialog box. The Shutdown button should be removed, because any user can bring your Workstation down without being logged on. This change can be manually executed by adding the following changes to the Registry:

> Hive: `HKEY_LOCAL_MACHINE\SOFTWARE`
>
> Key: `\Microsoft\Windows NT\Current Version\Winlogon`
>
> Name: `ShutdownWithoutLogon`
>
> Type: `REG_SZ`
>
> Value: `0`

■ *Password Length.* C2-level security requires a minimum password length of five characters. I recommend you configure a number larger than six characters. This is also configurable through Account Policies within the User Manager.

■ *Guest Account.* C2-level security requires the disabling of the Guest account. This is also configurable through the User Manager.

■ *Networking.* C2 compliance requires that no networking software be installed on the workstation.

■ *Drive Letters & Printers.* This security measure allows administrators to assign drive letters and printers. This is not a C2 requirement.

■ *Removable Media Drives.* Allocating the floppy and CD-ROM drive(s) at logon prevents programs started by other users from accessing them. This is not a C2 requirement.

■ *Registry Security.* C2-level security requires that you have the ability to assign ACLs to the system Registry keys.

■ *File System Security.* C2-level security requires you to have the ability to assign ACLs to the system directories.

■ *Other Security Items.* These are requirements of C2-level security that cannot be detected by the C2 Configuration Manager. These include the presence of a BIOS password, a secure system partition (RISC systems only), changing the User Manager program icon, and restricting the user rights in accordance with the C2 security guide.

File System

The NT file system allows you to define permissions and ownership on files, directories, and file shares at a user and group level. A lot of files and directories have full control permissions given to the Everyone group, and, by default, all file shares are created with full control granted to the Everyone group. To rectify this takes a bit of careful configuration. To change permissions on files or directories, kick off Explore and right-click on the file or directory whose permissions you want to change and then select Properties from its menu (see Figure 10.30). For more on the NT file system, refer to Chapter 12, "Working with the NT File System."

FIGURE 10.30.

Select properties of a directory within Explore.

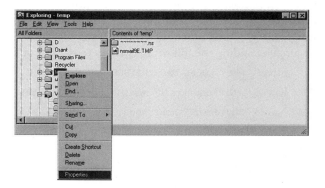

You are now presented with a properties dialog box. Select the Security tab to reveal the security settings on the directory or file (see Figure 10.31).

FIGURE 10.31.

The Security tab within a file or directory properties dialog box.

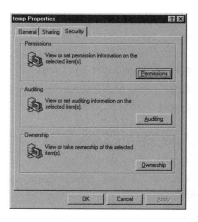

Click Permissions to reveal the permissions on a file or directory (see Figure 10.32).

NOTE

You can also see two other buttons marked Audit and Change Ownership. Again, as with all other objects within NT Workstation, you can audit files and directories and record successful and failed operations such as read, write, execute, change permissions, and take ownership.

Figure 10.32.

*The Directory
Permissions dialog box.*

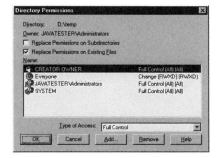

You can use the Permissions dialog box to amend permissions on any file or directory.

Start by securing the system files, giving them permissions as follows:

Directory	Permissions
\Winnt	Administrators: Full Control
	CREATOR OWNER: Full Control
	Everyone: Read
	SYSTEM: Full Control
\Winnt\FONTS	Administrators: Full Control
	CREATOR OWNER: Full Control
	Everyone: Read
	SYSTEM: Full Control
\Winnt\HELP	Administrators: Full Control
	CREATOR OWNER: Full Control
	Everyone: Read
	SYSTEM: Full Control
\Winnt\INF	Administrators: Full Control
	CREATOR OWNER: Full Control

continues

Directory	Permissions
\Winnt\PROFILES	Everyone: Read
	SYSTEM: Full Control
	Administrators: Full Control
	CREATOR OWNER: Full Control
\Winnt\REPAIR	Everyone: READ
	SYSTEM: Full Control
	Administrators: Full Control
\Winnt\SYSTEM	SYSTEM: Full Control
	Administrators: Full Control
	CREATOR OWNER: Full Control
\Winnt\SYSTEM32	Everyone: Read
	SYSTEM: Full Control
	Administrators: Full Control
	CREATOR OWNER: Full Control
\Winnt\SYSTEM32\CONFIG	Everyone: Read
	SYSTEM: Full Control
	Administrators: Full Control
	CREATOR OWNER: Full Control
\Winnt\SYSTEM\DHCP	Everyone: List
	SYSTEM: Full Control
	(Delete this directory if you are not running DHCP)
\Winnt\SYSTEM32\DRIVERS	Administrators: Full Control
	CREATOR OWNER: Full Control
	Everyone: Read
\Winnt\SYSTEM32\RAS	SYSTEM: Full Control
	(Delete this directory if you are not running RAS)
\Winnt\SYSTEM32\OS2	(Delete this directory if you are not running OS\2)
\Winnt\SYSTEM32\SPOOL	Administrators: Full Control
	CREATOR OWNER: Full Control
	Everyone: Read

Directory	Permissions
	PowerUsers: Change
	SYSTEM: Full Control
\Winnt\SYSTEM32\VIEWERS	Administrators: Full Control
	CREATOR OWNER: Full Control
	Everyone: Read
	SYSTEM: Full Control
\Winnt35\SYSTEM32\WINS	(Delete this directory if you are not running WINS)

You can tighten up the following files off the root directory by applying the following permissions:

File	Permissions
\AUTOEXEC.BAT	Administrators: Full Control
	EVERYBODY: Read
	SYSTEM: Full Control
\BOOT.INI	Administrators: Full Control
	SYSTEM: Full Control
\CONFIG.SYS	Administrators: Full Control
	EVERYBODY: Read
	SYSTEM: Full Control
\NTDETECT\COM	Administrators: Full Control
	SYSTEM: Full Control
\NTLDR	Administrators: Full Control
	SYSTEM: Full Control

With all other application directories, you should set the following permissions with propagation:

Administrators: Full Control
SYSTEM: Full Control
USERS: List

You might also consider replacing the Everyone group with an equivalent Everyuser substitute account for these permissions.

Because each of the directory file shares created on NT gives full control to the Everyone group, you might also consider reviewing them to ensure that this is still not the case. To review the permissions on a directory file share, right-click each shared directory from within Explore and select Properties from its menu. Next, select the Sharing tab from within the Properties dialog box (see Figure 10.33).

FIGURE 10.33.

The Browsers Properties Sharing dialog box of a directory.

Click the Permissions button to display the Access Through Share Permissions dialog box (see Figure 10.34). You can add users and groups by using the Add Users and Groups dialog box, accessed by clicking Add. To remove groups or users, simply highlight whatever object you want to remove and click the Remove button.

FIGURE 10.34.

The Access Through Share Permissions dialog box of a directory.

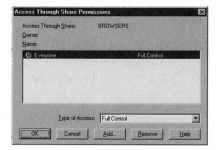

NT also creates hidden shares on each of the NTFS volumes and the system root within its system, by default. These are well-known shares because they are called after the drive letter (for example, the hidden share on the C drive is c$). These shares can be accessed only by administrators, and permissions to them cannot be altered. If this configuration bothers you, you might consider disabling drive shares completely by removing all users and groups from Access this computer from the network. This, however, prevents anybody from connecting to your NT workstation. Alternatively, you might consider using a batch job that would run at boot time. You can use the net share statement to delete these predefined shares. Here's an example:

```
net share admin$ /delete
```

RAS

As I mentioned earlier, RAS is yet another access point to your workstation, but it can also be a vehicle to carry users onto your network. Users who connect via RAS can be confined to your workstation only and can be prohibited from making connections beyond it.

NOTE

You can restrict connection to the workstation only when the RAS service is enabled to accept incoming calls. This is done by choosing the appropriate setting from the Configure Port Usage dialog box, which is accessed by clicking the Configure button from the Remote Access Setup dialog box.

This option is configurable under the RAS service entry within the network applet in Control Panel, which can be accessed as follows:

1. Open the Control Panel (click Start and then select Settings | Control Panel).
2. Click the Network applet.
3. Click the Services tab.
4. Highlight the RAS service entry and click the Properties button to be presented with the Remote Access Setup dialog box (see Figure 10.35).

FIGURE 10.35.

The Remote Access Setup dialog box.

5. Click the Network button to open the Network Configuration dialog box.
6. In the Server Setting frame, there is a check box for each of the network protocols you are running on the workstation. Users can connect under any one of these protocols, so you have to click the associated Configure button for each loaded protocol. Then once inside the RAS protocol configuration dialog box, restrict connection to this workstation by selecting the This computer only radio button. See Figure 10.36 for an example of the protocol dialog box for TCP/IP.

FIGURE 10.36.

Restricting network access under TCP/IP to the workstation.

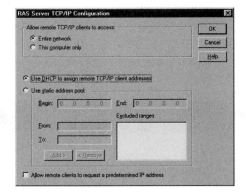

As a further security precaution, you should consider using Point to Point Tunneling Protocol (PPTP) with RAS. PPTP is a new feature with NT Workstation 4, and it allows you to secure your RAS connections by encrypting communications from end to end. For more on PPTP, see Chapter 25, "Remote Computing with Remote Access Service."

TCP/IP Filtering

The final aspect I will discuss in this chapter is TCP/IP filtering. This is another new feature to NT Workstation 4; it allows you to define security at a protocol level. Described as the poor man's firewall, you can use TCP/IP filtering to configure NT to either allow or reject packets through the network interface card at a protocol level. Configuration of TCP/IP filtering is hidden deep within the Network dialog box. To reach the TCP/IP Security dialog box, you must do the following:

1. Click the Network applet within the Control Panel.
2. Select the Protocol tab.
3. Highlight TCP/IP from the Network Protocols pane and click Properties.
4. Click the Advanced button within the IP Address tab of the Microsoft TCP/IP Properties dialog box.
5. Check the Enable Security check box and then click Configure in the Advanced IP Addressing dialog box.

You are finally presented with the TCP/IP Security dialog box, as shown in Figure 10.37.

Within the TCP/IP Security dialog box, you can configure filtering to a particular network interface by selecting the desired adapter from the Adapter drop-down list. Having selected your intended adapter, you can restrict packets at a TCP or UDP port level or at an IP protocol level. Once you add a port or protocol to be permitted, all other ports or protocols will be denied by exclusion from the list.

FIGURE 10.37.
*Configuring TCP/IP
filtering.*

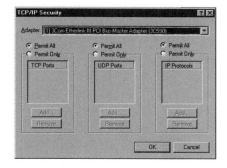

To add a port or protocol, take the following steps:

1. Check the Permit Only radio button associated with the TCP or UDP port or IP
   protocol list you are adding to.
2. Click the Add button to present the Security Add dialog box (see Figure 10.38).

FIGURE 10.38.
*The Security Add
dialog box.*

Enter the port or protocol number in the text field and click the Add button. You are returned
to the TCP/IP Security dialog box, and the port or protocol you have just added appears in the
associated list box. To remove a port or protocol, simply highlight one within a list box and
click the Remove button located below it. The port or protocol is removed from the list and is
no longer permitted through the selected network adapter. For more on TCP/IP filtering, see
Chapter 26, "Windows NT Networking Protocols."

Summary

NT Workstation "straight out of the box" is not a highly secure operating system. You have to
affect configuration changes to the system to tighten the many NT security features. In this
chapter, you looked closely at security, C2 certification, the NT security model, and securing
an NT workstation. You learned step-by-step procedures to strengthen the main components
of a workstation, such as the following:

- Users and groups
- The Registry
- The file system
- Policies and auditing

These security measures should be a part of an overall security policy enforced by you or your company. All that is set out in this chapter might not suit your environment, but you should try to execute as many recommendations as are applicable.

The NT Registry

by Mike Sheehy and Thomas Wölfer

CHAPTER 11

IN THIS CHAPTER

The Registry has long been regarded as the inner sanctum of NT, and many have felt too daunted to change it or even look at it. The Registry is a database that stores the system configuration data in one secure place. In this chapter, you'll take a close look at the NT Registry. You'll learn the purpose of the Registry, what it contains, and how you can administer it.

Prior to the Registry, Microsoft stored system and application data in .INI files, small human-readable files with bracketed headings and entries underneath those headings. Although some applications placed their .INI files in private directories, most of these files could be found in the \Windows\System directory. Because .INI files were to be easily accessed, they basically contained text; sometimes an application would store binary data in a hex format, but most did not.

The most important .INI files were WIN.INI and SYSTEM.INI, the central configuration files used by Windows. Some applications did store their configuration information in WIN.INI and SYSTEM.INI, which added to the confusion already created by the multitude of .INI files.

With the introduction of Windows NT and Windows 95, Microsoft replaced the .INI file mechanism with a more centralized way for storing configuration information: the Registry.

Who and What Uses the Registry?

As I stated earlier, the Registry is a centralized database where all system configuration data is stored. This configuration data includes everything that heretofore was stored in .INI files. Configuration data that could be found in the AUTOEXEC.BAT and CONFIG.SYS, application-specific data, hardware-specific data, device driver data, and network protocol and adapter card settings are all placed in the Registry.

Apart from manual changes made by authorized users, there are a number of processes that use and make changes to the Registry. These processes, as illustrated in Figure 11.1, include the following:

- *Ntdetect.com.* When NT Workstation boots, the Ntdetect.com routine starts and attempts to detect whatever hardware is installed. Once this list is complete, Ntdetect.com writes this list to the Registry.

- *Ntoskrnl.exe.* Also at boot time, the NT Kernel, Ntoskrnl.exe, writes to the Registry, informing it of details such as the Kernel version and other configuration data. As well as adding to the Registry, the Kernel also queries the Registry to find out what device drivers to load and the order in which it should load them.

- *Administrative tools.* The Control Panel applets (see Chapter 9, "Advanced Control Panel Tools") write to and query from the Registry. Because these applets are used to configure the system, it is no surprise that there is interaction between them and the Registry. Many of the tools that administrators use to troubleshoot and analyze NT Workstation take their data from the Registry.

■ *Device drivers.* Device drivers write load parameters, resource usage, and configuration data to the Registry so that the Registry can, in turn, report this information to other device drivers and applications. This enables informative and useful installation and configuration programs.

FIGURE 11.1.

Components interacting with the Registry.

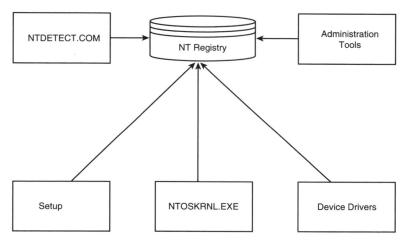

It is now easy to see why users are so reluctant to tinker with the Registry, because any mistake can bring a system to its knees. This also emphasizes why you need to secure the Registry. You can refer to Chapter 10, "Fine-Tuning NT Security," for an in-depth look at securing the Registry.

Though the Registry is perceived to be one single data store, it is not. The Registry is information gathered from a number of data stores. When users access the Registry by using either of the Registry editors, Regedit or Regedt32, they are presented with a single database ordered in a hierarchical fashion. Because of this, it doesn't really matter where the information comes from. The Registry editors take care of gathering all the information from the appropriate places and transparently ensure that changes are written back to the correct files. In addition to this, all operations executed on the Registry are *atomic*. This means that there is an all-or-nothing policy that prevents changes being half propagated to the Registry. Atomicity is even ensured against system failure due to hardware or software problems.

Although the Registry is located in fixed locations on the hard drive, it also resides in an area of memory when in use. Because the size of the Registry can grow, it is necessary to limit the area of memory that the Registry can hold. This limit is dictated to by a value set within the Registry itself. The RegistrySizeLimit value limits the area of memory that the Registry can consume. This value is located under HKEY_LOCAL_MACHINE\System\CurrentControlSet\Control and has a type of Reg_DWORD. By default, the Registry size is set to 25 percent of the available area of memory. The system tries to ensure that the RegistrySizeLimit remains within a minimum value of 4MB and a maximum value of 80 percent of the allocated area of memory. The size of this area of memory, called the *page pool space*, is defined by the Registry value `PagedPoolSize`, which is located at `HKEY_LOCAL_MACHINE\System\CurrentControlSet\Control\Session Manager\Memory Management`.

The Registry Hierarchy

There will come a time, however, when the applets within the Control Panel will not do everything you require and you will have no alternative but to go directly to the Registry. Before you start blindly editing the Registry, you should first become familiar with its key components. The Registry can be perceived as a hierarchical structure whose starting point is its root. At the root of the Registry are *subtrees*, each of which is a set of *subkeys*. Each of these subtrees is prefixed with `HKEY_`. Figure 11.2 illustrates the hierarchical organization of the Registry.

FIGURE 11.2.

The Registry hierarchy.

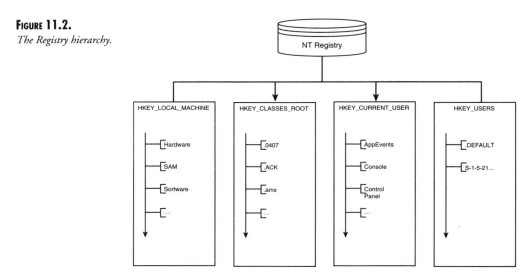

The hierarchy contains data as well as *keys*. Keys are equivalent to folders in the file system, and they build up the actual hierarchy. That is, keys might contain other keys as well as data. *Data* is the element that makes up the hierarchy's leaves. Each data item has a name that describes the item, a data type, and the actual value of the item. There are five data types exposed by Regedt32 and three data types exposed by Regedit. Both editors know about string values, binary values, and DWORD values, which represent data as a 4-byte number. Only Regedt32 knows about the data types `REG_EXPAND_SZ` and `REG_MULTI_SZ`. Apart from these extra data types, I prefer to use Regedt32 because it allows you to configure security and auditing on keys, a function not as yet supported under Regedit.

String values are ordinary strings; that is, they might store information such as a username and street address. These values can easily be edited. Binary values contain data an application chooses to store in binary format and, thus, are hard to change or even read. DWORD values basically are numbers. For example, they are used to store options, where a 1 reflects the option being turned on and 0 means the option is turned off. REG_EXPAND_SZ is a special type of string that can contain environment variables. When an application requests such a data type from the Registry, the system replaces the embedded environment variable with the current setting from the system Control Panel applet. REG_MULTI_SZ is another type of string, where the data item can contain more than one string. (A string, in this context, is one from a programmer's point of view. That is, it is text that is terminated by a special symbol represented by the value zero. REG_MULTI_SZ can have more than one of these zero-terminated strings.)

In Regedit, the Registry's root is split into six parts, whereas Regedt32 is split into five. However, the actual content of the Registry is split into four different roots. These are HKEY_LOCAL_MACHINE, HKEY_CLASSES_ROOT, HKEY_CURRENT_USER, and HKEY_USERS. HKEY_CURRENT_CONFIG and HKEY_DYN_DATA (the last one displayed by Regedit) are not used to store configuration information but have other purposes that I will explain later in this chapter. Figures 11.3 and 11.4 illustrate the default view of the Registry offered by Regedt32 and Regedit, respectively.

FIGURE 11.3.

The Registry through Regedt32.

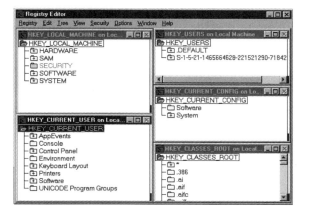

FIGURE 11.4.

The Registry through Regedit.

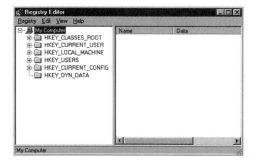

Just by looking at the cryptic names used in the Registry, you can see that it isn't actually intended as a tool for the end user; it is more a tool to be used by programmers. Although the Registry is a single database, the information within it is not stored in a single file. In fact, when NT Workstation is installed in a Windows NT domain and roaming user accounts are enabled, it is even possible that parts of the Registry aren't stored on the local hard drive, but rather on the server. (A *roaming user account* is a user account that enables a Windows NT user to use the same configuration settings regardless of the machine he/she uses to log in.)

Hives

As I mentioned earlier, though the Registry is perceived to be one database, it is made up of constituent components stored in different locations on the hard drive. These components, called hives, are permanently part of the Registry, and they differ from those subkeys and subtrees that are dynamically created at boot time. These hives can be mapped to files on the hard drive. The standard hives are as follows:

- HKEY_LOCAL_MACHINE\SAM
- HKEY_LOCAL_MACHINE\Security
- HKEY_LOCAL_MACHINE\Software
- HKEY_LOCAL_MACHINE\System
- HKEY_CURRENT_CONFIG
- HKEY_USERS\DEFAULT
- HKEY_CURRENT_USER

You can trace these hives back to physical files residing in the <winnt40>\system32\config directory and <winnt40>\profiles\<username> directory.

The hive files are as follows:

- Sam
- Security
- Software
- System
- Default
- Userdiff
- Ntuser

The hives also have other associated files whose filenames are made up of the hive name plus the following file extensions:

- .alt—This file extension is associated only with the HKEY_LOCAL_MACHINE\System hive and is its backup copy.

■ `.log`—These files log the changes to keys and values of a hive.

■ `.sav`—These files contain a copy of the hives.

Figure 11.5 shows the hive files through Explorer. Notice, also, the `.log`, `.alt`, and `.sav` files.

FIGURE 11.5.
The hive files.

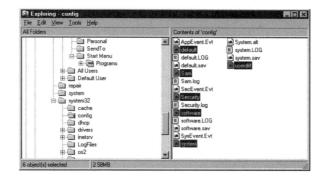

Windows NT Subtrees

There are a number of subtrees off the root of the Registry. Let's look at each of these in turn, and I will explain its purpose within the Registry.

HKEY_LOCAL_MACHINE

The `HKEY_LOCAL_MACHINE` part of the Registry contains configuration information relevant to the local computer. For example, the hardware configuration information collected by NT during boot time is stored here. `HKEY_LOCAL_MACHINE` also contains installed drivers, their settings and configuration data, and the security accounts database. The information from `HKEY_LOCAL_MACHINE` is used by the system regardless of the currently logged-in user.

`HKEY_LOCAL_MACHINE` is divided into five sections. These are `HARDWARE`, `SAM`, `SECURITY`, `SOFTWARE`, and `SYSTEM`. Here is an explanation of each of the subkeys:

■ The `HKEY_LOCAL_MACHINE\HARDWARE` subkey stores the physical configuration of the computer. The information in this subtree is created at boot time and contains specifics on device drivers, resource maps, and device maps (see Figure 11.6). The information in this subkey is also used by the Windows NT diagnostic program, `WINMSD.EXE`, through which it is presented in a far more readable format.

■ The `HKEY_LOCAL_MACHINE\SAM` subkey contains the Security Account Manager (SAM). On an NT workstation, SAM contains information on user and group accounts. Administrators use the User Manager and the Permission dialog box of Explorer (using an NTFS partition) to access and maintain SAM information.

■ The `HKEY_LOCAL_MACHINE\SECURITY` subkey contains even more security information pertaining to policies and user rights. This information, however, is used locally by the security subsystem only.

> **NOTE**
>
> As you can see in Figure 11.6, the SAM and SECURITY subkeys are disabled, thus denying you direct access to them through the Registry. You will have to use the User Manager to access these subkeys.

■ The HKEY_LOCAL_MACHINE\SOFTWARE contains system-wide software configuration data. For example, a vendor might choose to supply a default configuration that is used each time a new user starts an application. Also, a vendor might store path information about installed products on a system, which doesn't change when a new user logs on. This kind of information is also stored in the SOFTWARE section.

■ The SYSTEM section contains information about the way NT is configured to boot. It also contains information on NT services, required device drivers, and other behavioral aspects of NT.

Figure 11.6 illustrates the HKEY_LOCAL_MACHINE subtree.

FIGURE 11.6.

The
HKEY_LOCAL_MACHINE
subtree.

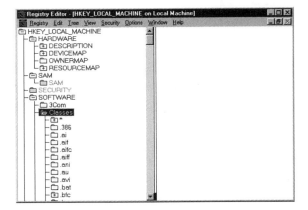

HKEY_CLASSES_ROOT

The HKEY_CLASSES_ROOT part of the Registry is available only for compatibility reasons. It provides the same information as did the REG.DAT file in 16-bit Windows 3.*x*.

HKEY_CLASSES_ROOT contains the OLE file associations on the local computer. That is, when the File Types dialog box from Explorer's options is used to associate a file extension with an application or when an association is made during an application installation, the association information is stored here.

11

THE NT REGISTRY

Windows applications that are 32-bit do not use HKEY_CLASSES_ROOT, but rather an identical copy of this section that can be found under HKEY_LOCAL_MACHINE\Software\Classes (refer to Figure 11.6). If you manually change an entry in either of these subkeys, the Registry Editor ensures synchronization by updating the other to reflect your manual changes.

There are two distinct types of subkeys within the HKEY_CLASSES_ROOT:

■ *Filename extensions.* As you can see from Figure 11.7, which illustrates the HKEY_CLASSES_ROOT, there are a number of subkeys beginning with a dot plus a three-letter extension. These are definitions of filename extensions that allow applications to be associated with file types. These file type associations are defined during application installations and also manually through the use of the File Types tab within Explore.

FIGURE 11.7.
The
HKEY_CLASSES_ROOT
subtree.

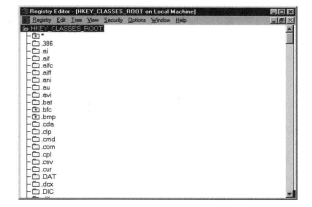

Figure 11.8 shows an example of the definition of the .doc file type.

FIGURE 11.8.
The .doc *file type*
within the
HKEY_CLASSES_ROOT
subtree.

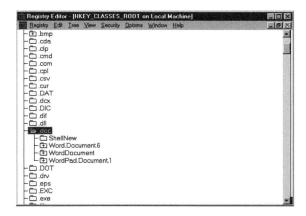

Apart from application installations or manual entries to the Registry, you can use the File Types tab within Explorer to map applications to file types. The File Types tab is accessed from the Options entry of the View menu within Explorer. Figure 11.9 shows the Options dialog box and the File Types tab selected to the .gif file type. The application presently associated with .gif file types is Internet Explorer. This association allows you to double-click on a .GIF file and view it by invoking Internet Explorer. Notice also that you can define an icon with a file type. This icon association determines what icon Explorer will display with a file type.

FIGURE 11.9.

The File Types tab within Explorer Options.

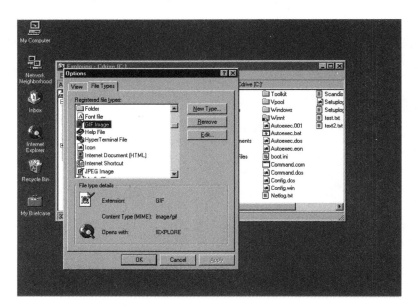

■ *Class definition.* Class-definition subkeys contain information on Component Object Model (COM) objects. Subkeys define specific COM properties, such as dynamic data exchange (DDE). Figure 11.10 shows the subkey for Microsoft Word 6 and the subkeys defining the DDE commands of open and print.

HKEY_CURRENT_USER

HKEY_CURRENT_USER holds the currently logged-in user's profile. A profile contains system settings as well as application-specific information. For example, the desktop's layout, available network resources, mapped drives, the contents of the Start menu, and screen colors are stored here.

Most of the entries in HKEY_CURRENT_USER are created by installed applications and, thus, differ from system to system and from logged-in user to logged-in user.

FIGURE 11.10.

The Class definition for Microsoft Word 6.

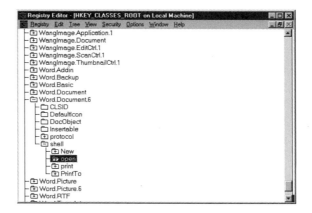

However, there are some default subkeys created by Windows NT that are always available (see Figure 11.11). These are AppEvents, Console, Control Panel, Environment, Keyboard Layout, Network, Printers, and Software. The following list describes these default subkeys:

- ■ AppEvents defines application events. Application events are user-defined events that occur for particular events. For example, each time the machine boots up you can configure a particular sound bite to play.

- ■ Console defines the look and feel of character-mode applications such as the Windows NT command prompt. Console can also define the size and position of program group windows.

- ■ Control Panel contains user-specific settings from—you guessed it—the Control Panel. This corresponds to information that was stored in the WIN.INI and CONTROL.INI files under Windows.

- ■ Environment holds the user's environment variables that have been set via the System applet in the Control Panel. These settings correspond to user settings that were held within the AUTOEXEC.BAT file in DOS.

- ■ Keyboard Layout defines the language of the current keyboard layout. To change this setting, you must use the Keyboard applet within Control Panel.

- ■ Network is a subkey that is no longer in use.

- ■ Printers contains a description of all printers available to the user. To change these values, you must first click Start and then select Settings | Printers.

- ■ Software is the most interesting subkey because it holds all application settings for the current user. This includes system applications and Windows NT settings (for example, Task Manager preferences). This subkey has the same structure as HKEY_LOCAL_MACHINE\Software. Again, under earlier versions of Windows this information would have corresponded to application-specific information from the WIN.INI file.

- ■ The UNICODE subkey is not used unless the installation of NT 4 was an upgrade.

FIGURE 11.11.

The Registry
HKEY_CURRENT_USER
subtree.

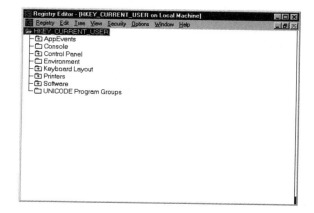

HKEY_USERS

HKEY_USERS contains all locally available user profiles, which basically look like the HKEY_CURRENT_USER profile and differ only in the actual values for the data items found within.

When users log in, their personal configuration is copied from their personal subkey under HKEY_USERS to HKEY_CURRENT_USER. During logout, information from HKEY_CURRENT_USER is copied back to the user's personal subkey in HKEY_USERS.

There are at least two subkeys in HKEY_USERS (see Figure 11.12):

- .Default. When a user logs on to Windows NT for the first time, the system uses the .Default subkey to create the initial user profile. In other words, the .Default subkey can be used by the workstation's administrator to preconfigure settings for all new users of a machine. For example, a company logo could be used as the default background image for all new users. The .Default subkey has the same structure as HKEY_CURRENT_USER. The .Default subkey is also used when no user is logged on to the workstation.

- SID_#. All other subkeys apart from .Default are Security ID (SID) strings of the user they apply to. That is, the user's settings are not identified by username, but rather by a string supplied by NT security. However, it is possible to resolve a username from this Security ID string by looking into HKEY_LOCAL_MACHINE\Software\Microsoft\WindowsNT\CurrentVersion\ProfileList, where the usernames are listed below the Security ID strings.

FIGURE 11.12.
The Registry
HKEY_USERS *subtree.*

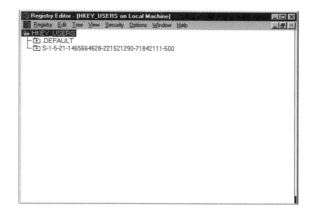

HKEY_CURRENT_CONFIG

HKEY_CURRENT_CONFIG is not really a separate Registry section, but rather a shortcut to the currently used hardware configuration from HKEY_LOCAL_MACHINE\SYSTEM\CurrentControlSet\ Hardware Profiles\Current. (Hardware configurations, also known as *hardware profiles*, are created with the System applet from Control Panel.) The HKEY_CURRENT_CONFIG subtree is new to the Windows NT 4 Registry and was added for compatibility reasons. The HKEY_CURRENT_CONFIG subtree corresponds directly to the HKEY_CURRENT_CONFIG subtree within the Windows 95 Registry (see Figure 11.13). This allows applications to run under both Windows NT and Windows 95. This subtree contains details on the current hardware profile being used by NT. Hardware profiles are sets of configurations governing devices and services that will be executed by NT when loading.

FIGURE 11.13.
The
HKEY_CURRENT_CONFIG
subtree.

Hardware profiles are most useful for laptop computers. For example, one configuration is used while the laptop is docked to a docking station, and the other configuration is used while the machine is undocked. When you do have several hardware configurations on your computer, you can select the one to use when the machine boots. Hardware profiles are created through the System applet within Control Panel. From within the System applet, click Hardware Profiles. (See Chapter 9 for more on the System applet.)

All hardware profiles are stored within the `HKEY_LOCAL_MACHINE\System` subtree. Even the current hardware profile is stored here under `CurrentControlSet\Hardware Profiles\Current`.

HKEY_DYN_DATA

Just like `HKEY_CURRENT_CONFIG`, `HKEY_DYN_DATA` isn't really a separate section in the Registry. Instead, as the name implies, it is a collection of dynamic data (meaning the data can change at any time). For example, the current state of plug-and-play devices can be found here.

Also, `HKEY_DYN_DATA` makes up the Performance Registry. That is, measurement tools such as Performance Monitor use the data available in `HKEY_DYN_DATA`; the information needed for performance measurement is logged to this place.

However, because plug-and-play technology is not yet part of Windows NT and because performance data is available only via tools such as Performance Monitor, `HKEY_DYN_DATA` appears to be empty and unable to be edited. In fact, depending on your user rights, `HKEY_DYN_DATA` might not even be displayed in the Registry editor.

Registry Administration

As mentioned previously, there are two editors you can use to edit the Registry. This section discusses both editors. Also, I will detail how you traverse through the Registry and how you add and remove keys to suit your environment. In addition, you'll look at remotely administering the Registry when things go wrong.

> **WARNING**
>
> I cannot emphasize enough the caution you should take when making changes within the Registry. Any mistakes within the Registry could prove detrimental to your workstation.

Why two editors? Traditionally, Microsoft supplied Regedt32 as the Registry editor until Windows 95 was written. With Windows 95 came Regedit, a Registry editor with an Explorer-type interface. Both editors are installed by default with Windows NT, and both allow you execute the basic editing functions of add, change, and remove. The main difference between the editors is that you are unable to use the security features of auditing keys (assigning permissions to keys) when using Regedit.

Regedit

Regedit is accessed by typing `regedit` from the Run window of the Start menu. The Regedit screen is split into two vertical panes:

- The left pane displays the Registry root, denoted by My Computer, with six subtrees hanging from it. Each of these subtrees was explained previously in detail.

- The right pane is divided into two columns under which the Value Name and Value Data are displayed for the selected key in the left pane. Figure 11.14 shows the `HKEY_CURRENT_USER\Console` key selected on the left pane and its associated Value Names and Value Data displayed on the right.

FIGURE 11.14.

The Registry through Regedit.

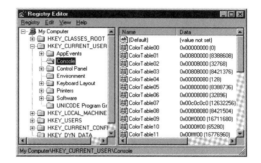

Regedit will always display both panes, but you can adjust the split between them either by clicking it with the mouse or by selecting Split from the View menu. Once you have high-lighted the split (denoted by a change in the cursor), hold the left mouse button down and drag the split left or right to suit your needs. The View menu also has an entry to refresh the display. This can also be executed by selecting the F5 key on your keyboard.

Traversing the Registry

Traversing through the Registry is the same as traversing through the file system using Explorer. You can use either the arrow keys on the keyboard or the mouse to get around the Registry. Within the View menu is an option to display a status bar at the base of the window. This status bar is helpful because it displays your current position within the Registry. You can en-able the status bar by selecting Status Bar from the View menu. To expand a subtree, you must select it using the mouse or the arrow keys. Once the subtree is selected, you can expand it by double-clicking it with the mouse or by hitting the Enter key from the keyboard. To collapse a subtree, you again use the Enter key from the keyboard on the selected subtree or double-click a subtree with the mouse. Regedit also supports the right-click features for editing keys and value entries.

Adding a Key

To add a key to the Registry, you must do the following:

1. Position your cursor at the point in the Registry where you want to add the key.

2. From the Edit menu, select Add | Key.

3. A new subkey is immediately added under your current position. This key is called `New Key #1` and is highlighted and ready for editing. Type the correct name for the new key and press Enter.

4. Now you must add a value entry for the key. Again, make sure you are positioned on the key to which you want to add the value entry. From the Edit Menu select New and then String Value, Binary Value, or DWORD Value, depending on the value entry you want to add.

5. The new value entry now appears on the right pane and is highlighted and ready for editing.

6. Edit the value entry to reflect the value you want. Press Enter to save the change.

7. To edit the value entry, select Modify from the edit menu. Ensure that the correct value entry is highlighted before you do so.

8. You are now presented with the Edit dialog box. Enter the value into the Value Data text box.

You can also rename keys and modify data values by highlighting the key or data value and selecting Rename or Modify from the Edit menu.

Deleting a Key

To delete a key from the Registry, you must highlight the key you want to remove and then select Delete from the Edit menu. The same procedure applies for the removal of value entries.

> **NOTE**
>
> You cannot remove the predefined subkeys from the Registry.

Finding a Key

It can be difficult to locate keys and value entries within the Registry by hand. To ease your search efforts, select Find from the Edit menu. Figure 11.15 shows the Find dialog box. The Find operation will commence only from your current position within the Registry to the end of that branch.

11

FIGURE 11.15.
The Find dialog box.

The Find dialog box is made up of the following items:

- The Find what text box, where you enter the string you want to find.
- The Look at frame, which includes a check box for Keys, Values, and Data. When these boxes are checked, the Find operation will look in these associated areas.
- The Match whole string only option will determine whether the Find operation is to look for an exact or partial string match.

Saving the Registry

With Regedit you have the ability to save the Registry keys and their subkeys to a text file with a .reg extension. This can be a useful option, because it allows you to store a copy of the Registry elsewhere, and you can later use it to rebuild a Registry key or subkey. To do so, you must perform the following steps:

1. Select the Registry key you want to save.
2. Select Export Registry File from the Registry menu.

   You are now presented with the Export Registry File dialog box, as shown in Figure 11.16.

FIGURE 11.16.
Saving Registry keys.

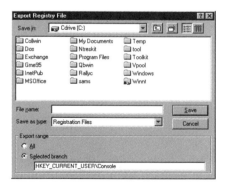

3. The top half of the dialog box enables you to name the text file and also to determine where it will be saved. In the Export range frame, select the All radio button to save the entire Registry. To save the selected key or subkeys, select the Selected branch button.

Restoring Registry Keys

As well as exporting the Registry to a text file, you can import that same text file back into the Registry. The following is a description of how to restore a Registry key:

1. Select Import Registry File from the Registry menu.
2. From the Import Registry File dialog box, locate the file you want to restore.
3. Select the file and click Open.

Connecting to a Remote Registry

In NT you have the ability to remotely administer a Registry. Provided you have permission to connect remotely to a remote Registry, you can see the remote Registry as if it were local. This is an invaluable option that can help an administrator troubleshoot problems remotely. To connect to a remote registry, select Connect Network Registry from the Registry menu and type in the name of the remote computer whose Registry you want to administer. For more information on securing a connection to the Registry remotely, see Chapter 10.

Regedt32

Regedt32 is accessed by typing `regedt32` from the Run window of the Start menu. You can see that the Regedt32 screen is quite different from that of Regedit. (See Figure 11.17.)

FIGURE 11.17.

The Registry through Regedt32.

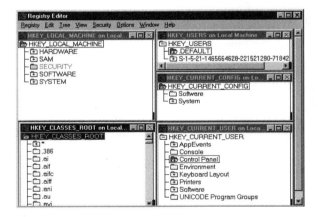

Figure 11.17 shows a sample Registry through Regedt32. As you can see, Regedt32 displays the HKEY_ subtrees in separate windows. The Windows menu allows to you tile, cascade, arrange, and switch windows. You can also minimize and maximize each of them for ease of use. Because Regedt32 presents each of the subtrees in separate windows, any customization changes you make to one window will not be reflected in the others. Unlike Regedit, Regedt32 allows you to decide between views of the tree only (corresponding to the left pane in Regedit), the data only (corresponding to the right pane in Regedit), or a combination of both. These options are set under the View menu and only correspond to the currently selected window. Again,

as with Regedit, you can define the split between the tree and data panes by either clicking it with the mouse or by selecting Split from the View menu. Once you have highlighted the split (denoted by a change in the cursor), hold the left mouse button down and drag the split left or right to suit your needs.

Traversing the Registry

Traversing under Regedt32 is the same as traversing under Regedit. First of all, select the window you want to traverse through. You can use either the arrow keys or the mouse to move up and down the tree. Under the Tree menu there are options for expanding the tree or current branch or for collapsing the current branch. Remember again that this is on a per window basis. Alternatively, you can use either the mouse or the arrow keys. Once selected, a branch or tree can be expanded by double-clicking it with the mouse or by pressing the Enter key from the keyboard. To collapse a tree or branch, you press the Enter key with the tree or branch selected or double-click it with the mouse. Regedt32 does not support the right-click features for editing keys and value entries.

Adding a Key

To add a key to the Registry under Regedt32, you must perform the following steps:

1. Select the key under which you want to add the new key.
2. From the Edit menu, select the Add Key entry.
3. The Add Key dialog box appears. Type the name of the new key into the Key Name text box.
4. Leave the Class box blank until later.

Deleting a Key

To delete a key from the Registry under Regedt32, you must highlight the key you want to remove and then select Delete from the Edit menu. The same procedure applies for the removal of value entries, as well.

> **NOTE**
>
> You cannot remove the predefined keys from the Registry.

Finding a Key

The Find Key option in the View menu allows for the searching of keys only. Figure 11.18 shows the Find dialog box. The Find operation will commence from your current position within the Registry and will go to the end of that branch.

FIGURE 11.18.

The Find dialog box.

Unlike the Find operation in Regedit, Find Key does not search entry values or data values. It does, however, allow you to search in a particular direction, either up or down, and can search on case also.

Saving Registry Keys

This is the same Save operation as described previously for Regedit. In Regedt32 you can save Registry keys to a different location and restore them at a later date. To save a Registry key, you must perform the following steps:

1. Select the Registry key you want to save.

2. Select Save Key from the Registry menu.

    You are now presented with the Save Key dialog box, as shown in Figure 11.19.

FIGURE 11.19.

Saving a Registry key in Regedt32.

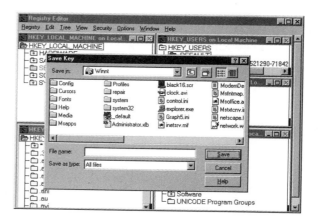

3. Enter the name of the file and select its destination. Once completed, click Save.

> **NOTE**
>
> IF you are saving over the network, remember to enter the UNC path (for example, *servername**sharename**filename*) rather than the network drive K:*filename*.

Restoring the Registry Keys

Once saved to a safe location, the Registry key can be restored at a later date. The following is a description of how to restore a Registry key:

1. Select the key you want to restore from the hive file.

2. Select Restore from the Registry menu.

3. Enter the filename and location of the stored hive in the Restore Key dialog box and then click Open.

Connecting to a Remote Registry

In Regedt32, to connect to a remote registry, choose Select Computer from the Registry menu. You are presented with the Select Computer dialog box. You can enter the name of the remote computer into the Computer text box, or you can browse your way to it via the Select Computer Server/Workstation list. (See Figure 11.20.)

FIGURE 11.20.

Connecting to a remote registry.

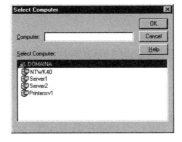

Using Hives Remotely

There is an alternative to connecting to a registry remotely with Regedt32. Regedt32 allows you to load entire hives that were saved from a remote registry. This is ideal if you cannot connect to a remote registry over the network, because now you can save a hive from the troublesome machine onto a floppy and transfer it anywhere.

To load a remote hive, you must perform the following steps:

1. First of all, you must save the hive by using Save key from the Registry menu (see the previous section, "Saving Registry Keys").

2. Once you have saved the file, you can load the hive into another registry. To load a hive, you must first select either the HKEY_LOCAL_MACHINE or HKEY_USERS subtree.

3. When either of these are selected, choose Load Hive from the Registry menu.

4. Through the Load Hive dialog box, you can point to the location of the saved hive and load it. Again, if this is over the network, you'll have to use a UNC pathname.

Once you have finished with the hive, you can unload it as follows:

1. Select the top of the hive.
2. Choose Unload Hive from the Registry menu.

Summary

The Registry has long been an area of NT that only experienced administrators worked with. In an effort to break down some of the mystique surrounding the Registry, this chapter covered the purpose of the Registry and shows how you can use it to suit your needs. You have seen that the Registry is a collection of data stores brought together in a hierarchical structure. The Registry stores configuration information about the computer, its hardware, its software, and security information (among other things). You looked at what made up the Registry and where it fits in with NT. Also contained in this chapter were examples of using both the Registry editors—Regedit and Regedt32—to modify the Registry. You also took a close look at remote administration of the Registry and the saving and restoring of Registry keys.

PART

III

IN THIS PART

Working with Windows NT Workstation

Working with the NT File System

by Paul Cassel

IN THIS CHAPTER

CHAPTER 12

A hard disk is logically divided into concentric rings, called *tracks*. Each track is divided into logical sections called *sectors*. Each sector either contains stored data or is vacant awaiting data. The sector is the smallest unit of disk storage space. A sector can technically be any size, but it's almost always 512 bytes.

Aside from the Multiple Zone Recording (MZR) type disks, the number of sectors in each track remains the same because sector density increases as the tracks approach the center of the disk. As the tracks vary in size depending on their location on the disk itself, the sector density rises in relation to a track's nearness to the center of the disk. Figure 12.1 shows a simplified schematic of the logical structure of a hard disk.

FIGURE 12.1.

A hard disk is divided into sectors, usually of 512 bytes.

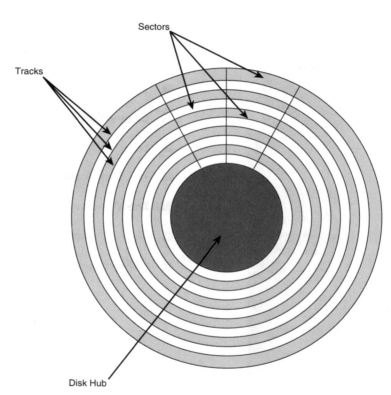

A computer's file system distributes and tracks data according to clusters made up of one or more sectors. A cluster can contain only one file. It can't have parts of various files in it. In other words, there's only one cluster for each file or part of a file. For example, if your computer has a cluster size of two sectors, each having 512 bytes, it can store a file of up to 1,024 bytes in a single cluster. As soon as the file size exceeds the size of a single cluster, it gets a whole new cluster even if the file doesn't fully populate the cluster.

Take a computer with the cluster size of 1,024 bytes. A file of 1,000 bytes will take up just about a whole single cluster. If the file grows to 1,100 bytes, it takes up all of one cluster plus a second one for the bytes above 1,024. Most of the second cluster doesn't contain any data, but it's lost for further data storage because the file system can't assign data storage to part of a cluster. The amount of cluster area unavailable for data storage is the disk's *overhang*, or *overhead*.

The file system assigns contiguous clusters when you store a file. This works all right until a file grows from its original size or you start erasing files. Here's what happens in those cases. Suppose you create and save a file to disk. The file system assigns clusters 20–30 to this file. Next, you create and save another file. This gets assigned clusters 31–45. If you open and increase the size of the original file, the file system needs more clusters, but the next in the series are occupied by file number 2. Therefore, it goes to the next free space starting with cluster 46. This causes file number 1 to be split between two noncontiguous clusters.

Similarly, if you erase file number 1 and then write another larger file to its clusters, the file system will use up its original clusters and then go searching for more wherever it can find them. This splitting of files across noncontiguous clusters is called *file fragmentation*.

The makers of a file system have to decide on some tradeoffs. A large cluster size will work against fragmentation, but it will be inefficient due to a large amount of overhead. In addition, all file systems are limited to the amount of clusters they can address. If a disk capacity is such that the cluster numbers threaten to climb beyond the addressable number, the cluster size must grow.

The FAT System

FAT stands for File Allocation Table, the central feature of this system. It was originally designed for early hard disks that were quite small compared to today's disks. The designers of the FAT system were looking at disks typically between 5 and 20MB. In all likelihood, they didn't consider today's storage needs, where even a moderately powerful computer will have a disk exceeding 3GB in capacity.

Figure 12.2 shows the structure of a FAT system for a particular partition. There are two copies of the actual file allocation table, an early attempt at ensuring data integrity. This FAT system was introduced with the IBM XT in the early 1980s. Today, it survives in the forms of FAT16 and the new and improved FAT32.

The File Allocation Table contains the following information about cluster usage:

- Cluster numbers
- Clusters available for files
- The files assigned to clusters and whether this is the last cluster for the file or a pointer to the next cluster containing a file
- Whether the cluster is marked as unusable

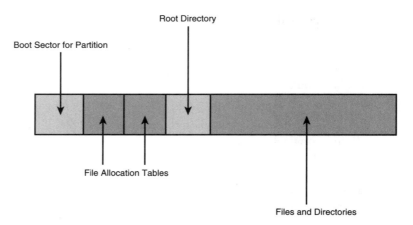

The FAT system can address a partition size of up to 4GB. As the partition grows, so does the cluster size. The format program assesses the partition size and creates the FAT structure, as shown in Figure 12.2. In the process of creating this structure, it decides how many sectors to assign per cluster. Table 12.1 shows how the format program assigns sectors.

Table 12.1. FAT's cluster sizes.

Partition Size	Cluster Size in Bytes	Sectors in a Cluster
To 32MB	512	1
33–64MB	1,024	2
65–128MB	2,048	4
129–255MB	4,096	8
256–511MB	8,192	16
512–1,023MB	16,384	32
1,024–2,047MB	32,768	64
2,048–4,096MB	65,536	128

As you can see, larger partitions yield cluster sizes that quickly grow inefficient. A partition of 1,500MB, hardly unusual today, will use up a full 32,768 bytes of disk space to store a file of only a few bytes. A quick bit of division will show you that each partition can contain roughly 64,000 clusters or a maximum of 64,000 files, assuming the unlikely situation of one file per cluster. The rule of thumb for disk overhead is number of files × .5 × cluster size. Therefore, theoretically a partition can have an overhead of 50 percent of its entire size. In practice, the overhead is a good deal less, but in some extreme cases you'll encounter overheads approaching 40 percent.

People disagree on how large a partition having a FAT file system should be, but most agree that 511MB is about it. The newer FAT32 system is more efficient when it comes to overhead, but its use isn't as widespread as FAT16. From time to time, you might hear the term VFAT. This is a FAT system with the capacity for long filenames (LFN).

You access FAT partitions under Windows NT Workstation just as you do under MS-DOS, Windows, and Windows 95.

Overview of the NT File System

The Windows NT File System (NTFS) is the successor system to the FAT, VFAT, and High Performance File System (HPFS) systems. The latter system was developed for OS/2 and supported by versions of Windows NT prior to 4.

NTFS meets the needs for a secure file system with the performance needed for the much larger volumes seen today, as compared with the time that inspired the FAT system. Similarly to the UNIX file system, NTFS allows access privileges down to the file level.

NTFS uses the cluster scheme seen in FAT for data allocation, but at any given volume size it has less overhead. Table 12.2 shows NTFS's cluster sizes.

Table 12.2. NTFS's cluster sizes.

Partition Size	Cluster Size in Bytes	Sectors in a Cluster
To 512MB	512	1
513–1,024MB	1,024	2
1,025–2,048MB	2,048	4
2,049–4,096MB	4,096	8
4,097–8,192MB	8,192	16
8,193–16,384MB	16,384	32
16,385–32,768MB	32,768	64
To 16 exabytes	65,536	128

The structure of an NTFS volume is similar in look to FAT, but the details vary significantly, as you can see in Figure 12.3.

The Master File Table (MFT) is somewhat analogous to the FAT, but it contains much more information than the earlier system. Figure 12.4 shows the structure of a typical entry in the MFT.

FIGURE 12.3.

The NTFS structure superficially resembles the FAT system; however, the information kept and its format is significantly different in the two systems.

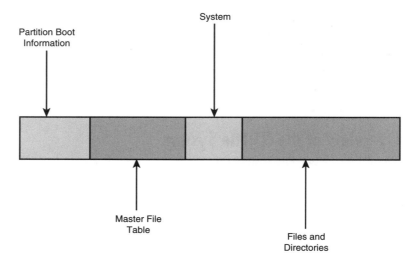

FIGURE 12.4.

The MFT contains information well beyond what's found in the file allocation tables of a FAT system.

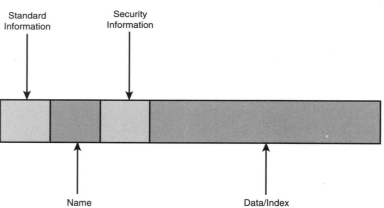

From a user's view, the single greatest addition to the MFT over the FAT is the security section. This contains information about a file's ownership and who has permissions to perform file procedures. FAT has nothing even slightly analogous to NTFS's security.

In addition, the MFT has a log file that keeps a record of disk activity. In the event of a system crash, NT can restore its integrity using this log file. The log file's size depends on the volume size—it can grow to 4MB on very large volumes.

NTFS uses a new-for-PC structure called *streams*, although a similar scheme, dual forks, has been in use in the Macintosh since that machine's inception. A stream identifies some data attribute. This allows, for example, a program to track different modifications to a file using a different stream for each. Within the MFT, a colon separates the file from the stream. For this reason, the colon is an illegal character in a filename.

NTFS supports file-by-file compression but doesn't support, nor can it read, volume compression schemes such as DoubleSpace, DriveSpace, or Stacker. The maximum volume size where you can use any kind of compression in NT is 4GB.

The only system that can read NTFS volumes is Windows NT. You can't "see" or access files on an NTFS volume from Windows 95, previous Windows versions, or any version of MS-DOS. There is at least one utility available, NTFSDOS, that allows limited read-only file access on an NTFS volume from either MS-DOS or Windows 95.

12

WORKING WITH
THE NT FILE
SYSTEM

> **TIP**
>
> You can increase NTFS performance by telling it not to create short (8.3) MS-DOS format filenames. Do this only if all your applications can see LFN. To do this, change the value of `NtfsDisable8dot3NameCreation` in `HKEY_LOCAL_MACHINE\System\CurrentControlSet\Control\FileSystem` from its default of 0 to 1.

FAT Versus NTFS

FAT is surely the *lingua franca* of file systems. Most personal computer operating systems from UNIX to NT can read and even write to it. NTFS is exclusive to Windows NT, but it is more efficient in larger volumes and has safety and security features FAT has never heard of. Table 12.3 is a summary chart for these two systems.

Table 12.3. The pros and cons of file systems.

Application	*NTFS*	*FAT*
Volumes < 200MB	Poor	Good
Volumes 200–500MB	Fair	Good
Volumes 500–4,000MB	Good	Poor
Volumes > 4,000MB	Good	N/A
Security	Good	N/A
Recoverability	Good	N/A
Undelete erased files	N/A	Good
Full access on dual boot machines	N/A	Good
Long filenames	Good	Good
Compatibility for Macintosh files	Good	N/A
File compression	Good	N/A in NT
Volume compression	N/A	Good
Maximum partition size under Windows NT	4EB	4GB

Note that at least one utility, Norton Utilities for Windows NT, adds an unerase capacity to Windows NT.

Converting FAT to NTFS

The easiest way to install Windows NT Workstation to a new installation is to use FDISK to create the volume structure you want, format the volumes to FAT, and then run SETUP. Windows NT setup will ask you whether you want to convert any of the existing volumes from FAT to NTFS prior to installing Windows NT Workstation.

If you failed to do the conversion during setup, don't worry: You can convert existing FAT volumes to NTFS at any time, although the process can take several hours on volumes with a lot of data. You can't convert a full FAT volume to NTFS, because the conversion process requires up to 110MB free for temporary storage.

The Command Line Interface (CLI) has, among its utilities, CONVERT, which is the program that does the conversion from FAT to NTFS. Once you convert to NTFS, you can't return to FAT without reformatting the partition. This process erases data on the volume, so a full backup is required beforehand. Although the conversion of FAT to NTFS has a good deal of redundancy built in, it's a good idea to have a full backup before proceeding anyway.

To convert a volume from FAT to NTFS, start a CLI session by choosing Command Prompt from the Start | Programs menu. Enter convert [*volume*] /FS:NTFS [/v], substituting the drive letter you want to convert to NTFS for the [*volume*] parameter. The [/v] parameter is optional. It produces a verbose output for the conversion process.

If your system is on the volume you want to convert, or for any other reason CONVERT can't get exclusive access to the volume, the program will tell you that it can't proceed until next bootup. If you agree to let it, the program will run the next time you boot up.

Figure 12.5 shows the CONVERT program, offering the option to do a conversion at next startup.

Keep in mind that NTFS volumes require a certain amount of "wasted" space for security features. This space grows as the volume grows, but it isn't proportional to volume size. This makes small volumes in NTFS very inefficient compared to FAT for two reasons:

■ FAT doesn't have a serious overhead problem until volumes exceed 511MB.

■ NTFS uses up a proportionally large part of small volumes for its security feature.

Although NTFS volumes can and do grow fragmented, this file system generally handles fragmentation better than FAT. Also, the physical layout of directories (folders) in NTFS enables faster file access than FAT, especially in larger volumes. However, file creation is slightly faster in FAT, because NTFS has the added job of setting security attributes—something lacking in FAT.

FIGURE 12.5.

If the conversion program can't gain exclusive access to the target volume, it will offer to schedule the conversion at next startup.

Lazy and Careful

Previous to NTFS, there were two general types of file systems: the low-performance, *careful write* types and the gung-ho, *lazy write* types. The original versions of MS-DOS use careful write technology. This performs disk write requests in a serial fashion, as they're asked for. This soaks up computer time because the machine essentially halts while the disk is being written to. Although this type of scheme works all right for a single-process operating system such as MS-DOS, it tends to slow down excessively a system with many processes running, or a system with a virtual memory store, or both. However, this system is safe. If a system crashes, only the disk write in progress will be affected. Although this can cause some disk integrity loss, the loss will be fairly small in most cases.

The second type of file system is the lazy write system. This system saves write information to a RAM cache and during processor idle time commits the cached information to the disk. Microsoft added a lazy write cache (also called a *write-behind cache*) to MS-DOS 6.0. It caused havoc with users not familiar with this new and improved feature. Although the disk performance of the new cache speeded up not only MS-DOS but, more importantly, Windows 3.1, users assuming their systems still had a careful write scheme turned off their systems before the write from cache to disk. This caused serious data loss and disk corruption in many cases.

Microsoft changed the caching default from lazy write to careful write in subsequent versions of MS-DOS 6.*x*, leaving lazy write as an option for knowledgeable users. Although this made MS-DOS and Windows 3.1 safer to some extent, it did exact a performance hit.

With NTFS, Microsoft has combined the safety of careful write with the speed of lazy write systems. The trick is NTFS's recoverability. This system uses transaction processing to ensure the volume's integrity, because the system can always roll back transactions to a previously good state in the case of a system crash. Although some user data might still be lost, the volume should be accessible, except in the instance of corruption to the system areas of a volume.

In transaction processing, a write request remains in cache like a lazy write system, but a record of the request gets logged to a log file. It's this log file that allows rolling back of partially completed disk writes. This is similar to lazy write, but in that scheme a partial disk write is possible, thus corrupting an entire volume. If the NTFS system senses a partial write upon startup after a crash, it will go to the log file and roll back the disk transactions to the point of having no partial or bad writes. Microsoft calls this system *lazy commit* to distinguish it from the older and less reliable lazy write systems. The lazy commit system in NTFS is virtually as fast as lazy write and as safe as a careful write. Although nothing can prevent user data loss in the case of an unplanned shutdown, as occurs in a power loss scenario, NTFS comes as close as any file system in use today.

Rollback of transactions upon startup after a crash is completely automatic. It requires no user input.

NTFS also has a facility called *cluster remapping*, which moves data from a cluster reported bad to NTFS to a good one. The file system then marks the cluster as bad in a bad cluster file, preventing its use again. This facility is similar to the third-party utilities that do the same thing for FAT.

The Disk Administrator

The Disk Administrator is a graphical utility useful for various disk management tasks. By default, it's under the Start | Programs | Administrative Tools menu choice. Using it, you can do the following tasks:

- Create partitions
- Delete partitions
- Monitor and display volume information
- Format volumes
- Scan and repair volumes for disk errors
- Extend volumes by adding regions of free space

Figure 12.6 shows the Disk Administrator launched on a computer with a small FAT and a medium NTFS volume.

FIGURE 12.6.

The Disk Administrator combines many of the features of Fdisk, format, *and* chkdsk, *along with some unique capabilities of its own.*

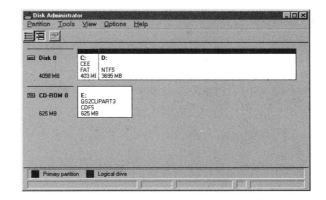

You need to be logged on with Administrator rights to use the Disk Administrator. The first time the Disk Administrator starts, it flashes a message saying it's dealing with a newly discovered disk configuration. This message is harmless. Click the OK button and the message will go away. You'll not see it again unless you install Windows NT cleanly.

Creating and Preparing Partitions

To create a new partition, follow these steps:

1. Choose the free space you want to convert. This, by default, shows up as a crosshatch bar in the graphical display.

2. Pull down the Partition menu and choose Create. The Disk Administrator will respond with a dialog box showing the minimum and maximum partition sizes available to you. Also, this dialog box contains a text box that allows you to specify the size you want.

3. Click OK. The Disk Administrator will whirl around for a while doing the job you used to have to use Fdisk to do.

4. After it's done, choose the Commit Changes Now entry under the Partition menu to write the changes to the file system.

5. Choose the Format option from the Tools menu to format the new partition to either FAT or NTFS.

   The Format command has a quick option, similar to the /q switch in the CLI FORMAT command. If you choose this option, FORMAT will skip the error-checking process. Instead, it will just create the volume structure. Don't use this option unless you're in a hurry, because the error checking will ensure data integrity.

   Click OK and then click OK again in the message box indicating the completion of a successful operation.

You've just created a new formatted partition where none was before.

Adding a New Disk

You also can extend a single partition to include free space from a newly added disk drive as long as the partition you want to extend doesn't hold NT itself. Proceed as before, but select more than one area by pressing the Ctrl key as you click on the existing partition and the new area. This enables the Extend Volume Set command on the Partition menu. Choose this and you'll extend the current volume to include the newly added disk space.

Deleting Partitions

To delete a partition, click on the partition you want to rid yourself of and then choose Delete from the Partition menu. You can't delete the boot partition or Windows NT system partitions. Remember that deleting partitions is permanent. Once they're gone, so is the data once stored there (except for backup sets).

Viewing and Monitoring

The Disk Administrator is capable of two views of your disk. The default view is called Disk Configuration. You can also choose the Volumes view either from the View menu or from the toolbar. Figure 12.7 shows the Volumes view.

FIGURE 12.7.

The Volumes view of the Disk Administrator shows disk information in a numerical format rather than the graphs in the default view (Disk Configuration).

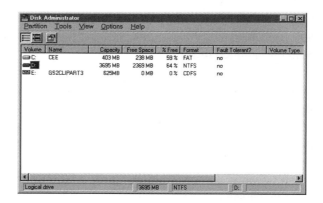

One advantage of the Volumes view is the ability to sort on any column by clicking the volume heading. Figure 12.8 is the same display as in Figure 12.7, but it is sorted by free space. Clicking again on the column head will sort the display in the reverse order.

There is a compromise in the graphical Disk Configuration view: You can choose how the Disk Administrator shows the regions. To make this choice, select the Regional Display entry in the Options menu. The Disk Administrator will pop up a dialog box, as shown in Figure 12.9.

FIGURE 12.8.

The Volumes view allows easy sorting of any disk characteristic by clicking the appropriate column head.

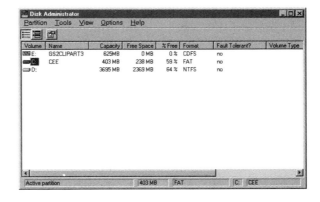

FIGURE 12.9.

The Regional Display Options dialog box allows user choices for the graphical Disk Configuration display.

In a similar way, you can vary the way the Disk Administrator shows just the disks by choosing the Disk Display entry in the Options menu. Figure 12.10 shows this dialog box.

FIGURE 12.10.

The Disk Display Options dialog box permits configuration of only the disk displays.

The Colors and Patterns dialog box (shown in Figure 12.11 and available under the Options menu), allows quite a bit of customization of the way the Disk Administrator looks. Why Microsoft chose to include so many cosmetic options in such a utilitarian program as the Disk Administrator remains somewhat of a mystery, but you might as well use the supplied options to make your program look just as you want it to.

The Disk Administrator will show two types of free space using subtly different displays. The first type of free space is a part of a defined partition that has yet to be included in a volume. The second kind is a disk that hasn't had any preparation at all. The easiest way to tell what exactly the graphic means is to click on it and then look at the status bar, which will show details in plain text. The status bar yields information not even shown in Volumes view.

FIGURE 12.11.

You can vary the colors and patterns that make up the Disk Administrator to just about anything you want.

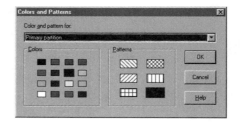

The final customizable part of the Disk Administrator is the toolbar. Figure 12.12 shows the dialog box for adding and removing buttons from this bar.

FIGURE 12.12.

The Customize Toolbar choice from the Options menu allows you to add or remove buttons from the toolbar.

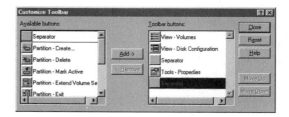

Changing Drive Letters

You can change the assigned drive letters for a volume by right-clicking the volume in either view and choosing Assign Drive Letter. You can also choose the menu selection Assign Drive Letter from the Tools menu. Be careful changing drive letters for volumes with installed programs, because altering this option won't change the settings in Windows NT Workstation's Registry or any initialization (.ini) files needed by installed programs.

By assigning a drive letter rather than letting NT assign it using MS-DOS conventions, you make the drive letter "sticky." That is, it won't change as you add or remove volumes. This prevents applications from getting lost as you add or remove volumes. For example, if you assign a letter L: to a particular volume, that volume will remain L: until you intentionally change it. Windows NT will not move the drive up or down the alphabet as you add or remove other volumes.

This eliminates the havoc wrought by automatic drive letter reassignment, which began with MS-DOS and still exists in non-NT Windows.

Properties

Within either view of the Disk Administrator, you can right-click a volume and then choose Properties from the context menu or you can choose the Properties button from the toolbar. This brings up a tabbed dialog box similar to the one shown in Figure 12.13. The computer shown has Norton Utilities for Windows NT installed and therefore has an extra tab. Other utilities, such as disk defragmenters, can also modify this dialog box.

Figure 12.13.

The tabbed Properties dialog box will differ from computer to computer, depending on the software installed.

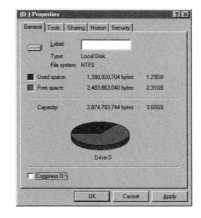

Although the name of the dialog box in Figure 12.13 is Properties, it also has access to some tools. For example, you can use the first tab on this dialog box to either change a volume label or compress the entire drive. Keep in mind that compressing a volume isn't technically the same as full drive compression (such as DriveSpace). Rather, this is a file-by-file compression done over the entire drive.

Additionally, the Tools menu has access buttons to start the NT version of CHKDSK, to run the NTBACKUP routine, and to compress the drive if you have a program installed to do this.

Figure 12.14 shows the Tools tab in the Properties dialog box.

Figure 12.14.

The Tools tab has buttons triggering backup, disk checker (diagnostic), and, if installed, a third-party compression routine.

The computer shown in Figure 12.14 does have a third-party compression program as part of the Norton Utilities for Windows NT; however, Symantec, the maker of the program, has chosen to install a new tab for its programs rather than attach its Speed Disk for NT to the Tools tab button.

The last tab of the Properties dialog box has access triggers for setting permissions for volumes, taking ownership of them, and starting or ending auditing. To start the latter, you must have the auditing option turned on in the User Manager before assigning a user or group to be audited here. Figure 12.15 shows the Security tab of the Properties dialog box.

FIGURE 12.15.

The Security tab is for accessing the auditing and permissions of a particular volume. You also can assign ownership of a volume for a particular group of users from this tab.

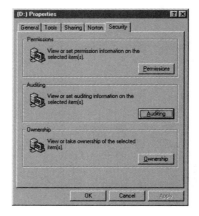

To take ownership of a volume, click the Security tab of the Properties dialog box and then click Ownership. This will let the logged on user take ownership of an entire volume, but like directory and file ownership, will not allow assignment of ownership to another user or group. Figure 12.16 shows this process.

FIGURE 12.16.

The person running the Disk Administrator can take ownership of an entire volume using the Ownership button on the Security tab.

If you've allowed auditing in the User Manager for a group, you can use the Auditing button to access the dialog box to add, delete, or modify auditing features for the highlighted volume. Figure 12.17 shows the dialog box for auditing.

To add a group for auditing, click the Add button, which results in the dialog box shown in Figure 12.18.

The Add button in the Directory Auditing dialog box features an optional display of users in all groups. This is a handy reminder feature that has the actual capability of doing some User Manager tasks, such as organizing your user groups. Figure 12.19 shows the display of the group members within the Add Auditing procedure.

FIGURE 12.17.

The Auditing button lets you change auditing parameters for groups over an entire volume.

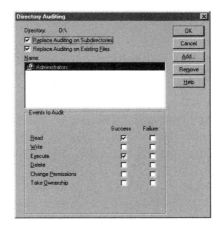

FIGURE 12.18.

To add a group to audit, click the Add button in the dialog box shown in Figure 12.17.

FIGURE 12.19.

This dialog box, brought up by clicking the Show Users button in Figure 12.18, is the Users group on the \\PAUL computer. It has two members.

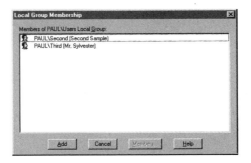

> ## BOOTS AND SYSTEMS
>
> The boot partition of a Windows NT Workstation installation is the primary partition containing the boot files such as NTLDR, NTDETECT, and the boot.ini configuration file. The system partition is the partition containing the Windows NT system, itself. This is, by default, in the WINNT directory.
>
> Many installations, especially dual boot ones, boot from a FAT primary volume, but they have Windows NT, itself, on an NTFS partition other than the boot one.
>
> The computer shown in the figures for this chapter uses a FAT volume C: as the primary and boot partition. It contains the boot loaders for MS-DOS and Windows NT. The same FAT volume also contains the system files for Windows 95. The large volume D: is an NTFS volume containing the Windows NT Workstation system under the WINNT directory.

The Windows NT Explorer

The Explorer for Windows NT resembles the Explorer for Windows 95, but it has security and compression extensions similar to the Disk Administrator. In fact, the Explorer for Windows NT includes the features of the Disk Administrator's security, except at the folder (directory) and file levels instead of the volume level.

Figure 12.20 shows the Explorer opened to an NTFS volume containing the Windows NT Workstation system files.

FIGURE 12.20.

The primary tool for working with files and folders in Windows NT is the Explorer.

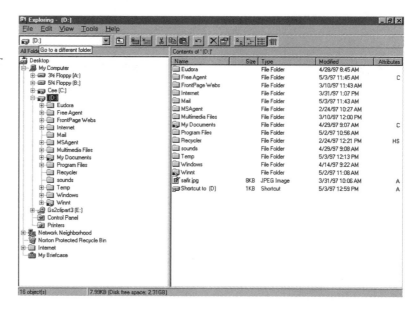

The Explorer has two panes. The left pane shows folders and drives, whereas the right shows the folders and files under those shown in the left pane.

File Associations

By default, the Explorer adheres to the document-centric approach to computing introduced in Windows 95. This approach is aimed at making novices comfortable by eliminating some display complexity. So, for the sake of simplicity, Explorer suppresses the display of file extensions for which there is an association in the Registry and system files such as .dll, .sys, and .vxd.

This might make a few novices more comfortable, but it seems to upset just as many. It doesn't do anything for intermediate-and-up users. To change the default display of files, open the Explorer and click the menu choice Options in the View menu. Figure 12.21 shows the Options dialog box.

FIGURE 12.21.

The Options dialog box can control the display of certain system files, file extensions, and other minor options.

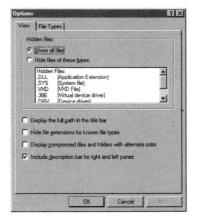

The second tab in the Options dialog box controls file associations. Windows NT, like previous versions of Windows, associates files with applications according to the file extension. Traditional file extensions were limited to three legal DOS (almost always letters only) characters. Windows NT can handle longer extensions, but tradition holds that most applications still use the shorter file extensions. This has a practical reason. If you set Windows NT Workstation to keep an MS-DOS (8.3) filename along with the standard long filename (LFN), it will truncate the filename to the left of the dot, but not the extension to the right of the dot.

Therefore, the file

```
My letter to you.doc
```

has the short filename

```
mylett~1.doc
```

assigned to it by Windows NT Workstation. If moved to a non-LFN computer, it will still be associated with the program linked to the .doc extension. However, if the file has the name

```
My letter to you.longdoc
```

the short filename is

```
mylett~1.lon
```

and so it loses its association.

To associate a file with an application, click the File Types tab on the Options dialog box. Like previous Windows versions, Windows NT uses the file extension to associate files with applications. Figure 12.22 shows this tab.

Figure 12.22.

The File Types tab of the Options dialog box affords you a place to add, delete, and edit file extensions.

The list box in the middle of the tab has a list of the file types and their associations. You can scroll through this list to see the file type you want to edit or delete. Once you've found the entry you want to alter or delete, highlight it and click the Remove or Edit button. Removing or deleting an association means that when you double-click the file having that extension in the Explorer, you won't have the associated application swing into action.

For the most part, you'll delete associations only for those applications that no longer exist on your computer. However, you'll have many needs to edit an entry.

Windows NT setup programs can, in the course of setting themselves up, associate file extensions with their applications. You rarely have control over this process. So, for example, say you have the file extension .pcx associated with the application Picture Publisher and you install a new program also able to open the .pcx file type. That new application might, as part of its setup, disassociate the .pcx extension from Picture Publisher and grab the extension as its own.

This might not be your intention. The Edit button on the File Types tab is the place to reassociate Picture Publisher with the .pcx extension.

The following example takes the files having the .pcx extension currently associated with the WANGIMG program and changes that association to the Paint Shop Pro 4.1 program.

The first thing to do is find the .pcx extension in the list box shown in Figure 12.22. Once located, click the Edit button. This brings up a dialog box shown in Figure 12.23.

FIGURE 12.23.

The Edit File Type dialog box is the starting point for adding, deleting, and editing actions associated between a certain file type and an application.

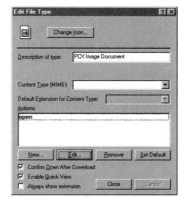

Figure 12.23 shows that the WANGIMG application has a single action associated with the .pcx file types: Open. To add another action, such as Print, click the New button at the bottom of the dialog box. To edit the actions, click Edit. To Remove an action, highlight it and click Remove. To set a particular action as default, highlight it and click Set Default.

The Edit button can change the association but keep the action as Open. Clicking Edit results in the dialog box shown in Figure 12.24.

FIGURE 12.24.

The Editing action for type dialog box is similar to the New dialog box, but it only allows editing for the application, not an addition of actions for the application.

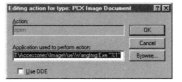

To change the application, you can enter the path to the application or browse for it. Figure 12.25 shows browsing the file structure to locate the Paint Shop application.

FIGURE 12.25.

Browsing for an application is similar to browsing for anything in the Windows NT Explorer.

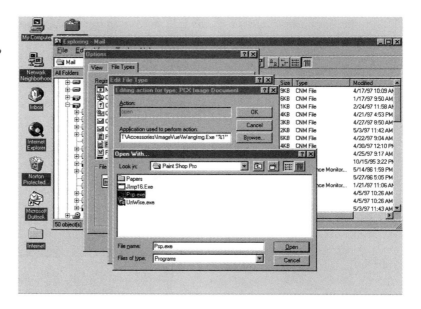

Once you've found the application to associate, double-click it. This will associate the application with the Open action for the file type specified. Paint Shop Pro uses DDE (Dynamic Data Exchange) as a way to open specific files; therefore, in this case, the user had to check the Use DDE check box and add the DDE Message [open("%1")] as a command for Paint Shop Pro to open the specific file rather than just opening itself and loading a series of thumbnails. Figure 12.26 shows the finished dialog box.

FIGURE 12.26.

Most applications can open a file directly, but some need a DDE message. This example edited the path to the application according to MS-DOS conventions.

Adding a new action is similar to editing a current one, but you start by clicking the New button and adding an action, such as Print, and then browsing to the associated action. The actions affect the context (right-click) menu in the Explorer. For example, if you have two actions, Open and Print, associated with a file extension, those two actions will appear on the context menu when you right-click that file type. Adding more actions adds more entries to the context menu.

File Manipulation

You can open a CLI session in Windows NT Workstation and use the old MS-DOS commands for moving, copying, and deleting files, but most people prefer the graphical method using the Windows NT Explorer. You can do all these operations in a variety of ways.

To copy a file from one drive to another, locate the drive in Explorer, click it, and then drag it to its new location. To move the file from one drive to another (not leaving a copy in two places), press the Shift key as you drag the file.

If you drag a file from one directory to another on the same drive, Explorer will, by default, move the file rather than copy it. To copy the file (end up with two copies), press the Ctrl key while dragging. When copying a file, Explorer will show a small plus sign next to it. When moving a file, Explorer will not show this plus sign. Figure 12.27 shows moving a file from one directory to another. Note the lack of a plus sign, indicating that this is a move operation.

FIGURE 12.27.

Explorer can copy, delete, or move files via dragging. The lack of a plus sign near the dragged file indicates this is a move operation.

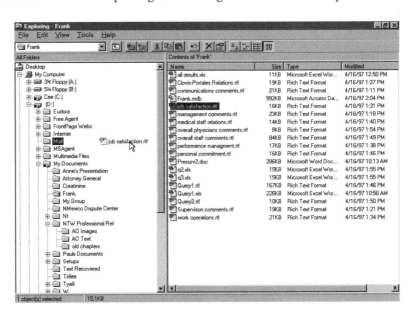

To delete a file, drag it to the recycle bin. This will move a file from its location to the recycle bin. To delete a file without moving it to the recycle bin, press Shift while dragging to the bin. You can also press Delete to delete a file or set of files.

If you don't like dragging, Explorer will let you move, copy, or delete a file other ways. You can right-click a file and then cut it, delete it, or copy it. If you copy or cut it, you can right-click in another drive or directory to paste it. When cutting or copying in a Windows application such as Word or Excel, Windows actually copies an item to the clipboard. The actual file isn't copied in Explorer, but the effect remains the same.

The Edit menu has the cut and copy options as part of it. It also has an undo command for the last undoable action. This is handy if you've accidentally dropped a dragged file to an unknown directory. Just click Edit | Undo Move, and your file pops back to its former location.

Explorer offers two ways to rename files. You can click, then pause, then click on a file in the Explorer, which sends the graphic display into edit mode. This is a bit tricky. Some people never seem to get the hang of this click, pause, click, and they end up double-clicking the file. The second way to rename a file is to right-click it and then choose Rename from the context menu. This will instantly take you into Edit mode. Figure 12.28 shows the Explorer in Edit mode.

FIGURE 12.28.

If the click, pause, click routine ends up frustrating you, you can enter Edit mode for a filename by choosing Rename from the context menu in Explorer.

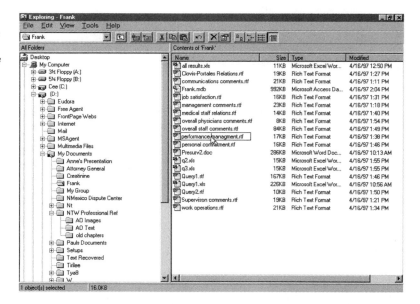

As in all noun-verb style GUIs, highlighting the items you want to take action on is an important part of Explorer file manipulation. Highlighting individual files is as simple as clicking them. Highlighting all files in a directory is simple, too. Just get to the target directory and select Edit | Select All from the Explorer menu. You can also press Ctrl+A to choose all files.

If you want to select a bunch of contiguous files (contiguous in the Explorer, not necessarily in the MFT or FAT or volume), select a file at one end of the block and then press Shift while clicking on the file at the end of the block. If you want to select a series of noncontiguous files, press Ctrl while clicking the files.

Figure 12.29 shows a block of files selected by the Shift+click method.

FIGURE 12.29.

The Shift+click method results in highlighting a block of contiguous files in the Explorer. Use the Ctrl+click method for noncontiguous files.

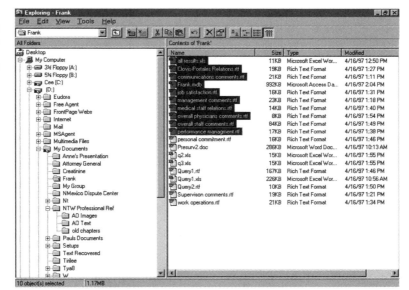

You can combine your use of Shift and Ctrl to select two or more noncontiguous blocks. The selection in the following figure came about by using the usual Shift+click method to highlight the first block, then Ctrl+click to highlight one file of the next selection, then Shift+Ctrl+click on the last file of the second selection. Figure 12.30 shows this technique.

The Edit menu of Explorer has a very handy option called Invert Selection. This selects whatever is currently unselected. Figure 12.31 shows the selection from Figure 12.30 inverted.

FIGURE 12.30.
You can choose noncontiguous file blocks within Explorer.

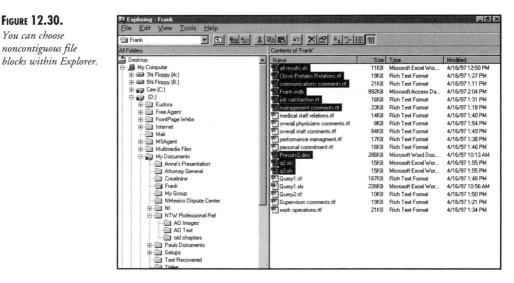

FIGURE 12.31.
Select the files you don't want to take action on and then choose the Invert Selection option from the Edit menu to select your target files.

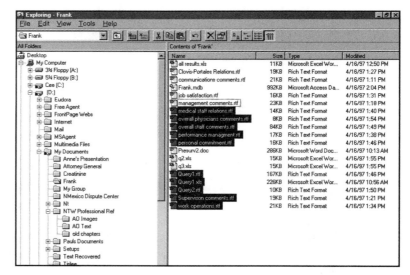

Viewing

Explorer has four possible views. The easiest way to choose different views is to make the toolbar visible by selecting Toolbar from the Tools menu (if it's not visible). The four buttons to the far right change the way Explorer shows files. The buttons are, from left to right:

■ *Large icons.* Each file has a large icon with its name underneath. This is similar to the display in the Control Panel.

■ *Small icons.* Each file has its applications icon (if known) to the left of the filename. Files are displayed in a wide format.

■ *List.* Similar to small icons, but files are listed vertically.

■ *Details.* Shows details such as type of file (or a guess), file time, date, and size.

Figure 12.32 shows the directory from Figure 12.31 in the Large Icon view.

FIGURE 12.32.

The Large Icon view of Explorer is similar to the Program Group default display or the display in the older style Program Manager.

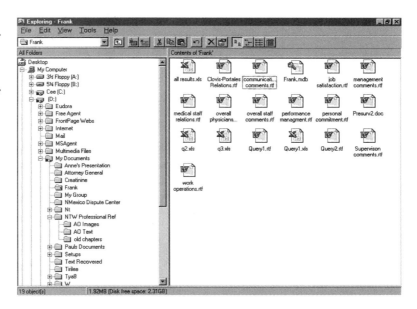

You can select and manipulate files in an identical fashion within any of the four views.

Shortcuts

During the early stages of the Windows NT Workstation 4 GUI, shortcuts were called *links* because they provided a link or a pointer to an actual file. The name *link* survives today in the extension of a link fileL: lnk. A link or shortcut is a way to access a file from a location that's different from the file's actual whereabouts.

Figure 12.33 shows the location of the executable file to launch Microsoft Access.

This file, MSACCESS.EXE, is in the standard location:

```
\\Program Files\Microsoft Office\Office\MSACCESS.EXE
```

However, you will likely want to launch it from another location such as the Desktop or the Start menu, or both. This is what a shortcut does. To make a shortcut, right-click on the file, drag it to a new location, and then drop it. Choose Create Shortcut (Here) from the pop-up menu. You can also make a shortcut by choosing New | Shortcut from a context menu, such as the context menu of the Desktop.

FIGURE 12.33.

Files under the new Windows NT Workstation interface physically, and logically reside in the same location.

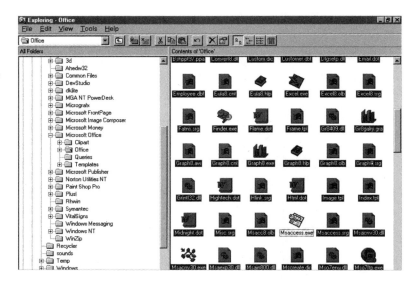

Figure 12.34 shows a shortcut to Access on the Desktop. By right-clicking the shortcut and choosing Properties, you can view the tabbed dialog box, which is also shown in Figure 12.34.

FIGURE 12.34.

Note the target for this shortcut is the MSACCESS.EXE file shown in Figure 12.33. This shortcut allows you to launch the program from a different location than the actual file.

You can open a Properties dialog box for a shortcut by right-clicking on the shortcut and then choosing Properties from the context menu. The Shortcut Properties dialog box allows you to do many manipulations on a shortcut, such as setting its permissions (Security tab), locating its target, changing its attributes, or altering its icon. Figure 12.35 shows a change of icon for the shortcut shown in Figure 12.34.

> **NOTE**
>
> Setting permissions and other security items for a shortcut does not set or alter them for the target file.

FIGURE 12.35.

The properties you can alter for a shortcut vary from the serious, such as permissions and ownership, to the trivial, such as displayed icon.

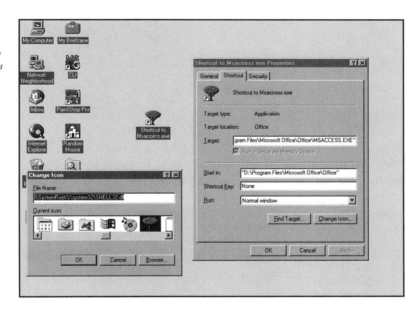

Security

Just as the Disk Administrator allows anyone with Administrator rights to take ownership, set auditing, and set permissions for a volume, the Explorer allows the same, but at the directory and file levels.

To change any security-related item for a file or directory from the Explorer, select the item or items you want to operate on and then right-click and choose Properties from the context menu. The Security tab has three buttons:

- *Permissions.* Allows anyone with the necessary security level to set access control for selected items.
- *Auditing.* Allows adding or removing auditing (and type of auditing) for groups.
- *Ownership.* Allows taking, but not giving, of ownership of selected items.

For example, to eliminate access to a file for a group of users, first select the file you want to restrict. Right-click and then choose Properties from the context menu. Choose the Security tab and then click the Permissions button. Figure 12.36 shows the resulting dialog box.

Figure 12.36.

Setting permissions for a file starts with this dialog box.

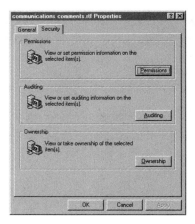

If the group you want to restrict doesn't appear in the list box, click the Add button. This button adds a group, not a set of permissions. Figure 12.37 shows the adding of the group. You can see the filename in the title bar of the Properties dialog box at the top-left of the figure.

Figure 12.37.

You can add a group with a type of access from the Add dialog box. This dialog box shows the addition of the Users group from the computer \\PAUL added with no access rights to the file communications comments.rtf.

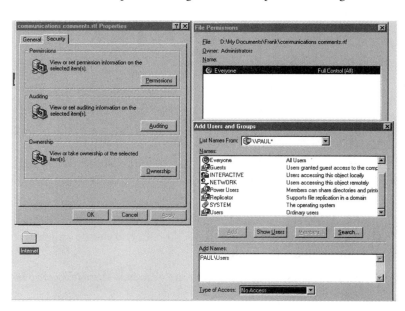

You can set the permissions for the added group as you add the group by clicking the Type of Access combo box and choosing the level of security you want to set. To find a group not listed in the groups listing, scroll down using the arrow keys or the scroll bar at the right of the list box.

From this point on, any person logging on from the Users group on \\PAUL will not be able to access the file communications comments.rtf in any way.

Using identical techniques, you can set permissions for volumes, file groups, and directories. Similarly, you can set auditing for these files or take ownership for your group.

Sharing and Mapping

Sharing a file, a directory, or a volume means you allow others on a network to gain access to those resources. It does not mean sharing with others logged on to the workstation with the shared resources. This latter capability is handled through security.

Mapping a file, directory, or volume means you map, or alias, another's shared resource to a volume letter on your workstation. As with many other Windows NT operations, you set security options when sharing, whereas you must have the requisite permissions to map.

Sharing

To share a file, directory, or volume from Explorer, right-click the target object and then choose Sharing from the context menu. Alternatively, you can highlight the object and choose Properties from the File menu and then choose the Sharing tab from the Properties dialog box. The context menu option is a direct jump to the Sharing tab of the Properties dialog box. Figure 12.38 shows this tab.

FIGURE 12.38.

You can jump directly to the Sharing tab of the Properties dialog box through the context menu, or navigate there from the Explorer menu choices File | Properties.

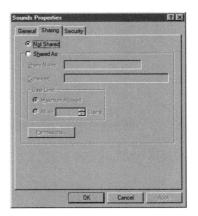

The Sharing tab has information about the shared status of Explorer objects. To share an object, choose the Shared As option button; then, if you choose, fill in a name or label to share the object as. Figure 12.39 shows the D:\Sounds directory from Figure 12.38 shared as Wild Sounds.

FIGURE 12.39.

Clicking the Shared As option button will give you a default name or label to share an object as. You can also fill in your own choice.

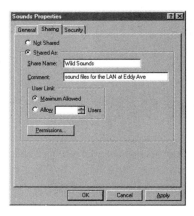

Setting permissions for a shared object has as many options, and it has a familiar look, as do most other Windows NT Workstation security dialog boxes. In Figure 12.40, the default permission of Full Control for Everyone (effectively no security) has been deleted. In its place, the Users group has been granted Read (only) permission.

FIGURE 12.40.

The Permissions button from the Sharing tab has the usual dialog boxes for adding, deleting, and editing the permissions of users and user groups.

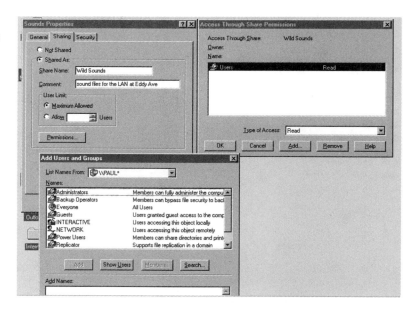

NOTE

The Shared As name, Wild Sounds, isn't valid from workstations without LFN enabled. If you use LFN in shared resources, make sure all the potential users of those resources have LFN enabled. If not, or if you're unsure, stick to the MS-DOS naming conventions.

When you click OK through the various dialog boxes to accept the sharing you've just done, Explorer will visually indicate the shared resource by changing its icon to one with an extended hand. Figure 12.41 shows the Sounds directory shared.

FIGURE 12.41.

Explorer has a visual clue to shared resources—the extended hand. Other shared directories in this computer's D: drive are My Documents and Winnt.

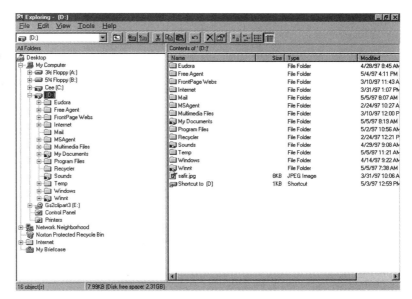

Mapping

To map a shared resource, you first locate it and then assign it a drive letter as an alias. You don't need to map a resource to use it, but if you regularly use, say, a directory on a network, mapping and then connecting to that resource upon startup will save you some time. It's also easier to access a mapped resource than to browse for it.

Figure 12.42 shows Excel saving a spreadsheet to a shared resource, a directory called `Tirilee's Documents` on the computer `Tirilee`.

FIGURE 12.42.

You don't need to map a shared resource to use it. In this case, the user found the shared resource, `Tirilee's Documents`, *on the server* `Tirilee` *through the Network Neighborhood option in the File | Save As dialog box.*

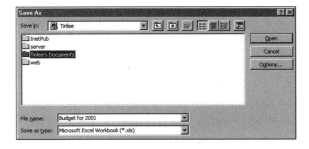

There are several ways to map a resource to a drive letter. Here's the one used most: From the Explorer, click the Map Network Drive button from the toolbar or make that choice from the Tools menu. The network shown in this series of screens has been simplified by limiting the display to a workgroup named WORKGROUP that has only two members. Normally, a workgroup will have more clients and servers than shown here. Clicking the Map Network drive will bring up a dialog box like the one shown in Figure 12.43.

Figure 12.43.

Mapping a resource to a drive letter starts with choosing the Map Network Drive option from the toolbar or the Tools menu.

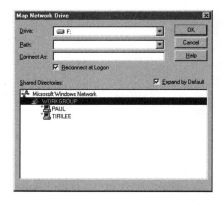

The dialog box will have as the default the next available drive letter using MS-DOS conventions. Locate the resource you want to map and then highlight it. In this case, the resource is the Tirilee's Documents directory in the F: drive of the computer TIRILEE. Figure 12.44 shows the process of locating a computer you wish to map.

Figure 12.44.

Navigating to the resource you want to map starts by finding the computer with the resource and then finding the resource in the directory structure.

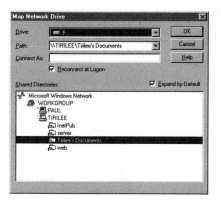

Change the file letter designation if you want to and then click OK to make your choice of mapping stick. After you do, the new drive alias will appear in the left pane of your Explorer. Figure 12.45 shows the newly mapped drive alias and the file it contains.

FIGURE 12.45.

After mapping a resource, you can see it in the left pane of the Explorer and in the pull-down drive list. At this point, you can use a mapped resource just like any local drive to the extent of your permissions.

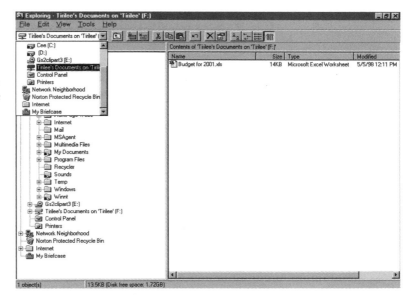

Other Context Menu Tricks

The context menu in Explorer contains quite a few options to make your computing experience easier or more convenient. Microsoft has allowed hooks into this menu for developers, so the screens shown here might not agree with the ones on other computers. Notably, the utility WinZip has been installed on the demo computer, so options to zip or unzip files appear on all the file or directory context menus.

Viewing and Editing

If you have Quick View installed (through Setup), you can view many types of files in a read-only form through the context menu. Figure 12.46 shows the context menu for the file Job Satisfaction.rtf.

This is a file type associated with the Microsoft Word application.

Choosing Quick View from the context menu will bring up a type of dialog box containing the highlighted document, as shown in Figure 12.47. In this example, the associated application is Microsoft Word. You can see a button to launch Word with this file loaded at the far-left of the toolbar.

The buttons on the toolbar allow you to launch the associated application, reduce or increase font size, and replace the window with new files.

FIGURE 12.46.

The context menu in Explorer will vary from computer to computer, depending on the Windows NT setup and installed applications.

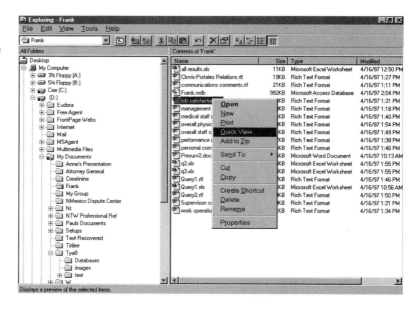

FIGURE 12.47.

The Quick View dialog box contains a read-only view of a file with an option to launch the associated application.

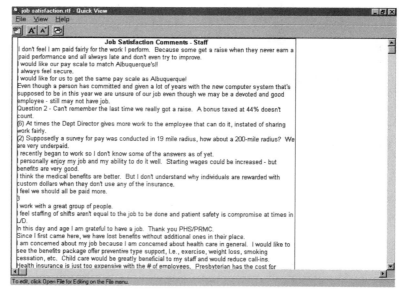

Printing

You can use the Print choice from the context menu to send a file to the default printer. There is no real trick here. To print the file, Windows NT Workstation calls up the application and then asks the application to print the document. A document printed this way will not appear on the MRU (Most Recently Used) file list of an application, so it's a sort of stealthy way to print something. It will appear on the Documents menu of Start, however.

Sending To

You can send files or other Explorer objects to various devices or services through the SendTo option of the context menu. The devices and services in the SendTo entry of the context menu are those that are there by default, plus those that appear in the SendTo directory. Figure 12.48 shows the SendTo directory. This is a directory subordinate to the system directory, usually \Winnt.

FIGURE 12.48.

The SendTo directory contains entries that will allow you to direct files from the context menu.

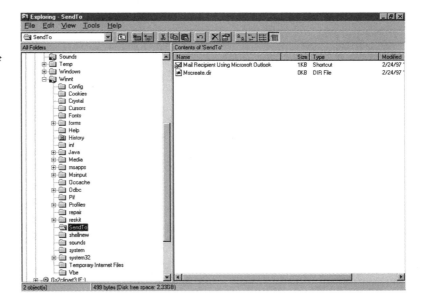

If you want to add an object to SendTo, add it to the directory or add a shortcut. Figure 12.49 shows a shortcut to the current drive F:, which is

```
Tirilee's Documents on Tirilee
```

or

```
\\Tirilee\Tirilee's Documents
```

The shortcut was created by right-dragging the entry for drive F: from the left pane of Explorer to \Winnt\SendTo and then dropping it and choosing Create Shortcut (Here) from the pop-up menu. The name of the shortcut was then changed to `Tirilee's Documents`.

Figure 12.49 shows the SendTo context menu entry without any additions to the SendTo directory.

FIGURE 12.49.

You can add many devices and services to your SendTo context menu entry by adding them or their shortcuts to the SendTo directory.

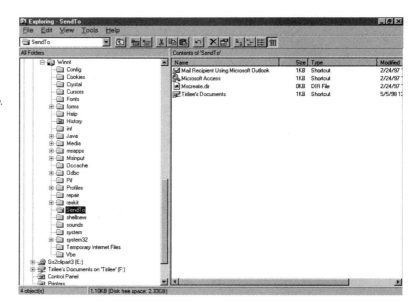

In a similar way, you can add applications or devices to this directory and then see them appear in the Send To entry of your context menu.

Summary

The FAT file system has the advantage of being as close to a universal file system as exists in computers today. However, it lacks modern capabilities such as ensuring disk integrity and security. Also, it's not efficient in volumes greater than about 500MB and is limited to comparatively small volumes. The NT File System (NTFS) fills the need for a modern, secure file system created by the shortcomings of FAT.

The chief graphic tool for administering the file system is the Disk Administrator. Using it, you can create, delete, view, and manipulate volumes and partitions. The Disk Administrator also allows you to add or edit security for volumes as well as take ownership of them.

The Explorer is the chief graphic tool for manipulating files and directories. Using it, you can share, map, set security, copy, rename, delete, move, view, as well as other such options available in your SendTo entry of your context menu.

Installing Applications on NT

by Paul Cassel

IN THIS CHAPTER

Windows NT, like other Windows versions, uses the open architecture concept for itself and its applications. In a nutshell, this means the operating system and its native applications are made up of many components in a manner similar to a brick wall being made up of individual bricks.

The advantage of the open architecture is that many applications can share common parts and that the parts of either Windows NT Workstation or its applications (or both) can be updated rather easily. The downside of all this openness is extremely complex installation and deinstallation routines. Applications often replace parts of Windows with newer components. When running, they are actually, in a way, part of Windows, not just running under it.

If this weren't enough potential confusion, most applications require multiple entries in the Registry to run properly or at all. When removed, these programs need to have their registration entries removed also or Windows will malfunction or, at best, flash numerous warning messages at hapless users.

Vendors working in conjunction with Microsoft have come up with fairly standardized installation and deinstallation (or *uninstallation,* as some prefer) programs, but they aren't foolproof. They can't be. Here's just one scenario of why that's the case.

Suppose a program, FastWord, uses a component, Fancy.dll, as part of its component package. Upon installation, FastWord's setup copies Fancy.dll to the [%windows32%]\system32 directory and registers itself along with Fancy.dll in the Registry. In a perfect world, deinstallation would remove Fancy.dll from [%windows32%]\system32 and from the Registry. However, what if another program, GreatCalc, also needs to use Fancy.dll and has installed it into [%windows32%]\system32? There aren't two copies of this file, because FastWord's version overwrote GreatCalc's during its setup.

If the deinstallation of FastWord removed Fancy.dll from [%windows32%]\system32, it would cause GreatCalc to malfunction. On the other hand, if FastWord is the only application to use Fancy.dll and deinstallation fails to remove it from the machine, FastWord leaves an orphaned piece of itself behind.

If that weren't enough, the Windows components suffer from version madness (VM). A component will retain the same name through many version changes. Each change should be a superset of the component and usually is, but that doesn't prevent another setup program from overwriting a newer version of the component with an older one. This results in a subset of the component's total abilities replacing the whole set of the original component. Usually this causes some sort of malfunction with the application needing all the component's features.

Until the application calls on the component to supply the (now) missing functions, this malfunction won't appear. So the installation of Application20 might ruin the existing installation of Application12, but in such a way that it doesn't show up for weeks or months. Worse, Application12 won't flash a message saying "Application20's install of Fancy.dll has ruined my spell checker." It won't even flash a message hinting at the problem. Instead, it will just start acting bizarrely.

RegClean

Microsoft has a utility called RegClean, which will go through your Registry trying to locate orphaned entries. It then offers to clean your Registry of these entries. After running, it creates a .reg file with the entries it deleted. Double-clicking this file in Explorer will restore the deleted entries, so in the vast majority of cases, running RegClean can't land you in worse shape than not running it.

You can find RegClean at Microsoft's Web and FTP sites as well as the usual places that contain Microsoft utilities. Figure 13.1 shows a .reg file from running RegClean. This is an example of the output of running RegClean on a well-functioning machine. The resulting .reg file is 7KB, meaning RegClean found a lot of entries it felt were spurious or injurious.

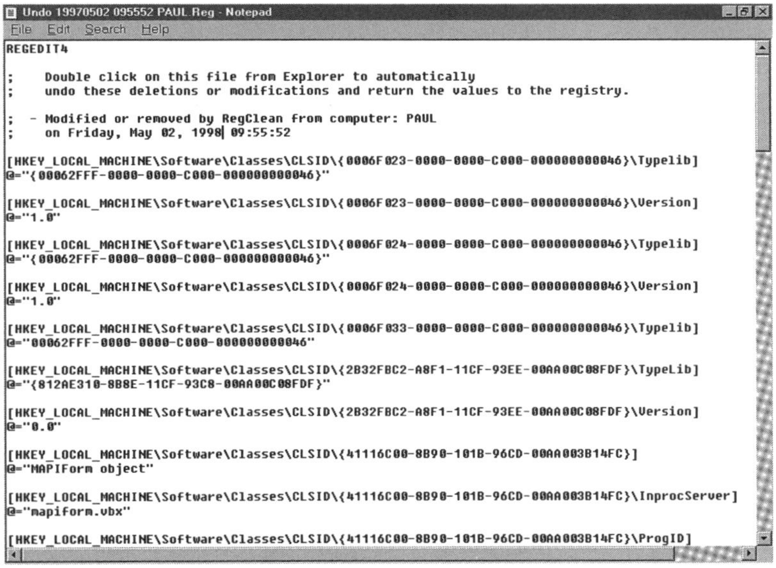

```
REGEDIT4

;    Double click on this file from Explorer to automatically
;    undo these deletions or modifications and return the values to the registry.

;  - Modified or removed by RegClean from computer: PAUL
;    on Friday, May 02, 1998 09:55:52

[HKEY_LOCAL_MACHINE\Software\Classes\CLSID\{0006F023-0000-0000-C000-000000000046}\Typelib]
@="{00062FFF-0000-0000-C000-000000000046}"

[HKEY_LOCAL_MACHINE\Software\Classes\CLSID\{0006F023-0000-0000-C000-000000000046}\Version]
@="1.0"

[HKEY_LOCAL_MACHINE\Software\Classes\CLSID\{0006F024-0000-0000-C000-000000000046}\Typelib]
@="{00062FFF-0000-0000-C000-000000000046}"

[HKEY_LOCAL_MACHINE\Software\Classes\CLSID\{0006F024-0000-0000-C000-000000000046}\Version]
@="1.0"

[HKEY_LOCAL_MACHINE\Software\Classes\CLSID\{0006F033-0000-0000-C000-000000000046}\Typelib]
@="00062FFF-0000-0000-C000-000000000046"

[HKEY_LOCAL_MACHINE\Software\Classes\CLSID\{2B32FBC2-A8F1-11CF-93EE-00AA00C08FDF}\TypeLib]
@="{812AE310-8B8E-11CF-93C8-00AA00C08FDF}"

[HKEY_LOCAL_MACHINE\Software\Classes\CLSID\{2B32FBC2-A8F1-11CF-93EE-00AA00C08FDF}\Version]
@="0.0"

[HKEY_LOCAL_MACHINE\Software\Classes\CLSID\{41116C00-8B90-101B-96CD-00AA003B14FC}]
@="MAPIForm object"

[HKEY_LOCAL_MACHINE\Software\Classes\CLSID\{41116C00-8B90-101B-96CD-00AA003B14FC}\InprocServer]
@="mapiform.vbx"

[HKEY_LOCAL_MACHINE\Software\Classes\CLSID\{41116C00-8B90-101B-96CD-00AA003B14FC}\ProgID]
```

FIGURE 13.1.
To restore Registry entries deleted by RegClean, double-click the file the utility creates.

RegClean will run and not make any changes to the Registry if you tell it not to. This doesn't make much sense, because there's no reason to run it just for the sake of running, but the utility does offer you a way to back out, as you can see in Figure 13.2.

FIGURE 13.2.

RegClean will diagnose your Registry and then give you an option to apply its diagnosis.

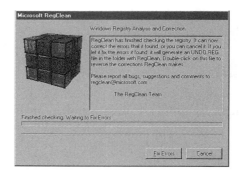

Safe Installs

There isn't a sure way around all setup problems. The only real solution, and it's a poor one, is to practice defensive installation, just as you would practice defensive driving. Defensive driving assumes that the other person will make errors. You take the responsibility of avoiding the potential resulting collisions. Defensive installation assumes a problem with a setup routine but also means that you can restore your system to a preinstallation state in these cases.

Here are the steps to take in a defensive installation:

1. Make a new ERD.
2. Back up the system and installation target volumes, including the local Registry. This backup should include any .ini files.
3. Make sure you have a boot disk, although having a setup go so bad that you need this is a rare occurrence.
4. Install the new application.

This will allow you to return to your previous state in case the setup of a new application goes awry. This routine isn't too effective in the case of an installation's problems showing up weeks after running setup, but it will allow you to return exactly to the pre-setup state. And that's better than nothing.

If you want to take the trouble, you can create a before and after listing of directories to see what files have been added, written over with changed versions, or—in odd cases—deleted. To do this, start a command session (CLI).

To create a simple text file consisting of a sorted directory listing, navigate to that directory and enter

```
dir /on > filename.txt
```

If you want to suppress directory listings, enter

```
dir /a-d /on > filename.txt
```

Do this list for at least the home system directory and the subdirectories \system and \system32. If you want, you can create a huge listing of the home system directory and all its subdirectories by including the `/s` switch in the `DIR` command, but doing so creates an unwieldy file due to its size.

After running setup, you can compare the before and after status of the directories using the `FC` (File Compare) command-line utility. The `FC` command takes the following parameters:

`/a`	Displays the start and ending lines for each difference
`/b`	Does a binary comparison
`/c`	Case-insensitive compare
`/l`	ASCII compare
`/LB`*n*	Stops the compare after finding *n* hits
`/n`	Line number display of mismatches
`/t`	Ignores tab expansion
`/w`	Removes whitespace (20H) characters
`/u`	Compares files as Unicode

To use `FC`, enter this at the command prompt:

```
FC [parameters] Filename1 Filename2
```

Figure 13.3 shows a \system32 directory listing made with the following command in Notepad:

```
dir /a-d /on > before.txt
```

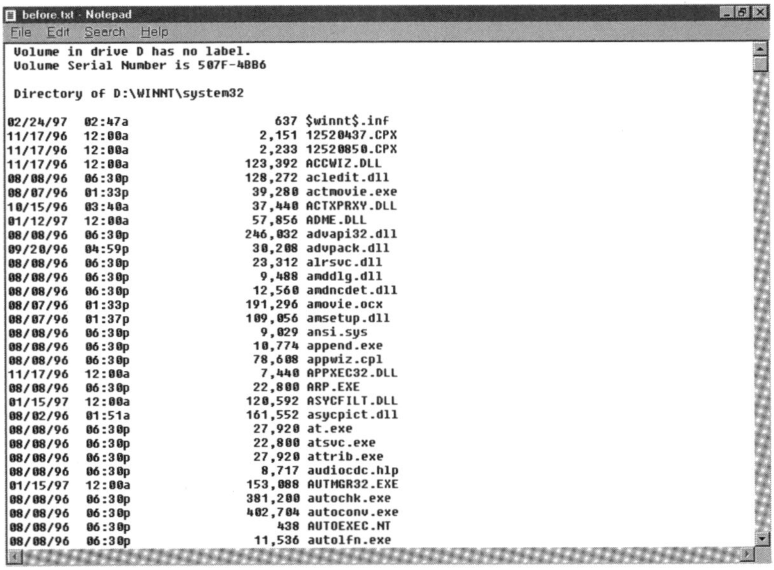

```
Volume in drive D has no label.
Volume Serial Number is 507F-4BB6

Directory of D:\WINNT\system32

02/24/97  02:47a                   637 $winnt$.inf
11/17/96  12:00a                 2,151 12520437.CPX
11/17/96  12:00a                 2,233 12520850.CPX
11/17/96  12:00a               123,392 ACCWIZ.DLL
08/08/96  06:30p               128,272 acledit.dll
08/07/96  01:33p                39,280 actmovie.exe
10/15/96  03:40a                37,440 ACTXPRXY.DLL
01/12/97  12:00a                57,856 ADME.DLL
08/08/96  06:30p               246,032 advapi32.dll
09/20/96  04:59p                30,208 advpack.dll
08/08/96  06:30p                23,312 alrsvc.dll
08/08/96  06:30p                 9,488 amddlg.dll
08/08/96  06:30p                12,560 amdncdet.dll
08/07/96  01:33p               191,296 amovie.ocx
08/07/96  01:37p               109,056 amsetup.dll
08/08/96  06:30p                 9,029 ansi.sys
08/08/96  06:30p                10,774 append.exe
08/08/96  06:30p                78,608 appwiz.cpl
11/17/96  12:00a                 7,440 APPXEC32.DLL
08/08/96  06:30p                22,800 ARP.EXE
01/15/97  12:00a               120,592 ASYCFILT.DLL
08/02/96  01:51a               161,552 asycpict.dll
08/08/96  06:30p                27,920 at.exe
08/08/96  06:30p                22,800 atsvc.exe
08/08/96  06:30p                27,920 attrib.exe
08/08/96  06:30p                 8,717 audiocdc.hlp
01/15/97  12:00a               153,088 AUTMGR32.EXE
08/08/96  06:30p               381,200 autochk.exe
08/08/96  06:30p               402,704 autoconv.exe
08/08/96  06:30p                   438 AUTOEXEC.NT
08/08/96  06:30p                11,536 autolfn.exe
```

FIGURE 13.3.
This is a listing of the before setup status of the \system32 directory. To see what's changed after setup, you can run the `FC` *utility on this and the* `after` *directory listing.*

After the listing shown in Figure 13.3 was run, this Windows NT Workstation installation got first a setup then an uninstall of an electronic camera. After the uninstall program ran, the user entered

```
Dir /a-d /on > after.txt
```

to create an after-install/uninstall listing of \system32. To see if the uninstall left any detritus, the user entered

```
FC before.txt after.txt > compare.txt
```

to compare the two directory listings and enter the results in a file called compare.txt. Making a file is an easier way to view the output of FC than the console display. Figure 13.4 shows the file compare.txt in Notepad. After eliminating the false hits caused by the after.txt file itself, you can see that two entries remain different from before and after the installation of the electronic camera's software. These files are twaindrv.dll and pwrshot.cnt.

FIGURE 13.4.

The output of FC *redirected from the console and into a text file, shown here in Notepad.*

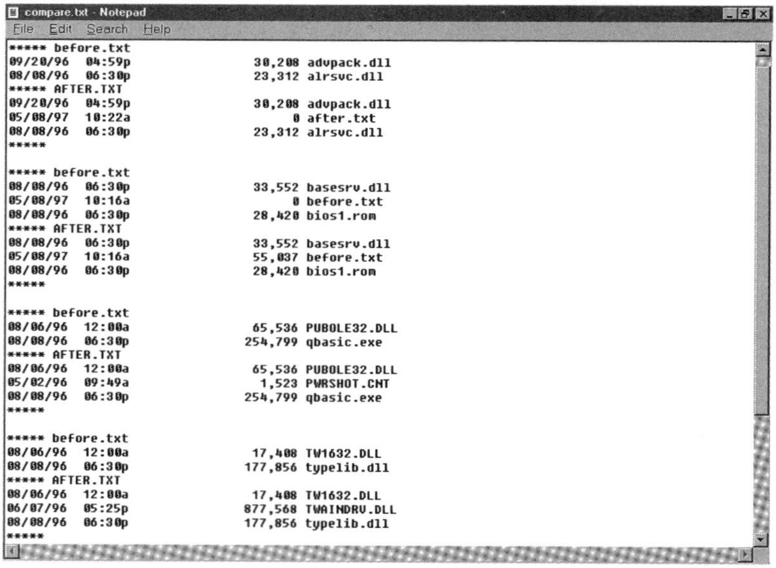

The output from FC takes a little getting used to. It not only shows mismatches but also surrounding text. There is one false hit here caused by the existence of the redirected .txt file itself, but ignoring that shows the clear problem of having two additional files in the after listing that weren't there in the before listing. The reason the command

```
FC before.txt after.txt
```

worked all right is because the FC utility defaults to an ASCII compare of the output suitable for this task. Therefore, it required no optional parameters.

At this point, you can delete these files, or more safely, use Explorer to move them to the Recycle Bin. If you're fairly sure they're benign or are serving some useful purpose, leave them in.

Altering Windows NT

You can add or remove Windows NT Workstation's components using the Add/Remove Program Wizard. This works similarly to the Custom installation option you might have opted for during Windows NT setup. Figure 13.5 shows the Control Panel for a machine lacking the Accessibility Options applet.

FIGURE 13.5.

This machine lacks the Accessibility Options applet.

To add these options, or to add or remove any optional Windows NT Workstation components, click Add/Remove Programs in the Control Panel. This brings up the Add/Remove tabbed dialog box with a listing of currently installed applications, as shown in Figure 13.6.

FIGURE 13.6.

The Add/Remove dialog box launches with a list box showing all the currently installed applications.

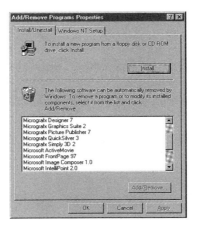

The Windows NT Setup tab will show all the currently installed optional portions of Windows NT Workstation, as shown in Figure 13.7.

FIGURE 13.7.

The Windows NT Setup tab is similar to the Custom option of the initial setup program. It also serves an identical purpose.

To add Accessibility Options to this workstation, click the blank check box next to this option and then click OK. If you haven't done so already, you'll need to place your distribution CD-ROM in the drive or point to where on the network Windows NT can find the distribution files. Figure 13.8 shows Windows NT asking for the location of its setup files.

FIGURE 13.8.

Setup needs to know where the distribution files reside. This is usually on the distribution CD-ROM or the network. In any case, you need to guide Setup to these files.

After setup accesses and installs the files, it closes down its File Copy dialog box, leaving you at the Install/Remove applet, where you can install or remove other applications or components. In this case, the next time Control Panel was launched, it had the Accessibility Options applet as part of the panel. Figure 13.9 shows the newly revised Control Panel.

You can also run Windows Setup from the distribution CD-ROM. Insert the CD-ROM in the drive and it should start up, giving you the screen shown in Figure 13.10.

To run the Add/Remove routine, choose the third option from the splash screen, Add/Remove Software. This adds or removes portions of Windows NT, not application programs.

To remove optional portions of Windows NT Workstation, use the same technique but clear the check boxes for those components you want to remove.

FIGURE 13.9.

After running Setup from the Windows NT Setup tab, this workstation has Accessibility Options as part of Control Panel.

FIGURE 13.10.

The Autostart feature of the distribution CD-ROM will launch this screen when you insert the CD-ROM into the drive during a Windows NT Workstation session.

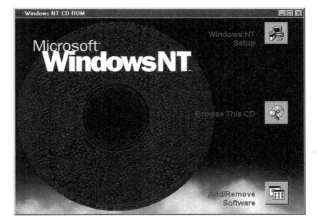

Adding Applications

Adding 32-bit applications is similar (or can be) to adding Windows NT Workstation components. The vast majority of the applications you'll encounter will have one of a few standardized installation programs. To run them, you can use the Add/Remove Applications applet in Control Panel. If you prefer, you can use the Explorer to locate their Setup.exe program on the distribution CD-ROM or disks. Double-click Setup.exe and then follow the instructions, which usually consist of some or all of these choices:

- Which directory to install the application into
- The program group (if any) to create for convenient program launching
- The parts (components) of the program to install

In many cases, application distribution CD-ROMs will have an Autorun routine. As soon as you insert the CD-ROM, you'll launch into the setup program.

The actual screens for program installation will differ, depending on the particular install program used to create the installation routine and the needs of the application.

Figure 13.11 shows the start of the setup program for Microsoft Office 97 on a machine with an existing version of Office 97. Because there is an existing Office 97, this screen shows the currently installed components. This gives information to the user, allowing intelligent addition or deletion of Office components.

Figure 13.11.

Office 97, like many applications, allows the adding or removing of components from existing installations.

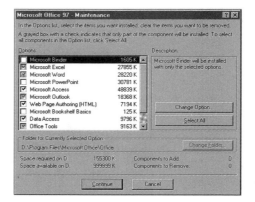

This screen in Figure 13.11 has a similar function to the screen shown in Figure 13.7. The difference is that here the component options are for Office 97; in Figure 13.7, the options are for Windows NT Workstation.

Adding or Removing 16-Bit Windows Applications

The method used to add or remove 16-bit applications depends upon the application itself. Few, if any, of these applications, even Windows native ones, use a Setup or Install routine compatible to Windows NT Workstation's native expectations. Instead, Windows NT Workstation tries to conform to the expectations of these older-style programs.

Many of these programs use .ini files or modify the two application-usable .ini files, system.ini and win.ini, that are the precursors of the Windows NT Registry.

Windows NT has a directory of the system folder called \system that serves as an analog to \system32 for shared 16-bit components. It is also able to use the files system.ini and win.ini. Some 32-bit applications use these files also. Figure 13.12 shows both these files for a Windows NT Workstation setup.

FIGURE 13.12.

In theory, the Registry should hold configuration information for all 32-bit applications, leaving win.ini and system.ini for 16-bit applications only. However, theory and practice often diverge. Some 32-bit programs use either or both of the older .ini files.

To add a 16-bit Windows program, take the following steps if you want to play it very safe:

1. Back up everything.
2. Create a "before" directory listing using any technique you prefer. Earlier on, you saw the use of the `dir /a-d /on > before.txt` routine. You'll need to do this for the [windows]\system directory and the Windows directory (often \Winnt40).
3. Create backup copies of win.ini and system.ini.
4. Setup the application.
5. Create an "after" directory listing using any technique you prefer.

To remove a Windows 16-bit application that doesn't have an automated uninstall program (few do), take these steps:

1. Remove the application directories and contained files.
2. Remove any application-added entries to win.ini and system.ini. Do this by either editing the two files or restoring the files from their backups. Don't restore from backups if you've installed subsequent applications, because restoring might adversely affect these applications.
3. Run `FC` or in any other way determine any added files to the [windows] and \system directories. Remove them if you're sure they aren't shared by another application.
4. Remove any .ini files related to the application. These almost always exist in the \windows directory.

5. Remove any shortcuts from Start | Programs, the Desktop, or any other location you or the setup program might have created for them.

The good thing about 16-bit Windows applications is that rarely, if ever, will their partly installed components (or partly uninstalled bits and pieces of these applications) adversely affect Windows NT Workstation or 32-bit applications.

DOS Applications

Few, if any, DOS applications you run will be aware of Windows NT's existence. To install these older style applications, run their install programs (if they exist). Many DOS programs are installed by copying the contents of their distribution disks to a directory.

What the Setup Programs Do

Setup programs for 32-bit applications perform three broad services:

- Creating an application directory structure and install the needed files in that structure.
- Adding shared, or potentially shared, components to the appropriate folder. This is usually \system32.
- Making the appropriate Registry entries.

The setup program also often creates a file containing information about the installed components. If so, the uninstall program uses this information as a checklist. Often, if an uninstall routine fails mysteriously, it's because this file is missing or corrupted.

There's nothing unusual or different about the first two tasks of setup programs: creating a directory structure or installing files. Adding Registry entries is the real kicker. It's somewhat analogous to making .ini entries in the old system.ini and win.ini files or making an application's own .ini files. However, due to the complexities of Windows NT (and Windows 95, too), the Registry entries are likewise complex.

CLSID or GUID

You'll see a long 16-digit (16 bytes or 128 bits) hexadecimal (base16) number as part of many Registry entries. This is the GUID, or CLSID. GUID stands for Globally Unique Identifier, whereas CLSID stands for Class ID. Although the numbers are the same, whether they're referred to as a GUID or a CLSID depends on the context.

A GUID is a unique identifier for a Registry entry. Unique in this context means the application entry has that number for itself. The number remains the same in all registries, but no other application, or application part, can use the same GUID for itself.

Microsoft distributes a "random" number generator, GUIDGEN.EXE, as part of its Software Developer's Kits (SDKs) for making GUIDs. Developers use the generated numbers to uniquely identify their applications. The uniqueness is supposed to be guaranteed by the impossibility of generating two identical numbers of that length. However, Microsoft maintains a database of assigned GUIDs developers can check and register their GUIDs with just in case.

The Registry Entries

The type of entries made in the Registry by a setup program depends on the capacity of the program and what interactions it expects to have with other installed programs and Windows itself. Microsoft Excel is a good example of a program with many Registry entries. Following are three (of many) of them with their explanations.

Figure 13.13 shows one entry for Excel 97. The program, along with the other parts of Microsoft Office 97, are versioned as 8, but are marketed at 97. This entry is under HKEY_LOCAL_MACHINE \SOFTWARE\Microsoft\Office\8.0\Excel\InstallRoot.

FIGURE 13.13.

The Registry entry for Excel telling Windows NT and any other interested party the home or root folder for this application.

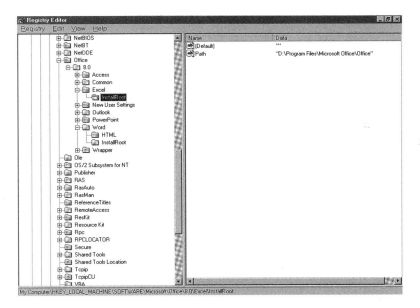

Similarly, the setup program enters information about the file extensions associated with that program. The Registry area, HKEY_LOCAL_MACHINE\SOFTWARE\Classes\, shown in Figure 13.14, is this area.

A very important part of the Registry is the SharedDLLs section. Windows NT is, like all Windows versions, a component operating system. That is, the exact variant of Windows NT you run is a core set of routines, with added services depending on your hardware and installed or running options/services.

FIGURE 13.14.

Here is the file extension area of the Registry. Users can add, modify, or delete entries found here through the View-Options menu entry in Explorer on the File Types tab.

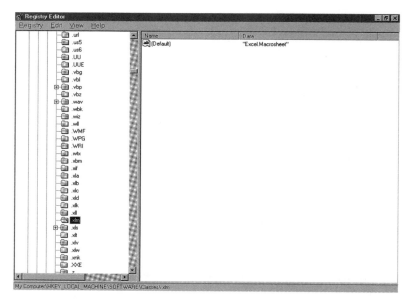

In the same way, applications running under Windows NT are component applications. They, too, are a core set of routines with extensions often shared among other applications. The advantage of this system is that only one of each shared extension (file) needs to be present on a machine (or network in some cases) or loaded into memory.

For example, the routines to convert one file format to another for Microsoft applications have the extension .cnv. The file to convert Excel file extensions is Excel32.cnv. More than one application uses this file as part of its Save As routine.

The first application to have the Excel file format as a part of its import or export (Save As) needs to install the Excel32.cnv file. Subsequent applications don't need to install this file, because it already exists. Doing another installation of an identical file, Excel32.cnv, will, at best, just overwrite an existing file or, at worst, install itself at a new location, thus wasting disk space.

Rather than having this scenario, the first application to install Excel32.cnv enters it in the SharedDLLs section of the Registry with a value of 1. Each time an application capable of Save As an Excel format file is added to a computer, it increments the value of this entry. Each time an application that uses Excel32.cnv uninstalls, it decrements the entry's value. If an uninstall that includes Excel32.cnv finds a value of 1 in the SharedDLLs section, it notifies the user that it's about to remove a shared component. This dialog box gives the user an option to continue or to retain the component.

Figure 13.15 shows the SharedDLLs section of the Windows NT Workstation Registry HKEY_LOCAL_MACHINE\SOFTWARE\Microsoft\Windows\CurrentVersion\SharedDlls.

Figure 13.15.

Here is the SharedDLLs *section of the Registry. This workstation has four registered applications that use the Excel32.cnv file format converter.*

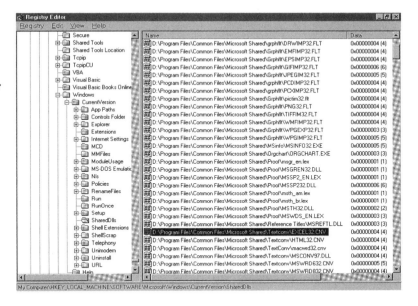

The idea of the SharedDLLs section of the Registry is a good one, but it doesn't always work out. Uninstall routines fail, people uninstall programs manually without decrementing the SharedDLLs section, and other things go bump in the night to conspire against this facility. It's better than nothing, however.

Troubleshooting Setups and Uninstalls

The following are some commonly encountered problems with suggested solutions.

Problem: After uninstalling a 16-bit application, you get the message that Windows NT can't locate a part of that application.

Solution: Search system.ini and win.ini for orphaned entries related to the uninstalled application. Also, search for any other .ini file that might have been created at the time the program was installed.

Problem: An error message for a 32-bit uninstalled program pops up upon startup. This message can be that Windows NT Workstation can't find the application or a service failed during startup.

Solution: Look in the Startup groups for orphaned shortcuts. Similarly, examine the Run and Load lines of Win.ini. In the case of a service, search the Registry for the entries and delete them. Make sure you've backed up your Registry before deleting any keys or altering values unless you are very sure you understand what you are about to do.

Problem: Setup leaves a mysterious directory such as ~Mssetup.t.

Solution: These are temporary directories that Setup should have deleted before ending. Some problem prevented Setup from doing so. You can delete these directories if you're sure Setup has finished running.

Problem: You try to uninstall a 32-bit application. You get an error message saying uninstall can't continue. The application exists on your machine.

Solution: You've probably lost a pointer file, such as DelsL1.isu, that uninstall needs to proceed. You'll need to uninstall the application yourself manually. Delete the installation's directory structure with the accompanying files. Back up the Registry. Remove unique entries in the Registry by searching for them and then deleting them. If you feel ambitious, decrement the application's entries in SharedDLLs. If you feel very ambitious, remove any unneeded .dll files and other shared components from \system32.

Problem: An application uninstalled and inactive on your computer still exists in the Install/Uninstall dialog box.

Solution: Remove the entry from the Registry from HKEY_LOCAL_MACHINE\SOFTWARE\Microsoft \Windows\CurrentVersion\Uninstall. Figure 13.16 shows this section.

FIGURE 13.16.

A section of the Registry is dedicated to tracking applications that should uninstall. Sometimes an application uninstalls but leaves itself in the Registry.

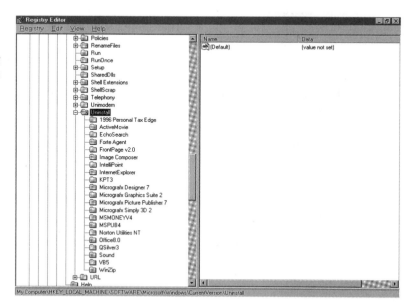

Figure 13.17 shows the installed applications list for the computer shown in Figure 13.16.

FIGURE 13.17.

*The installed
applications section of
the Add/Remove applet
reflects Registry entries.*

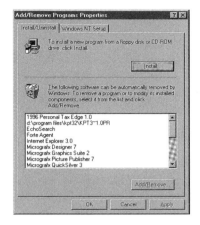

Summary

Installing applications in Windows NT Workstation is similar to other versions of Windows, especially Windows 95. The chief tool for doing installations is the Add/Remove applet in Control Panel. This applet has two tabs in its dialog box. The Install/Uninstall tab controls applications, whereas the Windows NT Setup tab controls Windows NT Workstation's optional components.

Installations usually go well, but things do go awry. The only way to assure yourself that you can return to a preinstallation profile is to back up your system so you can restore it if necessary.

Setup programs perform three broad functions. They create and populate a directory (folder) structure for the application, add common components to another folder (usually \system32), and make needed Registry modifications.

Sharing with OLE and ActiveX in NT

by Paul Cassel

IN THIS CHAPTER

Object Linking and Embedding, or OLE, was originally marketed as an interprocess communications protocol to replace the barely functional Dynamic Data Exchange (DDE). The older DDE allowed blind piping of information from one process (application program) to another, but it was slow, unreliable, and inflexible. Microsoft's plan for OLE encompassed addressing all these problems.

Before OLE grew to full interprocess reliability, Microsoft extended its scope to be the foundation of a component-based operating system. Once again, before Microsoft fully implemented a component-based operating system (or even got a good start on a commercial version), OLE was extended to become ActiveX. This is one significant branch of Microsoft's Internet strategy.

Today, OLE (or ActiveX) is the Windows-specific standard for interprocess communications and data exchange. One of its competitors is Java, although Java has a vastly different technical background. However, to many folks, Java applications and ActiveX components look and act the same. The other competitor is OpenDoc, a standard once promoted by IBM and Apple chiefly, but now abandoned by both because they yield one part of the battle to OLE and join the Java wave using the resources once applied to OpenDoc.

This chapter is a light treatment of OLE. The topic, from a programming viewpoint, is among the most complex in computing and well beyond the scope of a short chapter. However, from a user viewpoint, or an administrator viewpoint, using OLE and even creating simple OLE applications using macro tools, isn't terribly complicated.

Again, from a user viewpoint, there are two sides to an OLE exchange. One side is the server side. An OLE server is an application capable of being controlled by another application. An OLE controller, often mistakenly called an *OLE client*, is a program capable of controlling an OLE server. Therefore, if you embed an Excel spreadsheet in a Word document, Word acts as the controller while Excel acts as the server. Most people refer to this arrangement by its network-like description, where Word becomes the OLE client and Excel the OLE server.

Figure 14.1 shows a simplified diagram of the relationship between an OLE automation server and controller.

FIGURE 14.1.

An OLE, or ActiveX, communication has two sides: the controller side, or client, and the server side. The OLE object exists within a container in the controller document.

Although technically speaking, you don't need automation to have an OLE relationship, most uses of OLE today use such automation. OLE automation is the interface where one application controls another. For example, the Excel chart in a Word document example means that Word can control Excel or use Excel's resources to modify the chart used in its document.

Creating Compound Documents

Once you've inserted a document or object in another document, you've created a compound document. Doing this with OLE-enabled applications is fairly simple. Using a link is one way of many.

The Link

The process of making an OLE link starts with creating the document you want to have inserted in another. This example uses an Excel chart and a simple Word memo type document to create a compound document. Figure 14.2 shows the chart done in Excel.

FIGURE 14.2.

You can create a compound document many ways. This example starts with a simple chart in Excel. Excel will be the server application in this exercise.

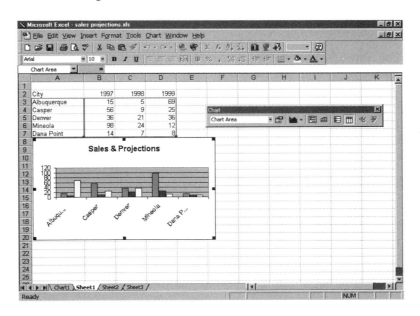

Highlight the chart by clicking it and then right-click and choose copy. You can also choose the Edit | Copy menu commands or press Ctrl+C. This will copy the chart object to the Clipboard.

Open up Word, create the host document, and then choose Edit | Paste Special from the menu. This brings up the dialog box shown in Figure 14.3.

FIGURE 14.3.

The Edit \ Paste Special command will allow hot, warm, or cold linking of an object copied from an OLE automation server.

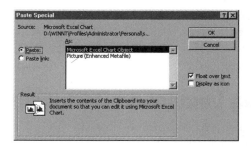

The two option buttons and two formats for pasting give you a great deal of flexibility in how your compound document will behave.

The two choices for the Microsoft Excel object are Paste and Paste Link. Here's what they do:

- *Paste.* This adds the chart to the document and maintains an on-demand link to that object. You can edit and update the chart using Excel by double-clicking the chart.
- *Paste Link.* This creates a hot link to the object. As the object changes in Excel, those changes are reflected in the Word document.

The Paste Link option allows dynamic updating of the objects. This is very useful in situations where a workgroup creates objects that are part of a large compound document. As each person works on his or her parts of the document, those changes are reflected at other people's workstations.

The other option is to paste the chart as a metafile, or a picture. This breaks the link to Excel.

Once pasted, the chart appears to become part of the Word document, as you can see in Figure 14.4. This chart was Paste Link inserted, maintaining a hot link with the original Excel document.

Here's how the hot link works. In this example, the sales manager who created the spreadsheet made an error with the 1998 sales for Dana Point. Instead of 7, it should have been 70. Figure 14.5 shows editing that figure in the original Excel document.

As soon as the sales manager finishes his edit and presses Enter, Excel modifies the data for the cell and updates the chart, as you can see in Figure 14.6. The chart part that changes is the middle bar for Dana Point.

FIGURE 14.4.

Once pasted, the chart appears to be part of the Word document.

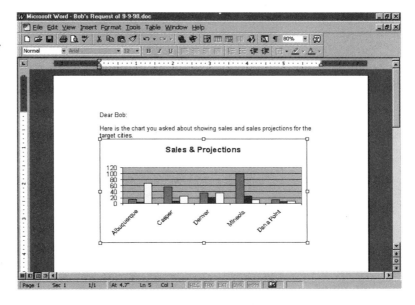

FIGURE 14.5.

The sales manager made an error in data entry. Here, he edits the sales figures for Dana Point to the right amount.

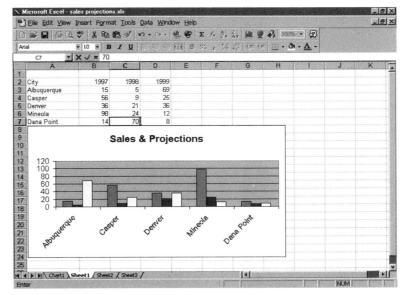

FIGURE 14.6.

Excel automatically updates charts when the underlying data changes. In this case, the sales figure for Dana Point in 1998 changed from 7 to 70, and the corresponding bar in the chart grew to ten times its original size.

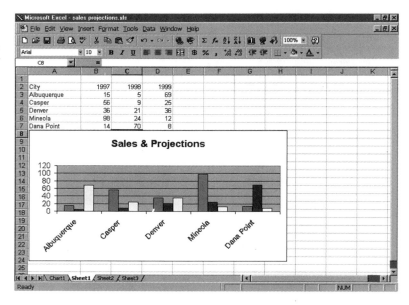

Without any user intervention, the chart in the hot linked Word document also changed, as you can see in Figure 14.7.

FIGURE 14.7.

The hot link allowed the ripple of change to work its way to the Word document chart, as well.

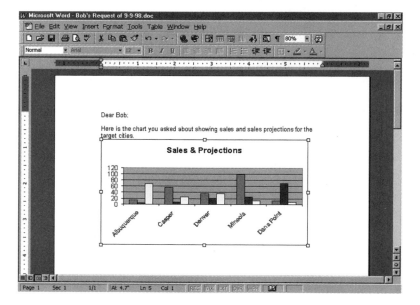

This change occurred instantly (or nearly so) because all the documents existed on a single computer. Had this been a network, the ripple would have taken a few seconds. Naturally, you can see no changes if either the host computer to the server or controller application is offline or if the compound document on the controller host isn't open.

Modern OLE allows you to modify the links in a compound document. The Edit menu in Word has a full set of such options, whereas the context menu for the linked object has one set.

To examine and optionally modify the link properties for the chart in the Word document, choose the menu selections Edit | Links. This brings up the dialog box shown in Figure 14.8.

FIGURE 14.8.

The Edit | Links menu choice allows modification of inserted OLE objects.

Here are the options in this dialog box:

- *OK.* Accept changes.
- *Cancel.* Forget the whole thing.
- *Update Now.* Force changes in the server document to the controller document.
- *Open Source.* Launch the server application with the server document loaded.
- *Change Source.* Alter the linked file for the object.
- *Break Link.* Change linked object to an image. Once you've broken a link, the only way to get it back is to copy/paste the object again.
- *Update Automatic.* Hot linking that ripples changes in the server document automatically to the controller (compound) document.
- *Update Manual.* Update only upon user command.
- *Locked.* Object is frozen. Changes to the server document can't be reflected in compound document.

Linking and Embedding

OLE has the capability to link or embed objects. A *linked object* is one that has pointers from the destination file (in the controller application) to the source file (made in the server application). A linked object never becomes part of the destination file. Here are the advantages of a linked object:

■ The size of the destination, or host file, isn't greatly increased, because it gets only link information (a container and a pointer) rather than the file itself.

■ Changes to the source file or object can be reflected either manually or automatically in the destination (compound) document.

The chief disadvantage of a linked object is that the controller application doesn't really have absolute control. For example, a user having sufficient rights can delete the file with the source object, thus destroying the compound document.

An embedded object becomes part of the destination or host file or document. An embedded object can retain links to the source application just as a linked object can. For example, to edit an embedded object, double-click it. This brings up the server application, and you can begin editing.

Here's the advantage of an embedded object:

■ The object becomes part of the host document. This simplifies distribution and makes the compound document less sensitive to unauthorized or unintentional fiddling.

The chief disadvantage of a compound document with an embedded object is that the size of the document grows alarmingly as it gets the object embedded in it. A file with an embedded object not only grows by the size of the embedding, but it also gains some overhead.

Creating an Embedded Object

You can create a document with an embedded object as easily as one with a linked object, but the steps vary. Figure 14.9 shows a letter in Word that hosts an embedded object—again an Excel document.

The right side of Figure 14.9 shows the document; the left side shows the Windows NT Explorer with the Explorer view of the saved file. Note that at this point, it's about 19KB large.

To start to embed an object, choose the menu selection Insert | Object. This brings up the dialog box you see in Figure 14.10. Click the Create New tab to see the exact screen in Figure 14.10.

The list of server programs that appear on any given computer will vary depending upon the applications installed. Locate the type of file you want to embed by hunting around in the Object Type list box. Only server applications supporting linking and embedding will appear in this list box.

FIGURE 14.9.

You're not committed to a type of link or even whether your compound documents are linked.

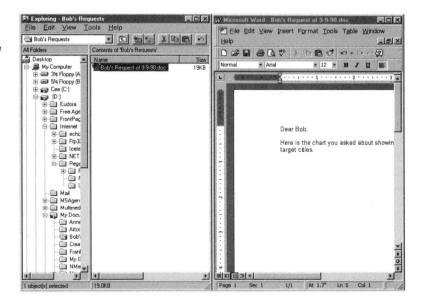

FIGURE 14.10.

The start of the embedding process is the Insert | Object menu command.

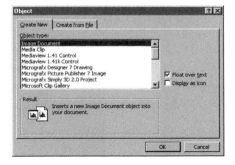

After you choose the type of file you want to embed by clicking on that type, click OK and Word will call on Excel to create and then embed a placeholder object. For example, if you choose an Excel Chart object, you'll get an object that looks like the one shown in Figure 14.11.

At this point, you can edit the Excel document to create the chart you want.

Let's say that instead of creating a new object, you want to insert a previously made file, as in the earlier link example. To do this, click the Insert from File tab in the Insert | Object dialog box and browse for the file containing the information you want to embed. If you know the path to the file, you can just fill it in at the text box.

FIGURE 14.11.

Asking Excel to embed a new object results in a placeholder object inserted in your document.

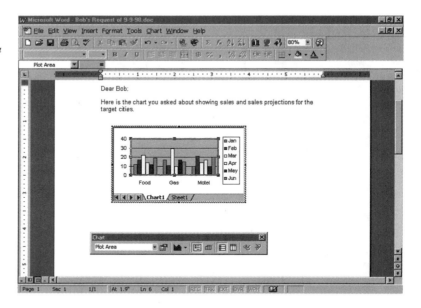

Figure 14.12 shows the dialog box for inserting an existing file with the filename added in.

FIGURE 14.12.

To embed an existing document, fill in its name or browse for it in the Create from File tab of the Object dialog box.

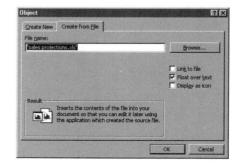

After you click OK, Word and Excel will work together to embed the named book into your document. Figure 14.13 shows this finished embedding.

To edit the chart within the Word document, double-click it. This brings up the entire Excel book, not just the worksheet with the chart on it.

Note in Figure 14.14 that the menu bar and toolbar have changed to those of Excel, even though the title bar clearly indicates that you are in Word and in the original Word document. At this point, within Excel, you can do just about any operation on this book that you can do within Excel. You can add or delete sheets, edit formulas, alter the chart, change the chart type, add Visual Basic "macros," and when finished, you can return to the Word document by clicking the text portion of the Word document. Figure 14.15 shows the Word document saved with the embedded object as well as an Explorer view of that file.

FIGURE 14.13.

An embedded file looks just like a linked one, but it is part of the host document, not just a link within it.

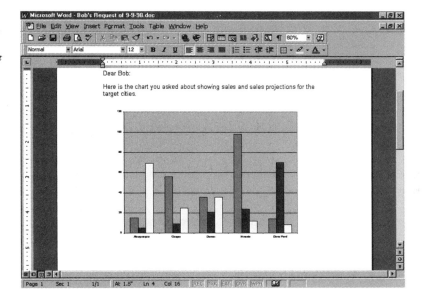

FIGURE 14.14.

Double-clicking an embedded object will allow editing of any part of that object. In this case, you can edit not only the chart and its source worksheet, but also any other sheet within the file.

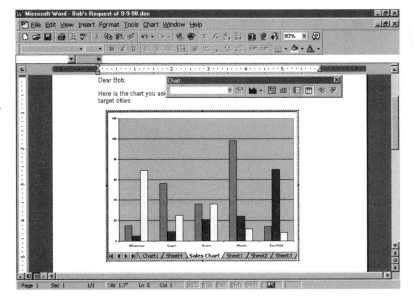

FIGURE 14.15.

Embedding an object (in this case, an Excel file) in a Word document makes the embedded object a part of the host file. This enlarges the host file by a little more than the size of the embedded object, due to some overhead cost.

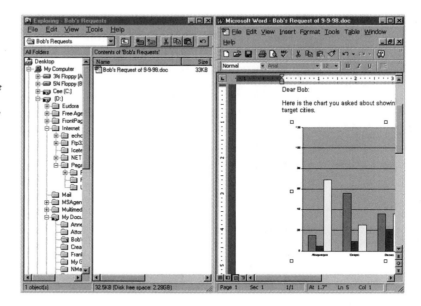

OLE Conversions

You can convert embedded objects to inserted graphics quite easily. There is no way, short of reinserting it, for a graphic to revert to an OLE object, however. To convert an object to a graphic, highlight (click on) the object and then press Ctrl+Shift+F9.

You can also change the type of object and how it's activated. Choose the Convert choice from the Worksheet Object entry in the context menu for the OLE object. As an alternative, you can choose the menu entry Edit | Worksheet Object | Convert. Figure 14.16 shows the context menu way.

Figure 14.17 shows a new Excel Chart object inserted into the memo file and then converted to a graphic. Note the floating toolbar to edit this object is now the Picture toolbar, clearly indicating this object has been altered from an embedded one to a plain graphic.

FIGURE 14.16.

*The Worksheet Object |
Convert menu choice
starts the process of
converting an object.*

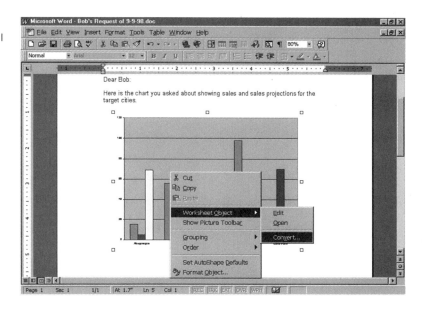

Double-clicking the object in Figure 14.17 brings up the Picture Editor from Word (or
Office, really) rather than Excel. Figure 14.18 shows the graphic editing process.

FIGURE 14.17.

*The plain tip-off as to
what kind of object
you're dealing with is
the type of toolbar the
controller application
brings up when you
activate the object.*

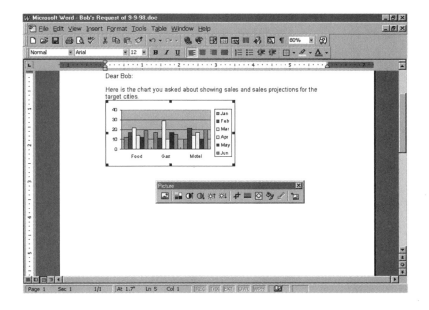

14

**SHARING WITH
OLE AND
ACTIVEX IN NT**

FIGURE 14.18.

Once an object has been converted to a graphic, double-clicking it brings up the server program appropriate to graphics rather than the original server program.

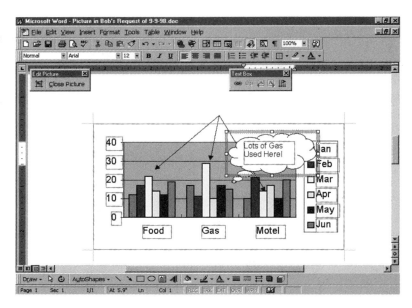

After you're finished editing the graphic, you exit the editing program the same way you exited the other server application, which results in a saving of your edits, as you can see in Figure 14.19.

FIGURE 14.19.

Exiting the graphics editing routine results in changes in your original document.

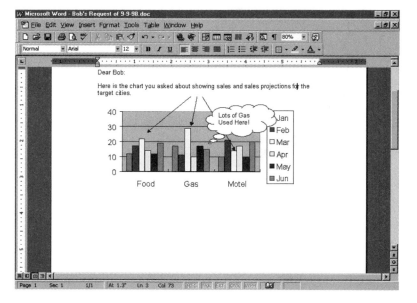

Scraps on Your Desktop

A less well-known capability of OLE is the creation of *scraps*, which are parts of documents you can drag from an application to your Desktop—or anywhere else for that matter. When people first encounter scraps, they often think of them as almost miraculous, but they're just a new document made from part (or all) of an existing one with the OLE link intact.

This example uses Word to make a scrap and puts it on the Desktop. Figure 14.20 shows the Word document with a section highlighted. This section will become the scrap.

FIGURE 14.20.

Highlighting a selection is the start of a Desktop scrap. This example uses Word, but any OLE server application can do the same thing.

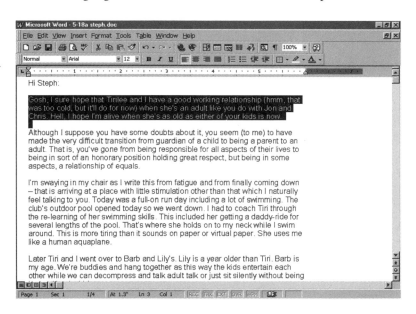

To make the scrap, drag the highlighted section from the document to the Desktop. Figure 14.21 shows the dragging process in progress.

After you release the mouse button, Windows NT Workstation creates the scrap with the label reading the first part of your selection. You can see this in Figure 14.22.

FIGURE 14.21.
Drag the highlighted selection from the document to the Desktop. This copies the selection rather than moving it.

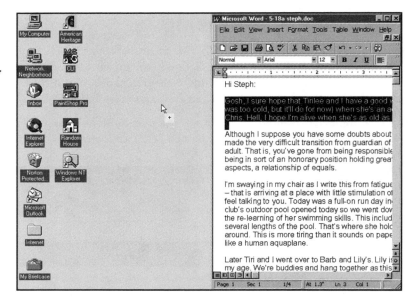

FIGURE 14.22.
Windows NT Workstation identifies the scrap by the first few words of the selection.

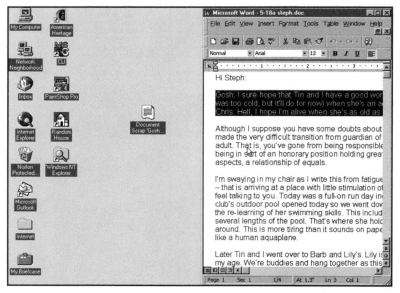

The scrap is really a type of Word document. Double-clicking it will bring up Word and insert the scrap, as you can see in Figure 14.23. Note that the title bar in Figure 14.23 clearly indicates that this is a scrap loaded into Word rather than the entire file.

FIGURE 14.23.

Double-clicking a scrap brings up the server application. The title bar is the giveaway that this is a scrap rather than a regular Word document, although there is no functional difference between the two.

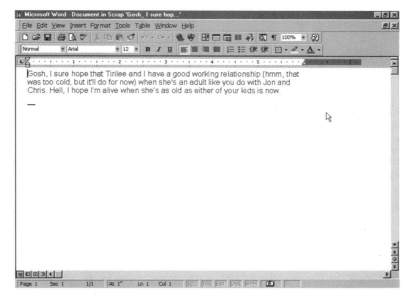

Creating an ActiveX Control

Until very recently, creating anything in OLE or ActiveX was one of the most difficult projects for a Windows programmer. This has recently changed dramatically with a new generation of tools. The current versions of Borland and Microsoft C++ as well as Borland's Delphi and Microsoft's Visual Basic 5 make this a feasible undertaking for regular humans. You still need to have an idea of what you want to do and how to do it, but the grunt work is now a lot less "grunty."

The following example is trivial, but it does show how easily one can create a genuine OLE custom control for use in host programs. This example uses Visual Basic 5 Enterprise Edition, arguably the fastest path from OLE darkness to ActiveX enlightenment.

Launch Visual Basic 5 and choose an ActiveX control as a new project (see Figure 14.24). This tells Visual Basic to line up all the needed ducks for an ActiveX control.

FIGURE 14.24.

The start of an ActiveX control in Visual Basic is telling the program where you want to go today.

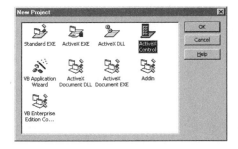

Clicking OK gets you to the workplace where you'll do the actual work constructing your control. Figure 14.25 shows the Visual Basic workspace with a single form having a picture box control added to the single form that's the whole of this project. This control will do nothing except show a picture. Although this is a trivial example, the basics of making a control of any complexity are the same—you just add code.

FIGURE 14.25.

This project's only function will be to show a picture. To create a more complex control, just add your imagination and some code.

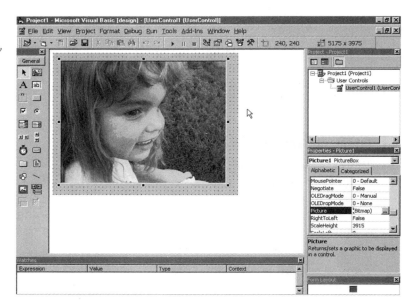

Save the project and tell Visual Basic to convert the project into an ActiveX control from the File menu. Figure 14.26 shows the making of an OCX or ActiveX file from the project.

If this creation of an ActiveX control seemed too easy, it was. The total time was roughly 45 seconds. Naturally, an ActiveX control that does something useful will take a little longer to make.

FIGURE 14.26.

Once you've finished your project, Visual Basic can turn it into an OCX, EXE, DLL, or some other type of file with one menu command.

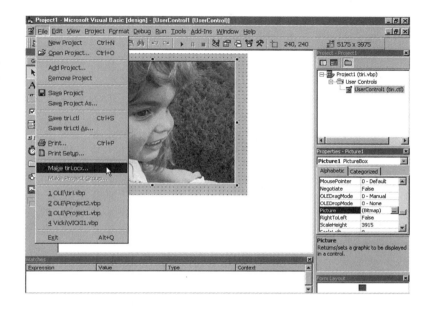

The next step is to see if the ActiveX control works. Microsoft Access will be the test bed for the trial. Figure 14.27 shows Microsoft Access open to a new form created with the idea of inserting the ActiveX control in it.

FIGURE 14.27.

This is the form that will host the ActiveX control made earlier in this chapter. Previous to this, Access registered the control using its Tools \ ActiveX Controls menu command and dialog box.

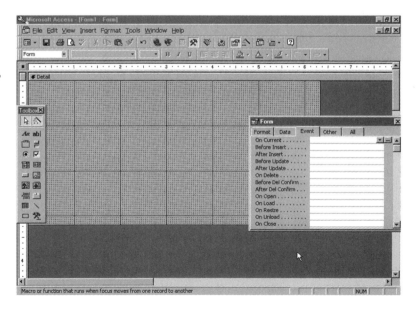

To insert the new ActiveX control, choose the More Controls tool from the toolbox. This brings up a list showing all the registered controls. Figure 14.28 shows the list with the newly made control highlighted.

FIGURE 14.28.

The list of controls available will vary, depending on Registry entries.

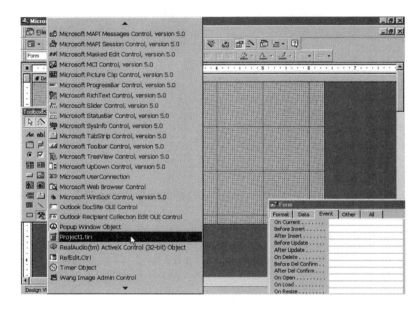

Click the control and then drag a rectangle to contain the control somewhere on the form. You can see the result in Figure 14.29.

FIGURE 14.29.

Tell Access where to insert the control and then let go of the mouse button. The program will insert the ActiveX control into the form.

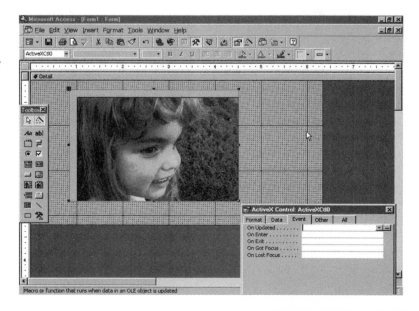

This example was a bit silly, because you could have achieved the same effect by pasting a graphic onto the form. However, the principle is clear. Although this ActiveX control doesn't do much of anything other than display a picture, a little programming (which is beyond the intended scope of this chapter) could make this control into anything you want it to be.

This was a genuine example of making an ActiveX control. It even has assigned its own GUID (Class ID) and a Registry entry of `HKEY_CLASSES_ROOT\CLSID\{52DFA336-D60C-11D0-A788-002018325237}`. Figure 14.30 shows the Registry with this control added.

FIGURE 14.30.

The control is fully registered and working. It has its own GUID. Access inserted this control in the Registry.

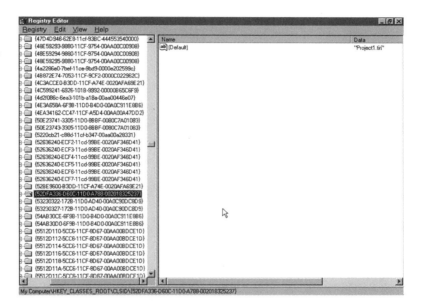

Summary

OLE or ActiveX is primarily an interprocess communications protocol. Using it, you can link or embed documents from server applications into client or controller application documents. A linked document isn't part of the host document, whereas an embedded one is. You can link hot, warm, or cold, or you can break the links entirely. You can also convert an embedded object into a graphic.

Similarly, you can use OLE to create scraps on your Desktop or anywhere else you should choose. Scraps are parts of documents that are still associated with their server processes.

Creating an ActiveX control was once a chore for only the hardiest. Modern tools such as Microsoft's Visual Basic and Borland's Delphi make it just a matter of painting in a form and then adding some code. How difficult it turns out to be depends on how complex the duties are that you want your control to perform.

CHAPTER 15

Exploring the Command-Line Interface

by Paul Cassell

IN THIS CHAPTER

Windows NT Workstation was designed from the outset to have a graphical user interface (GUI). Many people think of it as only having such an interface, but it also has integrated into the Command Line Interface (CLI).

The CLI for Windows NT Workstation is similar to late versions of MS-DOS minus those commands that aren't appropriate. Additionally, Windows NT has many CLI commands exclusive to it and never found in previous Microsoft operating systems.

Although the CLI of Windows NT has less variety than other competing operating systems, such as various shells of UNIX, the most important commands are all there. Also, many of the operations required from the command line in UNIX are possible through the GUI of Windows NT. Even so, some UNIX fans who enjoy playing "stupid" shell tricks find the subset of commands in NT to be restrictive. There are third-party add-ons mimicking some of the common UNIX shells for those people. Also, some releases from Microsoft, such as the Resource Kit, add some interesting utilities. The Resource Kit even has a Rexx interpreter for OS/2 immigrants.

What's In and Out of the CLI

Here's a list of the commands found in later versions of MS-DOS but deleted in Windows NT Workstation, with an explanation and alternative, if known and existing, respectively:

- Assign: Very dangerous in an NT environment.
- Choice: A mysterious deletion. The reason for its deletion is a good topic for debate over Jolt colas.
- CTTY: You must issue commands from the console only.
- Dlbspace: This compression scheme is unrecognized by Windows NT Workstation due to data integrity concerns. Use the file compression routine native to Windows NT in its stead.
- Defrag: Use third-party defraggers such as Disk Keeper or Norton Utilities.
- Dosshell: Windows NT Workstation uses explorer.exe as a shell.
- Drvspace: *See* Dlbspace.
- EMM386: Purposeless, given Windows NT Workstation's architecture.
- Fdisk: Use the Disk Administrator.
- Include: You have one DOS and only one DOS configuration.
- Interlnk/Intersrv: Purposeless with Windows NT Workstation inherently providing a superset of these services. MS-DOS clients can connect to Windows NT using a net start disk or RAS.
- Join: NTFS and DOS capacity to handle larger volumes makes this command obsolete.
- Memmaker and supporting files: Facilities automatically done in NTVDMs.
- Menu[color][default][item]: *See* Include.

■ Mirror: Make and use an ERD.

■ Msav: Use third-party utilities. DOS and similar virus checkers aren't effective under Windows NT.

■ MSBackup: Use the surviving and still unreliable backup and restore if you're masochistic and don't really care about your data anyway. Use NTBackup if you're normal or loss of your data will be troubling.

■ Mscdex: Windows NT Workstation virtualizes the CD-ROM drive, eliminating the need for real-mode drivers it can't use anyway.

■ Msd: Use Windows NT Workstation's diagnostics utility.

■ Numlock: You need to press the key yourself if you don't like the way things have turned out when turned on. Often, this utility exists as part of your firmware's setup.

■ Power: Windows NT Workstation doesn't support this utility. This doesn't mean it's power-less in any large sense. Expect support for this or a similar utility in subsequent versions of Windows NT.

■ Scandisk: NTFS volumes tend to be self-healing. You can use scandisk from Windows 95 or MS-DOS for FAT volumes by booting to DOS. Use third-party utilities.

■ Smartdrv: Windows NT Workstation automatically and dynamically manages the disk cache. A Smartdrv for Windows NT would impinge on this hard-won sovereignty.

■ Submenu: *See Menu.*

■ Sys: Windows NT is too big to Sys from or to a floppy disk.

■ Undelete: Files deleted from the Explorer are generally undeletable. Files deleted from the CLI aren't unless a third-party utility protects your computer.

■ Unformat: Don't format anything you don't want to stay formatted.

■ Vsafe: *See MSAV.*

Starting and Configuring the CLI

To start a CLI session, choose the Start | Command Prompt entry. This brings up a screen similar to Figure 15.1.

FIGURE 15.1.

The CLI should be familiar to anybody having seen MS-DOS, SCO UNIX, OS/2, or similar command-line operating systems.

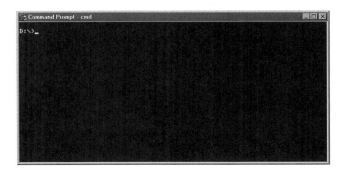

The title bar tells you that you're at the command prompt and the command you executed is cmd. cmd is the command interpreter (shell) for Windows NT. Windows NT Workstation also contains a shell for DOS called, not surprisingly, Command. In most cases, it doesn't make any difference which shell you launch, but keep in mind that some DOS programs can become severely confused if launched under cmd. Also remember that Command is DOS-like, not NT-like.

You can configure the window for your CLI using the same tools as under later DOS versions with some interesting additions. To see a menu for configuring the CLI, click the MS-DOS icon in the upper-left corner of the CLI window or press Alt+spacebar. This will drop down a menu, as shown in Figure 15.2.

FIGURE 15.2.

Configuring the CLI isn't as much fun as a holiday on ice, but you can't fall through and get wet either.

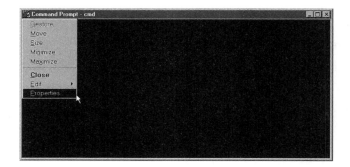

The Move and Size commands on this menu are real head-scratching bafflers. You can move the window by clicking its title bar and dragging it just like any window. You can size it by clicking a border and dragging with the mouse.

The Maximize command will not really maximize the window but rather will only maximize it to its full size as a window. To make the window a real full-screen CLI, press Alt+Enter. This is a toggle. To get back to a window again, press Alt+Enter. This works only on Intel boxes, because Alpha systems lack a full-screen mode.

The real action from this menu comes from the last entry, Properties. Click on that and you'll bring up a tabbed dialog box, as shown in Figure 15.3.

Here are the choices for the first and most useful tab, the Options tab:

- *Cursor Size.* This is how big that flashing thing is, not how large the command prompt appears to be. Choose large and the cursor becomes a block just about as big as a character box. If you change this option, the Properties dialog box will allow you to make the modifications for all instances of this shortcut or only this session.

- *Display Options.* Start in window or full screen? This is whether you need to hammer the session down to a window with Alt+Enter or you need to blow it up with the same key sequence. This option is only for Intel boxes.

■ *Command History.* Windows NT Workstation has the equivalent of DOSKEY built into its command shell for recalling commands. This property controls how many commands it keeps in its buffer and how big that buffer is. The larger the buffer, the less room available for programs, but not by much.

■ *Quick Edit Mode.* Enables use of the mouse to highlight, copy, and paste. If unselected, you need to use the Edit subcommands from the pull-down menu. To use the Quick Edit, highlight the area you want to copy using the mouse and then press Ctrl+C. Ctrl+V pastes at the cursor.

■ *Insert Mode.* The default for the line editor in the shell is overtype. Check this box if you prefer to be in Insert mode. The Insert key (INS) toggles this option in the editor.

FIGURE 15.3.
No shocks here. The Properties entry brings up a tabbed dialog box.

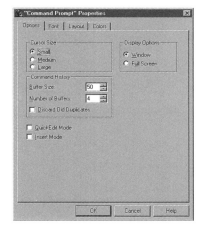

The Font tab allows setting of the font type and size in either this session or all sessions. Figure 15.4 shows the Font tab and the setting of the font for this session to a larger true type rather than the default raster.

The Font tab will change the size and appearance of the prompt and any text displayed in the CLI window.

The command prompts aren't as flexible as the old DOS prompt with ANSI.SYS cocked and loaded, but you can still rock out. As in times of yore, you can alter the prompt by entering the prompt command followed by a parameter. Here are some parameters:

$A	& (Shift+7)
$B	¦ (vertical line used for piping)
$C	(
$D	System date

$E	The Esc character
$F	)
$G	>
$H	Backspace
$L	<
$N	Drive
$P	Path
$Q	=
$S	Space or ASCII 32 (20h)
$T	System time
$V	Windows NT version
$_	CRLF
$$	$
[Any Text]	Any text

So, if you want to create a prompt that says

```
My Computer
Leave Alone
```

and show the time, you would enter

```
Prompt My Computer$_Leave Alone$_$t
```

at the prompt and press Enter or Return. You can see the command and the results in Figure 15.5.

Figure 15.4.

Changing the font size and type for a CLI session or shortcut will affect the size of the window the CLI occupies. Changes in this tab won't affect the full-screen mode (if available) of the CLI.

FIGURE 15.5.

You can get just about as silly with CMD *as you can with ANSI.SYS. To return to the default prompt, enter the command* prompt *with no parameters and then press Enter or Return.*

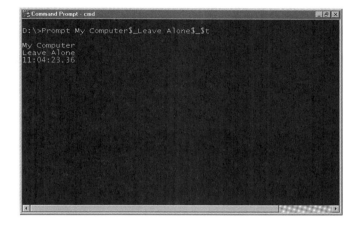

Windows NT has two prompt commands with no analogs in DOS:

$+[more +'s]	Reflects pushed directories in the stack.
$M	Displays the remote name associated with a network drive letter. This is null in a local drive.

The Layout tab lets you configure how wide and how deep (in characters) your screen will be. It also allows you to set a default position for the CLI window. Figure 15.6 shows this tab.

FIGURE 15.6.

The Layout tab allows the setting of screen width, depth, and placement.

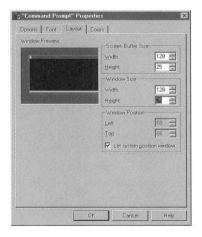

Figure 15.7 shows the results of setting the Screen Buffer and Window Size to 128 characters. Because the Windows NT display is only 80 characters wide, the CLI session responds by placing scrollbars in the window.

FIGURE 15.7.

You can set the Layout of the CLI window to be larger than 80 characters. Doing so has somewhat doubtful utility.

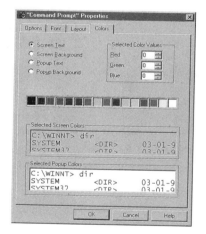

```
Command Prompt - cmd
D:\>dir/w
 Volume in drive D has no label.
 Volume Serial Number is 507F-4BB6

 Directory of D:\

[Eudora]            [Free Agent]        [FrontPage Webs]    [Internet]
[MSAgent]           [Multimedia Files]  [My Documents]      my log.csv
[Sounds]            [TEMP]              [WINDOWS]           [WINNT]
             16 File(s)         288,538 bytes
                             2,461,093,376 bytes free

D:\>
```

The final tab in the Properties dialog box allows you to set the colors of the CLI. This is where newbies tend to set the foreground and background colors to the same color, thereby making the session's commands invisible. You can set colors both for the regular screen and pop-up text. Figure 15.8 shows this tab.

FIGURE 15.8.

The Colors tab not only allows selection of colors but also shows a preview of what you'll get when you click OK.

You can choose from the basic color bar in this dialog box or mix up your own colors using the RGB mixer at the upper-right corner. For some reason, newbies tend to set the colors for the screen text and screen background the same. This makes reading the CLI somewhat problematic.

You can also change the title in the title bar by entering the command title with some following text. Figure 15.9 shows this command in action.

FIGURE 15.9.

The title *command allows you to title your CLI window to a text of your choosing.*

Configuring the Shortcut or Program

The same options and more that are available to you from the CLI menu are available through the Properties tabbed dialog box of the program or shortcut itself. Figure 15.10 shows this dialog box for a shortcut to the Windows NT CLI, CMD.EXE.

FIGURE 15.10.

The Properties tabbed dialog box for a shortcut to the CLI has a superset of the options available from the menu within the CLI.

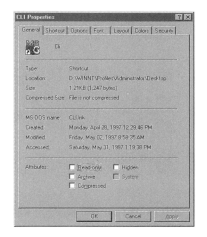

Here are the three major differences between setting options at the shortcut level and the menu level:

- The shortcut options will have effect on all instances of the CLI unless explicitly canceled or countermanded by a menu configuration.
- The shortcut dialog box has options for the shortcut itself, just like other shortcuts.
- The shortcut Properties dialog box contains a Security tab with buttons for Permissions, Auditing, and Ownership.

To get to the Properties tabbed dialog box, right-click the shortcut and choose Properties from the context menu.

15

EXPLORING THE
COMMAND-LINE
INTERFACE

Piping, Redirection, and Conditional Symbols

MS-DOS allows some piping and redirection of input and output. Windows NT takes this a bit further. Adding the following symbols to your commands or batch files can add considerable power and flexibility to them. Here's a list of the command symbols you can use on your command line or in batch files:

- ■ >: Redirection, usually from the console to a device or file. This works the same as DOS. For example, the following line:

  `w.bat > myfile.txt`

  redirects the output of the batch file `w` to a file `myfile.txt` rather than the console.

- ■ >>: Same as > but will append output if the named file exists. This works the same as DOS. For example, the following:

  `v.bat >> myfile.txt`

  will create `myfile.txt` and direct the output into that file. If `myfile.txt` exists, it will append the output of `v.bat` to the file.

- ■ 2>: Redirects only error output. This works the same as DOS. For example, the following:

  `w.bat 2> error.fil`

  will direct any errors stemming from running `w.bat` to the file `error.fil`.

- ■ <: Places input from a source (usually a file) to a command capable of accepting the input. This works the same as DOS. For example, the following:

  `[command] < myfile.txt`

  runs the file `myfile.txt` through the `[command]` program. Thus, to sort a file and dump the output to a new file, you would enter

  `sort < myfile.txt > sorted.txt`

- ■ ¦: Pipes the output of one command to another command. This works the same as DOS. For example, the following:

  `dir ¦ sort`

  will run the output of the `dir` command through the `sort` command.

- ■ ¦¦: Executes the command to the right of the symbol if the command to the left failed. For example, the following:

  `Type myfile ¦¦ echo no type radio`

  echoes `no type radio` if the `Type` command fails (for instance, if it can't find the file).

- ■ 2>>: Same as 2> but will append output if the file exists.

- ■ ^: Interprets the next character as a literal, not a command. This allows you to use command symbols in file names or parameters. For example, the following:

```
Dir ^&file.txt
```

allows the use of the Dir command with the file named &file.txt.

- ■ ; or ,: Separates parameters, feeding them individually to a command. For example,

```
Dir myfile.txt;yourfile.txt
```

will execute Dir against the parameters myfile.txt and yourfile.txt, sequentially.

- ■ (): Groups multiple commands.
- ■ &: The AND of the CLI. Executes a series of commands sequentially from left to right. For example, the following:

```
DIR A:&DIR B:
```

will run DIR twice, once with the A: parameter and once with the B: parameter.

- ■ &&: Executes the command to the right if the command to the left is successful. (The inverse of the ¦¦ symbol.) For example, the following:

```
DIR A:&& DIR B:
```

will run DIR B: only if DIR A: worked.

Figure 15.11 shows the use of the ampersand (&) on a command line. Here, the command line dir *.log & dir *.jpg executed the DIR command first with the parameter *.log and then with the parameter *.jpg. The output is the console display, showing files with both extensions. The command dir *.jpg & *.log will not yield the same output. Instead, it will err on the *.log parameter.

FIGURE 15.11.

The ampersand (&) is the AND *symbol of the CLI.*

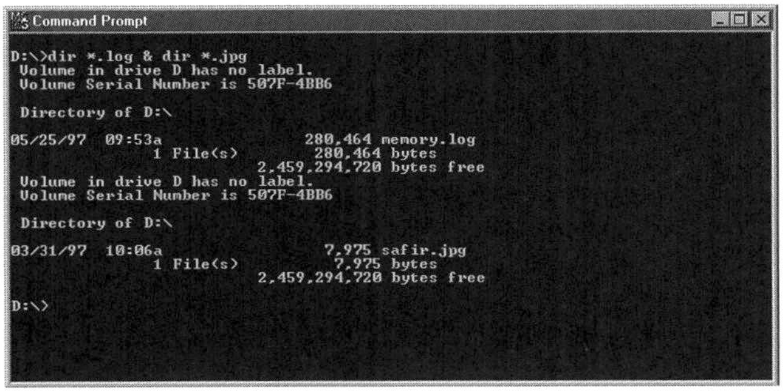

Operating the CLI

If you've spent any time with MS-DOS, including the command-line interface of Windows (that's DOS, too) or with a text-based UNIX system such as SCO UNIX or even Amiga DOS, you should be quite comfortable with the CLI of Windows NT Workstation. The basics of using a CLI are that you enter a command with parameters (sometimes) and then press the Return or Enter key to tell the system to execute (or try to execute) the command. The subtleties of a CLI are enormous, however.

MS-DOS is a bone-simple operating system that's been around in one form or another for over 15 years. Even so, there are people still discovering new twists or tricks with commands, or batch files, or both. This is partly due to newer versions of DOS and DOS successors (such as Windows 95) being slightly different in implementation, giving rise to a lore of DOS-dom similar to the nitpickers of *Star Trek*.

Throw in a more complex command set such as the one found in most UNIX shells (all today) plus a language or two to interact with that shell (such as AWK or Rexx), and you end up with one of those almost infinite fields of study. If you want to delve into these complex but rewarding areas, you can use the native Windows NT shell or buy a shell extending the NT command set. Two such shells are the 4DOS-type shell from J.P. Software and the Korn-like shell from MKS System. The latter especially is a real-time sink, but it's a lot of fun, too.

However, most people have all they can handle with the native Windows NT command set. Oddly enough, Microsoft has, for some reason, documented the command set fairly well.

Getting Information on the CLI

Appendix D, "NT Command Reference," is an expanded reference with examples for the more commonly used commands of the native Windows NT CLI.

The Help command from the Start menu is the main entry to the GUI Help system for Windows NT Workstation. Searching this system on the keyword Command will bring up an alphabetical listing of most of the CLI commands. Though generally okay, this listing isn't perfect, nor is it right all the time. Figure 15.12 is the GUI listing for the diskperf command. Note that the command-line parameters are

```
diskperf [-y¦-n] [\\computername]
```

This isn't entirely right. There is an e parameter, too, for use when the ftdisk service is running.

FIGURE 15.12.

The online help system for the CLI in Windows NT is a good idea and well implemented, but it's incomplete in some areas.

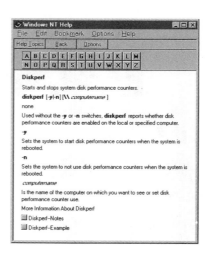

Figure 15.13 shows the command-line Help system for the diskperf command. This gives the proper and complete information for this command. Presumably, Microsoft is updating the Help system at all times so that later versions of Windows NT Workstation might have this and some other Help anomalies sorted out by the time you get your copy. The diskperf Help oddity appeared in a very early commercial version of Windows NT Workstation.

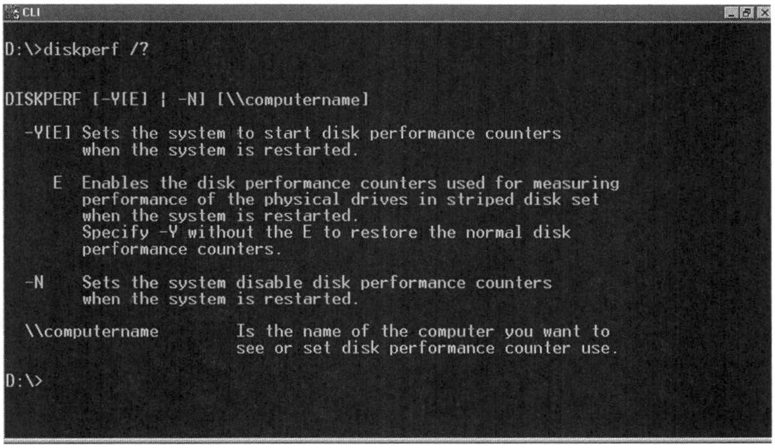

FIGURE 15.13.

The command-line Help for the diskperf *command gives information about the missing parameter— missing from the GUI help system, that is.*

```
D:\>diskperf /?

DISKPERF [-Y[E] | -N] [\\computername]

    -Y[E]  Sets the system to start disk performance counters
           when the system is restarted.

       E   Enables the disk performance counters used for measuring
           performance of the physical drives in striped disk set
           when the system is restarted.
           Specify -Y without the E to restore the normal disk
           performance counters.

    -N     Sets the system disable disk performance counters
           when the system is restarted.

    \\computername      Is the name of the computer you want to
                        see or set disk performance counter use.

D:\>
```

To see the command-line Help text for any listed command, enter

```
[command] / ?
```

and press Return or Enter where *[command]* is any listed command.

Slashes and Dashes

Commands need some way to know what you mean by the entries following them on the command line. For example, consider the following simple Directory (dir) command:

```
dir d
```

This will return a display to the console of any files named d in the current directory. Figure 15.14 shows the outcome of running this command.

Change this command line to

```
dir /d
```

and the results will be the display shown in Figure 15.15.

The difference between the two command lines is a simple slash. This tells the command interpreter (CMD.EXE, in this case) that the following character or characters form a switch rather than a variable.

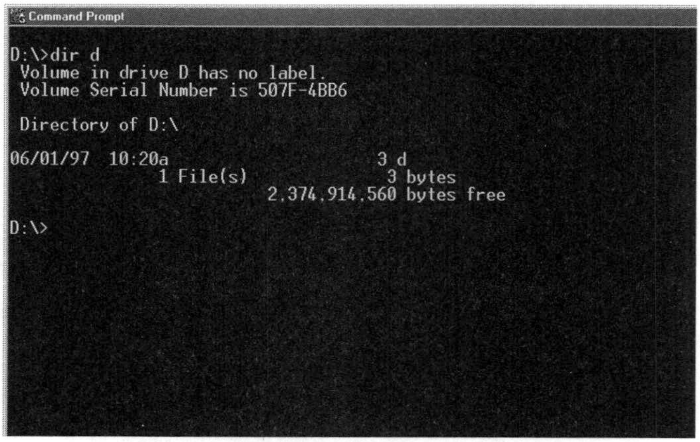

FIGURE 15.14.

Without any symbols, the dir *command takes the* d *in this command line to be a request to display any files named* d.

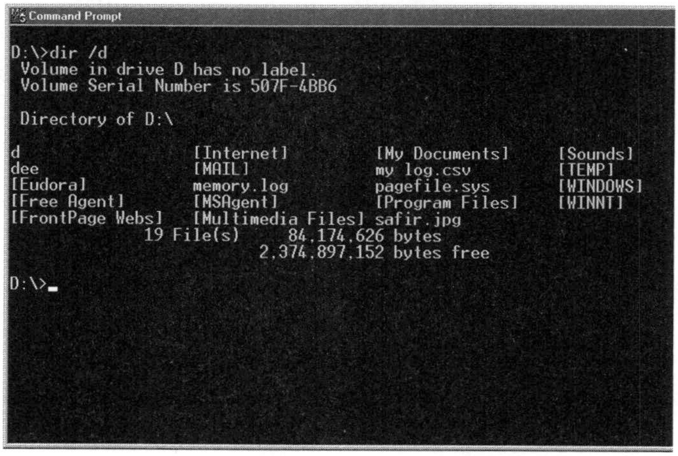

FIGURE 15.15.

Add a slash to the d *and the* dir *command understands that you mean a command-line switch rather than a file specification.*

The vast majority of commands in the CLI take switches. However, different commands require different switch symbols. As a general rule, the DOS-derived commands, such as dir, format, and find, want forward slashes as a switch symbol. The TCP/IP commands need dashes and will often try to interpret the slash as a variable.

For example, if you enter

help ping

on the command line, Windows NT Workstation will respond as shown in Figure 15.16.

FIGURE 15.16.

Seeking help on the ping *command will elicit a suggestion that you try the standard method to get help on an individual command.*

```
D:\>help ping
This command is not supported by the help utility.  Try "ping /?".

D:\>_
```

However, if you enter

ping /?

on the command line, the command will try to ping a computer named /?. Few networks have computers named /?, and that's probably not what you were after anyway.

Figure 15.17 shows the results of entering ping /? on the command line. This screen shows the ping command ended by a Ctrl+C.

FIGURE 15.17.

Giving a slash rather than a dash to ping *confused the utility. Here, it tried mightily to echo a ping off a computer named* /?. *Although it's not apparent in this screen,* ping *spent a lot of time trying to find a computer named* /?.

```
D:\>ping /?
^C
D:\>_
```

The problem is that ping doesn't see the slash as a symbol to interpret the following string as a switch. Instead, it sees the entire string /? as a variable. This is because in the land of ping's origin, UNIX, the slash is a delimiter for directory navigation. A directory structure in UNIX, like other operating systems such as AmigaDOS, looks something like this on the command line:

```
usr2/etc/med
```

On the other hand, Windows NT (or DOS) looks like this:

```
winnt\system32\user1
```

It works or fails to work the other way, too. If you want to see online help for ping, you need to follow its UNIX conventions and enter

```
ping -?
```

on the command line. Figure 15.18 shows the results of entering this command line. If you tried to follow Help's suggestion of using *ping /?* rather than the *ping -?*, then you know how eternal optimists sometimes feel. Note that all *ping* switches require a dash rather than a slash. If you use the slash rather than the dash, *ping* will dash your hopes for success as it slashes your chances for a predictable outcome.

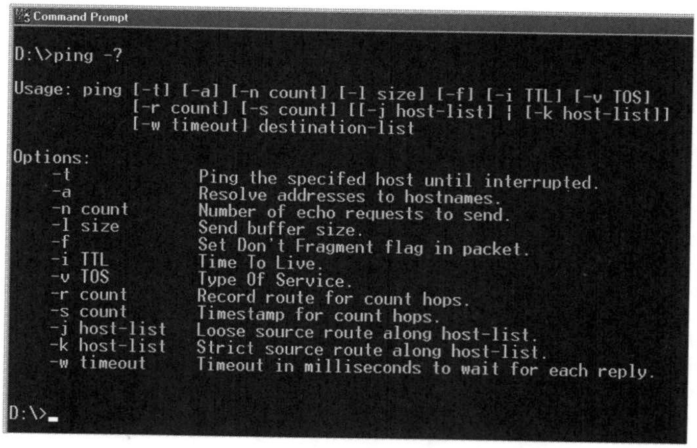

FIGURE 15.18.

ping and the other UNIX-derived commands will joyously give up their secrets if you have been initiated into the knowledge of how to coax them along.

To add to the confusion, the DOS-derived commands won't accept dashes as switches but will, like ping's interpretation of the slash, interpret the dash as a variable. Figure 15.19 shows one example of how dir gets fooled by a dash. There are two files starting with the letter d in the directory shown in Figure 15.19, but none named -d.

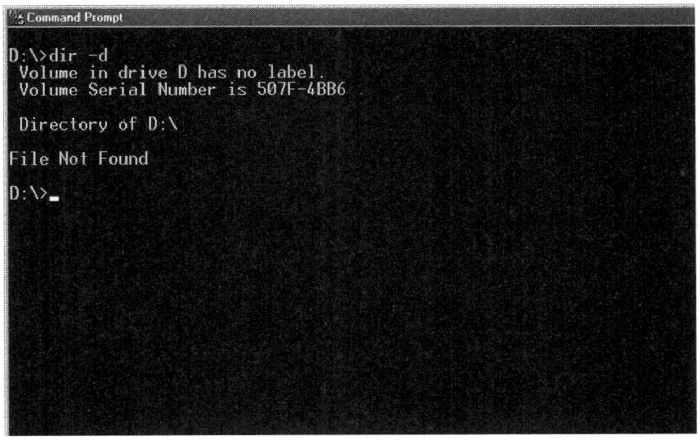

FIGURE 15.19.

dir *seeks a slash to separate the variables from the switches. It won't accept a dash for a slash. In other words, the dash isn't part of* dir*'s knowledge stash. Use it, and your commands will end up as ash while your teeth gnash.*

```
D:\>dir -d
 Volume in drive D has no label.
 Volume Serial Number is 507F-4BB6

 Directory of D:\

File Not Found

D:\>_
```

If there's a rule about when the slash will work or crash or when the dash will prevail or bash, nobody seems to know what it is (or they're not telling). If you've drifted through the UNIX or TCP/IP world, you can pretty well rely on any identically worded action-type command in Windows NT Workstation to need the dash.

Online Help is a real saver here because it always gives the switches correctly within the specific Help for a command.

The Batch Files

A batch file is a text file containing one or more commands that are executed upon the execution of the batch file, itself. For example, the batch file containing the text

```
DIR d
DIR d*
```

will first execute the DIR command with the variable d and then with the variable d*. Batch files do have rudimentary flow control using primarily the FOR and GOTO commands. Virtually any command available on the command line can be run in a batch file. However, the FOR and GOTO commands have no existence outside of these specialized files. Batch files require either the .bat or the .cmd extension for Windows NT Workstation to recognize them as batch files.

Although you can use batch files for any purpose you can think of, under Windows NT Workstation, most people use them for backups.

For example, the file mybackup.cmd containing

```
Ntbackup d:\winnt /a /b
Ntbackup d:\my documents /a
```

will, when executed, first back up the winnt directory along with the local Registry, appending the backup to the existing tape, and then backup the my documents directory and append that, too, to the tape.

Many users combine the AT command with a backup command set in batch files to start unattended backups after hours.

CMD, Command, and Environments

You can launch a CLI by starting either the CMD.EXE or the Command.com applications supplied with Windows NT Workstation. CMD.EXE is a native Windows NT application just like any other Windows NT applet. Running Command.com will launch an NTVDM (Windows NT Virtual Device Machine).

CMD.EXE will allow you to run native DOS programs under it, but when you do so, you "convert" it from a native NT application to an NTVDM.

There are two files, Autoexec.nt and Config.nt, that will let you automatically configure the CLI or DOS programs upon their launch. These files act just like the autoexec.bat and config.sys files from DOS and Windows days, except for the limitations and extensions of running them under Windows NT.

Optimizing DOS

The simplest way to optimize a DOS program for use in Windows NT Workstation is to use the Properties dialog box. If you're a masochist or just hate to let go of any once-useful knowledge set, you can also create those crazy old .pif files from Windows and Windows 95 heritage. Windows NT doesn't care.

Don't overlook the wealth of options Windows NT gives you when running these older-style programs. Most problems with business-oriented DOS programs under Windows NT stem from people not configuring them right (or even not knowing that they can be configured). Figure 15.20 shows the tabbed (surprise!) dialog box for a DOS program.

FIGURE 15.20.

The tabbed Properties dialog box for DOS programs under Windows NT has a blizzard of useful options. Somewhere in there exists the combination to make just about anything run well.

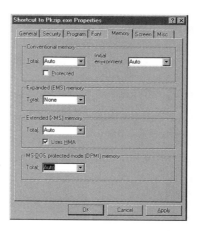

The Properties area of the program PKZIP 2.04g, shown in Figure 15.20, has had the XMS option altered from None to Auto. As you can see from the figure, the memory options for a DOS program are many and varied. They include the normally problematical DPMI type of memory.

Windows NT is pretty good about accommodating the often bizarre needs of DOS programs, but it can't do it all automatically. Properties is the place to show that you're smarter than NT.

One greatly overlooked place to configure a DOS program is the Windows NT button on the Program tab. This will allow you to specify two configuration files for this program. These files take the place of the DOS config.sys and autoexec.bat. By default, Windows NT will configure the NTVDM using `[%systemroot%]\system32\config.nt` and `[%systemroot%]\system32\Autoexec.nt`. Click the Windows NT button to change this default. You can specify different configuration files for every DOS program on your system. Figure 15.21 shows the dialog box revealed when you click the Windows NT button on the Program tab of the Properties dialog box for an NTVDM. Within the world of Windows NT, you have the freedom to make your NTVDMs any way you want them. How you use that freedom depends on you.

FIGURE 15.21.

You can specify as many NTVDM configuration programs as you want.

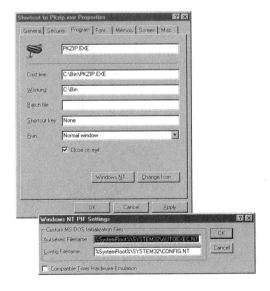

If you experience trouble with a DOS program under Windows NT and can't get the configuration right, try the following:

■ Under the Screen tab, try running in a full screen rather than a window.

■ Under the Screen tab, uncheck the Fast ROM emulation and the Dynamic memory allocation options.

- Check your documentation to see whether your program requires DPMI or XMS memory. If so, locate and select the appropriate settings under the Memory tab.

- Under the Memory tab, specify the amount of memory to assign to the program rather than leaving this to the Auto daemon-like routine.

- Under the Misc tab, deselect the Always Suspend and Screen Saver options one at a time.

- Under Misc, try selecting the Mouse | Exclusive mode option.

- Study the documentation for your program and configure files to replace the recommended config.sys and autoexec.bat files; then use the Windows NT button on the Program tab to point at those files.

- If all else fails, run the program in a DOS boot session.

Summary

The Command Line Interface (CLI) for Windows NT Workstation is both a subset and a superset of the CLI for previous versions of Windows and for MS-DOS itself. To start a CLI session, run CMD.EXE, Command.com, or a shortcut to either from the GUI.

Although the variety of shell commands native to Windows NT isn't as rich as those found in most UNIX shells, it is richer than previous operating systems from Microsoft. You can increase the CLI environment by using third-party add-ons from vendors such as J.P. Software or MKS. With or without those add-ons, you can pipe, redirect, and use some conditional symbols on the command line.

Be careful to use the right switch symbol for each command you choose. Commands derived from UNIX TCP/IP action commands generally use the dash, whereas others insist on the slash. Commands will do what you say, not what you mean.

CMD.EXE is a native Windows NT applet, whereas the DOS work-alike command.com runs always as an NTVDM. You can optimize the way DOS or OS/2 programs work under Windows NT by making a .pif file for them or by exercising options under their Properties dialog box. Each program can have its own configuration programs. Windows NT will, by default, use Autoexec.nt and Config.nt for CLI configuration files.

CHAPTER 16

Printing with Windows NT

by Paul Cassel and Thomas Lee

IN THIS CHAPTER

Installing and configuring printers in Windows NT follow other Windows versions closely. However, the underlying principles of printing vary significantly due to NT's architecture. If all you want to do is configure a printer and know how to do so under Windows, all you need to do is get the right driver and install. If you want to understand the way Windows NT handles printers, this chapter provides a short introduction.

Printers

Printing in Windows NT has always been a mixture of good news and bad news. The bad news is that the internal architecture is rather complex, but the good news is that printing works. Almost all the problems you'll find in printing are simple to fix. For example, the hardware isn't plugged in, connected, or turned on, or you have the wrong drivers. Remember that Windows NT needs its own drivers for printers. Previous drivers for other operating systems such as Windows 95 or even previous versions of Windows NT usually don't work or don't work well.

Printing Basics

You need to understand the basics of printing on NT and the following NT-specific definitions:

- The *printer device* is the output hardware. It might be a physical printer or a virtual printer such as a fax adapter.

- The *printer* is the software interface between the application and the printing device. That is, the application prints to a printer, and NT handles the transition to the printing device.

- The *printer spooler* is the list of jobs waiting to print at a printer. The actual list of jobs is the print queue. The spooler is a service that can be stopped or started like any service. Technically, it is a set of dynamic link libraries (DLLs) that receives, schedules, and distributes the printing chores.

- The *print monitor* is the software component that routes the final output from the printer to the printing device.

- The *print server* is the NT system on which the printer is defined and on which the print monitor runs.

- The *port* is the place where the print monitor sends the output. Usually, it is your system's parallel or serial port. However, it can also be a network port—for example, an HP printer with a Jet Direct card.

These definitions might be different from other systems you've used, such as UNIX, but they are the definitions used with NT, so you would be well served to learn them. Also, the way a print job moves from an application to an output device is NT's own and differs in at least a few details from other systems.

The following is an overview of how a job moves from an application to a printer:

1. The user of an application (such as Word or WordPerfect) chooses the print option for a document.
2. The application processes the document for printing and passes it on to the spooler. The spooler stores the print job to disk.
3. The local print provider analyzes the print job, altering as necessary for proper printing.
4. The provider passes control to the page processor, which can add a cover page to the job.
5. The disk feeds the job to the print monitor.
6. The hardware device receives the job for physical output.

Creating a Printer for Windows NT

Before your application can do any printing, you first have to define a printer on your system, either by creating a printer on your machine or connecting to a printer somewhere on your network. After you create or connect to the printer, your applications can then use the printer, although you might want to modify the printer's configuration.

The Printers folder in Windows NT Workstation is the place where all printing-related configuration and management are carried out. You can access the Printers folder in one of the following three ways:

- Opening the My Computer folder
- Choosing Start | Settings | Printers
- Selecting the Printers applet from the Control Panel

The Printers folder is the same, no matter which method you choose to invoke it. The Printers folder on my system is shown in Figure 16.1.

Figure 16.1.

The Printers folder is the starting place to define (install and set up) a new printer or modify the settings of an existing printer.

To set up a new printer on your system or connect to a printer on the network, you should use the Add Printer Wizard. Using the wizard is a quick, easy, and almost foolproof way to define the printer. To start this wizard, double-click the Add Printer applet in the Printers group, shown in Figure 16.1.

Only a member of the Administrators local group can create a new local printer. The process of setting up a new local printer is illustrated in Figures 16.2 through 16.11 and involves the following steps:

1. Specify whether the printing device is managed locally or is connected via the network, as shown in Figure 16.2.

FIGURE 16.2.

Telling the wizard whether the new printer will be a local one or one you will access through a network.

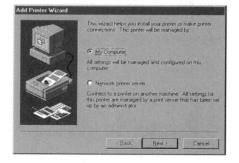

2. Specify the port to which the printing device is connected. For a local printer, it is usually either a serial or parallel port, as illustrated in Figure 16.3. The last option in the Port column, File, allows you to send the image of a print job to disk.

FIGURE 16.3.

In this wizard dialog box, you can specify the printer port and whether the printer will use the spooler.

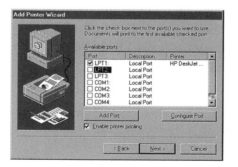

3. Choose the manufacturer and model of the printing device, as shown in Figure 16.4. In many cases, your printer isn't listed as part of the supplied drivers, or you have an updated driver. In these cases, you should have a driver CD-ROM or disk. Choose the Have Disk button and point Windows NT to that location.

Figure 16.4.
*You need to tell the
wizard what type of
printer you want to
install.*

4. Give the new printer a (local) name and specify whether it is the default printer for
Windows applications running on this system, as shown in Figure 16.5. Most of the
time, you can use the supplied name, but you can let your imagination run wild if you
prefer such whimsy as part of your computing experience.

Figure 16.5.
*You need to name your
printer to uniquely
identify it.*

5. You next specify whether the printer is shared across the network and which printer
drivers are loaded onto your system, as shown in Figure 16.6. If the printer is shared,
you can also give it a share name used by others when they connect to this printer.

Figure 16.6.
*You can specify whether
a printer is shared,
what operating systems
you anticipate will
access it, and its shared
name in this dialog
box.*

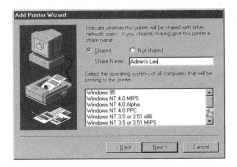

6. Finally, you get the opportunity to print a test page, as illustrated in Figure 16.7. You should always perform this useful test. If Windows NT can't find the printer driver on the hard disk, it asks for the distribution CD or the disk with the drivers, as shown in Figure 16.8.

FIGURE 16.7.

Windows NT's Add Printer Wizard gives you a chance to try a test page. Testing is always a good idea and worth the cost of some toner and paper.

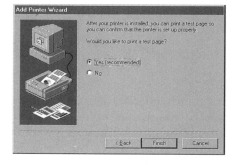

FIGURE 16.8.

If Windows NT can't find the needed drivers on the hard disk, it asks you for their location.

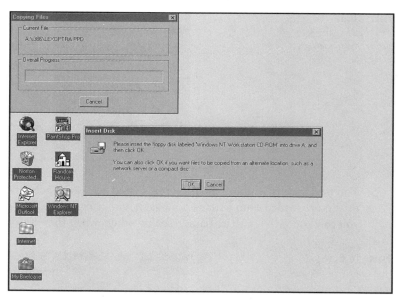

7. After Windows NT prints the test page as far as it can tell, it opens a confirmation dialog box, as shown in Figure 16.9, in which you can confirm that the page has printed successfully.

FIGURE 16.9.

After Windows NT prints a test page, it asks you whether the page looks all right. If you click the Yes button, the wizard closes normally.

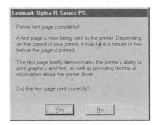

8. If you're unhappy with the print job, you can click the No button. Doing so brings up a Help service called the Printer Troubleshooter, as shown in Figure 16.10. It offers not only a few helpful suggestions to fix your printing problems, but it also offers hot links to other help topics. The last entry in this figure, No, hot-jumps you to another Help topic with more troubleshooting suggestions.

The Printer Troubleshooter walks you through the various parts of installing and setting up a printer to make sure all is right. In the end, if nothing works, the Printer Troubleshooter suggests you just start over. Sometimes this approach works because a file might have been copied wrong. If the Troubleshooter runs out of ideas, it'll suggest you do the entire installation over, as shown in Figure 16.11. This works a surprising percentage of times.

FIGURE 16.10.

The Printer Trouble-shooter is part of Windows NT's Help system.

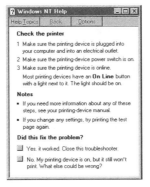

You can access the Printer Troubleshooter by choosing the "troubleshooting" entry under Printers in the standard Help system. The entry point is a little different than from the Printer Setup Wizard, but the effect is the same.

Besides choosing the wrong drivers, printer errors are mundane: the printer isn't turned on; the parallel or serial cable is not connected; the printer is out of paper; and so on. For the most part, troubleshooting these problems is very simple.

FIGURE 16.11.

The final step of the Printer Troubleshooter is a "do over" suggestion. If you had clicked the No button at the bottom of the screen, Help would have admitted that your problems were beyond its ken.

> **TIP**
>
> If you are responsible for Windows NT Workstation support and users phone you with printer problems, tell them to try the Printer Troubleshooter first and call you back only if it fails to resolve the problem. Most printing problems can be resolved by using the Troubleshooter, but of course, your mileage in this situation may vary.

Network Printing

Setting up network printing is almost as easy as setting up local printing. If you're going to share your printer on the network, the previous instructions are all you need. If you want to connect to an existing printer on the network, you also use the New Printer Wizard. If you want to connect to a new printer on the network, you must define this printer first, using the steps outlined previously. This process, illustrated in Figures 16.12 through 16.15, includes the following steps:

1. Start the Add Printer Wizard from the Printers folder. Select Network printer server, as shown in Figure 16.12.

FIGURE 16.12.

Adding a printer from the network starts by telling the wizard this is your intent.

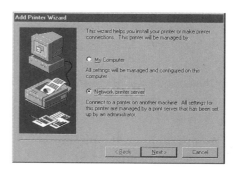

2. Locate the machine and the printer you want to add to your printer options. You can see this step in Figure 16.13.

FIGURE 16.13.

Locate the printer and the machine to which it's locally connected by using the familiar network browser utility.

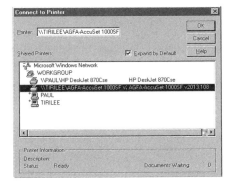

3. Choose whether the new printer should be the default printer for Windows applications, as shown in Figure 16.14.

FIGURE 16.14.

The network version of the Add Printer Wizard gives you the default option, just as the local Add Printer Wizard does.

After you complete these steps, you get a final confirmation dialog box, as shown in Figure 16.15.

FIGURE 16.15.

The network setup version of the Add Printer Wizard is much shorter than the local setup version.

The network printer setup is much simpler than the local printer setup routine because the only task you're performing is attaching to a printer. All the tough work, such as making sure the printer works and the drivers are correct, has been done during local setup at the server.

Networked Printer Drivers

Setting up any printer is quick and easy, although you need to get the drivers somehow. These drivers are typically on your Windows NT Workstation 4 CD-ROM. Alternatively, you might get them on a disk with new printers, or you can download them from the Internet, especially from the manufacturer's Web or FTP site.

When you create a local printer, Windows NT loads the printer drivers for local printing. For network printing, NT gets clever; when you connect to a network printer, Windows NT simply downloads the printer driver for you from the machine on which the printer was initially created. That's it!

NT achieves this by sharing the %SYSTEMROOT%\System32\Spool\Drivers folder as PRINT$. When a remote system wants to get print drivers from your system, it merely connects to \\*YOURSYSTEM*\PRINT$ (where *YOURSYSTEM* is the NetBIOS machine name, defined in the Network applet). Directly below, Windows NT creates one extra folder for each hardware platform for which drivers are held.

The only real issue to resolve is which printer drivers you should have located locally. A printer driver is a specialized form of an executable program, typically a DLL, designed to run on a particular version of Windows and hardware. If you define a printer for use by other users on the network, you need to hold all the printer drivers for all the various combinations of systems that are likely to access it. If Windows NT fails to find the correct drivers on the remote machine, it simply prompts for a location to find them, and when fed the appropriate disk, CD-ROM, or network share point, it can then load the drivers for this alternative location.

With NT Workstation 4, you can automatically load printer drivers for other NT systems as well as for Windows 95, as illustrated in Figure 16.6.

If you access the printer via Windows for Workgroups, Windows 3.*x*, or DOS, you have to load the printer manually on each of the client systems. Also, if you connect from your system to a printer defined on a non-Windows NT system (for example, Windows 95), you also must load printer drivers manually.

Printer Ports

Most printing is done via a system's parallel or serial port, and these ports are usually specified for local printing, as shown in Figure 16.3. Windows NT also supports other ports, including the Digital Network port, HP Network port, Lexmark DLC Printer port, Lexmark TCP/IP port, and the LPD port (for printing to UNIX printers).

These ports enable you to directly connect a printer to the network for your Windows NT system to print directly to the printer. This setup requires a different print monitor, which is loaded automatically when you define the appropriate network. To print to a UNIX printer, you must load the TCP/IP printing services.

Printing from DOS Applications

If you're using DOS applications, printing becomes slightly more difficult. Each DOS application requires its own printer driver. One of the greatest advancements Windows brought was the idea of defining one printer for all applications. DOS printer drivers are always application-specific. They must be obtained from the application manufacturer in almost all cases. In some rare instances, user groups maintain and create drivers for the programs that define their existence. However, finding drivers for current production printers can be impossible for older programs. Most vendors in the DOS business are either long gone or have stopped supporting their DOS applications as they have moved all their resources to their new Windows programs.

DOS applications also have a weak—if any—concept of sharing. They tend to "sit on" a configured LPT or COM port and dump their output, which is not much help when the printer is remote. To enable DOS applications to print successfully, you need to use the NET command from the CLI on the client system. Go to the command line and use the following syntax:

```
NET USE LPT2: \\server\remoteprinter
```

LPT2 is the port your DOS application uses, and *server* is the machine on which the printer shared as *remoteprinter* is located.

After you use this command, you must tell your DOS application to use the port (LPT2:) you just set up by the USE command. Printing across the network should now work.

You can view the printers you're currently using by typing net use at the command line. Figure 16.16 shows this command used without parameters to show network connections.

Managing and Reconfiguring Printers

After you define the printer, you might want to update the printer properties or manage the printing process. You can carry out both of these operations from the Printers folder.

To modify a printer's parameters, you either select the printer and choose File | Properties, or you right-click the printer and choose Properties from the context menu. You then see a dialog box that is specific to the printer being managed so that you can review and amend the printer's properties. The Properties dialog box for my installed DeskJet 870Cse printer is shown in Figure 16.17.

FIGURE 16.16.

The CLI net *command with the* use *suffix displays all current network connections.*

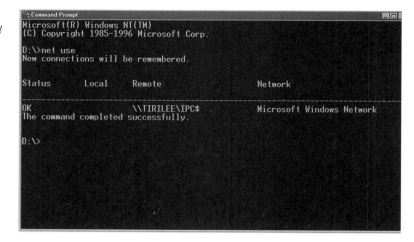

FIGURE 16.17.

Choosing Properties from the context menu brings up a dialog box with a combination of the usual tabs, such as Security, as well as specialized tabs such as Ports and Scheduling.

Advanced Configuration Options

Windows NT Workstation has a number of additional advanced printing features you might want to use. These features, which are set from the printer's Properties dialog box, are as follow:

- *Separator Page:* Whenever Windows NT sends a job to be printed, you can print an optional separator, or cover page, at the head of the print job.

- *Scheduling:* Because a printer (from a software point of view) is the interface between the system and the printing device, you can make a printer available only during certain times of the day. Also, you can actually define two printers to print to a single print device and give one printer a higher priority. You do so by using the printer's Scheduling tab, as shown in Figure 16.18.

FIGURE 16.18.

*On the Scheduling tab,
you can restrict the time
a printer is available
for use and its priority
level.*

- *Printer pools:* A printer pool is the place where you have multiple printing devices attached to a single printer. It is ideal for situations in which a single printing device is unable to print all the documents sent to the related printer, which could happen in a word processing department, for example.

- *Printer device settings:* The printer drivers enable you to configure a wide range of printing features. The Device Settings tab enables you to configure features of your specific printer.

Printer separator pages are useful for highly used printers shared by many users where jobs might pile up in the output tray, although the feature is rather wasteful of paper and toner. The three separator pages loaded by default are PCL.SEP, PSCRIPT.SEP, and SYSPRINT.SEP. PCL.SEP is used for HP LaserJet Printers and switches the printer into PCL mode. PSCRIPT.SEP switches the printer into PostScript mode but does not actually print a separator page. SYSPRINT.SEP simply prints a page before each document. If you have an HP printer, use PCL.SEP.

Printer pools are easy to set up. About the only drawback is that they must either be the same actual model or be able to emulate the same model.

Security

In Chapter 10, "Fine-Tuning NT Security," you learned about the general security model for NT. In summary, all NT resources are owned, and the owner of the resource can enable other people to use that resource at his or her discretion. Additionally, any resource can be audited so that the use of the resource is logged to NT's Event Log. Printers are just another resource, like directories and files, that you can secure. All security settings are configured from the printer's Security menu, part of the printer's properties, as shown in Figure 16.19.

FIGURE 16.19.

The Security tab of the Properties dialog box contains the familiar three buttons.

The first security issue to address is who can create a printer. Only members of the Administrators or Power Users groups can create a local printer unless you define another group with this permission. Any user has the right to connect to a remote printer, subject to the printer's access controls.

The person who created a printer owns it. The owner has full control of the printer and can set the rights for every other user, from full rights to denying access.

A user who has sufficient privileges can take printer ownership, as in files and directories. This person is typically a member of Administrators. Any user with the full control permission on that printer can likewise change ownership.

The owner of a printer can give any other group or user defined on the system access to the group by using the printer's Owner dialog box, shown in Figure 16.20.

FIGURE 16.20.

The Ownership button of the Security tab reveals a dialog box familiar to those used to Windows NT security.

You can give four different permissions to a printer: Full Control, Manage Documents, Print, and No Access. When applied to a group or user, these permissions define what the user can or cannot do with the printer. Table 16.1 summarizes the printer permissions.

Table 16.1. Printer permissions.

Permission	Full Control	Manage Documents	Print	No Access
Change document settings	X	X		
Change printer permissions	X			
Change printer properties	X			
Change printer settings	X			
Delete printer	X			
Pause/resume, restart, delete documents	X	X		
Pause/resume printer	X			
Print documents	X		X	
Purge printer	X			
Take ownership of a printer	X			

As you can see from the table, although you can print to a printer, you can't do much else unless you have the Full Control permission.

Printer Auditing

As with any other secure object, Windows NT allows you to audit a printer, which means you can tell who did what to the printer and when. You set up printer auditing by clicking the Auditing button on the Security tab. The Printer Auditing dialog box then appears, as shown in Figure 16.21.

With auditing, you first have to decide who to audit and then what to audit. You can audit any or all users or groups defined on your system by choosing the Add button. You can also remove users or groups by using the Remove button.

After you decide who to audit, you have to decide which events to audit. When Windows NT audits a printer, it is, in effect, recording the use of the rights summarized in Table 16.1.

FIGURE 16.21.

*The Auditing button
on the Security tab
allows you to log printer
events to the Event Log.*

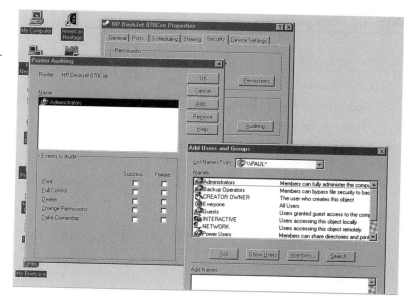

Summary

You can easily set up printing and get working. Properly securing the printer takes a bit more
work, but all the permissions are consistent with NT's overall security model.

Windows NT Fonts

by Paul Cassel

IN THIS CHAPTER

The Macintosh wasn't the first personal-type computer capable of doing page layout chores, but it popularized the notion of Everyman as a typographer. For many years, Windows and DOS were poor also-rans in the personal typesetting race.

In recent years, however, the tools once exclusive to the Macintosh for performing the common document layout chores have either moved to Windows or have their equivalents in native Windows programs. Windows NT, with its capability of harnessing powerful computer systems, is a natural for doing layout-type work on a PC. Even people who aren't interested in true layout work want their documents to look good. A familiarity with how Windows NT handles fonts is part of the knowledge set most people need to accomplish this or the more ambitious goal of actual typesetting.

What's a Font?

A font is a single typeface. A typeface is a family of characters, numbers, letters, punctuation marks, and so forth that share certain characteristics such as width of stroke, presence of a serif, and general shape. The word "font" usually means a family of characters apart from certain attributes, such as bold or italics. Figure 17.1 shows a few fonts or typefaces in Microsoft Word.

FIGURE 17.1.

Different fonts have different looks. Most computer systems have a choice of over 20 fonts.

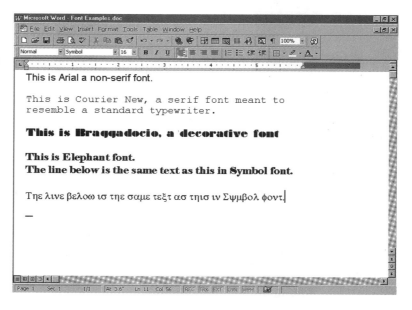

Although too many fonts can impede performance and eat disk space, many people have as many as 100 fonts available to them.

A font family is a group of similar typefaces. Windows NT recognizes the following five font families:

- Decorative
- Modern
- Swiss
- Roman
- Script

A font in Windows NT Workstation has the following three possible appearances:

- *Font style:* Examples are italic or bold.
- *Font size:* The point size of a font.
- *Font effects:* Effects include underlining.

Figure 17.2 shows these appearance characteristics.

17

WINDOWS NT FONTS

FIGURE 17.2.

A font's appearance depends on its style, size, and effects.

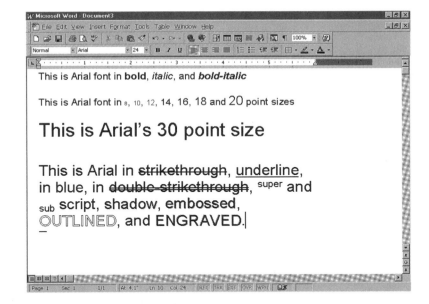

You can mix appearance attributes with fonts. For example, nothing prevents you from combining bold with strikethrough if you have a need for that type of display.

Windows NT uses the following additional terms to describe the final appearance of a typeface:

■ *Weight:* Indicates how heavy the stroke is. The weight goes from light to extra bold.

■ *Serif or non-serif:* Indicates whether the characters have a "tail" or projections that lead the eye from one character to another. Courier is a serif font and is generally easy to read. Arial is a non-serif or sans serif font. This type of font appears to most people as classier or neater in page layout schemes.

■ *Pitch:* Indicates how much horizontal space is taken up by a character. This metric applies to fixed-pitch fonts such as Courier.

■ *Spacing:* Indicates whether the characters all take up the same horizontal room per font size or whether they're proportional based on the layout of the face. Figure 17.3 shows a fixed and proportional font.

FIGURE 17.3.

The serif in Courier New extends naturally thinner letters such as I to be as wide as letters such as R. In Arial, the fonts take up space proportional to their spacing needs.

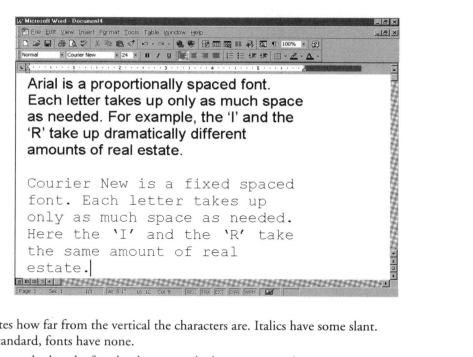

■ *Slant:* Indicates how far from the vertical the characters are. Italics have some slant. Roman, or standard, fonts have none.

■ *Width:* Indicates whether the font has been stretched or compressed.

■ *X-height:* Indicates the height of half-line characters such as *e* and of the lower part of lowercase characters such as *h*.

Printer Fonts and Screen Fonts

In a perfect world, a font would just be a font, but this isn't yet a perfect world. Therefore, you can choose from two broad categories of fonts: printer and screen.

Printer fonts are created in the printer. Often, you can install these fonts into your Windows NT Workstation system using distribution disks from the printer manufacturer. These fonts come in the following three flavors:

- *Downloadable soft fonts* usually reside on your hard disk and are installed with your printer. This way, Windows NT Workstation can display fonts specific to the printer.
- *Device fonts* are built into the hardware (firmware, really) of the printer.
- *Printable screen fonts* are fonts that Windows NT uses for screen displays, and they can also be interpreted by the printer to look the same.

Screen fonts are fonts Windows NT uses to display information on the screen or monitor. They don't necessarily have to be the same (although they might be named the same) as the fonts your printer can produce.

The symbol for each font is its *glyph*. Glyphs are either raster or vector. Two types of vector glyphs are of special interest to Windows NT users.

- *Raster fonts* are bitmaps. Each pixel or screen dot is stored in memory for display or printing. Bitmaps resist scaling and rotation. Figure 17.4 shows a bitmap of three letters.

FIGURE 17.4.

Bitmaps don't scale or rotate well. Here you can see the jagged look (jaggies) caused by scaling the small ABC to a larger size and then rotating it.

■ *Vector* or *outline fonts* are objects described by mathematical expressions. The computer doesn't remember each dot's or each pixel's placement, but it obeys a command like "draw a line from point A to point B of 1 point thickness," where the points are previously agreed-upon coordinates. Figure 17.5 shows an example of a vector font. This image is of lesser quality than it would be if printed, because of technical limitations in the production of images and the reproductive process used in book publishing.

FIGURE 17.5.

Vector fonts scale and rotate well because in doing so the computer need only change the mathematical expression.

■ *TrueType fonts* are outline fonts with hinting. *Hinting* is information designed to skew the fonts, thus making them look better scaled and rotated than without the intelligent skewing. In the section "TrueType Technology," you learn more details about this important topic.

■ *Adobe Type 1 PostScript fonts* are hinted outline font types. Windows NT can handle this type of font. Originally, Adobe Type 1 PostScript fonts were the only quality font type, but a licensing dispute between Adobe and the rest of the world led to the need for TrueType fonts, which now technically equal Type 1 fonts. However, the true quality of the font depends on the font vendor. TrueType fonts vary more in quality than genuine Adobe-vended Type 1 fonts.

Generally speaking, raster fonts are developed for one size and orientation. They are also generally used for one device, printer, or screen. Windows NT can scale raster fonts, but they don't look very good if scaled too far from their intended size. Similarly, you can rotate these fonts, but they appear ugly in most unintended orientations.

If your printer has a close match to a raster font, you can print it satisfactorily. The key here is "close match," a rather nebulous term and one utterly unsatisfactory for exacting work. To resolve the problem of making a printed sheet look just like the Print Preview screen, some applications convert the entire document to a huge bitmap and then send it down the wire to the printer. This process ensures that the Preview and the actual printed image match exactly, but it increases rendering and printing time.

Vector fonts installed in Windows NT reside in a series of GDI calls. Although accurate and easily scaleable, they take a long time to generate because the computer must process strokes.

TrueType Technology

TrueType is a special type of font technology. Rather than the font shape being stored as a bitmap as with raster fonts, or being generated by calls like vector fonts, TrueType fonts are stored as glyph primitives or glyph shapes. That is, they are a series of points and scaling hints. When an application requests a font, Windows NT responds by supplying the hinted shape at the requested size.

The first call for a particular TrueType font causes Windows NT Workstation to generate that font (from its outline and hints) to a bitmap. That bitmap gets placed in a cache for later use. This process works similarly to a disk cache. As long as the cache space isn't exceeded, subsequent requests for the font come from the cache and therefore require much less processing than the first call. This caching capability makes TrueType font use quite efficient.

Windows NT Workstation uses TrueType fonts both for screen display and printer output. The fonts used for both are the same, giving true matching between the screen and printer when the fonts are used exclusively. If a document has non-TrueType fonts mixed in, the result can be a mismatch between the screen and output.

You can see the fonts available for your workstation by opening the [%system%]\fonts folder. Figure 17.6 shows a listing for one system.

Figure 17.6.

You can see a file listing for fonts in the Fonts folder.

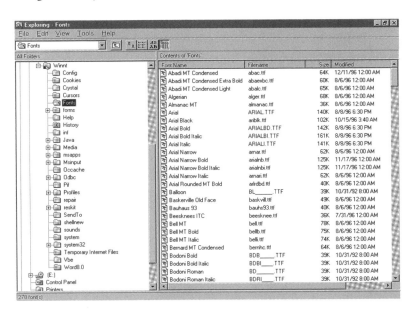

You can see a more useful list of the fonts through the Control Panel. To see it, open the Control Panel by choosing Start | Settings | Control Panel; then double-click the Fonts applet. Figure 17.7 shows this display with the menu choice View | List Choice by Similarity selected. This lists fonts proximate to other fonts that they resemble. Using this facility, you can see what duplicate fonts you have masquerading under different names and also get an education on font relationships. If you have the toolbar open, this button is the third from the left in the View options.

FIGURE 17.7.

You can view your installed fonts sorted by similarity. You select the font you want compared in the combo box that currently shows Arial.

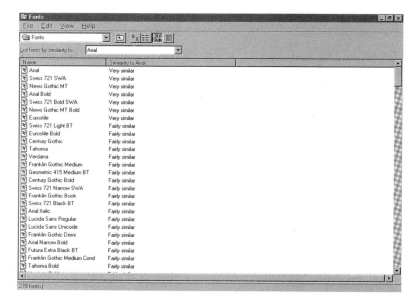

Windows NT provides an icon telling you what kind of font each is in the listing. The icons to the left of the font name all show that the fonts listed in Figure 17.7 are TrueType fonts. Other font types are available for this computer, but they are all below the bottom font shown in this figure.

You can see a good display of the font by double-clicking its entry in the screen shown in Figure 17.7. Figure 17.8 shows the compared font changed to a Zapf Calligraphic variant.

Figure 17.9 shows the results of double-clicking the Zapf Calligraphic font chosen for comparison in Figure 17.8. Figures 17.10 and 17.11 show the same display for the two fonts Windows NT considers closest to the compared font.

FIGURE 17.8.

Changing the compared font also changes the sort of the font listing, bringing the newly similar fonts to the top of the list.

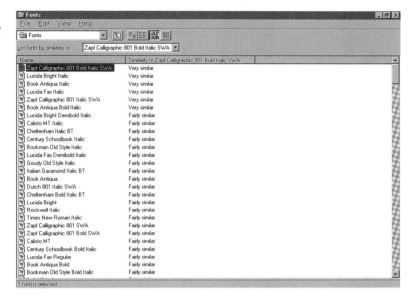

17

WINDOWS NT
FONTS

FIGURE 17.9.

Double-clicking the Zapf Calligraphic font entry in the Control Panel display brings up a display showing how the font will look in various sizes and for various characters.

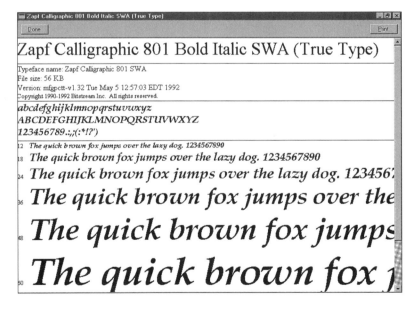

FIGURE 17.10.

Windows NT considers Lucida Bright to be very close to Zapf Calligraphic. Most people would agree. In fact, most people would be hard pressed to tell the difference.

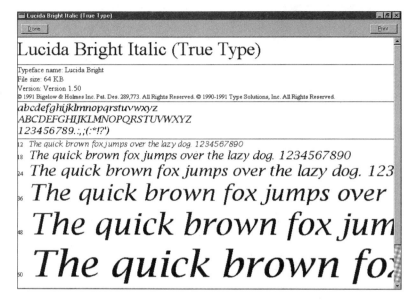

FIGURE 17.11.

Book Antigua is next on the similar font list. As with Lucida Bright, most people can't tell the difference from Zapf Calligraphic or wouldn't care if this font were used instead in a document.

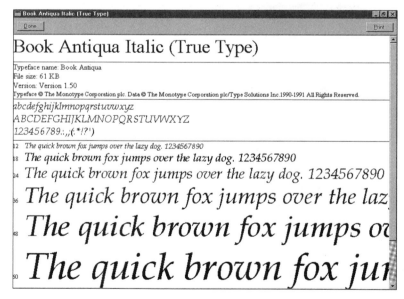

Even Cheltenham, listed as "Fairly similar" in the Fonts listing, would be acceptable to most people for use where Zapf Calligraphic is called for. Figure 17.12 shows this font in the expanded Fonts display.

FIGURE 17.12.

Cheltenham is only "Fairly similar" to Zapf Calligraphic but close enough for most people's use.

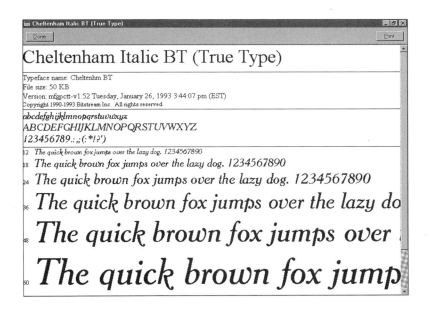

When viewing these fonts in separate screens, most people see little or no difference between the fonts. Figure 17.13 shows the four fonts displayed in 24-point size in one document.

FIGURE 17.13.

Windows NT looks at the font information and tells you what it's similar and dissimilar to. If you want to see the specific differences, nothing is as illustrative as putting the various fonts on the same page.

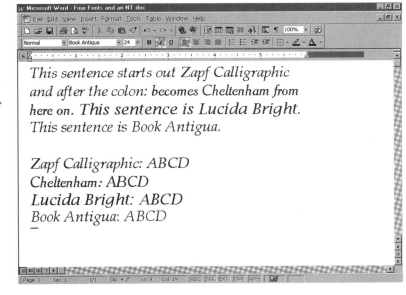

If you look at the first paragraph in Figure 17.13, the one that contains the four fonts, you might conclude that the only difference between them is stroke width. Book Antigua looks finest, closely followed by Zapf, with Lucida Bright being significantly wider and Cheltenham the widest of them all. Either Cheltenham or Lucida Bright could pass as a bold version of Book Antigua.

Next, look at the four separate lines in the lower part of the figure. Examine the letter *B* for all the fonts. Note that the Cheltenham *B* is significantly fatter in the outline forming the front or the rounded part of the letter. This is the key to why the Fonts listing had Cheltenham as only "Fairly similar" to Zapf and the others. The bolder look of Lucida Bright didn't disqualify it from being "Very similar" to Zapf. Stroke width is less important than outline shape when considering font similarity.

When you're looking at these screens, remember that the printed versions of these fonts lay out the same as the screen but look significantly smoother because of screen display limitations.

Going All TrueType

Windows NT Workstation needs some non-TrueType fonts for system use, but most people can live very comfortably choosing only TrueType fonts for their documents. Using only TrueType fonts speeds processing and assures that your screen layouts print as you expect them to. Also, installing TrueType fonts exclusively (other than NT's system fonts) takes up less disk space because the fonts are scaleable. Therefore, one font file has the information available in it to create many fonts effectively. What's really occurring is that the system scales a font to different sizes with different characteristics.

To instruct Windows NT Workstation to display only TrueType fonts in your applications, choose View | Options from the Fonts display, as shown in Figures 17.7 and 17.8. Then choose the TrueType Fonts tab, shown in Figure 17.14, and check the box Show only TrueType fonts in the programs on my computer.

You need to restart your computer before this option takes effect.

FIGURE 17.14.

You can opt to show only TrueType fonts in your applications. This option is good for most users to choose.

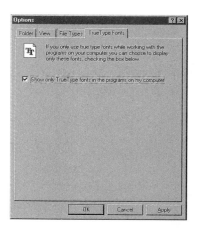

Installing and Deleting Fonts

Unless you have very exacting or special needs, you reduce your system overhead by eliminating appearance-like fonts and telling Windows NT Workstation to use only TrueType fonts. The former action frees some disk space; the latter makes your machine most efficient by using the most efficient font technology.

To delete a font, choose File | Delete in the Fonts display, as shown in Figures 17.7 and 17.8. Figure 17.15 shows the confirmation dialog box opened when you choose this option.

FIGURE 17.15.

Deleting a font from the Fonts list deletes the entry from Fonts and from your application font selection list. It also deletes the font file from the Fonts folder but doesn't move the file into the Recycle Bin. This action makes the deletion fairly permanent without a backup or a distribution list.

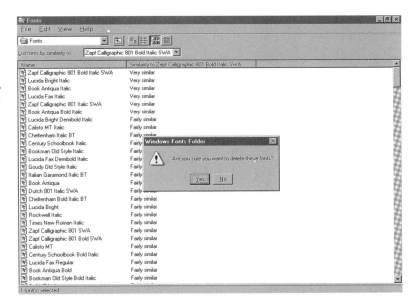

To add fonts from the Fonts display, choose File | Install Fonts. You need to browse to find the fonts. Figure 17.16 shows how to browse for new fonts to install.

FIGURE 17.16.

You need to have the fonts you want to install on hand. After you do, installing them is as easy as browsing for them and choosing the ones you want to have available to your programs.

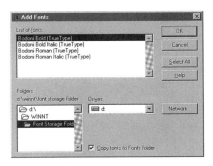

Many installation or setup programs install their own set of fonts, either after seeking your approval or by stealth. Unfortunately, some of these programs either complain or even refuse to run if they don't find the fonts they expect when they launch. If you've deleted these fonts, you might run into problems even though the programs have identical (if not identically named) fonts available to them. If one of these programs is especially cranky, you might need to re-install it, accepting the overhead of the extra fonts as some additional cost of the program.

Figure 17.17 shows a warning box about missing fonts. This application isn't overly sensitive about its missing fonts, but it clearly would be more content if they were available.

Figure 17.17.

Some programs just have to have their own fonts to be perfectly content.

The American Heritage Dictionary is able to muddle through without its fonts, as you can see in Figure 17.18. Not all applications show such resiliency in the face of adversity.

Figure 17.18.

The American Heritage Dictionary can not only make do without its fonts, but it also can define the expression.

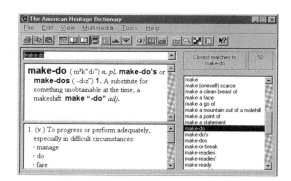

Extra Symbols and Decorative Fonts

Any given font or typeface contains only certain characters. Most contain the letters from a to z in both lower- and uppercase, plus all the numbers and common punctuation marks. They take up only part of the available characters in a set. What's left is up to the vendor of the font. As a result, the particular character you need is often left out. For example, the question mark character (?) isn't available in every font.

In some cases, the entire font set is given over to special characters. The following two lines are the same ASCII characters. The first line is in Courier New. The second is in Symbol.

```
This is a line of text.
```

Τηισ ισ α λινε οφ τεξτ.

As you can see, Courier New uses the Roman or common U.S. English character set, and the Symbol font uses the Greek alphabet.

The Character Map, which is an applet within Windows NT, displays the entire character set for a font. Figure 17.19 shows the Character Map for Courier New.

FIGURE 17.19.

The Character Map shows all the available characters for any given font. Using this applet is a quick way to know what's available for each font and to get a special character into your document.

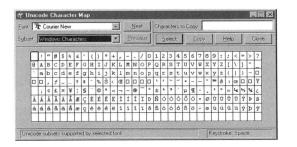

To see the Character Map, choose Start | Programs | Accessories | Character Map. If you don't see the Map, it likely wasn't installed as part of your Custom option or push install. You can install the Character Map from your Windows NT CD-ROM through the setup program.

You can get a special character (non-keyboard) from the Character Map or the font set into your document in the following three ways:

- ■ Double-click the character you want to insert.
- ■ Click the character in the Map, and click Select or press the Enter or Return key on your keyboard.
- ■ Enter the ASCII code for the character by holding down the Alt key and then entering the numeric code from the numeric keypad (not the keys above the regular key set). When you click a character (really a character place) in the Character Map, the status line tells you what the ASCII code for that character is.

Using the first two techniques, you then need to click the Copy button to copy the character or characters to the Clipboard, where you can paste them into your application.

Each font has its own set of special characters. Figure 17.20 shows the Curlz MT font. Note that this font has no common alphanumeric characters at all and that the selected symbol is character 240. You can tell by examining the status bar at the bottom right of the Character Map.

FIGURE 17.20.

Some fonts such as
Curlz MT and Symbol
have no ordinary
alphanumeric
characters. These fonts
exist only to supply
special characters for
your documents.

The limit of what you can do with fonts is bounded by your imagination. Figure 17.21 shows the character 240 from Curlz MT entered into Micrografx Designer 7, blown up to about 600-point size and then given a double gradient fill. Using fonts this way, you can take a simple font character and change it to a minor work of art.

FIGURE 17.21.

Fonts can be fun. You
can start with the basic
font and alter it in any
way if you have the
software.

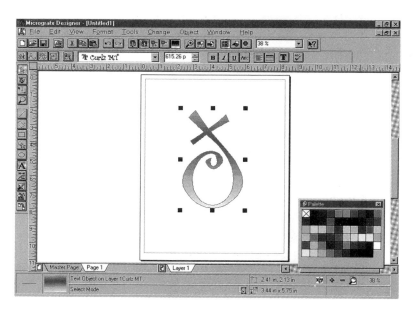

In Figure 17.21, Micrografx Designer 7 takes a regular font from Curlz MT (see the font name in the combo box in the toolbar), expands it to almost a full page in size, and then gives it a double gradient fill. Creating this effect took about five seconds' work in this version of Designer.

Although you can't easily change the installed characters in a font set, you can modify them if you have a few simple tools. Figure 17.22 shows the character 240 from Curlz MT first copied to a new document and then warped. I completed this effect in Micrografx Designer 7.

FIGURE 17.22.

To change a character from any set, copy it to a drawing program and then use the tools supplied to change it any way you choose. This transformation took place in Designer 7 using the Warp tool.

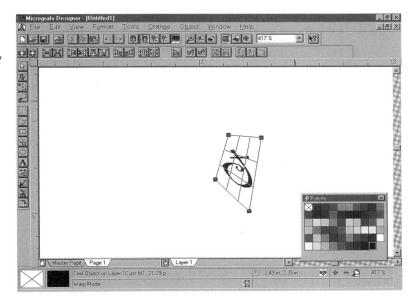

Figure 17.22 still shows a character, but it's changed somewhat. To make the changes effective in other documents, you need to convert it to a graphic. To do so, you choose the Convert to Curves option in Designer. You can then copy it in a document, as you can see in Figure 17.23.

FIGURE 17.23.

After you modify the image of a character, alter it to a graphic; then it's available for use in any appropriate Windows NT application. Here, the Curlz MT character 240 is used in a letter from an artist to her agents.

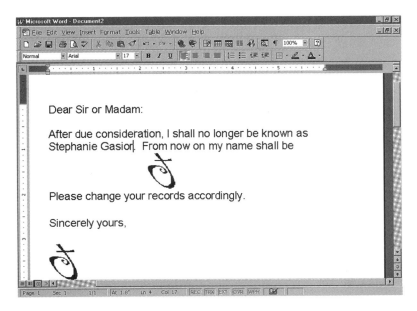

Summary

Windows NT Workstation can use a variety of fonts. Raster, vector, and TrueType outline fonts are all equally at home in Windows NT. However, the technology behind TrueType fonts makes them the right choice for the vast majority of uses. Many users need only TrueType fonts for their applications, although Windows NT itself requires some ASCII and Symbol fonts.

You can add or delete fonts through the Fonts applet and also see what fonts you have and their similarity to each other. Some applications rudely add fonts to your system without your approval. In some cases, these applications don't run without such fonts.

The Character Map is a good place to view all the character symbols for each font. Using a bit of creativity and a drawing program, you can exercise quite a bit of latitude on how you display fonts and where you can use them.

Using NT on Laptops—Really!

by Joshua Allen

IN THIS CHAPTER

Window NT Workstation 4, with its abundance of enterprise-oriented services and performance capabilities, has established itself as the operating system of choice for expensive, high-end workstations. You are probably aware of NT's reputation as a desktop operating system; however, you might be surprised to find that NT could also be the best operating system you can install on your laptop. In the past, the choice was clear: use NT on your workstations and Windows 95 on your portable machines. Today, however, you should seriously consider standardizing on one platform for all of your machines.

In this chapter, we'll discuss the advantages and disadvantages of using NT Workstation 4 as your laptop operating system. You'll find detailed instructions to help you install and use NT 4 on a laptop, and you'll be given tips for dealing with many of the common problems that are peculiar to portable computing. Finally, you'll read about some of the issues you'll encounter if you are responsible for supporting NT 4 laptops in a corporate environment, and you'll be presented with some useful tips to help you avoid common pitfalls and make your laptop easier to use.

Why Use NT on Your Laptop?

The first decision you must make before installing NT on your laptop is whether you even want to use NT as your laptop operating system. Although NT 4 includes new features specifically aimed at laptop use, there are some limitations that might make NT 4 unattractive for use on your laptop. Currently, you might want to consider using Windows NT Workstation 3.51 or Windows 95 as your laptop operating system instead. Both NT 3.51 and 95 have advantages and disadvantages compared to NT 4; you'll learn those pros and cons here.

Perhaps the most important factor you should consider is that Windows NT 4 does not have native support for hot-swapping of PC card devices and does not support power management for you to get more life out of your battery. Having to reboot your machine each time you switch from modem to LAN can become a real hassle, and if you travel frequently, power management support could be an influential decision criterion. Don't throw out NT 4 just yet, though. Many laptops support power management through the BIOS, and if you have purchased your laptop recently from one of the major vendors of mobile computers, vendor-specific extensions to Windows NT may address your power management qualms. Some of the more popular laptop manufacturers have begun to package custom add-on software with their NT 4 laptops that compensate for NT's weaknesses and support hot-swapping and power management. Contact your vendor to find out if they can give you these add-ons. One final point worth mentioning is that NT 4 does not support the infrared driver API natively. You probably will not be able to use any accessories that use an infrared interface for communication.

As an answer to its inadequacies, NT 4 holds forth a handful of unique features that make it attractive as a laptop operating system. Foremost is NT 4's new and improved list of automatically supported hardware. NT 4 supports significantly more hardware out of the box, which means you have to spend less time on the phone and less time scouring the Web for updated drivers. You stand a much better chance of having the install program for NT 4 properly detect your video and other peripherals than you do with Windows 95 or NT 3.51.

In addition to the expanded compatibility list, NT 4 supports briefcase replication and hardware profiles—both of which are lacking in version 3.51. Briefcase replication, as you may know from using Windows 95, allows you to easily synchronize changes that you make on your laptop with files that are stored on the machines at your home or office. The use of hardware profiles makes it easy for you to switch between different configurations of your laptop. For example, you might have one profile that you would select for using the laptop over an ISDN line from home, and another that you would select while using it in your docking station at home. The last major technical feature that makes NT 4 a good choice for laptop users is its built-in support for Point To Point Tunneling Protocol (PPTP). With PPTP, you can use a local Internet dial-up from anywhere in the country to open a secure, encrypted communication channel with the computers at your office. In this way, you can stay connected with your office while avoiding high-cost long-distance phone charges and eliminating costly dial-in modem pools. Review Table 18.1 for a concise comparison of the benefits and drawbacks of using NT 4 on a laptop.

Table 18.1. Pros and cons of NT 4 for laptop users.

Feature	*NT 4*	*NT 3.51*	*Windows 95*
PPTP	Yes	No	Yes (not native)
Briefcase replication	Yes	No	Yes
Hot-swap PCMCIA	Maybe	No	Yes
Power management	Maybe	No	Yes
Hardware profiles	Yes	No	Yes
Widest hardware support	Yes	No	No
Infrared support	No	No	Yes
NTFS security	Yes	Yes	No

18

USING NT ON
LAPTOPS—REALLY!

In addition to the technical reasons listed earlier, you may be influenced by other, less technical criteria. If your corporation has chosen to standardize on a single platform in order to avoid the cost of supporting multiple operating systems, you might be forced to use NT 4. If you work in a large corporation, though, your most important question will be whether your commonly used applications will work on the operating system. In a large company, you almost certainly use applications that are tailored to your specific environment and do not have the wide platform independence that mass-market applications need to be successful. Some of your critical business applications might be written exclusively for NT 4 and will not run on the other 32-bit operating systems. And, even if all of your applications work on both versions of NT today, don't automatically assume that the software vendor will continue to support an older operating system in future releases. In any case, it is wise to check the operating system requirements for the various corporate applications that you'll be using before you decide.

Installing NT 4 on Your Laptop

Once you've decided to use NT 4, you'll need to make sure that it is installed properly on your laptop. If you have not yet ordered your laptop, the best thing you can do is ask the vendor to send it preloaded with NT 4. It is much easier to let the vendor ensure that all of the correct drivers are loaded and tested, and they might even throw in power management and PC card management utilities while they are loading your machine. If a vendor-loaded machine is out of the question, though, you'll have to go through the normal installation process.

Before You Install

Before attempting to install to your laptop, you should check the Hardware Compatibility List (HCL) to make sure that your hardware is included. You can download the most recent HCL from `ftp://ftp.microsoft.com/services/whql/hclnt4.exe`. If your laptop is not listed in the HCL, it might still be possible to load NT 4. Call your laptop vendor (or check their Web site) to see whether there are any problems that you'll need to address while installing NT 4.

If you are planning to use a docking station or port replicator, you probably won't find any listed in the HCL. This is because docking stations aren't really something that the operating system will have to support, because a docking station is just an extension of the system bus. If the peripherals (network adapter, and so on) contained in your docking station are supported, your docking station will be supported.

Finally, you should make sure that your computer exceeds the RAM, processor, and disk space requirements of NT 4, as described in Chapter 3, "Installing Windows NT Workstation."

Next, you should make a checklist of the components listed in this paragraph that will be relevant to your laptop install. Careful planning of the order in which you install the various components can save you quite a bit of grief later in the process. First, are you going to be using your laptop as a standalone machine, as a docked machine, or will you be alternating between both configurations? Will you be using a network? Will the network adapter that you use be a PC card adapter or an adapter in the docking station, or both? Will you need to use a modem, Remote Access Service (RAS), or PPTP? If you are going to be switching between various configurations, such as LAN/Dialup or Docked/Undocked, you should pay particular attention to the caveats listed in the following paragraphs so that you will be prepared for the setup described in the section on hardware profiles, later in this chapter.

Installation

Getting at the Windows NT 4 source media might end up being the trickiest part of the installation process. If your laptop doesn't have a CD-ROM drive, your options for a workaround are more limited than if you were installing a desktop machine. If an operating system is already loaded on the machine, use it to open a network or direct cable connection with a machine that has a CD-ROM drive and copy the entire i386 directory from the CD-ROM to your local hard disk. If you have no suitable operating system installed, you might want to use a different computer to build a network boot disk to connect your laptop to a shared source. The procedure for creating network boot disks is described in Chapter 27, "Windows NT Network Services." Even if you have a CD-ROM drive, it is best to copy the full i386 source to your hard drive and install from there.

You'll launch the installation procedure by issuing a command such as `c:\i386\winnt /b /s:c:\i386` from a DOS prompt. Before you press the Enter key, though, remember the list you made earlier! If you intend to use your laptop in more than one configuration, such as LAN/Dialup or Docked/Undocked, you should make sure your laptop is fully disconnected from any relevant peripherals during the initial installation process. In other words, leave your laptop disconnected from its docking station and remove any modem or LAN card, PC card adapters before you begin. This might seem like a strange request, but it will make things much more clean and manageable when you get around to setting up hardware profiles.

If, on the other hand, you'll be using your laptop in only one configuration, you should make sure that all peripherals you'll be using are on the laptop before you begin the install. Your laptop should look, at least from a hardware perspective, exactly as it will look when you are using it. This allows NT 4 to detect and configure all of your devices up front.

At last, you are ready to begin the install. From here, just follow the normal installation procedure discussed in Chapter 3. At this point, you shouldn't be disappointed if NT does not detect your PC card devices while loading. You'll be able to install them through the Control Panel as soon as the loading procedure is complete.

Performance Tuning for Laptops

Once the initial load is complete, but before you add any further components, you might want to tweak some settings to get the best performance out of your laptop.

In particular, you'll probably want to select Control Panel | Services and then turn off the Server service (see Figure 18.1). Click the Startup button and set the startup setting to Disabled. This will also shut down the Browser service, which you'll manually want to set to Disabled. Of course, you might want to use the Server service with this laptop, but normally you can leave this feature off for laptop users.

FIGURE 18.1.

Disabling the Server service.

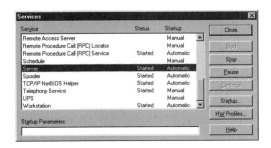

If you have any other services that you do not need, disable them now. If you are accustomed to keeping large NTFS security logs in Event Viewer, you can probably safely abandon this practice with your laptops. Take time also to make sure that you have the correct video drivers from the manufacturer. Laptop video displays are still quirky enough that your performance can depreciate significantly just from using a video driver that isn't optimized. More general performance tuning tips can be gleaned from Chapter 8, "Tuning Windows NT Performance."

If this laptop is going to be used primarily in one configuration, you can skip ahead to the section on configuring PCMCIA devices. If you'll be switching between different configurations, however, keep reading for a discussion of hardware profiles.

Setting Up Hardware Profiles

If you are planning to alternate between different configurations for this laptop, NT 4's hardware profiles will help you make your transitions smoothly. Hopefully, at this point you have installed NT 4 fresh with no network or other peripheral components installed. In the following example, we'll assume that you are going to be alternating between two primary configurations: docked to a docking station connected to the LAN through a PCI network card, and undocked, connecting through a PCMCIA Modem/Ethernet adapter. You'll see step-by-step instructions for configuring your machine so as to flexibly shift between these two setups:

1. Begin by selecting Control Panel | System | Hardware Profiles. Alternatively, you can just right-click the My Computer icon and select Properties and then the Hardware Profiles tab. (See Figure 18.2.)

FIGURE 18.2.

The Hardware Profiles properties sheet.

2. Notice that there is only one profile currently installed. This profile is the bare-bones profile that you'll build upon to create your other profiles.

3. Select Original Configuration in the list and then click Copy.

4. When prompted for a name, type in a relevant name. In this case, use `Docked - PCI Network Adapter`.

   Keep in mind that we are merely setting up templates to which we'll add different components later, so don't worry if you are not actually connected to a docking station right now.

5. Make another copy of Original Configuration, but this time name it `Undocked - Xircom PC-Card`. Your Hardware Profile list should appear, as shown in Figure 18.3.

FIGURE 18.3.

The Hardware Profiles list with blank profiles.

Now that you have the two actual profiles you'll be using most often, you can decide what to do with the Original Configuration profile. It's a good idea to keep this profile around as a starting point for new profiles, and in this case there is another use for it—you'll set it up as the profile to be used when the laptop is completely disconnected from any network in standalone mode.

6. Highlight Original Configuration in your list and then click the Properties button.

7. Select the Network tab and check Network-disabled hardware profile. (See Figure 18.4.)

   Now, when you select Original Configuration at system startup, your system will load peacefully without attempting to load network drivers or restore permanent mappings. Of course, you'll have to remember to clear this check box on any further copies that you make if you want to add any more network-enabled profiles.

8. Before you begin customizing the profiles, use the up and down arrows at the right side of the Hardware Profiles properties sheet to rearrange the profiles in whatever order makes sense to you.

9. In this example, move Undocked to the top, Docked second, and Original Configuration at the bottom.

18

USING NT ON LAPTOPS—REALLY!

FIGURE 18.4.

Setting up a profile for standalone use.

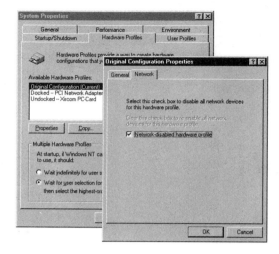

10. Close out your System Properties menu and shut down the machine. Windows NT 4 likes to be shut down when PCMCIA devices are inserted. You can insert any PC card devices that you would like to install now, before you restart your laptop. Later, you'll see how to install the drivers for your PCMCIA device.

11. Once your card is inserted, restart your computer.

    During the text mode portion of system startup, you'll be presented with a menu allowing you to choose between the three hardware profiles that you created earlier.

12. In this case, accept the default choice, Undocked. You can press Enter here or wait until it is automatically chosen and the startup continues. The default selection timeout is configurable through the Hardware Profiles properties sheet.

13. When your machine has finished loading, go back to Control Panel | System | Hardware Profiles and observe that the list now shows a new profile as being current. (See Figure 18.5.)

Any changes you make from now until the next reboot will affect this profile only and will leave your other two profiles untouched. Before installing your PC card device, though, you should configure the docking status of all three profiles. Follow these steps:

1. Select Undocked in your profiles list and click the Properties button.

2. Set the docking state as shown in Figure 18.6.

3. Set the appropriate state for the Docked profile as well and set Original Configuration to Undocked.

Having done this, NT 4 might be able to help you switch between profiles automatically now (but don't expect any miracles). Now close your System Properties window. Next, you'll add a PCMCIA network adapter to your Undocked profile.

FIGURE 18.5.
Rebooted with a new profile.

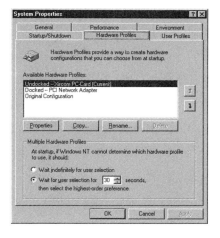

FIGURE 18.6.
Setting Docked/ Undocked status.

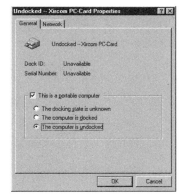

Installing PC Card (PCMCIA) Devices

First, let's assume that the PCMCIA card you want to install was inserted into the PCMCIA slot previous to the last restart. Now, follow these steps:

1. If your PCMCIA card has not been inserted yet, insert it into a PCMCIA slot now and then restart your laptop.

   Once NT 4 has had a chance to compensate for its lack of hot-swap prowess, you can get around to detecting and installing the PCMCIA device.

2. Double-click the Control Panel and then the PC card icon. Immediately upon opening, the Configuration applet will attempt to detect your card.

3. If the system detects a card for which it does not yet have drivers, you'll be prompted to install them (see Figure 18.7). Just select the OK button.

FIGURE 18.7.
PC card installation.

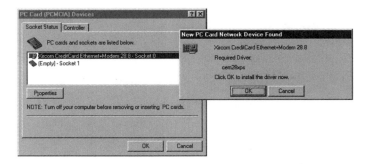

4. As soon as NT 4 has finished installing the components it needs for this device, you'll be presented with a driver-specific configuration screen, such as the one shown in Figure 18.8.

FIGURE 18.8.
PC Card properties configuration.

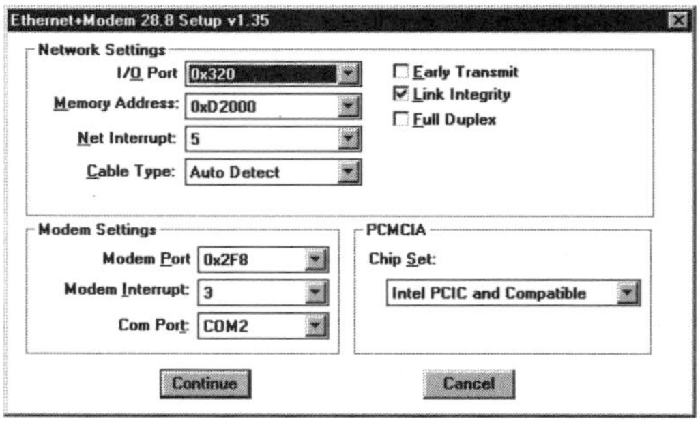

This configuration dialog box is generally the same one you would see by pressing the Properties button on the Socket Status properties sheet with your PC card selected. In most cases, you can just accept the defaults here. Sometimes NT 4 will ask for this configuration information one more time after you reboot, so do not worry if you see this screen again after the next reboot. If you get the screen a third time, though, you might be in for some troubleshooting.

WARNING

Windows NT Workstation 4's PC Card Configuration applet detects new PC card devices by using information stored in the PCMCIA subkey of the Registry. Information in this Registry area tells NT 4 which device drivers to use for a particular card. Unfortunately, you cannot assume that the drivers listed in this database are actually written for NT 4. Some of the drivers that NT 4 appears to detect and install automatically were actually written for NT 3.51. These drivers will often work, but they can cause perplexing errors that can be difficult to diagnose later. If you are experiencing trouble with a particular PC card, try installing from a manufacturer-sanctioned drivers disk.

In this example, the PC card is a modem as well as a LAN adapter, so you need to take the extra step of detecting and configuring the modem now. Double-click Control Panel | Modems (see Figure 18.9). The process of installing and configuring a modem is covered more completely in Chapter 21, "Setting Up Your Modem."

FIGURE 18.9.

Detecting your PCMCIA modem.

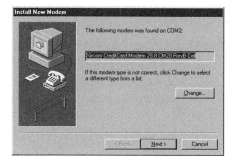

Now that your undocked profile has been customized, you can reboot your machine into the docked configuration and configure your docking station's devices. When configuring your docking station, the only tool you'll probably need to use is the Add New Hardware Wizard, which is discussed in Chapter 5, "Not-Ready-for-Plug-and-Play Hardware." You'll simply connect your machine to the docking station, boot the machine up in the Docked profile, and then use the Add New Hardware Wizard to detect all of the peripherals.

If you are using a PCI bus, however, you might have to reboot once and run the Add New Hardware Wizard a second time to catch all the devices. Be sure to select Docked again on the Profiles menu while booting or else you might be surprised to find that all your recently detected hardware has disappeared! When you have shut down your machine, you'll have a computer that is capable (through the use of hardware profiles) of switching effortlessly between Docked, Undocked, and Standalone configurations. Congratulations!

Remote Computing Features

Your laptop is now able to function on the LAN whether docked or undocked. What else could you want? The answer, of course, is to be able to connect to your network remotely—from your home or the hotel. If you have a modem installed, you certainly want to configure your computer to take full advantage of it. Following the previous example, you'll now reboot the machine and select the default Undocked profile from which the PCMCIA modem is available.

The most common feature you'll be using to connect to your network or the Internet from remote locations is the Remote Access Service (RAS). You can install this service from the Control Panel | Network | Services tab by pressing the Add button. Alternatively, this component can be installed when you install software from an Internet Service Provider (ISP), such as Microsoft

Network (MSN). A complete discussion of how to install Remote Access Service and your dial-up connections can be found in Chapter 20, "Talking to Another Computer: Direct Cable Connection." You might want to study Chapter 20 before continuing, or if you do not intend to use Point To Point Tunneling Protocol. The following discussion of Point To Point Tunneling Protocol does not, however, require that RAS be installed. You'll see how to accomplish both tasks together in the discussion that follows.

Installing Point To Point Tunneling Protocol (PPTP)

Point To Point Tunneling Protocol (PPTP) is a new feature of NT 4 that allows you to use practically any public dial-up to connect to your corporate network. PPTP allows you to "tunnel" through any number of public networks using encryption, thus creating a virtual private network that is secure from snooping. If you have an Internet connection at your office and do not want to install a modem pool for dial-ups or want to avoid long-distance telephone charges, PPTP is probably the best way to provide remote connectivity to your company network. You can purchase a third-party ISP account from a company such as UUNET or Netcom with local dial-ups in virtually every area code and then use that account to tunnel into your corporate network from almost anywhere at very low cost.

Here's how to install PPTP:

1. Double-click the Control Panel and then the Network icon. Select the Protocols tab.

2. From here, press the Add button to select PPTP from the list. (See Figure 18.10.)

FIGURE 18.10.

Installing PPTP.

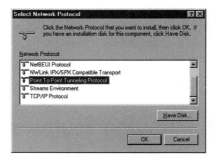

3. After you press OK and the operating system finishes installing the driver components, you are given an opportunity to select the number of virtual private networks (VPN) you'll be using.

   If you plan to connect to only one PPTP server at a time, then one will be sufficient. (See Figure 18.11.)

4. Select OK after choosing a number of VPNs.

FIGURE 18.11.
*How many virtual
private networks
do you need?*

PPTP works by tunneling through an existing dial-up networking connection. You have to be dialed in to a regular RAS connection before your PPTP connection will work properly, so naturally PPTP requires that RAS be installed before it will agree to work for you.

If you have not yet installed RAS, the PPTP Installation applet politely offers to help with this job (see Figure 18.12). After you have installed RAS, you'll be presented with the dialog box shown in Figure 18.13.

FIGURE 18.12.
*Installing Remote
Access Services.*

FIGURE 18.13.
*Adding your VPN
as a RAS device.*

If you installed RAS prior to this, you'll need to select the Services tab of your Network Settings dialog box, double-click Remote Access Service, and then click Add Device to get this dialog box. Select your VPN and click OK. Use this procedure to make sure that all your modems and VPNs are included in the list of RAS devices.

NOTE

This chapter concentrates on the PPTP client primarily. Installing a PPTP server is done exactly the same way, though. If you have a RAS server already configured, you can turn it into a PPTP server by following the directions given for client installation and then selecting Accept Incoming Calls in the RAS properties for the VPN adapter. This process is described in Chapter 11 of the Windows NT Server 4 Networking Supplement Manual.

Adding a PPTP Connection Entry

Now that PPTP is installed on your laptop, you need to configure a Dial-Up Networking entry to point to your company's PPTP server. This is accomplished in much the same way as adding a connection to your ISP, but with some important differences.

To begin, follow these steps:

1. Double-click the My Computer icon.

2. Double-click the Dial-Up Networking icon.

3. If you have already created some dial-up connections, you'll need to double-click the Add Entry icon. If this is your first entry, you'll automatically be asked to enter a name for the new connection.

4. Once you have selected a name, you'll be allowed to choose an adapter with which to associate your new connection (see Figure 18.14). Notice that the PPTP VPN appears in the list as if it is just another internal modem.

FIGURE 18.14.

Using a VPN as a dial-up networking adapter.

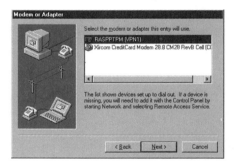

5. Select your VPN adapter and press Next.

6. When you are prompted for a phone number, enter the IP address of your PPTP-enabled server instead, as shown in Figure 18.15.

FIGURE 18.15.

PPTP uses an IP address instead of a phone number.

Tunneling Through to Your Corporate Network

Before you attempt to open a virtual private channel to your corporate network, you'll need to be dialed in on some sort of TCP/IP network that is connected to the Internet. This can be CompuServe, Netcom, MSN, or any other ISP connection. You can also tunnel a VPN through a local Ethernet, if that Ethernet is connected to the Internet. For example, you might want to connect to a PC in your office and download a few files, but you are stuck in meetings at a customer site where you have connected your laptop to their LAN in order to use their printers. If their LAN is connected to the Internet, you'll be able to tunnel out through the Internet and establish a private connection to your home network.

> **TIP**
>
> To find out whether you are going to be able to open a VPN with your home network, try using the `Ping` command from wherever you are. For example, if your PPTP server's IP address (phone number) is `199.201.210.2`, you can check your connection by typing `Ping 199.201.210.2` at a command prompt. If the connection times out or fails, PPTP will not be able to open a VPN. Chapter 22, "Setting Up TCP/IP Protocol Access," gives you advice about troubleshooting TCP/IP connections.

Once you are connected to a TCP/IP network that is visible to your laptop as well as your PPTP server, follow these steps:

1. Open a VPN by double-clicking the icon that represents that connection in your Dial-Up Networking folder (in the My Computer icon).

2. From this dialog box you may also modify the VPN settings by selecting More | Edit entry and modem properties (see Figure 18.16). Just press the Dial button here.

FIGURE 18.16.

"Dialing" a PPTP server.

18

USING NT ON LAPTOPS—REALLY!

3. Next, you'll be prompted to enter a username, password, and domain name for connecting to your company's network. This is not the same as the username and password used to connect to your dial-up service provider account—this is actually the username and password that you use when logging in at your office. Figure 18.17 shows the credentials dialog box.

FIGURE 18.17.

PPTP credentials for the remote domain.

4. Press OK at this prompt, and you'll be connected to your company network over a securely encrypted channel. (See Figure 18.18.)

FIGURE 18.18.

Opening a new tunnel.

Until you disconnect, you'll be able to access your office's network resources as if you were sitting at the office.

Support for Offline Use

Despite the plentitude of features that NT 4 offers to users who want to be constantly connected to their network resources, there will be times when you cannot be connected to any sort of network, or do not want to be connected. Traveling on an airplane is one example. Of course, you could swipe your platinum card through the phone in your seat and hope that AT&T doesn't hang up on you when your credit is exhausted. But what's the point, when all you really want to do is make a few changes to your sales analysis to prepare it for printing when you return? Fortunately for you, NT 4 has a few features even for you, the offline user. This chapter discusses Briefcase replication and deferred printing—two features designed to make your life easier as you carry your work with you.

Preparing Briefcase Replication

The first thing you should do before you take your laptop on the road is drag any files that you might need into your Briefcase—that is, the My Briefcase icon that sits on your desktop. Figure 18.19 shows the Sales Analysis document being dragged from the Network Data folder into the Briefcase. While you have some free time on the airplane, you can make modifications to the Sales Analysis file by double-clicking the My Briefcase icon and then double-clicking the document in your Briefcase.

FIGURE 18.19.

Put your papers in your Briefcase before you travel.

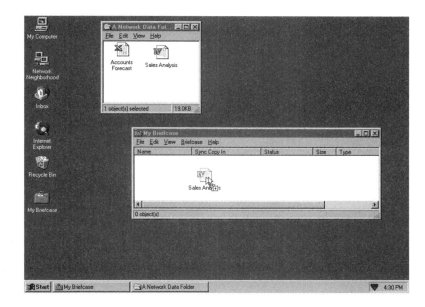

Deferred Printing

After making a few changes, you might become concerned that the copy of your sales analysis sitting back at the office has become out of date, and you do not want to forget to copy over your changes. You can relax, though, because you know that the Briefcase will take care of all of that for you. Before you get back to your office, however, you have decided to print a copy of your sales analysis executive summary pages. First, select Settings | Printers from the Start menu and select the icon for the office printer to which you want to send the printout. The Printer Configuration window is shown in Figure 18.20. From the Printer menu in this window, select Work Offline. Now you can go ahead and send as much as you want to the printer without worrying about the fact that the printer is currently unavailable.

FIGURE 18.20.

Configuring a printer for deferred printing.

> **TIP**
>
> If you switch between working standalone and logging into a Windows NT domain, you should be careful to avoid problems with mandatory user profiles. If your normal machines are configured to allow login only to a domain controller, you probably don't want to extend this policy to your laptops. You might become very frustrated when you discover that you cannot access the data on your hard drive just because you do not have a network connection!

Back at the Office

When you return to the office and boot up your machine with a network connection, NT 4 will ask you whether you would like to print out all your pending documents and will then finish the job for you. If you double-click your Briefcase, you'll see a screen similar to Figure 18.21, telling you that the Sales Analysis document needs to be synchronized. If you right-click the document and select Update, you'll be given a confirmation dialog box, as seen in Figure 18.22.

FIGURE 18.21.

Briefcase needs updating.

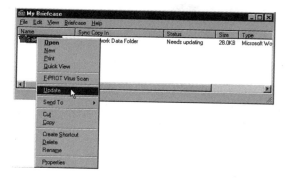

FIGURE 18.22.

Briefcase update confirmation message.

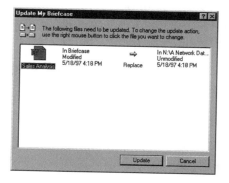

> **NOTE**
>
> What do you do if both the network copy and the copy in your Briefcase have been modified? If both documents have been modified, the Briefcase first checks the Registry to find if a reconciliation handler has been defined for that file type. If there is a reconciliation handler defined, Briefcase passes control to the reconciliation handler, which attempts to merge the differences between the two files. In many cases, there will be no reconciliation handler, and you'll receive an error like the one shown in Figure 18.23. One popular application that does supply a powerful reconciliation handler that can merge changes by many different users is Microsoft Access. If you are interested in making your Microsoft Access databases replicable through the Briefcase, check out Knowledge Base article Q136134 at http://www.microsoft.com/kb.

FIGURE 18.23.

Irreconcilable differences.

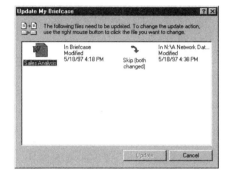

Support in a Corporate Environment

Even with all of the laptop-specific features that NT 4 provides, making sure that your laptop is a productivity aid rather than a productivity drain can be a challenging task. If this task is challenging for you, a computer professional, just imagine what it is like for your corporate users. Most corporate users of laptops are nontechnical, managerial types, who expect excellent service and minimum headaches from their tools. Laptops, by nature, are complex and prone to problems. Therefore, if you are assigned to manage the support for the laptops within your corporation, you can be sure that this is not a commission to be taken lightly. There are a number of things you can do to protect your paycheck in this capacity, while offering the best service to your demanding customers. If you are not involved with corporate support of NT 4 laptops, the following section might be rather boring for you. You can skip to the section on security for some tips that apply to individuals as well as corporations, or you can skip directly to the "Final Tips" section.

Rollout

If you work within a relatively large organization, you know that organizational units are fond of making standards and mandating strategies. You might receive the mandate that all future laptops will be supplied with NT 4 preinstalled and preconfigured to meet certain corporate standards. Or you might actually be in a position to make this policy yourself. In any case, your job as a corporate support person for laptops will almost certainly involve your spending much time making sure that NT 4 laptops are installed properly. The rest of this chapter offers some ideas for keeping this activity from stealing ever-larger amounts of your time.

To put it simply, standardization is the key to ensuring that you have time to spend on more important activities. Chances are, if you've installed NT Workstation 4 on five dissimilar laptops, then you've had to learn five different workarounds during the installation processes. Multiply this on a daily basis, and you'll find yourself spending a lot of time looking for new ways to circumvent installation problems, while spending very little time actually getting laptops loaded. If you can standardize on one manufacturer, one set of possible laptops from which your corporate customers can choose, then you'll be able to get increasing returns from your earlier learning experiences. This is just plain common sense in the case of desktop computers, but it is even more valid when considering the complexity inherent in laptop computing. Reducing the number of "standard" vendors has a payoff in two ways. First, you automatically reduce the number of models that you need to support. Second, such a strategy eases your burden considerably by reducing the complexity you must deal with in getting vendor support. All the time that you spend looking for vendor support phone numbers, support account codes, remembering which representative was the easiest to talk to, you could be doing other things. As you build up a support relationship with just one or two primary vendors, you find that you spend less time getting the answers that you need. Of course, you'll be pressured from a customer satisfaction standpoint to support as many different types of laptops as possible, and you might not be able to reduce the amount of complexity as much as you would like. However, your willingness to build a compromise between the two conflicting positions of wide support and reduced complexity will ensure that you can offer the most effective service.

Troubleshooting Problems

Once you have mastered the rollout procedure, the next major area to tackle is troubleshooting. Many problems will be highly individual and will require considerable effort on your part to solve satisfactorily, but there are some steps you can take to minimize your burden in this area, too. The first thing you should do is begin educating your users on how to use Briefcase replication and recommend that they store all of their data files in one or two easily backed-up directories on the hard drive. When the user's data is easily backed up, that means the machine can be reloaded without causing excessive user anxiety. Also, knowing that a machine can be reloaded from scratch, if necessary, will reduce your anxiety about experimenting.

In troubleshooting, as in loading, simplicity pays off—but don't take this cookie-cutter approach too far. If many of your laptops are the same model with identical peripherals, you might be tempted to make a disk image of one well-configured laptop and use this image to reload laptops that are broken. At first glance, this appears to reduce the time required for a reload from over an hour to just five minutes. However, the strategy soon runs into problems. The most significant problem is that NT 4 randomly generates two security identifiers (SIDs) while installing. These SIDs are used locally and throughout the network to manage permissions. Having machines with duplicate SIDs is not recommended by Microsoft and can cause problems that might be very hard to diagnose.

If your budget supports it, it might be wise to have one or two standard load laptops sitting around at all times. If a customer comes to you with a misconfigured laptop, you can give her a replacement laptop so that she doesn't have to sit idle while you troubleshoot. Customers generally appreciate it when you are considerate of their time.

Security

Laptops provide some unique reasons for corporate security persons to be concerned. The people within your company who use laptops frequently are the people who are working with just the sort of data that your competitors would like to see. Most users of laptops dial into the corporate network frequently, using unsecured telephone lines. Laptops by nature are not as easy to secure physically, either. It's much easier for a thief to steal a lightweight laptop from a busy airport than it is for him to lug your desktop machine from your twentieth floor office. Some simple precautions can minimize the risk to which you invariably are exposed when your users travel with laptops.

One simple first step is to make sure that your drives are formatted with NTFS and that all local accounts have passwords. If a laptop is stolen, the use of NTFS does not prevent all thieves from getting at your files, but it can prevent most of the less-technical criminals from stealing sensitive information. Show your users how to format their floppies with NTFS, also. Educating your users on other security issues is also a good idea, though not a panacea. Although you may instruct your users to not store sensitive information such as corporate credit card numbers or PBX long-distance phone calling codes on their machines, you can be sure that some of them will. At the very least, stress the importance of keeping passwords separate from the machine. It is ridiculously common for users to write their relevant passwords on a little sticky note and place it somewhere inside the laptop case. This makes it relatively simple for a thief to plunder not only the laptop hard drive, but the corporate network as well. If your users must write down their passwords, at least convince them to keep the note separate from the laptop. The same holds true for such hardware solutions as SecureID. If a thief steals one of your users' laptops, he generally gets that user's SecureID card in the case, and often the PIN number as well. Introduce your users to the wisdom of storing the SecureID card somewhere other than the laptop case.

Dial-up connections in particular pose a challenge. If your users cache their dial-up networking passwords, you might be opening up your entire corporate network for perusal. The same is true if your users are in the habit of using the same password for all of their accounts. Another pitfall to consider is the use of credit card accounts for long-distance chargeback. You might save large amounts of money in exorbitant hotel telephone charges by configuring the Use Credit Card option in Dialup Networking Properties, but you also stand the risk of having your credit card or phone card numbers stolen along with the laptop. None of the options for avoiding this risk are really very attractive, but at least be aware of the risk and make sure that the machine is protected with NTFS and good passwords. Finally, to protect against silly mistakes by your more technical users, think about making PPTP available. Many of your users will have their own private Internet accounts through services such as Netcom or CompuServe. There are many reasons why a user would choose to dial in to an ISP rather than your corporate network dial-ups while traveling. For example, the user might want to check her CompuServe e-mail before sending out copies of her report, or she may simply want to use a local connection and avoid the long-distance cost of dialing directly to your company's lines. In any event, problems arise when your users begin to transact company business over a public network. If your users send company-related e-mail from this connection, transfer files via FTP, or log in to any company systems using telnet, your corporate security is threatened. Telnet and FTP do not encrypt the passwords that are sent over the network, and e-mail, too, is not encrypted. It is a relatively simple task for someone with the proper knowledge to intercept these transmissions and steal your passwords. This is especially disturbing if your competitors happen to be companies that own any of the network hosts through which your transmissions must travel. Installing PPTP on your users' laptops will allow them to log in to their private ISP accounts and tunnel through to your corporate network using a VPN, which encrypts the transferred data.

Final Tips

Now that you've learned how to evaluate, install, configure, support, and secure NT Workstation 4 in a laptop environment, I'll leave you with a few tricks to help make your life easier.

My favorite tweak to add to laptops is the "StickyKeys" feature found under accessibility options in the Control Panel (see Figure 18.24). If your laptop is anything like most laptops, the Shift, Ctrl, Alt, and Delete keys are placed in positions that maximize their difficulty of use. Especially frustrating is the fact that the Ctrl+Alt+Delete (or three-finger salute) combination cannot be accomplished with three fingers of the same hand as it can on most desktop keyboards. This means that you have to set down your drink on a shaky airline seat-back tray to free up your other hand every time you want to pull up your task list. By using StickyKeys, you can press the Ctrl, Alt, and Delete keys one at a time, and the computer will know what you mean. You might want to examine some of the other accessibility options as well. In particular, FilterKeys can help you reduce the frustrations created by working on a cramped, disorganized keyboard.

18

USING NT ON
LAPTOPS—REALLY!

FIGURE 18.24.
Enabling StickyKeys.

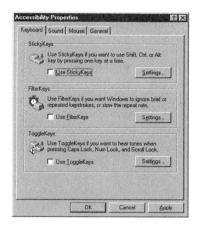

One last tool that will help you cope with laptop screens that are usually smaller than you would like is the MultiDesk (Multidsk.exe) utility included on the Windows NT Workstation 4 Resource Kit CD-ROM. This utility allows you to use a larger desktop than is visible on one screen. You can keep your screen at a more readable resolution while viewing just the areas of the desktop on which you are currently working. You might find it useful to configure your video display for a docked profile at a higher resolution to take advantage of the docking station's monitor and then configure a more readable resolution in conjunction with MultiDesk for your undocked hardware profile.

Summary

Now that you are familiar with all the laptop-friendly features that Windows NT Workstation 4 brings to the table, you can see that using Windows NT for your mobile computing needs may be more enticing than you once thought. Support for multiple hardware profiles, Point To Point Tunneling Protocol, and Briefcase Replication makes NT Workstation an attractive choice for laptop use. NT's inability to support Power Management and PCMCIA hot-swapping are less important now that these deficiencies have largely been addressed by hardware vendor add-ons. Finally, careful planning of your installation and support processes can ensure that your use of NT on laptops is trouble-free.

Configuring Multimedia Devices

by Paul Cassel

IN THIS CHAPTER

CHAPTER 19

Windows NT Workstation isn't usually thought of as a multimedia platform, but it does quite well as a system. Many legacy hardware devices lack Windows NT drivers, or at least drivers for the current version of NT; however, due to the burgeoning popularity of NT, most current hardware has or soon will have the proper drivers.

Windows 95 and that family of operating systems introduced Plug and Play (PnP) to the IBM-compatible family of computers. When used with PnP-specification hardware, these operating systems dynamically configure the hardware, making themselves aware of it and ensuring a lack of conflicts.

Conflicts have historically been a real problem with PCs. The theory of configuring devices is simple—each device added to a computer can have one or more of the following resources:

- *IRQ (or Interrupt Request number).* Originally, the PC had a total of eight of these. Today, computers cascade the interrupt controllers to provide a total of 16.
- *DMA channel (Direct Memory Access channel).* DMA allows device communications that bypass the processor. It does so by using several channels that act similarly to the channels on a TV. That is, they are pipes that keep the communications discrete.
- *I/O port addresses.* This consists of a base address and a range.

In a perfect world, no two devices in any computer would ever use the same resource. In the real world, however, devices often do. This usually isn't a problem as long as the devices don't operate at the same time.

For example, a tablet digitizer can share an IRQ with a modem just as long as both aren't in use at the same time. If they do become active at the same time, a signal from or for one will often interfere with the other.

Although a working system can perhaps tolerate a digitizing tablet and a modem on the same IRQ, it most likely can't tolerate a mouse and a modem on the same one. It's wildly unlikely that the user would never use the mouse during a modem session. Doing so would knock either the modem or the mouse (or both) out for that booted session.

True PnP uses the Configuration Manager and a compliant BIOS (mainboard firmware) to manipulate the devices. In rough cut, here's how PnP works at bootup:

- The Configuration Manager queries the buss enumerators to query any compliant PnP devices the busses have plugged into them.
- The buss enumerator reports back information about its installed devices.
- The Configuration Manager takes this information and then locates and installs the proper driver for each device.
- The Configuration Manager uses the resource arbitrator to check and resolve any resource conflicts. It then assigns resources for each device.

Figure 19.1 shows a simple graphic of this process. It sounds easy—and it is, from a user standpoint. In theory, if you plug in a new board, the Configuration Manager will detect it during the next bootup, configure it, and either install a driver from its library or request that the user insert a diskette or CD with the driver. In the cases of hot installable hardware, PnP will detect and configure without a boot. At least, that's the theory.

FIGURE 19.1.

The Configuration Manager is the key player in the PnP bootup process.

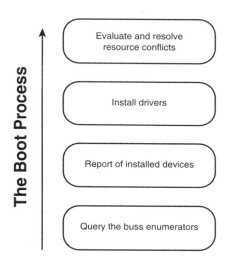

The practice is a little less ideal. First, there are many noncompliant or only partially compliant PnP devices running around out there. PnP either can't address these or makes mistakes when it tries.

Second, an incredibly high percentage of early PnP computers mistook one piece of hardware for another or "discovered" nonexistent hardware during the bootup process. Although nonexistent hardware (or ghost hardware) usually wasn't a functional problem, many users were (and still are) annoyed by these phantoms in the machinery. Convincing a PnP operating system that it has made an error and needs to rethink its ideas about what hardware is actually there can be frustrating or even impossible.

There is no way to turn off PnP, although in many cases you can configure the installed devices to not be PnP and then manually configure them yourself. This removes some of the allure of PnP, but it also removes all the configuration hassles. However, this step should only rarely be necessary.

Windows NT Workstation isn't truly PnP, because it won't dynamically enumerate or configure hardware upon bootup or hot installation. Later versions of Windows NT might be fully PnP-compliant, which might turn out to be a mixed blessing. Although adding hardware in Windows NT today isn't fully automatic, it's not nearly as fully frustrating as in times past.

Windows NT has a detection routine and a good diagnostic to help you install devices without much trouble. More importantly, the lack of a Configuration Manager means Windows NT Workstation will never try to install a phantom piece of hardware. For the most part, if there is a device conflict or misidentification in Windows NT, it's the doing of a human, not the system.

The downside is that you must determine the configuration of all your devices and track them yourself. In many cases, devices won't conflict. For example, video cards will never try to over-write the I/O port address or address space of serial ports. However, some conflict (especially with serial devices and IRQs) is more than possible.

The Multimedia Applet

Multimedia has gone from a buzzword to a reality. The explosive growth of the Internet has helped to fuel the development of increasing numbers of multimedia-capable applications. Users have come to expect software that can talk to them, play music, or show them video clips in real time. Software companies continue to find newer and more innovative ways to exploit the interactive potential of multimedia.

This trend has caused multimedia hardware to become a *de facto* standard part of virtually every computer sold in recent history. Windows NT, like other software offerings, provides comprehensive support for this new and exciting capability.

Multimedia devices within Windows NT are added and configured from the Multimedia applet of the Control Panel. Figure 19.2 shows the Multimedia applet.

FIGURE 19.2.

The Multimedia applet takes the form of the familiar tabbed dialog box showing various aspects of this applet.

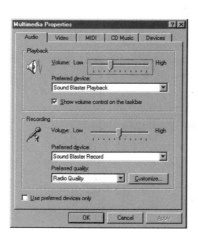

The Multimedia applet is the usual tabbed dialog box with tabs across the top. The Audio, Video, MIDI, and CD Music categories all have a tab. These four tabs configure the user preferences for installed devices of the specified type.

The Devices tab, farthest to the right, shows, installs, and configures device drivers for new or existing multimedia devices. This tab is somewhat similar to the Devices dialog box in Windows 95, but is technically quite dissimilar.

Using the Multimedia Applet Devices Tab

Figure 19.3 shows the Devices tab of the Multimedia applet. The applet has five tabs, each concerned with configuring certain aspects of multimedia. Using the Devices tab, you add, remove, or install drivers for installed hardware.

FIGURE 19.3.

The Devices tab of the Multimedia applet shows installed devices and, optionally, their properties.

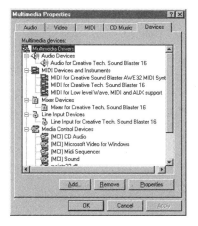

Note that there is a line for every category of multimedia device known to the system. Double-clicking any category or highlighting the category and then clicking Properties produces a list of devices of the selected type. Highlight a device and click Properties to see general information about the device. Figure 19.4 shows the properties for the popular SoundBlaster AWE32 MIDI device. The message box at the bottom of the screen (the box that looks like a pre-NT 4 box) contains version information from Creative Labs, the maker of the SoundBlaster AWE32 board.

The type of information displayed varies somewhat, depending on the device type. If the device has configurable settings, you can display or modify them by clicking the Settings button. Figure 19.5 shows the settings for the SB16 part of the auto board shown in Figure 19.4.

Settings are device-specific and dependent on the hardware characteristics of the device. If your device can be software-configured for different I/O addresses or IRQs, use the Settings button to display a configuration dialog box. You cannot modify the settings for some devices; therefore, the Settings button has no effect on them. Figure 19.5 shows a device that's set to auto-configure. The resource setting combo boxes appear but aren't enabled.

FIGURE 19.4.

The Properties button for a device can lead to another tabbed dialog box and even an About-like screen from the manufacturer.

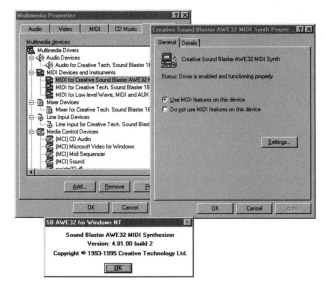

FIGURE 19.5.

The Properties and Settings buttons for the basic audio board show configurable resource settings when applicable to the device.

Using the Multimedia Applet Audio Tab

Windows NT 4 supports multimedia audio extensions. The Audio tab is shown in Figure 19.6. The upper part of the Audio tab controls audio playback characteristics. You can set the playback volume and the preferred playback device for audio output. The volume controls are unavailable if your audio device's volume can't be controlled by software.

The lower part of the Audio tab, shown in Figure 19.6, controls audio recording functions. You can configure the volume, preferred audio recording device, and preferred recording quality. The setting of the Preferred Quality box has a very large impact on the way your system records sound and the size of the sound files that are produced. You can see the extremes with two of the built-in modes. The 8kHz, 8-bit monaural mode uses about 7KB of disk space per second of recording. That is about what telephony-grade recording requires. (Telephony actually uses slightly less.) A CD-quality sound track in 16-bit stereo at 44.1kHz uses a whopping 172KB per second. That is an increase of more than 2,400 percent in disk utilization.

FIGURE 19.6.

The Audio tab controls both recording and playback of sound. By clicking the Customize button, you can choose from preselected recording configurations or make one of your own.

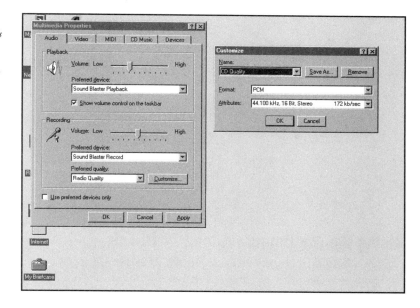

Using the Multimedia Applet Video Tab

The Video tab of the Multimedia applet is shown in Figure 19.7. The Video tab configures characteristics of the display when it is used to play back AVI files or other video information.

You can choose to display video clips either in full-screen mode or in a window. Video clips might be grainy when displayed in full-screen mode, so you might want to use a windowed mode to enhance readability. Selecting the Window button allows you to choose one of several zoom factors for your displayed video clips. The applet tries to simulate what the video will look like in different screen sizes. The picture of the skier in Figure 19.7 looks coarse, and so would video played at full screen.

Selecting the Advanced button of the Video tab allows you to configure your video system to be compatible with the older 16-bit AVI standard. This is sometimes slower than using 32-bit AVI, but it helps to eliminate incompatibilities between Windows NT 4 and older video applications.

19

CONFIGURING
MULTIMEDIA
DEVICES

FIGURE 19.7.

The Properties button for a device can lead to another tabbed dialog box and even an About-like screen from the manufacturer.

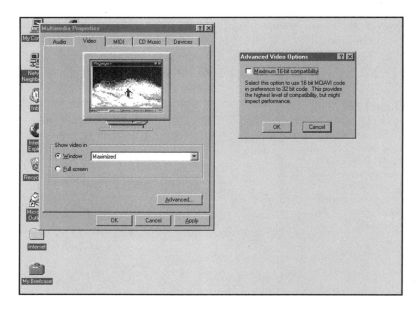

Using the Multimedia Applet MIDI Tab

The *Musical Instrument Digital Interface (MIDI)* standard specifies electrical interconnections and communications configurations that allow you to use your computer to control and play digital musical instruments. Most keyboards today support the MIDI standard.

MIDI can allow you to control up to 16 instruments at once by assigning each instrument to a separate channel. For instance, you might have both a keyboard and a drum module attached to your system. Many MIDI devices are capable of producing very high-quality sound, particularly if you use external MIDI instruments instead of playing MIDI output directly through your sound card.

Figure 19.8 shows the MIDI tab on a system with a MIDI board installed. This tab of the Multimedia applet allows you to use the default settings for your MIDI computer device or to install new instruments manually. Clicking the Add New Instrument button brings up a wizard. The first step of this wizard is shown to the right of the MIDI tab.

Output is configured to use a single MIDI instrument—in this case, the integrated sound capabilities of the SoundBlaster card. You can change the output device by selecting the new device from the list box. If output is assigned to the MIDI port output, you see a list of configured MIDI devices. Selecting a configured device directs future MIDI output to the chosen instrument.

FIGURE 19.8.

MIDI is a specialized area of multimedia. It provides communication between musical hardware and certain software such as sequencers and composition aids.

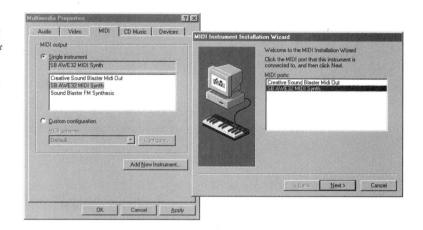

It is also possible to create a custom configuration for MIDI output. Custom configurations can use multiple concurrent instruments. Click the Custom Configuration button if you want to configure more than a single instrument for MIDI playback. Selecting Configure allows you to create your custom configuration. Figure 19.9 shows the MIDI configuration dialog box.

FIGURE 19.9.

The Configure button allows adding one instrument at a time and saving the configurations with a user-specified name.

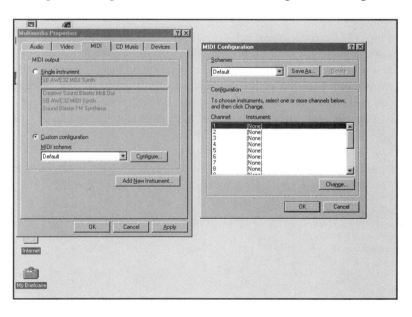

19

CONFIGURING
MULTIMEDIA
DEVICES

You use the top area of the dialog box to select or create a MIDI configuration scheme for editing. You can enter the name of your scheme in the entry box. After you have configured all the instruments for this scheme, click Save As to record the scheme. You can delete an existing scheme by highlighting it and clicking the Delete key.

You use the lower part of the dialog box shown in Figure 19.9 to select the channels and instruments for your new playback scheme. Highlight a channel that you want to configure and then click the Change button. You'll see a dialog box like the one shown in Figure 19.10.

FIGURE 19.10.

You can change the configuration of a MIDI device to add any installed instrument.

Select the instrument that you want to assign to the channel using the combo box; then click OK. You are returned to the display in Figure 19.9. Repeat the instrument configuration procedure for each channel that you want to use in your scheme and then select OK.

Using the Multimedia Applet CD Music Tab

You can usually use the same CD-ROM devices that are used for data devices for music playback as well. Many sound cards have a connector going from the CD player to the sound card that allows CD-ROM music to play back through the sound card amplifier. Most CD-ROM drives are also equipped with a front panel jack that can directly drive headphones or a speaker.

The CD Music tab shown in Figure 19.11 controls the playback of music through a CD-ROM drive. If you have more than one CD-ROM drive connected to your system, select the drive that you want to use for playback using the combo box. You can use the slide control to set the volume of the output at the CD-ROM drive's headphone jack. Note that most drives are also equipped with a hardware volume control. The hardware control and dialog slide control can work against one another; therefore, many times, it is easiest to set one to the maximum volume and always set the volume using the other.

FIGURE 19.11.

The CD Music tab of the Multimedia applet allows you to set the drive letter and the volume of the CD music playback.

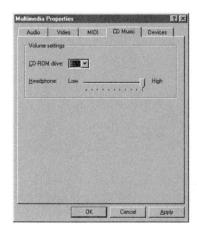

When Things Go Wrong

The best way to install new multimedia hardware is to make sure no conflicts arise in the first place. To see what resources are used in your system, check out the Windows NT Diagnostics program that is part of Start | Programs | Administrative Tools.

This gives you a very good picture of your system. Examine your new device to see what settings it can use and juggle it between the cracks of the currently used resources. Figure 19.12 is the Windows NT Diagnostics program showing currently used IRQs.

FIGURE 19.12.

The Windows NT Diagnostics applet can show used and free IRQs, I/O addresses, DMA channels, and more. This display shows the used IRQs for one system.

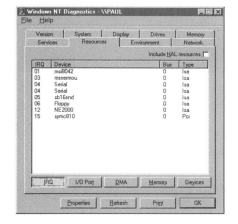

The system shown in Figure 19.12 is configured with a possible conflict. Two serial ports use the same IRQ. This can lead to real problems down the road. In this case, the two serial devices connected aren't ever used together, so there is no practical problem (although it's a bad idea to leave the situation this way as a general rule).

Chapter 5, "Not-Ready-for-Plug-and-Play Hardware," discusses configuration, installation, and troubleshooting of hardware and the use of the Windows NT Diagnostics program.

Summary

Windows NT Workstation 4 isn't PnP, but future versions might be. PnP has a Configuration Manager and a compliant BIOS that allows dynamic detection and configuration of hardware upon startup or hot installation of parts that are hot-installable.

The Multimedia applet is the place to install and configure multimedia devices. It has five tabs: Audio, Video, MIDI, CD Music, and Devices. The main tab is, perhaps, Devices, where general configuration and installation occurs. The other tabs fine-tune existing devices. The MIDI tab allows you to add new instruments using a wizard.

19

CONFIGURING MULTIMEDIA DEVICES

IV
PART

Windows NT Goes to the Internet

Talking to Another Computer: Direct Cable Connection

by Mike Sheehy

IN THIS CHAPTER

CHAPTER 20

How many times have you encountered the need to transfer information from a standalone workstation that is not connected to the network? You don't want to go to the trouble of finding and installing a network card in the workstation and then spending more time getting it onto the network and adding it to a domain. You might not even have a network card available. Is there an alternative?

Direct cable connection (DCC) is a useful method of connecting two workstations together through a null modem cable. If you do not have a network card available and you need to transfer large amounts of data from a standalone workstation, direct cable connection fits the bill. There is no documented information available from Microsoft on DCC under NT 4; therefore, this chapter will take you through the necessary steps to prepare the two workstations for DCC. Be warned that DCC is very unforgiving and will not work if you stray from the outlined steps (which I learned the hard way).

Before you attempt to initiate DCC, I recommend that you acquaint yourself with Chapter 25, "Remote Computing with Remote Access Service," and Chapter 26, "Windows NT Networking Protocols." In addition to this, decide which of your workstations will be the RAS server receiving the calls and which one will be the RAS client initiating the calls.

Null Modem Cable

The null modem cable is the main piece of equipment used to link two workstations together. A null modem cable is a serial cable that has certain lines swapped so that the send and receive lines are correctly routed to each machine. When you are connecting two pieces of data terminal equipment (DTE), which computers are, you need to replace a standard serial cable with a null modem cable.

Figure 20.1 outlines the cabling requirements for a 9-pin and 25-pin null modem cable.

FIGURE 20.1.

Cable requirements for null modem cables.

9 PIN Null Modem		25 PIN Null Modem	
3	2	2	3
2	3	3	2
7	8	4	4
8	7	5	5
6,1	4	6,8	20
5	5	7	7
4	6,1	20	6,8

Ports

There are a number of preparatory steps required for making a DCC. The first of these steps includes the configuration of the COM ports on both machines. Both ports must be running at

19,200bps. Although Microsoft states that DCC can go up to speeds of 15,200bps, I repeatedly encountered errors when I set the speed to anything beyond 19,200. To confirm the speed of your COM ports, open the Control Panel and select the Ports applet, as shown in Figure 20.2.

FIGURE 20.2.

The Ports applet in the Control Panel.

Once you have selected this applet, you are presented with a list of all the workstation's configured ports (see Figure 20.3). Highlight the port you intend to use DCC with and then click the Settings button.

FIGURE 20.3.

The Ports applet lists all the workstation's ports.

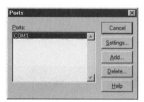

Once you have selected the Settings button, you are presented with the Settings dialog box for the selected port. This dialog box allows you to configure the major aspects of the port (see Figure 20.4). From the Baud Rate drop-down list, select 19,200. While you are in the Settings dialog box, take note of the other settings (such as parity, flow control, and stop bit values). If these values are not the same on both workstations, you can get errors. Repeat the baud rate selection of 19,200 on the other workstation and confirm that the other settings are in sync. For more on COM ports, see Chapter 9, "Advanced Control Panel Tools."

FIGURE 20.4.

The Settings dialog box for a COM port.

Installing a Microsoft Loopback Network Card and TCP/IP

If you are connecting two standalone workstations, you have to install virtual adapters to which you bind a network protocol. This virtual adapter is called the Microsoft Loopback adapter. Complete the following steps to install the virtual adapter and TCP/IP on your workstations.

To install the Microsoft Loopback adapter on the workstation, open the Control Panel and select the Network applet. Then, select the Adapters tab, as shown in Figure 20.5.

FIGURE 20.5.

The Adapters tab in the Network applet.

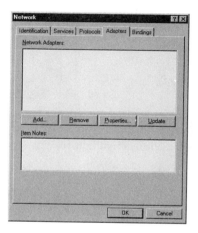

> **NOTE**
>
> You do not have to install the Loopback adapter if a network Interface card is already installed on the workstation.

Click the Add button to be presented with a list of possible adapters. Scroll down the list and select MS Loopback Adapter and then click OK to continue (see Figure 20.6). Once NT copies files to your hard drive, the setup routine displays the MS Loopback Adapter Card Setup dialog box (see Figure 20.7). Select a frame type and configure the other workstation with the same frame type. Enter the path to the NT distribution media when prompted. The new adapter will appear on the Adapter list.

FIGURE 20.6.

Adding the MS Loopback Adapter.

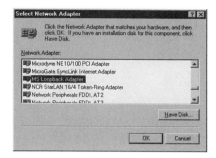

FIGURE 20.7.

Setting the frame type for the Loopback adapter.

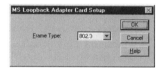

Presumably, you have no network protocols installed on the RAS client or on the RAS server if both are standalone. When using DCC, you'll need to install a common network protocol on each of the workstations so that they can communicate. I have found TCP/IP to be the most reliable to use with DCC. To install TCP/IP on a workstation, open the Network applet from within the Control Panel. Select the Protocols tab, as illustrated in Figure 20.8.

FIGURE 20.8.

The Protocols tab of the Network applet.

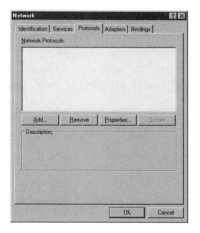

Click the Add button to be presented with a list of additional protocols you can install. Scroll down the list and select TCP/IP Protocol (see Figure 20.9). Click OK to continue.

20

TALKING TO
ANOTHER
COMPUTER

FIGURE 20.9.

*Selecting the TCP/IP
Protocol.*

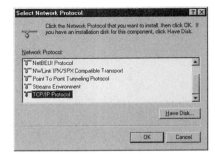

The setup routine will prompt you for the path to the NT distribution media. Enter the path and click OK to copy the necessary files. Once the files are copied, you'll be prompted by the setup routine and asked whether a Dynamic Host Configuration Protocol (DHCP) server is present on your network. DHCP allows a workstation to lease an IP address from a DHCP server. Click Yes for the RAS client workstation so that all the required TCP/IP settings will be taken from the RAS server on connection. On the RAS server workstation, click No to manually set the TCP/IP settings yourself. You'll be presented with the TCP/IP Protocol dialog box with the IP Address tab selected (see Figure 20.10). If the RAS server is already connected to a network and has TCP/IP installed, click OK to exit the Network applet. You'll be presented with the IP Address tab.

Once within the IP Address tab, you'll need to select the Loopback adapter from the drop-down list of adapters to configure its values. On the IP Address tab of the RAS server, enter an IP address and a subnet mask for the DCC interface. This can be any valid IP address you want. If the two workstations are not on a network, it does not matter what IP addressing scheme you choose. If, on the other hand, one of the workstations is on a network, you will have to choose an addressing scheme that fits the local network.

FIGURE 20.10.

The IP Address tab.

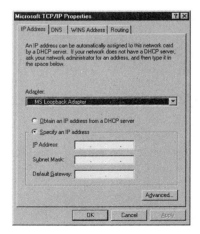

Again, if this RAS server is connected to an existing network, enter the same default gateway address that is used by your network adapter. If you intend to allow the client workstation to connect to the entire network, you'll have to enable the workstation to route traffic onto the network. To configure this, you must select the Routing tab and check the Enable IP Forwarding check box, as illustrated in Figure 20.11. For more on TCP/IP, see Chapter 22, "Setting Up TCP/IP Protocol Access."

FIGURE 20.11.
Enabling IP forwarding.

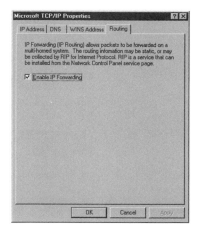

This completes the configuration of the MS Loopback adapter and the network protocol TCP/IP. The workstation will prompt you to reboot so that the new configuration changes can be applied.

Installing Remote Access Service

At this stage, TCP/IP is installed on both workstations; the next step is to install Remote Access Service (RAS) on each of the workstations in turn. RAS is a network service that allows remote users to dial in over a modem and connect to an NT RAS server. One of the workstations has to be configured to call out only, and the other has to be configured to receive calls only. To install RAS, you need to open the Network applet from the Control Panel. Select the Services tab, which is shown in Figure 20.12.

To install an additional service, such as RAS, click the Add button. Clicking the Add button displays a list of additional services you can add. Scroll down the list and highlight the Remote Access Service entry, as shown in Figure 20.13. Then click OK.

You are now prompted for the path to the NT workstation distribution media. Enter the correct path and click Continue.

FIGURE 20.12.

*The Services tab in the
Network applet.*

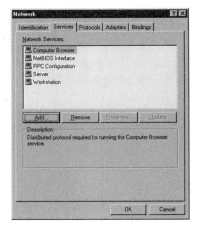

FIGURE 20.13.

*Adding the Remote
Access Service.*

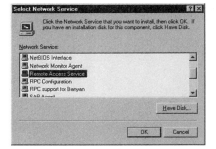

Once NT has finished copying the files, it will present you with the RAS setup routine, which allows you to configure RAS to your needs. If you have not installed an RAS-capable device, you'll have to do so at this point. Traditionally, this has always been a modem, but under DCC you'll have to install a virtual RAS device.

Figure 20.14 shows you the RAS Setup dialog box that you'll be presented with. If you have not already done so, you'll be prompted to install an RAS-capable device. This is done either through the Modem applet, within the Control Panel, or now within the RAS setup. Because you're not installing a real modem, choose the option to manually select the modem. Because you are installing a virtual modem (the null modem cable), NT will fail to auto-detect it— hence the manual option.

When manually selecting a modem, you'll be presented with the dialog box shown in Figure 20.15. Select Standard Modem Types from the Manufacturers list and Dial-Up Networking Serial Cable between 2 PCs from the Models list. The dial-up networking serial cable is the virtual modem that DCC will use to route traffic through RAS to the remote workstation. Click Next to continue.

FIGURE 20.14.
Detecting your modem.

FIGURE 20.15.
Manually selecting the virtual modem.

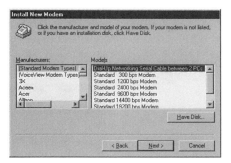

Once you have selected the modem, you must tie it to an available COM port. Figure 20.16 displays a list of available ports. Choose the correct port and select Next. Clicking Next will bring you to the final dialog box of the New Modem setup. Click Finish to proceed with the RAS configuration. For more on installing a modem, see Chapter 21, "Setting Up Your Modem."

NOTE

When you install the direct cable modem, it always defaults to 19,200 but does not alter the baud rate of the COM port it is attached to. You must do this manually.

FIGURE 20.16.
Selecting a port for the virtual modem.

20

TALKING TO ANOTHER COMPUTER

The next dialog box you'll be presented with is the Add RAS Device dialog box (see Figure 20.17). The newly created virtual modem is visible in the list of RAS-capable devices. Select the virtual modem and port and then click OK.

FIGURE 20.17.

Selecting the virtual modem as an RAS-capable device.

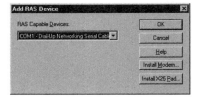

Figure 20.18 shows the installed modem in the Remote Access Setup dialog box after you click OK. Now that you have installed the virtual modem, you must configure it for dialing and a network protocol.

FIGURE 20.18.

The virtual modem installed under RAS.

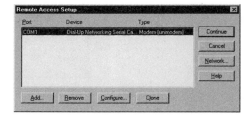

Selecting the Configure button from the Remote Access Setup dialog box produces the configuration dialog box shown in Figure 20.19. You can configure the port for incoming calls, outgoing calls, or both. Click OK when you have selected your option, and you'll be returned to the Remote Access Setup dialog box. As I mentioned earlier, there are two workstations involved in a DCC connection, and one has to be configured to dial out only and the other to dial in only. At this point, you must decide which of your NT workstations will make the call and which will receive the call.

FIGURE 20.19.

Configuring the RAS-capable device to dial out.

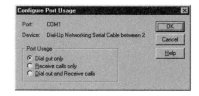

Once you have set the configuration option, you must select a network protocol that will be used with RAS. Click the Network button within the Remote Access Setup dialog box. If you are on the workstation that you have configured to dial out, you'll be presented with a dialog box of available dial-out protocols, as shown in Figure 20.20. Because you have already installed TCP/IP on the workstation, check the TCP/IP box and click OK.

Figure 20.20.

RAS dial-out protocol selection.

If you are on the workstation that will receive calls, you'll be presented with the options shown in Figure 20.21.

Figure 20.21.

RAS dial-in protocol selection.

Checking the TCP/IP check box will enable its Configure button. Click this button to be presented with the RAS Server TCP/IP Configuration dialog box, as shown in Figure 20.22.

Figure 20.22.

The RAS Server TCP/IP Configuration dialog box.

20

TALKING TO
ANOTHER
COMPUTER

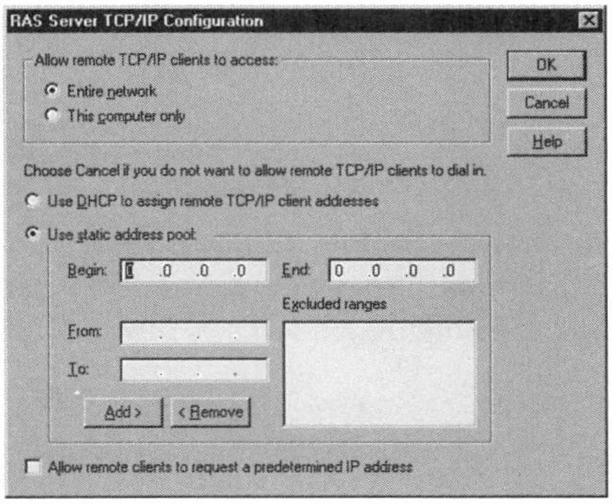

This dialog box is used to specify addressing and accessibility options for connecting clients. Within this dialog box, you can define what the connecting workstation can access. The connecting workstation can be restricted to access either the RAS server only or the entire network—that is, if the RAS server is connected to a network.

Because you have chosen to use DHCP on the RAS client, you must configure the RAS server to allocate IP addresses to the connecting client. Select the Use static address pool button to define a range of valid TCP/IP addresses for your incoming RAS connection. Enter the beginning address of the desired range in the Begin box. Enter the last address of the desired range in the End box. Make sure that the addresses entered are on the same subnet that you configured earlier for the Microsoft Loopback/Network adapter on the RAS server.

This completes the RAS configuration on the RAS server. Click OK to save any changes and reboot the workstation. You are informed that the Remote Access Admin is added to the Start menu under Administrative Tools (Common). For more on TCP/IP RAS configuration, see Chapter 25.

Remote Access Admin

Now that the RAS server is configured, you must allow users to dial-in and connect to it. Once the RAS server workstation restarts, click Start and select the RAS Admin tool by selecting Programs and Administrative Tools (Common). This is a newly added program entry, which is illustrated in Figure 20.23.

FIGURE 20.23.

The Remote Access Admin dialog box.

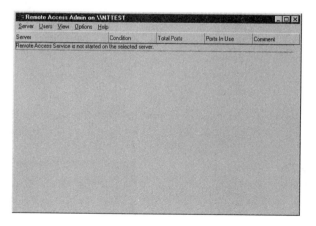

Usually RAS does not start automatically. To start RAS on the workstation, select Start Remote Access Service from the Server menu. You'll be presented with the Start Remote Access Service dialog box. (See Figure 20.24.)

FIGURE 20.24.

Starting RAS.

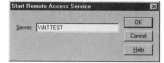

Enter the name of the RAS server and click OK. RAS will start and the Remote Access Admin dialog box will appear. (See Figure 20.25.)

FIGURE 20.25.

The Remote Access Admin dialog box with RAS started.

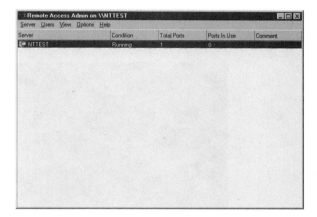

Now that RAS is started, you must allow users to connect via RAS. From the Remote Access Admin dialog box, select Permissions from the Users menu to activate the Remote Access Permissions dialog box (see Figure 20.26). Here, you can see a list of users and whether they have permissions to dial in via RAS. Highlight the username you want to grant access to and check the Grant dialin permission to user check box to allow RAS connection from that user. Click OK to return to the Remote Access Admin dialog box. This completes the configuration on the RAS server side. For more on Remote Access Admin, see Chapter 25.

FIGURE 20.26.

Giving users dial-in permission.

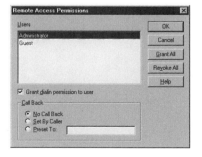

20

TALKING TO ANOTHER COMPUTER

Configuring Remote Access Service Client (Dial-Up Networking)

All that remains now is to configure a dial-up networking session so that the RAS client can connect to the RAS server via DCC. Dial-up networking (DUN) is primarily used to dial a RAS server or an Internet service provider (ISP). Because you are using a virtual modem and RAS, DUN can be used to establish an RAS connection via DCC.

To start DUN, click Start | Programs | Accessories | Dial-Up Networking. This is shown in Figure 20.27.

FIGURE 20.27.

Invoking the dial-up networking client program.

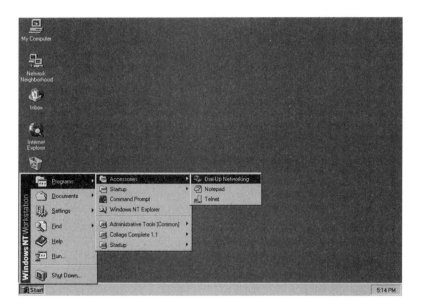

If this is the first time you have started DUN, you'll be asked to create a new phonebook entry. Click OK to create a new entry. (See Figure 20.28.)

FIGURE 20.28.

The initial Dial-Up Networking dialog box.

Creating Simple RAS Client Phonebook Entries

Selecting OK causes DUN to create a new phonebook entry for you. You have two choices at this point: to allow the wizard to create the DUN session for you or to configure it yourself. For first-time users, I suggest that you let the wizard do the legwork for you. (See Figure 20.29.)

FIGURE 20.29.

The New Phonebook Entry Wizard.

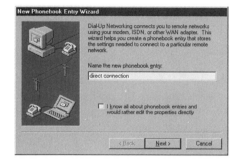

Enter a descriptive name for the session (for example, Direct Cable Session). Click Next to be presented with the next dialog box in the setup. (See Figure 20.30.)

FIGURE 20.30.

Defining the DUN characteristics.

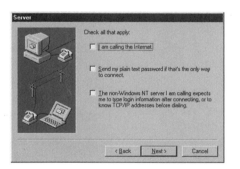

None of the options are really applicable for a DCC session, so just click Next to proceed to the next dialog box. The next dialog box is for entering a phone number for the server you want to call (see Figure 20.31). This should remain blank because you are not making a phone call.

20

TALKING TO
ANOTHER
COMPUTER

FIGURE 20.31.

Entering phone numbers in the Phonebook Wizard.

Clicking Next presents you with the next and final dialog box, as shown in Figure 20.32. Once you click Finish, you are presented with the Dial-Up Networking dialog box, as shown in Figure 20.33. The details of the newly created session are displayed.

FIGURE 20.32.

The final Phonebook Wizard dialog box.

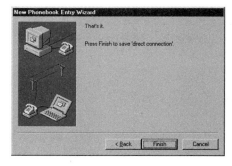

FIGURE 20.33.

The Dial-Up Networking dialog box.

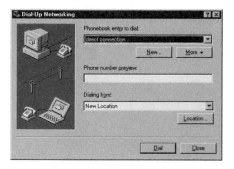

There is further configuration required for the newly created phonebook entry before it becomes ready for use. Click the More button and select Edit entry and modem properties from the menu. This activates the Edit Phonebook Entry dialog box (see Figure 20.34). This dialog box contains five tabs; those relevant to DCC are covered in the following sections.

FIGURE 20.34.

The Basic tab on the Edit Phonebook Entry dialog box.

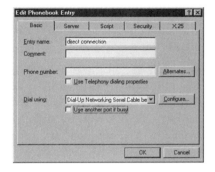

The Basic Tab

Through the Basic tab, you can rename the session and determine what RAS-capable device the DUN session will use to connect to the RAS server. In Figure 20.34 you can see that the virtual modem is selected. To configure the virtual modem, click the Configure button to be presented with the Modem Configuration dialog box. (See Figure 20.35.)

FIGURE 20.35.

The Modem Configuration dialog box.

As I said earlier, I found only the 19,200 speed to be reliable when connecting two NT workstations via DCC. Set the initial speed to 19,200bps. Click OK to be returned to the Basic tab.

The Server Tab

Now select the Server tab. This tab allows you to configure protocol settings. (See Figure 20.36.)

FIGURE 20.36.

The Server tab in the Edit Phonebook Entry dialog box.

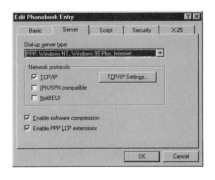

The scroll box at the top of the dialog box allows you to select the remote server type. Here, you are connecting to an NT workstation, so you should select the dial-up server type PPP: Windows NT, Windows 95 Plus, Internet.

Because you are using TCP/IP, click the TCP/IP Settings button to configure the TCP/IP protocol options. The PPP TCP/IP Settings dialog box is shown in Figure 20.37. Here again, you have the ability to define how the RAS client will pick up an IP address. Because you are using the RAS server as a DHCP server, the default setting of server-assigned addresses suits our example's requirements. You can, however, assign specific values if you prefer.

Figure 20.37.

Configuring the TCP/ IP protocol options.

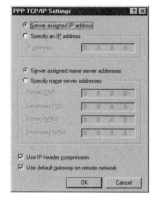

Click OK to finish your TCP/IP protocol configuration.

The Security Tab

The Security tab allows you to select from a number of different security options (see Figure 20.38). If, as in this case, you are connecting to another NT system, select all of the Microsoft encryption options.

> **NOTE**
>
> When you install RAS to receive calls, security defaults to accepting only Microsoft-encrypted authentication. When you install RAS to dial out, security defaults to requiring only encrypted authentication. Make sure that these settings are in sync on both machines.

FIGURE 20.38.

The Security tab.

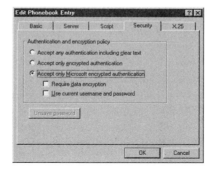

Callback options can also be set on this tab, but it does not make sense to configure callback for DCC. For more on DUN, see Chapter 25.

Making a Direct Cable Connection

Once you are satisfied with the settings on your dial-up session for DCC, click OK to save changes and return to the main DUN dialog box. To initiate a direct connection to the remote workstation, click the Dial button located at the base of the DUN dialog box. You'll be presented with a logon window, as shown in Figure 20.39. Enter a username and password to connect. If you are connecting to a remote NT domain, enter the domain name also. Click OK to authenticate with the remote workstation. Once authenticated, the connection is complete. If you are connecting to a domain, you'll be registered on the network and you'll be able to see the entire domain and its members if you have configured the RAS server to allow access to the entire network.

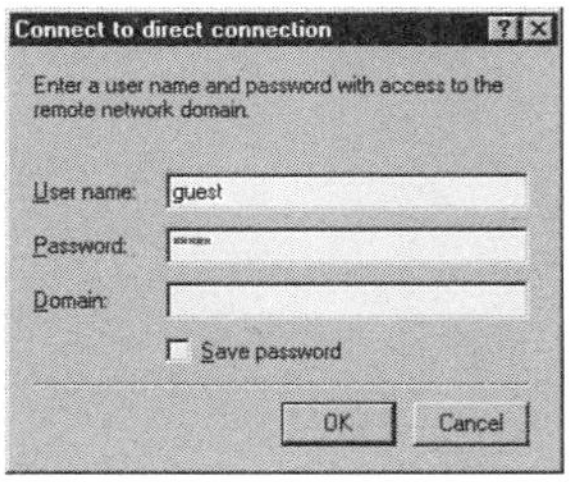

FIGURE 20.39.

The Logon Window.

Summary

In the absence of a network card, Direct Cable Connection (DCC) allows you to transfer data between two NT workstations. DCC uses RAS and a null modem cable to create a link between the two computers. DCC is neither quick nor easy to install because it requires the installation of RAS and a network protocol on both participating machines. If you stray from the required settings, DCC will not work. Having said that, if you are stuck without a network card and require connection between two computers, DCC is for you.

This chapter covered the preparation of both machines by installing and configuring RAS, a virtual modem, a virtual network card, and a network protocol (TCP/IP). You learned the steps required to configure a dial-up networking (DUN) session and to make a direct connection to a remote machine.

CHAPTER 21

Setting Up Your Modem

by Mike Sheehy

IN THIS CHAPTER

In this chapter, you take a close look at the modem and how it works with Windows NT Workstation. The modem has become an important tool over the last few years. The emphasis these days is on mobile users, telecommuters, and dial-up Internet users—none of which would be possible without the modem. Recently, we have seen the speed of modems rise to 56Kbps. If you are a mobile user, telecommuter, or simply a home user who dials an ISP for Internet access, you'll need to be *au fait* with installing, configuring, and troubleshooting your modem.

Installing Your Modem

It's important when buying a modem to choose one that is included in the Hardware Compatibility List (HAL) for Windows NT 4. Installing your modem is done through the Modems icon, which is located in the Control Panel. To install a modem, follow these steps:

1. Double-click the Modems icon, which is contained within the Control Panel (see Figure 21.1). The Control Panel can be accessed either by opening the My Computer program group or through the Start menu (that is, selecting Start | Settings | Control Panel).

FIGURE 21.1.

Accessing the Modem icon.

2. When you double-click the Modems icon, you are presented with the Modems Properties dialog box (see Figure 21.2). This properties dialog box contains a large pane that lists all currently loaded modems. It lists the type of modem and the COM port it is attached to. Currently, there is nothing in the list because no modems are loaded. To install a modem, click the Add button.

3. You are now presented with the Install New Modem dialog box (see Figure 21.3). The installation routine will attempt to detect your modem automatically. NT scans all the workstation's COM ports in turn for a modem. Before you continue, NT suggests that you check to see that the modem is connected correctly and is powered on. It also

advises that you quit any programs that may be using the modem. If you do not want NT to detect your modem and instead would prefer to select it from a list yourself, check the Don't detect my modem; I will select it from a list check box. I prefer to manually select the modem, because I find that NT sometimes returns a standard modem as the result of its findings. At least when you select the modem yourself, you are forcing NT to install that modem. Click the Next button.

FIGURE 21.2.

The Modems Properties dialog box.

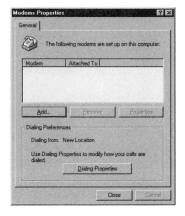

FIGURE 21.3.

The Install New Modem dialog box.

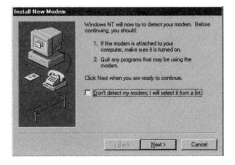

4. The next setup dialog box appears, listing all the modem manufacturers that NT supports (see Figure 21.4). Scroll down through the list of manufacturers and select the manufacturer of the modem you are about to install. When you select a manufacturer, that manufacturer's modems appear in the list on the right. Again, scroll down through the list of models and select your particular modem model. Once you have selected your manufacturer and model, click Next to continue. If you cannot find your manufacturer or model on the list, click the Have Disk button to be presented with the Install From Disk dialog box (see Figure 21.5). Enter or browse to the path of the manufacturer's distribution disk and click OK. You will now be presented with the manufacturer's list of models, as shown in Figure 21.4.

FIGURE 21.4.

Selecting the manufacturer and model of your modem.

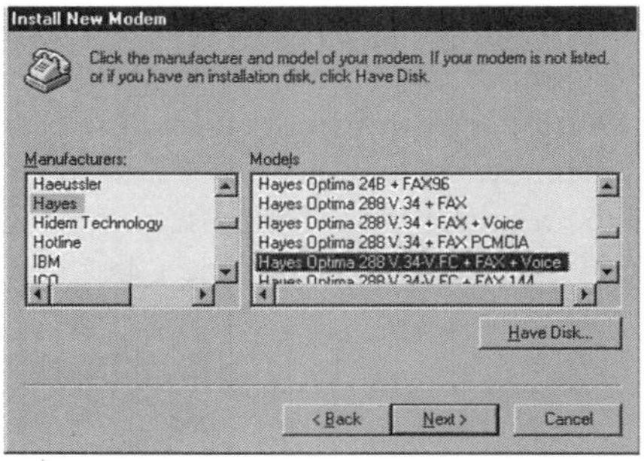

FIGURE 21.5.

The Install From Disk dialog box.

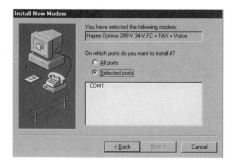

5. Once you have selected a manufacturer and modem model, you are now presented with the next dialog box in the setup (see Figure 21.6). On the top of the dialog box is the name of the modem you chose in the previous step. You must now select the COM port that the modem is attached to. Choose the Selected ports radio button and highlight the COM port that the modem is connected to.

FIGURE 21.6.

Selecting a COM port.

6. Once you have selected the correct COM port, click Next. NT now installs your selected modem on your chosen COM port. The final dialog box in the setup routine informs you of the successful installation of the modem (see Figure 21.7). You can change the properties of the installed modem at any time by selecting the Modems icon within the Control Panel. Click Finish to return to the Modems Properties dialog box.

FIGURE 21.7.

Confirmation of a successful installation.

7. You can now see your newly installed modem listed in the Modems Properties dialog box (see Figure 21.8), as well as the COM port it is attached to.

FIGURE 21.8.

The newly installed modem.

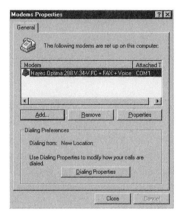

Configuring Your Modem

Sometimes when you install a modem, the COM port that the modem is attached to is also changed to reflect the speed of the modem. To confirm whether the COM port is set correctly for your modem, use the Ports applet within the Control Panel. You will be presented with a dialog box similar to the one shown in Figure 21.9.

Highlight the COM port that the modem is using and click the Settings button. As you can see from Figure 21.10 (which shows an example of a Settings dialog box for a COM port), there is a drop-down list that you can use to select the baud rate of the COM port. If this value is not the right one, you can select the correct value from the drop-down list. For more on COM ports, see Chapter 9, "Advanced Control Panel Tools."

FIGURE 21.9.

The Ports applet.

FIGURE 21.10.

Confirming COM port settings.

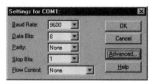

Once you are sure of the COM port settings, return to the Modems Properties dialog box and click the Properties button to configure your modem (see Figure 21.8). You will be presented with the Modems Properties dialog box, which has four tabs: General, Connection, Address, and Forwarding.

General

The first of these tabs is the General tab; it is usually the selected tab by default. Figure 21.11 shows you an example of the General tab. The tab confirms the name of the modem and the COM port it is attached to. You can configure the volume of the modem by positioning the speaker volume slider. You can also set the maximum speed of the modem by choosing its speed from the Maximum speed drop-down list located at the bottom of the tab. In addition to selecting the maximum speed, you can force the modem to connect only at this maximum speed. To configure this option, check the Only connect at this speed check box. If the modem cannot connect at this speed, the call will be terminated. If this option is not checked, the modem will drop down its speed to meet the speed of the remote modem. Forcing the modem to connect only at the maximum speed is advisable only if you know that the remote modem you are dialing can support your maximum speed.

FIGURE 21.11.

The General tab of the Modems Properties dialog box.

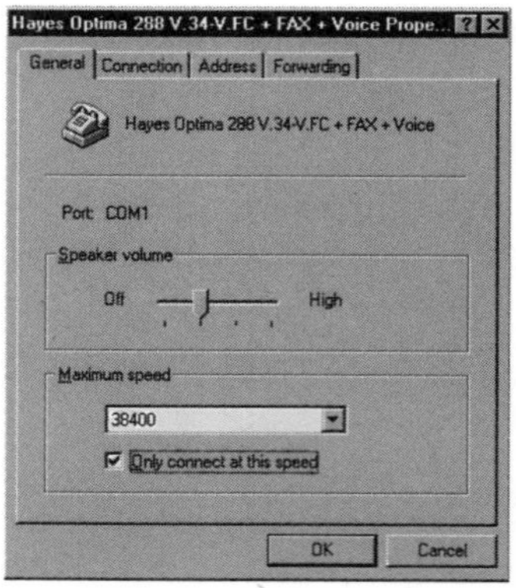

Connection

The next tab in the Modems Properties dialog box is the Connection tab (see Figure 21.12). You can use this tab to configure your connection and call preferences.

FIGURE 21.12.

The Connection tab of the Modems Properties dialog box.

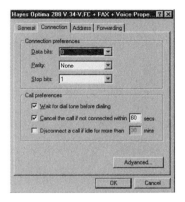

The first frame on the Connection tab is the Connection preferences frame. Within this frame you can set the number of data, stop, and parity bits your connection will use. Your modem has to support this feature, of course. There is little or no need to change any of these settings unless you are dialing in to a private network whose connection settings are different.

The Call preferences frame allows you to configure some preference settings for your calls. Checking the Wait for dial tone before dialing check box forces the modem to wait until a dial tone is detected before it dials the destination's phone number.

You can configure the modem to disconnect if it has not connected within a given number of seconds. To set this preference, check the Cancel the call if not connected within check box and enter a value in seconds that the modem will wait before terminating the call.

The next option is useful for those of you who regularly forget to close dial connections and return an hour later and remember you are still connected long distance. To enable this option, check the Disconnect a call if idle for more than check box and enter a value for the idle period in minutes, after which the call will be disconnected.

Click the Advanced button to configure advanced connection settings. You will be presented with the Advanced Connection Settings dialog box. (See Figure 21.13.)

This dialog box allows you to drill further down to configure advanced options, such as error control. The first frame within the dialog box is Use error control. This frame, when checked, allows you to use error control with your modem connections. Within the frame are options to force error control on connection, to compress data (thus increasing the throughput of your modem connection), and to support cellular protocol for cellular phones. Your modem has to be able to support these options, however.

FIGURE 21.13.

The Advanced Connection Settings dialog box.

The Use flow control option, when checked, allows you to choose hardware or software flow control between your modem and your computer. Flow control adjusts for discrepancies between the speeds of your computer and your modem.

The Modulation type drop-down list allows you to use standard or nonstandard modulation types. Most modems use the standard modulation type for signaling, but if you are having trouble connecting to the remote modem, you might consider changing the modulation type to nonstandard.

The Extra settings text box allows you to enter extra AT initialization commands that might be required by your modem.

The final check box, Record a log file, allows you to log the modem to a file called modemlog.txt that will be placed in your systemroot directory. This can be useful for troubleshooting modem problems. Once you are happy with the advanced connection settings, click OK to return to the Connection tab on the Modems Properties dialog box.

Address

The Address tab (see Figure 21.14) allows you to associate rings with incoming call types. Your phone has to support Distinctive Ring Services for this option to be of any use to you.

FIGURE 21.14.

The Address tab.

Check the This phone line has Distinctive Ring Services check box to activate the frame. There are three ring patterns that you can assign to incoming calls: single, double, and triple. You can associate each of these with voice, fax, data, or unspecified types of incoming calls by selecting the correct entry from the drop-down menu.

Forwarding

The final tab on the Modems Properties dialog box is the Forwarding tab (see Figure 21.15). This tab allows you to enter activation and deactivation codes for call forward. Once you have completed configuring the modem properties to your liking, click the OK button to return to the main Modems Properties dialog box.

Figure 21.15.

The Forwarding tab.

Dialing Properties

At the base of the Modems Properties dialog box is the button Dialing Properties (see Figure 21.8). Clicking this button allows you to define dialing from and dialing to criteria. If you are a mobile user, this can be an invaluable set of options, because dialing is not the same from country to country. Figure 21.16 shows an example of the Dialing Properties dialog box. The My Locations tab allows you to create and choose settings for when you are dialing from different locations.

The default location is already created for you. To create a new location with its own settings, click the New button. The creation of the new location is confirmed by a dialog box message. (See Figure 21.17.)

Edit the name of the location, the area code, and the country to suit your new location. In addition, you must fill in the bottom frame, which defines how your modem dials from the selected location. If there is a digit you have to dial to get an outside line, enter this digit value in the first dial text box. Again, if an additional digit is required to make a long distance call, enter that number in the for long distance text box. If you are using a long distance carrier and want to pay by calling card, you can do so by checking the Dial using Calling Card option and select your carrier by clicking the Change button. You will be presented with the dialog box shown in Figure 21.18. Choose your calling card from the drop-down list and enter your personal identification number (PIN).

Figure 21.16.

The Dialing Properties dialog box.

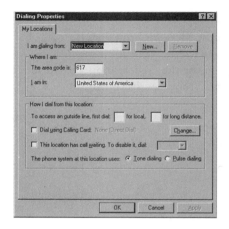

Figure 21.17.

Confirmation that a new location has been created.

Figure 21.18.

Selecting a calling card.

If your carrier is not on the list, simply click the New button to be presented with the Create New Calling Card dialog box (see Figure 21.19). Enter a descriptive name for the entry and click OK.

Figure 21.19.

Enter a name for the new calling card.

You are next required to enter the rules that are associated with this calling card for dialing local, long distance, and international calls (see Figure 21.20). Enter the rules and click OK. Calling rules are available from your carrier. Enter characters to specify particular rules. These characters can be found by pressing the F1 function key and activating the context help for the Dialing Rules dialog. Figure 21.20 shows an example of the characters specifying rules.

FIGURE 21.20.

Enter the rules for the new calling card.

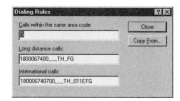

To remove any calling card entry, select it from the list and click the Remove button. Once you have selected the calling card of your choice and have entered your PIN, click OK to return to the Dialing Properties dialog box. If the location you are dialing from supports call waiting, you can disable it by checking the appropriate check box and entering the correct digit sequence to disable this feature. The last option that needs to be set is the dial tone—choose whether the location you are dialing from has pulse or tone. Once you have finished configuring this location's settings, press the Apply button. Figure 21.21 shows an example of a completed location configuration.

FIGURE 21.21.

A completed location configuration.

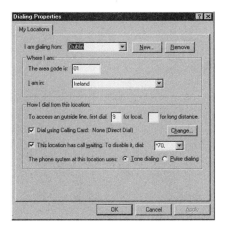

Click OK to return to the main Modems Properties dialog box. Click the Close button to exit this dialog box.

Summary

In this chapter, you explored the installation and configuration of a modem under Windows NT 4. Also, you stepped through the configuration of the modem, drilling down to the level of error control and flow control settings. Finally, you looked at how mobile users might define and save dialing locations. In each country, dialing properties are different. To meet these differences, NT allows you to create and call up dialing location settings that suit your present location. For more on dial-up connectivity, see Chapter 25, "Remote Computing with Remote Access Service."

Setting Up TCP/IP Protocol Access

by Mike Sheehy

IN THIS CHAPTER

CHAPTER 22

From its inception as a United States Defense project in the mid-1970s, TCP/IP is now firmly established as the most popular networking protocol. Its popularity is largely due to the success and growth of the Internet. The Defense Advanced Research Project Agency (DARPA), which developed TCP/IP, started with a project goal to develop a packet-switched network to provide communication between the many research institutions dotted around the United States. Even in the early days of the project, it was clear to everyone the potential that packet-switched networks could have.

In this chapter, you will look a little closer at TCP/IP. I will briefly discuss layering protocols and the concept of IP addresses. I will also step you through the initial installation of TCP/IP on an NT workstation and guide you through the configuration required to get your NT workstation communicating on a TCP/IP network. You will also learn about some simple utilities you can use to troubleshoot your TCP/IP network.

Protocol Layering

The concept of protocol layering has been around for a long time. You can visualize protocol layering as the stacking of protocols on top of one another to produce a *protocol stack*. Each protocol within the stack passes information up and down the stack to the protocols above and below it. Through this interprotocol communication, hosts talk to each other across the network. Information gets passed from a user's application down the stack, across the network medium, and up the remote host's protocol stack to the remote application layer, thus supplying end-to-end communication over the network.

In the late 1970s, the International Organization of Standards (ISO) developed the Open Systems Interconnect (OSI) model, which is a protocol layer model to be used as a blueprint in the development of open systems. Any developer wanting to implement an open systems network has to adhere to the OSI model. Although the Department of Defense (DoD) model does deliver the same functionality as the OSI model, it does not match the OSI model layers exactly (see Figure 22.1).

As you can see from Figure 22.1, the DoD Network access layer corresponds to the Physical and Datalink layers of the OSI model. The DoD Internetwork (IP) layer corresponds to the Network layer in the OSI model. The DoD Host-to-Host (TCP) layer corresponds to the OSI Transport layer. Finally, the DoD Process/Application layer corresponds to the Session, Presentation, and Application layers of the OSI model.

So what does each of the DoD layers do? Let's take a look at each of them in turn:

1. *Network Access Layer.* The lowest layer represents the cables, network cards, and LAN access protocols such as Ethernet or token ring, and so on. The Network Layer groups bits into frames and transmits these frames over the physical communication channel. The Network Access layer is the first layer to provide node-to-node connectivity.

FIGURE 22.1.

The OSI and DoD models.

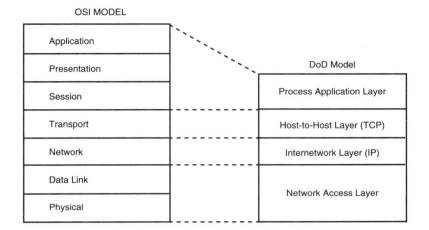

2. *The Internetwork Layer.* This layer builds on the Network Access layer by providing routing capabilities. With routing comes the capability to cater for congestion and flow control. The Internetwork (IP) layer uses network addresses to deliver data to the correct remote node.

3. *Host-to-Host Layer.* Again building on the layer directly beneath it, the Host-to-Host (TCP) layer gives reliable data delivery between hosts. The TCP layer can determine whether packets were lost and can ensure that they are re-sent. If the layers below the TCP layer are not reliable, the TCP layer has to work harder to deliver reliable data. Although the data is delivered to the correct node, it must now be delivered to the correct software element on that node. To identify the correct software element, TCP uses port numbers to deliver data to the correct application. These port numbers are well known, and applications are tied to particular ports. See Appendix B, "Well-Known Service Ports," for a list of well-known addresses.

4. *Process Application Layer.* After the three preceding layers successfully deliver data over the physical medium, through the network, to the correct node, and finally to the correct port within the remote node, the Process Application Layer opens and maintains sessions between the user interface applications.

Figure 22.2 shows a graphical representation of the information flow through the protocol stacks between two hosts over the network.

FIGURE 22.2.
Data flow between two protocol stacks.

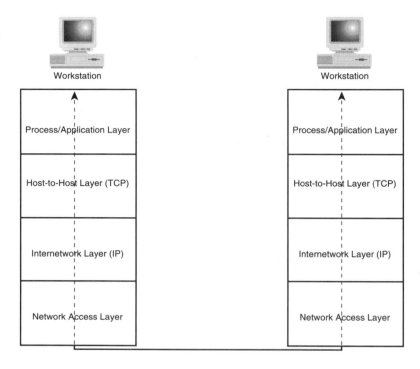

Internet Addresses

The IP address with a port address enables data to be delivered across the network to a specific application running on a remote node. The IP address is crucial to TCP/IP networks, and your having a clear understanding is important in gaining an insight into TCP/IP networks.

The IP address is a unique 32-bit integer assigned to every machine within an IP network. Here's an example of an IP address:

```
10000000 00001001 00000010 00010101
```

This address is rather difficult to remember, especially if you have to administer a network with hundreds of nodes. IP addresses are usually split into four octets, separated by a period, and are represented in decimal form.

The usual representation of an IP address is as follows:

```
127.34.2.1
```

This address is far easier to remember and is more intuitive. The IP address is used to represent both the network address and the host address of a machine. The following are the different types of networks:

■ *Class A.* These networks have IP addresses that are made up of 7 bits to represent the network number and 24 bits to represent the nodes within that network. Mathematically, given a 32-bit integer, you can have 127 class A networks with 16 million nodes each.

■ *Class B.* These networks have a 14-bit network number and a 16-bit node number. You therefore have 16,383 class B networks with 65,000 nodes each.

■ *Class C.* These networks have a 21-bit network number and an 8-bit node number. You therefore have 2,000,000 class C networks with 254 nodes each.

■ *Class D.* These broadcast-based networks are currently being researched.

If you want to connect your network to the Internet, you have to apply for a series of network addresses for your nodes from the Network Information Center (NIC) or its equivalent. You will probably get a class C set of addresses unless you can justify anything bigger. If you just want to implement a TCP/IP network and do not intend to connect it to the Internet, you can use either illegal IP addresses (addresses that are not forwarded through the Internet), or you can use any of the preceding IP address schemes. However, remember that someday your network might be connected to the Internet, and you will be forced to change the addresses.

IP Subnets

So that the assignment of IP addresses and the size of routing tables on gateways could be minimized, the concept of dividing, or *subnetting*, networks was introduced. The division of networks allows IP addresses to reside in multiple physical networks. The key to subnetting is the *subnet mask.* The subnet mask is a 32-bit integer, like an IP address, that determines the division of the network. The IP address coupled with the subnet mask determine the topology of an IP network. The subnet mask is set so that it reflects the subnetting of the network. When you use a logical AND to join the subnet mask with an IP address, you can determine which subnet that IP address belongs to.

Consider a simple class C network such as 192.12.124.0, where the first three octets always describe the network and the fourth octet describes the hosts within that network. You have addresses 0 to 255; however, two of these addresses are unusable because 192.12.124.0 identifies the network and 192.12.124.255 is used as the broadcast address to broadcast to all nodes on the network. You therefore have 254 usable addresses.

The subnet mask for an undivided class C network is 255.255.255.0, which in binary form is 11111111.11111111.11111111.0, where the 1s signify the network grouping. When this subnet mask is AND-ed to an IP address from the class C network, the result is always 192.12.124.0 — the network. Try the following:

```
        192.17.124.18    11000000.00010001.01111100.00010010
AND     255.255.255.0    11111111.11111111.11111111.00000000
        192.17.124.0     11000000.00010001.01111100.00000000
```

To subnet a class C network means that part of the fourth octet describes both the subnetwork and the host. The degree to which it describes the subnetwork is determined by the subnet mask.

Table 22.1 shows subnet masks and the subnetworks and hosts they give you for a class C address scheme.

Table 22.1. How subnet masks divide a class C network.

Subnetmask	*Subnetworks*	*Number of Hosts on Each Subnetwork*
255.255.255.192	2	62
255.255.255.224	6	30
255.255.255.240	14	14
255.255.255.248	30	6
255.255.255.252	62	2

> **NOTE**
>
> After you start subnetting, you start to lose node addresses. This happens because, for every subnetwork you create, two addresses are unusable; they are used to describe the subnetwork address and the broadcast address for that subnetwork.

Table 22.2 shows the division of a class C network using a subnet mask of 255.255.255.224, which divides the network into 6 subnets containing 30 hosts each.

Table 22.2. A class C network subnetted into 6 subnets.

Subnetwork	*Hosts*	*Subnetwork Broadcast Address*
192.17.124.32	33–62	192.17.124.63
192.17.124.64	65–94	192.17.124.95
192.17.124.96	97–126	192.17.124.127
192.17.124.128	129–158	192.17.124.159
192.17.124.160	161–190	192.17.124.191
192.17.124.192	193–222	192.17.124.223

Installing TCP/IP on an NT Workstation

Now that you have covered the background to TCP/IP and have examined the major concepts of an IP network, you're ready to apply it to your NT workstation. If you have not already added your network card, refer to Chapter 26, "Windows NT Networking Protocols," for assistance.

Selecting Your Network Protocol

To install TCP/IP protocol support, use the following procedure:

1. Open the Network applet. You can do so either by right-clicking Network Neighborhood and choosing Properties, or by opening the Control Panel and selecting the Network Applet.

2. In the resulting Network dialog box, select the Protocols tab, as shown in Figure 22.3.

FIGURE 22.3.

The Protocols tab of the Network dialog box.

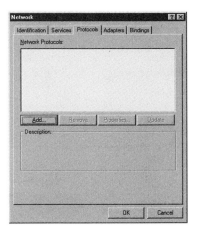

3. Click the Add button to open the Select Network Protocol dialog box, as shown in Figure 22.4.

FIGURE 22.4.

The Select Network Protocol dialog box.

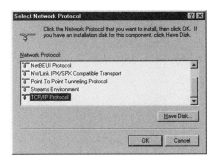

4. Scroll through the list of possible protocols and select the TCP/IP Protocol. Then click OK.

5. The setup routine asks you whether a DHCP server exists on the network, as shown in Figure 22.5. If you choose Yes, the setup routine configures the TCP/IP protocol to receive its settings from the DHCP server. For the sake of this example, I chose No.

FIGURE 22.5.

Does your network possess a DHCP server?

> **NOTE**
>
> A Dynamic Host Configuration Protocol (DHCP) server leases out IP addresses to DHCP clients. Clients, when they boot, request an IP address from the DHCP server. The duration of the lease is determined by the DHCP server. In addition to giving an IP address, the DHCP server also informs the client of the network topology. The DHCP can inform the client of information such as where to find the DNS and WINS servers, what the Internet domain name is, and also what the IP address of the Default gateway to the outside world is.

6. In the resulting Windows NT Setup dialog box, shown in Figure 22.6, enter the path to the NT Workstation distribution media and click Continue. Windows NT Setup then starts to copy files to your system drive.

FIGURE 22.6.

Enter the path to the distribution media.

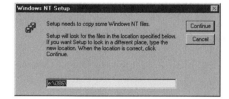

7. After the file copy is complete, you can see the TCP/IP protocol added to the list of loaded protocols in the Network Protocols list of the Network dialog box, as shown in Figure 22.7.

8. At this stage, you have added the TCP/IP protocol. Click Close in the Network dialog box.

FIGURE 22.7.

The TCP/IP protocol is added to the list of loaded network protocols.

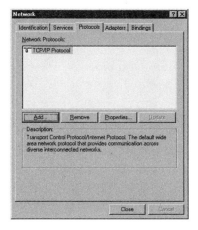

Configuring the TCP/IP Protocol

Once the protocol is added, it must be configured to suit the network around it. When you close the Network dialog box, NT displays the Microsoft TCP/IP Properties dialog box, the contents of which must be configured (see Figure 22.8). The following steps outline the configuration of the TCP/IP protocol:

FIGURE 22.8.

The TCP/IP Properties dialog box.

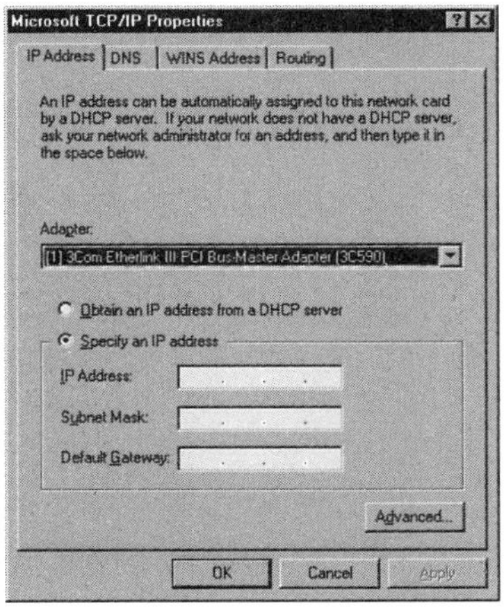

1. The IP Address tab is displayed by default, as you can see in Figure 22.8. Notice the drop-down list of adapters on this tab. NT allows you to have a *multi-homed* machine, in which more than one adapter card can be loaded. This capability is ideal if you want your NT workstation to act as a router or gateway. First, you need to determine whether your network has a DHCP server. Check the appropriate radio button.

2. If your network does not have a DHCP server, you must manually configure each of the TCP/IP elements by hand. To do so, select the Specify an IP address radio button.

3. Selecting the Specify an IP address radio button enables the IP Address, Subnet Mask, and Default Gateway text boxes. At this stage, you should have a fair indication of what these values should be. Remember that you're setting the IP address, subnet mask, and default gateway for the currently selected adapter. Now enter the appropriate information for the adapter.

Configuring Advanced Settings

There are a number of advanced settings that must also be configured for the TCP/IP protocol. These settings are for experienced users and should not be undertaken unless you know what you are doing. The following steps are required to configure the advance options for TCP/IP:

1. Click the Advanced button. The Advanced IP Addressing dialog box then appears, as shown in Figure 22.9.

FIGURE 22.9.

The Advanced IP Addressing dialog box.

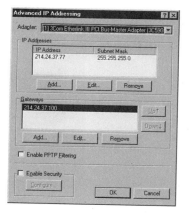

2. On this dialog box, you can configure some advanced TCP/IP options on your workstation. It displays the settings you entered in the preceding section. The options you set here affect only the currently selected adapter. The first of these options is the IP Addresses frame. NT Workstation allows you to set five IP addresses for an adapter. This capability is useful if you have set up multiple logical IP networks.

To add a new IP address, click the Add button. The TCP/IP Address dialog box then appears, as shown in Figure 22.10. Enter an additional IP address and subnet mask for the adapter. Then click Add to return to the Advanced IP Addressing dialog box.

To edit an existing address, just select one from the list in the IP Addresses frame, and click Edit to open the same dialog box, shown in Figure 22.10. Edit the values to suit

your needs. Click the OK button from the TCP/IP Address dialog to return to the
Advanced IP Addressing dialog.

To remove an IP address, select one in the IP Addresses frame, and click Remove.

FIGURE 22.10.

*TCP/IP Address
dialog box.*

3. The next Advanced option in the Advanced IP Addressing dialog box is contained
   within the Gateways frame. This frame allows you to specify multiple gateways.
   Again, you can specify up to five default gateways, thus providing greater fault
   tolerance within your network. If the first gateway on the list is unreachable, then the
   workstation tries to reach the next gateway on the list.

   To add a second gateway, click the Add button to open the TCP/IP Gateway Address
   dialog box, as shown in Figure 22.11. Enter the IP address of an alternative gateway.
   Then click Add to return to the Advanced IP Addressing dialog box.

   To edit an existing gateway's IP address, select it and click the Edit button to open the
   TCP/IP Gateway Address dialog box again (see Figure 22.11). Once you have edited
   the gateway address, click on the OK button to return to the Advanced IP Addressing
   dialog.

   To remove a gateway, first select it and then click Remove.

   You can use the up and down arrow buttons to the right of the Gateways frame to
   change the order in which the alternative gateways are tried when the default becomes
   unreachable.

FIGURE 22.11.

*TCP/IP Gateway
Address dialog box.*

4. If you're implementing a Virtual Private Network (VPN), check the Enable PPTP
   Filtering check box in the Advanced IP Addressing dialog box (refer to Figure 22.9).
   Selecting this option configures the workstation to receive only PPTP packets. For
   more information on PPTP, see Chapter 25, "Remote Computing with Remote
   Access Service."

5. If you check the Enable Security check box, you can then choose the Security button.
   The TCP/IP Security dialog box then appears, as shown in Figure 22.12. This new
   addition to NT enables you to define which packets your workstation will accept and
   reject. The TCP/IP Security dialog box contains three lists that allow you to define

ports and protocols through which you will accept packets. The three lists are for TCP and UDP ports and for IP protocols. You can permit all ports and protocols by selecting the appropriate radio buttons. However, note that when you add a port or protocol to a list, all other ports and protocols are excluded. To add a port or protocol, simply click the Permit Only radio button associated with the list you're adding to. Then click the Add button under the list to open a dialog box similar to the one shown in Figure 22.13.

FIGURE 22.12.

TCP/IP Security dialog box.

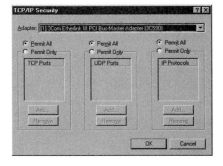

FIGURE 22.13.

A Security Add dialog box for TCP.

6. After you set your filtering configurations and close the Security Add dialog box, click OK to close the TCP/IP Security dialog box and return to the Advanced IP Addressing tab. Click OK again to return to the main Network dialog box. Remember that the packet filtering you configure applies only to the currently listed adapter. To configure another adapter, select it from the adapter list.

Configuring DNS

If you have not configured the workstation for DHCP, you must also configure it manually for DNS. This is done from the DNS tab. The following steps outline what is required to configure the DNS settings:

1. Select the DNS tab from the Network dialog box, as shown in Figure 22.14. Domain Name Service (DNS) provides the ability to resolve IP names into IP addresses and vice versa. DNS has done away with the old method of maintaining host files on each machine. These host files contained IP names and their corresponding IP addresses. Each computer resolved IP addresses locally, but the downside was that a single change had to be executed on all host files. This process was time-consuming and a nightmare to maintain. Finally, the idea of a DNS server evolved in which computers

went to a third party and asked it to resolve IP addresses. The host files are now contained in one place. DNS servers themselves can have secondary DNS servers to which they automatically replicate information at regular intervals. Secondary DNS servers can also resolve IP address requests from clients.

FIGURE 22.14.

The DNS tab.

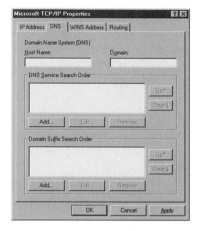

2. Usually, NT picks up your NetBIOS name and places it within the Host Name text box. Having your NetBIOS names and your TCP/IP names match makes life a lot easier. You can change it if you want by editing the contents of the Host Name text box.

3. Enter your IP domain name in the Domain text box. Don't confuse this name with your NT domain name if you are a member of an NT domain.

4. In the DNS Service Search Order frame, you can enter names of three DNS servers. Click the Add button to open the TCP/IP DNS Server dialog box, as shown in Figure 22.15. Enter the IP address of the DNS server and click Add to return to the DNS tab.

   To edit a DNS server entry, select it in the DNS Service Search Order frame, and click the Edit button to change the server's IP address.

   To remove a DNS server, select it and click the Remove button.

   To arrange the order in which NT Workstation queries the servers listed, use the up and down arrow buttons to the right of the frame to list the servers in order of preference. If you selected Yes to using a DHCP server earlier, these settings are filled from the DHCP server when you restart the workstation.

FIGURE 22.15.

TCP/IP DNS Server dialog box.

5. In the Domain Suffix Search Order frame of the DNS tab, you can enter six extra domain names to be tagged to hostnames when sending a name's resolution request to your DNS server. Configuring this option is good if you can identify domains that you regularly visit. Notice that DNS is not configured on an adapter basis.

Configuring WINS

The next tab, WINS, allows you to configure a network adapter for Windows Internet Name Services (WINS). WINS is to NetBIOS what DNS is to TCP/IP. WINS is used to resolve NT NetBIOS names. The history of WINS is the same as that of DNS. At first, an LMHOSTS file containing NetBIOS names and IP addresses was kept on every computer. Eventually, this evolved into a third-party service supplied by a WINS server. Under NT Server 4, DNS and WINS are tightly coupled services. Execute the following steps to configure an adapter for WINS:

1. Select the WINS Address tab of the TCP/IP Properties dialog box, as shown in Figure 22.16.

FIGURE 22.16.

The WINS Address tab.

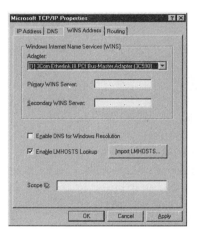

2. Enter the IP address of your primary and secondary WINS servers in the appropriate text boxes. If the workstation fails to contact the Primary WINS server, it tries to contact the secondary server instead. Notice that the adapter drop-down list, WINS, is configured on an adapter basis.

3. Check the Enable DNS for Windows Resolution check box if you want to use DNS after a failure is returned from a WINS server. If the WINS server returns a failure for a resolution request, the NT workstation sends the query to its DNS server, tagging its domain to the end of the NetBIOS name. The other suffix domain names are tried in turn if configured.

4. If you're also maintaining a local LMHOSTS file, check the Enable LMHOSTS Lookup check box.

5. Click the Import LMHOSTS button to import an LMHOSTS file from anywhere in the network. The LMHOSTS file normally resides in the systemroot\system32\ drivers\etc directory. For more information on LMHOSTS files, see Chapter 26.

6. The Scope ID box, located at the bottom of the WINS Address tab, is usually left blank. Computers can talk to one another only if they have the same Scope ID.

Configuring Routing

If your NT workstation is acting as a router, you might want to configure the routing option in the Routing tab.

Click the Routing tab, which is shown in Figure 22.17, to view the routing settings. Routing is the last of the TCP/IP configuration tabs.

FIGURE 22.17.

The Routing tab.

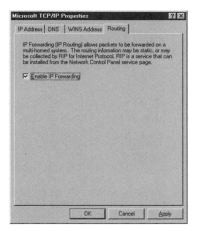

If your NT workstation has more than one network adapter card loaded, you can use it to route traffic. Check the Enable IP Forwarding check box to enable IP routing. By default, it supports static routing, but you can load Routing Information Protocol (RIP) as a service and get your workstation to support dynamic routing.

To define static routes, you can use the command-line utility route. From the DOS prompt, enter the following syntax for the route command:

```
route [-f] [-p] [command [destination] [mask subnetmask] [gateway] [metric
➡costmetric]]
```

For more on the route utility, type route at the DOS command line.

After you finish configuring all the TCP/IP settings, click the Apply button at the bottom of the TCP/IP Properties dialog box to update any changes you have made. NT then performs some high-level checks on the configurations and reports any erroneous settings. You are returned to the main Network dialog box. When you click OK to exit the Network dialog, NT prompts you that you need to restart the workstation before any of the changes can take effect, as you can see in Figure 22.18. Choose Yes to restart the workstation.

FIGURE 22.18.

Restart the workstation for network changes to take effect.

Confirming TCP/IP Is Running Properly

When the workstation restarts, you need to determine that it can now communicate with other computers on the network and that TCP/IP is loaded properly. Provided that no TCP/IP errors are displayed when NT starts and there are no TCP/IP errors within the event log, it is safe to assume that the installation of TCP/IP has succeeded. The only other problem you might have is with the configuration settings. To check the validity of these settings within your network, you can use the command-line utilities described next.

ipconfig

The ipconfig command-line utility shows you the current network settings of your workstation. Type ipconfig /all at the DOS prompt, and you see output like the following:

```
Windows NT IP Configuration
Host Name . . . . . . . . . : javatester.mydomain.com
DNS Servers . . . . . . . : 192.67.42.5
Node Type . . . . . . . . : Hybrid
NetBIOS Scope ID. . . . . :
IP Routing Enabled. . . . : No
WINS Proxy Enabled. . . . : No
NetBIOS Resolution Uses DNS : Yes
Ethernet adapter El59x1:
Description . . . . . . . : Fast Ethernet Adapter
Physical Address. . . . . : 00-20-AF-F6-BC-A7
DHCP Enabled. . . . . . . : No
IP Address. . . . . . . . : 192.67.42.77
Subnet Mask . . . . . . . : 255.255.255.0
Default Gateway . . . . . : 192.67.42.151
Primary WINS Server . . . : 192.67.42.135
```

The /all option gives you the complete settings. Typing ipconfig on its own gives you only the workstation's IP address, its subnet mask, and the IP address of its default gateway.

ping

By far the most useful and easy-to-use utility available to administrators is ping. It is a command-line utility that confirms connections between remote computers. Many GUI versions of this application have been developed over the years, but they really don't give you anything over the command-line version. Connection is verified by sending ICMP echo packets to a remote computer and then listening for a reply. The ping utility prints the number of packets sent and received. By default, ping sends four packets containing 64 bytes of data and waits 1 second for a reply.

You either ping a remote computer by its IP address or by its IP name. Using the IP address is better, if you can remember it, because using an IP name brings an extra variable into the mix. What if your DNS server is not up and you start pinging by IP name? You never get a response from the DNS server, and your ping fails.

The following is an example of a ping to www.microsoft.com's IP address:

```
C:\>ping 207.68.156.52
Pinging 207.68.156.52 with 32 bytes of data:
Reply from 207.68.156.52: bytes=32 time=101ms TTL=243
Reply from 207.68.156.52: bytes=32 time=100ms TTL=243
Reply from 207.68.156.52: bytes=32 time=120ms TTL=243
Reply from 207.68.156.52: bytes=32 time=120ms TTL=243
```

You can change the number and size of packets that ping sends by setting them at the command line. After you confirm that you can ping by IP address, you can then consider pinging by IP name. This operation also confirms that you can reach your DNS server and that it is resolving properly.

tracert

Sometimes you can ping computers in your local subnetwork but cannot reach anything beyond that. To determine where the breakdown in communication is, you can use the tracert utility. It, too, is a command-line utility. The tracert utility displays each network hop it takes on its route to the remote computer. After it hits a network error, it responds with a time-out message. You should always try to tracert by IP address first. The following is an example of using tracert:

```
C:> tracert 192.56.139.5
Tracing route to 192.56.139.5 over a maximum of 30 hops

  1    160 ms    170 ms    201 ms   147.223.24.1
  2    191 ms    190 ms    190 ms   147.223.24.18
  3    210 ms    200 ms    211 ms    192.56.139.5
Trace complete.
```

The tracert utility also displays DNS hostnames for the nodes it meets on the route—that is, if they have hostnames.

nbtstat

The utility nbtstat checks the status of NetBIOS over TCP/IP connections. You can also use it to view and flush a workstation's NetBIOS name cache.

Typing nbtstat at the DOS command line gives you all the command-line options.

One of `nbtstat`'s options, `nbtstat -a computername`, gives you a list of the remote computer's name table. It lists the name of the computer, its domain or workgroup, and what role it plays within the NT network.

The following is a sample listing returned from `nbtstat -a computer`:

```
c:> nbtstat -a Javatester
NetBIOS Remote Machine Name Table
    Name          Type    Status
------------------------------------
MAC Address = 00-20-AF-F6-BC-A7
JAVATESTER       <00>    UNIQUE
DOAMINA          <00>    GROUP
JAVATESTER       <03>    UNIQUE
JAVATESTER       <20>    UNIQUE
DOMAINA          <1E>    GROUP
```

netstat

The `netstat` command-line utility can give you protocol statistics and confirm the state of current TCP/IP connections. For more options on `netstat`, type `netstat /?` at the DOS command line. The following is an example of the information returned for the local host when you type `netstat` at the command line:

```
C:>netstat
Active Connections
Proto  Local Address        Foreign Address        State
TCP    javatester:1026      localhost:1027         ESTABLISHED
TCP    javatester:1027      localhost:1026         ESTABLISHED
TCP    javatester:1030      SHEEHY:nbsession       ESTABLISHED
```

Summary

In this chapter, you learned the background to TCP/IP and looked at the concepts of IP addresses and subnetting. You also stepped through the installation and configuration of Microsoft's TCP/IP network protocol. Finally, after installing TCP/IP, you examined utilities that you can use to confirm that the NT workstation is configured and communicating properly under TCP/IP.

Using Microsoft Internet Explorer 4

by Mike Sheehy

IN THIS CHAPTER

CHAPTER 23

For some time now, the battle of the browsers has raged as Microsoft redirected its corporate focus toward the Internet. Because enough has already been written on this epic struggle to capture the browser market, this chapter concentrates on the task of investigating the nuts and bolts of Internet Explorer 4, Microsoft's latest offering into the Web browser arena.

If you're not familiar with browsers or the Web, let me give you a little background. The World Wide Web (WWW) is primarily an information service on the Internet. Web sites dotted around the Internet store information, text, graphics, sounds, and so on. These sites use an underlying technology called HyperText Markup Language (HTML) to format and present the information. On each user desktop is a browser, which is an application that can request information from a Web site, interpret it, and present it to the user in a nice, graphical fashion. Information is transferred from the Web site to the user desktop via an IP protocol called HyperText Transfer Protocol (HTTP).

Kicking Off Internet Explorer 4

Version 4.0 of Internet Explorer does not come pre-installed with Workstation. You must download and install version 4.0 over the existing version of Internet Explorer. Internet Explorer is freely available from Microsoft's Web site. After you download and install Microsoft Internet Explorer 4 (IE4), you can configure it by kicking off the setup wizard the first time you start IE4. You can access IE4 by selecting it from the Start menu. To do so, choose Start | Programs | Internet Explorer Suite | Internet Explorer, as shown in Figure 23.1.

FIGURE 23.1.

Accessing IE4 from the Start menu.

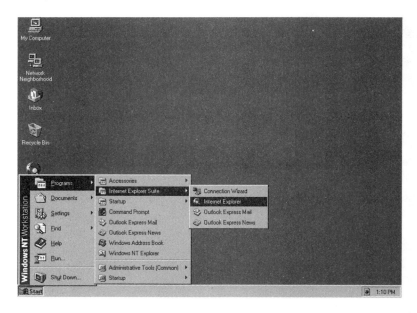

If this is the first time you have started IE4, you are presented with the Internet Connection Wizard dialog box, as shown in Figure 23.2.

FIGURE 23.2.

*The Internet
Connection Wizard.*

In this first dialog box, you can define how your Workstation will connect to the Internet. Choose your preferred connection method and click Next to proceed.

If you choose to connect via a modem, the setup wizard takes you through the detection, installation, and configuration of the modem and also the installation and configuration of the Remote Access Service (RAS) client. For more information on adding a modem and RAS, refer to Chapter 21, "Setting Up Your Modem," and Chapter 25, "Remote Computing with Remote Access Service."

If you choose to connect via a LAN, you are asked whether you connect via a Proxy server, as you can see in Figure 23.3. Choose the correct option and click Next to continue.

FIGURE 23.3.

Are you using a proxy?

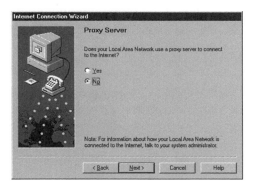

If you choose Yes, you have to fill in the correct proxy values for the services you are using. Figure 23.4 shows the Proxy Server Name dialog box. Enter the name or IP address of the proxy server in the Proxy to use column and enter the port number in the Port column for that service. After you enter your proxy settings, click Next to continue.

If you're not using a proxy, the next dialog box asks whether you want to set up your Internet mail account, as you can see in Figure 23.5. To set up your account now, choose Yes and then click Next to continue. Your e-mail account, as with all other IE4 settings, can be configured later if you choose.

23

USING MICROSOFT INTERNET EXPLORER 4

FIGURE 23.4.

Enter the Proxy values.

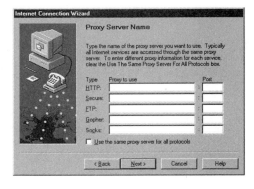

FIGURE 23.5.

Set up your e-mail account.

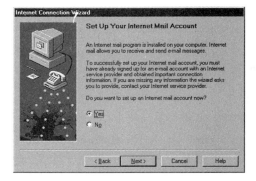

If you choose Yes, the next wizard dialog box requests your Internet mail account name, as you can see in Figure 23.6. You can enter any name you want that will be a descriptive name to represent your Internet service. Enter a descriptive name now and click Next to continue.

FIGURE 23.6.

Enter your Internet mail account name.

The next wizard dialog box, shown in Figure 23.7, requires you to enter your full name. This name will be displayed in the From field of all your outgoing messages. Enter your name and click Next to continue.

FIGURE 23.7.

Enter your display name.

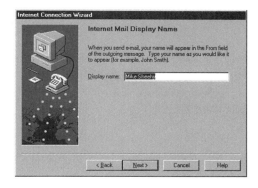

In the next wizard dialog box, shown in Figure 23.8, you must enter your e-mail address. After you're done, click Next to continue.

FIGURE 23.8.

Enter your e-mail address.

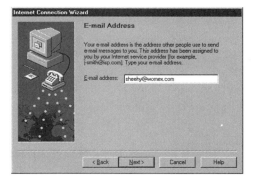

In addition to your e-mail address, the setup wizard requires you to enter the type of mail server you're using, as you can see in Figure 23.9. Select the correct type of mail server from the drop-down list. Also enter the name or IP address of your incoming and outgoing mail servers. Then click Next to continue.

FIGURE 23.9.

Enter e-mail server addresses.

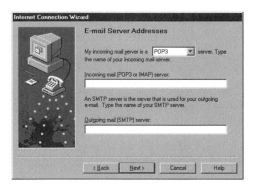

After you enter the e-mail server details, the next dialog box, shown in Figure 23.10, requires you to choose how you will be authenticated by the e-mail server. You can choose from two possibilities:

■ Log on using a username and password.

■ Log on using Secure Password Authentication (SPA). This capability has to be supported by your ISP.

FIGURE 23.10.
Internet Mail Logon.

After you choose how you will log on, click Next to be presented with the next wizard dialog box, shown in Figure 23.11. This dialog asks whether you want to set up your Internet news account.

FIGURE 23.11.
*Set up your Internet
News Account.*

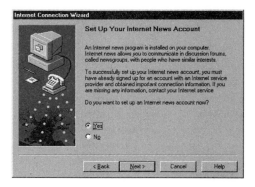

If you choose Yes and then click Next, you are presented with the Internet News Account Name dialog box, as shown in Figure 23.12. In this dialog box, enter a name for the news provider and click Next to continue.

The next dialog box, Internet News Display Name, requires you to enter a display name for news. By default, IE4 displays the display name you entered for e-mail, as you can see in Figure 23.13. You can change this name to whatever value you want. Then click Next to continue.

FIGURE 23.12.

Enter your news provider.

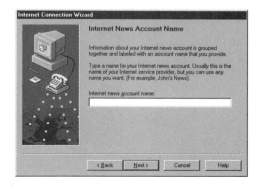

FIGURE 23.13.

Enter your news display name.

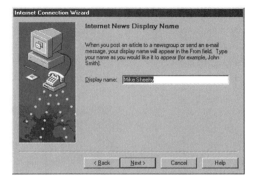

The next wizard dialog box requires you to enter an e-mail address for news. Again, IE4 picks up the e-mail address you specified earlier for e-mail, as you can see in Figure 23.14. You can change this value if you prefer. Click Next to continue.

FIGURE 23.14.

Enter an e-mail account for news.

The next wizard dialog box, shown in Figure 23.15, requires you to enter the name of the news server you will be using. If you have to log on the news server, check the My news server re-quires me to log on check box. Then click Next to continue.

Figure 23.15.

Enter the news server name.

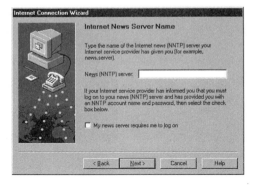

If you do not choose the option to log on to your news server, you are presented with the final dialog box in the setup, as shown in Figure 23.16. If you do have to log on to your news server, you are presented with a dialog box, like the one in Figure 23.10, that requires you to specify how you will log on to the server. After you enter these values and continue, you are presented with the final dialog box. Click Finish to complete the setup.

Figure 23.16.

Configuration complete.

When you start IE4 again, you go to the IE4 section of the Microsoft Web site.

The IE4 User Interface

Before going any further, let me explain the main areas of the IE4 User Interface (UI). These areas include the following:

- *Menu bar.* The menu bar located at the top of the UI allows you to configure and use the browser by selecting entries from the appropriate menu. I describe each of these menu entries in turn later in the chapter.

- *Toolbar.* Below the menu bar is the toolbar. The toolbar contains buttons that represent many of the menu options.

■ *Address.* In the Address list box, you can enter locations of Web sites you want to see. The Address list box keeps a history of the sites you have visited. To revisit any of them, simply scroll down the list and select the one you want.

■ *Links.* The Links bar is used to store preselected Web sites. You can toggle between the Address list and the Links bar by clicking either the Address or Links button.

■ *Page.* Below the Address is a large pane. This pane is used to display the information sent back from the Web site. Web sites divide their information into pages.

■ *Status bar.* At the base of the UI is the status bar that displays the current status of the browser. The status bar displays information such as the page it is accessing, what percentage of the page is left to download, and so on.

■ *Logo.* Another area of the UI is the logo that is located on the top right-hand side of the browser. This logo also represents the status of the browser. If the browser is downloading or opening a page, the logo moves. If the browser is inactive, this status is represented by a static logo.

Address

To access a Web site, you must enter its address in the Address list box. Web sites are represented by Uniform Resource Locators (URLs). These URLs can be as general or as specific as you require. Through URLs, you can specify either an entire Web site, or you can drill down and specify a particular page within it. A URL is always preceded by a prefix to define the data type it represents. For example, if a URL is preceded by a prefix of `http://`, it signifies a scheme of HTML files. Other schemes are outlined in the Table 23.1.

Table 23.1. URL definition schemes.

Scheme	*Data Type*	*Example*
file	Data files	`file://ftp.microsoft.com/download/ie4.exe`
http	HTML files	`http://www.womex.com`
news	newsgroup	`news:news.womex.com`
telnet	Telnet	`telnet://hp1.mydomain.com`
wais	WAIS	`wais://wais.mydomain.com:8080`

As you can see from Table 23.1, a URL consists of a scheme prefix and a host and IP domain name. A host and IP domain name is a means of representing an IP address in a more intuitive way. For example, a machine might have an IP address of `192.168.12.10`, yet might possess a DNS name of `myhost` and might be a member of the `mydomain.com` IP domain—for example, `myhost.mydomain.com`. As you can see, a DNS name is easier to remember than an IP address. There is nothing stopping you from entering an IP address for a URL instead of a DNS name. For more information on DNS, see Chapter 26, "Windows NT Networking Protocols."

Look at the example of the http entry from Table 23.1—http://www.womex.com. This general
URL points to the index page for the entire site, as you can see in Figure 23.17.

FIGURE 23.17.

A general URL.

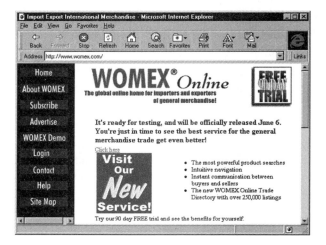

To drill down further, you either need to enter a more specific URL, as shown in the Address
list box in Figure 23.18, or follow a hypertext link.

FIGURE 23.18.

A specific URL.

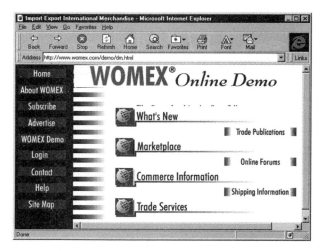

As I mentioned previously, the Address list keeps a history of the sites you visit. To go to any
of these sites, simply scroll down through the list and select a site you want to visit.

Toolbar

The toolbar, which is located beneath the menu bar, is useful for quickly accessing various tools and features within IE4. Toolbars are primarily used to present menu options to users in a graphical fashion. When the main menu options are displayed in a prominent position on the toolbar, users can select options quicker. The main toolbar buttons are outlined later in this chapter. The IE4 toolbar contains navigation buttons that allow you to navigate your way through sites. You can use the Back and Forward buttons to navigate between pages you have previously visited. Usually, Webmasters place hypertext links to preceding and succeeding pages within the pages themselves. You use the Stop button to interrupt the loading of a page, site, file, or other multimedia object.

To refresh the display, click the Refresh button. This action builds the page from IE4's cache. To force IE4 to reload from the site directly, hold down the Shift key and click Refresh.

The Home button, when clicked, takes you to your user-defined home page. When you start IE4, it always loads this home page. Later in this chapter, you learn how to set this page to be whatever you want.

The Search button splits your page and displays a search page, as shown in Figure 23.19.

FIGURE 23.19.
The search page.

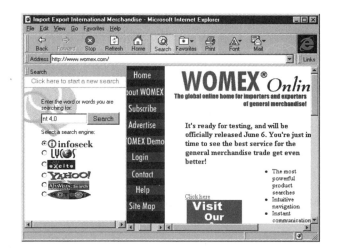

This search page contains a list of possible search engines you can use and a text box into which you can enter a keyword or phrase to search for. Click the Search button on this page after you select a search engine and keyword. The search engine searches the Internet and returns a list of sites containing the keyword or phrase you're looking for, as you can see in Figure 23.20.

FIGURE 23.20.

A search result.

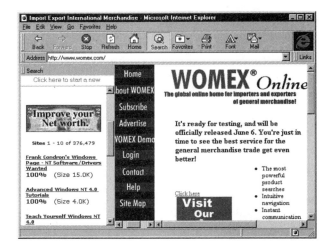

To go to any of those sites, simply click the hypertext link. To remove the split and close the search page, click the Search button on the toolbar. If you think that having the two pages side-by-side is a little cramped, you can open the search page within a window of its own by right-clicking the search bar at the top of the search window and selecting the Open in Window option.

Favorites

The Favorites button on the toolbar contains a menu for configuring and selecting your favorite sites. Click it to activate the menu, which is shown in Figure 23.21.

FIGURE 23.21.

The Favorites menu.

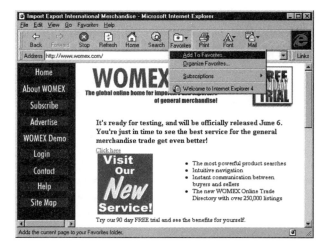

To add the current URL to your list of favorites, simply choose Add To Favorites from the menu.

You can manage your favorites by choosing the Organize Favorites option. The Organize Favorites dialog box then appears, as shown in Figure 23.22.

FIGURE 23.22.

The Organize Favorites
dialog box.

Your favorites are stored within the Favorites folder of your profile folder. The buttons at the base of the Organize Favorites dialog box can aid you in the management of your favorites.

The Move button allows you to move a selected favorite to a subfolder underneath the favorites folder. After you choose the Move button, the Browse for Folder dialog box appears, as shown in Figure 23.23. In this dialog box, you can select a new destination for your folder. After you decide on a destination, click OK to return to the Organize Favorites dialog box.

FIGURE 23.23.

Browse for Folder
dialog box.

The Rename button in the Organize Favorites dialog box allows you to rename a selected favorite to whatever name suits you. Choosing the Delete button removes the favorite from the list. To open a separate IE4 window with the selected favorite, click the Open button. To close the Organize Favorites dialog box and return to IE4, click the Close button.

At the base of the Favorites menu are the current favorites. When you select any one of them, IE4 takes you to that site.

Subscriptions

The next option on the Favorites menu is Subscriptions. Through the Subscriptions submenu, you can subscribe to a Web site and configure IE4 to pull down any updates to the site automatically. This feature is useful because you can download the pages by night or when your workstation is idle. You can view the updated site either online or offline at your convenience.

To subscribe to a site, simply choose the Subscribe option from the Subscriptions submenu. The Subscription dialog box then appears, as shown in Figure 23.24.

FIGURE 23.24.

The Subscription dialog box.

This dialog box lists the details of the subscription. If you're not happy with any of the subscription details, click the Properties button to change them. Doing so activates the Properties dialog box for your newly created subscription. This dialog box, shown in Figure 23.25, is divided into four tabs, the first of which is the General tab.

FIGURE 23.25.

The General tab of the Subscription Properties dialog box.

The General tab outlines the details that you see on the main Subscription dialog box. The following details are included on the General tab:

- The name of the site you're subscribing to
- How you will be notified of updates
- When IE4 will seek updates
- When you subscribed
- When the next update will occur
- When IE4 last updated the site
- The status of the last update

On the Schedule tab, shown in Figure 23.26, you can define when IE4 seeks an update from the site.

FIGURE 23.26.

The Schedule tab.

You can set IE4 to update daily or weekly, or you can customize IE to update when you require. If you select Custom and click the Edit button, the Custom Schedule dialog box then appears, as shown in Figure 23.27.

Here, you can get more specific with scheduling and download when it best suits you. Select a schedule and click OK to return to the Properties dialog box.

You need to set one final configuration option on the Schedule tab of the Properties dialog box. If the remote site requires a username and password, click the Login Options button. The Login Options dialog box then appears, as shown in Figure 23.28.

In this dialog box, enter your username and password for the site. Click OK to return to the Properties dialog box.

FIGURE 23.27.
The Custom Schedule dialog box.

FIGURE 23.28.
The Login Options dialog box.

The next tab within the Properties dialog box is the Delivery tab, as you can see in Figure 23.29.

FIGURE 23.29.
The Delivery tab of the Subscription Properties dialog box.

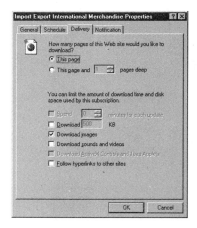

On this tab, you can control how much is downloaded from the remote site. You can download a single page or a user-defined number of pages below the current level if you want. You can also place a cap on the total size of pages, in kilobytes, that can be downloaded. In addition, you can decide whether to download graphics, sound, and video. You can configure IE4 to follow links to other sites automatically and download its contents also.

The last tab within the Properties dialog box is the Notification tab, which is shown in Figure 23.30.

FIGURE 23.30.

The Notification tab of the Subscription Properties dialog box.

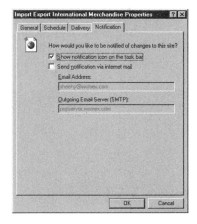

On the Notification tab, you decide how IE4 will notify you of changes to your subscribed site. The options are either a notification icon on the Taskbar or via Internet mail. Notice that IE4 has already displayed your e-mail details. Select the appropriate method of notification and click OK to return to the main Subscription dialog box (refer to Figure 23.24). If you are now happy with the subscription settings, click OK to close the Subscription dialog box.

To view your currently subscribed sites, choose View All from the Subscriptions submenu. You then are presented with the Subscriptions dialog box shown in Figure 23.31.

FIGURE 23.31.

Viewing current subscriptions.

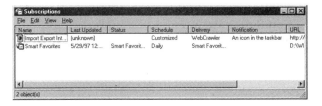

This dialog box lists all your current subscriptions, when they were updated last, how often they are updated, how they are delivered, how you are notified, and finally the URL for the site. You can visit any of these sites by double-clicking their entry from the list.

Also within the Subscriptions submenu is the Update All option, which forces IE4 to update all your subscribed sites.

The final option on the Subscriptions submenu, called Options, allows you to set global options for all your subscriptions. When you choose this option, the Global Properties dialog box appears, as shown in Figure 23.32.

23

USING MICROSOFT INTERNET EXPLORER 4

FIGURE 23.32.

The Global Properties dialog box.

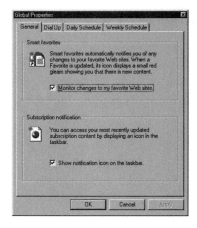

The first tab on the Global Properties dialog box, General, allows you to configure IE4 to monitor changes to your favorite sites and notify you immediately (see Figure 23.32). Through the General tab, you can also access the most recently updated content through an icon displayed on the Taskbar.

The Dial Up tab, shown in Figure 23.33, applies if you're connecting to the Internet via a dial-up connection.

FIGURE 23.33.

The Dial Up tab of the Global Properties dialog box.

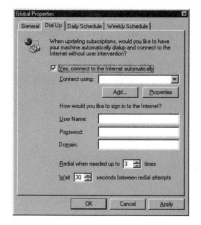

You can get NT to make a dial-up connection to the Internet automatically without user intervention. By selecting Yes, connect to the Internet automatically check box, you enable all the settings on the tab. You can define or create a dial-up session that IE4 will use. This brings you through the creation of a phonebook entry within Dial-Up Networking (DUN). For more information on DUN, see Chapter 25. If you're logging onto an NT domain when you connect to the Internet, you can enter your username, password, and domain name here so that it is submitted automatically for you. At the base of this dialog box are options you can set to define the number of times NT will re-dial to make a successful connection. Additionally, you can set a waiting period between each attempted re-dial.

On the Daily Schedule tab, shown in Figure 23.34, you can customize your daily schedules. You can define a period of time within which the update must start, a repeat interval, and a termination time.

FIGURE 23.34.

The Daily Schedule tab of the Global Properties dialog box.

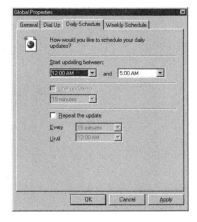

The Weekly Schedule tab, shown in Figure 23.35, gives you the same options but at a weekly level. In addition to the options offered under the Daily Schedule tab, the Weekly Schedule tab also allows you to choose days of the week for updating.

FIGURE 23.35.

The Weekly Schedule tab of the Global Properties dialog box.

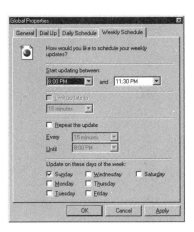

After you finish setting the global options for your subscriptions, click Apply to update your changes. To exit the Global Properties dialog box, click OK.

File Menu

In addition to the toolbar, a user can choose to use the menu bar, located at the top of IE4. The first menu on the menu bar is the File menu. By choosing the Open option from the File menu, you can open a URL. This approach is equivalent to entering the URL in the Address list box. When you choose Open, the Open dialog box appears, as shown in Figure 23.36. Here, you enter the URL for the site you want to visit and click OK. Notice that the Open dialog box keeps a history of URLs you have previously entered within its drop-down list. A history list containing previously visited sites is also maintained within the File menu itself. You can also browse to a saved URL by choosing the Browse button. To save the current URL you're visiting, simply choose File | Save. You can also choose the Save As option to determine where the URL is saved.

FIGURE 23.36.

The Open dialog box.

If you choose File | Properties, the Properties dialog box for the currently displayed URL appears, as shown in Figure 23.37. The General tab of the Properties dialog box lists the page header, its protocol, its document type, its URL, its size, and when it was created, modified, and updated.

FIGURE 23.37.

The Properties dialog box for a page.

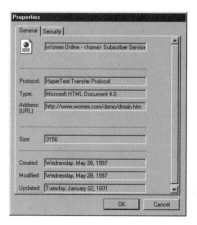

The Security tab of the Properties dialog box, shown in Figure 23.38, lists the security information for the current page. To close the Properties dialog box, simply click OK.

23

USING MICROSOFT
INTERNET
EXPLORER 4

FIGURE 23.38.

Security information on the current page.

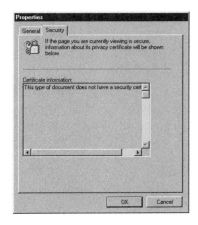

The Browse offline option on the File menu allows you to traverse through pages that you downloaded earlier through a scheduled update. You do not have to be online because these pages are all on your workstation. If you try to traverse to pages that are now held locally, the mouse pointer changes to a prohibited sign to signify that you have to be online to visit that particular hyperlink.

Edit Menu

The Edit menu allows you to cut, copy, and paste selected objects to and from pages. You also can choose the Find option, which searches the current page for a word or phrase you enter.

View Menu

You use the View menu to enable or disable the toolbar and status bar. You can also use it to view the source of a page in raw HTML format. Figure 23.39 shows the HTML equivalent of the page shown in Figure 23.17.

FIGURE 23.39.

A home page in raw HTML.

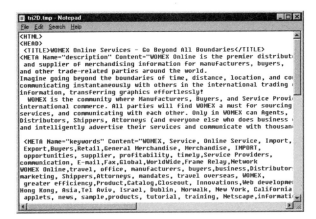

Options

By choosing View | Options, you can configure IE4 to a look and feel that suits you. Figure 23.40 shows the General tab of the Options dialog box that appears.

FIGURE 23.40.

The General tab of the Options dialog box.

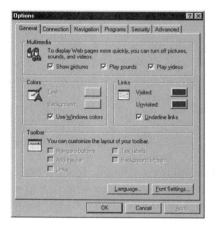

From the Multimedia frame, you can enable or disable IE4 from playing sounds and videos and showing pictures. In the Colors frame, you can define your own color scheme for the text and the background. The Links frame allows you to define which colors are associated with visited and unvisited links. You can also specify that links be underlined.

Choosing the Language button activates the Language Preference dialog box, as shown in Figure 23.41. Many sites offer their content in multiple languages. If you have multiple languages loaded, the page is displayed in the order of languages you have loaded matching one supported by the providing site. If you want to add a language, simply click the Add button and select a language from the list. To change the priority of languages, select a language and use the Move Up and Move Down buttons to reorder them. Click OK to return to the Options dialog box.

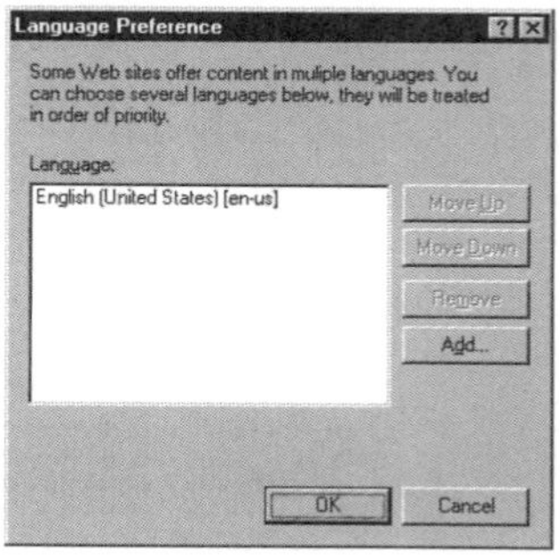

FIGURE 23.41.

The Language Preference dialog box.

Selecting the Font Settings button on the General tab invokes the Fonts dialog box, as shown in Figure 23.42. Here, you can set which proportional and fixed-width fonts to use and at what size. You can also set the default character set. Click OK when you're happy with the font settings.

FIGURE 23.42.

The Fonts dialog box.

On the Connection tab of the Options dialog box, shown in Figure 23.43, you can set a proxy for IE4. Checking the Connect through a proxy server check box turns on the Settings button.

FIGURE 23.43.

The Connection tab.

If you choose the Settings button, the Proxy Settings dialog box appears, as shown in Figure 23.44. On this dialog box, you can enter proxy values for services. You should be aware of the ports these services use. Consult Appendix B for a full list of ports. To disable the use of a proxy server for certain IP addresses or domains, you must enter the IP addresses and domains in the Exceptions box located at the base of the dialog box. You can use wildcards here to describe networks and so on. Click OK to return to the Options dialog box.

FIGURE 23.44.

The Proxy Settings dialog box.

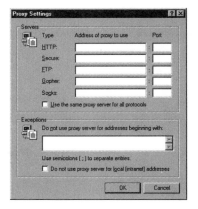

If you want IE4 to go to a location and read the configuration information from a file automatically, clicking the Automatic Configuration button on the Connection tab displays the Automatic Configuration dialog box, as shown in Figure 23.45. Here, you enter the URL to the configuration file. Click OK to return to the Options dialog box.

FIGURE 23.45.

The Automatic Configuration dialog box.

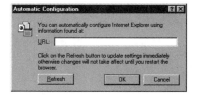

On the Navigation tab of the Options dialog box, shown in Figure 23.46, you can configure the Links bar. Every option within the Page drop-down list is associated with a name and address displayed in the text boxes below the Page drop-down list. You can customize all five links yourself. Simply select them from the Page list and change the Name and Address to whatever you want.

In the History frame, you can set the number of days pages remain within the history. To view the current history list, click the View History button to activate the History dialog box, which is shown in Figure 23.47. The History dialog box lists all the sites visited, their titles, when they were last visited, and when they were last updated. To clear the contents of the history, click the Clear History button on the Navigation tab.

FIGURE 23.46.

The Navigation tab.

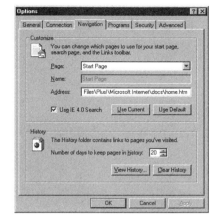

FIGURE 23.47.

The History dialog box.

On the Programs tab of the Options dialog box, shown in Figure 23.48, you can configure programs to use with IE4. The Mail and news frame is used to configure what mail and news program IE4 will use. When you're selecting files from the Internet, you can get IE4 to open them automatically with an associated program. Within the Viewers frame, click the File Types button to display the current file type associations (see Figure 23.49). They are the same as the file type associations mentioned in Chapter 11, "The NT Registry." As you can see from Figure 23.49, a JPEG image file is opened with IE4.

FIGURE 23.48.

The Programs tab.

FIGURE 23.49.

File type associations.

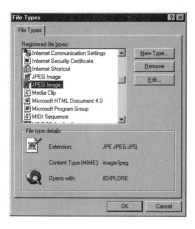

On the Security tab of the Options dialog box, shown in Figure 23.50, you can set restraints on the use of IE4.

FIGURE 23.50.

The Security tab.

You can place restraints on the content being downloaded to your workstation by invoking the Content Advisor. This ratings advisor is protected with a password of your choice when first activated. To activate the Content Advisor, click the Enable Ratings button. After you set a password, click the Settings button to configure the Advisor. After you enter the correct password, the Content Advisor dialog box then appears, as shown in Figure 23.51.

This dialog box has three tabs: Ratings, General, and Advanced. On the Ratings tab, shown in Figure 23.51, are categories of Language, Nudity, Sex, and Violence; you can restrict this content by sliding the ratings bar located beneath the Category box.

FIGURE 23.51.

The Content Advisor.

The General tab of the Content Advisor, shown in Figure 23.52, allows you to set restrictions on sites that have no rating and to override a closed page by typing the correct password. You can also change the Content Advisor password by clicking the Change Password button.

FIGURE 23.52.

The General tab.

On the final Content Advisor tab, Advanced, you can define or change the ratings company the Content Advisor uses (see Figure 23.53).

Click the Rating Systems button on this tab to activate the Ratings System dialog box, which is shown in Figure 23.54.

FIGURE 23.53.

The Advanced tab.

FIGURE 23.54.

The Rating Systems dialog box.

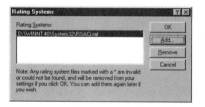

You can add or remove rating files obtained from ratings companies from within this dialog box. After you select your preferred ratings company, click OK to return to the Content Advisor dialog box. Remember to click Apply to update your changes. You then return to the Security tab of the Options dialog box.

The Certificates frame of the Security tab allows you to configure IE4 for certificates (refer to Figure 23.50). These digital certificates are used to secure communication made between nodes on the Internet. Clicking the Personal button allows you to see what personal certificates you have. If you choose the Sites button, you can view only certificates from selected sites. Figure 23.55 shows you the Site Certificates dialog box with the names of the companies who issue the certificates. Click Close to return to the Security tab.

FIGURE 23.55.

The Site Certificates dialog box.

The Publishers button in the Certificates frame allows you to define what publishers of software you trust. The Authenticode Security Technology dialog box, shown in Figure 23.56, appears when you choose the Publishers button. You can trust all publishers by selecting the Consider all commercial software publishers trustworthy check box. Click OK to return to the Security tab.

FIGURE 23.56.

The Authenticode Security Technology dialog box.

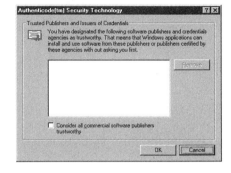

In the Active content frame on the Security tab, you can enable or disable the following:

- Allow downloading of Active content
- Enable ActiveX controls and plug-ins
- Run ActiveX scripts
- Enable Java programs

Choosing the Safety Level button at the base of the frame activates the Safety Level dialog box, as shown in Figure 23.57. Here, you can select a security method that suits you; your choices are High, Medium, or None. After making your selection, click OK to return to the Security tab.

FIGURE 23.57.

The Safety Level dialog box.

The final tab within the Options dialog box is Advanced, which is shown in Figure 23.58.

23

USING MICROSOFT INTERNET EXPLORER 4

FIGURE 23.58.

The Advanced tab.

You use the Temporary Internet files frame to manage the cache of temporary files that IE4 stores on your hard drive. To view them, click the View Files button. You then see a list of all the files currently stored within IE4's cache, as shown in Figure 23.59.

FIGURE 23.59.

The IE4 cache.

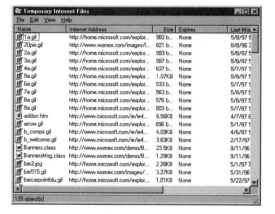

Choosing the Settings button from the Temporary Internet files frame displays the Settings dialog box, as shown in Figure 23.60. Here, you can manage the cache.

Within the Settings dialog box, you can force IE4 to verify its cache in the following ways:

- Every visit to the page
- Every time you start Internet Explorer
- Never

FIGURE 23.60.
The Settings dialog box.

Using the slide gauge, you can define what percentage of your drive can be occupied by your cache. The present location of the cache is also detailed. If you want to move, view, or empty the cache, choose the appropriate button. When you're happy with the cache settings, click OK to return to the Advanced tab of the Options dialog box.

Within the Advanced frame of the Advanced tab, you can also set options on Browsing, Cryptography, Imaging, Java, Printing, Searching, and Warnings. By selecting the appropriate radio buttons or check boxes, you can tailor these features to suit your environment.

Go Menu

Through the Go menu, you can traverse backward and forward through pages, access any of your links, and also kick off Outlook's Mail and News clients and Windows Address Book applications.

Favorites Menu

The Favorites menu on the menu bar is the exact same as the Favorites menu within the toolbar. See the section earlier in this chapter for details.

Links

To access a number of sites quickly, you can use the Links bar. The Links bar shares the same area on the user interface as the Address list box. To toggle between them, simply click either the Address or Links button. Figure 23.61 shows the IE4 UI with Links selected. As I mentioned previously, you can set the contents of the Links bar through the Navigation tab of the Options dialog box. You access the Options dialog box via the View menu; see the "View Menu" section.

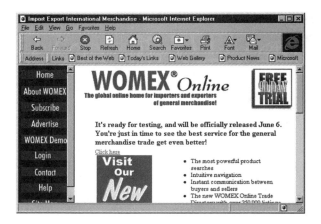

IE4 Tips and Tricks

To complete this look at IE4, I'll give you some tips and tricks to help you to get more from your browsing.

Drag to Links

You can drag a URL from a page and drop it on your Links bar. You can change the link's settings later by choosing View | Options.

Context Menu

Right-clicking any page gives you the right-click, or context, menu (see Figure 23.62). With the right-click menu, you can traverse backward and forward, select all, create shortcuts, add the current page to your favorites, View the document source, select the default language, print the current page, refresh the current page, and view the properties of the current page.

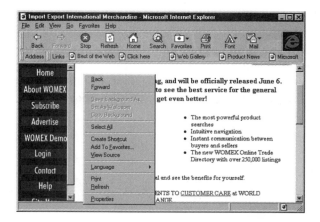

Powerful Printing

In IE4, options have been added to the standard print options. Figure 23.63 shows the Print dialog box with the two extra frames: Print What and Linked Documents. The Print What frame allows you to print either the select frame or all frames. This capability is useful if you're visiting a site with HTML frames. The other frame, Linked Documents, allows you to print all linked documents also. Be careful with this option because your current page could be linked to many more pages.

FIGURE 23.63.

Extra print options.

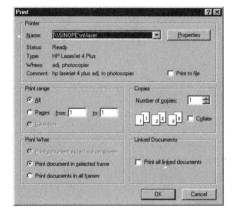

Moving Favorites

You can drag and drop favorites within the Favorites menu and the Favorites toolbar entry. If you have several favorites, you can organize them so that the most popular ones are always on top.

Back and Forward

If you right-click the Back or Forward buttons, you get a list of the recent sites you visited. Select one, and IE4 takes you there directly.

Dragging Bars

By default, the Address and the Links bar share the same space. You can move either of them to a separate line by clicking its left side and dragging and dropping it, as shown in Figure 23.64.

FIGURE 23.64.

Dragging bars.

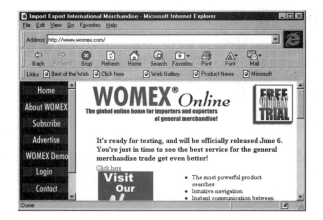

Summary

As the battle of the browsers rages, Microsoft's latest response comes in the form of Internet Explorer 4 (IE4). This chapter covered the initial setup of IE4 and took you through this feature-rich browser. The chapter concluded by covering some tricks and tips you can employ to leverage off IE4's many features.

Using the Microsoft Exchange Client

by Mike Sheehy

CHAPTER 24

E-mail is now firmly established as one of the most popular media for information exchange. Windows Workstation NT 4 comes with its own e-mail client, Microsoft Exchange client. This version of Exchange client is not the full-blown version that comes with Exchange Server. Nonetheless, it still has more than enough functionality to meet your needs because this version is crammed with options.

In this chapter, I will describe Microsoft's Exchange client, walking you through the steps required to send and receive e-mail. I will try not to drill down too much because a full discussion on the Exchange client on its own could fill a book (such as *Microsoft Exchange Server 5 Unleashed*, Sams, 1997). After you're comfortable with these basic tasks, you will learn how to customize Exchange client to suit your needs. I will show you how to generate and maintain your own Address Book and how to queue e-mail for delayed delivery if you work offline.

Starting Exchange Client

To start Microsoft's Exchange client, follow these steps:

1. Double-click the Inbox icon located on your desktop. If this is the first time you've executed this operation, the system prompts you to install Windows Messaging, as you can see in Figure 24.1.

FIGURE 24.1.
Installing Windows Messaging.

2. Choose Yes to start the Exchange client installation. You then are prompted for the Windows NT Workstation distribution media.

3. Insert the CD, and type or browse to the Workstation files. The system begins copying the necessary files required by the Exchange client.

4. After the file copy operation is complete, double-click the Inbox again. This time, double-clicking the Inbox starts the Windows Messaging Setup Wizard, as shown in Figure 24.2.

FIGURE 24.2.
The Windows Messaging Setup Wizard.

5. By default, two information services are checked for use in the first dialog box of the setup wizard: Microsoft Mail and Internet Mail. If you do not have a requirement for either of these services, uncheck the appropriate box and click Next to continue. If you're an experienced end user, you can choose to configure the information services manually by selecting the Manually configure information services radio button located at the base of the dialog box.

NOTE

Exchange client is primarily intended for use as a POP3 Internet mail client. However, there is good news if you do not have an Internet connection or any messaging system in place. Microsoft also includes Workgroup Postoffice (WGPO), which is a simple messaging system that can be used in-house. Exchange clients support both POP3 and WGPO. To configure Workgroup Postoffice, you use the Microsoft Mail Postoffice applet in the Control Panel.

---

6. On the next dialog box of the setup wizard, shown in Figure 24.3, enter the path to the Microsoft Postoffice. Then click Next to continue. Even if you cannot connect to the Postoffice, the setup wizard continues to configure the Exchange client for a WGPO.

FIGURE 24.3.

Enter the path to the Postoffice.

7. In the next dialog box, shown in Figure 24.4, identify your postoffice account. Select your account and click Next.

8. In the next setup wizard dialog box, shown in Figure 24.5, enter the password to the WGPO account to confirm you are who you say you are and then click Next.

FIGURE 24.4.

Identify your WGPO account.

FIGURE 24.5.

Enter your WGPO password.

9. Now you must configure the Internet Mail information service. The next dialog box of the setup wizard, shown in Figure 24.6, gives you a choice of connections to the Internet: Modem or Network. Select whichever is applicable to you and click Next. (For this example, I chose to connect via a network.)

FIGURE 24.6.

Define your connection to the Internet.

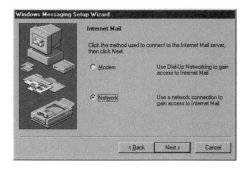

NOTE

If you choose to connect via a modem, the setup wizard takes you through the Dialup Networking (DUN) configuration. See Chapter 21, "Setting Up Your Modem," for more details on DUN.

10. In the next setup wizard dialog box, shown in Figure 24.7, enter either the name or IP address of your POP server and click Next.

FIGURE 24.7.

Enter the name or IP address of your POP server.

11. In the next setup wizard dialog box, shown in Figure 24.8, you have to choose how messages get transferred to and from your POP server. If you chose to connect via a modem, the Off-line option is more suitable because you can define when to send and receive e-mail. The alternative, Automatic, is more suitable to network-based connections. Select an appropriate choice and click Next.

FIGURE 24.8.

Define transferring mode.

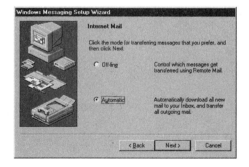

12. Supply your Internet e-mail address and your full name in the next dialog box, shown in Figure 24.9. Then click Next.

FIGURE 24.9.

Enter your Internet address and your full name.

13. In the next dialog box, shown in Figure 24.10, enter your mailbox name and password. Then click Next.

FIGURE 24.10.

Enter your mailbox name and password.

14. In the next setup wizard dialog box, enter the name and location of your new Address Book and click Next.

15. In the next dialog box, enter the name and location of your personal folder file and click Next. The setup wizard then shows you the Information services you configured for confirmation. Click Finish to complete the installation. The Exchange client is then automatically launched on completion.

The Inbox

After you complete the setup, you are presented with the Inbox window, as shown in Figure 24.11. Next, I'll describe the various parts of this window.

FIGURE 24.11.

The Inbox window.

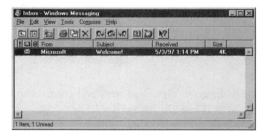

Columns

The default view of the Inbox shows a large pane in which all the inbound mail appears. The pane is divided into seven columns. You can remove all these columns and add others by choosing View | Columns. The Columns dialog box then appears, as shown in Figure 24.12.

FIGURE 24.12.
The Columns dialog box.

The following is a list of the default columns (shown on the right in Figure 24.12) and what they signify:

- *Importance.* When an exclamation mark appears on this column, it signifies that the mail is important.
- *Item Type.* Describes what type of a message it is.
- *Attachment.* Indicates whether an attachment is included with the message.
- *From.* Tells who sent the message.
- *Subject.* Tells the subject of the message.
- *Received.* Tells when the message was received.
- *Size.* Indicates the size of the message.

You can add 37 more columns, so you are bound to find a mix that suits you. To add a column, simply select one from the Available columns list and click the Add button. It then appears in the Show the following list. You can set the order of the columns by using the Move Up and Move Down buttons to rearrange them. You can also set the column width of each by entering the number of pixels in the Column Width pixel box.

Folders

Managing your messages so that you can easily find them in the future is important. The best way to manage them is by grouping messages on a particular subject into a folder. The Exchange client comes with a number of predefined folders. To view these folders, choose View | Folders. The messages pane of the Inbox then splits into two parts. The left side is occupied by a number of folders, and your messages occupy the right side. Figure 24.13 shows the predefined folders.

24

USING THE
MICROSOFT
EXCHANGE CLIENT

FIGURE 24.13.
Viewing folders.

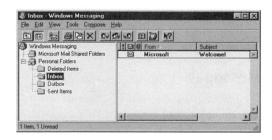

The folders are organized into a tree structure. You can collapse and expand this folder tree by clicking the +/- box at its root. In Figure 24.13, notice that the Inbox is selected and that all the messages contained in the Inbox appear on the right side of the pane. Selecting any folder displays its contents in the pane on the right.

The four personal folders are as follows:

- *Deleted Items.* Messages deleted from other folders are placed here.
- *Inbox.* Received messages are placed here.
- *Outbox.* Outgoing messages are placed here.
- *Sent Items.* Sent messages are place here.

> **NOTE**
>
> If you're working offline, the Outbox contains messages queued for sending until you get online.

You can drag and drop messages between folders at will. Alternatively, you can choose File | Move or File | Copy. Choosing either of these commands opens a dialog box similar to the one shown in Figure 24.14 (in this case, a Move dialog box).

FIGURE 24.14.

Moving a message.

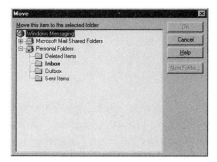

In this dialog box, you can create a new folder and store messages pertaining to a particular subject. You can choose the New Folder button within the Copy or Move dialog boxes, or you can select File | New Folder directly. Simply enter the name of the new folder in the text box of the New Folder dialog box that appears and click OK. You can rename and delete these folders at a later stage if you want.

Viewing Messages

Now you know how to organize your folders and how to group your messages. Next, you're ready to view, create, reply, and forward these messages. When you start Exchange client, one message from Microsoft is already waiting for you in your Inbox. Double-click the message to view its contents, as shown in Figure 24.15.

FIGURE 24.15.

Viewing a message.

As you can see, the message text takes up the majority of the window. You can use the scrollbar to traverse up and down the message. At the top of the window is listed the sender of the message, when it was sent, to whom it was sent (in this case, you), and the subject of the message.

Across the top of the window is a toolbar that contains various tools you can execute on the message. These tools include the following:

■ *Print.* Sends the message to the printer.

■ *Move.* Moves the message to another folder. Choosing this tool activates the Move dialog box (refer to Figure 24.14).

■ *Delete.* Moves the message to the Delete folder.

■ *Reply.* Sends a reply to the sender.

■ *Reply All.* Sends a reply to both the sender and all recipients.

■ *Forward.* Forwards the message to another user. The Reply, Reply All, and Forward options activate a message similar to a newly created message dialog box. These messages contain the original message plus anything else you want to add. They are, in essence, new messages.

■ *Previous.* Shows the previous message in the folder.

■ *Next.* Shows the next message in the folder.

■ *Help.* Provides context help on any area of the message.

In addition to the toolbar located here, these tools also reside on the main Exchange client window.

File Menu

The File menu allows you to execute the following tasks:

■ *Save and Save As.* These options allow you to save the message as a text file anywhere on the network.

24

USING THE
MICROSOFT
EXCHANGE CLIENT

■ *Move and Copy.* These options allow you to move and copy the message between folders.

■ *Print.* This option allows you to print the message.

■ *Delete.* This option moves the message to the Delete folder.

■ *Close.* This option closes the message.

■ *Properties.* This option activates the Properties dialog box for the message. This dialog box has two tabs. The General tab contains general information about the message, such as what the subject is, how big it is, and so on. Figure 24.16 shows an example of the General tab.

The second tab, Recipients, lists who sent and who received the message. Figure 24.17 shows an example of a Recipients tab.

FIGURE 24.16.

The General tab of a message's Properties dialog box.

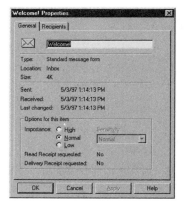

FIGURE 24.17.

The Recipients tab.

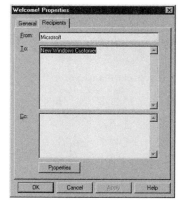

Edit Menu

The Edit menu allows you to execute the usual edit functions: Undo, Cut, Copy, Paste, Paste Special, Select All, Find, Replace, Links, and Objects.

View Menu

The View menu allows you to enable or disable the status bar, the toolbar, and the Formatting toolbar. In addition, you can access the previous and next messages in the folder by selecting the Previous and Next options. The Formatting toolbar contains tools that allow you to manipulate the text of the message. Figure 24.18 shows the message with the Formatting tools enabled.

FIGURE 24.18.
Enable the Formatting tools.

The Formatting tools enable you to change the color and font of the text, to indent and bullet the text, and to add bold or underline, and to align the text, among other changes.

Insert Menu

The Insert menu allows you to locate and insert messages, files, or objects into the message. Figure 24.19 shows the Insert File dialog box. As you can see, you can insert files as text, attachments, or links.

If you choose Format | Font, you can change the font of the highlighted text. If you choose Format | Paragraph, you can align a selected paragraph and optionally include a bullet point at its start.

24

USING THE MICROSOFT EXCHANGE CLIENT

FIGURE 24.19.

Inserting a file.

Tools Menu

The Tools menu allows you to define what tools appear in the toolbar. You do so by choosing Toolbar | Customize Toolbar. In the Customize Toolbar dialog box that appears, as shown in Figure 24.20, you can add and remove tools from the toolbar. You use the same method you used previously for adding and removing columns. You learn about the Services option later in this chapter.

FIGURE 24.20.

Customizing the toolbar.

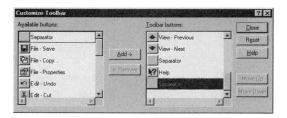

By choosing Tools | Options, you can configure the Exchange client to suit your needs. The resulting Options dialog box has six tabs; the first is the General tab. Of these six tabs, three of them—Services, Delivery, and Addresses—can be accessed through the Mail applet in the Control Panel. This applet, by the way, was added after the initial setup of the Exchange client.

General

On the General tab of the Options dialog box, as shown in Figure 24.21, you can configure general settings for the Exchange client.

In the When new mail arrives frame, you can configure events that will inform you of the arrival of new mail. You can play a sound, briefly change the pointer, or display a notification message.

FIGURE **24.21.**
The General tab.

The Deleting items frame allows you to configure a warning whenever an attempt is made to delete messages and also to empty the delete folder after you exit the application.

The When starting Windows Messaging frame allows you to configure which user profile is used by the application. The choices are to always use a predefined profile or to prompt the user for a profile.

At the bottom of the tab are two options to enable titles and to enable the selecting of entire words.

Read

On the Read tab of the Options dialog box, as shown in Figure 24.22, you can set options that will be associated to messages being read.

FIGURE **24.22.**
The Read tab.

The first frame on this tab, After moving or deleting an open item, defines whether the message above or below will be opened or whether the user is returned to the main messaging window. In the When replying to or forwarding an item frame, you can set the Exchange client to include and indent the original text, close the original message, and select a font for the test.

Send

On the Send tab of the Options dialog box, as shown in Figure 24.23, you can configure options that relate to sending messages.

FIGURE 24.23.

The Send tab.

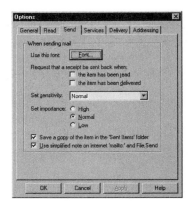

Apart from defining what font is used, you can trigger a message to be sent to you when the mail is delivered or when the mail is read. You also can set a sensitivity and importance level on the message.

Services

On the Services tab of the Options dialog box, as shown in Figure 24.24, you can add, remove, and configure information services with the loaded profile. You can also access this tab by choosing Tools | Services.

FIGURE 24.24.

The Services tab.

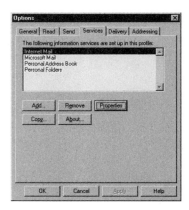

You add and remove information services by choosing the Add and Remove buttons, respectively. To view the properties of an information service, select the service and click Properties.

Figure 24.25 shows an example of the properties for the Internet Mail information service. This Properties dialog box has two tabs of its own: General and Connection. The General tab contains the information you supplied during installation. The Connection tab, as shown in Figure 24.26, allows you to select your mode of connection, modem or network, and also to determine whether mail transfer will be offline. When you select to connect via a modem, the Dial using the following connection drop-down list and the Add Entry, Edit Entry, and Login As buttons are enabled. You have to select a dial-up connection to be used when you dial. You also have to select the Login As button and enter a username and password combination to be used to authenticate your dial-up session.

FIGURE 24.25.

Information Service properties dialog box.

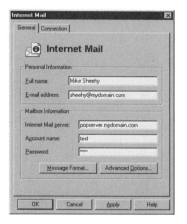

FIGURE 24.26.

Connection tab for Internet Information service.

To save changes to the configuration, click the Apply button.

You can view the properties of the other loaded information services also.

Delivery

The Delivery tab of the Options dialog box configures changes that have an impact on the delivery of messages. In Figure 24.27, you can see how to determine where new mail gets delivered and the order in which the recipient addresses are processed.

FIGURE 24.27.

The Delivery tab.

Addressing

The Addressing tab of the Options dialog box governs the use of Address Books and address names. Within this tab, shown in Figure 24.28, you can select which address list will be displayed first, where personal addresses will be kept, and the order in which address lists will be used to check names when sending messages.

FIGURE 24.28.

The Addressing tab.

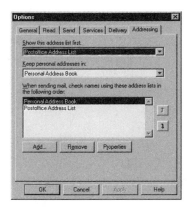

Compose Menu

The Compose menu allows you to create new messages, reply to messages, reply to all, and forward messages. These operations are the same in principle, so I'll discuss creating a new message.

After you choose Compose | New Message, the New Message dialog box then appears, as shown in Figure 24.29.

FIGURE 24.29.

Composing a new message.

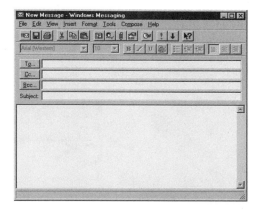

Type the address of the recipient in the To text box, or pick a name from your Address Book by clicking the To button. This action activates the Address Book, which is shown in Figure 24.30.

FIGURE 24.30.

The Address Book.

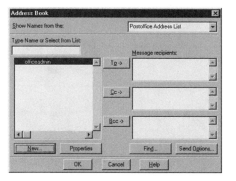

Using the Address Book, you can easily add and store users and their addresses in one place. Through the Address Book, you can add users to the recipient list of a message.

The Address Book window is divided into a number of list boxes. The Show Name from the list box displays the name of the Address Book being used currently. The main list box on the left of the Address Book window shows the users defined in the current Address Book. On the right side are three list boxes that contain the names of addressees on the To list, the Cc list, and the Bcc list. The To list is a list of people to whom the message is primarily directed. The Cc list is a list of people who receive a carbon copy of the message, and the Bcc list is a list of people who also receive a carbon copy but their names do not appear on the distribution list. To populate any of these lists, simply select a user from the left list box and click either the To, Cc, or Bcc buttons to add them to the appropriate list.

To add a user to an Address Book, click the New button located at the base of the Address Book window. The New Entry dialog box then appears, as shown in Figure 24.31. You then must decide the type of address you want to create, whether it will be added to the Address Book or whether it will be just used for this message.

FIGURE 24.31.

The New Entry dialog box.

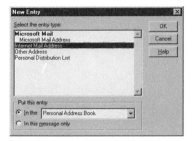

After you select the type of address to create and click OK, you have to fill out the properties of the new address. The example shows the creation of an Internet address. Figure 24.32 shows the dialog box you must complete if you're creating an Internet address.

FIGURE 24.32.

The SMTP tab on the New Internet Mail Address Properties dialog box.

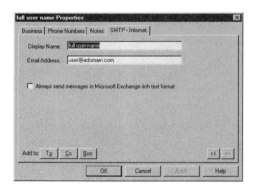

The New Internet Mail Address Properties dialog box has four tabs. On the SMTP tab, you can enter a descriptive name and the e-mail address of the addressee. The other three—Business, Phone Numbers, and Notes—are used for storing additional information about the person. At the base of each of these tabs is a series of buttons that allow you to add the address to the To, Cc, and Bcc lists. As you can see in Figure 24.33, I have created an address in the Personal Address Book and have added that address to the To list.

FIGURE 24.33.
The new address is added to the To list.

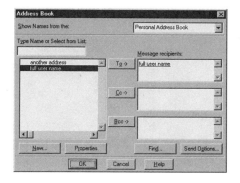

After you compile your distribution lists, click OK to exit the Address Book window. You then return to the New Message dialog box with the addresses added to the distribution windows. In the Subject text box, you then can enter the subject of your message. Type the body of the message in the lower window. You can also set the importance level on the message by selecting the appropriate button on the toolbar. As with all the toolbars within Exchange client, you can add and remove tools by choosing Tools | Customize Toolbar.

Finally, to send the message, you can either choose File | Send or select the Send icon from the toolbar. The message then appears in the Outbox, as shown in Figure 24.34. If you're working offline, the message remains in the Outbox until it is sent, and then it is sent to the server and moved to the Sent box.

FIGURE 24.34.
The Outbox contents.

Now you can take a closer look at the main Windows Messaging window.

Remote Mail

If your connection to the Internet is via a modem, then you might consider using Remote Mail. Remote Mail allows you to write messages offline and queue them for sending until you're connected to the Internet and ready to send them. As you learned earlier, you choose Remote Mail in the Connection tab of the Internet Mail Information service. To get your mail from the server, you must use the Remote Mail dialog box, as shown in Figure 24.35, after you establish a dial-up connection to your server.

FIGURE 24.35.

The Remote Mail dialog box.

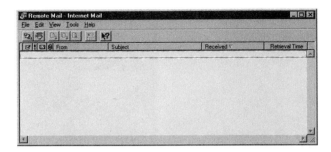

The Remote Mail dialog box is similar to the Windows Messaging window in that it lists who the message is from, what the subject is, when it was received, and so on. Although you are connected to the Internet, you must also connect to your mail server. Connecting to your mail server gives you a list of message headers that are waiting for you on the server. During connection to the server, any mail queued for delivery also is sent. You connect to the mail server by choosing Tools | Connect or by selecting the appropriate icon from the toolbar. After the Remote Mail client connects with the mail server, it retrieves the list of message headers, as shown in Figure 24.36.

FIGURE 24.36.

Getting a list of message headers.

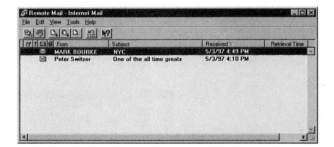

You can mark all or any of the messages for retrieval by selecting the appropriate option from the Edit menu, toolbar, or right-click (context) menu of a message. Other options include retrieval of a copy, which keeps a copy of the message on a server but also copies one locally. You can also delete a message from the server. After you select a message for retrieval, it is marked with an icon as in Figure 24.37.

FIGURE 24.37.

Message marked for retrieval.

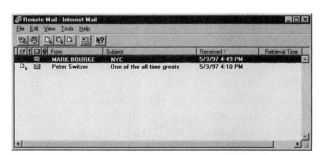

When you connect with the server again, the message marked for retrieval is copied into your Inbox. As with the main Windows Messaging window, you can customize it to suit your needs, adding and removing columns, sorting and filtering incoming messages, and so on. From the main Windows Messages window, you can schedule Remote Mail Delivery by choosing Tools | Microsoft Mail Tools | Remote Mail Delivery. The Scheduled Remote Mail Delivery dialog box then appears, as shown in Figure 24.38.

FIGURE 24.38.

The Scheduled Remote Mail Delivery dialog box.

To schedule a remote delivery, first click the Add button to open the Add Scheduled Session dialog box, which is shown in Figure 24.39.

FIGURE 24.39.

Adding a delivery session.

A delivery session requires the name of a dial-up networking session, how often it is supposed to run, and when. After you decide on these variables, click OK to save the session parameters. The newly created session is then added to the Currently scheduled sessions list in the main Scheduled Remote Mail Delivery dialog box.

Summary

In this chapter, you looked at the Exchange client. You stepped through its initial setup and learned how to add information services. The chapter covered the basics of organizing your mail, and viewing, creating, and deleting your mail. In addition, you looked at Remote Mail and how you might use Exchange client to connect to an Internet mail server via a modem.

Remote Computing with Remote Access Service

by Mike Sheehy and Eric D. Osborne

IN THIS CHAPTER

Today's computer users live in an increasingly interconnected world. The typical business user in today's environment works on a workstation attached to a LAN. Each of these desktops is in turn connected to the rest of the enterprise and, subsequently, to the Internet. The need for connectivity can often make it impossible for modern workers to perform effectively unless connected to networked resources. And, because many of today's workers are mobile, there is a corresponding need for networking technology capable of providing those mobile users with transparent and simple access to centralized facilities. Field engineers, sales personnel, and other travelers in today's competitive business environment require continual access to e-mail and corporate databases. The growing ranks of telecommuters require cost-effective and reliable access to corporate facilities. Even on the home front, the explosive popularity of the Internet and the World Wide Web all contribute to the need for connectivity.

Remote Access Service (RAS) is Microsoft's answer to this need. Microsoft has designed RAS to provide simple, effective, and reliable wide area networking. RAS is not new to Windows NT 4. It has been a part of Microsoft's operating system offerings since the introduction of Windows NT 3.1. Since that time, the technology focus of RAS has changed substantially.

The basic functionality provided by RAS essentially consists of an on-demand wide area networking transport and authentication service. Other facilities associated with RAS, such as file and print sharing, involve higher level protocols that layer on top of the RAS transport mechanism.

Microsoft has embedded RAS into all its current windowing operating system offerings. Windows 95 and, to a lesser extent, Windows for Workgroups are both capable of acting as RAS clients. Windows NT can act as both a RAS client and server. Windows NT Server is capable of supporting many concurrent incoming RAS connections. Windows NT Workstation can provide the same RAS server functionality, but only for one incoming connection at any given time.

The RAS client can be viewed as software for turning your COM port and modem (or other supported device) into a network adapter. Establishing a RAS connection can be generalized to the following simple steps:

1. The user determines a need for some remote resource.
2. A connection, typically through a modem and telephone line, is established to a RAS server.
3. The user provides authentication (password) information to the server for verification.
4. Once authenticated, the user has access to server facilities and can then attach file shares or use Internet applications such as Netscape Navigator or Microsoft Internet Explorer.

You should note that client systems always initiate RAS sessions. Therefore, the RAS server software must *always* be running and waiting on the server system. The RAS server can provide a myriad of services for a connected client, including the following:

- Providing access to disk or printer resources local to the server
- Providing access to disk or printer services on other servers within the server's domain
- Providing routing of TCP/IP or IPX/SPX packets to non-RAS resources on the server LAN
- Routing the user's packets to the Internet for access to Web and other services

Connection Technologies Supported by RAS

The connection technologies supported by the RAS client software include standard asynchronous modems, X.25 packet-switched networks, and ISDN (Integrated Services Digital Network) adapters. All these technologies provide the user with wide area networking capabilities through the telephone system.

Each has specific advantages. Modems, for example, are relatively inexpensive and portable, and they can be used from essentially anywhere. Modern modems, supporting uncompressed data rates of up to 28,800bps, provide sufficient throughput to support the needs of a very large percentage of users. The low cost, portability, compatibility with standard telephone lines, and ease of use of modems make them ideal for travelers or for low-cost home use.

ISDN provides much higher speeds than can be achieved through modems—up to 128 kilobits of uncompressed data per second (128Kbps)—but it requires more costly equipment and higher fees. ISDN does not run across standard analog telephone circuits. ISDN circuits are available in Basic and Primary Rate variants. A Basic Rate ISDN connection is a digital interface, but it can be run across standard telephone wire. Basic Rate interfaces have a pair of 64Kbps data channels (B channels) and a 16Kbps control channel (D channel). Attempts are currently being made to utilize the D channel for downloads from the Internet, leaving the B channels free for browsing. The two B channels can be aggregated into a composite 128Kbps channel. Primary rate connections are composed of many channels and have a composite bandwidth of 1.44Mbps. Because ISDN connections require special connections to the telephone company, ISDN interfaces don't work for traveling users, but they are ideal for the professional programmer who telecommutes from home. Many locals within the United States still don't have telephone switches capable of supporting ISDN traffic. ISDN is extremely popular in certain European countries.

X.25 packet-switching networks are available as a moderately priced wide area networking technology. X.25 networks predate the development of either TCP/IP or the ISDN standard. Most telephone switching networks are X.25 packet-switching networks. Therefore, ISDN connections actually layer other protocols (such as PPP) on top of X.25 packet switching. This way, these higher level protocols can traverse the existing telephone network.

RAS connections over X.25 rely on devices called Packet Assembler/Disassemblers (PADs) to frame user data into X.25-compliant packets. X.25 can be used across dial-up lines, but the end user commonly arranges for a dedicated telephone circuit to be installed. The circuit is often permanently connected to a network service provider. Because the connection is commonly made through a dedicated circuit, it often seems like a LAN connection (but slower) to the end user. X.25 is not commonly used in the United States (except by telephone companies), but it is still very popular in Europe.

Like RAS client, RAS server supports all the previously mentioned technologies. In addition to them, RAS server also supports connection via TCP/IP across a LAN. The reason that RAS server supports LAN connections is largely economic. A modem-attached RAS server intended to support a number of concurrent dial-up users would require a large number of COM ports and attached communications devices. Maintaining and administering these devices and their associated telephone lines can be too expensive or difficult for some organizations.

Microsoft has added a new protocol called Point To Point Tunneling Protocol (PPTP) to Windows NT 4 to address this problem. PPTP encapsulates and encrypts PPP packets from the client PC and transmits across a LAN or WAN to a server system. The effect is to create a private "tunnel" through a public network. The tunnel isolates the systems at each end of the connection, effectively establishing a private network contained within a larger network such as the Internet. PPTP is further explored in the section "RAS and the Internet," later in this chapter.

These kinds of private connections are sometimes called *Virtual Private Networks*, or *VPNs*. Both Windows NT 4 Server and Workstation support the PPTP protocol. PPTP allows a user to connect to an Internet Service Provider and then have a private, encrypted PPP session through the ISP to a remote RAS server. This eliminates the need for the RAS server to be equipped with a large pool of dedicated dial-in modems because the remote RAS client can be assured of secure, encrypted connections even when connecting through an arbitrary Internet Service Provider.

I previously mentioned that Windows NT Workstation supports RAS in both client and server modes. This means that the user can use RAS not only to dial out to a remote host, but also to provide a secure incoming interconnect to the workstation. This facility can be extremely helpful to users such as the telecommuting programmer described earlier. Consider the situation in which a user has traveled to a seminar or trade show, for example. The telecommuter might have much of his or her work stored on a home system instead of the corporate RAS server. If the need arises, either the telecommuter or any other authorized user could dial into the telecommuter's workstation and copy files or access other information.

Installing Remote Access Service

Remote Access Service can be installed during a custom installation of Windows NT, or at any later time from the Network Services dialog box of the Network applet in the Control Panel. Figure 25.1 shows the Network applet with the Services tab selected. You can see all the services already installed on the workstation. To install RAS, click Add.

FIGURE 25.1.

*Examining installed
network services.*

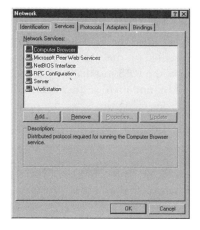

Clicking the Add button produces a list of additional services you can install. Scroll down and highlight the Remote Access Service selection, as shown in Figure 25.2. Then click OK.

FIGURE 25.2.

*Adding the Remote
Access Service.*

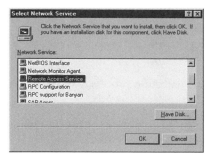

The Setup program displays a dialog box, as shown in Figure 25.3, requesting a path to the NT installation media (normally your CD-ROM drive). Enter the correct path and click Continue. Remember to include the processor type as part of the pathname. The correct path would be *drive-letter*:\i386 for Pentium, i386, or i486 processors.

FIGURE 25.3.

*Installing RAS from the
Network applet.*

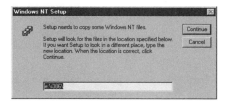

Adding Modems to Your System Configuration

After setup has installed files, the RAS installation process checks to see whether any RAS-capable devices are installed on the system. Unless such a device has been previously installed for some other purpose, the RAS installation program asks whether you want to install a RAS device. Click Yes to add a modem to your configuration. You can install additional modems or modify modem properties using the Modem applet of the Control Panel at any time in the future.

> **TIP**
>
> Depending on the type of modem that you have, you might need manuals or other technical information about your modem to complete this step.

The next step in configuring a modem is shown in Figure 25.4. As you can see, you can either select your modem from a list or have Windows NT try to detect it automatically. The built-in list of modems in Windows NT covers most popular brands and models, so you stand a very good chance that NT will correctly determine your modem type automatically. Simply click Next to have NT determine your modem type. You might need to select the Don't detect my modem; I will select it from a list check box if any of the following conditions apply to your system:

- The automatic detection process fails.
- Your modem is an external modem and is powered off.
- You simply want to configure the modem manually.

FIGURE 25.4.

*The modem detection
dialog box.*

If you choose to select a modem type manually, the selection dialog box shown in Figure 25.5 appears. The selection box on the left is a scrollable list of modem manufacturers. The list on the right is a list of modem models made by that manufacturer. Select the desired manufacturer and model of modem and click Next. If you have a driver disk from the modem manufacturer, click the Have Disk button.

Figure 25.5.

*The modem manual
selection list dialog box.*

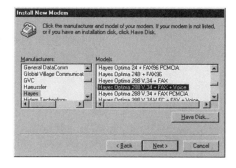

The automatic modem selection process, if successful, determines which port your modem is connected to. If you have manually selected a modem type, the modem installation utility displays a list of available ports, as shown in Figure 25.6. Select the correct port and click Next. If you want to configure identical modems on all the available ports, click the All ports radio button before clicking Next. The installation of the modem is now complete, so when you are presented with the final setup dialog box, click Finish. For more information on installing a modem, see Chapter 21, "Setting Up Your Modem."

Figure 25.6.

*The modem installation
port selection
dialog box.*

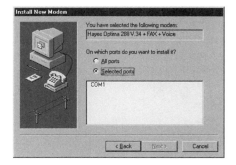

Selecting Communications Devices to Be Used by RAS

After you choose a port for your modem, you return to the RAS installation process. The dialog box shown in Figure 25.7, Add RAS Device, allows you to choose a RAS-capable communications device. If you have configured a modem according to the preceding steps, it is visible in the RAS Capable Devices scroll box. Select the desired modem and port information and click OK. If you want to use an X.25 Pad instead of a modem, click the Install X.25 Pad button.

FIGURE 25.7.

Selecting a RAS-capable device.

Figure 25.8 shows the installed modem in the Remote Access Setup dialog box. You can configure the connection type and protocol options at this point. To remove or add additional RAS-capable devices, click the Add or Remove button as appropriate.

FIGURE 25.8.

The Remote Access Setup device configuration dialog box.

Clicking the Configure button from the Remote Access Setup dialog box produces the configuration dialog box shown in Figure 25.9. You can configure the port for incoming calls, outgoing calls, or both. Click OK after you select your option.

FIGURE 25.9.

The RAS options dialog box for the selected port.

NOTE

A port must be configured for outgoing calls to use the RAS client software. A port must be configured for incoming calls to use the RAS server software (unless RAS is accessible through a LAN). If the same modem must be used for both RAS client and server functionality, make sure to configure the port to dial out and receive calls.

Now you must select network protocols to be used with RAS. Click the Network button within the Remote Access Setup dialog box. If you configured the RAS port to dial out only, you are presented with a dialog box of available dial-out protocols, as shown in Figure 25.10. Most people should select TCP/IP; it is the most widely used network protocol suite in the world. The Internet runs across a TCP/IP backbone.

FIGURE 25.10.

RAS dial-out protocol selection.

IPX/SPX is a protocol designed by Novell, and as such it is useful to most people only when connecting to corporate NetWare servers.

NetBEUI is Microsoft's NetBIOS Extended User Interface. Microsoft's NetBEUI protocols were designed long before Windows NT existed. The NetBEUI protocols were never intended to be used in wide area networks. NetBEUI relies heavily on broadcast packets for communication between hosts and is by definition a very "chatty" protocol. These broadcast packets work well enough within a LAN but generally don't pass through routers. The fact that NetBEUI can't be routed restricts its use to local LANs. NetBEUI was originally the only protocol supported by RAS. Older clients, such as Windows for Workgroups, still require NetBEUI by default.

Microsoft still supports NetBEUI on both the RAS client and server software, but TCP/IP is clearly the future of RAS.

NOTE

Although Windows for Workgroups must (by default) use NetBEUI to connect to a RAS server, you can use third-party software to overcome this limitation. Packages such as TechSmith's Foray PPP Client allow Windows for Workgroups to attach to RAS servers through either a direct modem connection to an NT system or through an Internet Service Provider using TCP/IP.

If you configured RAS to receive and dial out, you are presented with a Network Configuration dialog box, as shown in Figure 25.11.

25

REMOTE COMPUTING WITH REMOTE ACCESS SERVICE

FIGURE 25.11.

The Network Configuration dialog box for dial in and dial out.

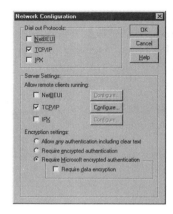

Additional Steps Required for Incoming RAS Connections

The Server Settings frame of the Network Configuration dialog box allows you to define network protocols for incoming RAS clients. As with dial-out, you can choose a combination of NetBEUI, TCP/IP, and IPX/SPX.

NetBEUI

Selecting NetBEUI enables its Configure button. Click NetBEUI's Configure button to open the RAS Server NetBEUI Configuration dialog box, which is shown in Figure 25.12. Through this dialog box, you can define whether a RAS client can access the RAS server only or the entire network via NetBEUI. Choose the appropriate setting and click OK to return to the Network Configuration dialog box.

FIGURE 25.12.

The RAS Server NetBEUI Configuration dialog box.

TCP/IP

If you check the TCP/IP check box in the Network Configuration dialog box and click its Configure button, the RAS Server TCP/IP Configuration dialog box then appears, as shown in Figure 25.13.

Figure 25.13.

*The RAS Server TCP/
IP Configuration
dialog box.*

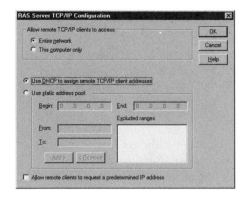

In this dialog box, you can specify addressing and accessibility options for connecting clients. TCP/IP is a routable protocol, which means that messages can find a path, or *route*, through interconnected LANs. This functionality is the basis of the Internet. If routing is disabled, a RAS client can use only those resources residing on the RAS server. When routing is enabled, the client can connect to any TCP/IP resource that the server can see. You can restrict connecting the client to the RAS server only, or you can extend access to the entire network.

The RAS server allows two methods for defining the IP address of a connected client. You select either option from the Server TCP/IP Configuration dialog. The first (and default) method uses the Dynamic Host Configuration Protocol (DHCP) to assign addresses. Therefore, a DHCP server must be available on your network. Note that a Windows NT Workstation 4 system cannot act as a DHCP server. That functionality is available only on Windows NT Server systems and some UNIX servers. If you're installing RAS in server mode on your NT Workstation 4 system, make sure that a DHCP server is available on your network before selecting the Use DHCP to assign remote TCP/IP client addresses radio button.

Alternatively, you can still have the RAS server on your NT Workstation 4 and have it allocate client addresses, even if your workstation is not attached to a LAN with a DHCP server. To do so, select the Use static address pool radio button to define a range of valid TCP/IP addresses for your incoming RAS connection. Enter the beginning address of the desired range in the Begin box. Enter the last address of the desired range in the End box. Make sure that the addresses entered are valid addresses within the subnet in which the Windows NT Workstation 4 host resides.

NOTE

If you're installing Windows NT Workstation 4 at home, you almost certainly don't have a DHCP server available. In this case, select the Use static address pool radio button. Even if

continues

> *continued*
>
> your system can support only one incoming RAS connection, you need to define a range
> of at least two addresses because one of the addresses is allocated to the incoming port
> on your NT Workstation 4 system. The other address is allocated to the connecting RAS
> client system.

You can exclude ranges of addresses from the static address pool. This way, RAS can accommodate address ranges that might have a few addresses occupied by hosts or network components. To exclude a range of addresses, enter the address of the first address to be excluded in the From box. Enter the address of the last address to be excluded in the To box. Then click Add. You can remove the excluded range by selecting it in the Excluded ranges box and then clicking Remove.

If you choose, you can also allow the calling client to define its own IP address. Select the Allow remote clients to request a predetermined IP address check box to enable this functionality. The client must be configured (via the Dial-Up Networking facility) to use a static IP address within the correct subnet.

At the base of the Network Configuration dialog box is the Encryption settings frame. In this frame, you can define constraints on the authentication of dial-in RAS clients. You can choose from three possible settings:

- The Allow any authentication including clear text option allows connection using any authentication protocols (MS-CHAP, PAP, SPAP). This option is useful for a diverse client base.
- The Require encrypted authentication option permits connection using any authentication requested by the client except PAP. This option requires encrypted passwords.
- The Require Microsoft encrypted authentication option permits connection using MS-CHAP authentication only. The Require data encryption check box ensures that all data sent over the wire is encrypted. Windows NT RAS provides data encryption using the RSA Data Security Incorporated RC4 algorithm.

IPX

Adding the IPX protocol and clicking its Configure button in the Network Configuration dialog box opens the RAS Server IPX Configuration dialog box, as shown in Figure 25.14.

FIGURE 25.14.

The RAS Server IPX Configuration dialog box.

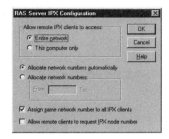

Again, as with the other protocols, you can restrict an IPX client to accessing either the RAS server or the entire network. In addition, you can configure the following:

- *Allocate network numbers automatically.* The client is assigned an IPX network number not currently in use by the RAS server.

- *Allocate network numbers.* The RAS server can allocate an IPX network number to clients from a pool of numbers. This capability is useful if you want to identify clients on the network. When you enter a network number in the From box, RAS automatically determines the To value based on the number of available ports.

- *Assign same network number to all IPX clients.* RAS gives the same network number to all RAS clients.

- *Allow remote clients to request IPX node number.* You can allow a RAS client to select its own IPX node number rather than use the node number provided by the RAS server.

Remote Access Admin

After you complete the installation of RAS and reboot the Workstation, a new tool, called Remote Access Admin, is added to the Start menu to aid you in administrating the RAS server for dial in. To access the Remote Access Admin tool, choose Start | Programs | Administrative Tools (Common). The Remote Access Admin displays the name of the RAS server, the status of the service, the total number of ports, how many of these ports are in use, and a comment, as shown in Figure 25.15.

The RAS service is not configured to start automatically, so you have to start it manually each time or configure it to start automatically from the services applet within the Control Panel. For more details on configuring services, see Chapter 9, "Advanced Control Panel Tools." To start the RAS service from within Remote Access Admin, choose Server | Start Remote Access Service. In the Start Remote Access Service dialog box, shown in Figure 25.16, enter the name of the workstation into the Server text box. After you click OK, NT tries to start the RAS service.

FIGURE 25.15.

The Remote Access Admin dialog box.

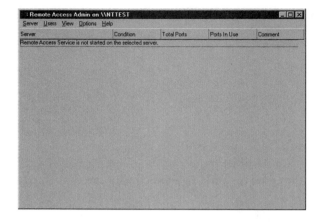

FIGURE 25.16.

Start the RAS service.

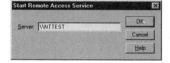

After the service successfully starts, the Remote Access Admin dialog box appears, as shown in Figure 25.17.

FIGURE 25.17.

The Remote Access Admin with RAS started.

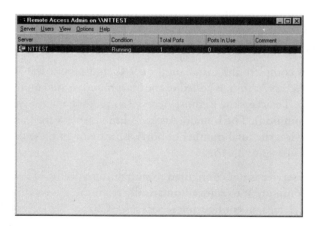

Other options within the Server menu include the ability to stop, pause, and continue the RAS service. You also can choose to administer a RAS server remotely by choosing Server | Select Domain or Server.

To view the communications ports that the RAS server is using, choose Server | Communication Ports. In the Communication Ports dialog box, shown in Figure 25.18, you can view details on a port-by-port basis. The dialog box details what port a user is connected to and when the connection was made. You can send messages to individuals or all connected users by clicking either the Send Message or Send To All button. You can also disconnect users by selecting their entries from the list and clicking the Disconnect User button.

FIGURE 25.18.

The Communication Ports dialog box.

If you click the Port Status button, the Port Status dialog box then appears, as shown in Figure 25.19. This dialog box details the RAS server's name, the condition of the modem, the condition of the line, and the bits per second on the line. The Port Statistics frame totals the number of bytes in and out on the line. The Connection statistics frame gives a further breakdown by detailing the bytes, frames, and the percentage compression both in and out on the connection. Any device errors are displayed in the Device errors frame. These errors include CRC, Timeouts, Alignment, Framing, Hardware Overrun, and Buffer Overrun errors. The final frame, Remote Workstation, lists the NetBEUI name and IP and IPX addresses of the remote workstation, if they exist. Click Reset to reset the displayed values. To return to the Communication Ports dialog box, click OK. Click OK again to return to the main Remote Access Admin dialog.

FIGURE 25.19.

The Port Status dialog box.

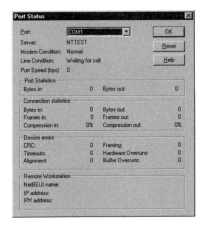

25

REMOTE COMPUTING WITH REMOTE ACCESS SERVICE

To grant or deny dial-in permission to users, you must use the Remote Access Permissions dialog box, which is shown in Figure 25.20. You access this dialog box by choosing User | Permissions on the main Remote Access Admin dialog box. The Users pane lists the currently defined users on the Workstation's local security database or on the local NT domain. To grant or deny access to a user, simply select its entry and check or uncheck the Grant dialin permission to user check box as appropriate. You can grant permission to or revoke permission from all users by clicking the Grant All or Revoke All buttons.

FIGURE 25.20.

Giving users dial-in permission.

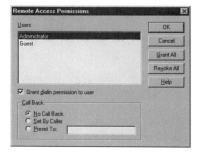

In the Call Back frame of the Remote Access Permissions dialog box, you can set callback options for a RAS client. Options include the following:

- *No Call Back.* The RAS server does not call back the client.
- *Set By Caller.* The RAS server calls back the client at a number set by the user.
- *Preset To.* The RAS server calls back the user at a preset number set in the Preset To box.

To return to the main Remote Access Admin dialog box, click OK. Now choose Users | Active Users to open the Remote Access Users dialog box, as shown in Figure 25.21. This dialog box lists the currently connected users, which server they are connected to, and the date and time of the connection. The User Account button, when selected, displays details on the highlighted user's account. As with the Communication Ports dialog box, you can send messages to all or individually connected users, and you can disconnect their connections from the RAS server. Click OK to return to the Remote Access Admin dialog box.

FIGURE 25.21.

Remote Access Users dialog box.

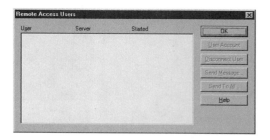

Configuring Remote Access Service Client (Dial-Up Networking)

The process of installing RAS performs most of the work of configuring the RAS server. The RAS client, however, requires substantially more information before you can use it.

NT 4 and Windows 95 refer to the RAS client as Dial-Up Networking (DUN). The DUN facility enables users to connect to NT servers, Windows for Workgroups servers, or Internet Service Providers. DUN allows users to define a list of known servers, maintaining separate configuration information for each. Configuration information is stored in a phonebook.

As an example of the reasons that a user might need separate configurations, consider the case of a professional programmer who is taking classes at a local university. This user might have separate accounts with an Internet Service Provider, on a UNIX server at the university where he or she is taking classes, and with an employer's corporate NT server. Separate configuration information, including telephone numbers, protocol specifications, usernames, and passwords would be necessary for each. Using the phonebook, this user could configure setups for any number of servers and then connect to any of them by simply selecting a server from a menu.

To configure DUN, begin by choosing Start | Programs | Accessories | Dial-Up Networking, as shown in Figure 25.22.

FIGURE 25.22.

Invoking the Dial-Up Networking client program.

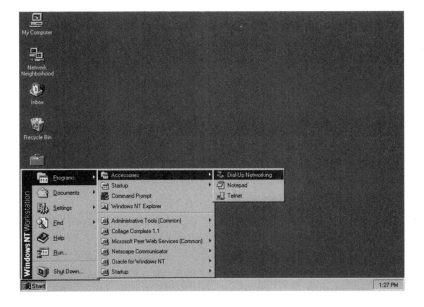

RAS maintains a list of servers that it knows, and configuration information about those servers, in a phonebook. Because the phonebook is empty until RAS is configured, the first time DUN is invoked, it asks whether you want to add an entry, as you can see in Figure 25.23.

FIGURE 25.23.

The initial Dial-Up Networking dialog box.

Creating Simple RAS Client Phonebook Entries

Choosing OK to the message about adding entries causes the system to begin the process of defining a phonebook entry. RAS presents you with two options at this point, as shown in Figure 25.24. Novice users can enter a name for a new phonebook entry and allow RAS to step through a setup wizard. More experienced users can choose to edit the phonebook entries directly by clicking the check box shown in this dialog box. The default choices made by the New Phonebook Entry Wizard work for most people, so use them to create an initial phonebook entry in this case. I discuss advanced editing of phonebook entries later in this chapter.

FIGURE 25.24.

The New Phonebook Entry Wizard.

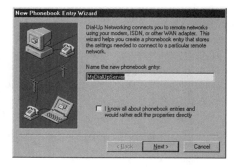

After entering the name of your phonebook entry, click the Next button. The dialog box shown in Figure 25.25 appears. The New Phonebook Entry Wizard uses the checked items here to determine protocol and security characteristics of the server that you want to call. You should check as many of the boxes as apply to your server.

■ Check the first box if you're calling an Internet Service Provider or any non-NT system such as a UNIX server.

■ The second box defines the characteristics of the password that will be sent to the server. Most newer servers use encrypted passwords, meaning that the password is encoded before being transmitted to the server. Some servers, however, accept passwords only in plain text. Plain-text passwords can represent a security risk because they can sometimes be detected by hackers who monitor the Internet. Check the second box if your server requires plain-text passwords.

■ If you're connecting to a non-NT server or if you're connecting to an NT server through an Internet Service Provider, you might need to enter passwords or perform other tasks prior to starting RAS. You might also need to perform some special security process before you can dial, such as authorizing a long distance telephone call. Selecting the third box allows you to pop up a terminal window or run a script to address these issues.

FIGURE 25.25.

Selecting server characteristics.

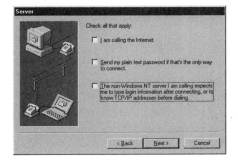

After selecting the options you want, clicking Next presents the dialog box shown in Figure 25.26. Enter in the designated space the phone number for the server that you want to call.

FIGURE 25.26.

Entering phone numbers in the Phonebook Wizard.

If you like, you can select the Use Telephony dialing properties check box, which changes the screen as shown in Figure 25.27. You can then enter in the indicated space the area code for the number you want to call.

Figure 25.27.

*Selecting Telephony
dialing properties in the
Phonebook Wizard.*

RAS allows you to enter multiple phone numbers for each server. If RAS fails to connect to the desired number because it is busy or otherwise unavailable, RAS automatically tries connecting to an alternative number. Figure 25.28 shows the dialog box for entering alternative telephone numbers. RAS dials the numbers in the order listed. You can use the Up and Down buttons to select the order manually for your list of phone numbers. If you select the check box at the bottom of the dialog box in Figure 25.28, RAS places the first successful number at the top of the list after dialing.

Figure 25.28.

*Entering alternative
phone numbers in the
Phonebook Wizard.*

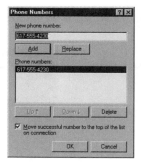

Click OK to close the Phone Numbers dialog box and then select the Next button, as shown in Figure 25.27. If you did not select a non-Windows NT server in the Server dialog box (refer to Figure 25.25), your configuration is complete and you are presented with the dialog box shown in Figure 25.29. Select Finish to complete your new entry. If you did select a non-Windows NT server in the Server dialog box, however, you are taken on a different route requiring further configuration.

FIGURE 25.29.
Completing the phonebook entry.

Figure 25.30 shows the first alternative dialog box you see.

FIGURE 25.30.
Completing the phonebook entry.

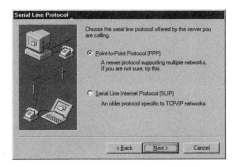

Here, you must confirm whether the connection to this non-NT server is either a PPP or a SLIP connection. Choose the appropriate option.

Clicking Next opens the next dialog box, as shown in Figure 25.31. You must now confirm whether the dial-up session with this server will require an interactive screen to allow you to enter logon details. The alternatives include using no terminal or using a script that automatically enters details where and when they are required. This capability removes the need for interaction. You can choose and edit the script of your choice (by clicking the Edit script button). After you finish, click Next.

FIGURE 25.31.
Login Script dialog box.

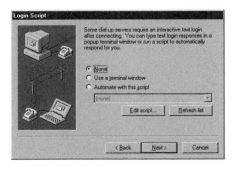

In the next dialog box, the IP Address dialog box shown in Figure 25.32, you can specify an IP address for the connecting client. Leave the default values as they are if the remote server provides you with an IP address on connection. Click Next to continue.

FIGURE 25.32.

The IP Address dialog box.

You next have to enter the IP addresses of the remote DNS server and WINS server in the dialog box shown in Figure 25.33. Again, if the remote server supplies this information, leave the default values as they are. Clicking Next brings you to the finish of the setup routine; click Finish to complete.

FIGURE 25.33.

Name Server Addresses.

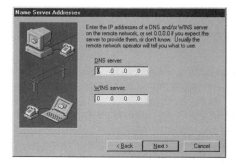

Advanced Editing of RAS Phonebook Entries

You also can directly edit Dial-Up Networking phonebook entries. If you always want to edit phonebook entries directly, you can turn off the New Phonebook Entry Wizard. Invoke Dial-Up networking by choosing Start | Programs | Accessories | Dial-Up Networking (refer to Figure 25.22). After the Dial-Up Networking dialog box appears, click the More button and choose User preferences from the menu, as shown in Figure 25.34.

FIGURE 25.34.

Choosing User preferences from the Dial-up Networking dialog box.

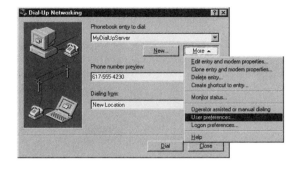

After the User Preferences dialog box appears, select the Appearance tab. The dialog box should then look like the one illustrated in Figure 25.35.

FIGURE 25.35.

The User Preferences dialog box.

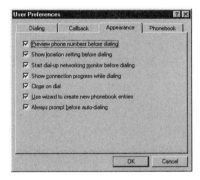

Make sure the Use wizard to create new phonebook entries check box is not selected. Here are the other options available for configuration:

- Preview phone number before dialing
- Show location setting before dialing
- Start dial-up networking monitor before dialing
- Show connection progress while dialing
- Close on dial
- Always prompt before auto-dialing

If you select the Dialing tab, the User Preferences dialog box looks like Figure 25.36.

FIGURE 25.36.

The Dialing tab of the User Preferences dialog box.

Within this tab, you can enable auto dialing from your defined locations so that RAS automatically dials whenever you reference a resource that is not local. You can also define the number of redial attempts RAS makes, the number of seconds between redials, and the number of idle seconds before RAS hangs up and terminates the connection. You can configure these values via their associated number boxes.

In the Callback tab of the User Preferences dialog box, as shown in Figure 25.37, you can configure your response to a request from the RAS server to determine whether you want to be called back. This capability is useful if you want the phone call to be billed from the server. This option must be granted from the RAS server side, however. You can either choose to decline the offer of callback each time you dial, configure the RAS client to ask you for a callback number, or alternatively set RAS to call you back at a predefined number(s). You select the appropriate radio button for each of these options. If you elect to be called at a predefined number, you can edit it by choosing the correct radio button and then by clicking the Edit button. Enter the new phone number in the text box that appears.

FIGURE 25.37.

The Callback tab of the User Preferences dialog box.

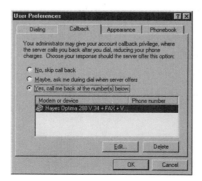

The final tab within the User Preferences dialog box is Phonebook, as you can see in Figure 25.38. Through this tab, you can decide to use the system phonebook that is located at %systemroot%\system32\rasphone.pbk. Alternatively, you can use a personal telephone book that is visible and accessible only to you—assuming that the workstation is installed on an NTFS file system and the proper file restrictions are set. Choosing the final alternative allows you to use a phonebook outside the system32 directory, maybe on another workstation.

FIGURE 25.38.

The Phonebook tab of the User Preferences dialog box.

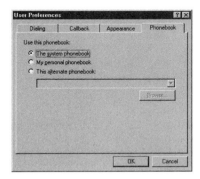

Click OK to return to the main Dial-Up Networking dialog box, as shown in Figure 25.34.

Also contained within the More button's drop-down menu are the following options:

- The ability to delete a highlighted entry
- The ability to clone a highlighted phonebook entry
- The ability to create a shortcut to a dial-up entry
- The ability to start the Dial-Up Networking Monitor
- The ability to enable operator-assisted dialing, which allows you to dial the number manually for RAS.
- The ability to set logon preferences, which are similar to the user preferences

Setting Phonebook Entry Basic Properties

You can now begin entering your new phonebook entries. Click the New button in the Dial-Up Networking dialog box to begin the process. The New Phonebook Entry dialog box appears, as shown in Figure 25.39. Note that this dialog box has several tabs. Make sure that the Basic tab is on top of the display; then enter the name of your phonebook entry and enter a telephone number. If you select the Use Telephony dialing properties check box, you can add the area code and alternative phone numbers. (This dialog box is similar to the Phone Number dialog box shown in Figure 25.26.) Also select a modem from the Dial using drop-down list.

Figure 25.39.

Entering basic information for a new phonebook entry.

Clicking the Configure button located at the base of the tab activates the Modem Configuration dialog box, which is shown in Figure 25.40.

Figure 25.40.

The Modem Configuration dialog box.

Through this dialog box, you can set the initial speed at which the modem negotiates a connection with the RAS server. This capability can be useful if your system has problems keeping up with extremely fast connections. Some COM ports, for example, do not have built-in buffering. If you don't have an extremely fast processor, your system might not be able to handle data at 57,600bps. Use this setting to reduce the speed to 38,400bps or 19,200bps.

You can also enable or disable the following:

- Hardware flow control
- Modem error control
- Modem compression
- Modem speaker

You should select the Enable hardware flow control check box for fast modems. Most users should also select the Enable modem error control check box. This causes your modem to try to automatically correct any data errors caused by noisy telephone connections.

Surprisingly enough, you might not want to select the Enable modem compression check box. RAS provides facilities for software compression of the data stream. Furthermore, PPP has built-in facilities for doing software compression of packet headers (often called VJ compression).

Enabling the RAS software compression and disabling the modem compression usually results in better throughput than modem compression can provide.

Finally, you can use this dialog box to disable the speaker on your modem. Doing so might save some wear and tear on your ears, but it can also make debugging failed connections somewhat more difficult.

After you're happy with the modem configuration for this phonebook entry, click OK to return to the Basic tab. Here, you can force RAS to use an alternative COM port if the selected one is busy.

Setting Phonebook Entry Server Protocol Options

Selecting the Server tab of the New Phonebook Entry dialog box allows you to configure protocol settings, as you can see in Figure 25.41.

FIGURE 25.41.

The Server tab in the New Phonebook Entry dialog box.

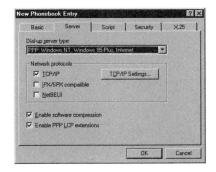

Using the scroll box at the top of the dialog box, you can select the remote server type. Select the PPP: Windows NT, Windows 95 Plus, Internet entry if the server you want to call is one of these types or if you don't know what it is. PPP is the most widely used of the available protocols, so it is most likely to be correct.

SLIP, or Serial Line Internet Protocol, was the first protocol designed to allow TCP/IP connections over dial-up modems. SLIP is a relatively low-overhead protocol, but it is somewhat lacking in error correction and security facilities. SLIP has largely been replaced by PPP, but some older Internet sites still use SLIP. If you need to connect to one of them, select the SLIP:Internet entry as your server type.

Select the Windows NT 3.1, Windows for Workgroups 3.11 entry if you're connecting to either of these older server types. You will have relatively limited functionality when compared to PPP connections.

Some PPP servers can support IPX/SPX-compatible connections. If you're connecting to a Novell server, it might require that the IPX/SPX compatible check box be selected.

NetBEUI is a local area protocol designed by Microsoft and IBM. It was the only protocol originally available for Windows for Workgroups clients and NT 3.1 servers. Unless you're connecting directly to a NetBEUI compatible server, you do not need to select the NetBEUI check box. For more details on network protocols, see Chapter 26, "Windows NT Networking Protocols."

The Enable software compression check box should generally be selected. If you have trouble communicating with a server after the modem makes a connection, try turning off this feature. If you can leave it on, you will probably get better performance.

The Enable PPP LCP extensions check box enables some of the newer protocol features of PPP. You should leave this feature enabled if possible. If you have trouble connecting to a server with this feature enabled, try turning it off.

If your server is using TCP/IP (using either SLIP or PPP), click the TCP/IP Settings button to configure the TCP/IP protocol options. The PPP TCP/IP Settings dialog box then appears, as shown in Figure 25.42. In most cases, the server assigns an IP network address to your client when you dial in. If you want to enter an address, select the Specify an IP address radio button and type one into the appropriate space. Make sure that the address you enter has been assigned by the network administrator at the site you want to call.

FIGURE 25.42.
Setting phonebook entry TCP/IP protocol options.

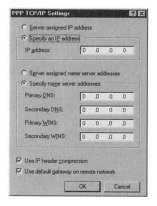

Setting Phonebook TCP/IP Options

Many systems exist on the Internet. Each of these systems has an individual network address number, but you don't have to know a system's network address to contact it. That's because the Domain Name Service, more commonly known as DNS, looks up system addresses. DNS uses a hierarchical approach in translating system names to network addresses. Suppose, for example, that in your Web browser you enter the address www.microsoft.com. The name consists of three parts. The first part, www, is the name of a specific system. The name www is used by convention as a default for an organization's Web server. The second part indicates that the system is part of Microsoft's corporate network. The third part indicates that the Microsoft network is part of a larger group of commercial enterprises. Government agencies within the USA have addresses ending with .gov, educational institutions have addresses ending with .edu, and so on.

Microsoft has created a variation of this model called Windows Internet Naming Service, or WINS. WINS serves the same functionality as DNS within NT domains by providing NetBIOS namespace to TCP/IP address translation. In a routed TCP/IP network, for example, WINS can tell a client where to look for a domain controller to authenticate a domain logon. NT DUN resolves NetBIOS names through WINS. So if you intend to mount file or print shares through a RAS connection to an ISP, you either specify a WINS server address or build an LMHOSTS file for your NetBIOS hostnames.

You'll need access to a DNS server to perform name resolution when using programs such as Netscape, Internet Explorer, FTP, or Telnet. In most cases, the PPP protocols allow the server to specify the address of the DNS name server for you. In some cases, you might want to enter DNS or WINS server addresses yourself.

If you want to enter the address of a DNS server, select the Specify name server addresses radio button in the PPP TCP/IP Settings dialog box. Note that you can enter the addresses for both primary and secondary servers of both types. You probably do not need a WINS server address unless you're connecting to another NT system or domain through an intermediary ISP without using PPTP. If you're connecting through an Internet Service Provider solely to use Internet applications, the DNS server may or may not be needed. Ask your ISP to be sure. For more information on DNS and WINS, see Chapter 26.

Selecting the Use IP header compression check box enables the so-called VJ header compression on TCP/IP packets. This is used both on PPP and on a SLIP variant called CSLIP (Compressed SLIP). You get better performance on your connections if this box is left selected, but if you have problems connecting to your RAS server, try turning it off.

Finally, connecting with any host other than the one you dial into requires that your network packets be routed through a gateway machine (either a host or a dedicated network router). If you select the Use default gateway on remote network check box, your connections are automatically forwarded through the default router on the network that you dial into. You should normally leave this box selected.

Click OK to finish your TCP/IP protocol configuration and return to the New Phonebook Entry dialog box.

Using Scripts Within Phonebook Entries

The Script tab of the New Phonebook Entry dialog box enables you to build customized programs for logging into remote servers. This capability can be required when the remote server requires special security provisions or when the telephone system has special requirements for dialing a number. As you can see in Figure 25.43, the three basic options on this tab are as follows:

25

**REMOTE COMPUT-
ING WITH REMOTE
ACCESS SERVICE**

■ If the None radio button is selected, RAS dials the target telephone number and tries to authenticate using the entered password. The authentication method is negotiated with the PPP server and can be either CHAP, MS-CHAP, or PAP. All these methods encrypt the previously entered password and pass a secure encrypted token to the remote server for verification.

■ If the Pop up a terminal window radio button is selected, RAS establishes a connection to the remote modem and then opens a terminal window. The user can then manually type any commands required to complete authentication and connection.

■ If the Run this script radio button is selected, RAS connects to the remote modem and then runs the script named in the box just below this button. Scripts can be used to wait for prompts from remote systems and to send complex responses. Several sample scripts are included with RAS.

FIGURE 25.43.

Configuring scripts within phonebook entries.

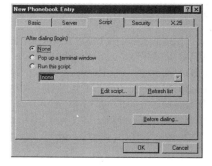

Selecting the Before Dialing button presents a list of options identical to those described in the preceding section, but the options are applied before the modem dials the target number.

RAS Security

Because RAS allows remote connections into the NT 4 system, security is an issue of some concern to most network and system administrators. RAS security is implemented at multiple levels. Remember that RAS on NT Workstation 4 has both server and client features. The RAS client always connects to the RAS server through a wide area networking technology such as a modem, an ISDN adapter, or an X.25 Pad. The RAS server can use any of these devices to accept the connection. If the client connects using the PPTP protocol, the server views the connection as a RAS client connection. Alternatively, the client can connect through an Internet Service Provider or other network agent using routed TCP/IP. In this case, the RAS server's view of the connection is essentially identical to that of local LAN connections.

RAS provides security facilities to address all these connection schemes. Point-to-point devices such as ISDN adapters or modems attached to RAS servers should be configured to use the most secure authentication method possible. If the RAS clients can support these features, this requires both MS-CHAP password encryption and data encryption. These options are set in the Network Configuration dialog box of the Network Control Panel applet.

RAS client security options are set in the phonebook. Figure 25.44 shows the Security tab of the New Phonebook Entry dialog box. The security options must be set to match the server being called. Again, if the targeted server is another NT system, select all the Microsoft encryption options.

FIGURE 25.44.

Setting RAS security options on phonebook entries.

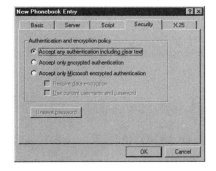

You can set callback options to further enhance security. When callback is enabled, a user calls the RAS server from a remote site. Upon successfully authenticating the call, the RAS server notifies the caller that he or she will be called back. The server can either hang up immediately and call back at a predetermined number, or it can query the user for a phone number that the server can call back on.

If the server is set to call back to a predetermined number, the overall security of the system is greatly enhanced. Even if a user's password is stolen or broken, an intruder cannot get access to system resources without being physically present at the callback number.

Note that, in some senses, callback schemes that allow users to enter a callback number are worse than no callback at all because an intruder with a stolen password could call from a hotel, or other temporary number, and then get your system to call back. Not only would this situation compromise your system, but it would potentially cause you to incur telephone charges in the bargain.

You set callback security options in the User Manager or in the Users menu option of the Remote Access Administrator applet found in Administrative Tools.

X.25

In the X.25 tab of the New Phonebook Entry dialog box, shown in Figure 25.45, you can configure options for your X.25 Pad. Through this tab, you can configure the name of the X.25 network, its address, and additional details such as user data and parameters.

FIGURE 25.45.

The X.25 tab of the New Phonebook Entry dialog box.

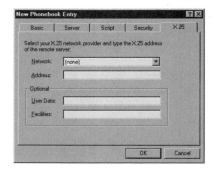

Click OK after you configure the X.25 options. You've completed the configuration of the phonebook entry. You're now ready to dial the remote RAS server.

Making a Connection and Using the Dial-Up Networking Monitor

From the main Dial-Up Networking dialog box (refer to Figure 25.34), click the Dial button after you select the phonebook entry from the scroll box. In the resulting dialog box, shown in Figure 25.46, enter your connecting username, password, and domain name; then click OK. The RAS client opens the COM port and dials the remote server, which authenticates your username and password and connects you to the remote server.

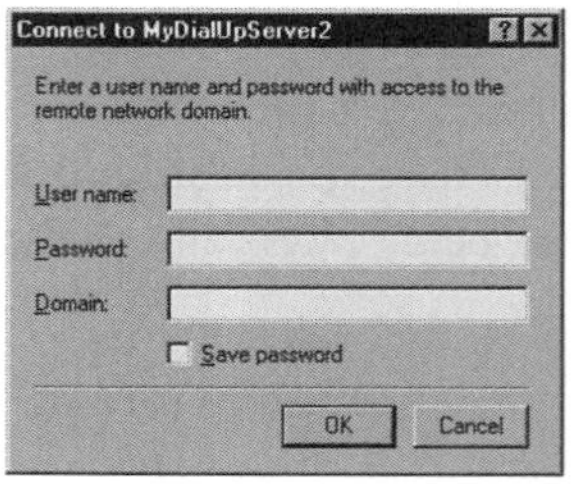

FIGURE 25.46.

Dialing a remote RAS server.

You then are given the option to hide the phonebook when the connection is made, as you can see in Figure 25.47. Click OK to continue.

FIGURE 25.47.

Hiding the phonebook during connection.

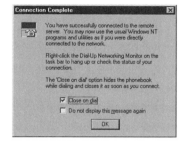

If you disabled the dial-up monitor from starting when you dial, you can invoke it by selecting the Dial-up monitor applet in the Control Panel or by choosing it from the More button's menu in the Dial-Up Networking dialog box. If the dial-up monitor is open and minimized in the system tray area of the Taskbar, you can execute several right-click operations to open the monitor or dial or hang up a phone entry (see Figure 25.48).

FIGURE 25.48.

Using the dial-up monitor from the Start tray.

After the Dial-Up Networking Monitor is activated, you can see that it has three tabs: Status, Summary, and Preferences.

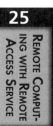

Status Tab

The Status tab of the Dial-Up Networking Monitor, which is shown in Figure 25.49, contains the following details:

- What device is being used to make the remote connection
- What the status of the connection is
- Throughput in bits per second on the connection
- The duration of the connection
- How many bytes are being transferred in and out on the device
- How many bytes are being transferred in and out on the connection
- How many frames are being transferred in and out on the connection
- The percentage compression in and out on the connection
- Device errors such as CRC, Framing, Timeout, Hardware overruns, Alignment, and Buffer overruns

FIGURE 25.49.

The Status tab of the Dial-Up Networking Monitor.

If you have more than one RAS device loaded, you can select it from the Device scroll box and view its status. To get additional details, click the Details button located at the base of the Dial-Up Networking Monitor. A Details dialog box then appears, as shown in Figure 25.50.

The Details dialog box lists the device being used and the frame encapsulation. The dialog box also lists some details by network protocol. For example, it displays the RAS server and client IP addresses for TCP/IP. Click OK to return to the Dial-Up Networking Monitor.

FIGURE 25.50.

The Details dialog box.

Summary Tab

The Summary tab of the Dial-Up Networking Monitor, which is shown in Figure 25.51, lists which networks and remote users are connected and which devices are in use.

FIGURE 25.51.

The Summary tab of the Dial-Up Networking Monitor.

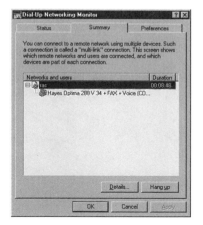

Preferences Tab

The Preferences tab of the Dial-Up Networking Monitor, which is shown in Figure 25.52, allows you to configure the DUN Monitor to suit your needs.

You can configure the generation of a sound when

- A connection is made
- A connection is dropped
- Data is sent or received
- A line error occurs

25

REMOTE COMPUT-ING WITH REMOTE ACCESS SERVICE

FIGURE 25.52.

The Preferences tab of the Dial-Up Network-ing Monitor.

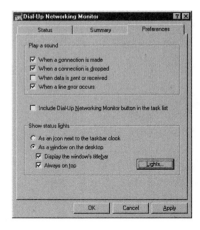

Also, you can configure the Dial-Up Networking Monitor to appear in the task list. If you just have to see lights, you can display the connection's activities through LED-type displays on the desktop or near the Taskbar clock. Clicking the Lights button opens the dialog box in Figure 25.53. In the Status Lights dialog box, you can configure LED displays for either the installed modem or all devices.

FIGURE 25.53.

Configuring lights for all devices and the modem.

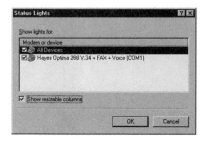

Figure 25.54 shows an example of the LED display.

FIGURE 25.54.

The LED display.

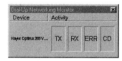

Click Apply to save changes made to the Dial-Up Networking Monitor. To exit the Dial-Up Networking Monitor, click OK.

RAS and the Internet

RAS enables your Windows NT system to connect as a client to the vast resources of the Internet. All that is required to use your computer to access the Internet are the following:

- A modem
- A valid account with an Internet Service Provider or NT RAS server that is connected to the Internet
- The RAS client software

Create a phonebook entry as described previously. If you have properly configured your entry, you establish a PPP connection to your remote server. At that point, you have effectively made yourself a part of a wide area TCP/IP network. Unless you are constrained by the network or server security facilities, you should be able to access essentially any other node on the Internet. Network browsers and other Internet-capable utilities such as Telnet and FTP work across the RAS connection.

If you have connected through an Internet Service Provider, you still can use file and print shares on other remote Windows NT systems. As long as you can reach the resource in question via TCP/IP, you have correctly configured your LMHOSTS file (or have access to a WINS server), and you have the proper passwords, you can reach out to NT systems anywhere on the Internet. This means that a single RAS dial-up connection from your home (or anywhere else) can be used to access Web pages, file shares, and logons to remote systems simultaneously. You can establish secure sessions through PPTP, which is discussed next.

PPTP

Point To Point Tunneling Protocol (PPTP) is a new feature that has been incorporated into RAS under Windows NT 4. PPTP allows you to route PPP packets securely over an IP network by encapsulating or tunneling any of the LAN-based network protocols within PPTP packets. PPTP supports the encapsulation of NetBEUI, IPX/SPX, and TCP/IP packets. The obvious advantage of using PPTP is that all communications are encapsulated and encrypted. With PPTP, you can also establish a corporate WAN using the Internet as your backbone. PPTP has a huge cost saving associated with it because you can call a local number and establish a secure connection to another office easily and quickly.

Because PPTP is a new protocol, information is only now becoming available, and many of the misunderstandings are disappearing. A PPTP connection requires two dial-up connections: the first to your ISP or corporate RAS server and the second to your PPTP server. The following steps help you install, configure, and connect through a PPTP tunnel from an NT Workstation. I'm assuming you have already set up up a DUN phone entry to either your ISP or your RAS server. The only other configuration required is to PPTP-enable RAS and create another DUN phone entry to the PPTP server. The configuration required to create a PPTP connection is straightforward and follows similar lines to the creation of an ordinary dial-up session:

1. Install the PPTP protocol. To do so, open the Network applet from within the Control Panel. Select the Protocols tab, as shown in Figure 25.55.

FIGURE 25.55.

The Protocols tab in the Network applet.

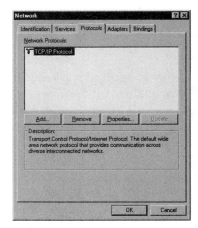

2. Click the Add button. In the next dialog box that appears, shown in Figure 25.56, select Point To Point Tunneling Protocol and click OK.

FIGURE 25.56.

Add the Point To Point Tunneling Protocol.

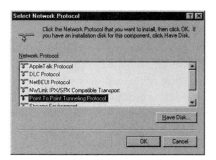

3. You then are asked to enter the path to the NT Workstation distribution media, as you can see in Figure 25.57. Enter the path and click Continue.

FIGURE 25.57.

Supply the path to the NT Workstation distribution media.

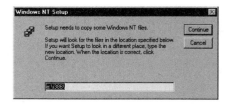

4. The setup routine copies files to your hard drive and opens the PPTP Configuration dialog box, as shown in Figure 25.58. In this dialog box, set the number of tunnels you want to define on your workstation. Click OK after you select the number of tunnels from the drop-down list.

FIGURE 25.58.

Define the number of tunnels for your workstation.

5. The setup routine then asks you to reconfigure you RAS settings for PPTP, as you can see in Figure 25.59. Click OK.

FIGURE 25.59.

Configure RAS for PPTP.

6. When the Remote Access Setup dialog box appears, as shown in Figure 25.60, click the Add button to add the Virtual Private Network (VPN) device. Notice the modem already installed within RAS.

FIGURE 25.60.

Add the Virtual Private Network device.

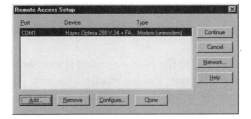

7. In the Add RAS Device dialog box, shown in Figure 25.61, select the RAS PPTP modem (RASPPTPM) device from the RAS Capable Devices drop-down list. Click OK to continue.

FIGURE 25.61.

Select the RASPPTPM.

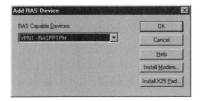

25

REMOTE COMPUT-
ING WITH REMOTE
ACCESS SERVICE

8. Now you must configure the RAS port. From the Remote Access Setup dialog box, highlight the newly added virtual RAS device and click the Configure button to configure the port. The Configure Port Usage dialog box then appears, as shown in Figure 25.62. Here, you can see the name of the port and the device it uses. Select the Dial-out only radio button. Click OK to return to the main Remote Access Setup dialog box.

Figure 25.62.

Configure the port usage.

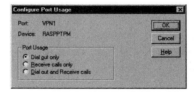

9. Again from the Remote Access Setup dialog box, click the Network button to select the dial-out protocols to be tunneled. In the Network Configuration dialog box, shown in Figure 25.63, ensure that the appropriate protocols are checked. Click OK to return to the Remote Access Setup dialog box.

Figure 25.63.

Choose the network protocols to be tunneled.

10. After you configure the port usage and the network protocols, click Configure at the bottom of the Remote Access Setup dialog box. After the setup routine copies files and binds the newly added Point To Point Tunneling Protocol, you can see it added to the list of loaded protocols in Figure 25.64. Click Close to exit the Network applet. You then are prompted to reboot the Workstation so that the changes can take effect. You've now completed the RAS configuration of the tunnel client. Now you must create a DUN phone entry for the tunnel.

11. Open the Dial-Up Networking dialog box either through the My Computer program group or by choosing Start | Programs | Accessories | Dial-Up Networking. In this dialog box, shown in Figure 25.65, click the New button to create a new phonebook entry. Notice an entry for dialing into a RAS server is already present.

12. In the resulting New Phonebook Entry dialog box, shown in Figure 25.66, enter the name for the connection on the Basic tab. For the phone number, enter the IP address for the remote PPTP server. By the time you use this connection, you will already have established a connection to your RAS server or ISP. From there, you now have to get to your PPTP server. From the Dial using drop-down list select the RASPPTPM virtual device. Note that the other tabs in this dialog box are configured as though you

were configuring an ordinary dial-up connection. If you need a refresher, refer to the "Making a Connection and Using the Dial-Up Networking Monitor" section earlier in this chapter. After you enter all the configuration details for the PPTP dial-up connection, click OK to save the details. Now you've completed the client configuration steps.

FIGURE 25.64.

PPTP is listed among the loaded protocols.

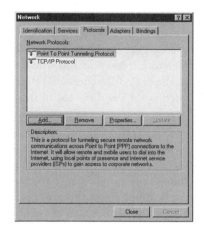

FIGURE 25.65.

Create a new phonebook entry.

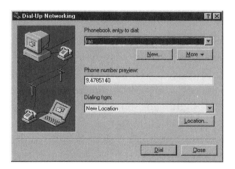

FIGURE 25.66.

Adding the basic details for the PPTP entry.

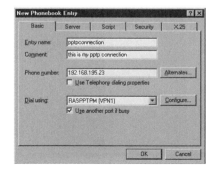

13. Now you must configure the PPTP server. If you use an NT workstation for your PPTP server, it can support only one port for incoming calls. Hence, the workstation cannot support the initial RAS connection and the PPTP connection. An NT workstation can support a PPTP connection only via its network card; the first connection is established either through an ISP and then connected to the PPTP server through the Internet or, if you're using RAS, another RAS server on the local network. On the PPTP server side, you must again have RAS and the PPTP protocol installed. You must also add the VPN device to the PPTP RAS server (refer to step 7). Next, you must configure the port usage on the VPN to accept incoming calls and configure the Network settings as you would for any other incoming RAS connection. As I said before, the only differences PPTP brings to RAS and DUN are the addition of the VPN device in RAS and the use of the IP address for the phone number in the DUN.

14. Now that the configuration of the server and client is complete, you can initiate a tunnel connection. Open the DUN on the client side, and dial into your ISP or RAS server. After this connection is established, dial the PPTP connection you just created. You are again asked for your username and password as you would be for a normal dial-up connection. Enter your username and password to be authenticated by the PPTP server. You've now completed the tunnel connection.

Summary

The Internet is fast becoming a part of everyday life. This trend will continue and accelerate as time goes on. The ability to connect systems into global information networks is critical to any modern computing system. Windows NT 4 has risen to meet that challenge by providing robust and user-friendly tools for connecting to remote networked resources. Furthermore, Microsoft has taken significant steps toward improving the flexibility and security of Remote Access Services by incorporating support for the Point To Point Tunneling Protocol in both NT 4 Workstation and Server. This chapter covered the installation and configuration of RAS both as a server and as a client via Dial-Up Networking (DUN). It also detailed the configuration requirements for creating and establishing a PPTP tunnel.

V

PART

Networking Windows NT Workstation

Windows NT Networking Protocols

by Mike Sheehy and Sean Mathias

CHAPTER 26

IN THIS CHAPTER

In this chapter, you will learn how to install Windows NT Networking. You will first look at the installation of a network interface card (NIC), which prompts the installation of network components of NT. This discussion will be followed by a detailed description of the Network applet, which is the main tool used for configuring the network components of NT. Finally, you will finish the chapter by looking at the installation and configuration of the three most common network protocols, namely Microsoft's NetBEUI, Microsoft's NWLink Compatible Transport IPX/SPX, and TCP/IP.

Installing NT Networking

You can install Windows NT Networking during the initial installation of Windows NT itself or at a later time. The fact that you can delay this process until after initial installation can be helpful when a problem arises with the networking portion of setup. You then can cancel the networking setup and finish installing the rest of the operating system rather than quit the setup of Windows NT and solve the networking issue.

In this chapter, you learn how to install Windows NT Networking after the initial Windows NT setup has been completed. Although the processes are identical for installing networking components during or after setup, I always prefer to get the workstation up and running properly first, as a standalone machine, before I attempt to undertake the installation of the networking components.

First, let me once again emphasize my point: Use a network card that is listed on the Hardware Compatibility List (HCL). Yes, you can use unlisted cards if you can get Windows NT drivers for them, but save yourself the headache and use a supported card. You will find that even the cards listed on the HCL can be difficult to install because they might need a bit of work to get them functioning properly.

To begin installation of Windows NT Networking (assuming it has not already been installed), right-click the Network Neighborhood icon on the desktop and choose the Properties option. You are presented with a dialog box, as shown in Figure 26.1, informing you that Windows NT Networking has not been installed and asking whether you would like to install it now.

FIGURE 26.1.

The Network Configuration dialog box.

To be prepared for this process, be sure to know which network protocols are used at your location. Also, know the network protocol's appropriate configuration settings, the type of network adapter you're using and its settings, and the services you want to install. If you are in doubt, ask your IS group for the information.

Clicking Yes starts the Network Setup Wizard. This wizard briefly analyzes and inspects your system before presenting you with a dialog box asking how your computer should participate in the network—via local connection or using remote access. (See Figure 26.2.)

FIGURE 26.2.

The Network Setup Wizard configuration dialog box.

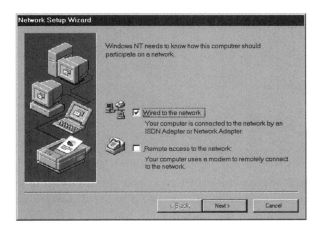

If you plan to access the network through an ISDN adapter or network adapter, select the Wired to the network option. If you plan to access the network remotely using a modem, select the Remote access to the network option, or select both if they are applicable to your situation. After you make the necessary selections, click Next.

Installing and Configuring a Network Card

The next step is to install a network adapter. The Network Setup Wizard presents an adapter installation dialog box. You can either let the Setup Wizard search your system to see whether it can detect a network card, or you can select the network card yourself.

To let Windows NT search your system for a recognized network adapter, click the Start Search button. Windows NT searches your hardware for any recognized network adapters. When it finds a network adapter, it stops and lists the adapter in the Network Adapters box. If you have more than one adapter installed in your system, click the Find Next button. Repeat this process until all installed adapters have been detected. Figure 26.3 shows an adapter that was detected by the Setup Wizard. If Windows NT does not find your adapter, you have to use the Select from list option and manually specify your network adapter.

FIGURE 26.3.

*The network adapter
installation dialog box.*

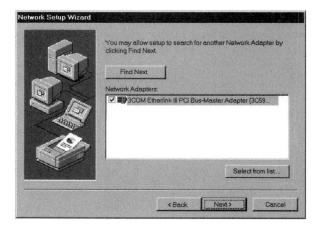

To select an adapter manually or specify an unsupported or unlisted adapter, click the Select from list button. Select the adapter that is installed in your system from the list in the resulting Select Network Adapter dialog box, as shown in Figure 26.4; or, if you have a driver for an unlisted adapter or an updated driver, select the Have Disk button and provide the path to the network adapter driver files. Click OK to return to the Setup Wizard dialog box.

FIGURE 26.4.

*Manually selecting a
network card for
installation.*

After all installed network adapters have been specified, click the Next button.

Choosing the Right Protocols

NT supports the ability to load multiple network protocols. The next step in the Network Setup Wizard is to specify the protocols you want to use. This option depends on the protocols in use at your location, your networking needs, and your environment.

By default, the Network Setup Wizard lists the three most common protocols—TCP/IP, NWLink IPX/SPX Compatible Transport, and NetBEUI—with TCP/IP being the only protocol selected (evidence again of Microsoft's focus on the Internet). This dialog box is shown in Figure 26.5.

26
WINDOWS NT
NETWORKING
PROTOCOLS

FIGURE 26.5.
*The Network Setup
Wizard protocol setup
dialog box.*

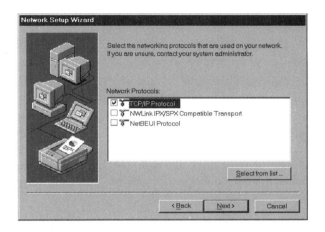

The following is a description of each of these protocols:

- *TCP/IP:* The Internet protocol suite. This suite of protocols was originally designed to link diverse network and systems architectures over public and switched networks. This protocol is fairly efficient and flexible, although given the explosion of the worldwide Internet, it is reaching its limits in its current version (IPv4).

- *NWLink IPX/SPX Compatible Transport:* A NetBIOS-enabled implementation of IPX/SPX used for connectivity and communications with Novell NetWare servers.

- *NetBEUI:* This is the long-standing protocol of choice for Microsoft networking. It is a very fast and efficient NetBIOS protocol, but it is not routable (except in rare circumstances of token ring networks with source routing enabled). Therefore, NetBEUI is typically used only in small, non-routed networks or departments.

To select or deselect a listed protocol, check or remove the check from the appropriate check boxes. To add additional protocol support, click the Select from list button. A dialog box of installable network protocols then appears, as shown in Figure 26.6.

FIGURE 26.6.
*NT supports additional
network protocols.*

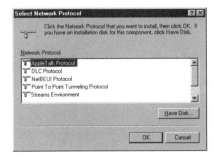

Windows NT offers the following additional protocol support:

■ *AppleTalk Protocol.* This protocol is used for communications with Macintosh computers or on Macintosh networks.

■ *DLC Protocol.* This protocol, used in a Windows NT environment, is primarily for communicating with and facilitating network printers using HP JetDirect cards.

■ *Point To Point Tunneling Protocol.* This new protocol was developed by an Internet Engineering Task Force (IETF) Working Group and implemented by Microsoft in Windows NT 4 to facilitate the use of the Internet as a secure medium of interconnecting systems or sites. This protocol establishes a secure virtual circuit (tunnel) between the interconnected systems and provides encryption at the protocol level for security.

■ *Streams Environment.* This interface protocol is used to provide network data stream support (similar to the STREAMS protocol in UNIX systems).

You can follow a few general guidelines to determine which protocols to install and use. First, use as few protocols as necessary. This way, you can reduce network overhead and response time while increasing performance. To determine the protocols to use, take a look at the systems to be connected and the functionality needed.

If relatively few computers must be connected and they all use Microsoft operating systems (Windows for Workgroups, Windows 95, Windows NT) and don't need to connect to other systems, the clear choice is NetBEUI. It provides the best performance in this situation.

If you need to communicate with systems on a Novell NetWare network, install the NWLink IPX/SPX Compatible Transport. It allows communications with these systems, provided the necessary application or gateway support is available.

If you are in a large or routed network environment or are connected to the Internet, you need to install and configure TCP/IP. Any one of these protocols can be used independently, or any combination of them can be used together as needed.

After you select the necessary protocols, click OK to close the Select Network Protocol dialog box and return to the Network Setup Wizard dialog box. Then click Next to continue with the installation.

Installing and Configuring Network Services

The next Setup Wizard dialog box you are presented with is the network services dialog box, as shown in Figure 26.7. By default, during Windows NT Network installation, a group of standard services are selected for installation and cannot be deselected. These services, which are shown in Figure 26.7, are described in the following list:

■ *RPC Configuration.* This service is the Windows NT networking method of communications between systems (similar to the interprocess communication, or IPC, service

on local systems) and distributed applications. It allows NT to make procedure calls to remote machines.

■ *NetBIOS Interface.* This interface is another interprocess communication mechanism for use by distributed applications.

■ *Workstation.* This service allows Windows NT to act as a network client to other systems on the network and to access network resources.

■ *Server.* The Server service provides the opposite functionality of the Workstation service and enables Windows NT Workstation to share resources on a network.

FIGURE 26.7.

The Network Setup Wizard network services dialog box.

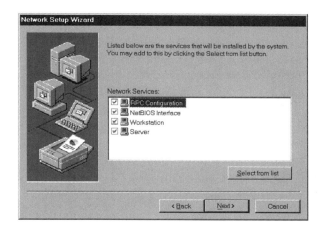

As before, you can add a service that is not listed by clicking the Select from list button. In the Select Network Service dialog box that appears, as shown in Figure 26.8, you can choose from a list of installable network services. Again, consistent with other installation routines in Windows NT and Windows 95, the Have Disk button is helpful if you have a third-party network service to install.

FIGURE 26.8.

The installable network services list in the Select Network Service dialog box.

The installable network services provided by Windows NT Workstation are described here:

■ *Client Service for NetWare.* This service provides access to file and printer resources on NetWare servers.

■ *Microsoft Peer Web Services.* This service provides a platform for Web-based intranets or Internets similar to Microsoft's Internet Information Server. See Chapter 29, "Using Peer Web Services."

■ *Microsoft TCP/IP Printing.* This service provides a TCP/IP-based print gateway. A shared printer can be created to provide Microsoft Networking clients access to a TCP/IP-enabled printer or, conversely, to provide UNIX clients access to a TCP/IP-enabled printer that is connected to a Windows NT system.

■ *Network Monitor Agent.* This remote agent supports the Microsoft Network Monitor (or `Bloodhound`), which is bundled with Microsoft Systems Management Server (SMS) or the scaled-down version included with Windows NT Server.

■ *Remote Access Service.* This service is the equivalent of dial-up networking in Windows 95. This service is installed by default when you're configuring a system with the Remote Access to the Network option in the Network Setup Wizard. If the system is not configured for this option, RAS is not installed by default but can be selected using the Select from list button.

■ *RPC Support for Banyan.* This service provides RPC support for distributed applications located on Banyan VINES networks and servers.

■ *SAP Agent.* This Service Access Protocol agent makes SAP-compatible broadcasts across the network.

■ *Simple TCP/IP Services.* This collection of client software is for services such as Character Generator, Daytime, Discard, Echo, and Quote of the Day.

■ *SNMP Service.* This service provides a mechanism for the system to be managed and monitored remotely using tools such as HP OpenView.

After you select the network services you want, click OK to close the Select Network Service dialog box to return to the Network Setup Wizard dialog box. Then click Next. At this point, you can either backtrack, by clicking Back, and amend any choices you made or continue with the installation by clicking Next. If you proceed, you are prompted for the path of your Windows NT Workstation files. Provide the correct path and click Next.

After you provide the necessary configuration information for your network card, protocols, and services (described in greater detail later in the chapter), and Windows NT has finished copying files, you are presented with a bindings dialog box, as shown in Figure 26.9.

FIGURE 26.9.

The wizard's bindings dialog box.

From the bindings dialog box, you can enable or disable specific network protocol and service bindings on a per-adapter card basis. This capability can be useful in some respects for security purposes. For example, you can disable NetBIOS over an interface that is connected to the Internet to eliminate a potential intrusion point. Note, however, that you can impair or disable your network by arbitrarily disabling bindings. You should have a good understanding of networking and Windows NT before making these modifications.

After you make all binding changes (if any), click Next. You are then instructed to click Next to start the network. After you do so, Windows NT tries to start the network. If errors occur, you are informed so that you can go back to reconfigure the device, protocol, or service that caused the error.

Workgroups and Domains

The Network Setup Wizard then opens the dialog box shown in Figure 26.10. Here you specify a network name for the system and decide whether this system will participate in a workgroup or a domain. Computer names are limited to 15 alphanumeric characters, and I recommend not using spaces, underscores, periods, or hyphens if possible (because they tend to present problems on the Internet and with various network applications).

Let me take time out to explain workgroups and domains. Workgroups and domains, although logically similar, serve two distinct purposes and are implemented in different ways. The decision as to which model you choose largely depends on whether an existing network is in place at your location and which model it is using. The following sections describe workgroups and domains with their relevant characteristics, capabilities, and limitations.

FIGURE 26.10.

*The computer name
and network model
dialog box.*

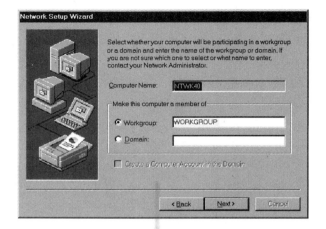

Workgroups

Workgroups are really nothing more than a logical grouping of computers that belong to the same business unit, perform similar functions, or are somehow related in purpose or proximity. In a workgroup, each Windows NT computer maintains its own user and group account information and security policies.

Workgroups are best suited for small networks that do not require a dedicated server or central management of resources. Workgroups quickly become ineffective as the number of systems grows because each system must have an account created for each user who needs access to its resources.

These accounts must be maintained on each individual system, which makes for quite an administrative task to keep accounts synchronized across multiple systems. Adding a single system to the workgroup can increase the administration factor exponentially.

Domains

Windows NT domains are similar to workgroups in function and purpose, but they provide centralized management of users and resources on the network as well as sadvanced security features. Windows NT domains are created and controlled by a single, authoritative Windows NT Server, called a Primary Domain Controller (PDC).

A given domain can have only one PDC, but it can have many Backup Domain Controllers (BDC) to distribute the load of user authentication and security across a domain. A PDC maintains a master list of user accounts, passwords, and security policies for a domain and replicates the list to the BDCs periodically. This process provides consistent security to user accounts automatically across all systems in a domain and greatly reduces the amount of administrative overhead involved with maintaining those accounts.

Domains are the obvious choice for networks that consist of more than a handful of systems with users sharing resources. Using domains allows for maximum flexibility and management.

Now back to the network installation procedure: If you choose to participate in a workgroup, specify the name of the workgroup in the Make this computer a member of the frame, as shown in Figure 26.10. If the workgroup name you specify cannot be found on the network, it is created for you. There are no prerequisites to becoming a member of a workgroup.

If you choose to participate in a Windows NT domain, you must provide the name of the domain that you want to join in the Domain text box. Windows NT computers, like users, must have accounts on the domain to join. To create an account on the domain, either request that your domain administrator create one for you, or check the Create computer account in the Domain check box near the bottom of the dialog box.

If you choose to create the computer account, you are prompted to provide a username and password for an account in the domain that has administrative rights or sufficient rights to add workstation accounts to the domain. Click Next to continue to the next step in the setup routine, which allows you to configure your chosen network protocols via the Network applet.

The Network Applet

You can at any time add, remove, or reconfigure network protocols from your workstation. You execute changes to the existing network components through the Network applet. Before you undertake any changes to the network components, you should be familiar with the Network applet. You can access it in two ways:

- First, you can right-click the Network Neighborhood desktop icon and choose Properties from its menu.
- Alternatively, you can access the Control Panel and select the Network applet.

No matter which route you choose, you see the dialog box shown in Figure 26.11.

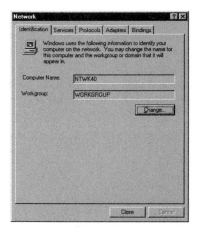

FIGURE 26.11.
The Network applet.

The Identification Tab

The Network applet always opens on the Identification tab, as shown in Figure 26.11. This tab has only two pieces of information, which are probably already filled in based on data you supplied when you installed Windows NT Workstation. You can use this tab to change this information at any time, which might be necessary if you skipped the data when installing, if you have a conflict with another machine on the network, or if you want to alter the name of the workstation for personal reasons.

Each machine on a network is uniquely identified to every other machine by a number of pieces of information, some of which are transparent to you. The most common identification method is through an IP address (used in TCP/IP networks). An IP address is unique to your network and your machine and can be used to route information over the network to or from your workstation. Some other network protocols rely on computer names or names that are mapped to numbers to identify your machine.

To change the existing computer name or workgroup/domain, click the Change button to open the Identification Changes dialog box, which is shown in Figure 26.12.

In the Identification Changes dialog box, you enter both a machine name and either a workgroup or domain name. The machine name is unique to your machine and should not be the same as any other machine on the network. The machine name can be anything that will help others associate your machine with you, such as your name, or with a function that the workstation serves. The workgroup or domain name is used by some networks to identify which network or subnetwork your machine belongs to.

FIGURE 26.12.
*The Identification
Changes dialog box.*

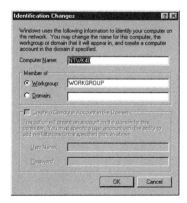

Make sure both of these pieces of information are supplied and that no errors occur when you click the OK button to register your entries. If you want to choose membership to a domain, you can create an account for your workstation by selecting the Create a Computer Account in the Domain check box and by entering a username/password combination. The username you enter must have privileges within the domain to add machine accounts. Your workstation tries to communicate with a Primary Domain Controller (PDC) for that domain to determine the validity of the username and password.

> **NOTE**
>
> Computers and users must have accounts defined for them within an NT domain.

The Services Tab

The Services tab of the Network dialog box shows a list of all the network services that are currently installed on your workstation, as you can see in Figure 26.13. The list shows only the services that are installed and configured, not all the services available to you.

Your workstation uses several types of services. Some services let you share your directories and peripherals, whereas others provide automatic functionality such as backups and name lookups.

Most services have configuration details associated with them. You can usually see these details by highlighting the service name in the Network Services window and clicking the Properties button. This action opens a Configuration dialog box, such as the one shown in Figure 26.14 for the RPC (Remote Procedure Call) service. After viewing this dialog box and making any necessary changes, click OK to return to the Services tab.

FIGURE 26.13.

The Services tab shows all network services installed on the workstation.

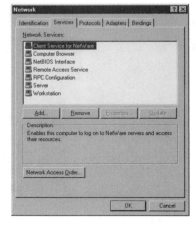

FIGURE 26.14.

Most services have configuration information associated with them.

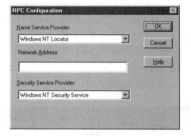

A few services do not have configuration information, so you cannot configure any changes to them. These services have the properties grayed out or disabled. To add new services to your system, click the Add button below the Network Services list on the Services tab. A list of all services that Windows NT Workstation has available to you is then compiled. The Select Network Service dialog box appears with the full list, as shown in Figure 26.15.

FIGURE 26.15.

The Select Network Service dialog box shows all services available to the workstation.

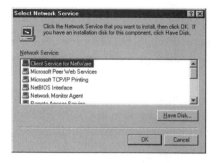

Selecting a service from this list and clicking on the OK button starts the installation and configuration process, after which the service appears in the list of installed services. (Later in this chapter, you will add some services to match the network requirements.)

Notice the Network Access button located at the bottom of the Services tab. This appears only if you are a member of more than one network—that is, you are a member of both a Novell network and an NT network. It allows you to arrange the order in which your workstation accesses services from the network. After you click this button, simply select a network service and change its order by clicking the Move Up or Move Down buttons in the Network Access Order dialog box, which is shown in Figure 26.16.

FIGURE 26.16.

Changing the order of network services.

The Protocols Tab

The Protocols tab of the Network dialog box shows the protocols that are currently installed on your workstation. Many protocols can be installed, although they don't all have to be used. An icon to the left of the protocol name shows that the protocol is used by the network. Figure 26.17 shows the Protocols tab with a single protocol (TCP/IP) in use by the workstation.

FIGURE 26.17.

The Protocols tab shows all the network protocols that are in use by the workstation.

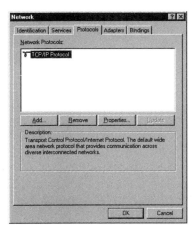

As with the Services tab, a property sheet is attached to each protocol on this tab. You can see the property sheet and, hence, all the configuration information for each protocol by selecting a protocol in the list and then clicking the Properties button. As you look at several network protocols later in this chapter, you will use the property sheet to provide all the configuration information the workstation needs for using the network.

You also can obtain a list of all protocols that the workstation knows about by clicking the Add button on the Protocols tab. A list of available protocols is then generated and displayed in a dialog box, as shown in Figure 26.18. You can install protocols other than the ones shown in this list, as long as you have the software drivers for the network. Some specialty networks have to be configured in this manner. You perform this type of configuration through the Have Disk button. Click OK to return to the Protocols tab.

FIGURE 26.18.

The Select Network Protocol dialog box lets you choose which network protocols to install on the workstation.

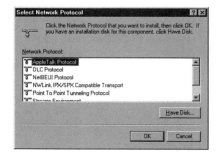

The Adapters Tab

As you might expect, the Adapters tab of the Network dialog box, as shown in Figure 26.19, lists all the network adapter cards that are configured and recognized by the Windows NT Workstation. You saw how to add and configure network adapters earlier in the chapter.

FIGURE 26.19.

The Adapters tab lists all network adapters that are recognized by Windows NT Workstation.

The particular system shown in this figure is configured with a single network adapter—3COM EtherlinkIII PCI BusMaster adapter.

As with the Services and Protocols tabs, a property sheet that identifies the card's IRQ and memory address is associated with each network card. The EtherlinkIII card is nonconfigurable, so when you click the Properties button to view its properties, you see a message box similar to the one shown in Figure 26.20.

FIGURE 26.20.

Unable to configure the PCI EtherlinkIII PCI BusMaster adapter.

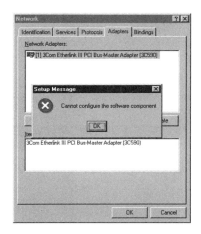

The Bindings Tab

On the Bindings tab of the Network dialog box, you tie together adapters, protocols, and services. A selection list box at the top of the tab lets you see bindings for all services, adapters, or protocols. You can start with the services bindings, as shown in Figure 26.21. The list of bindings on this tab shows the order in which the workstation tries to resolve requests for network services. By putting the most frequently used binding first, you can minimize the amount of time your workstation requires to accomplish network tasks. If you have several networks connected to your workstation, or you use multiple protocols on your system, selecting the proper order for use is important because performance can be affected.

You can alter the order of bindings on this list, changing the way in which your computer deals with network services, by using the Move Up and Move Down buttons below the list. You can also disable or enable bindings by using the Enable and Disable buttons below the list. A disabled binding is ignored by the workstation when a network service is to be resolved.

The icon next to the name of each binding on the list shows you the status of the binding. A computer screen icon (such as the one shown in Figure 26.21) means that the binding is enabled and active. Disabled bindings have a red cross symbol next to them, as shown in Figure 26.22, where two bindings are disabled. There are two disabled states. A red icon means the entire binding has been disabled, and a yellow icon means that some of the bindings are disabled and some are enabled.

FIGURE 26.21.

The Bindings tab lists connections between services, protocols, and network adapters.

FIGURE 26.22.

A red or yellow cross icon next to a binding name means the binding is disabled completely or partly, respectively.

To the left of the Bindings list is a small box with either a plus sign or a hyphen in it. If a plus sign appears in the box, it means that underlying levels of detail to the binding can be shown by clicking either the box or the binding name. Figure 26.23 shows expansions of some of the bindings shown earlier. You can use this feature to expand or compress the Bindings list for better legibility or to provide details of all the services or protocols bound to each entry.

Property sheets are not attached to each service, adapter, or protocol shown in the Bindings tab. The properties must be changed on the proper tab in the Network dialog box. For example, if you want to change your machine's IP address, you can't do so by clicking the TCP/IP Protocol entry on the Bindings tab, so you must go through the Protocols tab and select Properties there, as you learned earlier.

FIGURE 26.23.

Several levels of binding information can be available, depending on the icon to the left of the binding name.

As I mentioned before, the Bindings tab contains a selection list box that enables you to display the services or the bindings for each network adapter or network protocol. Changing the selection alters the Bindings list, as shown in Figures 26.24 and 26.25, which show the adapters and protocols bindings, respectively. In both of these figures, the lists have been expanded to show information below the top level.

FIGURE 26.24.

The adapter bindings show the protocols bound to each adapter card.

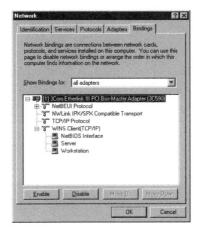

FIGURE 26.25.

The protocol bindings show the adapters to which each protocol or service is bound.

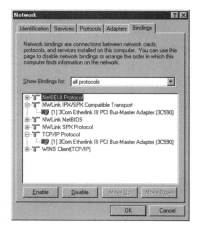

The three types of bindings lists let you see how the adapters, protocols, and services installed on your workstation interact. You will probably use all three bindings lists at one time or another to see how your workstation handles network functions.

You can now use the five tabs of the Network dialog box to configure your Windows NT Workstation machine for several different networks. Click OK to close the Network Applet. In each case, as you already know, adding your workstation to a network is a matter of simply configuring the adapter, protocol, and service to work with the rest of the network. Usually, this process is much easier to say than do, although a little experimentation usually sets things right quickly!

NetBEUI

IBM first developed Network Basic Input/Output System (NetBIOS) to provide a fast and efficient communication transport between PC-based and host-based systems. The NetBIOS specification consisted of 17 commands. The NetBIOS Enhanced User Interface (NetBEUI) protocol is a redefined set of NetBIOS commands. This protocol really is an excellent transport, providing fast speed and very low overhead, but it suffers from a few key design and implementation limitations.

> **NOTE**
>
> NetBEUI refers to a transport protocol, whereas NetBIOS refers to an actual set of commands.

At the time NetBEUI was developed, most networks were Ethernet (10Base-5 or 10Base-2) and were connected using bridges. Routers were not nearly as common at that time. Because of this fact, NetBEUI was designed as a nonroutable protocol (with one exception) to minimize its overhead and improve performance.

NOTE

The exception to NetBEUI's nonroutable design is an IBM token ring network with source routing enabled. This all ties in together because IBM developed NetBEUI and the token ring technology—so it essentially designed a low overhead protocol for use on its token ring topology.

NetBEUI operates at layers 3, 4, and 5 of the OSI model. NetBEUI is a broadcast-based protocol, which means that computers on a NetBEUI network communicate through broadcasts rather than a direct point-to-point communication link. For this reason, NetBEUI is often referred to as a "chatty" protocol. Every machine on a NetBEUI network sees all traffic.

NetBEUI, as I stated previously, is an extremely efficient protocol with minimum overhead. Its limitations stem from the underlying architecture of NetBIOS. The most important limitations are that this protocol is not routable in mainstream network architectures (those without IBM token ring and source routing enabled) and that NetBIOS imposes a 15-character, name-space limitation. You can, however, configure your routers to forward NetBIOS traffic, but doing so defeats the purpose of segmenting your network traffic in the first place.

With the growing concept of internetworking—whether using the global Internet or a large, private corporate network—any given protocol must necessarily provide support for routing capabilities. Along these same lines, identification becomes an issue with ever-growing networks. NetBIOS's 15-character name-space limits the capability of identifying a large number of systems descriptively across an enterprise. This might seem to provide an adequate supply of names (36^{15} possibilities or 2.21^{23} using only alphanumeric characters); however, people typically prefer meaningful names rather than the alphanumeric combinations that machines prefer. This requirement dramatically reduces the number of practical possibilities, especially when you try to implement standardized or meaningful naming conventions.

In a small- or medium-sized company, NetBEUI is the appropriate choice for its simplicity and efficiency, as long as you do not want Internet or public network connectivity.

Even the installation and configuration of the protocol is simple and straightforward. To install NetBEUI, follow these steps:

1. Open the Control Panel and start the Network applet.
2. Choose the Protocols tab and click the Add button.
3. From the list of available protocols that appears, select NetBEUI and click OK.
4. Provide the path to your Windows NT installation files and click OK.
5. After you finish copying files, click OK.
6. Restart your computer when prompted.

This procedure is simple, and you don't have to configure anything for NetBEUI other than providing a name for your computer that is unique on the network (which is done during the installation process).

NWLink IPX/SPX Compatible Transport

The NWLink IPX/SPX Compatible Transport was included initially with Windows for Workgroups 3.*x* to provide connectivity to Novell NetWare networks. It has subsequently been bundled with Windows 95, Windows NT 3.*x*, and now Windows NT 4.

The NWLink IPX/SPX Compatible Transport is a fairly good mainstream transport for private networks. This protocol is fully routable and does not incur any major transition overhead. The reason for its limited implementation is its lack of widespread public standardization. This transport is fully compatible with Novell NetWare IPX/SPX but never gained the acceptance of TCP/IP, due to the fact that it was designed and developed by a private corporation (Novell) and thus was limited in function and flexibility by design.

If your organization wants to run its own private network and does not need a transport such as TCP/IP, NWLink IPX/SPX Compatible Transport is an excellent choice because it is routable and can be used to wrap or transport other protocols.

Installing NWLink IPX/SPX Compatible Transport

To install NWLink IPX/SPX Compatible Transport, use the following procedure:

1. Open the Control Panel and start the Network applet.
2. Choose the Protocols tab and click the Add button.
3. From the list of available protocols that appears, select NWLink IPX/SPX Compatible Transport and click OK.
4. Provide the path to your Windows NT installation files and click OK.
5. After you finish copying files, click OK.
6. Restart your computer when prompted.

After the software is installed, you can opt to restart your computer later to configure the newly installed protocol.

Configuring NWLink IPX/SPX Compatible Transport

To configure the NWLink IPX/SPX Compatible Transport, perform the following steps:

1. Open the Control Panel and start the Network applet.
2. Choose the Protocols tab and select NWLink IPX/SPX Compatible Transport, as shown in Figure 26.26.

FIGURE 26.26.

The NWLink IPX/SPX Compatible Transport listed in the Protocols tab of the Network dialog box.

3. Click the Properties button. A dialog box similar to the one in Figure 26.27 then appears.

FIGURE 26.27.

The NWLink IPX/SPX Properties dialog box.

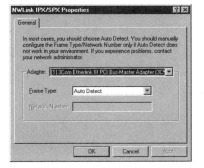

4. Select the adapter for which you want to configure the protocol, and select the Frame Type you want to use on the card. (The default, Auto Detect, does not always work well. If you experience problems, find out the correct frame type for your network and specify it explicitly.)

5. If you explicitly specify the Frame Type, you need to provide the Network Number for your network (see your system administrator).

6. When you're done, click Apply to save changes and then click OK to close the NWLink IPX/SPX Properties dialog box.

7. You are now returned to the Protocols tab of the Network applet. Click Close to exit the Network applet. NT will now bind the new changes and prompt you to restart your computer.

> **NOTE**
>
> You might notice that when you installed the NWLink IPX/SPX Compatible Transport, it also installed and listed the NWLink NetBIOS protocol. It is, effectively, NetBIOS over IPX. The difference is that it is installed by default and shows as a separate protocol. In previous versions, this protocol was simply an option to be enabled or disabled within the NWLink IPX/SPX configuration.

Included with Windows NT Workstation is the Client Service for NetWare, which is used to allow file and printer resources to be shared with NetWare servers. In addition, the Client Service included with Windows NT supports the Novell Directory Service (NDS).

Installing the NetWare Services

You install the NetWare Client Services through the Services tab of the Network dialog box. If this NetWare client was not loaded by default when you installed Windows NT, click the Add button on the Services tab to generate a list of all available services. From this list in the Select Network Service dialog box, select Client Service for NetWare (usually at the top of the list), as shown in Figure 26.15. Then click OK.

After you select Client Service for NetWare, Windows NT loads drivers from the distribution media (usually the CD-ROM). After the proper drivers are loaded and linked to the kernel, the Client Service should appear on the Network Services list in the Services tab, as shown in Figure 26.28.

FIGURE 26.28.

Client Service for NetWare has been added to the Network Services list.

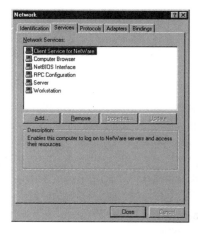

No property sheet is associated with the Client Service for NetWare. To configure the Client Service for NetWare, you must do so through the Control Panel using the Client Service for NetWare (CSNW) applet. See Chapter 9, "Advanced Control Panel Tools," for details.

Installing and Configuring TCP/IP

Transmission Control Protocol/Internet Protocol (TCP/IP) is fast becoming the enterprise network protocol of choice, due primarily to the rapid growth and use of the worldwide Internet. This reason is certainly not the only one, though. TCP/IP is a relatively efficient and flexible protocol that has been adapted to almost every network technology, such as Frame Relay and Asynchronous Transfer Mode (ATM), as well as to applications such as video conferencing and multimedia.

The Microsoft implementation of TCP/IP has matured significantly since its introduction in Windows for Workgroups 3.11 (Wolverine, the 32-bit TCP/IP stack for WfW 3.11) and is getting closer to a standards-compliant stack. Windows NT 3.5x introduced an improved implementation of TCP/IP, providing much better compliance and integration as well as some Microsoft-specific features such as Dynamic Host Configuration Protocol (DHCP) and Windows Internet Name Services (WINS).

With Windows NT 4, Microsoft has further extended its TCP/IP standardization and greatly enhanced its feature set to include native Domain Name System (DNS) name-resolution capabilities. Also new to the TCP/IP implementation is a security component that provides filtering capabilities (similar to a router access list or firewall) and Point To Point Tunneling (PPTP), facilitating the creation of Private Virtual Circuits (PVCs) over public-switched networks such as the global Internet.

With the integration of WINS and DNS capabilities, Windows NT can now seamlessly resolve names such as \\MYSERVER or www.myserver.com from the command line or any interface, as long as the DNS resolution is configured properly. The obvious benefit is ease of use for the user. This means that you can now map a drive to ftp.microsoft.com/data and access it through the Explorer rather than through a third-party application or the command line (see Figure 26.29).

FIGURE 26.29.

Mapping a TCP/IP-based volume to a network drive.

If you have not yet installed support for TCP/IP, use the following procedure to do so. If you have already installed the protocol, continue to the next section to configure TCP/IP for your network.

Installing TCP/IP Support

To install TCP/IP protocol support, use the following procedure:

1. From the Control Panel, open the Network applet, or right-click the Network Neighborhood icon on the desktop and choose Properties.

2. Within the Network applet, choose the Protocols tab and click the Add button.

3. Select the TCP/IP Protocol and click OK twice.

4. Restart your system when prompted.

Continue in the next section to configure TCP/IP for your network environment.

Configuring TCP/IP

Depending on your network environment and configuration, you can configure your TCP/IP support in several ways. The easiest, and preferred, method is to use a Dynamic Host Configuration Protocol (DHCP) server; the alternative is to configure your TCP/IP settings statically. On bootup, a DHCP client requests an IP address and a subnet mask from the DHCP server. The IP address and the subnet mask describe the subnetwork in which the DHCP client resides, but it needs more information about its network if it is to communicate fully with other computers. This extra information about the network can be configured on the workstation itself or can be obtained from the DHCP server.

DHCP is the preferred method to use for TCP/IP administration and configuration because all IP addresses and configuration parameters are administered and maintained centrally. If a configuration change is necessary, you need to make the change only once at the DHCP server rather than go around the network to each machine to bring about the configuration change.

Not all networks have a DHCP server, nor do all clients support the DHCP service, and sometimes you need to use a static configuration for TCP/IP, typically for hosts that offer Internet services.

To configure (or reconfigure) TCP/IP options, use the following process either during TCP/IP installation or at any time after installation. Open the Network properties page either by using the Network applet in the Control Panel or by right-clicking the Network Neighborhood icon and choosing Properties.

The TCP/IP Properties dialog box contains four tabs to help you configure the TCP/IP protocol to suit your environment; they are as follows:

■ *IP Address.* On the IP Address tab, as shown in Figure 26.30, you can configure your workstation's IP address. If your network is using DHCP, select the Obtain an IP address from a DHCP server radio button and click OK; you need not configure anything else unless instructed by your network administrator. The alternative to using DHCP is to give your workstation a fixed IP address. To choose a static configuration, select the Specify an IP address radio button and fill in the IP Address,

Subnet Mask, and Default Gateway fields. If you're not sure, check with your network administrator. I will discuss the Advanced Configuration button in the "Configuring TCP/IP Advanced Options" section later in this chapter.

FIGURE 26.30.

The IP Address configuration tab of the TCP/IP Properties dialog box.

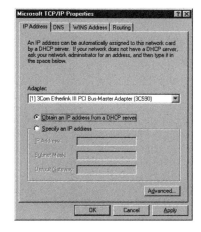

NOTE

The settings you choose in the IP Address tab apply only to the currently selected network card chosen in the Adapter list box. If you have more than one network adapter card installed, you can configure it by first selecting it from the Adapter list box.

■ *DNS.* On this next tab, as shown in Figure 26.31, you can configure the Domain Name Service (DNS). DNS server can resolve TCP/IP names with IP addresses. On the DNS tab, you have to set the TCP/IP hostname and domain for your workstation. The hostname, by default, is set to the computer name as defined during Windows NT installation; you should not need to change it, provided that it is compatible with TCP/IP naming conventions—that is, it does not include spaces, periods, and so on. Provide the name of your TCP/IP domain name in the Domain field. Consult your network administrator if you do not know.

Figure 26.31.

The DNS configuration tab of the TCP/IP Properties dialog box.

NOTE

A TCP/IP domain name is entirely independent of a Windows NT domain, and the two should not be confused. TCP/IP domain names are names such as isoc.org or microsoft.com. If you're not on the Internet, you might not have a TCP/IP domain name. You don't need to have one, so if you're unsure, leave this field blank.

In the DNS Service Search Order section, click the Add button and add the IP addresses for as many as three of the DNS servers that your network uses. When your workstation wants to resolve a TCP/IP name with an IP address, or vice versa, it sends a DNS query to these DNS servers. These DNS servers, in turn, resolve the IP address and return the results to the workstation. Use the Up and Down buttons to move the selected servers up or down in order of preference. The workstation will attempt to contact the first DNS server on the list and will attempt to contact subsequent DNS servers only if contact fails.

In the Domain Suffix Search Order section, provide a list of TCP/IP domain names to append to hostnames to create Fully Qualified Domain Names (FQDN) for use when a hostname is specified without a domain suffix. This parameter is optional but can speed up resolution for you if you are continually accessing the same remote domains. You can specify up to six domain names to use, and as with the DNS servers, you can change the order of preference by using the Up and Down buttons.

■ *WINS Address.* Windows Internet Name Service is a service for resolving NT names, and the client configurations are done through the WINS Address tab, which is shown in Figure 26.32. In the Windows Internet Name Services (WINS) section, select the adapter for which you are configuring WINS. Provide the addresses of a

Windows NT Networking Protocols

CHAPTER 26

611

26

WINDOWS NT
NETWORKING
PROTOCOLS

primary and secondary WINS server for your network. A WINS server maintains a database that maps computer (NetBIOS) names to IP addresses; this is different behavior from using a protocol such as NetBEUI in which communication is facilitated by mapping computer names to hardware (MAC) addresses. When you use TCP/IP, a computer name is resolved to an IP address, which is then resolved to a hardware address, and then a session between the systems can be established. Not all networks use—nor are they required to use—WINS services. This Microsoft-specific implementation further integrates Microsoft networking services with the TCP/IP protocol. At boot time, a workstation configured to use WINS informs its WINS server(s) of its NetBIOS name and IP address. The WINS server stores this information in its database so that it can resolve any queries on this name in the future. Even if a workstation picks up a different IP address from a DHCP server every day, it still informs its WINS server of its new address, thus ensuring that the WINS server is always up to date.

FIGURE 26.32.

The WINS Address configuration tab of the TCP/IP Properties dialog box.

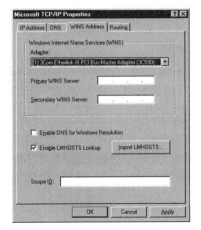

If appropriate, select the Enable DNS for Windows Resolution check box. This is typically used in place of WINS services. If you check this option, the system tries to resolve Windows names using DNS by getting the hostname and applying the default TCP/IP domain name to generate a Fully Qualified Domain Name and then attempts to resolve that name to an address.

If systems on your network use LMHOSTS files, select the Enable LMHOSTS Lookup check box. An LMHOSTS file is a text file with computer-name-to-IP-address mappings. This file can also include additional directives for specifying Windows NT domains and domain controllers. This method of name resolution is not adequate because it is static and does not take DHCP into consideration. It can, however, be a useful safety net if used properly. I usually enter the names of the domains PDC and BDC(s), which have fixed IP addresses, into the LMHOSTS file, thus building redundancy into the system. These entries in the LMHOSTS file can be loaded into the workstation's cache, ensuring fast resolutions for those machines regardless of whether the WINS servers are up or down.

If you choose to use LMHOSTS files, and you have a default LMHOSTS file available to you, you can click the Import LMHOSTS button and provide the path to the default file to import it into your system. A sample LMHOSTS file, called LMHOSTS.SAM, is available in the %systemroot%\system32\drivers\etc directory. You can edit this file and add entries for your network. The LMHOSTS file is parsed, and either an entry for the corresponding NetBIOS name is found and its IP address returned, or the resolution ends in failure. As the LMHOSTS file is parsed, you should remove all unnecessary lines to speed parsing. The following is a sample LMHOSTS file:

```
192.44.47.11   omnus     #PRE #DOM:philia # DOMAIN PDC
192.44.47.24   Bachaus   #PRE     # DOMAIN BDC
```

The two most important keywords used in the LMHOSTS file are

> #PRE: This keyword forces the preloading of the entry into the name cache.
>
> #DOM:DOMAIN_NAME: #DOM announces the entry as being the PDC for the domain DOMAIN_NAME.

If necessary, provide a scope ID for your computer. Scope IDs typically are not used anymore. They provide information for name resolution when a DNS server is not available. If you do specify a scope ID, you must be sure that it is the same on all the computers in your network that you want to communicate with because you cannot communicate with systems that have different scope IDs.

■ *Routing.* The last tab is the Routing tab, shown in Figure 26.33. The one option is for multi-homed systems that have more than one network interface card (NIC). If two or more network interfaces on a Windows NT computer belong to different IP networks or subnets, you can select this option to enable IP routing between the two interfaces, providing a path for systems on the two networks to traverse to the other networks. If you have only one NIC, leave this option unchecked. If you have more than one NIC, and they belong to different networks, you can check this option to have your system act as a router.

FIGURE 26.33.

The Routing configuration tab of the TCP/IP Properties dialog box.

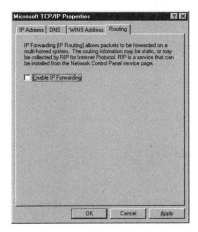

NOTE

Although you can use Windows NT systems as routers between different IP networks, you should consider a couple of issues. First, Windows NT (especially Workstation) is definitely not designed to act as a router. Consequently, the performance quickly diminishes as the size of the network traffic increases and the routing function is utilized more. Second, the system acting as a router experiences an impact on performance. The more route processing the system does, the fewer resources are available to the workstation component, affecting the unfortunate users sitting at the console trying to get their work done. However, despite these issues, routing is a useful feature to have available. Windows NT is best suited to be used as a router for connecting and segmenting relatively small (fewer than 50) IP networks or as an Internet gateway for a small number of users. If you do decide to use your workstation as a router, NT has a command-line utility, called `route`, to help you configure routes on your workstation. See Chapter 37, "Troubleshooting NT Workstation," for more details on `route`.

After you configure your TCP/IP parameters, you should not need to modify them often, if at all. You need to modify the settings only when a change occurs on the network or the system moves to another network.

Configuring TCP/IP Advanced Options

Windows NT Workstation also offers several advanced TCP/IP configuration options such as support for multi-homing (multiple IP addresses), filtering, and Point To Point Tunneling.

To access the advanced TCP/IP configuration options, open the Network dialog box and select TCP/IP Properties from the Protocols tab. From the IP Address tab of the TCP/IP Properties dialog box, click the Advanced button to display the Advanced IP Addressing dialog box showing configuration options, as shown in Figure 26.34.

FIGURE 26.34.

The Advanced IP Addressing dialog box.

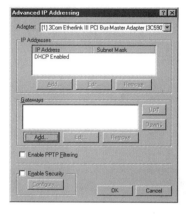

From the Advanced IP Addressing dialog box, you can configure settings on a per-adapter basis by selecting the appropriate adapter from the Adapter list box at the top of the sheet.

You can also add multiple IP addresses for a single card. Doing so is often desirable so that you can support TCP/IP domain name aliases, specifically for Microsoft Peer Web Services (discussed in Chapter 29). To add additional IP addresses, click the Add button in the IP Addresses section. You can provide the IP address and subnet mask for up to five addresses.

NOTE

To add support for more than five IP addresses, you must modify the Windows NT Registry directly. Again, caution is the number-one word when it comes to changing the Registry. For more details on the Registry, see Chapter 11, "The NT Registry."

To add more than five IP addresses, open the Registry Editor (regedt32.exe) and select the HKEY_LOCAL_MACHINE hive. From there, open the \SYSTEM\CurrentControlSet\Services branch. Next, find the key for your NIC. Usually, it is the driver name with an instance number such as tc50481 for a Thomas-Conrad PCI 5048, adapter number one, or EE161 for an Intel EtherExpress, adapter number one.

After you find the correct key, open the subbranch \Parameters\Tcpip. Select the IPAddress:REG_MULTI_SZ value; then choose select Edit | Multi String. For each IP address you want to add, enter it in dotted decimal notation (*xxx.xxx.xxx.xxx*), one per line. Also for each IP address, you must add a corresponding subnet mask. To do so, select the SubnetMask:REG_MULTI_SZ key and choose Edit | Multi String. Add the appropriate subnet mask for each IP address, in order, one per line.

Additionally, for networks with multiple routers or gateways, you can set a configuration option to specify more than one gateway. To add an additional gateway, click the Add button in the Gateways section and provide the appropriate IP address for the gateway.

Be aware that if the Enable PPTP Filtering check box is selected, only PPTP packets are allowed to traverse that interface; normal IP traffic is disallowed. For more details on PPTP, see Chapter 25, "Remote Computing with Remote Access Service."

Finally, one of the welcome new features of Windows NT is TCP/IP security, which you can access by selecting the Enable Security check box and then clicking the Configure button. The TCP/IP Security dialog box then appears, as shown in Figure 26.35.

FIGURE 26.35.

The TCP/IP Security dialog box.

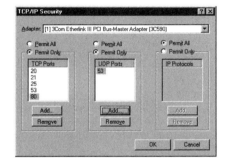

From this configuration dialog box, you can configure a packet-level filter (similar to a firewall). Using this configuration feature, you can allow, or effectively disallow, specific IP protocols and TCP or UDP ports.

For each of the three configurable categories—TCP Ports, UDP Ports, and IP Protocols—you have the option of permitting all port numbers or protocols or restricting the category to only specific ports or protocols.

The TCP and UDP Port categories are configured using port numbers as listed in the \SYSTEMROOT\SYSTEM32\Drivers\etc\services file. See Appendix B, "Well-Known Service Ports," for a full listing of the well-known ports. This file contains a listing of well-known services and their corresponding transport (TCP or UDP) with the assigned port number. Using this list, you can determine which TCP and UPD ports to allow and configure TCP/IP security appropriately.

For the IP Protocol category, the access restrictions are based on the \SYSTEMROOT SYSTEM32\Drivers\etc\protocol file. This file contains a listing of protocols and their assigned numbers. Access can be restricted to specific protocols by defining them in the IP Protocol category of the TCP/IP security configuration.

To restrict access to a given subset, click the Add button for the appropriate category and add a protocol or port number to allow. Repeat this step until you have defined all the ports and protocols you want. Do note, however, that if security is enabled on any of the three categories, that category exclusively permits the subset as you defined. There is no grace here; if security is enabled and a given port or protocol is not explicitly defined to have access, it is not passed.

Testing the Configuration and Connectivity: The `ping` Utility

After you install and configure the TCP/IP protocol and restart your system, you need to test its configuration and its connectivity. Typically, I advise that you do so in a progressive fashion so that, if the connectivity fails at some point, you can more easily pinpoint the error and resolve it.

First, open a command prompt window. At the command prompt, perform the following steps:

1. Type ping *xxx.xxx.xxx.xxx*, where *xxx.xxx.xxx.xxx* represents your local IP address. You should receive a reply similar to the following:

   `Reply from xxx.xxx.xxx.xxx: bytes=32 time<10ms TTL=128`

2. Type ping *xxx.xxx.xxx.xxx*, where *xxx.xxx.xxx.xxx* represents the address of your default gateway (router). You should receive a response similar to the preceding response. These first two tests determine whether TCP/IP is configured properly and whether you can communicate on your local network.

3. Type ping *xxx.xxx.xxx.xxx*, where *xxx.xxx.xxx.xxx* represents a DNS server for your network, preferably on a remote network. Again, the response should be similar to the preceding responses. This test determines whether you can communicate with the outside world.

4. Type ping *host.company.com*, where *host.company.com* is something like `www.microsoft.com` or `www.womex.com`. This final test determines whether your name resolution is working properly and whether you are correctly configured.

If your system passes all these tests, everything is installed and configured properly, and you can now use the resources available on your network and navigate the services of the Internet, if applicable. If one of these tests fails, something is configured improperly, and you need to coordinate with your system administrator to resolve the issue.

Summary

In this chapter, you looked closely at the networking components of NT. You explored the installation of a network interface card (NIC) and how you can add and configure network protocols such as NetBEUI, NWLink IPX/SPX Compatible Transport, and TCP/IP. You also learned additional protocols and how you add them or additional network services supplied by third parties.

Windows NT Network Services

by Mike Sheehy and Sean Mathias

CHAPTER 27

IN THIS CHAPTER

Windows NT network protocols provide a common language for computers to communicate with, but this capability does not provide much in the way of functionality. The network functionality of Windows NT is provided through various network services. Windows NT network services are modular components that sit on top of the network protocols. These network protocols can be added or removed as needed (except for some core components) and can coexist with each other.

The implementation of network services is consistent with the network and architectural model of Windows NT—providing a modular design that allows for various components to be rewritten, upgraded, added, or removed, without rebuilding the entire subsystem or recompiling the kernel as with some other operating systems.

In this chapter, you'll find detailed descriptions of each network service available in Windows NT Workstation 4. Services that are installed by default and are necessary for basic network functionality are shown in the following list. In addition to these services, the modular architecture of the Windows NT networking subsystem and open API set allow for third-party vendors to write their own Windows NT-compliant or compatible network services and integrate them seamlessly with the rest of the architecture.

Here are the default network services installed by Windows NT Network Setup:

- Computer Browser
- NetBIOS Interface
- RPC Configuration
- Server
- Workstation

Client Services for NetWare

Probably one of the most important services in the aspect of integration is the Client Services for NetWare. These services, along with the NWLink IPX/SPX Compatible Transport, provide access from a Windows NT Workstation computer to file and printer resources located on a Novell NetWare server.

Currently, the Client Services for NetWare are limited to accessing shared resources on a NetWare server. They provide no support for loading VLM-based applications, such as the netadmin.exe utility for administering NetWare servers, and no GUI-based tools to do so either, although Novell is rumored to be working on its own implementation of a Windows NT NetWare client service that bridges this gap.

To install the Client Services for NetWare, perform the following steps:

1. Open the Network applet in the Control Panel, or select the Network Neighborhood properties by right-clicking the icon on the desktop.

2. Choose the Services tab. You can see the default network services already loaded and listed in the Network Services list box. Click the Add button. In the resulting Select Network Service dialog box, you then see a list of available services that you can add, as shown in Figure 27.1.

FIGURE 27.1.

Adding additional network service support.

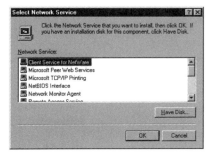

3. Select Client Service for NetWare. It should be the first service on the list. Then click OK. Next, you are asked to enter the path to your distribution media (usually your CD-ROM).

4. The necessary files are copied to your system, and if you have not yet installed the NWLink IPX/SPX Compatible Transport, you are prompted to do so. (See Chapter 26, "Windows NT Networking Protocols.") You can then see the Client Service for NetWare added to the list of loaded services along with the default network services on the Services tab, as shown in Figure 27.2.

FIGURE 27.2.

Client Service for NetWare is added to the list of loaded network services.

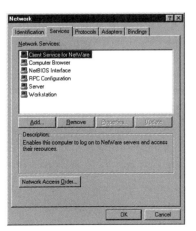

5. When prompted, restart your computer to make the changes take effect.

> **NOTE**
>
> In the Select Network Service dialog box is a button labeled Have Disk. By using it, you can install a third-party network service. Click the Have Disk button, provide the disk(s) when prompted, and proceed with the installation.

When your computer restarts and you log in, you see a secondary dialog box prompting you for a username, password, and preferred server or default tree and context to log in to, as shown in Figure 27.3. Note that you cannot change the username to log in, so that username must already exist on the NetWare network.

FIGURE 27.3.

Specifying a preferred server or default tree and context to log in to.

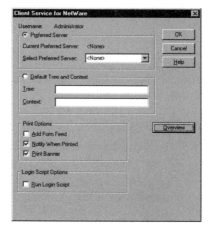

Provide the password for the user account and the preferred server or default tree and context to log in to; optionally, select the Run Login Script check box to execute the NetWare login script. Be aware that not all login script commands are supported under Windows NT Workstation 4—specifically, any commands that rely on VLMs being loaded.

Using the Client Service for NetWare (CSNW) applet in Control Panel, you can later modify these settings, if necessary, as well as specify print options such as adding a form feed, requesting print notification, and printing banner pages. For more details on the Client Service for NetWare (CSNW), see Chapter 9, "Advanced Control Panel Tools."

When you are logged in to a preferred server or to a default tree and context, you have access to file and print resources as well as any other resources. You can access them from the command line by mapping a drive, through Network Neighborhood or Explorer by browsing (see Figure 27.4), or in any other way that network resources are reachable.

FIGURE 27.4.

Browsing NetWare resources through Network Neighborhood in Explorer.

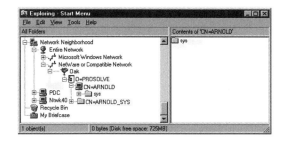

As with previous versions of Windows NT, after you connect to a resource and are authenticated, you can then share the resource on the network, providing access to it for other Microsoft networking clients by using a form of pass-through authentication.

Although the current implementation is somewhat limited, most prominently in the inability to provide access to NetWare management features for the administration of NetWare NDS trees, Client Services for NetWare provides the basic functionality and access to resources that most users need.

Computer Browser

The Computer Browser service is one of the default Windows NT networking services installed during the initial network configuration. This service provides two functions: a client-side function and a server-side function.

For the client-side function, the Computer Browser service maintains a local list of the current network, the computers on the network, and available resources. The service receives periodic updates from the domain master browser or a backup browser, systems responsible for discovering the available resources on the network and maintaining a current list of computers and their resources. If you stop this service, the local system cannot browse network resources in Network Neighborhood, Explorer, or a network-aware application. When you use the Network Neighborhood or any network-aware application, you are, in essence, querying a master browser for a list of resources.

The server side of this component enables the local system to act as a domain master browser or a backup browser, if necessary. By default, all Windows NT systems are configured to act as master browser computers. Windows 95 systems are configured to act as browse masters if they have Microsoft File and Print services installed and enabled. A number of different types of browser servers are available, and each has a different role to play in the browsing service. The term "server" here refers to any computer that uses NetBIOS and is capable of sharing its resources with other computers on the network.

Let me first outline the different types of browser servers:

- *Domain master browser.* At the top of the browsing structure is the domain master browser. The domain master browser is usually the Primary Domain Controller, and it has the highest election criteria of all browse servers. In other words, the domain master browser will always win a master browser election. Only one domain master browser exists for an entire domain. The domain master browser, at regular intervals, requests that the master browsers send it their browse lists. The domain master browser, in turn, compiles these lists to generate a complete list. All master browsers then request this complete list from the domain master browser.

- *Master browsers.* The master browsers are servers that maintain browse lists of all computers in their domains or workgroups. In segmented TCP/IP networks, each subnet has a master browser. Master browsers send an announcement of their existence to the domain master browser.

- *Backup browsers.* Backup browsers are the next level of browser servers. Backup master browsers step in if the master browser fails. Backup browsers request a full list from their master browsers every 15 minutes. If the backup browser cannot contact the master browser, it forces an election.

- *Preferred master browsers.* These servers are configured with an extra advantage that enables them to gain master browser status in an election. This configuration is a Registry key: HKEY_LOCAL_MACHINE\SYSTEM\CurrentControlSystem\Services\Browser\ Parameters\IsDomainMasterBrowser. If this key is set to TRUE, the server is given a greater advantage to win an election.

- *Potential browsers.* These browsers, as their name suggests, are computers that can be elected master browser. A server's ability to become a browser is again determined by a Registry key: HKEY_LOCAL_MACHINE\SYSTEM\CurrentControlSystem\Services\Browser\ Parameters\MaintainServerList. The values of this key can be NO, YES, and AUTO. If the value is set to YES, then on bootup the server tries to contact the master browser. If it fails to make contact, it forces an election and has the potential of becoming the master browser. If the value is set to AUTO, the server has the potential of becoming a master browser, but this depends on the other existing servers. The potential browsers can also become backup browsers if the ratio is favorable. This ratio is 15 clients to every backup browser.

To determine which system is the domain master browser, a computer sends out a broadcast when it comes online to determine whether a master browser currently exists. If it finds one, the computer passes this information to the client side to obtain and maintain its local list; if it does not find one, it attempts to become the master browser for the network. This process is imperfect, and often a system tries to become the master browser when one already exists. In this situation, an election is forced to determine which system becomes the domain master browser. The outcome of an election is based on the following criteria:

- The operating system of the browsers
- Whether the server is a PDC
- Whether the server is a preferred browser
- Whether the server is an existing master browser
- Whether the server is an existing backup browser
- Whether the server is a WINS client
- The Protocol election version

A subcriteria exists within operating systems. The following list details the operating systems in order of election weight:

- Windows NT Server
- Windows NT Workstation
- Windows 95
- Windows for Workgroups

A score is associated with having each of the preceding criteria. All these criteria go into the election mix until a master browser emerges.

Users familiar with Microsoft networking might notice (on a regular basis) while browsing the network that the system list is inaccurate; it lists systems that are no longer online, or it is missing systems that you know are online. This is especially true for segmented networks. Remember that the browsing service is run using directed datagrams and that no guarantee or fault tolerance is built into the service. This problem also occurs because a balance must exist between the accuracy of the browser and how much network bandwidth and system resources it uses to maintain the list. Maintaining a 100 percent accurate browse list at all times would put a burden on the master browser computer's resources and flood the network with discovery broadcasts, so you must settle on a less-than-perfect balance. Note, however, that most network operating systems face this dilemma; with Novell NetWare, having an overabundance of Service Access Protocol (SAP) broadcasts that serve basically the same purpose as the Computer Browser service is a common problem.

> **NOTE**
>
> For every network protocol you load on your network, a separate set of browser servers is associated with that protocol. Therefore, a server acting as a master browser could be so for multiple protocols and could be servicing queries from clients on each. This is yet another overhead associated with loading multiple protocols.

Microsoft TCP/IP Printing

The Microsoft TCP/IP Printing support service is yet another feature to further the enterprise integration of Windows NT. This service provides the capability of connecting to and sharing printers that are directly attached to the network via a network interface card and that are TCP/IP-enabled. You can also attach these printers directly to UNIX-based systems, thus providing the integration and access to disparate resources on a network. Note that Windows NT TCP/IP Printing supports only BSD-style TCP/IP printing and does not provide support for System V–style printing.

A computer that has TCP/IP Printing support installed and configured can print directly to the printers and act as a print gateway/server for other Microsoft networking clients on the network, thus extending the use of this resource to other computers on the network. A performance hit is incurred by the print gateway/server serving print requests from clients.

To install support for TCP/IP printing, follow these steps:

1. Open the Network applet in the Control Panel, or select the Network Neighborhood properties by right-clicking the icon on the desktop.

2. Choose the Services tab and click the Add button. The resulting Select Network Service dialog box lists available services.

3. Select Microsoft TCP/IP Printing, as shown in Figure 27.5, and click OK. If you have not installed the TCP/IP protocol on your computer, you are prompted to do so. (See Chapter 26.)

   The necessary files are copied from your distribution media to your system.

FIGURE 27.5.

Adding Microsoft TCP/IP Printing services.

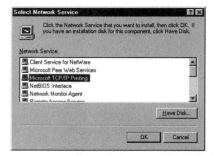

4. When prompted, restart your computer to make the changes take effect.

After you install Microsoft TCP/IP Printing support, you can create and configure TCP/IP network printers and share them on the network if you want. To do so, you must have the IP address of the network printer or the UNIX computer to which it is attached. (You can use the DNS name of the computer if you have configured support for DNS in the TCP/IP Protocol configuration.)

To create and configure a TCP/IP printer, perform the following steps:

1. Open the Printers folder in My Computer, select the Printers option from the Start Menu Settings item, or start the Printers applet in the Control Panel (so many choices!).

2. Start the Add Printer Wizard.

3. Select the My Computer radio button, as shown in Figure 27.6; then click Next.

FIGURE 27.6.

The Add Printer Wizard dialog box.

4. When you are presented with the port configuration dialog box, as shown in Figure 27.7, configure a port through which you will print. For the port configuration, click the Add Port button.

FIGURE 27.7.

Choosing a printer port.

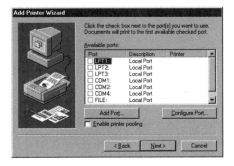

5. From the list of available ports that appears, as shown in the Printer Ports dialog box in Figure 27.8, select LPR Port and then click the New Port button.

6. In the Add LPR compatible printer dialog box, which is shown in Figure 27.9, enter the name of the server on which the printer resides or its IP address and the name of the printer. Click OK to close this dialog box and then click Close.

FIGURE 27.8.
Add an LPR port.

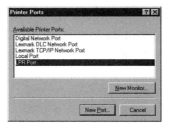

FIGURE 27.9.
Add an LPR-compatible printer.

7. When the IP address and name of the TCP/IP printer are listed as a configurable port in the Add Printer Wizard, as shown in Figure 27.10, select the corresponding check box. Then click Next.

FIGURE 27.10.
Select the newly added port.

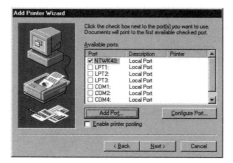

8. When you're presented with the list of printer manufacturers and printers, as shown in Figure 27.11, select the correct make and model of the printer you are connecting. Then click Next.

FIGURE 27.11.
Select the manufacturer and model of the printer.

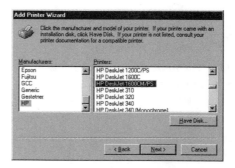

9. In the next wizard dialog box, provide a name for the printer.

10. If you want to share the printer on the network, select the Shared radio button and provide a share name for the printer, as shown in Figure 27.12. Select the appropriate operating systems that will use this printer so that the necessary drivers can be installed. After you finish, or if you are not going to share this printer, click Next.

FIGURE 27.12.

Sharing your printer.

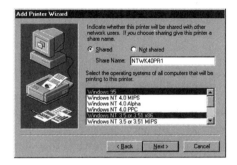

11. Choose Yes or No when prompted to print a test page and click Finish.

The necessary files are copied to your system, and if you elected to print a test page, you see a dialog box asking whether the test page printed properly. If it printed correctly, choose Yes; if it did not, choose No. Choosing No launches the Print Troubleshooting Wizard, which helps resolve the problem. When this is completed, the Printer Properties page opens; here you can configure the printer accordingly. (See Chapter 16, "Printing with Windows NT.")

In addition to connecting, printing to, and sharing TCP/IP and UNIX-based printers, you can also provide TCP/IP print services to UNIX-based clients. For printers attached to or managed by your system, you can start the TCP/IP Print Server service and allow UNIX-based clients to print to your printer. To enable this function, type `net start lpdsvc` at the command prompt, or select the TCP/IP Print Server service in the Services applet of the Control Panel. If this is a service you intend to offer to UNIX clients, configuring the service to start automatically at startup is a good idea. Also, keep in mind that this is a rudimentary implementation of the LPD service, and it might not behave as expected because of the vast assortment of UNIX varieties and their specific printing methods.

NetBIOS Interface

The Network Basic Input/Output System (NetBIOS) interface is an often misunderstood network service. Most people seem to equate it with NetBIOS Enhanced User Interface (NetBEUI), which is understandable. However, you should understand why they are not the same and know how they differ.

The NetBIOS interface is a session-level interface and interprocess communication mechanism, whereas NetBEUI is an actual network transport protocol.

In its current implementation, NetBIOS is typically encapsulated in either the NWLink IPX/ SPX Compatible Transport or TCP/IP to carry its traffic, providing NetBIOS over IPX or NetBIOS over IP (NBT). The Windows NT redirector is a NetBIOS-based application. The NetBIOS interface is responsible for establishing logical computer names on the network and for establishing sessions and providing reliable data-transport services for a given session.

Although the system allows you to remove this component, doing so is not recommended because removing it impairs interprocess communications and might result in unreliable or unpredictable network behavior. Some system services (such as the messenger service) rely on the NetBIOS interface.

Network Monitor Agent

The Network Monitor Agent is a component that gathers information and statistics from the local network interfaces. This agent is used by remote Windows NT Server systems running the Microsoft Network Monitor (also known as Bloodhound) or a Systems Management Server (SMS) system running the Network Monitor to gather information and monitor traffic on a remote interface or segment.

The Network Monitor Agent has no configuration options in Workstation.

Microsoft Peer Web Services

With the release of Windows NT Workstation 4, Microsoft has furthered its move toward an Internet-centric environment, not only by enhancing its TCP/IP Protocol suite and its integration but also by bundling Internet services as installable operating system components.

Windows NT Workstation 4 includes Microsoft Peer Web Services, a suite of Internet or intranet services that are almost identical to the server version, Internet Information Server 2.0, which is included with Windows NT Server 4.

Microsoft Peer Web Services are aimed at providing the framework for an intranet within an organization or department. Included are components to facilitate World Wide Web (WWW) services, file transfer (FTP) services, and information search and retrieval services (Gopher).

To install Microsoft Peer Web Services, perform the following steps:

1. Open the Network applet in the Control Panel or select the Network Neighborhood properties by right-clicking the icon on the desktop.

2. Choose the Services tab and click the Add button. The resulting Select Network Service dialog box lists available services.

3. Select Microsoft Peer Web Services and click OK. You are then prompted for the path to the distribution media. Enter the path and click OK.

4. Unlike the other services you have installed so far, Peer Web Services invokes its own external setup program. At the banner page, click OK to continue.

5. On the Microsoft Peer Web Services Setup dialog box, as shown in Figure 27.13, select or deselect the various components based on your specific needs and accept or change the installation directory. When you're satisfied, click OK to begin the installation.

FIGURE 27.13.

The Microsoft Peer Web Services Setup dialog box.

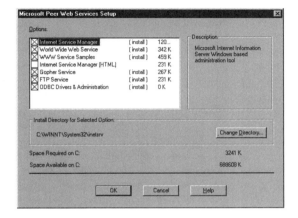

6. You are prompted to provide the location and directory root for each of the services you are installing, as shown in Figure 27.14. Provide the path to the location you want and click OK when you're satisfied with your selections. If the desired location does not exist, the Setup Wizard asks for permission to create it for you.

   The necessary files are copied to your system.

FIGURE 27.14.

The Peer Web Services directory path configuration dialog box.

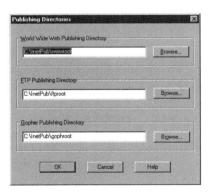

7. If you chose to install ODBC driver support, you are prompted to select the drivers you want to install. Select the desired drivers and click OK.

8. When you see a dialog box informing you that the setup has completed successfully, click OK.

The Setup Wizard also adds a program group within the Start menu to help administer the Peer Web Services (see Figure 27.15).

FIGURE 27.15.

A program entry added to the Start menu.

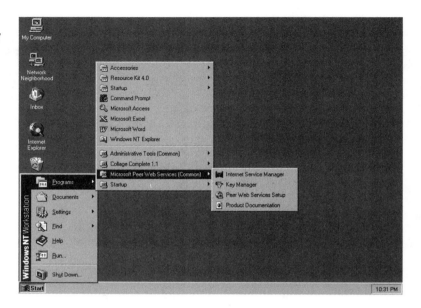

When the setup is finished, you don't need to restart the system. The services are installed, and you can start them by selecting them in the Services applet of the Control Panel and clicking the Start button. You can point your Web browser to the IP address of the local machine and use the online documentation, information, and samples to get started (if you installed the World Wide Web Publishing service).

For additional information about Microsoft Peer Web Services, refer to Chapter 29, "Using Peer Web Services." Because it is a fairly involved and extensive core component, an entire chapter is dedicated to its use and configuration.

Remote Access Services

Another old service with a new look and added functionality is the Remote Access Services (RAS). Remote Access Services provides a mechanism with which a user can connect from a remote location (thus the name) to a system running Remote Access Server on the corporate LAN, for example. Additionally, RAS supports the use of NetBEUI, IPX/SPX, and TCP/IP as well as Point to Point protocols (PPTP), which makes this single-client software component capable of connecting to another RAS server, a remote access device such as a Shiva LANRover, or an Internet Service Provider (ISP).

To install Remote Access Services, follow this procedure:

1. Open the Network applet in the Control Panel, or select the Network Neighborhood properties by right-clicking the icon on the desktop.

2. Select the Services tab and click the Add button. The resulting Select Network Service dialog box lists available services.

3. Select Remote Access Service and click OK.

   The necessary files are copied from the distribution media to your system, and the Setup Wizard determines the current network state of your Workstation.

4. If you have not yet installed a modem or other RAS-capable device, you are asked whether you want to invoke the modem installer to install one. Choose Yes. For additional information about installing and configuring modems, consult Chapter 21, "Setting Up Your Modem." After you install and configure a RAS-capable device, continue with the next step.

5. When the Add RAS Device dialog box appears, as shown in Figure 27.16, select the device you want to add and click OK.

FIGURE 27.16.

The Add RAS Device dialog box.

6. Back in the Remote Access Setup dialog box, which is shown in Figure 27.17, click the Configure button to change the RAS port configuration to support dial out only, receive calls only, or both (the default is dial out only). When you are done, click OK to exit the Configure Port Usage dialog.

FIGURE 27.17.

The Remote Access Setup dialog box.

7. To configure network support, click the Network button in the Remote Access Setup dialog box.

8. Depending on your choice for port configuration, you have network configuration options for dial out, receive calls, or both. Check the boxes next to the protocols you want to support. For receiving calls, click the Configure button next to the protocol to make the necessary configurations. Click OK to exit the protocol Configuration dialog and OK again to exit the Network Configuration dialog.

9. When you're finished, click Continue to exit the Remote Access Setup dialog. Then click Close to close the Network dialog box.

10. When prompted, restart your computer to make the changes take effect.

This process installs Remote Access with a basic configuration. For additional information, advanced configuration and usage guidelines, and instructions on how to create and use dial-up networking connections, refer to Chapter 25, "Remote Computing with Remote Access Service," which is dedicated entirely to this topic because it is a versatile and extensive application.

RPC Configuration

The Remote Procedure Call (RPC) Configuration is another core network component used for interprocess communication (IPC) and locating services on the network. RPC is unique in its method of IPC in that it uses other IPC media to establish a session between the client and server services. For network connections, it uses either Named Pipes, Windows Sockets, or NetBIOS to communicate between the systems. If the client and server services are located on the same system, it uses the Local Procedure Call (LPC) facility. Because it is implemented in this fashion, RPC has the highest degree of flexibility of all the IPC mechanisms.

The server component of a distributed or network-enabled application registers its services with the RPC Locator service, which manages the RPC Name database (a database of services available on the network). The client component in a distributed or network-enabled application queries the RPC Locator service to find the necessary server applications on the network.

By implementing an IPC in this fashion, the system has much more latitude in the type of application it can support and the features of that application. By utilizing the other IPC transports, RPC can satisfy almost any IPC request. For example, a given application might request a certain service from the IPC; when using RPC, it can make this request from a much wider variety of services and applications because of its broad support of Named Pipes, WinSock, and NetBIOS. This capability provides a much more open and expansive foundation on which to build in the future. Figure 27.18 shows the RPC Configuration dialog box, which you open by clicking the Properties button while RPC Configuration is highlighted on the Services tab of the Network dialog box. You should never need to change the setting here unless you migrate to a Distributed Computing Environment (DCE) network.

FIGURE 27.18.
The RPC Configuration dialog box.

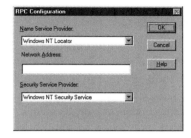

RPC Support for Banyan

The RPC Support for Banyan service is a new offering in Windows NT Workstation 4. This service provides an extension to the previous RPC Configuration mechanism, now incorporating support for Banyan systems IPC mechanisms and transports into the RPC subsystem. This addition extends network communications and incorporates the services available on Banyan VINES networks and servers into the RPC Locator service database.

SAP Agent

The SAP Agent is a NetWare-compatible Service Access Protocol agent that sends out broadcasts (SAP datagrams) announcing the services available on the local system for NetWare clients and servers. When you install this service, you are prompted to install the NWLink IPX/SPX Compatible Transport if it is not already installed. In some respects, this is similar to an RPC facility for NetWare networks.

Server

Windows NT Workstation 4 also includes a Server service. It is the network service that enables remote systems on the network to connect to the local system and for the local system to share resources on the network. Again, by breaking down the core network services into individual components, Windows NT maintains the modular architecture that allows you to easily modify and upgrade individual network services rather than the entire network subsystem. Windows NT Workstation has no configuration options for the Server service.

Simple TCP/IP Service

The Simple TCP/IP Service provides functionality for some older and less common TCP/IP utilities, most of which are entirely irrelevant to the normal operation and use of TCP/IP and TCP/IP applications. Provided with the Simple TCP/IP Service are the client software for the Character Generator, Daytime, Discard, Echo, and Quote of the Day services. If you install this service, the system can respond to requests from other systems that support these protocols. Probably the most common use of these services is using the Quote of the Day service to append a quotation to outgoing mail messages.

SNMP Services

The Simple Network Management Protocol (SNMP) component of Windows NT Workstation is an optional extension that you can install and configure to provide statistics, information, and alerts to a remote system running an SNMP management console application. In a limited fashion, this service also allows the system to be administered remotely by a system running an SNMP management console. If you install the SNMP service, performance counters for the TCP/IP protocol and services are also loaded and made available for use by the Performance Monitor.

To install the SNMP service, follow this procedure:

1. Open the Network applet in the Control Panel, or select the Network Neighborhood properties by right-clicking the icon on the desktop.

2. Select the Services tab and click the Add button. The resulting Select Network Service dialog box lists available services.

3. Select SNMP Service and click OK. If you have not installed the TCP/IP protocol or the NWLink IPX/SPX Compatible Transport on your computer, you are prompted to do so.

   The necessary files are copied to your system. You then see the SNMP Properties dialog box, as shown in Figure 27.19.

FIGURE 27.19.

The Microsoft SNMP Properties dialog box.

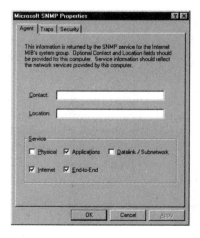

To configure the SNMP Service, perform the following steps:

1. On the Agent tab of the SNMP Properties dialog box, provide the name of the primary user of the system and the location of the physical location of the system.

2. Select which services for which you want to enable SNMP monitoring and functions. Your choices include the following:

- *Physical*: Choose this option if this system manages any physical network devices such as a hub (OSI layer 1).

- *Applications:* Choose this option if this system uses any TCP/IP applications. You should select it for all systems (OSI layer 7).

- *Datalink/Subnetwork:* Choose this option if this system manages any subnetworks or datalink devices such as a bridge (OSI layer 2).

- *Internet:* Choose this option if this is a multi-homed or gateway system (OSI layer 3).

- *End-to-End:* Choose this option if this system is a TCP/IP host. You should select it for all systems (OSI layer 5).

3. Choose the Traps tab, as shown in Figure 27.20. Here you can remove and add community names for the SNMP service by selecting the community name and clicking the Remove button or typing the name in the community name field and clicking the Add button.

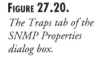

FIGURE 27.20.

The Traps tab of the SNMP Properties dialog box.

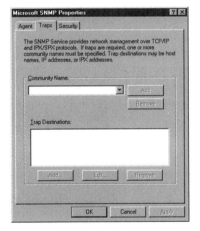

4. To add a trap destination, a host that is running an SNMP management console, click the Add button and provide the IP or IPX address of the trap destination. To change or remove a trap destination, select the trap destination and click the Edit or Remove buttons accordingly.

5. Choose the Security tab, which is shown in Figure 27.21, to configure the SNMP service security.

FIGURE 27.21.

The Security tab of the SNMP Properties dialog box.

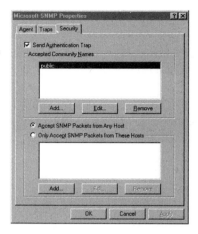

6. To configure the system to send an SNMP authentication trap to authenticate a session request from an SNMP management console, select the Send Authentication Trap check box.

7. Add to the list of Accepted Community Names all communities that are authorized to interact with the SNMP service and components. Edit or remove listed names as appropriate.

8. You can also configure the SNMP agent to accept SNMP packets from any host or from only explicitly specified hosts. To restrict access to defined hosts only, select the Only Accept SNMP Packets from These Hosts radio button. To add access for a host, click the Add button and provide the IP or IPX address of the host to allow. Repeat this procedure for each host from which SNMP packets should be accepted.

9. After you finish the configuration, click OK to close the SNMP Properties dialog box and then click Close to close the Network dialog box.

10. Restart your computer when prompted to make the changes take effect.

After you install and configure SNMP, you need some kind of management console or SNMP management application to use the SNMP service and remotely administer components of the SNMP-enabled system. Also note that to install and configure SNMP, you must be logged in as a member of the local Administrators group. This implementation of SNMP supports SNMP v.1 and Management Information Base (MIB) II.

Workstation

The Workstation service is another core network component, the counterpart to the Server service. This service provides the functionality necessary for Windows NT Workstation to act as a client on the network and to request and access network resources. The Workstation service has no configuration options and should not be removed.

Summary

The Windows NT Workstation network subsystem is broken down into modular components called services. This modularity provides for broad flexibility in implementation and allows you to add, remove, or update individual components without affecting other components or requiring the network core to be reconstructed.

Windows NT Workstation provides an open architecture that aids in integrating disparate network systems and allows for flexibility and coexistence with almost any network on the market today. Additionally, third-party vendors can write their own network services to further extend the functionality and increase the integration of Windows NT Workstation.

27

WINDOWS NT
NETWORK
SERVICES

Users and Groups on NT

by Mike Sheehy and Sean Mathias

IN THIS CHAPTER

CHAPTER 28

In this chapter, you will learn about users and groups and their significance within NT. Users and groups are an integral part of the NT security system. Information about users and groups provides a means of identifying users while they are on the system and, if auditing is enabled, you can record their actions. You also can associate a level of privilege to users so that NT knows exactly what those users are and are not allowed to do while logged in. You also will look at the main tool for maintaining user and group accounts, the User Manager, later in the chapter.

Users

When you try to use an NT workstation, you must first tell the workstation who you are. What you're really doing here is equating yourself with a user account defined on the workstation. Through this user account, you identify yourself to NT.

Built-In User Accounts

When you install NT Workstation, two user accounts are installed for you by default: the Administrator account and the Guest account. These accounts are created to simplify administration of the workstation.

The Administrator Account

The Administrator account is the first of the built-in accounts created during the system installation. This account is the most powerful account in NT and is equivalent to the root account in UNIX. By default, the Administrator account is a special account in that it cannot be deleted or disabled. From installation, the Administrator account has the following capabilities:

- Assigning user rights
- Creating and managing user accounts
- Creating and maintaining local groups
- Maintaining local profiles
- Sharing system resources
- Defining permissions to system resources
- Locking the server

The Guest Account

The Guest account is the second of the built-in NT accounts. This account is defined to facilitate the casual user of the workstation. A user can log on to a workstation as guest and work away under minimal privileges. The Guest account is more of a security headache than it is a useful account. Ideally, you should disable this account because it is better to be safe than sorry. For more details on NT built-in accounts, see Chapter 10, "Fine-Tuning NT Security."

User-Defined Accounts

If you want to define other accounts besides the default built-in accounts, you have to create them by hand. If you can identify users who regularly use your workstation, you should create an account for them and also define user rights within the system.

Groups

Groups are used to facilitate the administration of user accounts. They save on repetitive tasks such as assigning permissions on an individual basis. As administrator, instead of repeatedly having to give all users read permissions to a folder, for example, you can now with one operation define read permission to a group. You can really see the benefits of using groups when the number of users defined on the workstation is large.

The following are built-in groups defined on NT from installation:

- *Administrators.* Members of this group have full administrative rights over the local system and all of its resources. By default, the local Administrator account, which is created during Windows NT installation, is a member of this group.

- *Backup operators.* Members of this group are allowed special read and write access to all files and directories to perform backup and restore operations on the local system.

- *Guests.* This group has minimal rights on the system and is available for users who might be visiting for a few hours or a day and have a need to print a document or use a spreadsheet program. By default, the local user account Guest is a member of this group.

- *Power users.* This group is for users who might need to perform more advanced operations, such as system performance monitoring.

- *Replicator.* This group is used for accounts that perform file replication in a domain environment.

- *Users.* This is the default account for general users of the system. They have no special privileges.

- *Everyone.* This NT built-in group facilitates universal access to resources. However, this group is not listed in the User Manager along with the other groups. You see reference to the Everyone group only when you're defining permissions on an object or resource. Every account defined on the workstation gets automatically added to the Everyone group. File shares upon creation grant full control to the Everyone group.

User Manager

The User Manager is an administrative tool used by administrators for creating and maintaining users and groups on the system.

28

USERS AND GROUPS ON NT

You access the User Manager through the Start menu. First, choose Start | Programs | Administrative Tools (Common) | User Manager. You then see a User Manager dialog box similar to the one shown in Figure 28.1.

FIGURE 28.1.

The User Manager.

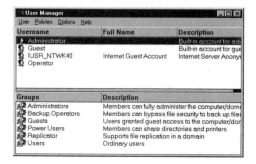

The User Manager is divided into two panes. The upper half of the dialog box lists users defined on the workstation, and the lower half lists groups defined on the workstation. Notice all the default users and groups listed in the User Manager.

A User Account

To view and modify an existing account's properties, you can either double-click the user account of your choice from the user accounts pane or select an account and choose User | Properties. Whichever route you choose, you open a User Properties dialog box similar to the one shown in Figure 28.2.

FIGURE 28.2.

The User Properties dialog box.

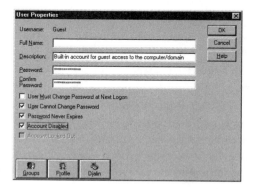

On this dialog box are a number of text boxes that allow you to edit the following User attributes:

■ *Full Name.* You can enter a user's full name here.

■ *Description.* You can enter a description of a user here.

- *Password.* This text box is for the user's password.
- *Confirm Password.* This text box is to confirm the user's password.

In addition to these text boxes are a number of check boxes:

- *User Must Change Password at Next Logon.* When this check box is selected, a user must change his or her account password at the next logon.
- *User Cannot Change Password.* When this option is selected, a user cannot change his or her password.
- *Password Never Expires.* When this option is selected, a user's password lasts indefinitely.
- *Account Disabled.* This option prevents the use of the user account.
- *Account Locked Out.* This option is selected when an account becomes locked out. This result usually occurs when a number of incorrect passwords are entered. This option becomes active only when an account is actually locked out, thus giving you the opportunity of unchecking it and unlocking the account. When the account is not locked out, this option is grayed out (dimmed) and is not accessible.

Also notice the series of buttons at the base of the User Properties dialog box:

- *Groups.* If you click this button, the Group Memberships dialog box appears, as shown in Figure 28.3.

28

USERS AND GROUPS ON NT

FIGURE 28.3.

The Group Memberships dialog box.

This dialog box lists the groups that this user currently belongs to and also what other groups he or she can join. The Member of list shows the groups with which the user account holds membership and the Not member of list shows all the groups with which the user account is not a member. You can add an account to a group by simply selecting the group from the Not a member of list and clicking the Add button. The group then appears in the Members of list. To remove a user from a group, simply select a group within the Members of list and click the Remove button.

- *Profile.* The second button at the base of the User Properties dialog box is Profile. Click the Profile button to open the User Environment Profile dialog box, as shown in Figure 28.4.

Figure 28.4.

The User Environment Profile dialog box.

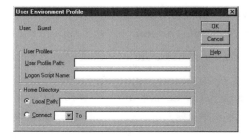

In this dialog box, you can set a path to the user's profile. A user profile determines the look and feel of the desktop tailored to the user. For more information on user profiles, see Chapter 9, "Advanced Control Panel Tools." You can also specify the path to a login script, which is a script or batch job that runs each time the user logs on. These login scripts are useful for connecting to network drives and so on.

In this dialog box, you can also define a home directory for the user. This home directory contains files and programs that the user uses. It is also used for the default directory for the Save As dialog box and for nonspecified working directories for applications. This home directory can be either a local directory on the user's system or a network directory on another system mapped to a network drive. To specify a home directory on the user's local system, select the Local Path radio button and specify the full path to the directory in the text box. To specify a network directory, select the Connect radio button and specify the drive letter to map the home directory to. Then enter the network path to that directory by using the Universal Naming Convention (UNC) name (\\servername\sharename).

NOTE

If your network has sufficient resources such as available disk space and bandwidth, using a network directory that can be backed up on a regular basis is advisable.

Also, avoid using the Z: drive letter for mapping home directories because the logon process temporarily uses this mapping for authentication and login script processing.

- *Dialin.* When you click the Dialin button on the User Properties dialog box, the Dialin Information dialog box then appears, as shown in Figure 28.5. In this dialog box, you define a user's RAS permissions.

  In this dialog box, you can grant a user permission to dial into a RAS server by selecting the Grant dialin permission to user check box. In the Call Back frame, you can configure the RAS server to call back the user at a number entered by the user or one you define, or you can disable the RAS server's ability to call back the user.

FIGURE 28.5.

*The Dialin Informa-
tion dialog box.*

If you are administrating a domain from your workstation and have loaded the User Manager for Domains, a couple of extra buttons appear at the base of the User Properties dialog box. These extra configuration buttons are covered in Chapter 10.

To rename a user account, select the account in the User Manager dialog box and choose User | Rename. When the Rename dialog box appears, as shown in Figure 28.6, enter the new account name in the Change To text box. You can also copy a user account by selecting an account in the User Manager dialog box and choosing User | Copy. A properties dialog box of the account appears with an extra text box that allows you to change the account name. The copied account holds onto all the settings the previous account had, except that the user rights and privileges are not copied over.

FIGURE 28.6.

*Renaming a user
account.*

Group Accounts

The lower half of the User Manager lists the currently defined groups. Double-clicking any of the groups gives you a list of the members of the group in the Local Group Properties dialog box, as shown in Figure 28.7.

FIGURE 28.7.

*The Local Group
Properties dialog box.*

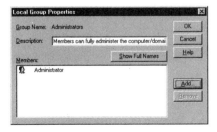

To delete a user account's membership of a group, select the user account in the Members pane of the Local Group Properties dialog box and click Remove.

28

USERS AND
GROUPS ON NT

To add a user account to a group, click the Add button to open the Add Users and Groups dialog box, which is shown in Figure 28.8.

FIGURE 28.8.

The Add Users and Groups dialog box.

As its name suggests, the Add Users and Groups dialog box allows you to select users and groups to be added to the group. You use this dialog box when you want to add users and groups to anything.

Simply select a user or group from the Names pane and click Add. After you finish selecting your users and groups, click OK to return to the Local Group Properties dialog box. Notice that the groups and users you selected have been added to the group. Click OK to return to the User Manager.

You create new local groups by choosing User | New Local Group. The New Local Group dialog box group appears, as shown in Figure 28.9.

FIGURE 28.9.

Adding a new local group.

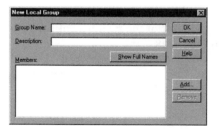

In this dialog box, enter the name of the new group and a description for it. To add users or groups to the new group, click the Add button to open the Add Users and Groups dialog box again (refer to Figure 28.8). Follow the procedures outlined previously for this dialog box, and then return to the User Manager.

You can copy a group by selecting it in the User Manager and choosing User | Copy. A properties dialog box of the group appears with an extra text box that allows you to change the group name. The copied group holds onto all the members of the previous group. The user privileges for the old group are not copied over, however.

Policies

Policies, accessed from the User Manager main menu, are constraints or configuration settings that you can enforce on users and groups. Policies have three constituents parts—Account, User Rights, and Audit—each of which is accessed from the Policies menu.

Account

You set account policies through the Account Policy dialog box, which is shown in Figure 28.10.

FIGURE 28.10.

The Account Policy dialog box.

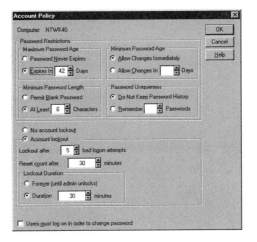

The Account Policy dialog box is primarily used to define constraints on account passwords and the user accounts. The upper half of the Account Policy dialog box concentrates on defining a policy for account passwords. You can limit the number of days a password can remain valid by selecting the Expires In radio button and by entering the number of days you want the passwords to remain valid. You configure this number in the Maximum Password Age frame. In the Minimum Password Age frame, you can define whether a user can change a password immediately or whether the user has to wait until the current password is at a certain age. You determine this age by configuring the Allow Changes In radio button and the Days list box. Through the Password Uniqueness frame, you can get NT to remember the last number of passwords a user chooses and force the user to choose one that the system does not remember. You should force users to define passwords that are not too short, thus making them more difficult to crack. You do so through the Minimum Password Length frame.

The Account lockout frame, when enabled, allows an administrator to lock out accounts in accordance with certain criteria. Criteria include locking out an account after a number of invalid passwords have been entered. Further constraints on the account lockout deal with how long the account will be locked out and whether administrative intervention is required to enable the account. At the base of the dialog box is a check box that, when selected, forces users to be logged on to change their passwords. For more details on Account Policy, see Chapter 10.

User Rights

Windows NT provides a set of network user rights that can be assigned on a per-user or group basis. Some rights are assigned to specific users and groups by default. Notice that at the bottom of the User Rights Policy dialog box shown in Figure 28.11 is a check box with an option to show advanced user rights.

FIGURE 28.11.

The User Rights Policy dialog box.

The standard user rights are as follows, along with a description and default assignments:

- *Access this computer from the network.* This right enables the specified users to make a connection with this computer across the network. This right is granted to Administrators, Everyone, and Power Users.

- *Back up files and directories.* This right allows users special access to all files on a system to perform backup operations. This right is granted to Administrators and Backup Operators.

- *Change the system time.* This right allows the user to change the system time. This right is granted to Administrators and Power Users.

- *Force shutdown from a remote system.* This right allows the user to shut down the system remotely. This right is granted to Administrators and Power Users.

- *Load and unload device drivers.* This right allows the user to add and remove hardware and components. This right is granted to Administrators.

- *Log on locally.* This right allows the user to log on to the local system from the system console. This right is granted to Administrators, Backup Operators, Everyone, Guests, Power Users, and Users.

- *Manage auditing and security log.* This right allows the user to view, delete, and change auditing settings and log settings, as well as examine the Event Log. This right is granted to Administrators.

■ *Restore files and directories.* This right allows users to restore from backup any files or directories. This right is granted to Administrators and Backup Operators.

■ *Shut down the system.* This right allows the user to shut down the system. This right is granted to Administrators, Backup Operators, Everyone, Power Users, and Users.

■ *Take ownership of files or other objects.* This right allows the user to take ownership of objects and files on the system, which the user does not own and might not have permission for. This right is granted to Administrators. Some users can use this option if the owner of a file grants them permission to take ownership of that file.

To grant or revoke a specific right for a user, select the appropriate right and choose the Add or Remove button.

The advanced user rights are as follows:

■ *Act as part of the operating system.* This right is granted to None.

■ *Add workstations to domain.* This right is granted to None.

■ *Bypass traverse checking.* This right is granted to Everyone.

■ *Create a pagefile.* This right is granted to Administrators.

■ *Create a token object.* This right is granted to None.

■ *Debug programs.* This right is granted to Administrators.

■ *Generate security audits.* This right is granted to None.

■ *Increase quotas.* This right is granted to Administrators.

■ *Increase scheduling priority.* This right is granted to Administrators and Power Users.

■ *Lock pages in memory.* This right is granted to None.

■ *Log on as a batch job.* This right is granted to None.

■ *Log on as a service.* This right is granted to None.

■ *Modify firmware environment variables.* This right is granted to Administrators.

■ *Profile single process.* This right is granted to Administrators and Power Users.

■ *Profile system performance.* This right is granted to Administrators.

■ *Replace a process level token.* This right is granted to None.

Advanced user rights should be assigned carefully because they typically are not needed by users (even administrators) and can be disastrous if used improperly. For more details on user rights, see Chapter 10.

Audit Policy

Because the security component of Windows NT is integrated into the operating system itself, auditing capabilities are integrated into the security subsystem. There are three separate auditing configurations: auditing for file and directory access, which is configured through File Manager; auditing of printer usage, which is configured through Print Manager; and user activity logging, which is configured through User Manager.

28

USERS AND GROUPS ON NT

This section covers the auditing of user activity. When you choose Policies | Audit from the User Manager menu bar, the Audit Policy dialog box shown in Figure 28.12 opens.

FIGURE 28.12.

The Audit Policy dialog box.

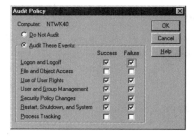

Initially, auditing is not enabled. To enable auditing features, select the Audit These Events radio button. You then need to configure which events to audit and whether to audit successes, failures, or both. Keep in mind the level of security necessary for your particular organization and the fact that, for auditing to be effective, someone must monitor the logs and interpret them to look for problems.

Also, because the audited events are written to the security section of the Event Log, you need either to closely monitor and maintain the log or modify its settings to accommodate the growth of the audit trail.

The following events can be audited for both success and failure:

- Logon and Logoff audits when a user logged on or off the workstation or made a network connection.
- File and Object Access audits when a user accessed a file or directory that has been configured for auditing or used a printer configured for auditing.
- Use of User Rights audits when the user exercised one of his or her user rights.
- User and Group Management audits when a change was made to the Security Account Manager database (add, remove, modify a user or group).
- Security Policy Changes audits when a change was made to the user rights or security policy.
- Restart, Shutdown, and System audits when the computer was shut down or restarted or a system event occurred.
- Process Tracking audits low-level process information such as duplicate handles or indirect object access.

Generally, you should be sparing in your selections so that you have a manageable audit trail, but not at the expense of compromising security. Choose the events that are important to you, and manage and track them closely; otherwise, this task can grow out of control or lose its value.

Also note that the more auditing features that are enabled, the higher the performance cost is on the system because the auditing process uses system resources.

Typically, I audit the failure of any of the events in the preceding list. But I also audit the success of User and Group Management, Security Policy Changes, and System Shutdown because being able to track when these events occur and who initiated them is a good idea. For more details on audit policy, see Chapter 10.

Summary

In this chapter, you learned about users and groups within NT and looked at the User Manager, which is the main administrative tool used for creating and maintaining users and groups. I discussed the built-in users and groups that are defined with NT Workstation by default, and I also discussed the three major components that make up policies—namely account policies, user rights policies, and audit policies.

Using Peer Web Services

by Joshua Allen

IN THIS CHAPTER

CHAPTER 29

No doubt you have heard of the World Wide Web (WWW) and have probably spent time browsing through the immense amount of information that can be obtained from the Internet. You might also be aware that a large number of the servers to which you connect while browsing the Internet are actually running Windows NT. In this chapter, you will be introduced to Peer Web Services (PWS), Microsoft's Internet server for Windows NT Workstation. You will get a picture of what PWS can and cannot do for you, and you will learn how to install, configure, and administer your workstation to be able to publish information to people within your company and across the world. This chapter gives you detailed, step-by-step instructions for using the information and security management features that make NT Workstation particularly suited for use as an Internet server.

What Can Peer Web Services Do for Me?

Peer Web Services is more than just a Web server for your Windows NT Workstation. PWS is a full-fledged Internet server suite with support for practically any feature that you find in use on the Internet today. PWS includes HTTP (Web), Gopher, and FTP servers. The Web server component of PWS will probably be the one you use most frequently. This server uses HyperText Transfer Protocol (HTTP) to answer requests from users across the network who are using a Web browser, such as Internet Explorer. (See Chapter 23, "Using Microsoft Internet Explorer 4," for more details about using Internet Explorer to read documents on HTTP servers.)

Suppose that your department wants to make a list of current activities, projects, and schedules available to other departments within your company and to your major clients. You could put this information in a spreadsheet on a file server somewhere and give a set of complicated instructions to anyone who wanted to read this information, or you could simply put PWS on your machine and tell your customers to point their Web browsers to a location such as `http://yourmachine.yourcompany.com/schedule.htm`. Your customers across the Internet and your customers across the hall can access the information in exactly the same easy way.

> **NOTE**
>
> Don't worry if your machine does not have an Internet or DNS name such as `www.mycompany.com`. Peer Web Services responds to local requests such as `http://yourmachine/doc.htm` without requiring a Fully Qualified Domain Name (FQDN). You don't even need to have an Internet connection at your company to experience the benefits of Peer Web Services. In fact, PWS shines best as an *intranet* server. Intranets are internal corporate networks of HTTP servers that are made to be used within the company itself to get work done rather than for publishing information to external users. You can find a full discussion of how to build an intranet in Chapter 30, "Setting Up an Intranet." In addition, Chapter 30 offers a more complete explanation of how to manage local machine names, Internet FQDNs, and other Windows NT naming services.

One of the more important benefits of publishing this way is the platform independence that you achieve. Web browsers are available for all major operating systems, including Windows, OS/2, UNIX, and the Macintosh OS.

Although most of the Internet is now built on HTTP, PWS supports other, less popular protocols as well. If you simply want to make files available to people, without the hypertext and graphics ability that a Web server offers, you can use File Transfer Protocol (FTP). Users can use an FTP client program to connect to your machine and PUT or GET files. FTP is one of the original Internet protocols, and still more machines are on the Internet with FTP clients than with Web browsers. If your intent is to make your files available to the widest number of people, you might want to make the files available using an FTP server, or a combination of FTP and HTTP. I will cover more details about combining FTP and HTTP services later in the chapter.

The final protocol supported by PWS is an older protocol known as Gopher. Before the WWW became popular, using Gopher became popular as a way of linking documents across different servers on a network. Gopher lacks many of the features that Internet users today take for granted. You can think of Gopher as a first attempt by the Internet community at building a WWW. If offered a choice today, nobody would use Gopher instead of HTTP. The only reason you might use the PWS Gopher server today is if you have to support legacy Gopher servers on your WAN and cannot convince your boss to just convert the servers to HTTP.

PWS Is the Superior Internet Server

In the past, most Internet servers were run on the UNIX operating system. UNIX boasts a much longer familiarity with TCP/IP (the underlying network protocol of the Internet) than do the other popular operating systems. But now that TCP/IP has swept the PC world as well, considering Windows NT as your server platform for Internet services makes sense. Although PWS is not the only Internet server available for Windows NT, you will probably do best to stick with PWS (or its cousin, IIS, on NT Server).

The most obvious factor is cost. PWS comes free with Windows NT Workstation. In addition, PWS will integrate better with your existing environment. Most of the browsers accessing your server will probably be running on some version of Windows rather than UNIX. Consider that PWS was developed by a company that is committed to the Windows operating system and was designed to run on a Windows server, and it is not surprising that PWS interacts more smoothly with your existing machines. For example, PWS taps into your existing Windows NT domain or workgroup security to make Internet security management a breeze. A PWS server can access files on Novell or Windows NT servers across your corporate network and make them available to users across the world who need not be running either protocol. Peer Web Services leverages Windows user-friendly concepts to make server administration from the server as easy as pointing and clicking. (For users on non-Windows machines, the server can still be administered through a Web browser interface.) Finally, using the ISAPI interface described later in this chapter, server-side programs can execute many orders of magnitude faster than similar CGI code on a UNIX server.

29

USING PEER
WEB SERVICES

THE IIS FAMILY OF SERVERS

Although PWS is available only on NT Workstations, Internet Information Server (IIS) is available as a part of Windows NT Server. In fact, PWS is really just a slightly scaled-down version of IIS. Microsoft rounds out the family of servers by making Personal Web Server (also called PWS) available for Windows 95 machines. For users who did not have PWS preloaded onto their Windows 95 machines, it is a free download from Microsoft.

When to Use PWS Instead of IIS

Although PWS is virtually identical to IIS, you should be familiar with a few slight differences. IIS is optimized to have many users retrieving information at once. Additionally, IIS can log all server activity to common database formats rather than the simple text file that PWS uses. IIS also can host multiple Web servers (www.somecompany.com, www.another.com) on the same machine. Finally, IIS allows you to strictly control the amount of network bandwidth that your server uses and block out particular remote addresses. These features make IIS ideal for an enterprise, high-volume server. Chances are, however, that you do not need any of the listed features that IIS provides. With PWS running on your personal workstation, you can take information from concept to published in less time than would be required if you were updating a remote IIS server. And the value of your corporate information network is increased as your flexibility and responsiveness are increased. Also, if you *are* required to update information to a remote IIS server, keeping PWS on your personal workstation still makes sense. Because PWS is virtually identical to IIS, you can do most of your troubleshooting and testing locally before you submit your work to the main server for publishing.

Installing Peer Web Services

In this section, you will see how to install Peer Web Services and its two essential add-ons, Active Server Pages (ASP) and Index Server.

Microsoft Peer Web Server

You can install Peer Web Services while you're loading the base operating system, or after, through the control panel.

1. Make sure that your drive is formatted with the NTFS filesystem. If you have already installed the operating system and have not used NTFS, you can do so by typing `convert c: /fs:ntfs` at a command prompt. (Of course, use something other than `c:`

if you're using a different drive for your data.) If you have to convert your drive to NTFS, you also need to reboot.

2. In the Control Panel, double-click Network (or just wait for the network configuration dialog box to appear, if you are loading the base operating system).

3. On the Services tab of the Network dialog box, click the Add button. When the Select Network Service dialog box appears, as shown in Figure 29.1, select Microsoft Peer Web Server from the list and click OK.

WARNING

If you're in the habit of using a network share point or a copied I386 directory as your source for NT 4 source, make sure that you have the files necessary for PWS installation. Normal NT 4 installations require only the files found in the root I386 directory, so there is a good chance that you have copied only the I386 directory to your network share or local hard drive. For PWS installation to be successful, however, you need to make sure that you have copied the INETSERV directory with your I386 source, as well.

FIGURE 29.1.

Adding Peer Web Server.

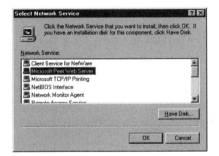

4. In the Microsoft Peer Web Services Setup dialog box that appears, as shown in Figure 29.2, choose which of the services you want to install (see Table 29.1). For example, you might want to clear the Gopher Service check box at this point if you don't plan to run a Gopher server (you can always add it later, if you change your mind). Additionally, if you use only one of the administrative interfaces (Internet Service Manager or Internet Service Manager [HTML]), you can install only that interface. Click OK to continue.

Part V

FIGURE 29.2.

*Choosing optional
components.*

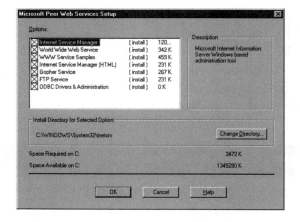

Table 29.1. Peer Web Services optional components.

Option	Description
Internet Service Manager	Administration tool that allows you to stop and start your Internet services and configure options such as security and performance.
World Wide Web Service	Allows your machine to operate as a WWW server and serve Web pages to users with Web browsers such as Netscape Navigator or Internet Explorer.
WWW Service Samples	Sample Web pages and scripts that you can use to model your own pages.
Internet Service Manager (HTML)	A Web-based version of the Internet Service Manager that allows you to administer and configure your Web server and other Internet services from any machine with a Web browser.
Gopher Service	Allows your Windows NT workstation to serve pages using the Gopher protocol, an older Internet protocol similar to the WWW protocol. Gopher servers are still in use within some organizations.
FTP Service	The FTP service configures your Windows NT Workstation to publish files using FTP, or File Transfer Protocol. FTP is widely used around the Internet to exchange files when the rich formatting capabilities of the WWW are not needed.

Option	Description
ODBC Drivers & Administration	Installs drivers and a control panel applet, which allow you to access databases from your Web pages. If you have already installed any database products, such as Microsoft Access, on your workstation, you may already have ODBC drivers installed. Later in the chapter, you will learn how to use ODBC to access databases from your Web pages.

5. You then are presented with an opportunity to choose the locations where your Internet files will be stored (see Figure 29.3). The Publishing Directories dialog box refers to the default location from which the Internet servers will read files for publishing, not the location of the actual server executables and code. For the rest of this chapter, I will assume that you have accepted the defaults here, but you might want to adjust these paths to a drive that has more space. After making your changes, click OK to continue.

FIGURE 29.3.
Where PWS looks for published documents.

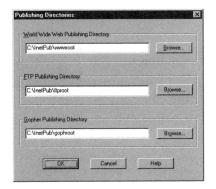

6. PWS Setup then offers you the opportunity to install ODBC drivers (see Figure 29.4). ODBC, which stands for Open DataBase Connectivity, is just a way to let applications access data from all different sorts of databases. The list in the Install Drivers dialog box is pretty skimpy, but don't worry if your favorite database is not listed. When you install the IIS 3.0 Active Server Pages later in this chapter, you can add more ODBC drivers. And PWS can use your third-party ODBC drivers to access your database, even if the drivers were not installed as part of PWS setup. Click OK to continue.

FIGURE 29.4.

The wimpy ODBC driver list.

7. That's it! PWS Setup has added icons to your start menu, as you can see in Figure 29.5. Notice the Peer Web Services Setup shortcut. By clicking this shortcut in the future, you can modify your existing installation by removing services that you do not need or adding new services.

FIGURE 29.5.

Peer Web Services shortcuts.

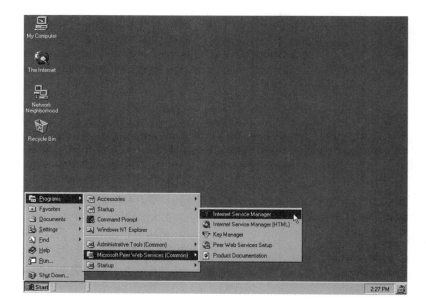

Active Server Pages

Active Server Pages, or ASP, is the free upgrade to PWS that was released by Microsoft after the NT 4 CD-ROMs had already been shipped. The PWS that comes with NT 4 is basically the same thing as IIS 2.0. ASP upgrades this to IIS 3.0. ASP introduces a few fixes and improvements to the basic Web server functionality as well as increases your options for publishing dynamic content. Even if you never use any of ASP's programmatic features (introduced later in this chapter), you probably should install ASP anyway, to keep your server up-to-date.

Here's how:

1. Download ASP. Just point a Web browser to http://www.microsoft.com/iis and click the IIS 3.0 download. You are given the opportunity to download many additional components, but ASP is all you really need to make your machine IIS 3.0. When you're prompted by your Web browser, choose Save to Disk, and remember the filename and location that you choose.

TIP

The ASP installation archive that you download is not IIS-specific. You can use the same archive to upgrade NT servers running IIS, NT workstations running PWS, and Windows 95 machines with PWS 95.

---

2. Launch ASP setup by double-clicking the name of the file that you downloaded.
3. Select the optional components that you want to install (see Figure 29.6). If you think that you might use ASP features, and you're not already an ASP programming expert, you should include the sample pages and documentation here.

WARNING

In rare cases, I have experienced a negative impact on existing database programs on a workstation by the addition of ODBC 3.0. If you never plan to use data access from your Internet servers, you would be wise to leave this option unchecked.

FIGURE 29.6.

Active Server Pages options.

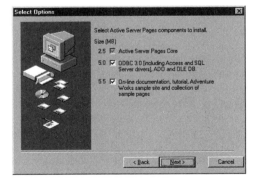

4. The rest of the installation proceeds uneventfully. Be aware that the ASP installation has to shut down the Web server temporarily while it modifies files and Registry locations, but it brings your server back up as soon as it is finished.

29

USING PEER WEB SERVICES

Index Server

Index Server is another free add-on for PWS and IIS. After you install Index Server, your Web server keeps track of any content that is added or removed and allows you to create simple search forms that enable users to quickly find any document that they are allowed to retrieve from your server.

To install Index Server, follow these steps:

1. Download Index Server from the following:

   `http://www.microsoft.com/ntserver/info/indexserver.htm`

   When you're prompted by your browser, choose Save to File and remember the filename and path to which you save.

2. Launch the setup by double-clicking the installation archive executable from within Windows NT Explorer.

3. You are asked for a directory for the Index Server Index files. Don't worry that the default here is the root of drive C:. When Index Server creates its index files, it cleanly stores them in a subdirectory beneath the path you choose. If you want, though, you can specify a different drive or path here.

4. Index Server needs to stop and start your Web server temporarily to install successfully. As soon as it finishes, it begins indexing your existing content. Index Server allows you to run searches immediately (described later in this chapter), but you might see an `Index Out of Date` message for the first moments while Index Server catches up. If you already have a considerable amount of content on your server when you add Index Server, you might have to wait for a few minutes.

Configuring and Administering Peer Web Services

Now that your workstation has been fitted with the essential Internet Server components, let's look at the tools and techniques that you will use to manage them.

Internet Service Manager

Although you might be tempted to configure the PWS service by choosing Properties from the Services tab of the Network dialog box, PWS does not support that interface. Instead, you must select the Internet Service Manager option from the Start menu (refer to Figure 29.5). Choosing this option opens the Microsoft Internet Service Manager dialog box, which is shown in Figure 29.7. The list at the bottom shows the servers that are running. Your HTTP server appears in the list as WWW. You can easily stop or start any service by clicking the toolbar buttons indicated in the figure.

FIGURE 29.7.

The Internet Service Manager.

FIGURE 29.7.

The Internet Service Manager.

Start selected service

Stop selected service

Key Manager

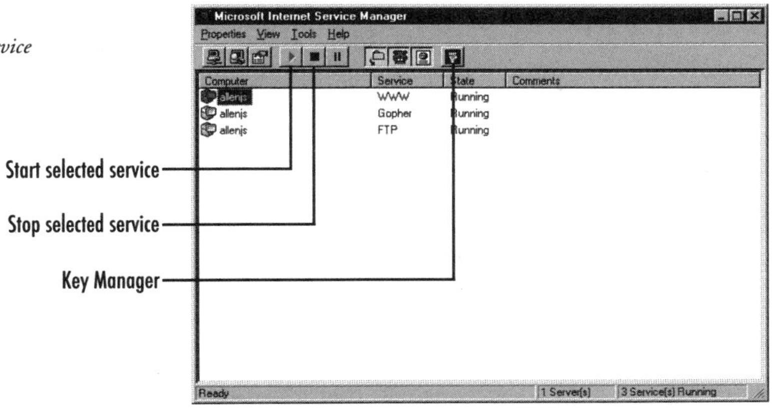

THE SERVICE LIST

You might have noticed that the service list in Figure 29.7 does not show ASP or Index Server. Index Server and ASP run as part of your WWW server rather than as separate servers. ASP is merely an association in the scriptmap section of your Registry (described later in the chapter). Index Server, too, adds a scriptmap association, but ties into the filesystem for dynamic updating of the indexes. Shutting down the WWW Service will take care of ASP and Index Server as well.

To configure options for any of the Internet Services, just right-click the service you want to configure; then choose Properties from the pop-up menu. An example configuration dialog box is shown in Figure 29.8. Discussion of how and when to configure the various available properties will be presented throughout the rest of this chapter.

FIGURE 29.8.

WWW Service Properties dialog box.

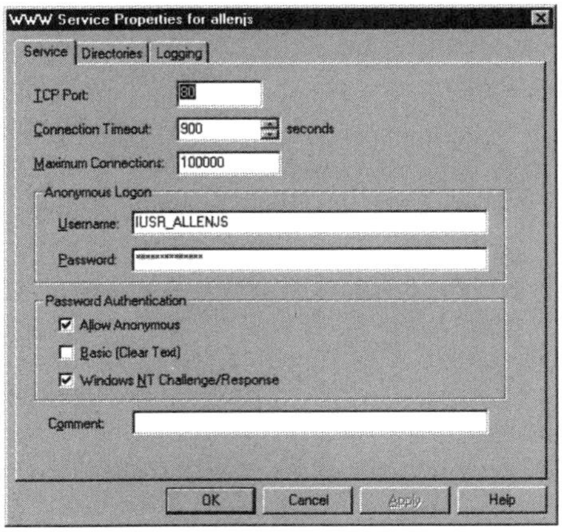

29

USING PEER
WEB SERVICES

Internet Service Manager (HTML)

In addition to the Windows-based administration utility, PWS enables you to administer your Internet Services through a Web browser. To see what this looks like, just select the Internet Service Manager (HTML) icon from your Start menu, or point your Web browser to `http://yourmachine/iisadmin`.

> **CAUTION**
>
> If you're trying to access the HTML Internet Service Manager from a remote machine, you might be denied access. To administer your PWS server, your login on the remote machine must be recognized as a member of the local Administrators group on the PWS server. This situation is ideal for a domain login using NT Challenge/Response authentication. If your server is using basic authentication instead of Challenge/Response, you can still administer it by entering a login ID and password that have administrative privileges on the PWS box when you are asked by your Web browser. This method is not recommended, though, because you will be transferring administrative passwords over the network without encryption. If you must use basic authentication, also make sure that you don't turn off basic authentication through the Service Manager; otherwise, your session will be disconnected! Read the section "Security: Controlling Who Sees What," later in this chapter, for more information.

Notice that the properties available through the HTML interface are grouped and presented in the same manner as with the Windows-based utility, but you can see one important difference: because the HTML interface is being served by your Web server, you cannot shut down and restart your Web server through this interface. Telling your Web server to turn on would require that your Web server be active, and it won't be active if you have told it to shut down!

Logging Server Activity

Peer Web Services records a log of all accesses or "hits" to your server. To configure this feature, follow these steps:

1. Open Internet Service Manager.
2. Right-click the service you want to configure (WWW in this example) and choose Properties from the pop-up menu.
3. On the Properties dialog box, choose the Logging tab and configure logging options as shown in Figure 29.9.

Depending on the frequency (Daily, Weekly, Monthly) that you choose for your log file, PWS opens new log files named according to the conventions that you see at the bottom of the property sheet next to Log file name:. The FTP, Gopher, and WWW services log all accesses to the same file and record information such as client's IP address, file requested, and time. The file, which is just a comma-delimited text file, is rather easy to understand.

FIGURE 29.9.

*The Logging options
property sheet.*

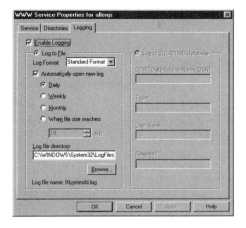

Notice that the Log Format drop-down box on this property sheet gives you the option of saving the log file in the NCSA format instead. NCSA HTTPD was one of the first popular Web servers on the Internet, and many third-party log file analyzer programs have been created to work with its style of log files. If you intend to use a freeware or third-party log file analyzer to summarize your log files, you might want to use the NCSA log file format.

Finally, notice that the database logging portion of Figure 29.9 is disabled. It is disabled because PWS on NT Workstation does not support this feature—if you were using a Windows NT Server running IIS, these options would be enabled.

Using Performance Monitor with PWS

Performance Monitor is another tool included with NT Workstation; it allows you to record scores of performance statistics over time and then graph or export this data for analysis. A full discussion of using performance monitor is included in Chapter 33, "Performance Monitor." If you're not familiar with this tool, you might want to skip ahead to Chapter 33.

After you install PWS, four new counter groupings are available in the Performance Monitor tool, including FTP, WWW, Gopher, and IIS Global. Files Sent will probably be one of the more useful statistics that let you detect trends in usage of your server. Another helpful counter could be Not Found Errors. You can glance at this chart periodically to check for spikes, which could indicate that a change or typographical error in one of your pages is pointing users to the wrong location.

Publishing Information to the World

After you master the basics of managing your Internet Service programs, you will probably want to begin publishing information right away. In this section, I will introduce you to many of the ways that information can be presented to network clients, starting with the most simple and progressing to more sophisticated methods.

Serving Files Directly

The easiest way to make a file available to someone is to serve it just the way it is. Any file that you place into c:\inetpub\wwwroot becomes available to Internet users as `http://yourmachinename/filename`. For example, try this procedure:

1. Use Notepad to create a new text document on your workstation that is running PWS. Type whatever you want into this file.

2. Save the file as `c:\inetpub\wwwroot\fun.txt`.

3. Now open a Web browser on your machine or another machine on your network, and point it to `http://yourmachinename/fun.txt`.

Simple, isn't it? Stay tuned, though; there is still more to learn. To start, consider what might happen if you create a subdirectory named `Test\` beneath the wwwroot\ directory and move fun.txt to that directory. You guessed correctly if you said that the new URL for the Web browser will be `http://yourmachinename/Test/fun.txt`. Notice that the URL never refers to the c:\inetpub\wwwroot part of the file's path because the Web server serves only files beneath its "home," which is the directory that you choose during installation (refer to Figure 29.3). PWS does offer a way around this restriction, which will be discussed in the next section. For now, though, continue by moving the file fun.txt from its location beneath c:\inetpub\wwwroot, and place it in c:\inetpub\ftproot. Now if you open an FTP session to your machine, using your favorite FTP client, you will see fun.txt sitting there in the root directory. Most Web browsers can now act as FTP clients, too, by using the `ftp://` URL syntax. For example, you could type `ftp://yourmachinename` to open a directory listing through your FTP server using a Web browser. Although you're using a Web browser in this case, this does *not* mean that the WWW service of PWS is taking any action. In fact, if you stop the WWW service right now, using Internet Service Manager, you would still be able to access fun.txt through your Web browser this way.

By now, you should have a pretty clear picture of where to place files for publishing and how to access them from a Web browser. You might have noticed that the data you place in the wwwroot directory is available only to users with Web browsers, whereas the files that you place in the ftproot directory are available to users with FTP programs and to users with Web browsers. You therefore might assume that the best place to put all your files is the ftproot directory. Placing your files here can sometimes be a good idea, but wait until you have read about virtual directories, in the next section, before deciding.

Now you have published a simple text file by directly placing it on your server, but what about not-so-simple file types? Try placing a Microsoft Word document in your wwwroot directory. If you're using a Web browser that supports OLE embedded objects, such as Microsoft's Internet Explorer, you see the embedded document within your browser when you access its URL. With most complex file types, however, the person accessing your file has to save the file to disk before viewing it; the file is not displayed within the Web browser. When you publish files by copying them directly into your wwwroot or ftproot directories, you make publishing easy, at the cost of sacrificing the flexibility and rich interface that tailored Web publishing offers. This approach will suit your needs adequately, though, if your primary intention is to have an easy way for customers to access copies of your files.

Virtual Directories

One of the more useful features of PWS is its capability of using *virtual directories* to publish data. With virtual directories, your Web server or FTP server can read and publish files from any directory on your machine and from any network drive to which your machine has access. To configure a virtual directory, follow these steps:

1. Open Internet Service Manager from your Start menu.

2. Right-click the service you want to configure (in this example, WWW) and choose Properties in the pop-up menu.

3. On the Properties dialog box, choose the Directories tab, as shown in Figure 29.10. Notice that several virtual directories for your WWW service have already been configured. Also notice the Enable Default Document and Directory Browsing Allowed check boxes. An explanation of these options will follow.

FIGURE 29.10.

The Directories tab of the WWW Service Properties dialog box.

4. To add another virtual directory definition, click the Add button. On the resulting Directory Properties dialog box, as shown in Figure 29.11, notice that the Virtual Server option is disabled for PWS. If you were configuring a Windows NT server running IIS, this option would be enabled.

FIGURE 29.11.

Adding a virtual directory.

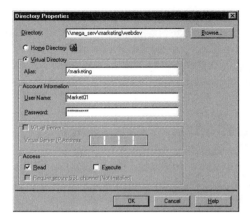

5. Type into the Directory text box the path from which you want to publish files. For example, if you have a particular directory on your drive to which you save most of your data, you might type `c:\data` here. You can also enter a UNC network path here (as shown in Figure 29.11) or a path that includes a mapped network drive. Generally, using a full UNC pathname rather than a network drive letter for networked resources is best because network drive mappings can change depending on who is logged in to the workstation.

    Notice that the Account Information section of the form automatically becomes enabled when PWS detects that you are entering a path that is not part of the local machine's file system. Just type in a username and password that PWS can use to read the network directory. You will learn more about the implications of this in the section on security, later in this chapter.

6. Make sure that Read access is selected in the Access section. Execute access will be discussed later in the chapter.

7. Select the Virtual Directory radio button, and choose an alias path for your files. You probably will never use the Home Directory radio button with PWS because you already selected the home location during installation. The Home option is really only useful with IIS servers, which can have multiple virtual servers and thus more than one Home directory.

8. You're done! Close out of the settings dialog box, and you can access the files in your newly configured directory from any Web browser. For example, if you had created the virtual directory configuration shown in Figure 29.11, a Web browser requesting `http://yourmachinename/marketing/prospect.xls` would be shown a copy of `\\mega_serv\marketing\webdev\prospect.xls`.

WARNING

You might be thinking about creating an alias for `c:\` named something like `/rootdir` and leaving it at that. This approach would certainly be an easy way to make all your files available, but this approach causes two major problems. Such an alias would expose your entire hard drive to any snoop who wanted to scan your files. And even if you protected your files with appropriate permissions, this strategy has another serious problem. As soon as you create any new virtual directory, Index Server immediately begins indexing all the content beneath that directory. Unless you have huge amounts of RAM and hard drive space, you probably don't want Index Server indexing your entire hard drive!

WWW Directory Browsing and Default Document

You might have noticed by now that you must always supply a full filename when accessing your WWW server. If, for example, you have a virtual directory named /marketing, and you type just `http://yourmachinename/marketing/` into your Web browser, you get a `Permission Denied` error, even if you have access to the individual files within the directory. In this case, you use the two check boxes on the Directories tab of the WWW Service Directories dialog box (refer to Figure 29.10). The first option, Enable Default Document, is probably already set. PWS always tries to return this file to a user if the user specifies a path without a filename. Each directory can have its own Default.htm (or whatever filename you specify in the Default Document text box). In the preceding example, if you had placed a file named Default.htm into your /marketing directory, it would have been referred to the user using the URL given.

By selecting the Directory Browsing Allowed check box, you can handle even the cases in which a directory has no Default.htm file. If PWS cannot find a Default.htm, or if the Default Document option is disabled, PWS then returns a directory listing of the directory specified, with underlined hyperlinks to all the files and sub-directories within that directory. Be sure to read about the security implication, though, in the section "Security: Controlling Who Sees What," later in this chapter.

Using Virtual Directories with FTP

Configuration of FTP service virtual directories is handled much like the management of WWW service virtual directories. Figure 29.12 shows an example of the FTP service virtual directories property sheet.

Notice that the Directory Browsing Allowed and Enable Default Document options are not available on the FTP property sheet because FTP, for the most part, does only directory listing and file retrieval. Disabling the directory listing would make no sense because then your server would no longer be an FTP server. (You can, however, disable directory listings for particular directories, using NTFS file permissions as described in the section on security.) Instead, you can choose UNIX or DOS directory listing styles. When your users open an FTP session to your server and execute a DIR command, they will see a UNIX- or a DOS-formatted listing of files, based on what you choose here. If you plan to use any third-party graphical FTP client programs, or if you plan to publish to the Internet at large, you should probably stick with the UNIX listing style. Most client software knows how to interpret the UNIX style listing, whereas ability to parse the DOS format is less common.

Figure 29.12.

The FTP service virtual directories property sheet.

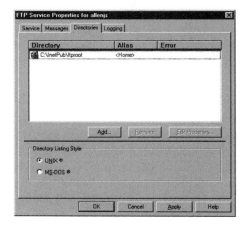

NOTE

Peer Web Services FTP Service permits you to customize the FTP session messages that people see when they connect to your server. You can change these messages on the Messages tab of the FTP Service Properties dialog box (see Figure 29.13). Because the FTP service that comes with PWS allows only a maximum of five simultaneous connections, you might want to type a descriptive error message that users will see if no connections are currently available. If your company has a policy regarding unauthorized use of company computing resources, you might want to include this information in the welcome message.

Finally, you should be aware of one particular problem that you will face with FTP virtual directories. As you would probably expect, a virtual directory named /shared_data could be accessed from your Web browser by typing the URL ftp://yourmachinename/shared_data/. However, if you were to open a normal FTP session to your machine and execute a DIR command from your home directory, you would not see the shared_data/ directory in your listing! You don't see it because the FTP service does not list virtual directory names in its directory listing. If you type CD shared_data from your home directory, you are placed in the correct directory, even though that directory does not appear in your original listing. The impact on you is that you have to inform all your users what the names of your virtual directories are because they cannot find them by browsing. The recommended way to work around this problem is to enable FTP server annotation and add annotations that describe the virtual directories. To do so, follow these steps:

1. Open the Registry Editor by typing `regedit` into the Start Menu's Run box and pressing Enter. (Registry editing is covered in detail in Chapter 11, "The NT Registry.")

2. Browse down through the Registry to `HKEY_LOCAL_MACHINE\SYSTEM\CurrentControlSet\Services\MSFTPSVC\Parameters`.

3. From here, choose Edit | New | DWORD Value from the pull-down menus.

4. Change the name of the newly created value to `AnnotateDirectories`.

5. Change the value (by double-clicking) to the number `1`.

6. Close the Registry Editor.

7. Use Notepad to create a text file listing the names of your virtual directories and some description information.

8. Save this file as `c:\inetpub\ftproot\~ftpsvc~.ckm`. Keep in mind that Notepad likes to append .txt to the end of files that it saves, so you might need to use Windows NT Explorer to rename the file correctly after you save it.

9. Test it! Different FTP client programs display annotations differently. Some present them as a dialog box to the user when he or she connects to your site, and others merely prepend the annotations to the directory listing. And yet other FTP client programs fail if they encounter annotations. In any case, testing your new annotations from the perspective of a potential user is a good idea so that you can be sure the behavior is acceptable.

FIGURE 29.13.

The Messages tab of the FTP Service Properties dialog box.

29

USING PEER
WEB SERVICES

You can add annotations to any of the directories that are accessed by your FTP server simply by creating a ~ftpsvc~.ckm in each directory.

HyperText Markup Language (HTML)

HyperText Markup Language, or HTML, is the most common file type that is transmitted by HTTP servers to browsers across the WWW. HTML allows for nicely formatted documents to be displayed directly within a user's Web browser. Additionally, HTML includes the capability to have hot spots, or hyperlinks, within the document, which, when clicked, redirect the user to a different page on the server or across the Internet. Because handling hypertext is one of the primary capabilities of browsers that make the WWW so powerful, you will probably want to include hypertext in your own publishing. Here, you will see just how simple hypertext publishing can be. Open Notepad and type in the text shown in Listing 29.1. Don't worry if your file is not formatted exactly the same as this one; it will work no matter how you format it, even if you type it all as one long line! Save this file as c:\inetpub\wwwroot\sample.htm.

Listing 29.1. sample.htm demonstrates basic HTML.

```
<HTML>
  <BODY>
    <FONT SIZE=+2 COLOR="red">
      This is <B>sample</B> HTML
    </FONT>

    <FONT SIZE=-1>
      Click <A HREF="http://www.microsoft.com">HERE</A>
      to go to Microsoft.
    </FONT>

    <IMG SRC="http://www.mcp.com/sams/images/sams_logo.gif">

  </BODY>
</HTML>
```

You can view this example by going to the location http://yourmachinename/sample.htm from within your Web browser. This example demonstrates several important features of HTML:

- HTML uses tags bracketed with < and > to format text. You indicate that you want to begin a certain style with an open tag, such as <B> for bold text, and end it with a close tag, indicated with a forward slash, such as </B>, to finish bold text.

- Tags can accept parameters. For example, the <FONT> tag in Listing 29.1 has parameters describing color and size.

- The <A> tag (meaning Anchor) is used to create a hyperlink. Add the HREF parameter to your opening anchor tag to tell where the hypertext reference should point.

- The <IMG> tag inserts a picture into your page. The SRC parameter to the <IMG> tag tells where the file is located. In this example, you see that the picture does not even need to be located on your server.

> **TIP**
>
> If you want to learn more details about how to write your own HTML code, go to the HTML Cafe, which has some excellent material for beginners, at `http://www.mcp.com/sams/home.html`. In addition, you can find a reference listing all available HTML formatting tags at `http://www.microsoft.com/workshop/author/newhtml/htmlref.htm`.

For more complex HTML code generation, you will probably want to use a program that helps you create the HTML files automatically. Most current word processing programs, such as Microsoft Word and WordPerfect, allow you to save your documents directly into HTML format. For more control, you can find plenty of HTML editor programs, such as Microsoft's FrontPage, which you can buy to create HTML documents easily without ever having to look at any HTML code.

Parsed HTML

If you save your HTML files with an extension of .STM, they will be preprocessed by PWS before being sent off to a user's Web browser. The Web server looks for certain preprocessing directives in your HTML code and then acts on them before sending the output. Listing 29.2 demonstrates this concept.

Listing 29.2. sample2.stm demonstrates parsed HTML.

```
<HTML>
  <BODY>

    Sample of including a file
    <HR>
    <!--#include file="x.htm"-->
    <HR>
    End of included file.

  </BODY>
</HTML>
```

When you load `http://yourmachinename/sample2.stm`, you see that the server inserts your previous example, `x.htm`, into the output. You will find this feature especially useful for boilerplate-type text, such as copyright notices or navigation bars, that must appear in many documents, but which could change at any time. You can take advantage of the parsed HTML feature to make changes easier by separating the repeated content into a single file and then using `#include` to repeat it. Future changes will then be made to the single file, but will appear in all documents that have the `#include`. You can find a more in-depth discussion of .STM capabilities at `http://yourmachinename/iasdocs/aspdocs/ssi`.

29

USING PEER WEB SERVICES

Common Gateway Interface

Peer Web Services WWW Service is a fully compliant Common Gateway Interface (CGI) server. CGI is a standard that developed during the early days of the WWW, and it allows you to execute programs on your Web server that return data back to a user. For example, try pulling up `http://www.proximus.com/cgi-bin/freemap?Address1=mcp.com` from your Web browser. Here's how it works:

- The remote server sees that your request is for a file beneath the cgi-bin directory.
- The server knows that freemap is an executable program, so it launches this program, passing the `?Address1=mcp.com` portion as a parameter.
- When the program is finished executing, the result is passed back to your Web browser. In this case, you get a quick map to the physical location of mcp.com.

So how can you configure your server to execute CGI programs? Here are a few basic steps you can take to tell your Web server that a particular file should be executed on the server rather than copied to the client's browser:

1. Open Internet Service Manager and select the WWW Service Properties.
2. On the Properties dialog box, choose the Directories tab, and view the properties for the directory that contains your scripts.
3. On the Directory Properties dialog box, make sure that the Execute permission is set (you don't need to enable the Read permission). See Figure 29.14 for an example.

FIGURE 29.14.

Setting Execute permission on a CGI directory.

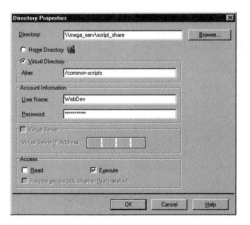

4. Now PWS recognizes this directory as a CGI-enabled directory. By default, PWS installs with the c:\inetpub\scripts directory as a directory for scripts and executables. The `http://yourmachinename/scripts` directory is analogous to the `http://servername/cgi-bin` directory on many UNIX HTTP servers.

5. In addition to the Directory configuration, PWS stores information about scripts in the Registry. Open your Registry by typing `regedit` in the Start menu's Run box.

6. Browse down to the `HKEY_LOCAL_MACHINE\SYSTEM\CurrentControlSet\Services\W3SVC\Parameters\Script Map` section, as shown in Figure 29.15.

FIGURE 29.15.

Script Map settings in the Registry.

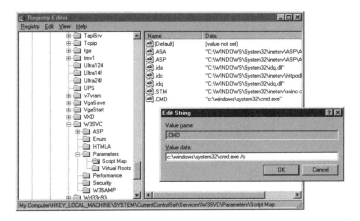

7. For files that are not normally recognized as executables (.COM and .EXE), this section of the Registry tells PWS how they should be executed. In Figure 29.15, you can see an association for .CMD (Windows NT Command Language) files being created. Now, if a user ever requests a URL such as `http://yourmachinename/scripts/somefile.cmd`, PWS will actually launch a copy of the command interpreter CMD.EXE to process the file.

TIP

The nice thing about CGI is that you can adapt tons of free CGI programs from the Web to your own server. Go to `http://www.mcp.com/sams/home.html` and check out Selena Sol's CGI script archive. If you're interested in writing your own CGI scripts, `http://hoohoo.ncsa.uiuc.edu/cgi` is the authoritative and original site. CGI is slower than some of the other options offered by PWS, though, so develop new applications with CGI only if you must be able to port the code across older UNIX servers.

Web Scripting: JavaScript, VBScript, and More

Today's most common Web browsers are becoming more sophisticated, and you have probably encountered many pages on the Web that take advantage of the scripting capabilities that they offer. Far from being just a pretty feature of modern Web browsers, though, scripting languages have evolved to become tightly integrated with the Web server, especially in the case of IIS and PWS. In common practice, scripts written using any of the popular scripting languages such as JavaScript are embedded in the HTML of a Web page. When the client Web browser opens the page, it can recognize and process the code contained in the script. Type in the sample HTML document in Listing 29.3, and save it as `c:\inetpub\wwwroot\jsamp.htm`. Then load `http://yourmachinename/jsamp.htm` into a JavaScript-enabled Web browser. For example, a recent version of Netscape Navigator or Internet Explorer will work.

Listing 29.3. jsamp.htm demonstrates JavaScript.

```
<HTML>
  <BODY>

  <SCRIPT Language="JavaScript">
    <!--
      alert("Hi there!")
      Document.Write(Date())
    //-->
  </SCRIPT>

  <INPUT type=button value="red background" onClick="Document.bgColor='red'">
  <INPUT type=button value="go to mcp.com" onClick="location='http://www.mcp.com'">

  </BODY>
</HTML>
```

This simple example should give you a taste of what is possible when you add scripting to your pages. Notice that you can write the code to become active while the page is loading (as in the <SCRIPT> tag here), or you can write it to activate when a certain event happens, like the onClick in the example. If you want to learn more about JavaScript programming, as well as find loads of sample programs to download, point your Web browser to `http://javascript.developer.com`.

JavaScript is not the only scripting language available in your Web pages, although it is probably the best one for you to use. VBScript, available for Microsoft Internet Explorer, allows you to write Visual Basic–style code into your HTML documents. VBScript allows you to take more control of the client Web browser and do some cooler things, but it does not work on Netscape's browsers. To achieve the widest compatibility, you are safer sticking with JavaScript.

> **WARNING**
>
> Internet Explorer actually supports Microsoft's JScript, which is written as a JavaScript-compatible language with a few extra features. If you're writing any JavaScript pages, though, you should be aware that a few JavaScript features are supported by Netscape but not supported by Microsoft's JScript. For a discussion of which features to avoid, check out `http://www.gmccomb.com/javascript/ie30.html`.

In fact, Microsoft's Internet Explorer and PWS both support the ActiveX Scripting model, which is a standard that allows them to use a scripting engine to support practically any scripting language. Scripting engines theoretically could be developed for any popular scripting language, such as Tcl or Python. In fact, fans of the Perl scripting language can download PerlScript, a free Perl scripting engine, from `http://www.activeware.com`.

Forms

Tightly associated with client- and server-side script processing and CGI is the ability to accept user input and process it with forms. PWS processes forms with whichever CGI program is specified in the `Action=` parameter to the `<FORM>` tag. Do you remember the example used to demonstrate CGI? Type in the short example shown in Listing 29.4, and save it as `c:\inetpub\wwwroot\fsamp.htm`. To test it, open `http://yourmachinename/fsamp.htm` and then enter the name of an Internet domain that you know, such as `microsoft.com`.

Listing 29.4. fsamp.htm demonstrates form processing.

```
<HTML>
  <BODY>

  <FORM ACTION="http://www.proximus.com/cgi-bin/freemap" METHOD="GET">
    <INPUT TYPE="TEXT" NAME="Address1">
    <INPUT TYPE="SUBMIT">
  </FORM>

  </BODY>
</HTML>
```

You must admit, this example is pretty simple. The browser tacks together the Action, input field name, and value to create something like `http://www.proximus.com/cgi-bin/freemap?Address1=microsoft.com`. It then calls the server directly, using that as a normal URL. Because your server probably stores the CGI scripts in the /Scripts virtual directory, your `ACTION=` parameter will probably be more like `http://yourmachinename/scripts/process.exe`, but otherwise the concept is the same.

> **TIP**
>
> Creating any but the simplest forms by hand can become frustrating. You will be much happier if you use some design aid here, such as Microsoft FrontPage. If you insist on doing things the hard way, though, `http://www.ncsa.uiuc.edu/SDG/Software/Mosaic/Docs/fill-out-forms/overview.html` will be an invaluable aid.

You can see that form processing takes two parts: the `<FORM>` tag in the HTML file and a CGI (or ISAPI, as you'll read later) program on the server. The example you just reviewed should show you that the CGI program and HTML file do not have to be running on the same server. If you don't want to write your own CGI form processors, you can always download many powerful programs from the Web (see Selena Sol's CGI archive at `www.mcp.com/sams/home.html`).

FrontPage Server Extensions

If you're using Microsoft FrontPage to design your HTML forms, you can use the FrontPage Extensions for Peer Web Services. Even if you already installed the FrontPage Server Extensions when you installed FrontPage, you should download the latest version (free) from Microsoft because there have been a few bug fixes since the original version was released. To do so, follow these steps:

1. Download the latest copy of the extensions from `http://www.microsoft.com/frontpage/softlib/current.htm`. You have to navigate through some licensing forms.

2. Use Windows NT Explorer to find the file that you have saved (fp97ext_x86_enu.exe, if you are using US English), and double-click it.

   FrontPage then installs a set of scripts onto your server. They allow you to process forms without knowing any CGI. Peer Web Services is temporarily stopped while this process takes place.

> **NOTE**
>
> If you have been using FrontPage on a number of machines, you may have noticed that FrontPage offers to install a Web server program if you do not already have one installed. FrontPage calls its Web server program Personal Web Server, but it is *not* the same as the Personal Web Server that is an add-on for Windows 95. The names of the two servers, to be correct, are Microsoft Personal Web Server and FrontPage Personal Web Server. FrontPage Personal Web Server is a very crippled server, lacking many of the IIS features of Microsoft Personal Web Server. Because the Microsoft Personal Web Server is a free download, you really don't need to use the one that comes with FrontPage, unless you just don't feel like taking the time to download the superior server.

If you have a form that you would like to have processed by your PWS WWW Service, take the following steps:

1. Load or create the form in Microsoft FrontPage.
2. Right-click somewhere inside the form on your screen.
3. Choose Form Properties from the pop-up menu.
4. In the Form Handler drop-down list, select the action that you want to take—for example, WebBot Save Results Component.

5. Click the settings button to set any options for the particular bot that you have selected. In this case, type in a filename where you want the results that the user enters into the form to be saved.

Internet Server API (ISAPI)

You can think of ISAPI as a really fast version of CGI, designed especially for Windows NT. The key to ISAPI is that it runs CGI programs as a Dynamic Link Library (DLL) that is loaded into memory only once, rather than an executable file that must be launched every time the process is called. Writing ISAPI applications can be quite a bit more complicated than writing similar CGI code, but from an administrative point of view, the process is identical. To enable an ISAPI application, do the following:

1. Place the ISAPI DLL in a scripts directory.
2. Make sure that the directory has the Execute Permission set (refer to Figure 29.14).
3. Configure any necessary script mapping file associations in the Registry (refer to Figure 29.15). Notice that several ISAPI DLLs are already configured in the Registry. For example, HttpODBC.DLL is an ISAPI program that allows you to export database information dynamically to client Web browsers.

If you would like a list of ISAPI programs that you can download for free or purchase, or if you want some information about how to write ISAPI programs, check out http://www.genusa.com/ isapi/.

Java

Java, not to be confused with JavaScript, is a fully compilable programming language that is designed to create programs that can be run with no change on many different operating systems. Java programs are loaded from the server but executed within the Web browser. So although you might expect to treat Java programs on your server as if they were CGI or ISAPI, you need to treat them more like HTML files. That is, any .java or .class files that you want to use on your server should be placed in Read directories as shown in Figure 29.11 instead of Execute directories like the one in Figure 29.14. The following steps show you how to install a Java applet on your server and reference it correctly from a Web page:

1. For this example, use Sun Microsystems's sample applet, Nervous Text. Just point your Web browser to http://java.sun.com/applets/NervousText/NervousText.class. When asked what to do with this file, just save it to c:\inetpub\wwwroot\NervousText.class.

2. Use Notepad to create a file containing Listing 29.5, and save it as c:\inetpub\wwwroot\javasamp.htm.

Listing 29.5. javasamp.htm loads the Java applet from PWS.

```
<HTML>
  <BODY>

    <APPLET CODE="NervousText.class" WIDTH=200 HEIGHT=50>
      <PARAM NAME=text VALUE="Unleashed!">
    </APPLET>

  </BODY>
</HTML>
```

3. Load `http://yourmachinename/javasamp.htm` into your Web browser. Notice that you can change the value of the text by adjusting the `<PARAM>` tag in the HTML code. If you want to choose from thousands of Java applets that you can download and use in your pages, check out `http://www.gamelan.com`.

Active Server Pages (ASP)

Active Server Pages, or IIS 3.0, is just an extension of the parsed HTML idea that you saw with .STM files. Basically, PWS processes .ASP files much like .STM files and modifies the output before sending the finished product to a Web browser. ASP goes far beyond the capabilities of .STM files, though, by allowing JavaScript and VBScript within the page to be processed by the server *before* it is sent to the client. This capability of PWS is very important because it allows you to take full advantage of VBScript or JavaScript without having to worry about whether your customer's Web browser supports scripting. Try typing the example shown in Listing 29.6 and saving it as `c:\inetpub\scripts\sample.asp`. Remember that ASP programs are really just processed by the ASP DLL, which is an ISAPI program. Therefore, you need to save your .ASP files in a directory that is set to Execute permission, even though the file looks like standard HTML.

Listing 29.6. sample.asp is a sample ASP page.

```
<HTML>
  <BODY>

    <% SET OBJbrowser=Server.CreateObject("MSWC.BrowserType") %>
    Your browser is <% = OBJbrowser.Browser %>
    <P>
    You are connected  from <% = Request.ServerVariables("REMOTE_ADDR") %>
  </BODY>
</HTML>
```

In Listing 29.6, you can see that ASP can determine what sort of browser a user is using as well as the IP address from which he or she is connecting. No doubt this opens up some powerful possibilities! If you want more information on ASP capabilities as well as a tutorial, simply choose Start | Peer Web Services and then select the Active Server Pages Roadmap shortcut.

NOTE

Much of ASP's ability to determine a remote user's browser type and capabilities relies on information stored in the browscap.ini file. To get the latest version of this file, point your Web browser to `http://www.microsoft.com/iis/UsingIIS/Developing/updates.htm`. Download browscap.ini and save it to the `c:\winnt\system32\inetsrv\asp\cmpnts` directory.

Index Server

The Index Server module of PWS is the final feature that I will discuss here. Index Server is designed to be hands-free, so you can or should do very little to configure or tweak the service. If you installed it, it is running right now and waiting for you to run a query. Load `http://yourmachinename/samples/search/queryhit.htm` into your Web browser and enter a search string. You'll get back a listing of every file on your Web server that contains that string. If the output looks like the output of a `www.microsoft.com` site search, that's because Microsoft's site uses Index Server, too! In most cases, the queryhit.htm form is more than adequate as a search form for your site. Of course, you might want to edit the HTML with Notepad or FrontPage to make the search form look a little better, but the basic form can stay the same. If you need a more customized search form, you can find better instructions by clicking the Index Server Online Documentation icon in the Index Server group on your Start menu.

Security: Controlling Who Sees What

PWS offers many features designed to make sure that your files are available to the right people and inaccessible to the wrong people. At the base of PWS security is the permissions that are applied to the NTFS files through Windows NT Explorer. In addition, PWS provides Secure Sockets Layer (SSL) functionality, to protect the data as it is sent over public networks.

Using NTFS File Permissions to Secure Your Files

In the old days, HTTP server administrators controlled access to their files by managing complicated sets of password lists and arcane access-control files with names like .htaccess. Today, you use the Windows NT User Manager and Windows NT Explorer to do the same. Here's how to control access to a file:

1. Make sure that you have an account for the user or group in question. The account does not necessarily have to be a local account on your workstation; it can be a domain account of a domain that you trust or are a member of. If you need help understanding users or groups, take a quick look at Chapter 28, "Users and Groups on NT."

29

USING PEER WEB SERVICES

2. Browse to the file to which you want to apply access control by using Windows NT Explorer. In this case, modify test.htm in the wwwroot directory.

3. Right-click the file and choose Properties from the pop-up menu.

4. In the Properties dialog box, choose the Security tab and then click the Permissions button.

5. In the File Permissions dialog box, shown in Figure 29.16, assign permissions as you want. In this example, I removed permissions for all users and groups except Sally Treadwell.

FIGURE 29.16.

Assigning NTFS permissions to a file.

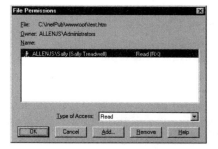

6. To test this arrangement, go to another machine and try to access the file with your Web browser. Unless you are logged on as the user to which you have granted permissions, you won't be allowed to see the Web page!

Windows NT Challenge/Response

If you tried the example in the preceding section from within a Windows NT domain, you may have been surprised that you were allowed to access the Web page without ever being prompted for a username or password. PWS is smart enough to determine the login ID of users who are logged in to its Windows NT domain or a trusted domain, by using Windows NT Challenge/Response authentication with your browser. The authentication process goes roughly as follows:

1. PWS checks to see whether the file has any special access restrictions.

2. If it does, PWS checks with your browser to see whether it supports Challenge/Response authentication.

3. If your browser supports Challenge/Response (currently only Internet Explorer supports this authentication), an encrypted exchange takes place and your Web browser tries to supply the appropriate credentials. If you are logged in under a username that is not granted access, you are given the chance to enter a valid username and password, as shown in Figure 29.17. This information, too, is authenticated using the secure Windows NT domain mechanism.

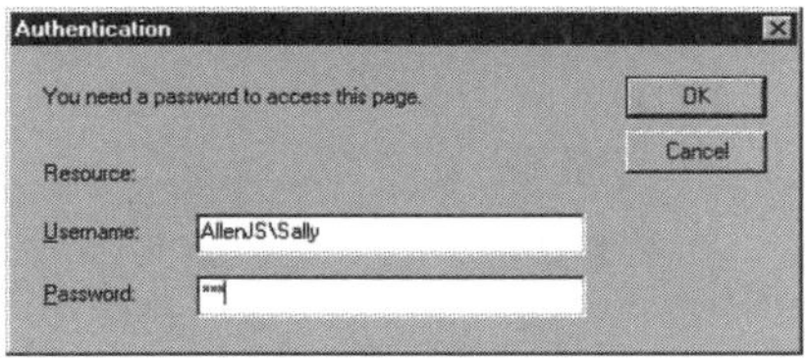

FIGURE 29.17.

*NT Challenge/Response
Authentication.*

4. If this process succeeds, you are given access.

5. For browsers that do not support Challenge/Response, you are presented with a
   similar dialog box for username and password entry but with one important difference. When you enter your username and password, it is sent in clear text over the
   network, where the PWS server then attempts to use the given credentials to access the
   file. If the credentials are good, the file is displayed.

> **NOTE**
>
> Notice the peculiar syntax of *MachineName\Username* in Figure 29.17. By default,
> Challenge/Response assumes that you are logging in to the current domain. If the account
> to which you have assigned permissions is a local machine account, as is the case with
> Sally Treadwell, you need to use the *MachineName\UserName* syntax to specify that the
> account is not a domain account.

From the preceding discussion, you can see that the PWS authentication process has some sticky
areas. Sending passwords and usernames over the Internet unencrypted is certainly not a good
idea, especially if those usernames and passwords are domain accounts within your corporate
Windows NT domain. Take a look back now to Figure 29.8. Notice that Internet Service
Manager allows you to disable the Basic Authentication feature of your HTTP server. If you
clear this check box, PWS allows access to controlled files for only those people who successfully complete a Challenge/Response negotiation. If the browser does not support Challenge/
Response, the user is simply denied access and is not given the opportunity to divulge his or
her passwords over the Internet. This security, however, costs you your ability to support other
Web browsers such as Netscape Navigator. Perhaps a better alternative would be to use SSL
(described later), which encrypts all Web traffic, including the Basic Authentication information.

> **NOTE**
>
> The problems of basic authentication are not unique to PWS. PWS basic authentication
> follows a long tradition of poor password security among the major HTTP servers. In fact,
>
> *continues*

continued

most HTTP servers support only basic authentication. The ability of PWS and IIS to use Challenge/Response authentication is a big step forward for Web security. Of course, SSL is another industry-wide method of protecting passwords and data, but SSL is not free. Refer to the section on SSL, later in this chapter.

The `IUSR_ComputerName` Account

Before PWS even attempts to use Challenge/Response or Basic Authentication, it first checks to see whether any authentication is necessary. One obvious case in which authentication would not be necessary is if the Everyone group had been assigned NTFS read permission to the file. More specifically, PWS checks to see whether the special account, `IUSR_ComputerName`, has access to a file before allowing it to be viewed. This account is automatically created and assigned a random password when you install PWS (see Figure 29.18). You can grant or deny access to certain files by granting or denying NTFS permissions for this account.

Figure 29.18.

User Manager, showing the `IUSR_ComputerName` *account (in this case,* `IUSR_ALLENJS`).

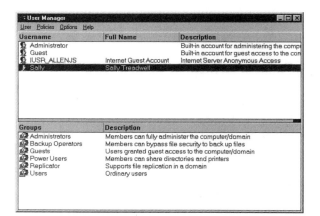

NOTE

You probably will never need to log in to the `IUSR_ComputerName` account, so it is not important that the password is randomly assigned. If, however, you ever need to re-create this account or change the password, you need to make sure that PWS knows that it has changed. The first place to modify this is the Services icon in the Control Panel, where you need to enter the new name and password for the Peer Web Server Service to run under. Next, you have to modify the Anonymous Connection information for your services, using Internet Service Manager. Figure 29.8 shows the appropriate dialog box for the WWW service, and Figure 29.19 shows the FTP service properties.

IUSR_ComputerName and FTP

Look at the FTP Service Properties dialog box, shown in Figure 29.19. You can see that the FTP Service handles nonauthenticated access much like the WWW service does.

FIGURE 29.19.

The FTP Service Properties dialog box, showing Anonymous access settings.

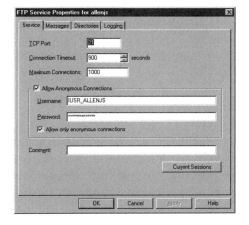

Authenticated access, however, is handled differently. Because there is no such thing as Challenge/Response for FTP, all authentication information is sent unencrypted over the network. Of course, PWS checks the NTFS permissions the same way and allows users to access only files that have permissions to the login that they have used to connect to your FTP server. For example, you could disable users from doing a DIR of a particular directory by revoking directory list permissions on that directory to the IUSR_ComputerName account. If you accept connections over the Internet, though, keeping the Allow only anonymous connections option checked is probably best. If you really have to allow people to log into your FTP server using secure accounts, you might want to think about setting up the accounts as local machine accounts on the PWS Workstation rather than using domain credentials. Use different passwords than the ones that you use on the domain so that damage will be minimized if your passwords are stolen.

> **NOTE**
>
> The username and password configured in the Allow Anonymous Connections section of the FTP Services Properties dialog box (refer to Figure 29.19) are not to be confused with Anonymous FTP login. The username and password that you type into this dialog box are the username and password that PWS uses to check file permissions, not the username and password that a user uses to gain anonymous access to your FTP server. To gain anonymous access, your users continue to use the username anonymous and the password email@machine.com that is standard for Anonymous FTP. In fact, if you try to log in to the server using IUSR_ComputerName and the appropriate password, the server tries to log you in as an authenticated user.

> **NOTE**
>
> Be careful of permissions for virtual directories that point to network shares such as Novell servers. The permissions for these resources are granted based on the permissions of the username and password that you specified when you created the virtual directory (refer to Figure 29.11) rather than the username and password of the user who is browsing the files. Naturally, you do not want to configure a virtual directory with a username and password that have more privileges than are absolutely necessary.

Secure Sockets Layer (SSL)

The final word in HTTP security is Secure Sockets Layer (SSL), a standard developed by Netscape. SSL uses public-key encryption to securely trade encryption information that is used during a session to protect all traffic from anyone who might be snooping. The standard SSL configuration is very secure. SSL protects your passwords from snoops, without even requiring Challenge/Response capability, but it goes even a step further. SSL encrypts *all* your data. If you're going to be exchanging credit card information or any other highly sensitive information, you need to use SSL. SSL is supported by PWS as a standard feature. To set up your server to use SSL, follow these steps:

1. Load Internet Service Manager, and click on the Key Manager toolbar button (refer to Figure 29.7).
2. Choose Key | Create New Key.
3. Fill in the dialog box, as shown in Figure 29.20. Click the Help button for more detailed instructions on what information is expected in these fields.

FIGURE 29.20.

SSL key generation.

4. Click OK and save the key. You have to verify the password that you typed into the dialog box.

5. If you're familiar with public key encryption, you know that the keys used for encryption come in pairs—a Public key and a Private key. For Web browsers to trust that you are who you say you are, your public key has to be digitally signed by some trusted third party. Your server cannot use SSL communications until your key has been signed by a trusted Certificate Authority, or CA. Point your Web browser to `http://www.verisign.com` to find out how to get your certificate signed. Certificate signing is not free, and must be renewed from year to year. Luckily, however, VeriSign gives you a two-week free trial of the signature before you have to pay, and the cost is not too high if you will be transferring sensitive data.

6. Paste your key file (in the example, c:\KeyCorpWWW.req), into the online request form and fill out the other appropriate information.

7. When you receive your signed certificate (basically a text file with a bunch of garbled characters in it), install it by choosing Key | Install Key Certificate from the pull-down menus of Key Manager.

8. Browse to the text file containing your signed key, which you received from VeriSign.

9. Enter the password that you used when generating the original key.

10. Choose Server | Commit Changes Now from the menu.

That's it! Users then can open files securely from your server by using the URL `https://` *yourmachinename*. (The `https://` protocol specifier tells the browser to connect using SSL to port 443 rather than the standard `http://` port 80.) Keep in mind, though, that users still have the option of connecting to your server with the `http://` port, thus bypassing your carefully configured SSL. If you have any directories that you absolutely cannot be accessed unencrypted, you should select the Require secure SSL channel check box at the bottom of the WWW Services Directory Properties sheet for that directory (accessed through Internet Service Manager). As Figure 29.11 shows, this option is disabled if SSL is not installed on your machine with a signed certificate.

Summary

In summary, Peer Web Services is a powerful suite of Internet Servers that you can install on your Workstation. Peer Web Services can be configured to publish nearly any type of content, from plain files to Java programs. PWS enables you to fully integrate with your existing network infrastructure, and its wide range of security features mean that you can be comfortable with even the strictest of access-control requirements. Though it lacks some of the enterprise scalability features of IIS, PWS makes a good Internet server and a great intranet server.

Setting Up an Intranet

by Joshua Allen

IN THIS CHAPTER

CHAPTER 30

Chapter 29, "Using Peer Web Services," showed you how to configure an individual Windows NT Workstation as an Internet server. At the most basic level, an *intranet* is just a collection of Internet-enabled machines within an organization. Users within the organization use Web browsers to access these internal corporate servers to retrieve information and do day-to-day work. This chapter gives you the information you need to begin tying your individual workstations together to create an easily accessible intranet. You explore the wide range of technologies that are available for creating your intranet and learn tips on integrating with existing systems within your enterprise.

What Good Is an Intranet?

Intranets are simply internal organizational networks that use Internet-style technologies to get work done. The growth of the Internet has taught us scores of new ways to get value out of widely separated machines in complex networks. Although you may be suspicious of the hype that surrounds intranets, there is solid evidence to support much of it. Far from the theoretical benefits that object technology and client/server offered, multitudes of real-world companies have already saved money and streamlined their operations by using intranet technologies.

WHAT-NET?

You have probably guessed that the word *intranet* was coined as a mutation of the word *Internet*, but you might not be familiar with the rest of the history behind these words. In the beginning, computer networks were LANs (Local Area Networks—networks within a building) and WANs (Wide Area Networks—networks that spanned across larger geographical regions). As universities and companies began to set up links between their networks and the networks of their partners, a new class of network emerged: *internets*. These internets (or *internetworks*) were just networks that joined different LANs and WANs together. These days, it is difficult to find a network that does not have a link to every other network in the world through some combination of internets. We call this ubiquitous network of internets the *Internet*. Notice that only the mother of all internets gets a capital *I*. Technically, an *intranet* is just a WAN or LAN that is configured to use common Internet technologies. As the boundaries between client/server and Internet begin to fade, it is becoming more difficult to tell the difference between a WAN and an intranet. Many companies like to use the term *infranet* rather than *intranet*, to denote that the network is used for infrastructure activities. Another fresh term is *extranet*, which refers to networks that are built by connecting portions of company intranets to other companies' intranets.

The simplest way to put a intranet to work for your organization is by using it to publish corporate documentation in electronic format. Many large companies today make their employee policy manuals available only through the internal network using a Web browser. The company saves money on printing costs, and employees gain by being able to search the online policies much more easily than browsing a paper copy. Companies save especially on printing costs by migrating those documents that require continual updating (company phone books or newsletters, for example). In the case of corporate newsletters, you can see that companies could also benefit from reduced duplication of effort by making the same document available to customers on the external Internet. Because intranets use standard Internet technologies, it is relatively easy for you to make internal resources available to the outside world, if you choose.

> **WARNING**
>
> The fact that intranets use standard Internet technologies makes it easy for you to offer corporate resources to the outside world, but it also means that it is easier for people in the outside world to get at data that you might not want them to see. If you are going to be connecting your intranet to the Internet, be sure to read the section titled "Connecting Your Intranet to the Internet," later in the chapter.

In the case of online phone listings, organizations can take advantage of more than just reduced printing costs. Most intranets allow the users to access data dynamically from existing company database systems. This means that you can continue to update your company information databases the way you currently do, and your users will always see the latest information through their Web browsers, without your ever having to regenerate a Web page. Figure 30.1 illustrates a simple network, with PC1 accessing a database directly and PC2 using a Web browser to see the data. Notice that the Web server acts as a gateway between the client Web browser and the database—the client never actually talks directly to the database server. One obvious benefit of this is that you can switch between different database architectures by making only one change on the server rather than multiple changes on each client; less obvious benefits become apparent when you use databases with distributed transactions. You can read more about this in the section titled "Database Access," later in this chapter.

FIGURE 30.1.

How databases interact with the intranet.

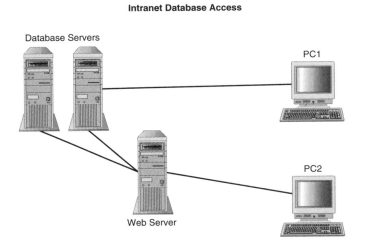

Intranet Database Access

Database Servers

PC1

Web Server

PC2

30

SETTING UP AN INTRANET

Of course, the database independence that placing a Web server between the client and database offers is not the only way to use an intranet to benefit from open standards. If you have been involved with any sort of client development using any of the popular tools today, such as Delphi, Visual Basic, or PowerBuilder, you already know that none of these products are compatible with one another. Web-based clients, on the other hand, all use HTML and can be used interchangeably. If Microsoft decides to start charging huge fees for its Web browser, you can switch to Netscape. Developing your clients for HTML rather than vendor-specific tools can help you avoid being locked in to a single vendor. Vendor-specific client-development tools often have another serious deficiency relative to Web-based applications: many of these products are available on only one operating system, or they have complicated porting procedures. Web browsers are available for every platform, meaning that you can write your intranet applications once and then use them on any operating system. In fact, many corporations today are using intranet technologies instead of the client/server tools they would have used two years ago to deploy critical systems such as accounts payable and order processing. For all practical purposes, you can think of an intranet as a client/server environment that uses totally open standards.

> **NOTE**
>
> Although client/server tool companies seem the most threatened by the advent of the intranet, most of these companies have responded in positive and innovative ways. Client/server giants such as PowerSoft and Borland now offer full integration with intranet technologies, competing on the basis of making your development job easier rather than on locking you into their own proprietary interfaces. Far from hurting these companies, the growth of intranet technology will probably make their products even more attractive to companies.

Putting the Intranet in Perspective

With the promise of universal open standards (and by extension, a way for developers to get work done without having to learn different competing development standards) you can see why IT managers are drooling over intranets. But be warned, intranets are not going to cure all of your ills. Although current intranets are often viewed as a way to harness the power of client/server without the hassles, there are still a few problems that you'll want to consider before deciding just how far to propagate this newfound wonder solution.

To begin, there are certain applications that you'll not want to be intranet-based. Applications that require very complex user interaction or processor usage, such as CAD programs, are not well suited to intranet deployment. Stick with traditional database-centric or workflow-centric applications for your intranet.

Another mistake that people often make when evaluating intranet usage is to assume that development and administration will be easier, just because intranets are easier for the general users to use. This is not always true, however. Using an intranet is easy for most users, because they have been using a Web browser at home for quite a while and are comfortable with this technology. But how many of your developers have been building intranets? You probably have more than a few COBOL programmers in your facility who are still resentful at being forced to learn C++. Changing the tables yet again is sure to be slow, painful, and expensive. Intranet-building expertise is still relatively rare, so even outsourcing intranet work can be very expensive today. As time progresses, the expertise required to build and administer intranets will probably become more common, but for now you should be realistic about how much it is going to cost. You might want to consider using intranet technologies that capitalize on developers current skills, such as Visual Basic or PowerBuilder. Of course, you save money on retraining costs, but you might stand to lose more by being locked into a vendor-specific solution. The benefits that you can gain by standardization on a single vendor technology are often at odds with the benefits that you gain by keeping your options open. In many cases, it can make sense to standardize on a vendor-specific solution, even though you sacrifice openness. Where you place the balance is up to you, but it should be decided carefully. The majority of this chapter will introduce the various technologies you can use to build your intranet and will give you a good idea of what tradeoffs each makes in terms of openness versus ease of use. These distinctions are complex and often very subtle; you'll want to evaluate carefully before committing to any of the available products.

A final problem that many corporations find with the intranet concept is that it does not lend itself well to a hierarchical management model. Although you could arrange your intranet servers in a pyramid-like structure, where lesser servers depended on more controlled, centralized servers, you probably would not be very successful. Intranets thrive best in an environment where responsibility for various servers is decentralized and dispersed across the organization. Chances are, much of the data on your intranet will be housed on Windows NT 4 workstations or servers located in various departments across the company. Links across servers tend to develop in a chaotic, Web-like fashion, rather than in a drill-down, outline fashion. In organizations with successful intranet projects, top management makes sure that the various segments fit nicely together and do not duplicate effort, but it does not attempt to engineer the entire system. If your company is more comfortable with a management style that is top-down and centrally engineered, you might want to stick with solutions that fit that model better.

Operating in an environment where servers and responsibility are decentralized presents new problems. No doubt you have seen pages on the Internet that purport to show current information but have not been updated for months or even years. When you allow various organizational units to be responsible for their own information, you also run the danger of having much of your data be perpetually out of date. You can address this issue by clever use of source-code control tools such as Visual SourceSafe or RCS, or you can try monitoring tactics like the one described in Chapter 29 in the section "Server Logging." You could also encourage your departments to use site management tools such as Microsoft Site Server. In any case, though, you should expect to expend significantly more energy keeping things current than you would in a more centralized system.

Another problem caused by the decentralized nature of intranets is that server management becomes very complex. Imagine, for example, that your accounting department is moving its intranet applications to a new server. Obviously, you'll have to tell all the users of the accounting applications to use the new URL. However, the real problem is less obvious—what do you do about all of the other departmental pages that have added hyperlinks from their pages to various pages on the accounting site? Each department in the company will have to search through their entire site and fix any hyperlinks that they have created or else risk having users get the dreaded HTTP/1.0 404 Object Not Found error. In fact, your accounting department need not move the server to cause this error; even relocating a directory on the server can cause these problems. This should make clear to you that it is wise to plan a reasonable directory structure *before* publishing information to the intranet. Once you have made data available, many departments within the company may begin depending on your directory locations, without implicitly notifying you. Any changes that you make could possibly cause grief to other departments that have grown to rely on your old conventions. To some degree, you can manage server moves by prudent use of WINS and DNS, as described later, and you can manage directory moves by using virtual directories as described in Chapter 29. Another trick you can use to ease a transition is illustrated in Listing 30.1. This sample HTML file shows how to redirect a user to a page's new location in a different directory or on a different server. Just save this file atop the old file, and change the URL to reflect the file's new location. Using this technique during a transition period can ease some of the problems that your move might cause.

Listing 30.1. redirect.htm: managing relocated documents.

```
<HTML>
<HEAD>
  <TITLE>Page Has Moved!</TITLE>
  <META HTTP-EQUIV=REFRESH CONTENT="1; URL=http://www.mcp.com">
</HEAD>
<BODY>
This page has moved to <A HREF="http://www.mcp.com">
http://www.mcp.com</A>
<P>
If your browser does not automatically transfer you
to the new location, please click the link above.
</BODY>
</HTML>
```

Intranet Building Blocks

Now that you know what you are getting into, it is time to discuss the various technologies that you'll use to build your intranet. At a basic level, you could put Internet Explorer (discussed in Chapter 23, "Using Microsoft Internet Explorer 4") on all of your client workstations and configure a few departmental workstations with Peer Web Services (discussed in Chapter 29) and then call it a day. However, an intranet is much more than the Web browsers and servers it uses. An intranet is built by making all your resources, including Web browsers,

Web servers, database servers, and legacy applications, work together. There are a number of technologies that you'll need to integrate into your Windows NT environment to build a successful intranet. This section discusses the various components that you need to understand, evaluate, and apply to create your intranet.

The Network

The way that you have configured your network will play a large role in determining the usefulness of your intranet. At the very least, all your client machines and intranet servers should be using TCP/IP. If you are using Windows NT as your server operating system on the network, you'll likely have already configured things to use TCP/IP. It is possible to operate an intranet over protocols other than TCP/IP by using protocol converter products built into proxy servers (see www.ftp.com, www.novell.com/border, www.microsoft.com/proxy); however, I don't recommend it. If your IT department doesn't have the expertise to move away from these older protocols, you probably shouldn't be building intranets.

Next, you should make sure that you're using WINS for name resolution on all of your Windows-based machines. Configure your DNS server to interface with your WINS server and consider using DHCP for dynamic addressing. For more details on installing WINS, DNS, or DHCP servers, refer to the Windows NT Server 4 networking supplement. Figure 30.2 illustrates the process of name resolution that takes place in a Windows NT 4 intranet.

FIGURE 30.2.

Intranet name resolution using WINS and DNS.

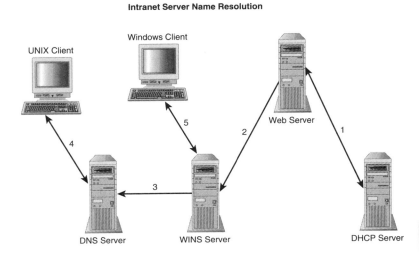

Intranet Server Name Resolution

Here's how it works:

1. When a Web Server (possibly a workstation with Peer Web Services enabled) is powered on, it requests an IP address from the DHCP server. The DHCP server responds by assigning a valid IP address. If your network uses static IP addressing, this step would be skipped, but the remaining steps are the same.

2. The intranet server then registers its name and IP address with the WINS server.

3. The DNS server is aware of the WINS server and is prepared to answer queries for the IP address of the newly booted machine.

4. Any non-Windows machines on your network will have to use a DNS name to access your server. This name will be something like `http://yourserver.yourcompany.com`. Figure 30.2 shows a UNIX machine requesting the IP address of the Web server from your DNS server. The DNS server returns the address that it has discovered through WINS, and the UNIX client is able to access your Web server.

5. When a Windows-based client, such as NT Workstation 4 with Internet Explorer, requests a connection using a name like `http://yourserver`, the IP address resolution is processed directly by the WINS server.

Clearly, you could leave the DNS server out of this picture if you do not need to support non-Windows clients. But even if your entire network is built of WINS-enabled clients, you still might want to leave the DNS service enabled. First, you'll need to have DNS enabled if you want to make any of your internal servers available to clients on the external Internet. Second, DNS enables you to do round-robin load balancing. For example, suppose that you have a server that is constantly being accessed and is having a hard time keeping up with the load. You could mirror the server to multiple machines, as shown in Figure 30.3. Then you would set up three records on your DNS server, each with the same name but with different IP addresses. The DNS server then distributes requests evenly across all the servers. This will work with DHCP and WINS, as well; you would simply have to point your DNS records to the WINS name rather than the IP address (of course, you would have to pick a DNS name that was not the same as any of the WINS names, in this case). You can find a detailed discussion of DNS configuration issues in the Windows NT Server 4 networking supplement.

If you can, avoid giving your machines names that include the underscore character. Although, Windows NT allows underscores in machine names, many programs based on Internet standards and ported to Windows NT still have difficulty with underscores in names.

Finally, you should plan carefully how you are going to manage access to your intranet servers. This is where you'll be especially glad that you are using a Windows NT network model. Peer Web Services and IIS are tightly integrated with Windows NT domain security. By default, the Local Administrators group includes the Domain Administrators group (see Chapter 28, "Users and Groups on NT"); therefore, you'll be able to administer any intranet server in any domain for which you have Administrator privileges. If your situation requires different parameters, you should devise an appropriate strategy for organizing permissions before you begin serious intranet development. If possible, you should configure all your intranet servers to require challenge/response authentication. Chapter 29 includes a full discussion of the pros and cons of this.

FIGURE 30.3.
Round-robin load balancing.

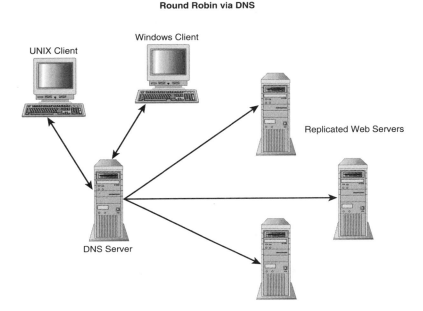

Round Robin via DNS

The Web Browser: Client Scripting
===

The Web Browser: Client Scripting

The next important component of your intranet is the Web browser. Specifically, you'll want to weigh the benefits that you might gain from using a particular browser against the benefits that you gain by developing vanilla code that works on any browser. Of course, all browsers support standard HTML, so that is not a problem. However, if you intend to do any serious intranet development, you'll need a browser that allows client-side scripting. Client-side scripting allows you to write code directly into your Web pages that is executed on the client machine when the user downloads the page. Chapter 29 introduces you to some of the things you can do with client-side scripting.

Today, the browsers that support serious client-side scripting are Internet Explorer, Netscape Navigator, and a few others. The level of scripting that each of the popular browsers supports is somewhat different, and the differences are significant enough to influence your intranet planning process. Recall from Chapter 29 that all of the scripting browsers support at least basic JavaScript. This is probably your best choice for intranet development if you are concerned about being locked into a specific browser. As far as your browser is concerned, though, it might not be such a terrible thing to be tied to one vendor, if that vendor is Microsoft. First, consider that Internet Explorer is free and will probably continue to be, because Microsoft regards it as part of the base operating system. Second, Internet Explorer enables you to use NT Challenge/Response authentication, which is going to make your job as an administrator much easier.

30

SETTING UP AN
INTRANET

Finally, IE supports VBScript, which will be a relief to your developers who know Visual Basic but have not taken the time to become fluent with Java or C++. Standardization of any software can also reduce your support and administrative costs considerably, especially when that software is a client piece that will be distributed to all the machines in your enterprise, such as a Web browser. Supporting two different brands of Web browser will cost your Help desk roughly twice as much as will supporting just one brand. On the other hand, if you have many UNIX clients, you'll probably want to stick with JavaScript, because your JavaScript code will behave nicely even on UNIX clients running Netscape Navigator.

The Web Browser: Client Programming (Plug-Ins and Java)

JavaScript or VBScript code is embedded directly in your Web page and executed by the browser when somebody accesses the page. This code is actually interpreted, however, and is not executed directly by the client operating system. If you want to take full advantage of the speed and capabilities of the client machine, you'll need to use some sort of plug-in. A *plug-in* is a piece of code that is compiled specifically for the client operating system and has special code that lets it tie into the Web browser. There are two popular plug-in standards for you to choose from: Netscape plug-ins and ActiveX. There is really not much difference between the two standards. Internet Explorer will allow you to use Netscape plug-ins or ActiveX plug-ins, and Netscape supports both also (ActiveX support for Netscape Navigator is a free add-on, available at `http://www.ncompasslabs.com`). The important thing to remember about plug-ins, though, is that they are platform-dependent. In other words, a plug-in built for 32-bit Windows (NT and 95) will not work on Windows 3.*x* or UNIX. Of course, this is the price you pay for having direct access to the features of the operating system.

If you need to have access to operating system features that are not available through your scripting language, but you want to have platform independence, you can use Java applets. Java applets are compiled like plug-ins, but they run on any operating system, unmodified. This can be more than a little misleading, though. If you take unquestioningly this description of Java applets and listen to all the hype surrounding Java, you could become very excited. In reality, however, Java is simply an intermediate step between a scripting language and a compiled language. If you have had any computer science courses (or even if you haven't), you might have been wondering how it is that a Java program can be compiled once and then run unmodified on any chipset or operating system. The answer, of course, is that Java is not really compiled in the same sense that normal plug-ins are compiled. Java code is compiled into a format that can then be executed by an interpreter on the client called a Java Virtual Machine. Of course, when you call it a "Java Virtual Machine" and it is separate from your Web browser, it is not so easy to think of it as an interpreter; thus, it is easy to become confused. To keep things clear in your mind, just think of Java applets as being both compiled *and* interpreted. Compiled means that you do not have to give out source code with your applets, and the applets run a little bit faster on the client. Interpreted means that it will run on any machine that has a Java interpreter (which means practically any machine that you buy today).

> **NOTE**
>
> As if the whole Java interpreted/compiled situation isn't confusing enough, hardware makers are rushing in to give us more to think about. Sun Microsystems is now manufacturing chips that execute Java code directly, without requiring a "virtual machine" to interpret the code. Other companies, including IBM, are also working on Java chips that will execute Java code directly. Of course, machines built on these chips will require an operating system, and at last check, Windows NT was programmed for the Intel and Alpha chipsets, but not the Sun Java chip. But wait—that seems to be the point! Sun is banking on the fact that a machine built on non-Microsoft operating system and non-Intel hardware will be attractive to consumers. Microsoft takes this threat very seriously, but it remains to be seen whether consumers will abandon their Microsoft/Intel infrastructures to adopt an operating system and hardware platform that is less than a year old.

The Web Server: Server-Side Programming

Chapter 29 introduces you to the concept of server-side execution of programs: CGI and ISAPI in the case of Peer Web Services. Server-side code is compiled specifically for the operating system and chipset on which the intranet server resides. This code is executed in response to a request from a Web browser, and the result is passed back to the Web browser for processing. In most cases, you'll not have to be very concerned about which server-side execution model you choose. For starters, you should probably be doing most of your server-side programming in a scripting language (this is discussed later in this section). Scripts are admittedly slower to execute than compiled programs, but this is not so important in the case of server-side code. Adding processing power to an individual server is much less expensive than adding resources to a multitude of clients, where the choice of compiled versus scripted code is more important. Also, compiled code is not really that much faster than scripted code on the server and can sometimes be slower (if you are using straight CGI). All of the popular Web servers for Windows NT support Common Gateway Interface (CGI). One problem with CGI, though, is that it requires the server-side CGI .EXE file to be launched every time that the client Web browser makes a request, which really hogs server resources. The popular Web server programs have addressed this issue by making available a form of CGI that uses Dynamic Link Libraries (DLLs), rather than executables, to service the client Web browser's request. This allows the program to be loaded once and then quickly accessed on subsequent requests. Here you need to tread carefully, though, because these DLL standards are all incompatible. Although they do basically the same thing, you'll have to use NSAPI with Netscape Servers, ISAPI with PWS and IIS, and WSAPI with WebSite. Don't let this scare you away from using these interfaces, though, if there is a clear need; the standards are similar enough that you could convert to a different server standard without too much effort.

Notice that all of the server-side programming mentioned so far is platform-specific, and especially specific to Windows NT. It is possible, however, to write platform-independent server-side code with CGI. Much of the CGI on the Internet is written using a language called Perl. Of course, Perl is an interpreted scripting language, but in common use, Perl programs are executed when a Web browser makes a request that launches a Perl interpreter as a CGI process on the server. On the server, the Perl interpreter is just an executable like any other and, thus, lends itself nicely to CGI. Excellent Perl interpreters are available at no charge for all versions of UNIX and Windows; therefore, Perl has often been chosen as a way to write server-side code that can be run on servers that reside on any operating system.

The Web Server: Server-Side Scripting

Your choice of a server-side scripting tool is probably the most important choice you'll make in choosing your intranet technologies. Server-side scripts are embedded in pages at the server and are processed by the server before the results are passed back to the client Web browser. The intranet programming model is very server-centric—most of the processing is done on the server, with the client Web browser being used only to collect input and display output. Because of this, most of the code for your intranet applications will reside on the server. Also, most of your server-based code will be created using some sort of server scripting language. To be sure, you want to be especially careful in your choice. With such an important choice to make, it is only natural that the available options are unnaturally complex with some wicked little subtleties to trip you up. The following paragraphs will give you a clearer picture of what the major offerings are so that you can ponder for yourself what your strategy will be.

Assuming that your intranet is built on Windows NT, you should consider Active Server Pages (see http://www.microsoft.com/iis). ASP is discussed in Chapter 29. ASP allows you to write your server-side scripts using VBScript, JavaScript, or any other ActiveX scripting engine (ActiveX scripting engines are also discussed in Chapter 29). ASP is tightly integrated with Windows NT and the rest of the BackOffice Suite. (For free sample applications that show you how to build intranet applications using ASP with such products as Microsoft Exchange Server and Microsoft SQL Server, check out http://www.microsoft.com/intranet.) ASP gives you access to any ODBC database. And finally, ASP is free with IIS. There is only one catch: all your ASP scripts will be useless if you ever move your Web server to a non-Windows operating system or a non-Microsoft Web server. Considering the effort that a conversion and retraining of developers would require, selecting ASP as your server scripting language is basically the same as saying that you'll always use Windows NT and IIS (or PWS) for your Web servers.

On the other hand, you could use Netscape's LiveWire (see http://home.netscape.com/comprod/server_central/product/livewire/). LiveWire uses JavaScript and runs on any Netscape server, including the ones that run on UNIX. LiveWire also supports ODBC access. LiveWire is free when you buy any of Netscape's servers. But here, too, there is a catch. LiveWire scripts are useless on any non-Netscape Web servers. Remember that the code you write on the server side is the most important component of your intranet. Considering that it would be very expensive to convert large amounts of LiveWire code to ASP or another scripting system, your choice to use LiveWire is basically the same as saying that you'll always use Netscape servers. Of course, you are no longer locked into using Windows NT, but you are also denied some of the great integration and other features that IIS and PWS offer. And it is a shame to waste those free licenses of PWS and IIS.

At first glance, both ASP and LiveWire seem very attractive. Both of these options can be very intimidating, though, when you realize the vendor commitments that you'll have to make with the code that forms the most important part of your intranet. Remember that one of the primary reasons for building an intranet is to isolate yourself from future vendor-specific changes. Depending on what your vision of the future is, either of the scripting environments we've discussed might seem so restrictive as to cancel out much of the perceived benefit of building an intranet.

A third option to consider is a third-party scripting package. Although Microsoft and Netscape get their profits by making sure that you stick with their servers, third-party software companies get money by making sure that their software works on any server that you choose. There are plenty of third-party intranet development packages available. Borland IntraBuilder (www.borland.com) is representative of the more popular packages. IntraBuilder is built to run on top of ISAPI, NSAPI, or WSAPI. This means that scripts you write with IntraBuilder can be run on Netscape, Microsoft, or O'Reilley servers without modification. IntraBuilder's scripting language is JavaScript, and it can interact with ActiveX or Java objects. IntraBuilder can access any ODBC database. Of course, third-party intranet scripting packages are not as tightly integrated with their Web servers as the vendor-specific languages are, and in the case of IntraBuilder, you don't achieve absolute vendor independence, because it won't run on UNIX. Also, as you move to lesser-known third-party solutions, you might have to deal with difficult-to-learn languages and shortages of qualified developers.

Finally, you might be thinking that the choices presented here are artificially restrictive. There is certainly no law that says that you cannot use more than one scripting technology on your intranet, and besides, your intranet is decentralized, so perhaps you should let your various departments decide which scripting model they will use. Especially given the possibility that your organization could end up dependent on one technology, it seems wise to cultivate expertise in more than one scripting environment. Of course, you'll waste company resources by duplicating effort in many areas, but this may be the insurance policy you need. When you are considering what route to take, also consider what impact each has on the previous technologies listed. For example, if you have decided to use VBScript as your client-side scripting model, but decide to use IntraBuilder for server-side scripts, your developers will have to be fluent in both JavaScript and VBScript. In any case, making this choice will be a thorough test of your decision-making skills.

30

Setting Up an Intranet

Database Access

The way in which you access corporate databases will be largely dependent on the server-side scripting model you choose. Listing 30.2 is an example of database access using ASP, which is free with Windows NT Workstation 4.

Listing 30.2. `dbtest.asp`: managing relocated documents.

```
<HTML>
<BODY>
<%
  If IsEmpty(Request("EmpID")) Then
    Response.Write("Enter an Employee ID to do a Lookup")
  Else
    Set EmpDB = Server.CreateObject("ADODB.Connection")
    EmpDB.Open "EmpTestDB"
    Qry = "SELECT * FROM Employees WHERE [Employee ID] = '" & Request("EmpID")
    ➥& "'"
    Set RSEmployee = EmpDB.Execute(Qry)
    If RSEmployee.BOF And RSEmployee.EOF Then
      Response.Write(Request("EmpID") & " doesn't exist")
    Else
      Response.Write(Request("EmpID") & " is " & RSEmployee("Employee Name"))
    End If
  End If
%>
<P>
<FORM METHOD="POST" ACTION="dbtest.asp">
  Enter an Employee ID:
  <INPUT TYPE="TEXT" NAME="EmpID">
  <INPUT TYPE="SUBMIT">
</FORM>
</BODY>
</HTML>
```

For an example of how this script works, follow these steps:

1. Open Microsoft Access and create a new database named `c:\test.mdb`. Create a new table named Employees and open it in Design View. (If you do not have Microsoft Access, you can follow along these steps with another ODBC database, but you'll have to modify Listing 30.2 to match your database.)

2. Modify the Employee table's design to include two fields, Employee ID and Employee Name, as shown in Figure 30.4.

3. Save the table's design and add a few records to the table with whatever Employee IDs and names you like.

4. Close Microsoft Access. ASP will have trouble querying the database if another program has it open in exclusive mode.

5. Open the ODBC applet by selecting Start | Settings | Control Panel and then double-clicking ODBC.

6. Select the System DSN (Data Source Name) tab and click the Add button. Choose Microsoft Access Driver (or whatever database type you are using) and press the Finish button, as shown in Figure 30.5.

FIGURE 30.4.

Creating the test.mdb *Employees table.*

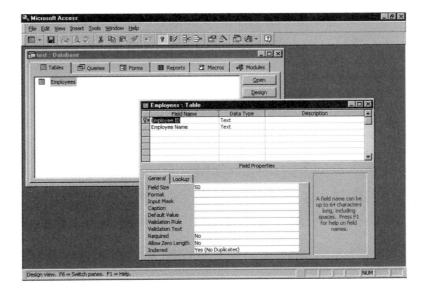

FIGURE 30.5.

Adding an ODBC system DSN.

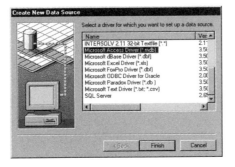

7. Enter EmpTestDB as the data source name and press the Select button to choose the location of the .mdb file, as shown in Figure 30.6.

8. Now save the text of Listing 30.2 as c:\inetpub\scripts\dbtest.asp.

9. Test it by loading http://yourmachine/scripts/dbtest.asp into a Web browser. Try typing an employee ID into the form and pressing the Submit button. If you are at all accustomed to writing database-access routines with Visual Basic or VBA, this should all seem pretty simple to you. In this example, you are using the ASP default VBScript to access the test database, so the syntax should be pretty much familiar to you.

30

SETTING UP AN
INTRANET

FIGURE 30.6.

Entering DSN parameters.

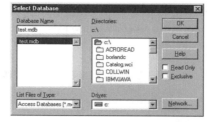

Although you might use a different scripting package than ASP, the general concept will be the same. Basically, you set up an ODBC name to point to a database and then you use your scripting language to translate Web browser requests into ODBC calls. Notice that this strategy allows you to migrate the test.mdb database to a remote Oracle server without ever having to change a single line of code on the Web server, simply by changing the DSN to point to the new Oracle database.

SQL, ODBC, AND JDBC

ODBC, or the Open Database Connectivity standard, is a set of standard functions that was developed to allow you to access databases from different vendors without having to use a different set of API function calls for each one. Regardless of which Web scripting model you choose, you'll probably be using ODBC to access your database. When you build a query or an update statement to the database, you write it using Structured Query Language, or SQL, a standard database query language developed a few decades ago. You pass the SQL statement (SELECT * from Customers, for example) to the ODBC driver, which then passes the request to the database server. SQL was intended to be a universal language for database access, but many database vendors use versions of SQL that are modified to take advantage of special features of their databases. ODBC gets around this problem by using its own version of SQL that offers a common denominator between the various databases. This means that you need to use ODBC SQL to access your Oracle databases, even if you are accustomed to using Oracle SQL. (In cases where you have to use a vendor-specific feature, ODBC allows SQL "pass-through," but this is not recommended because it sort of defeats the database independence of ODBC.) Finally, JDBC is the Java analogue to ODBC. If you are writing routines to read a database from a Java program, you'll need to use the JDBC API, which is really just a refinement of the ODBC specification. In fact, the Intersolv JDBC/ODBC bridge allows you to use ODBC database drivers from within your Java programs.

Whatever scripting package you choose will probably give you adequate access to your typical corporate databases. Even if you use any sort of distributed database transaction-processing middleware at your company, such as BEA Systems' Tuxedo or the new Microsoft Transaction Server, you'll not have too much trouble accessing your data because these products are basically transparent. Additionally, BEA Systems offers Jolt (`http://tuxedo.novell.com`) as a Web-based management piece for its Tuxedo servers, and Microsoft's Transaction Server is designed to integrate tightly with IIS.

Finally, you'll want some sort of report-writing software to help you with your more complex reports. None of the popular scripting products offer very sophisticated report-generating capabilities. There are a number of third-party solutions available. Try to choose a product that is not going to lock you in to any specific database of server vendor, if possible. If your company already uses a generic report writer, you should check to see whether the company that sells the reporting package has added extensions for intranet usage. Crystal Reports, for example, now has a version of its report viewer that runs as an ActiveX control within a user's Web browser. You can get this free by pointing your browser at `http://www.img.seagatesoftware.com/ActiveX`. This control is fully compatible with any reports that your company has probably already developed using Crystal Reports.

Getting to Legacy Data

Standard ODBC database access is fine for getting at your modern relational databases, such as Oracle or Informix, but what about the data that your company stores on mainframe or midrange systems? Many of your critical applications may be terminal or flat-file based applications running on older systems such as VAX VMS or CICS, possibly even on SNA networks. In fact, experts estimate that more than half of all critical data in corporations today still reside on these older systems. This section will give you tips for connecting your intranet to existing enterprise systems such as mainframe systems, terminal-based applications, vendor-proprietary solutions, and group messaging systems.

Much of your corporate data may be accessible only via SNA (IBM's Systems Network Architecture, a common architecture for large mainframe systems). For these systems, you'll need to build a gateway between your TCP/IP network and your SNA network. If your PCs are currently able to access the mainframe with 3270 terminal emulation, it is likely that you have already put such a gateway in place. If you want to tie your Web servers to non-3270 programs on the SNA network, such as the AS/400 APPN programming interface, you'll need to use a gateway product that translates CGI-style Web calls into equivalent AS/400 server calls. IBM's SNA gateway product, Communications Server, has extensions that allow you to make SNA APPN calls from any Java program or Web server. It also has hooks to allow your Web servers to easily access DB2 databases. For more information about using IBM Communications Server with Windows NT, check out `http://www.networking.ibm.com/ene`. Microsoft's SNA gateway product, SNA server, also adds Web hooks to most of its features by including Wall Data's Arpeggio (see `http://www.microsoft.com/sna`). In any case, it is unlikely that you'll be making the decision to buy an SNA gateway based on how well it integrates with your intranet development efforts. More likely, this decision has already been made, based on how well the SNA gateway does the other things it needs to do, such as connecting your legacy databases to your newer relational systems. Try to use an intranet connection strategy that ties in with your existing gateway—most such technologies are adequate.

For your 3270 terminal-based applications, the choice of gateway is not even a major issue. Whatever 3270 emulation solution you choose will work regardless of what SNA gateway you are using. IBM Host-on-Demand is a free Java program that runs a 3270 session within any Java-capable Web browser. You can download this from `http://www.ibm.com/java/applets_library.html`. IBM's Host-on-Demand is a pretty nice emulator, considering its price, but if your users want any of the more sophisticated features that they have grown to expect from their PC-based terminal packages, you'll have to go with a commercial solution. An example of such a package is White Pine's WebTerm. WebTerm embeds a 3270 session directly into the user's Web page. WebTerm can act as an ActiveX plug-in or a Netscape plug-in, and it can be automated using whatever scripting model your browser supports. If you are going to do any intranet automation of your 3270 sessions, a package such as WebTerm is essential. You can get a sample of WebTerm from `http://www.wpine.com`.

Even easier to access are your emulator-based legacy applications that reside on your non-SNA midrange systems. Generally, these are VT-based VMS or UNIX applications. WebTerm allows you to tie VT-based applications to your intranet, with capabilities ranging from simple display of a session within a user's Web browser to fully automating VT sessions from your scripting language.

If your organization is anything like the typical enterprise, much of your most critical business processes rely on vendor-proprietary systems built by companies such as SAP, PeopleSoft, or Oracle. When considering intranet connections, you should be primarily concerned about the parts of these systems that interface with normal users. For example, many of the common data-mining or warehousing packages are used mainly for behind-the-scenes processing, and the actual interfaces to these systems are used by few users, so you should not focus much effort on Web integration for these. On the other hand, your financial control systems or inventory processing systems are likely used by large numbers of corporate users and are therefore better candidates for intranet migration. Chances are, however, that you have relied on a company such as SAP or PeopleSoft to write the core of such systems for you. Manually converting the entire system to an intranet interface would negate the benefits that you gained by having the system basics outsourced in the first place. Luckily for you, the more popular vendors have already considered the need for intranet integration. Much of the new SAP code is built to tie in easily with any major Web server, and PeopleSoft, too, has added some very nice extensions to its products to let you tie interfaces into the Web. Of course, neither is quite ready for you to move your *entire* system to a Web-based interface, but neither is very far off, either. Also, you'll be able to do quite a bit with the extensions that are currently available. Oracle, on the other hand, does offer what could be considered a full intranet solution. The new release of Designer/2000 allows you to convert your existing (or new) Oracle client/server applications to pure Java applets. These Java applets can be placed on a Web server and run in any Web browser, with no need for Oracle software on the client. Besides Oracle, SAP, and PeopleSoft, many of the other popular corporate system developers now offer Web hooks. Check with your vendor for more information. Of course, you'll want to do some pretty extensive testing before you decide to convert any of your vendor applications to the Web. All these solutions will cost you some functionality, and they invariably end up being slower at either the server or the client side.

Finally, your existing corporate infrastructure likely includes some sort of group messaging or e-mail system (or systems). If your company is one of the many organizations that are still using PROFS, cc:Mail, QuickMail, and MS Mail, all at the same time, you might as well give up on trying to integrate your e-mail system with your intranet applications. If, however, you have standardized on one e-mail package, your chances of success are better. The simplest way to integrate your intranet with your existing e-mail system is to make sure that your e-mail system supports SMTP (Simple Mail Transfer Protocol) for incoming mail and POP3 (Post Office Protocol) for mail reading. Most Web browser packages support these protocols, and most packages do not support any other protocols. If your e-mail system supports SMTP, you can add a link to send e-mail with a line such as the following in your HTML:

```
<A HREF="mailto:president@mycompany.com>Send e-mail to the president!</A>
```

For more sophisticated messaging, though, you can't beat the capabilities of Lotus Notes or Microsoft Exchange Server. Both allow you to read e-mail and post to discussion groups directly from within your Web browser. Additionally, the other features of these systems, such as scheduling and voting, are available from any Web browser.

NOTE

Do you notice a trend? First, you move documentation to the Web browser; then you move new client server development to the same client, a Web browser. Next, you move all your database access to a Web browser client, and you use a Web browser to access all your terminal-based applications. Then you convert all your vendor-specific systems to run within a Web browser, and you begin to use our Web browsers for e-mail and groupware. Do you see now? If you build your intranet properly, the only application you'll need on your desktop will be a Web browser! User machines that consist only of a Web browser are naturally going to be less expensive to build and will be much easier to administer than the chaos that currently exists on the corporate desktop. This is why many vendors today are trying to sell you NCs (network computers) to replace your PCs. They figure that if you build your intranet right, you'll go for the Web-browser machine that is cheapest, easiest to administer, and offers the best performance, even if that machine does not use Intel or

continues

30

SETTING UP AN INTRANET

continued

Microsoft technologies. Check out http://www.sun.com/javastation for an example of one such product. Of course, solutions such as JavaStation assume that you are going to be able to convert your entire enterprise to non-Intel, non-Microsoft intranet technologies in one swoop. In my opinion, any organization that expects to do this is being very unrealistic. Both NCI (www.nc.com) and Tektronix (www.tektronix.com) offer NCs that allow some level of compatibility with existing Microsoft or Intel technologies. Microsoft and Intel, too, are betting that you won't want to or be able to abandon their technologies just yet. They address the whole NC issue by offering a number of technologies that give you many of the benefits promised by NCs, while allowing you to stick with your proven infrastructure. Check out www.intel.com/network/suite, www.microsoft.com.windows/zak, or www.microsoft.com/sms for more information. For a particularly interesting response to the NC challenge, look at www.citrix.com. Citrix WinFrame allows you to run Windows applications within your Web browser or on a NC-based terminal. Tektronix, among others, is hedging its bets by producing WinFrame-based (ICA architecture) NCs along with its Java-based NCs.

Connecting Your Intranet to the Internet

Eventually, you'll want to allow external Internet users to use certain resources on your intranet, and you'll want to let some of your internal users have access to the Internet for business purposes. You could very easily attain these benefits by adding a router between your intranet and an Internet Service Provider's digital line, but you would also attain some rather nasty headaches. For one, your entire internal network would be open to probing or sabotage by hackers and competitors all over the world. You would have no control over who accessed what, and if you tried to use authentication as described in Chapter 29, you would probably make things worse by exposing company passwords to Internet snoops (most authentication mechanisms are only effective within the context of your corporate Windows NT domain). Additionally, you would have no control over which users in your company used the Internet, and you would not be able to control the sites that they visited on company time. Clearly, there are risks involved with connecting your intranet to the Internet. You can, however, do this safely and effectively by paying attention to the tips offered in this section.

First, you should set up some sort of proxy as a barrier between your network and the Internet. Figure 30.7 illustrates your network with a proxy server connecting it to the Internet. The proxy server has two network interfaces (at a minimum): one that is connected to the internal network, and one that is connected to the Internet. When users within your company attempt to access the Internet, their requests must pass through the proxy, which can choose to reject them or log the request for management review. Outside users on the Internet will also have to pass through your proxy if they want to access any internal data.

FIGURE 30.7.

Connecting an intranet to the Internet.

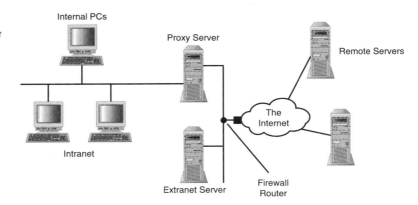

Some proxy server products that you can use are Netscape Proxy Server, Microsoft Proxy Server, and Novell BorderManager. Microsoft Proxy Server (www.microsoft.com/proxy) has the very nice capability of allowing you to assign Web access permissions by using existing login accounts within your domain, so you do not need to give your users separate passwords for Internet access. Novell's BorderManager (www.novell.com/border) gives you the same capability if you use NDS (NetWare Directory Services) for your primary authentication. Both Microsoft Proxy Server and Novell BorderManager add the option to proxy your protocol as well, so that you can have your IPX/SPX machines access the Internet without ever having to use TCP/IP on your network.

Although a proxy server will nicely manage your users' access to the Internet, your safest strategy for allowing external users to get at your intranet servers is to keep outside users on the other side of your proxy server. Any servers that need to be accessed by Internet users or that will be part of partners' extranets should be placed *outside* of the proxy, as shown in Figure 30.7. Because your proxy server uses two different network cards, and you have wisely disabled IP forwarding and routing on this machine, it will act as a one-way door, allowing internal users to get to the Internet, but preventing the Internet from seeing your internal network. Of course, segmenting your intranet like this (into an Internet-visible and an Internet-invisible portion) is going to make management a little bit difficult for you, but it is absolutely essential. The dangers of making your entire internal network open to the Internet are just too great to trust anything other than the one-way flow that a well-configured proxy server offers. Here are some of the hassles that you need to manage to make sure that your network is safe: First, your internal users will have to go through the proxy server to get at company resources that sit outside the proxy server. This will not be very difficult to manage, because most proxy servers have features to support this; but your proxy server could become a bottleneck for access to these resources. Second, your extranet, or Internet-visible servers, will not be able to access any databases that reside on the inside of your proxy server. Don't try to get around this by simply moving your databases to the outside of the proxy server. The rule here is "don't put anything outside the proxy unless you *must!*" As ugly as it may seem, you might have to set up a procedure to mirror small portions of your database to servers on the outside of your proxy.

30

SETTING UP AN
INTRANET

In addition to your network segmenting, remember that your Internet-visible servers, if using any sort of authentication at all, will probably be using an authentication scheme that is not very secure (see the section on security in Chapter 29 for a full discussion). Compensate for this by using Web-access usernames and passwords on your extranet servers that are valid only for the specific task used. In other words, don't use account names and passwords that could also be used to get into internal servers, and do not use account names and passwords that are valid on other extranet servers. If somebody steals one of your passwords, the amount of collateral damage that can be done will be minimized.

Last, you should further attempt to protect your Internet-visible servers by setting up a firewall between them and the Internet. Just because you have placed these servers outside of the protection your proxy server offers does not mean that you want your competitors to be modifying or sabotaging them. Configuring the router that connects you to the Internet to filter out all unnecessary ports will go a long way toward helping you protect these servers. Refer to your router configuration manual or talk to your Internet Service Provider for advice on this.

Summary

Building an intranet can help you make the most out of your Windows NT 4.0 infrastructure. A Windows NT environment offers you many options to consider when choosing the basic tools and technologies, and the long-term impact of your decisions here can be significant. The blend of technologies that you choose will depend on your particular current situation and your vision of the future. Finally, once you have begun to build your intranet, you can extend its usefulness by carefully making portions of your intranet visible to the external Internet.

VI
PART

Administering Windows NT Workstation

Disaster Recovery

by Paul Cassel

IN THIS CHAPTER

Computers are mechanical devices. They will fail. Even if they were faultless devices, they depend on electricity and the environment to exist. Although you can eliminate most power problems with a UPS (uninterruptible power supply) scheme of some sort, even these can have their limits. Any of the events in the following list can do a lot more than ruin your day:

- Fire
- Flood
- Sabotage
- A new virus that your anti-virus software fails to detect
- Theft of the computer or its data storage subsystem
- Catastrophic drive failure
- Lightning strike

That's just a partial list of things that can hit your system.

If you are unprepared for a disk crash, it can be catastrophic—particularly if you are a professional user who is vulnerable to financial damage when a system is down.

The external threats, such as viruses and hackers, make for good stories, but user error is easily the single most common cause for the deletion, loss, or modification of critical files. Of all the non-user–based problems, inconsistent power is the single greatest maker of lost data.

All these threats to the security of your precious data can be overcome by implementing a regular and carefully followed schedule for backing up your system.

> **TIP**
>
> If your data is really important to you, simply making backups isn't sufficient. If your home or office burns down and your backup tapes are in the building, you might have a bit of a problem recovering data from melted tapes. Maintain a copy of your data offsite. For small installations, simply renting a safe deposit box might be adequate for the purpose. Larger installations might want to investigate data archiving services that can provide fireproof vaults for storing offsite copies of their backups.

Even if you have the time and skill to reload your operating system and all your application software from scratch, loss of your documents, spreadsheets, e-mail, and other personal data can be extremely painful—and completely unnecessary.

DOS and Microsoft Windows did a poor job of addressing the issue of backups. The base operating system had no direct support for tape devices, so many people routinely backed up their files onto disks. Windows 95 did support some floppy-interface–based QIC tape drives that were barely sufficient for that operating system's needs.

Backing up to disk is a slow and cumbersome process that few people are willing to undertake regularly, even for small volumes. The problem is exacerbated by the ever-growing size of hard disks and the size of software applications. The type of system typical for Windows NT Workstation is clearly impractical for floppy disk backup due to its size. It is now common for a desktop system to be configured with more than 3GB of disk space. Fortunately, the NT backup facilities provide an excellent solution to the problem.

The ntbackup.exe program supplied with Windows NT is designed to address the higher capacities of modern computer systems. The NT backup philosophy has turned 180 degrees away from the older DOS and Windows 3.1 models. Unlike the Windows 95 backup routine, which uses various media options, NT's backup works only with tape devices. Tapes have the following advantages over other currently available storage media:

- *Low media costs.* Tapes provide by far the lowest cost per megabyte of the existing storage media. It is possible to buy 4- or 8-millimeter DAT tapes for under $10 each. DAT tape drives can be costly compared to QIC ones, however. Drives start at about $400 and range upward to several thousand dollars.

- *High capacity.* The capacity of tape drives varies widely with the technology, but even extremely low-cost cartridge drives can store several hundreds of megabytes. A 4- or 8-millimeter DAT or QIC tape drive can provide capacities of 2 to 8 or more gigabytes, with media costs sometimes falling below $10 per cartridge. That translates to storage at a cost of $1.50 to $5.00 per gigabyte. More exotic technologies, such as SCSI-attached Digital Linear Tapes, have capacities into the tens of gigabtyes. There are currently no other removable (or fixed) media devices that can provide that kind of capacity.

- *Speed.* Although the speed of a tape drive is dependent on the underlying technology, relatively inexpensive drives are capable of streaming at fairly high data rates. Furthermore, the high capacity of tape drives means that media changes need not occur frequently. This also means that backups can occur quickly and efficiently, without human intervention. It is possible to configure a backup system that works completely automatically, operating at some off hour. This saves the most important resource of all—your time.

- *Concurrency.* The backup program supplied with Windows NT Workstation will work in the background, allowing normal use of the workstation. The only restriction is that backup won't work on open files.

Tape isn't perfect. It does have some disadvantages:

- *Linear.* Tape is a linear storage medium. The files are stored logically in a long line on the tape. Restoration of a file or a few files can take a long time, because the software searches the entire tape for the file or files to restore. Most optical and all hard drives are random access, allowing much faster access to individual files.

- *One purpose.* Tape drives work only as backup devices. You can't open files on a tape from Windows NT Workstation. Other storage choices, such as spare hard drives or optical devices, can double as logical devices on your system.

- *Maintenance-intensive.* Tape drives need cleaning, fall out of alignment, and wear out. Hard drives and optical devices are much more robust.

- *The tapes.* The tapes themselves are somewhat more fragile and less long lived than some other technologies, especially optical.

- *Speed.* DAT, modern SCSI QIC, and DLT tapes are speed demons compared to the older QIC drives or disks, but they are sluggards compared to hard drives or most modern optical devices.

Supported Tape Technologies

The following paragraphs contain a brief overview of available tape technologies supported by Windows NT. Tape interface methods, media formats, and compatibility issues are discussed.

Tape Drive Interface Methods

Tape drives typically interface to PC systems via one of the following methods:

- Dedicated interface cards are sometimes used to connect tape drives. This was particularly true with some older cartridge tape units. Dedicated interfaces are decreasing in popularity, so it might be difficult to obtain drivers for these types of units.

- Many of the most popular low-end tape drives attach to the system floppy disk controller. Some tape drives of this type can also be driven by dedicated "accelerator" interfaces. Capacities and media formats vary for floppy–controller-based drives. Very inexpensive drives are available with capacities in the 800MB (compressed) range. Higher-end drives of this type can hold up to 3,200MB on a single compressed tape.

- Some tape drives can now be connected via EIDE disk interfaces. Again, these tend to be very reasonably priced drives with good speed and capacity.

- Many "external" or "portable" tape units attach to the system via a parallel printer port or a SCSI converter to that port. These drives have the advantage of easy portability, so they can be easily moved from one system to another. They are also compatible with laptop and notebook computers without the need for a docking bay or PCMCIA slot. External tape units that attach to the parallel port are usually QIC drives, although a few 4mm DAT units are available with parallel interfaces. You should be very careful to ensure that any external tape drive you are considering is actually supported by Windows NT. The tape drive vendor might provide NT drivers for externally connected tape units.

- Most of the higher-end tape drives on the market today use SCSI interfaces, which can attach a mixture of tape, disk, and CD-ROM devices to a single SCSI adapter. SCSI tape drives typically have much higher transfer rates than do floppy-disk–based or parallel-port–attached tape units. Some SCSI-attached units can be equipped with a magazine-fed auto-loader unit capable of holding hundreds of gigabytes or even terabytes of tape storage.

Tape Media Formats

A wide variety of tape media is available. When choosing a tape subsystem, it is important to make sure that the selected device meets your requirements for reliability, capacity, and performance. Media cost is also important—particularly if you won't be able to reuse media on a regular basis. This typically happens when you have to provide long-term archival storage of your backups. The most popular tape formats are shown in Table 31.1.

Table 31.1. Popular tape formats.

Type	Capacity	Comments
DLT	40GB (compressed)	Digital Linear Tapes are among the highest-capacity, fastest, and most reliable tape drives on the market. They are normally available with SCSI interfaces. DLT tapes are excellent backup devices, but both the drives and the media are expensive. Media can also be difficult to find.
4mm DAT	16GB	Very reliable, fast, low media cost, small form factor. Usually requires a SCSI interface. The drives are relatively expensive when compared to TRAVAN or QIC type drives, but lower media costs can make up for that over time. You can connect multiple SCSI tape drives to a single SCSI adapter.
8mm	7GB	Very inexpensive media. Slower and less reliable than 4mm DAT with higher soft error rates. Usually available as SCSI devices, these drives are losing popularity due to newer tape technologies. Therefore, if you don't already have one, you might not want one. The advantages of SCSI apply.
TRAVAN/QIC	4000MB	Very low drive cost. Media costs are 3 to 4 times that of 4mm or 8mm tapes, but if you don't need a lot of media, the low drive cost makes the higher media cost worthwhile. These drives are available with SCSI, floppy, or parallel-port interfaces.

Installing a Tape Device

Installing a tape device under Windows NT 4.0 is extremely simple. Invoking the Tape Drives applet of the Control Panel is usually sufficient to cause the system to detect the presence of the new tape drive. If SCSI, the system will often detect the drive upon startup. When the new tape drive is detected, the system will attempt to load the driver. This is shown in Figure 31.1.

FIGURE 31.1.

Installing a tape device.

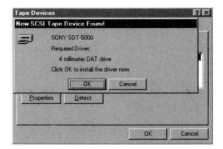

After your tape device is installed, you can begin using `ntbackup`, included with Windows NT Workstation 4. You invoke Backup by clicking Backup in the Administrative Tools Start menu. Upon launch, the display looks something like that shown in Figure 31.2.

Note that the display in Figure 31.2 has two distinct regions, with the Tapes window on the right and the Drives window on the left. Your system might initially size these windows differently, or it might not show both windows. You can tile the Tapes and Drives windows by selecting the Tile option of the Windows menu. If you have no tape in your drive, the Tape window will just contain a message to that end.

Note that the Tapes window shows the contents of any inserted tapes in addition to the current status of the tape device.

The general user interface of `ntbackup` is modeled somewhat after the File Manager supplied with older versions of Microsoft Windows and Windows NT. In simple terms, you select an item or items from one of the windows and then you choose an appropriate operation. In Figure 31.3, for instance, you can see that the check box for drive C: has been selected. The Drives windowpane has been moved to the right in this screen to show that the check box for Drive C: has been selected. The Operations menu shows that you can back up the selected disk or perform any of several administrative functions.

31

FIGURE 31.2.

The initial display for the Backup program under Administrative Tools.

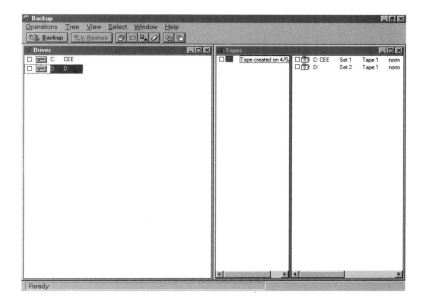

FIGURE 31.3.

The Operations menu enables those operations pertinent to the selections in the Drives or Tapes windows.

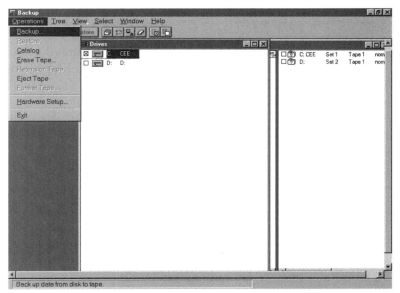

The specifics of backing up the system are covered at length in the "Backing Up Files, Folders, and Drives" section of this chapter. Each of the other options is discussed in the following list:

- The Erase Tape option does exactly what its name implies. This option is necessary before using some types of tapes, or if you want to ensure that sensitive material is removed from a tape.

- Certain tape formats can develop slack spots in the tape. This causes the tape to move at an inconsistent speed, which can result in tape errors. QIC cartridges are known to exhibit this behavior. The Retension Tape option causes the tape to fast forward to the end and then rewind in one continuous operation. This causes the entire tape to be wound at a consistent tension. Retensioning is not normally required with DAT or DLT tapes.

- After you have finished with a tape, use the Eject Tape option to remove it from your tape drive.

- NT tries to determine what tape devices are connected when the system boots, but if you have multiple tape devices, it can make wrong choices. You can use the Hardware Setup option to select the tape device you want to use from the list of units available on your system.

Backing Up Files, Folders, and Drives

Before you can start your backup, you have to choose the items that you want to preserve. Figure 31.4 shows an expanded view of the Drives window in Backup. In this screen, the Tapes window pane has been minimized to show Drives detail. As previously mentioned, it looks remarkably like the user interface of the Windows File Manager, with the addition of a small check box by the name of each object. The rule is simple: An object must be checked before it can be backed up.

Selecting the top level of a tree selects objects below it. The Tree options of the menu bar can be used to expand and collapse trees. You can also check (or uncheck) many items at once by highlighting them with the mouse and then clicking Check or Uncheck in the Select menu of the menu bar. Double-clicking on a drive or folder with a plus sign on it expands that object on layer.

You can also expand the entire volume tree by choosing Tree | Expand All.

TIP

Selecting the check box of a drive letter doesn't necessarily select all the files contained in the drive or volume. This is because Backup normally skips over any file that you don't have permission to access. Make sure that you are logged in with the correct permissions. Then, after highlighting a drive letter, click Check in the Select menu. That way, you will select all the files on the drive.

FIGURE 31.4.

You can expand the display of drives to show individual directories (folders) and files for selective backup.

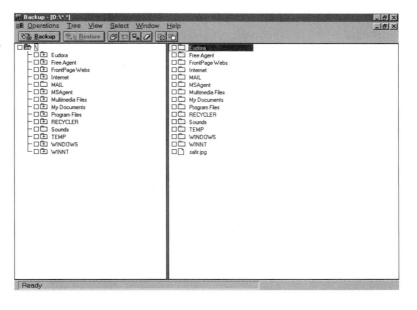

Running the Backup

After you've selected the items that you want to back up, click either the Backup option of the Operations menu or the Backup button on the toolbar. You should see the Backup Information dialog box shown in Figure 31.5.

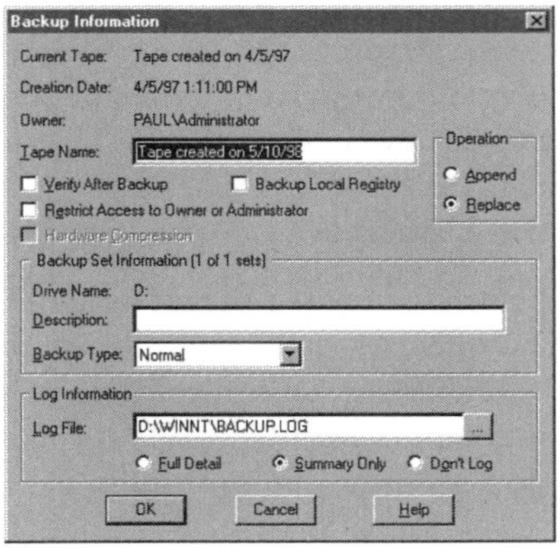

FIGURE 31.5.

Clicking the Backup button or selecting the Operations | Backup menu choice starts the backup process with an informational display.

31

DISASTER
RECOVERY

Notice that this dialog box is divided into three distinct areas. The top area is used to set options relating to the tape itself. If the tape is a new one, you must enter a Tape Name in the designated entry box. If the tape has been previously used by Backup, Backup reads in the name of the tape and displays it in the Tape Name box. The tape name must be less than 32 characters in length.

> **WARNING**
>
> Be careful when you are backing up to a tape that already contains backup sets. Backup, by default, selects the Replace button. If the Replace button is selected when the backup begins, all data on the tape will be lost. If you want to keep the existing data, select the Append button. Backup will try to append the current data to the end of the tape.

The Verify After Backup option causes the Backup program to verify the tape contents against the original files. Selecting this option helps to ensure the integrity of your backups but slows the backup process considerably.

Backing Up the Registry

Select the Backup Local Registry option if you are backing up the local disk containing your Windows NT Registry data. Backup must take special actions when backing up the Registry because many of the files comprising the Registry are open all the time. These open files would normally be skipped. Note that you can't back up the Registry information of a network resource. That one limitation is the reason that ntbackup can't be used as a general-purpose backup solution for your entire network.

You can set the Restrict Access to Owner or Administrator option if you want to make sure that the tape can be read only by an authorized person. Note that the Restrict Access option is available in the example shown in Figure 31.5. This is because the file system selected for backup is a NTFS file system. Because NTFS file systems have security information, the Restrict Access to Owner option is available for this backup. It would not be for a FAT volume.

Finally, if your tape device supports hardware compression, you can choose to make a compressed backup. This often greatly increases the capacity of the tape, but compressed backups are inherently less portable and sometimes less reliable than uncompressed backups. Use caution when selecting compression, particularly if you intend to use the tape on more than one computer. This tape device, an Archive Python, lacks hardware compression, so the option is not enabled.

The Backup Set

The middle of the Backup Information dialog box contains information on what is being backed up. The number of backup sets is shown, as well as the Drive Name (read from the disk label). A description of the backup can be entered for informational purposes.

Types of Backups

Pay particular attention to the Backup Type selector. NT Backup supports five distinct types of backups, and the contents of your tape can vary dramatically, depending on which type you select.

In order to understand the types of backups, it is necessary to realize that NT maintains a special flag for each and every file on the system. This flag (called the *archive bit*) can be used to mark files as they are backed up. The flag is set if the file is later modified in any way.

NT uses the archive bit as a way of keeping track of which files have changed since the last backup. That way, it is possible to back up only the modified data. Although that might not seem particularly important if you have a 4GB tape drive and a 3GB disk, it can be extremely important if you have many gigabytes of disk space online.

The five types of backup supported by NT are as follows:

- The *normal backup* copies all the selected files to tape, regardless of the state of the archive bit. As the files are copied, their archive bits are cleared. Normal backups are also referred to as *full backups.*

- *Copy backups,* like normal backups, copy all the selected files to tape. Unlike normal backups, however, the archive bits of the selected files are not modified.

- *Incremental backups* look at each file in the selected file set and copy only those with archive bits set. This allows you to make a quick backup of only those files that have been modified since the last full or incremental backup. The archive bits are cleared as the files are copied to tape. Windows NT Workstation sets the archive bit the next time the file is modified.

- The *differential backup* is a variation on the incremental backup. Differential backups copy only the files that have marked archive bits, but they do not change the files as they are copied. This is similar to a copy backup, but it only affects files with the archive bit set.

- Finally, you can use a *daily backup*. The daily backup copies only the files from the selected file set that have been modified that same day. This can be useful for grabbing a quick copy of your most recent work for transport to a home system.

You should make full backups of your system at regular intervals. One common strategy is to make a full backup once each week. You can then make incremental backups on a daily basis (as described in third item of the preceding list). The full backup ensures that you have a snapshot of your system in some known state. The incremental backups give you a way of quickly picking up the changed components of your system.

If your system usage doesn't justify backups this frequently, you can adjust the backup intervals to be more appropriate for your usage patterns. Remember, though, that restoring your system will require you to restore the most recent full backup and then apply incremental restores for each incremental backup that has occurred since the full backup. It's important to make sure that the full backups occur frequently enough to make this process reasonable.

Differential backups and copy backups are useful when you want to create an image of your system without modifying it. You can sometimes use this technique to replicate a set of directories and files. In most cases, you won't routinely use copy or differential backups.

Father, Son, Grandfather Backups

The *father, son, grandfather backup scheme* is a highly effective and well-used one. It requires a total of 10 tapes and saves files on a 12-week rotation. This means that any file should be available for as long as three months. If you don't notice a file is missing after that length of time, you likely don't need it all that much.

Here's how to do this routine. Take 10 new tapes and label them as follows:

1. Monday
2. Tuesday
3. Wednesday
4. Thursday
5. Friday A
6. Friday B
7. Friday C
8. Month A
9. Month B
10. Month C

Start this routine on Friday by following these steps:

1. Backup normal onto the Friday A tape.
2. On Monday, backup incremental to the Monday tape. Repeat this on Tuesday, Wednesday, and Thursday using the respectively labeled tapes.
3. On Friday, do a normal backup to the Friday B tape.
4. Repeat step 2 for the rest of the week.
5. On Friday, repeat step 3 using the Friday C tape.
6. Repeat step 4.
7. On Friday, perform step 5 using the Month A tape.
8. Repeat the cycle again but use the Month B tape when you get to step 7.
9. Repeat cycle again, but use the Month C tape when you get to step 7.

Consider storing the Friday or the Month tape(s) off premises. (If you are undergoing an EEO audit, name the backup scheme, mother, daughter, and granny.)

Logging Backup Results

The bottom of the Backup Information dialog box is used to set the log options for your backup. It is generally a good idea to log your backups—especially if, like most people, you don't plan to sit and watch the entire backup run. Select the level of detail using the radio buttons at the bottom of the dialog box. If you choose, you can also enter a pathname for the log file in the Log File entry box.

Clicking the OK button of the Backup Information dialog box initiates the actual backup process. At this point, a Backup Status dialog box appears. The Backup Status dialog box shows current information about backup operations. It also allows the user to abort the backup if so desired. As each backup set completes, you see information concerning the total number of files and the number of bytes that were backed up. You also see information about any files that were skipped. Files might be skipped if they are open for modification.

Recovery

If you're lucky, you won't need the recovery tools of Backup. If and when you do need to restore files, the operation of ntbackup is much the same as the operation described earlier for making backups.

Figure 31.6 shows an expanded view of the Tapes window of Backup. The Tapes window here has more than one tape in the left pane, because during the time the program was opened, three tapes have been inserted in the drive. Backup "remembers" all three tapes.

Note that it uses the same File Manager–like user interface that was described earlier. Select the desired tape and then select the Catalog option of the Operations menu. A full catalog of the available backup sets will be presented.

Double-clicking on any folder with a plus on it, such as My Documents (shown in Figure 31.6), expands the view to the display shown in Figure 31.7. If you want to restore an entire backup set, you don't need to expand anything, of course. Again, just as when selecting files for backup, clicking the check box for a folder causes items contained within the folder to be equivalently checked.

In Figure 31.8, the WINNT folder has been expanded to show its contents. The mouse has been used to highlight a set of files, and the Select option of the menu bar has been clicked. Clicking the Check option causes all of the highlighted items to be selected for restoration.

FIGURE 31.6.

The Tapes window shows the contents of any loaded tapes.

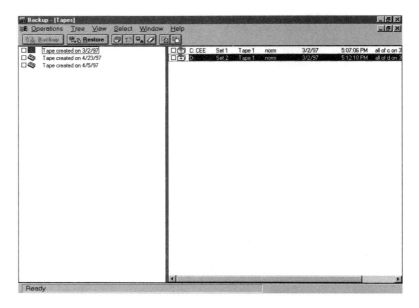

FIGURE 31.7.

A backup set from the Tapes window expands to look very much like the File Manager or Explorer.

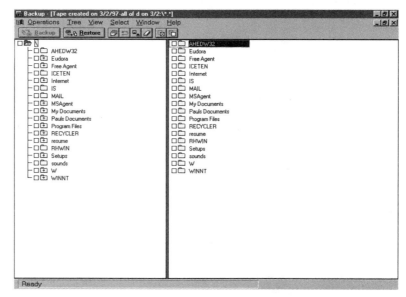

FIGURE 31.8.

An expanded directory with all files chosen for restoration.

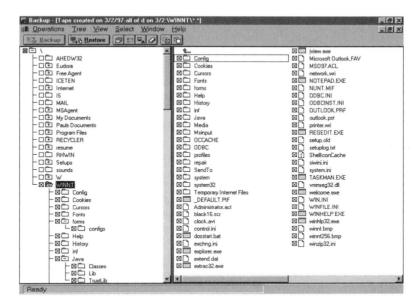

After selecting the files or folders that you want to restore, click the Restore button of the toolbar or the Restore option of the Operations menu to begin the restoration process. The Restore Information dialog box is displayed, as shown in Figure 31.9.

FIGURE 31.9.

The Restore Information dialog box is similar to the Backup Information dialog box.

Like the Backup Information dialog box, the Restore Information dialog box is divided into three sections. The top section contains information about the tape set or sets to be restored.

The middle section of the dialog box is used to set Restore options. By default, Backup restores the selected file sets to the same location from which they were originally copied. You can choose to specify a different drive or a different path within a drive. This allows files to be restored to disk without overwriting the copies already in place, which is sometimes useful for comparing files or folders.

If the file set that you are restoring contains Registry information, you can choose to have that restored as well. You can also check the Restore File Permissions box if you want the files restored with the permissions that they show on the tape. If you don't set this box, the files will inherit the permissions of the directory to which you restore them.

You can verify the integrity of the restore operation by checking the Verify After Restore box. If this box is selected, `ntbackup` first restores your data and then performs a verification pass that compares the restored files to the tape contents.

Restore Logging Options

Set any logging options using the Log Information area of the Restore Information dialog box. You can select the log detail level and pathname, just as you could when creating the backup set.

Clicking OK causes the restore to actually begin. A Restore Status dialog box appears, indicating the currently active operation. The dialog box also displays statistics concerning the number of files and bytes that have been restored. You can stop the restore operation by clicking the Abort button of the Restore Status dialog box.

Using a Command-Line Interface

There are times when you might want to use a command-line interface to run your backups. This can occur when you need to schedule the backup to run automatically, when you want to initiate a backup on one machine remotely from another system, or when you have some repeated set of backup options that you run frequently enough to justify using a script.

`ntbackup` provides a command-line interface for such cases. Most of the command-line options for `ntbackup` are intended to be used in batch files, so they require no user input. The two exceptions to this rule are the `/nopoll` and `/missingtape` options.

Use the `/nopoll` option to force `ntbackup` to skip any cataloging actions and immediately erase the tape. This option is particularly useful when a tape has become corrupted, because the cataloging operations might otherwise produce errors or cause `ntbackup` to abort.

Use `/missingtape` if you want to read only one volume of a multitape set, or if you have a multitape set with a damaged or missing tape. Backup scans each tape in order to rebuild the catalog information.

The `ntbackup` command-line interface is used like this:

```
ntbackup operation path options
```

The *operation* is required and must be either eject or backup. The *path* is required for backup operations. Multiple paths can be specified.

Available *options* are shown in Table 31.2.

Table 31.2. The ntbackup options.

Option	Explanation
/a	Sets append mode. The backup sets will be appended to the end of the tape. If this option is not set, the existing contents of the tape will be overwritten.
/v	Causes all operations to be verified.
/r	Restricts access to saved information to administrators or to the actual owners of the saved files.
/d "description"	Enables you to enter a textual description of the backup. Use the quotation marks if the description text contains any spaces.
/b	If the drive being backed up contains Registry information, specifying the /b switch causes the Registry information to be backed up as well.
/hc:{on/off}	/hc:on turns hardware compression on. /hc:off turns compression off. Compression sometimes greatly increases tape capacity, but it can slow the backup down or make the tape less portable.
/t {option}	The /t switch is used to specify the type of the backup. Available types are normal, copy, incremental, differential, and daily. The types of backups are explained in the "Types of Backups" section of this chapter.
/l "filename"	This switch is used to specify a pathname for a log file.
/e	If the /e switch is set, the log file will contain only exception information.
/tape:{n}	Used to select the tape drive number, where *n* is a number from 0 to 9.

Any or all of the listed options can be specified. As an example, a full backup of the F: drive could be made on a compressed archive by using the following command:

```
ntbackup backup F:\ /d "F: Full Backup" /hc:on /t:normal
```

Scheduling Automatic Backups

The command-line interface to ntbackup makes it relatively simple to automate the process of backing up your system. You can use the NT AT command to schedule tasks to be run at fixed times. If you place the `ntbackup` commands that you want to use into a script file, you can cause the script to be run by AT during some off hour. In this way, you can get an automated backup every night at the same time. Consider the following simple batch script:

```
REM backit.cmd - An automated backup script
@echo off
ntbackup backup C: /d "C: Backup" /t:incremental /r /a /b
REM Map network drive
net use x: \\server1\d$
REM Now back it up
ntbackup backup x: /d "Server1 D: Backup" /hc:on /t:incremental /a
net use x: /d
```

The preceding script runs an incremental backup of drive C: on the local system. It then connects the administrative share name \\server1\d$ to drive X: and runs an incremental backup of the remote drive. Finally, it disconnects the share from the local system.

Place the preceding commands into a file called `backit.cmd` and then run the following command:

```
at 01:00 /every:m,t,w,th,f,s,su backit.cmd
```

Every morning at 1 a.m., an incremental backup of drive C: and \\server1\d$ will be run. You can expand the script by adding additional paths to the `ntbackup` command. You can also put conditional logic into the script to cause the script to perform different actions on the basis of environment variables or the output of other programs.

NOTE

The AT command uses the Windows NT Scheduler service to run commands. In order for your backup to run correctly, you must be logged on to your workstation as an administrator or a member of the Backup Operators group. You must also have started the AT service.

Third-Party Backup Software

NT Backup is almost a complete backup solution. Its primary flaw lies in its inability to back up the Registry information of remote systems. A number of quality backup programs are available from third-party software vendors to address that inability. Three of the most popular are Backup Exec from Arcada/Seagate Software, Networker from Legato Systems, and Cheyenne Software's ARCserve. Each has its own set of strengths and weaknesses, but any of these applications is an excellent choice for backing up networked NT systems.

Emergency Repair Disk

Windows NT Workstation has a repair system built into its boot process. This system can be kicked into gear if you can't boot Windows NT from the Last Known Good control set. The most common reasons you might not be able to start from Last Known Good are as follows:

- Missing or corrupted system files
- Missing or corrupted Registry files
- Partition boot sector corruption

Working in conjunction with the distribution CD-ROM, an emergency repair disk (ERD) can fix these and similar problems; thus, returning you to the state you were before the problem occurred.

In many cases, either system corruption or missing files stems from a problem with a disk subsystem. Fixing the Windows NT Workstation installation without addressing the underlying problem will only result in a temporary restoration of function.

The Setup program for Windows NT Workstation will create an initial ERD if you let it. As soon as you install applications, change Windows NT's optional components or add new profiles, this disk becomes obsolete. The ERD can only restore the system as it was when the ERD was made. Think of it as a snapshot of your system. You need to update the ERD regularly—at least every time you make a major change to your system that would be inconvenient to lose.

The program that makes an ERD is the Rescue Disk utility (rdisk.exe). You can run rdisk from the Start | Run menu option or from the command-line interface (CLI). Figure 31.10 shows rdisk running from the CLI.

FIGURE 31.10.

The Repair Disk utility can update or create a new ERD.

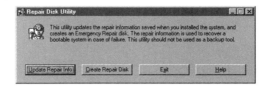

Disks are cheap, but the information contained on an ERD can be as valuable as the time you save using it rather than having to restore your Windows NT setup from scratch. Consider making duplicate copies of the ERD.

Using the ERD

To use the ERD when you can't boot from your hard disk or when you can't get Windows NT Workstation to launch, boot the computer with the Windows NT setup disk in the boot floppy drive. Insert the setup disk number 2 when its time has come. Choose the Repair option (press R) when you're presented with that option. This will launch the repair sequence.

You'll get a text-based option screen that gives you the following options:

- Inspecting the Registry
- Inspecting the boot environment
- Checking and verifying the Windows NT system files
- Inspecting the boot sector of the boot disk (Intel computers, NVRAM on Alpha)

Choose the options you feel you need to perform and then continue with the inspection.

The option to inspect the Registry is the most complex. It will inspect these sections by option:

- System
- Default user profile
- Security
- New user profile
- Software

The verification of system files uses a checksum routine to make sure all the needed system files exist and are in good working order. This information resides in the Setup.log file on the ERD. Figure 31.11 shows a section of a Setup.log from an ERD.

Figure 31.11.

The Setup.log file from an ERD contains the checksum information needed by Windows NT to verify the existence and integrity of its system files.

```
setup.log - Notepad
File  Edit  Search  Help

[Paths]
TargetDirectory = "\WINNT"
TargetDevice = "\Device\Harddisk0\partition2"
SystemPartitionDirectory = "\"
SystemPartition = "\Device\Harddisk0\partition1"
[Signature]
Version = "WinNt4.0"
[Files.SystemPartition]
ntldr = "ntldr","2a36b"
NTDETECT.COM = "NTDETECT.COM","b69e"
[Files.WinNt]
\WINNT\Help\31users.hlp = "31users.hlp","12bfc"
\WINNT\Help\acc_dis.cnt = "acc_dis.cnt","cc99"
\WINNT\Help\acc_dis.hlp = "acc_dis.hlp","b82c"
\WINNT\inf\accessor.inf = "accessor.inf","13070"
\WINNT\system32\acledit.dll = "acledit.dll","2be50"
\WINNT\system32\advapi32.dll = "advapi32.dll","408a5"
\WINNT\system32\drivers\afd.sys = "afd.sys","17142"
\WINNT\system32\alrsvc.dll = "alrsvc.dll","fa69"
\WINNT\system32\amddlg.dll = "amddlg.dll","4e1a"
\WINNT\system32\ansi.sys = "ansi.sys","2aa6"
\WINNT\Fonts\app850.fon = "app850.fon","14845"
\WINNT\system32\append.exe = "append.exe","448b"
\WINNT\inf\apps.inf = "apps.inf","11c5f"
\WINNT\system32\appwiz.cpl = "appwiz.cpl","1b943"
\WINNT\Fonts\arial.ttf = "arial.ttf","2d945"
\WINNT\Fonts\arialbd.ttf = "arialbd.ttf","2d595"
\WINNT\Fonts\arialbi.ttf = "arialbi.ttf","32fb1"
\WINNT\Fonts\ariali.ttf = "ariali.ttf","2e6e8"
\WINNT\system32\at.exe = "at.exe","99c1"
\WINNT\system32\drivers\atapi.sys = "atapi.sys","e3a9"
\WINNT\system32\drivers\atdisk.sys = "atdisk.sys","c769"
\WINNT\system32\atsvc.exe = "atsvc.exe","b4d5"
\WINNT\system32\attrib.exe = "attrib.exe","fe3e"
\WINNT\system32\audiocdc.hlp = "audiocdc.hlp","64b6"
\WINNT\system32\autochk.exe = "autochk.exe","5fee8"
```

The inspect boot sector option of the repair facility will verify the integrity of the Partition Boot Sector and will replace a bad or missing NTLDR. This facility only works for the first hard disk.

Restoring the Registry

There are four ways to restore the Registry or parts of it:

- For FAT systems, boot to MS-DOS and copy the Registry to a floppy or set of floppies using a disk spanning routine such as PKZip. Restore the Registry or parts of it by reversing the process.
- If you have possession of Regback.exe from the Resource Kit, use it to back up the Registry. This utility can restore keys selectively.
- Use the ERD and Windows NT setup.
- Use the Disk Administrator.

The Disk Administrator will only restore the System key after you have saved it. There is no reason to use it if you have an ERD because the ERD contains the System key. If, however, you don't have an ERD or it has become corrupted and you have saved your System key, you can try this.

To save your System key:

1. Launch Disk Administrator.
2. Choose the menu options Partition | Configuration.
3. Choose Save from Configuration.
4. Insert a floppy disk to receive the information.

To restore your System key:

1. Launch Disk Administrator.
2. Choose the menu options Partition | Configuration.
3. Choose Restore from Configuration.
4. Insert the floppy disk you made in the Save step.

If all else fails, you can try to use the Disk Administrator to search for your System key. This will overwrite your current System key, so use it with caution. Here are the steps:

1. Launch Disk Administrator.
2. Choose Partition | Configuration | Search from the menu.
3. Click OK at the Warning message.
4. If Disk Administrator finds another NT install, it will display its findings. Choose an option.
5. Click OK.
6. Disk Administrator will reboot Windows NT Workstation.

Re-creating the Master Boot Record

You can re-create or replace the master boot record (MBR) by using `fdisk`. To do this, boot from a floppy formatted with MS-DOS. You'll need the fdisk.exe file that runs with the version of MS-DOS you use to boot from. The DOS version must be 5 or greater for this switch to work. Follow these steps:

1. Boot using an MS-DOS floppy disk.

2. Enter `fdisk /mbr` at the A: prompt.

This will replace the MBR without affecting the partition table. Don't use this if you're using either of the following:

- A third-party disk manager such as Disk Manager from Ontrack Systems

- A multiple boot or some other utility that writes information between the partition table and the MBR

If nothing else works and you have the skills, you can copy the partition table and MBR from a good installation to your corrupted disk. The Windows NT Workstation Resource Kit contains a utility, DiskMap, that maps the structure of a disk. If you save this information, you can use it along with a low-level disk editor to restore a disk to working condition.

Figure 31.12 shows the DiskMap utility mapping a FAT volume. To make this screen, DiskMap was run on drive 0 (C) and then the output redirected to a file, d.txt. The file d.txt is shown here in Notepad. DiskMap is usually run from the CLI.

FIGURE 31.12.

The DiskMap utility's output can be part of a successful last-ditch recovery scheme when used with a low-level disk editor.

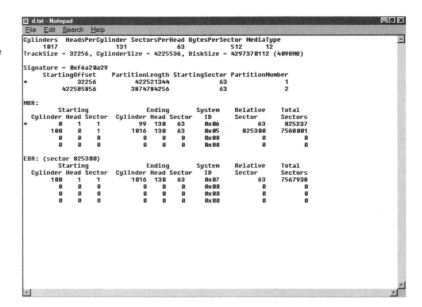

Summary

The single most catastrophic mistake made by both novice and advanced computer users is the simple failure to make routine backups. It's a dull, unexciting task that many users rarely find time for. Avoid that pitfall. A little forethought can make backups an automatic and painless process that can save you endless hours of frustration or financial hardship. NT's integrated backup facilities are easy to use and robust for standalone workstations, so there's no real need to defer the task. Take time today (if you haven't already done so) to plan a backup strategy. Start by immediately making a full backup of your entire system. If you ever need it, you'll realize that it was time well spent.

Also, make sure to regularly update your ERD. There's nothing like the feeling of confidence brought on by having a full backup and a current ERD. On the other hand, there's nothing like the empty feeling you get if you have neither and one day your system fails to start.

Event Viewer

by Paul Cassel and Thomas Lee

IN THIS CHAPTER

CHAPTER 32

The Event Viewer

In Windows NT Workstation, an *event* occurs whenever anything significant happens that either NT Workstation or a running application feels you should know about.

The definition of *significant* is left up to the developers. Thus, the events that you are notified about can vary enormously—from fundamental system errors, such as a network card not working or a fault-tolerant disk failure, to much less significant events, such as a service starting or a print job completing. Security events vary, depending on your needs, from meaningless to extremely important.

When a software component detects an event to be reported, it uses the ReportEvent API to pass details about the event to Windows NT. The Event Log service then posts these details to one of three event logs:

- *System log.* This log contains details about events that occur within the operating system, such as a driver failure.
- *Security log.* Security-related Audit events—such as when someone attempts to log on without the proper password—are stored in this log.
- *Application log.* This log contains details about events detected by applications running on your system. For example, a database application might record the failure to read a record.

All users can access the system and application logs, whereas only users with administrator rights can see the security log.

The Event Log service is responsible for writing event details to the event logs, and it is one of the standard NT services that is started each time you load Windows NT Workstation.

> **TIP**
>
> When the Event Log service starts, it reports this to the system event log. The event logged is event 6005, which can be very useful in troubleshooting. By looking for this event, you can determine when the system last rebooted and thus see all the events that have occurred since then. These events also show you how often Windows NT Workstation has been rebooted.

To view the information that has been logged, you use the Event Viewer application. Event Viewer is automatically installed when you load Windows NT Workstation.

Event Viewer enables you to perform the following tasks:

- See a summary of the events that have occurred
- See the details logged for each event

- Save event logs away for future analysis and view saved logs
- View the local event log and view event logs on remote systems (subject to security)

The Event Viewer is a powerful aid to troubleshooting and is usually a "first port of call" whenever a problem occurs on your system. Let's look at how you can use Event Viewer to diagnose problems in Windows NT Workstation. The Event Viewer is very straightforward to use. But getting the most out of it takes practice because there is no overall consistency in what is logged when events occur.

Suppose that a driver fails to start when you boot Windows NT Workstation. If this happens, you receive a message box after you start up, as shown in Figure 32.1.

FIGURE 32.1.
This message box tells you that there has been a driver startup failure, but it gives no specific information about the event.

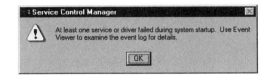

This message box tells you that something has gone wrong in the startup and that the Service Control Manager was not able to properly start one or more drivers. This message box, by itself, offers no indication as to what has happened; it only tells you that there has been a problem. If you've just changed or added a driver, this box alone might tell you what's wrong. However, often this is just the first hint that there's a problem. To determine what went wrong, you need to run the Event Viewer.

Event Viewer to the Rescue

With the Event Viewer application, you examine and manage the three event logs. When you install Windows NT Workstation, the installation process installs the Event Viewer application as %SystemRoot%\system32\eventvwr.exe and sets up a shortcut under the Administrative Tools (Common) group in the Start Programs menu.

SECURITY

Windows NT Workstation disables security logging by default. If you want this service, you must explicitly start it.

Running this application brings up the window shown in Figure 32.2.

FIGURE 32.2.
The Event Viewer application provides a summary of different kinds of events that have occurred.

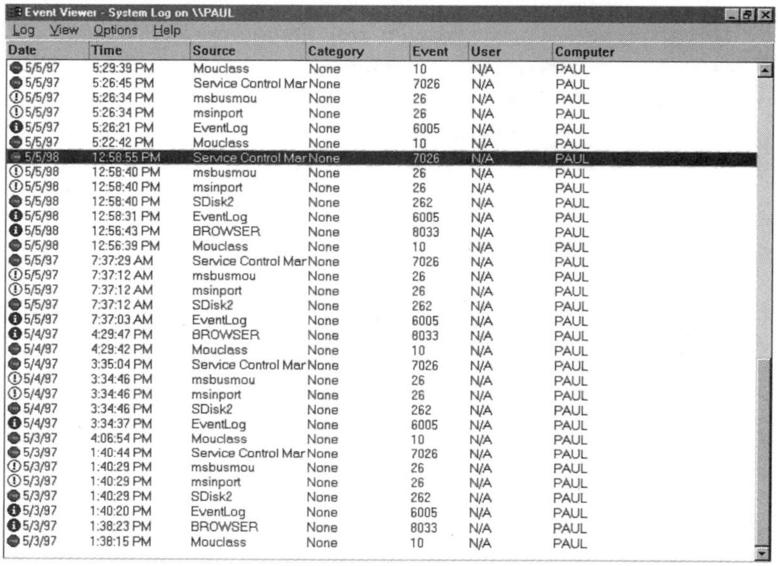

Date	Time	Source	Category	Event	User	Computer
5/5/97	5:29:39 PM	Mouclass	None	10	N/A	PAUL
5/5/97	5:26:45 PM	Service Control Mar	None	7026	N/A	PAUL
5/5/97	5:26:34 PM	msbusmou	None	26	N/A	PAUL
5/5/97	5:26:34 PM	msinport	None	26	N/A	PAUL
5/5/97	5:26:21 PM	EventLog	None	6005	N/A	PAUL
5/5/97	5:22:42 PM	Mouclass	None	10	N/A	PAUL
5/5/98	12:58:55 PM	Service Control Mar	None	7026	N/A	PAUL
5/5/98	12:58:40 PM	msbusmou	None	26	N/A	PAUL
5/5/98	12:58:40 PM	msinport	None	26	N/A	PAUL
5/5/98	12:58:40 PM	SDisk2	None	262	N/A	PAUL
5/5/98	12:58:31 PM	EventLog	None	6005	N/A	PAUL
5/5/98	12:56:43 PM	BROWSER	None	8033	N/A	PAUL
5/5/98	12:56:39 PM	Mouclass	None	10	N/A	PAUL
5/5/97	7:37:29 AM	Service Control Mar	None	7026	N/A	PAUL
5/5/97	7:37:12 AM	msbusmou	None	26	N/A	PAUL
5/5/97	7:37:12 AM	msinport	None	26	N/A	PAUL
5/5/97	7:37:12 AM	SDisk2	None	262	N/A	PAUL
5/5/97	7:37:03 AM	EventLog	None	6005	N/A	PAUL
5/4/97	4:29:47 PM	BROWSER	None	8033	N/A	PAUL
5/4/97	4:29:42 PM	Mouclass	None	10	N/A	PAUL
5/4/97	3:35:04 PM	Service Control Mar	None	7026	N/A	PAUL
5/4/97	3:34:46 PM	msbusmou	None	26	N/A	PAUL
5/4/97	3:34:46 PM	msinport	None	26	N/A	PAUL
5/4/97	3:34:46 PM	SDisk2	None	262	N/A	PAUL
5/4/97	3:34:37 PM	EventLog	None	6005	N/A	PAUL
5/3/97	4:06:54 PM	Mouclass	None	10	N/A	PAUL
5/3/97	1:40:44 PM	Service Control Mar	None	7026	N/A	PAUL
5/3/97	1:40:29 PM	msbusmou	None	26	N/A	PAUL
5/3/97	1:40:29 PM	msinport	None	26	N/A	PAUL
5/3/97	1:40:29 PM	SDisk2	None	262	N/A	PAUL
5/3/97	1:40:20 PM	EventLog	None	6005	N/A	PAUL
5/3/97	1:38:23 PM	BROWSER	None	8033	N/A	PAUL
5/3/97	1:38:15 PM	Mouclass	None	10	N/A	PAUL

The bar above the events has seven columns:

- Date
- Time
- Source
- Category
- Event
- User
- Computer

If you look at the event log, you can see that there are a number of error events (the ones with the red stop sign to the left). Looking back chronologically, you can see the first event (since the last reboot). Selecting that event and pressing the Enter key (or double-clicking the event) brings up the Event Detail dialog box, shown in Figure 32.3, which provides all the details that were logged.

FIGURE 32.3.

The Event Detail dialog box shows the greatest detail about the event in question, but sometimes it doesn't contain enough information for a full diagnostic.

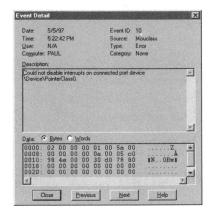

From this dialog box, you can see that the system could not disable the interrupts for the mouse it connected to the mouse port. Because on this machine the mouse functioned normally, this message makes little functional sense. After all, you can't fix what's not broken.

The type of event will give you a good indication of whether you should worry about the event or let it slide.

In other instances, the detail message actually does give you some information on a malfunctioning device. In this case, all you need to do is a full diagnostic and then fix the problem. However, this is usually easier said than done!

> **NOTE**
>
> In the Event Detail dialog box shown in Figure 32.3, the Service Control Manager is reporting that the device has failed to start and that it is not functioning. There could be an obvious reason and, thus, an obvious solution. However, the event details logged might not be all that helpful. Still, it's better than nothing!

The Event Viewer Application

The Event Viewer application is an important troubleshooting tool and is also very useful in administering networks of Windows NT systems. By examining the event log, you can solve the problems that occur, and, more importantly, you can identify and correct problems before they become more serious.

As you saw in Figure 32.2, the Event Viewer application has four menu items:

- *Log.* This enables you to choose which log to view and to manage the log.
- *View.* This option helps you to view the logs and find events within the logs.
- *Options.* This option enables you to change the font used in the application, control saving settings, and set up a low-speed connection.
- *Help.* This option provides standard Help facilities.

The remainder of this chapter covers these features and how to use them best.

What Information Is Logged?

Each event log entry contains parameters that are passed by the application to the RecordEvent API call. These are as follows:

- Source. This is the name of the software component that is reporting the event. The Source is either an application name or a component of a larger application.
- Event Identifier. This identifies the specific event and can be used by the support staff to aid them in determining the cause of the error. Event identifiers are unique to each Source.
- Type. Windows NT has five event types: Information, Warning, Error, Success Audit, and Failure Audit. Any event must be of only one of these event types.
- Category. To assist in organizing events (and to help users in reviewing the event log), a Source can define different categories. Although categories are not used much in the system or application logs, the security system uses several categories, including Logon/Logoff, File System Access, Privileged Actions, and Change in Security Policy.
- Description. This is a textual description of the event. The description is intended to provide you with the information needed to troubleshoot a problem, as opposed to programming details. The amount of helpful information included in the description varies significantly.
- Data. An event can have data associated with it. This could be a hardware error code, for example. Event data is not included for all events.

In addition to these parameters, each event log entry contains the time and date that the event was logged, as well as the system on which the event occurred. For security events, a user ID is also provided.

NOTE

When you view events in Event Viewer, the time and date shown will be the time on the local computer. To enable you to correlate events that occur on different systems, it is important to have a consistent time on all machines on a network. Use the NET TIME command, possibly as part of a logon script, to synchronize the clocks on all systems. Although the synchronized time might still be wrong, at least it's wrong over the entire network.

When viewing events with Event Viewer, the summary view (which you saw in Figure 32.2) shows Date, Time, Source, Category, Event, User, and Computer. In order to see the description and any included data, you need to look at the Event Detail.

As noted earlier, each event is categorized into one of five basic event types:

- *Information.* Information events are ones that are infrequent but successful. For example, the start of the Event Viewer is a useful event to note because it is usually the first event to occur when you boot the system. Information events are noted with a white exclamation point inside a blue circle. Information events are seen in the system and application logs.

- *Warning.* Warning events can reflect problems in the making. These are events that indicate a problem that is not yet serious—for example, the browser being unable to retrieve a list of domains from the browse master. This should usually resolve itself, but if it continues, the administrator might want to investigate and resolve this. Warning events are noted with a black exclamation point inside a yellow circle. Warning events are seen in the system and application logs.

- *Error.* Error events are events that usually represent a problem the user should be aware of, because these events usually indicate a loss of functionality. In the example in Figure 32.1, a network card failed to start; therefore, there will be no network functionality until the underlying cause is determined and rectified. Error events are noted by a red stop sign. Error events are seen in the system and application logs.

- *Success audit.* A success audit indicates that a successful audit event has occurred, such as a successful logon. A success audit event is noted with a key. Success audit events are seen only in the security log.

- *Failure audit.* A failure audit indicates that an unsuccessful audit event has occurred, such as a failed logon. A failure audit event is noted by a small padlock. Failure audit events are seen only in the security log.

System and Application Logs

The system event log contains events detected by the Windows NT Workstation operating system. The application log is used mainly to log events detected by applications running on your system. If possible, you should look at the logs on a regular basis. This enables you to spot problems before they become serious.

Here are some events that you are likely to see in the event log:

- *Event log startup.* Each time the system restarts, the Event Log service logs an information event. This tells you when the system restarted.

- *Driver startup failures.* If a driver fails to start, an error event is logged by the Service Control Manager to list the driver that failed. This can include error codes that can be very helpful to technical support staff but are not of much use to end users.

- *Device driver errors.* If a device driver encounters an error in operation, details of this error are written away to the system log. If a particular device is constantly logging errors, you should try to determine the source of the error. In such cases, the details logged in the system log might not be too much help in determining the error's cause.

- *Browser events.* The browser services tend to log a lot of events. Although these can usually be ignored, if multiple systems are constantly forcing browser elections, some reconfiguration of the network's browsing might be in order.

- *Service startup.* Some services, such as the SMNP service, log successful startups in the event log. You can usually ignore these events. However, if they don't occur when they should, their absence might be worth investigating.

- *Directory replication.* If your system is an import server, the Directory Replication service logs events in the system log. The details logged, in this case, are cryptic at best!

- *Printer events.* Whenever a new printer is added to your system or an existing printer driver is updated, Print Manager logs the event.

Most of these types of events result in clear and easy-to-understand system event log entries, although the Directory Replicator service is infamous for cryptic messages.

Security Log

The security event log is used to report security-related events. These events can indicate attempted or actual breaches of your system's security.

> **NOTE**
>
> In order to view all three event logs, you must be a member of the Administrator's local group. Without membership in this group, you can only view the system and application logs.

Unlike in the system and application logs, in the security log you determine which events are to be included. This is done by setting the audit policy and selecting events to audit.

Before you can get any security-related events recorded, you must first set the audit policy in User Manager. First, bring up User Manager; then select the Audit item from the Policies menu to bring up the Audit Policy dialog box, shown in Figure 32.4. You can also set audit policies for volumes and directories using the Properties dialog box for those objects. The audit policy dialog box is accessed via a button on the Security tab of the Properties dialog box.

FIGURE 32.4.

The Audit Policy dialog box from the User Manager is where you set audit policies for user groups.

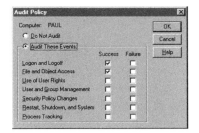

Before any security events can be logged, you must select the Audit These Events radio button. After you have set this option, you can select the specific security events to log and click OK to accept these options. There are three main places where you can set up audit events to be logged in the security log:

- General security events are set up in User Manager (as you saw in Figure 32.4).
- Registry-related security events are set up in the Registry Editor.
- File-related events are set up by using the file or directory Properties dialog box.

General security events are selected in the Audit Policy dialog box.

Selecting these events causes all occurrences of the event to be logged. Some events, such as the Use of User Rights or Process Tracking, can log a large amount of data and might not be very useful (unless you are developing and debugging an operating system component). The large amount of data logged also will slow down your system.

Using the Windows NT Registry Editor (regedt32.exe), you can log access to the System Registry by a user or group of users. Using the Audit item from the Security menu in regedit, you bring up the Registry Key Auditing dialog box, shown in Figure 32.5.

Unlike with general events, with Registry audit events you must select which users and/or groups should be audited. You do this by clicking the Add button and selecting the users and groups. Then you can select which audit events should be logged.

Audit events can be set up on any key or keys in the Registry. If you select Audit Permission on Existing Subkeys, you can replicate the auditing to all subkeys. Setting the auditing this way can take a lot of time, and if you set up very much auditing, you can generate many audit events. There also can be a significant performance impact of having to log the data.

FIGURE 32.5.

*You can set audit events
from the Registry
Editor, regedt32.exe.*

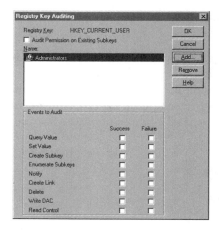

You can also log accesses by a user or group of users to any file or folder in your system. You set auditing by first selecting the folder or file to be audited and then right-clicking and bringing up the Properties dialog box for the object. From the Properties dialog box, select the Security tab, which is shown in Figure 32.6.

FIGURE 32.6.

*The NTFS Properties
Security tab has three
buttons: Permissions,
Auditing, and
Ownership.*

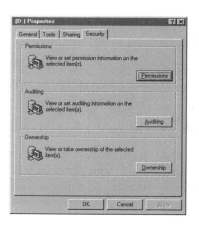

If you click the Auditing button in this dialog box, you bring up the Directory Auditing dialog box (if you are examining the properties of a folder) or the File Auditing dialog box (if you are examining the properties of a file). These two dialog boxes, which are very similar, are shown in Figures 32.7 and 32.8.

In both dialog boxes, you must first select the users whose access should be audited. Then you select which types of accesses you want to audit. It is not possible to log different audit events for different users in a single file or directory.

FIGURE 32.7.

The Directory Auditing dialog box allows setting of audit policies for an entire directory structure.

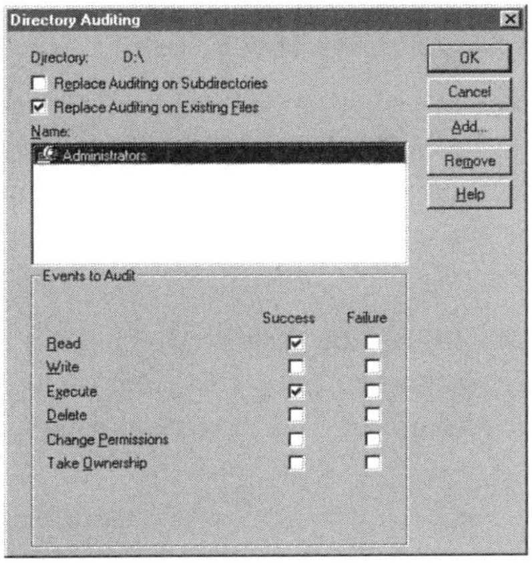

FIGURE 32.8.

The File Auditing dialog box is identical to the Directory Auditing dialog box, but its settings apply to files rather than directories.

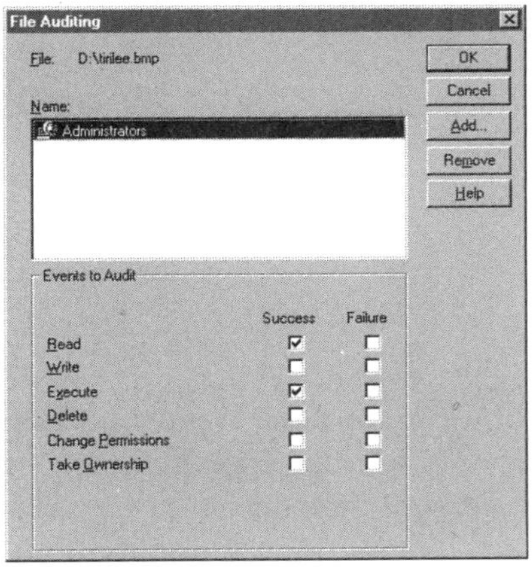

In the Directory Auditing dialog box, you can elect to replace the auditing information on all existing files within that folder, as well as to all the subdirectories.

> **WARNING**
>
> By default, the Directory Auditing dialog box replaces all existing audit events on all files in the chosen folder. If you have spent time setting up different levels of auditing on different files within a folder, clicking OK when viewing the Directory Audit dialog box overwrites all the audit events. This might not be what you want!

32

EVENT VIEWER

Viewing Logs Locally

When you start Event Viewer, it opens your local event log and displays whatever log was last being displayed (or the system log, the first time you run the application). Depending on what logging you have chosen and how long it has been since you cleared the event logs, you might find that the event logs are rather big. The View menu in Event Viewer has some options to assist you in finding events in the logs.

By default, all events logged are displayed. This can be a lot of data. Using the Filter Events item from the View menu brings up the Filter dialog box, shown in Figure 32.9. From here, you can reduce the amount of data to wade through.

FIGURE 32.9.

You can filter the events shown in the Event Viewer to focus on particular events.

Using this dialog box, you can select events that occurred between two times, as well as select which events to view. By selecting a specific source or user, you can see just the events generated by the related software component or by a specific user.

There are many Filter options available:

- *View From.* After a time or date.
- *View Through.* Up to and including a date or time.
- *Information.* The Information type event only.
- *Warning.* The Warning type event only.
- *Error.* The Error type event only.
- *Success Audit.* The Success Audit type event only.
- *Failure Audit.* The Failure Audit type event only.
- *Source.* The application, system component, or other object capable of being a source for an event.

- *Category.* Usually only for the security log. Filters by the category of the event, such as logons.
- *User.* The user name of the logged-on user during the event.
- *Computer.* The specific machine where the event occurred.
- *Event ID.* Shows only events bearing a particular ID number.

By default, Event Viewer displays the newest events at the top of the log and the oldest events at the bottom. You can change this order by selecting the Oldest First (or Newest First) option from the View menu. If you have Save Settings on Exit checked from the Options menu, whatever sort options you set will persist.

The Find item in the View menu can be used to find specific events. Selecting this option brings up the Find dialog box, which is shown in Figure 32.10. The combo box for the event source is expanded here with the 4mm tape drive highlighted. If selected, the Event Viewer will locate events for the drive.

FIGURE 32.10.

You can use the F3 key or View | Find menu command to locate particular events.

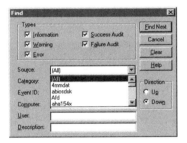

Using this dialog box, you select which items you are interested in seeing. Clicking the Find Next button finds the next occurrence of the event. If you are searching a large event log, you can press the F3 key to find the next occurrence.

If you are looking at a running system's log and events occur, you might not see them. To refresh the log, you can use the Refresh option on the View menu. The F5 key is a shortcut to this function.

Viewing Event Logs Remotely

As a Windows NT Workstation user, you will probably view only the logs on your computer system. However, in corporate networks, it might be useful to view remote event logs. Technical support staff, for example, might need to do this to diagnose problems remotely.

To view a remote system's event log, use the Select Computer option from the Log menu. This brings up a browse list containing systems you can select, as shown in Figure 32.11. You can also just type a machine name into the Computer name field.

FIGURE 32.11.

You select a system from your network by choosing the Select Computer choice from the Log menu.

> **NOTE**
>
> Before you can view a remote system's event logs, you must be able to log on to that system over the network. If you do not have those rights or you are not logged on as a user known to the remote system (with the right password), you get an error dialog box (Access is Denied).

After you select the remote system and get past the security, you can view the security logs on a remote system. Use the Log menu to choose which log to view and the View options to filter the log or find specific events.

Viewing the event logs on a remote system is as easy as viewing the logs on your own system.

If you are accessing a network via a slow connection (such as a modem), you might want to select the Low Speed Connection option. When this is selected, Windows NT will not enumerate all the computers on the network into the Select Computer dialog box. This can save you time if you're using a large network from a dial-up modem connection.

Managing the Event Logs

The event log can get to be rather large, and on most systems the vast bulk of the information logged is of little use.

To clear the Event Log, use the Clear All Events item from the Log menu. This clears the event log currently being viewed. Because the log might contain useful information, before

Windows NT clears the log, it offers you the opportunity to save the log. Because clearing the event log is an irrevocable event, Windows NT also asks for further confirmation before actually clearing the log.

To keep the event logs from getting too large, you can use the Event Log settings to set a maximum size for each log. Selecting the Log Settings item from the Log menu brings up the Event Log Settings dialog box shown in Figure 32.12.

FIGURE 32.12.

The Event Log Settings dialog box is the place where you set how long the archive exists and its size.

From this dialog box, you can select the maximum size of each of the three event logs. You can also use this dialog box to tell Windows NT what to do when the log fills up. You have three choices:

■ Overwrite events as required.

■ Overwrite events over a certain number of days. (The range is from 1 to 365 days.)

■ Do not overwrite events.

If you choose not to overwrite events, you need to manually clear the log in order to get new events logged. Most sites do not need to set this option.

Some users feel that the default font used by Event Viewer to display the logs is unattractive. You can change this font by using the Font option in the Options menu. If you choose a new font, this affects only the main event log screen (which you saw in Figure 32.2). Event details are still formatted in the standard system font.

Saving and Restoring Logs

Because of the importance of the event logs, you can choose to save them either when they get full or on a regular basis, rather than just clearing them, as discussed in the previous section.

To save a log, first select it from the Log menu. Next, select the Save As item from the Log menu. This brings up the Save As common dialog box, where you supply the filename and the format in which to save the log.

> **NOTE**
>
> Event log filtering has no effect on the log entries saved. Saving a log saves all entries, regardless of any filtering.

You have three choices of how to save the log:

- *Event log format.* This allows the saved log to be viewed by the Event Viewer application.
- *Text.* This saves the file as a simple text file.
- *Comma-delimited text.* Similar to Text, this format puts a comma between each field in the saved log.

Saving the log as comma-delimited text enables you to consolidate the saved log into a spreadsheet or database. Most spreadsheet or database programs support importing data from comma-delimited files.

> **NOTE**
>
> If you are going to import a saved event log into a spreadsheet or database, note that some description fields will contain commas. This might require extra work to ensure that all description fields are properly handled.

If you save an event log as an event log, you can later view the log using Event Viewer. If you use the Open item from the Log menu, you can open a saved event log and view it. A saved log can be filtered or searched in the same way as a live log.

Figure 32.13 shows an event log exported to a comma-delimited file and then imported into Microsoft Access. The conversion was handled automatically by Access.

The same table queried by Access can yield statistical information such as the number of each type of events. Figure 32.14 shows an example of this analysis.

ID	Date	Time	Event	Type	Category	Event ID	User
1	5/15/97	9:15:20 AM	msbusmou	Warning	None	26	N/A
2	5/15/97	9:15:20 AM	msinport	Warning	None	26	N/A
3	5/15/97	9:15:08 AM	EventLog	Information	None	6005	N/A
4	5/14/97	11:17:26 PM	BROWSER	Information	None	8033	N/A
5	5/14/97	11:17:19 PM	Mouclass	Error	None	10	N/A
6	5/14/97	10:01:44 PM	msbusmou	Warning	None	26	N/A
7	5/14/97	10:01:44 PM	msinport	Warning	None	26	N/A
8	5/14/97	10:01:33 PM	EventLog	Information	None	6005	N/A
9	5/14/97	5:35:05 PM	BROWSER	Information	None	8033	N/A
10	5/14/97	5:34:59 PM	Mouclass	Error	None	10	N/A
11	5/14/97	5:07:13 PM	msbusmou	Warning	None	26	N/A
12	5/14/97	5:07:13 PM	msinport	Warning	None	26	N/A
13	5/14/97	5:07:01 PM	EventLog	Information	None	6005	N/A
14	5/14/97	6:38:15 AM	BROWSER	Information	None	8033	N/A
15	5/14/97	6:38:07 AM	Mouclass	Error	None	10	N/A
16	5/14/97	6:21:33 AM	msbusmou	Warning	None	26	N/A
17	5/14/97	6:21:33 AM	msinport	Warning	None	26	N/A
18	5/14/97	6:21:22 AM	EventLog	Information	None	6005	N/A
19	5/13/97	1:34:16 PM	BROWSER	Information	None	8033	N/A
20	5/13/97	1:34:11 PM	Mouclass	Error	None	10	N/A
21	5/13/97	8:57:51 AM	msbusmou	Warning	None	26	N/A
22	5/13/97	8:57:51 AM	msinport	Warning	None	26	N/A
23	5/13/97	8:57:37 AM	EventLog	Information	None	6005	N/A
24	5/12/97	4:10:24 PM	Mouclass	Error	None	10	N/A
25	5/12/97	7:11:44 AM	msbusmou	Warning	None	26	N/A
26	5/12/97	7:11:44 AM	msinport	Warning	None	26	N/A

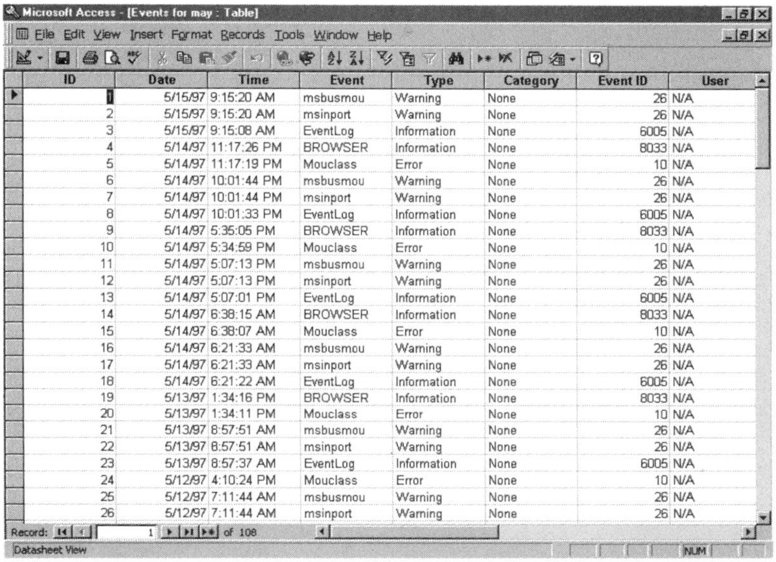

FIGURE 32.13.
Microsoft Access can easily create a table containing the event log using its Import facility.

Type	CountOfType
Error	29
Information	35
Warning	38

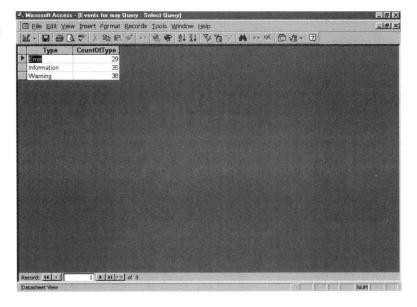

FIGURE 32.14.
A Totals query in Access (or a similar facility in Excel) can give you an analysis of your event log.

Summary

The Event Viewer application is a great place to start most troubleshooting sessions or to look for security violations. It is easy to use and can be very handy. Perhaps the biggest drawback is the quality of the messages that get posted—but this is not the Event Viewer's fault! All in all, this is a key application that any power user must be familiar and comfortable with.

Performance Monitor

by Paul Cassel

IN THIS CHAPTER

33

CHAPTER

The Performance Monitor

The Performance Monitor utility included with Windows NT is an extremely powerful and useful utility, and it is often overlooked or underused. Performance Monitor first and foremost provides a mechanism to monitor system performance on your or other networked computers in a general manner and provides the capability of isolating specific system components and monitoring them in minute detail to determine the root of a problem or cause of a bottleneck.

Using the Performance Monitor, you can

- View or change performance charts.
- Export data from Performance Monitor charts, logs, alerts, or reports to external programs such as Microsoft Access or Microsoft Excel.
- Set system alerts to either log those alerts or sound an alarm.
- Set a trigger to run a task based on system status.
- Create and append system logs for the local or other networked systems.
- View data from one or more computers.
- Save various settings or save the current global settings; then recall them as needed.

Performance Monitor has four separate components: Chart, Alert, Log, and Report. Each component monitors the performance of the specified components, but it handles the data in a different manner.

- *Chart.* The Chart utility charts the specified components at user-configurable intervals and presents the data in the form of either a graph or a histogram.
- *Alert.* The Alert utility enables the user to specify components to monitor and can be configured to send an alert and/or execute a program if the counter on a specified component goes over or under a defined threshold.
- *Log.* The Log utility logs to file the value of specified counters for components at specified intervals.
- *Report.* The Report utility generates a report based on the statistics of the specified counters.

Counters, Instances, and Objects

The Performance Monitor uses the terms objects, instances, and counters to identify its processes. An *object* is a system resource. Examples of objects are physical disks, processors, and memory. Some objects have instances that are duplicates. For example, a computer with two Pentium Pro processors has two instances of the object Processor.

A computer with only one processor has only one *instance* of that object. If a computer has four physical disks, it has that many instances of the object Physical Disk.

Counters are the statistical aspect of an object, a measurement unit as defined for a given component. For example, percentage of processor time is a statistic. It's expressed as `%Processor Time` in the Counter List Box of the Add to Chart dialog box shown in Figure 33.1.

Only Windows NT native (32-bit) programs appear named in the Performance Monitor. Non-NT programs, such as Windows 16 (Win16) ones run in a Virtual DOS Machine (NTVDM), appear as a VDM rather than with their executable name unless they're run in their own memory space.

Charting

The most common use of Performance Monitor, in my experience, has been to determine the cause of poor system performance. Unfortunately for most system administrator types, the time it takes to monitor system performance cannot be justified until a problem arises. If this is the case and a bottleneck exists in the system or the system just seems to be running poorly, the charting utility in Performance Monitor is the tool to use.

This utility charts the value of specified system components at any interval from 0 to 2,000,000 seconds, as defined by the user, which can give a good indication (in real time) of where the bottleneck exists. Typically, system slowness will be in one of four areas: disk I/O, processor resources, memory resources, or the network component (if installed).

To monitor a given component, Performance Monitor uses counters. Most Windows NT components have counters that can be monitored, although some must be installed manually. (To monitor TCP/IP performance, the SNMP feature of TCP/IP must be installed.)

To begin monitoring, you must specify the object that you want to monitor, the specific counters you want to monitor for that object (see Figure 33.1), and, if applicable, an instance of the selected object. To add objects and counters to a graph, click the Add to Chart option from the Edit menu. Each object counter can be customized in color, scale, line width, and style through the Add to Chart dialog box.

FIGURE 33.1.

To add objects and counters to a graph choose the computer, the object, then the counter specific to that object. This screen shows the computer \\PAUL, *object* Processor, *and counter* %Processor Time.

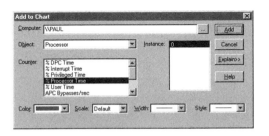

Typically, a good starting point for determining the area of the system causing the bottleneck is to use a general configuration, such as Total Processor Time, Memory Page Faults, Memory Bytes Available, and Paging File Usage.

If you have any questions about what a particular counter does, click on the Explain>> button. This will expand the dialog box to include a brief explanation of each counter. Figure 33.2 shows the Performance Monitor in operation after adding the counter shown in Figure 33.1.

FIGURE 33.2.

This is the Performance Monitor in operation after adding the counter shown in Figure 33.1.

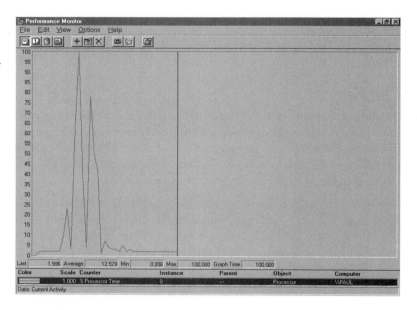

When you have determined which system component is the cause of the bottleneck, you can then customize your monitoring to drill down to the details of that subsystem and determine how to relieve the bottleneck. This does not always require a hardware upgrade; sometimes it is as simple as reconfiguring a system component, changing the paging file size, or tuning the working environment.

Other options are available for customizing the chart that are also available for the Alert, Log, and Report functions. Here is a summary of the options:

- *File Menu*

    New Chart (Alert, Log, Report) begins a new instance of the utility with new counters.

    Save Settings (As) saves the current settings so that they can be reused at a later time without having to define the settings again.

    Export exports the data to a delimited text file that can be imported to other applications and parsed as desired.

- *Edit Menu*

    Add to Chart adds object counters.

    Edit Chart Line edits the selected object counter.

Clear Display clears the gathered statistics and starts counting fresh.

Delete From Chart removes the selected object counter from the display.

■ *Options Menu*

Chart (Alert, Log, Report) displays the options for the utility, such as whether to display the legend and value bar, how to display data, and the time interval to collect statistics.

Data From allows the importing of previously collected data, and saved data can be loaded from a file to analyze.

Update Now causes the data to be updated immediately rather than waiting for the next specified interval.

Alerts

For those times when you are not actively trying to pinpoint a system performance problem, you can do other things to monitor ongoing system performance and be alerted to potential bottlenecks before they become critical, which gives you time to respond appropriately.

A very useful utility for this purpose is the Alert feature of Performance Monitor. Using this feature, you can specify object counters in the same way you did with the Chart previously. For each object counter that you want to monitor, you specify a threshold value for which an alert will be generated if that threshold is crossed.

When a threshold value is exceeded (or falls below the value), a record is written to the Alerts window in Performance Monitor (shown in Figure 33.3). Optionally, a program can be configured to run, an alert can be configured to be sent across the network to a specified individual or computer, and the occurrence can be written to the Windows NT Event Viewer Application Log.

33

PERFORMANCE
MONITOR

FIGURE 33.3.

The Alerts window in Performance Monitor shows when monitored system events exceed your set limits.

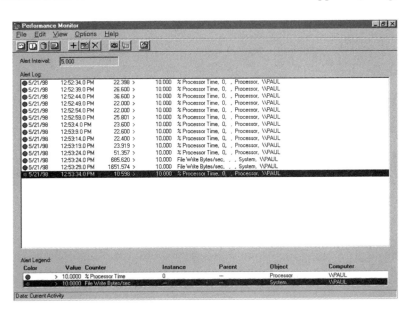

In the example shown in Figure 33.3, the Performance Monitor has been asked to create an alert if the processor works more than 10% or the system writes more than 10 bytes a second. Both those things occur regularly, so they have generated many alerts in a short time.

This utility provides a good method for monitoring system performance over long periods of time while under normal usage, providing a clear picture of how the system holds up under real-world usage over a period of time.

This can be helpful for situations such as monitoring a system throughout the course of a typical workday in order to determine when and why a specified object is pushed beyond its limits.

Monitoring Other Computers

You can monitor the objects on other computers at the same time you monitor local objects. To add another computer's objects to the Add to Chart dialog box, click the Add button to the immediate right of the Computer combo box. Figure 33.4 shows the browse network dialog box.

Figure 33.4.

To locate and add another computer to the Performance Monitor, you can browse for it using the familiar browse network dialog box.

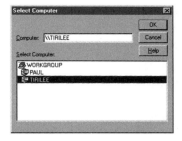

The dialog box in Figure 33.4 shows only two computers because a workgroup of two was constructed for this and other screen shots. Most working examples of networks have more than two computers.

Once you've located the network computer whose objects you want to monitor, you add those objects, instances, and counters just as you would those of a local computer. Figure 33.5 shows the simultaneous monitoring of the processor time on two different computers.

Logging

The logging utility in Performance Monitor is best used as a tool to gather system performance data over an extended period of time to export to another application for analysis.

Adding objects to the log is fairly similar to the other utilities, except specific counters cannot be specified; only objects can be specified. (By default, all counters for the selected objects will be logged.) Also, a log file must be specified (using the Options menu and Log item) to write the data to, and logging must be started manually by clicking the Start Log button.

FIGURE 33.5.

The Performance Monitor is tracking processor time used for two computers, \\PAUL *and* \\TIRILEE, *at the same time. The solid line represents* \\PAUL, *and the dashed line represents* \\TIRILEE.

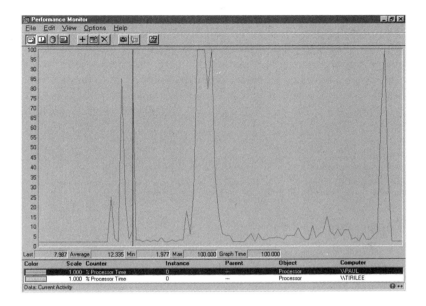

As mentioned earlier, this utility is designed to monitor performance data over an extended period of time. It is recommended that the log interval not be set at less than 15-second intervals, because the log file grows extremely fast and quickly becomes difficult to effectively parse and analyze.

When the log period is completed, the log file can be exported to a text-format comma-delimited file for use in other applications, such as Microsoft Access, or it can be imported into the Performance Monitor chart utility for interpretation.

You can set the logging parameters by choosing the Options | Log menu choices. Here, you can set the log name (so you can save and recall it), the logging interval, and the updating method. Figure 33.6 shows the creation of a new log.

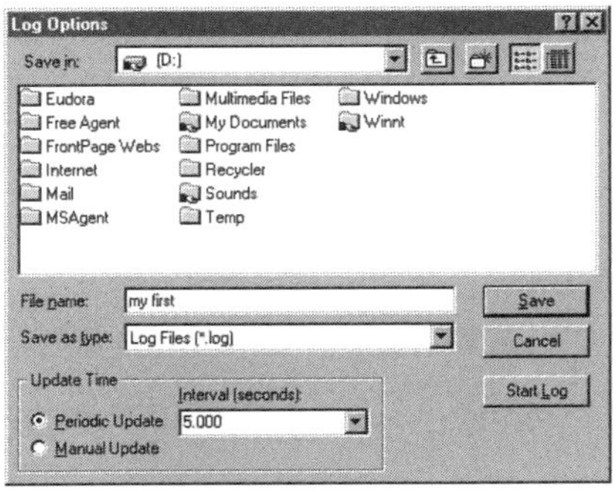

FIGURE 33.6.

The Options | Log menu choice brings up a dialog box allowing you to create as many log varieties as you choose.

Adding a Bookmark or Comment

You can add a bookmark or comment to a log file by clicking on the Commented Bookmark button on the toolbar, by choosing the menu options Options | Bookmark, or by pressing Ctrl+B. This brings up a simple input box allowing you to insert a comment, as shown in Figure 33.7.

FIGURE 33.7.

Adding a comment to the log file is as easy as pressing Ctrl+B, making a menu choice, or clicking on a toolbar button.

Reporting

The report view window in Performance Monitor is a very straightforward view of selected objects and counters. The selected counters and statistics are displayed in a report format similar to a spreadsheet-type report, providing a quick view of current activity and performance.

Figure 33.8 shows the report window of the Performance Monitor gathering information about three objects and one each of their counters.

FIGURE 33.8.

The report data window is a simple display showing, in this case, three counters and their momentary values.

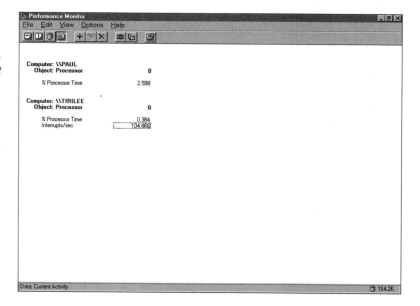

You can export the Report data to a comma-delimited file easily read by Microsoft Excel or Microsoft Access. To export a report, choose File | Export Report from the menu. Figure 33.9 shows an exported file brought up in Microsoft Excel.

FIGURE 33.9.

You can save one or a series of reports to a comma-delimited file for display or analysis in various programs, including Microsoft Excel.

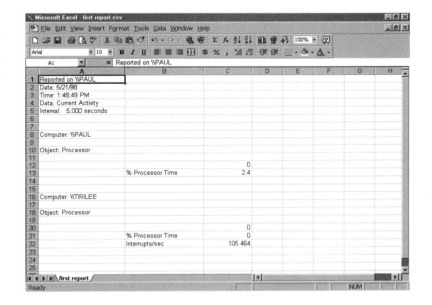

Summary

As you have seen here, Performance Monitor is a unique, very extensive application that can provide invaluable information about system performance and ways to improve it. This tool should be well understood and utilized by any Windows NT system administrator or person responsible for supporting Windows NT. It can save time and headaches if it is understood and utilized on a regular basis.

Task Manager

by Mike Sheehy

CHAPTER 34

IN THIS CHAPTER

How often have you posed the following questions: "How well is my workstation performing?" "Should I upgrade the spec of my workstation?" Up until NT 4 it was always difficult to back up your decision with facts. Sure, you could always use the Performance Monitor. The Performance Monitor itself is a powerful tool that encompasses performance measurements based on a wide range of criteria. The Performance Monitor can build a performance trend on your workstation or on any other NT servers or workstations simultaneously. The downside to the Performance Monitor, however, is that it requires setup, careful definition of your monitoring criteria, and time to build up a trend upon which you would base a final decision. On the other hand, the Task Manager, new to NT 4, concentrates on monitoring your applications and processes. The Task Manager allows you to view the applications and processes that are running on your system and also lets you see what impact they have on your workstation. The Task Manager is ideally suited to quick checks on your system and provides only basic counters. You should use the Task Manager as a precursor to the Performance Monitor. Armed with the Task Manager, you can rectify the obvious problems without having to go through the rigors of using the Performance Monitor. Tougher, more obscure problems, which you cannot pinpoint with the Task Manager, have to be weeded out by the Performance Manager. The Task Manager cannot monitor other workstations or servers, nor can it store data for later review.

Starting the Task Manager

You do not have to install the Task Manager, because it comes preinstalled by default. There are a number of different ways to access the Task Manager:

- You can press a combination of the Ctrl, Shift, and Esc keys.
- You can right-click on the Taskbar at the base of your screen and select Task Manager from the menu (see Figure 34.1).
- You can press a combination of the Ctrl, Alt, and Del keys to activate the Windows NT Security dialog. Click on the Task Manager from the dialog (see Figure 34.2).
- You can simply type `Taskmgr.exe` from the Run option (see Figure 34.3).

FIGURE 34.1.

Accessing the Task Manager from the Taskbar.

FIGURE 34.2.

Accessing the Task Manager from the Windows NT Security dialog.

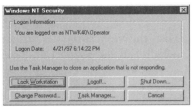

FIGURE 34.3.

Accessing the Task Manager from the Run option.

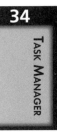

34

TASK MANAGER

Applications

Once you start the Task Manager, you are presented with the Windows NT Task Manager dialog. The Task Manager is divided into three tabs: the Applications tab, the Processes tab, and the Performance tab (see Figure 34.4).

FIGURE 34.4.

The Task Manager with the Applications tab selected.

The Applications tab lists the applications currently running on the workstation. The list has two columns: Task, which lists the applications, and Status, which reflects the status of the application.

You will notice three buttons located at the base of the Applications tab:

- The End Task button allows you to terminate the application that is currently selected from the Task list.

- The Switch To button allows you to switch to the application that is currently selected.

- The New Task button allows you to launch a new application. When clicked, the New Task button launches the Create New Task dialog (see Figure 34.5). You can browse to the application you want through the Browse button.

FIGURE 34.5.

The Create New Task dialog.

NOTE

The select list within the Create New Task dialog is the same history list of tasks that have been run from the Run box.

Right-clicking on any of the running applications from the Applications tab will enable a context menu, as shown in Figure 34.6.

FIGURE 34.6.

The context menu of an application within the Applications tab of the Task Manager.

This menu includes the following options:

- *Switch To.* This option allows you to switch to the selected application and make it the active application. The Task Manager minimizes to make way for the active application. You can also execute a switch-to operation by double-clicking on an application from the list.
- *Bring to Front.* This brings the currently selected application to the foreground. It differs from the Switch To option in that the Bring to Front option does not make the application the active application because the Task Manager remains maximized and active.
- *Minimize.* This option minimizes the currently selected application.
- *Maximize.* This options maximizes the currently selected application.
- *End Task.* This button allows you to terminate the currently selected application.
- *Go To Process.* This option allows you to switch to the Processes tab with the selected application's process highlighted. The Processes tab is explained further later in this chapter.

34

TASK MANAGER

Right-clicking on any area besides an application brings up a menu with the following options (see Figure 34.7):

- *New Task (Run).* This option launches a new application using the same Create New Task dialog described previously. The Create New Task dialog can also be invoked by selecting New Task from the File menu.
- *Large Icons.* This option configures the associated application icons to be large. The applications are arranged one after another with large icons.
- *Small Icons.* This option configures the associated application icons to be small. The applications are arranged one after another with small icons.
- *Details.* The Details option is the default view that arranges the applications in a list with the two columns, Task and Status.

FIGURE 34.7.

The context menu of the application area.

All the column widths can be resized as follows:

1. Simply move the mouse pointer over the split in the column headers until its shape changes (see Figure 34.8).
2. Hold down the left mouse and drag the column split left or right to suit your needs.

Clicking on the tab border of the tab will enable or disable the status and menu bars and the tab headers. Disabling these window elements will produce a nice compact view of the Applications tab (see Figure 34.9). Doubling-clicking the display border will toggle between the two views.

FIGURE 34.8.

Resizing the Task Manager columns.

FIGURE 34.9.

Disabling the status bar, menu bar, and tab headers.

The Options menu at the top of the Task Manager allows you to set the following preferences:

- *Always On Top.* This option will keep the Task Manager on top—that is, the Task Manager will always be visible even though it is not the active application.

- *Minimize On Use.* This option sets the Task Manager to minimize when you switch to another application.

- *Hide When Minimized.* This option removes Task Manager from the Taskbar. You can restore Task Manager by double-clicking it on the Task Tray (see Figure 34.10). As you can see from Figure 34.10, the Task Manager icon in the Task Tray also displays the CPU Usage when you bring the mouse pointer over it.

34

TASK MANAGER

FIGURE 34.10.
The Task Manager icon in the Task Tray.

The View menu has the following preference settings:

■ *Refresh Now.* This option forces Task Manager to refresh its display.

■ *Update Speed.* This option allows you to set the rate at which Task Manager will refresh its data. The sample rates are High, Medium, or Low. You can also pause the sampling by selecting Paused.

■ *Large Icons, Small Icons, Details.* These options allow you to choose how the applications appear within the list. Each of these options was explained previously.

The Windows menu allows you to set the following options:

■ *Tile Horizontally.* This option allows you to tile the running applications horizontally.

■ *Tile Vertically.* This option allows you to tile the running applications vertically.

■ *Minimize.* This option allows you to minimize the currently selected application.

■ *Maximize.* This option allows you to maximize the currently selected application.

■ *Bring To Front.* This option brings the currently selected option to the front.

Processes

Selecting the Processes tab brings up a list of processes (see Figure 34.11).

FIGURE 34.11.

The Processes tab.

The Processes tab window can display up to fourteen columns of data. By default, there are five columns displayed when you first select the Processes tab. Each of these columns is associated with a Performance Monitor Process Counter. Here is a list of the column headers and their associated Performance Monitor Process Counters; the first five are displayed by default:

- *Image Name.* The name of the process. This corresponds to the process name in the instance box of the Performance Monitor.

- *PID (Process Identifier).* A numerical value given to the process while it is running. This corresponds to the Performance Monitor Process Counter, ID Process.

- *CPU Usage.* The percentage of time the process used the processor since that last update was taken. This corresponds to the Performance Monitor Process Counter, %Processor Time.

- *CPU Time.* The processor time the process has used since starting.

- *Memory Usage.* The amount of main memory used by the process in kilobytes. This also corresponds to the Performance Monitor Process Counter, Working set.

- *Memory Usage Delta.* The change in memory since the last update. This can also reflect negative values.

- *Page Faults.* The number of page faults attributed to this process since it started.

- *Page Faults Delta.* The change in the number of page faults since the last update.

- *Virtual Memory Size.* What amount of the pagefile this process occupies. This also corresponds to the Performance Monitor Process Counter, Page File Bytes.

- *Paged Pool.* The amount of the paged pool occupied by the process. This also corresponds to the Performance Monitor Process Counter, Pool Paged Bytes.

34

TASK MANAGER

- *Nonpaged Pool.* The amount of nonpaged pool occupied by the process. This also corresponds to the Performance Monitor Process Counter, Pool Nonpaged Bytes.
- *Base Priority.* The priority of the process's threads. This also corresponds to the Performance Monitor Process Counter, Priority Base.
- *Handle Count.* The number of object handles in the process's object table. This also corresponds to the Performance Monitor Process Counter, Handle Count.
- *Thread Count.* The number of threads running under the process. This also corresponds to the Performance Monitor Process Counter, Thread Count.

The End Process button at the base of the Processes tab allows you to terminate the currently selected process. Different options appear under the menu headings when the Processes tab is selected.

Under the Options menu there is an extra option called Show 16-Bit Tasks. When checked, this menu option displays 16-bit processes on the process list.

Under the View menu, the final three options (Large Icons, Small Icons, and Detail) are replaced by Select Columns. This option allows you to choose which columns appear in the list. I mentioned previously that, by default, five columns appear on the process list. Under Select Columns, you can enable any of the fourteen columns to appear. When you choose this option, you are presented with the Select Columns dialog, as shown in Figure 34.12. The column headers are included by simply checking their associated check box.

FIGURE 34.12.

The Select Columns dialog.

Clicking on any of the column headers from the Processes tab will sort the list in ascending or descending order. If you right-click on a process from the process list, you can do the following:

- *End Process.* Terminate the selected process.
- *Debug.* Debug the selected process (if you have a debugger installed).
- *Set Priority.* Choose the priority under which the selected process's threads will run. This change is not permanent, however. The process threads will have the same priority, as set by the application code, the next time they run. There are four different priority levels to choose from: High, Medium, Low, and Realtime.

Again, as with the Applications tab, if you double-click on the border of the tab, the status bar, menu bar, and tab headers disappear.

Performance

The last tab on the Task Manager is the Performance tab. The Performance tab gives you an at-a-glance estimate of your workstation's performance (see Figure 34.13).

FIGURE 34.13.

The Performance tab.

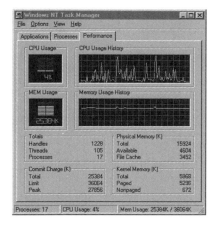

There are eight frames on the Performance tab:

- ■ *CPU Usage.* This is a graphical indicator that illustrates the CPU usage.
- ■ *CPU Usage History.* Again a graphical indicator, this illustrates the CPU usage over time.
- ■ *MEM Usage.* This frame graphically illustrates the memory usage of the workstation.
- ■ *Memory Usage History.* This frame graphically records the memory usage over time.
- ■ *Totals.* This frame keeps a running total of the number of handles, threads, and processes.
- ■ *Physical Memory (K).* This frame records the total, file cache, and available memory on the workstation.
- ■ *Commit Charge (K).* This frame records details on the Commit memory. Commit memory is memory allocated to programs and/or the system. Detail figures include total, limit, and peak values.
- ■ *Kernel Memory (K).* This frame records memory allocated to the operating system. Details include total, paged, and nonpaged.

Double-clicking anywhere on the Performance tab will maximize the CPU Usage and CPU Usage History (see Figure 34.14).

Figure 34.14.

Maximizing the CPU frames.

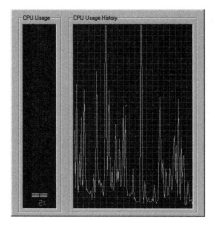

Again, as with the two previous tabs, there are extra options in the menus pertaining to the Performance tab. Under the View menu, there are two entries—CPU History and Show Kernel Times—that appear at the base of the menu when the Performance tab is selected. CPU History applies to multiprocessor machines and allows you to get a disparate graph for each CPU. Show Kernel Times, when selected, adds a graph line representing the memory usage by the kernel.

As you selected each of the tabs, the Status Bar remained constant at the base of the Task Manager. The Status Bar displays the number of processes, the CPU Usage, and the Mem Usage counters.

Summary

In this chapter, you looked closely at the Task Manager and saw how you could use it to help evaluate your workstation's performance. The Task Manager requires no setup or configuration and is installed by default on your workstation. The Task Manager is an excellent precursor to the Performance Monitor and allows you to monitor applications and processes and determine possible system bottlenecks. Through the Task Manager you can launch, switch between, and close applications and processes. You also can monitor the impact an application or process has on your workstation.

Server Manager

by Mike Sheehy

IN THIS CHAPTER

CHAPTER 35

In this chapter, you will look at another of NT Workstation's administration tools. The Server Manager does not come installed with Windows NT Workstation by default, but needs to be taken either from the NT Workstation Resource Kit or from the Windows NT Server CD-ROM. The Server Manager allows you to administer other servers and workstations remotely. Through the Server Manager, you can view and administer the shares and services on a remove server or workstation. The Server Manager can also be used administer domain membership and is ideal for gaining a quick snapshot of what users are doing over network connections.

Loading the Server Manager

On the NT Workstation Resource Kit, an executable file (srvmgr.exe) is located in \srvtools\winnt\i386 on the NT Server CD-ROM. To load the Server Manager onto your workstation, complete the following steps:

1. Open Explorer and go to the Server Manager executable.
2. Right-click on srvmgr.exe and select Copy from its menu.
3. Traverse to the Winnt\system32 directory on your workstation, right-click anywhere in the directory area and select Paste from the menu. Figure 35.1 shows the Server Manager copied to the systemroot directory.

FIGURE 35.1.

Copy the Server Manager to the systemroot directory.

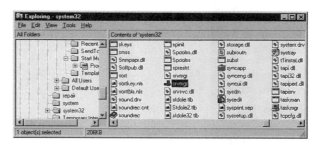

4. To add the Server Manager to the Taskbar, first select Start and then select Settings | Taskbar (see Figure 35.2).
5. Once you have activated the Taskbar Properties dialog, select the Start Menu Programs tab (see Figure 35.3).
6. Click on the Add button and enter the path to the Server Manager executable or browse to it using the Browse button (see Figure 35.4).
7. Click Next and you are presented with the Select Program Folder dialog. Select or create the folder you want the Server Manager to reside in (see Figure 35.5).
8. Click Next to be presented with the Select a Title for the Program dialog (see Figure 35.6). Click Finish to complete the addition to the Task menu.

FIGURE 35.2.
Accessing the Taskbar.

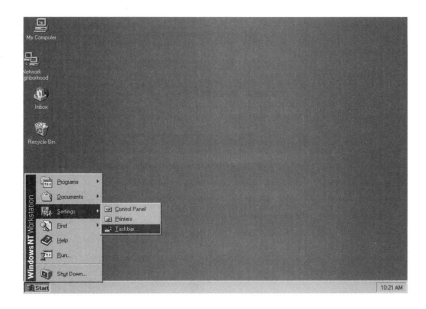

FIGURE 35.3.
*The Start Menu
Programs tab.*

FIGURE 35.4.
*Enter or browse to the
Server Manager
executable.*

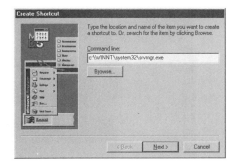

35

**SERVER
MANAGER**

FIGURE 35.5.

Determine the Server Manager's folder location.

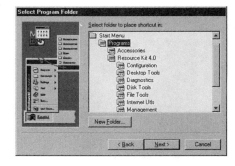

FIGURE 35.6.

Give a title for the program.

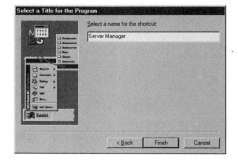

Figure 35.7 shows the addition of the Server Manager in the Task menu.

FIGURE 35.7.

Server Manager added to the Task menu.

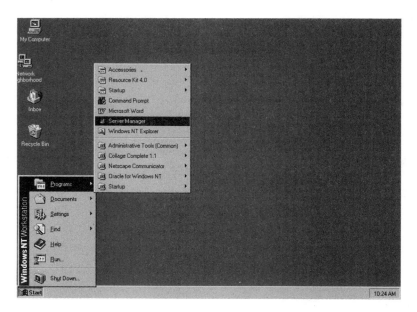

Viewing Computers Within the Server Manager

When you activate the Server Manager, you are presented with a browse list of all the computers within the domain or workgroup (see Figure 35.8). The list contains columns for the computer's name, type, and description.

FIGURE 35.8.

The Server Manager window.

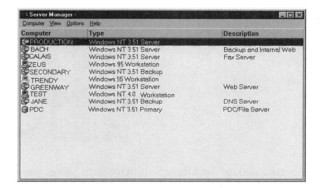

There are a number of different types of computers within an NT network, and these are represented by the different icons located to the left of each computer listing, as shown in Figure 35.8. The following are two types of computer that can exist within an NT network:

- *Servers.* Servers are either Primary Domain Controllers (PDC) or Backup Domain Controllers (BDC). The PDC stores the security database (SAM), which gets periodically replicated to BDC(s). When users log on to a domain, they are authenticated by either the PDC or a BDC.

- *Workstation.* Workstations are either non-PDC/non-BDC NT servers, NT workstations, Windows 95 computers, or Windows for Workgroups computers.

You can specify the view Server Manager presents to you by selecting your choices from the View menu. You can choose to view either Servers only, Workstations only, All computers, or Domain members only. You can refresh the list by selecting Refresh from the View menu or by pressing F5 on the keyboard.

> **NOTE**
>
> Notice the different types of icons associated with the different types of computers on the list. Notice also that when computers are not activated, those icons are gray in color.

Computer Properties

Now that you know how to set the scope of your network view, what can you do with the Server Manager? To be presented with a computer's properties, select any computer from the Computer window and choose Properties from the Computer menu. Figure 35.9 shows you a sample Properties dialog for a workstation. These Properties dialogs are the same for workstations as they are for servers.

FIGURE 35.9.

The Properties dialog.

In the Properties dialog, the Usage Summary frame gives you a summary of the following:

- *Sessions*. The number of users who are remotely connected to the workstation.
- *Open Files*. The total number of files open through those remote connections.
- *File Locks*. The total number of file locks by connected users.
- *Open Named Pipes*. The total number of named pipes open on the workstation. A *named pipe* is a communication channel that allows processes to communicate either locally or remotely with one another.

Below this frame there is a Description text box into which you can enter a description of the workstation to appear on the main Server Manager list. There are also five buttons that allow you to further configure the workstation.

Users

The first of these buttons is the Users button. When you select the Users button, you are presented with the User Sessions dialog (see Figure 35.10).

FIGURE 35.10.

The User Sessions dialog.

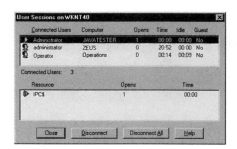

The upper half of the dialog gives you a breakdown of connections by user. This pane details the connected users, the computer from which the connections were made, the number of open connections, the duration of the session, the time since the user initiated an action, and whether the connection was via the Guest account. The lower pane lists how many open resources a selected user has and the time since the resource was opened.

There are four resources that a user can have open:

- A shared printer
- A shared directory
- A named pipe
- A communication device queue

You also can disconnect a selected user or all users by clicking on the Disconnect or Disconnect All button. To exit the dialog, click on the Close button.

Shares

The Shares button activates the Shared Resources dialog, illustrated in Figure 35.11.

FIGURE 35.11.

The Shared Resources dialog.

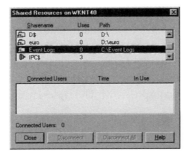

The upper half of the dialog lists the shared resources defined on the workstation, how many connections are open to each shared resource, and the path associated with the share. When you highlight an entry in the upper pane, a breakdown of the connected users to that resource appears in the lower pane. The lower pane details the user connected to the resource, when the session was opened, and whether a user has a file open on the share. Again, as with the User Sessions dialog, you can disconnect a selected user or all users from the shared resource.

In Use

When you select the In Use button, you activate the Open Resources dialog (see Figure 35.12). This dialog lists the resources open through remote connections.

FIGURE 35.12.

The Open Resources dialog.

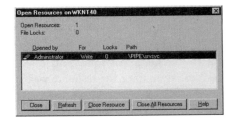

At the top of the dialog appears the total number of open resources and file locks on the workstation. The main pane within the dialog lists the user who opened the resource, what permissions it was opened with, the number of locks on the resource, and the path to the resource. Again, you have the ability to close selected or all open resources with the buttons located at the base of the dialog.

Replication

The Replication button launches the Directory Replication dialog. This dialog allows you to configure a set of directories between computers. These directories are exported from an export computer and are imported to one or more import computers. Replication is ideal if you have to maintain exact copies of files and directories across a number of different computers. With replication, you have to maintain changes only on the export or master computer and Replication will take care of replicating the changes to the import computers. The root for the export and import directories starts at `systemroot\system32\repl\export` and `systemroot\system32\repl\import`, respectively. Unfortunately, Windows NT Workstation can act only as an import computer, which renders it unable to act as a master or export computer.

In the Directory Replication dialog (see Figure 35.13), you are presented with two radio buttons that control whether the workstation will import files and directories.

FIGURE 35.13.

The Directory Replication dialog.

Once you select the Import Directories button, the import path is inserted into the To Path: text box. To further manage where the imported files and directories will reside below this directory level, you must select the Manage button. Selecting the Manage button activates the Manage Imported Directories dialog (see Figure 35.14).

FIGURE 35.14.

*The Manage Imported
Directories dialog.*

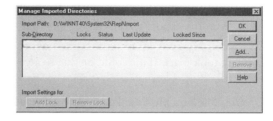

This dialog allows you to create a sub-directory into which you can place the imported data.
Selecting the Add button activates the Add Sub-Directory dialog (see Figure 35.15), which
allows you to define such a sub-directory.

FIGURE 35.15.

*The Add Sub-Directory
dialog.*

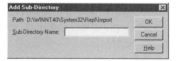

Enter a name for the sub-directory and click on OK. The new sub-directory now appears on
the Manage Imported Directories dialog, as in Figure 35.16.

FIGURE 35.16.

*The new sub-directory
added to the Manage
Imported Directories
dialog.*

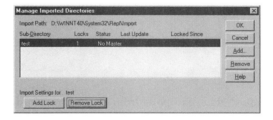

Other displayed attributes associated with the newly added directory include the following:

- *Locks.* Prevents imports being made to an import directory. If the value of Locks is not
  zero, an import will not occur. You can apply numerous locks on a directory by
  clicking on the Add Lock button located at the base of the dialog. To decrease the
  number of locks, click on the Remove Lock button.

- *Status.* Reflects the state of replication to this sub-directory. A directory can have a
  number of states:

    A sub-directory can have a state of blank, which means that replication never
    took place; that could be the result of a misconfiguration at either the import or
    export side.

    A state of OK indicates that the import computer is receiving data from the
    export computer and both contain identical data.

A state of No Master indicates that the import directory is not receiving any data from the export server.

A state of No Sync indicates that the import computer received data but no update took place. This could be due to a communication error, open files, and so forth.

- *Last Update.* The time that the last update was made to a file in the import sub-directory.
- *Locked Since.* The date and time of the oldest lock.

To remove a sub-directory, highlight its entry in the pane and select the Remove button within the Manage Imported Directories dialog. Once you have defined your import sub-directory, click on OK to return to the main Directory Replication dialog. You must now define from where the import sub-directory will be fed its data. To do this, click on the Add button located at the base of the Directory Replication dialog. You are now presented with a list of domains or computers, similar to Figure 35.17.

FIGURE 35.17.

The Select Domain dialog.

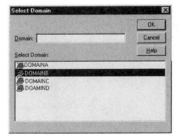

You can choose to receive imports from a domain or from an NT server, depending on how the export server was configured. If replication takes place over a WAN link, the outcome might not always be successful.

Alerts

The last button on the main Server Manager dialog is the Alerts button. Selecting it will activate the Alerts on dialog (see Figure 35.18).

FIGURE 35.18.

The Alerts on dialog.

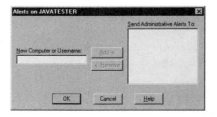

You can add names of computers or users who will be sent an administrative alert. Add users or computers by typing their names in the New Computer or Username text box. Names can be added and removed at will. On the source workstation, the Alerter and Messenger services must be running to generate and send the alert. On the destination computer, the Messenger services must be running to receive the alert.

The Alerts button concludes the Properties you can configure and view. So what else can you do with Server Manager?

The Computer Menu

The Computer menu at the top of the Server Manager dialog allows access to the other configuration functions. The following sections cover each of the entries within the Computer menu.

Shared Directories

The first of these entries besides Properties is Shared Directories. When you select this option, you activate the Shared Directories dialog, which allows you to create, maintain, and remove shared directories for the selected computer (see Figure 35.19).

FIGURE 35.19.
The Shared Directories dialog.

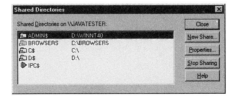

The main pane in the dialog lists those shares that have already been created and also lists their associated paths in the local filesystem. To stop sharing any of these shares, simply highlight the share and click on the Stop Sharing button. To view or change the properties of a share, highlight the share and click the Properties button to activate the Share Properties dialog. Figure 35.20 shows an example of a Share Properties dialog for one of NT's predefined shares, ADMIN$. This shares the systemroot directory to the administrators group, and permission to this share cannot be modified. The dollar sign after the share renders it invisible on a resource list; nonetheless, it is a well-known share.

FIGURE 35.20.
Share Properties on the ADMIN$ *share.*

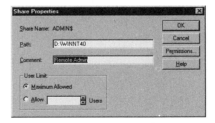

35

SERVER MANAGER

The Share Properties dialog lists the name of the share, the path to the share on the filesystem, a commentary on the share, and the user limit. The user limit allows you to define a limit on the number of users who can use the share simultaneously. When you are creating a new share, you must supply these details and must also define what users can use the share. You also can use the dollar sign at the end of the share name to hide the share from a resource browse list. Definition of the share permissions is done through the Access Through Share Permissions dialog, which is activated by choosing the Permissions button from the Share Properties dialog. The Access Through Share Permissions dialog in Figure 35.21 shows you the default permissions that are defined on all shares by default.

FIGURE 35.21.

The Access Through Share Permissions dialog.

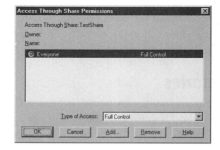

If you need to redefine the permissions to a share, use the Add and Remove buttons at the base of the dialog. To remove a user or group, simply highlight the user or group and click on the Remove button. To add users or groups, select the Add button to activate the Add Users and Groups dialog (see Figure 35.22).

FIGURE 35.22.

Giving user and group permissions to a share.

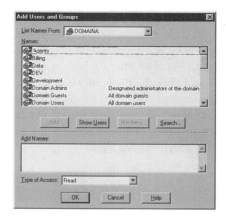

Users and groups are added in the usual manner.

Services

Another option on the Computer menu is Services. When you select this option, you are presented with the Services on dialog, which lists the services loaded on the computer you selected (see Figure 35.23).

Figure 35.23.

The Services on dialog.

This is the same dialog that appears when you select the Services applet from the Control Panel. For more on the Services applet, see Chapter 9, "Advanced Control Panel Tools." The Services on dialog lists all the services loaded on the computer. To stop, start, pause, or continue any of the services, simply highlight one and click on the appropriate button. To view the startup properties for a service, highlight one and click on the Startup button to reveal the Service on dialog (see Figure 35.24).

Figure 35.24.

The Service on dialog for the Alerter service.

With this dialog, you can configure the service's state at bootup. There are three settings you can configure for a service's startup:

- *Automatic.* When Automatic is set, the service will start automatically when the workstation starts.
- *Manual.* Manual requires you to manually start the service by using the Start button.
- *Disabled.* When Disabled is set, the service is prevented from starting.

The Log On As frame at the base of the Service dialog allows you to associate a user account with the service. Once associated with a user account, the service will run under the permissions and user rights inherited from that user. By default, services run under the System Account.

The HW Profiles button activates a dialog that allows you to enable or disable a service under a particular hardware profile. Figure 35.25 illustrates an example of the Alerter service being enabled to run under the original hardware profile on the workstation.

FIGURE 35.25.

The Alerter service enabled under the original hardware profile.

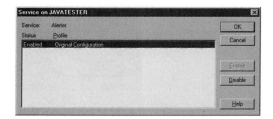

Send Message

The Send Message option activates the Send Message dialog, which allows you to send a text message to all users connected to the highlighted computer (see Figure 35.26). This is useful if you want to forcibly disconnect users from a computer.

FIGURE 35.26.

The Send Message dialog.

In order to send and receive a message, the Messenger service must be enabled.

Domain Functions

The remainder of the entries in the Computer menu are associated with domain functions. The first of these is the Add to Domain option. This is used when you wish to add a computer to a domain. When you select the Add to Domain option, you activate the Add Computer To Domain dialog (see Figure 35.27).

You must first declare whether the computer is a simple workstation or server or, alternatively, a Backup Domain Controller (BDC). Choose the appropriate radio button and enter the name of the computer in the text box. Then click on the Add button. Adding a computer to a domain is a restricted action, and only authorized users can do so.

FIGURE 35.27.

Adding a computer to a domain.

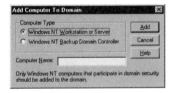

The Remove from Domain option is used to terminate a computer's membership with a domain. Highlight the computer you want to remove and select the Remove from Domain option from the Computer menu. Again, only authorized users can do this. You are given a warning of the consequence of this action (see Figure 35.28).

FIGURE 35.28.

Removing a computer from a domain.

When you highlight any of the BDCs, the Promote to Primary Domain Controller option on the Computer menu becomes active. This is used to promote a BDC to a PDC and is useful in case the PDC has crashed or is offline. When a BDC is promoted to a PDC, changes to its SAM database will not be replicated to the PDC when it comes back on line.

The Synchronize with Primary Domain Controller option on the Computer menu again is activated when you highlight a BDC. When this is selected, the SAM database on the PDC is replicated to the BDC. This usually takes a few minutes to complete.

The Select Domain option on the Computer menu allows you to switch to another domain and administer its computers with the Server Manager—that is, if you have permission to do so.

One other option worth noting is the Low Speed Connection setting under the Options menu. The setting is useful if you are communicating with a computer over a communication link that offers low transmission rates.

Summary

In this chapter, you explored the Server Manager, which is an administration tool that lets you view and configure remote computers' resources. Directory shares can be created, configured, and removed through the Server Manager. You can also kick off the Services applet from within Server Manager and add computers to and remove computers from domain membership. You can also remotely administer other domains, via the Server Manager, provided you have sufficient authority.

35

SERVER MANAGER

NT Diagnostics

by Mike Sheehy

IN THIS CHAPTER

CHAPTER

36

NT Diagnostics is based on the old MSD.exe utility that has been given a revamped look and a great deal of enhancement. NT Diagnostics, as the name suggests, is a tool used to aid with the diagnostics of your workstation. In its current version, NT diagnostics is a useful and powerful tool that can help you troubleshoot many NT system problems.

Accessing NT Diagnostics

To access NT Diagnostics, select from the Start menu, Programs | Administrative Tools (Common) | Windows NT Diagnostics (see Figure 36.1).

FIGURE 36.1.

Accessing NT Diagnostics through the Start menu.

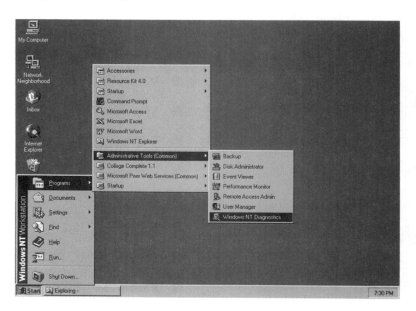

Alternatively, you can type `winmsd.exe` from the Run option (see Figure 36.2).

FIGURE 36.2.

Accessing NT Diagnostics through the Run option.

The Windows NT Diagnostics dialog appears, as in Figure 36.3, and is divided into nine tabs. The following sections investigate each of these tabs in depth.

FIGURE 36.3.
*The Windows NT
Diagnostics dialog.*

Version

The Version tab is selected by default when you open NT Diagnostics (refer to Figure 36.3).
The information detailed in the Version tab is always useful if you ever have to open a support
ticket; it contains information always asked for by support engineers to establish what type of
system you are running. Version details whether you are running Microsoft Server or Workstation, the version of the operating system, its build numbers, the build architecture, the number
and type of processors, and the product ID. In addition to this, Version also details the name
and company of the registered owner.

System

The System tab (see Figure 36.4) gives more detailed information on your workstation.

FIGURE 36.4.
The System tab.

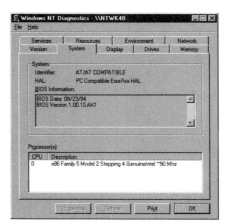

The top half of the tab contains the System frame, which lists the identifier for the processor and the Hardware Abstraction Layer (HAL). In addition to this it also lists details on the BIOS information, including the BIOS date and the BIOS version. Right-clicking on the data within the BIOS Information window activates the context menu. From this menu, you can select the BIOS information by selecting Select All. All the BIOS information is now highlighted. Activating the context menu again allows you to copy the highlighted information to the system Clipboard (see Figure 36.5). This is an easy way of gathering BIOS information to be sent to a support engineer.

FIGURE 36.5.

Copying the BIOS Information to the Clipboard.

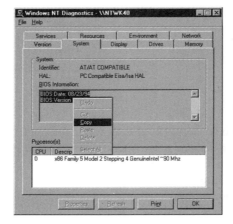

The base of the tab lists the CPUs loaded on the system and a description of each.

Display

The Display tab describes the video display and its driver (see Figure 36.6).

FIGURE 36.6.

The Display tab.

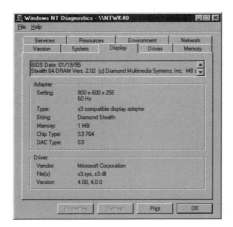

At the top of the tab, there is a scrolling text box that contains the BIOS information on the video display, including the date, version, and manufacturer. The Adapter frame contains the following video adapter information:

- *Setting.* Describes the resolution, refresh frequency, and number of colors that are currently selected for the adapter.
- *Type.* The type of video adapter.
- *String.* A description of the video adapter.
- *Memory.* The memory contained on the adapter.
- *Chip Type.* The type of chip on the adapter.
- *DAC Type.* Digital-to-analog converter type.

The Driver frame details information on the current display driver, including the vendor, the filename of the driver, and its version.

Drives

The next tab, Drives, lists the system drives (floppy, hard disk, and CD-ROM) and any network drives that may be mapped. You can list the drives by drive letter or by drive type as illustrated by Figure 36.7 and 36.8, respectively. Either of these views can be selected by clicking on the Drives by type and Drives by letter buttons at the base of the tab.

FIGURE 36.7.

The Drives tab by drive letter.

As you can see in Figure 36.8, you can expand the drive type tree to reveal the drives by clicking on the plus boxes on the drive type tree.

You can view the properties of a particular drive by either double-clicking on the drive or by highlighting the drive and clicking on the Properties button on the base of the tab. A dialog appears detailing the properties on the drive (see Figure 36.9). There are two tabs within the properties dialog: General and File System.

Figure 36.8.

The Drives tab by drive type.

Figure 36.9.

The General tab of the drive properties dialog.

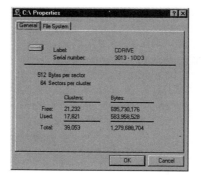

The General tab details the following:

- *Label.* Lists the current label on the drive. This is also displayed on the File System tab.

- *Serial number.* Lists the serial number of the drive. This is also displayed in the File System tab.

- *Bytes per sector.* Lists the number of bytes per sector.

- *Sectors per cluster.* Lists the number of sectors per cluster.

At the base of the tab is a table of the free, used, and total number of clusters and bytes on the system.

The File System tab (see Figure 36.10) lists details on the file system loaded on the drive. These details include the following:

- *File system used on this volume.* Lists whether the drive is FAT, NTFS, and so forth.

- *Maximum number of characters in a filename.* Lists the maximum number of characters allowed in a filename.

FIGURE 36.10.

The File System tab of the drive properties dialog.

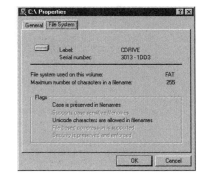

The Flags frame details features supported by the file system for this drive:

- Case is preserved in filenames.
- Case-sensitive filenames are supported.
- Unicode characters are allowed in filenames.
- File-based compression is supported.
- Security is preserved and enforced.

The features that are supported by the current file system are in black, and those that are not are in gray.

Memory

The Memory tab details information on the system's memory (see Figure 36.11).

FIGURE 36.11.

The Memory tab.

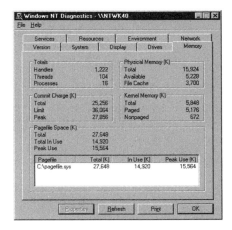

The Memory tab is divided into five frames:

- *Totals.* The totals frame keeps a running total on the number of handles, threads, and processes.
- *Physical Memory (K).* This frame records the total, file cache, and available memory on the workstation.
- *Commit Charge (K).* The Commit Charge frame records details on the Commit memory. Commit memory is memory allocated to programs and/or the system. Detailed figures include total, limit, and peak.
- *Kernel Memory (K).* This frame records memory allocated to the operating system. Details include total, paged, and nonpaged.
- *Pagefile Space (K).* The Pagefile Space frame details the total size of the pagefile, the amount of the pagefile in use, and the peak use in kilobytes.

Network

The Network tab gives information on the network components of the workstation. There are four buttons at the base of the tab; selecting them gives you different details on the loaded network components. When you select the Network tab, the General button is depressed and its information is displayed by default (see Figure 36.12).

FIGURE 36.12.

General information on the Network tab.

General

The General window includes NT network details on currently logged on users:

- *Your Access Level.* Level of access the user has.
- *Workgroup or Domain.* Is the user logged into a workgroup or a domain?
- *Network Version.* The version of the Network components (operating system).

- *LanRoot.* Location of DOS LAN Manager files.
- *Logged On Users.* Number of users logged on.
- *Current User (1).* The current user.
- *Logon Domain.* The name of the domain where the user is logged on.
- *Logon Server.* The name of the authenticating server.

Transports

Pressing the Transports button reveals information on the transport protocols currently loaded on the workstation (see Figure 36.13).

FIGURE 36.13.

Transports on the Network tab.

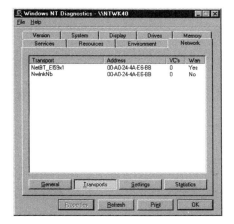

The Transports window lists the currently loaded network protocols, the MAC address of the associated network interface card, the number of virtual circuits currently used, and whether the network protocol is in a WAN.

Settings

The Settings button reveals in-depth details on the network components, such as cache time out, network errors, sessions errors, and so forth. The window is divided into two columns listing the setting and the current value of the setting (see Figure 36.14).

Statistics

The Statistics button, when selected, gives you a list of the network statistics. These statistics include the total number of bytes sent and received, the number of network errors, the number of session errors, and so forth. Figure 36.15 shows the Statistics window divided into two columns: the statistic that is being recorded and its current value.

FIGURE 36.14.

Settings on the Network tab.

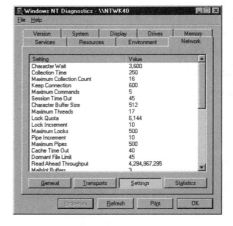

FIGURE 36.15.

Statistics on the Network tab.

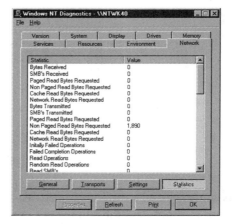

Environment

The Environment tab displays a list of the current global environment variables (see Figure 36.16).

The Environment tab displays values for such variables as number of processors, type of processor, operating system, and so forth. All these environment variables are configurable within the System applet of the Control Panel. You will notice that the System button is depressed, giving the default view of the system environment variables. There is a second button, Local User, that gives you the environment variables specific to the current user (see Figure 36.17).

FIGURE 36.16.

The Environment tab.

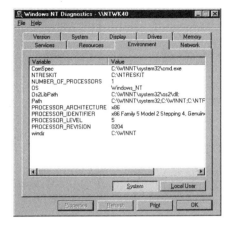

FIGURE 36.17.

Local User on the Environment tab.

Resources

The Resources tab displays the assignment of system resources to loaded devices. The information displayed on this tab is very useful when troubleshooting system faults. The Resources tab has five buttons located at its base (see Figure 36.18).

IRQ

The IRQ window is the default view of the Resources tab. As you can see from Figure 36.18, the IRQ window lists the IRQ assignments, device to which they are assigned, bus, and type.

FIGURE 36.18.

*IRQ on the
Resources tab.*

You can include Hardware Abstraction Layer (HAL) devices by checking the Include HAL resources check box. You can get a more in-depth view of the IRQ assignment by selecting an IRQ and clicking on the Properties button. The Properties dialog for an IRQ looks similar to Figure 36.19.

FIGURE 36.19.

*The Properties dialog
for an IRQ.*

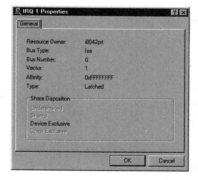

The Properties dialog lists the resource owner, bus type, bus number, vector, affinity, type, and share disposition for the IRQ assignment.

I/O Port

The I/O Port button, when selected, will display the memory I/O address assignments. The window lists the memory address range, device, bus, and type (see Figure 36.20). As before, you can include HAL devices by checking the appropriate check box.

FIGURE 36.20.

*I/O Port on the
Resources tab.*

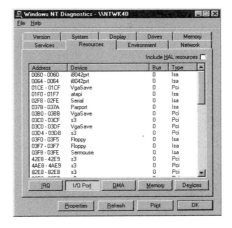

As with the IRQs, you can also view the properties on an I/O Port assignment by double-clicking on an entry from the list or by highlighting one and selecting Properties. The Properties dialog for the Port appears, as in Figure 36.21.

FIGURE 36.21.

*I/O Port Properties
dialog.*

The Properties dialog lists the resource owner, bus type, bus number, address, length, and share disposition for the I/O Port assignment.

DMA

The DMA listing details the assignment of DMA channels. The DMA window includes the channel, port, device, bus, and type for the DMA assignment (see Figure 36.22). Again, you can include HAL devices as described previously.

FIGURE 36.22.
DMA on the Resources tab.

To view the properties of a DMA assignment, you must invoke the Properties dialog. Figure 36.23 shows a sample DMA Properties dialog that details the resource owner, bus type, bus number, channel, port, and share disposition for the DMA assignment.

FIGURE 36.23.
DMA Properties dialog.

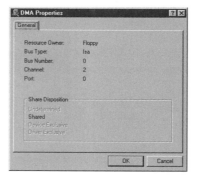

Memory

The Memory button displays the extended memory ranges. These are usually memory ranges that are exclusively mapped to devices that require dedicated memory. Figure 36.24 illustrates the memory window listing the address range, device, bus, and type on which they can be located. The inclusion of HAL devices is also possible.

The Memory Properties dialog (see Figure 36.25) details the resource owner, bus type, bus number, address, length, access type, and share disposition for the memory assignment.

Devices

The final button on the Resources tab is the Devices button. When you select the Devices button, you are presented with a list of loaded devices on the system (see Figure 36.26).

FIGURE 36.24.

Memory on the Resources tab.

FIGURE 36.25.

Memory Properties dialog.

FIGURE 36.26.

Devices on the Resources tab.

The properties of any device can be viewed by selecting the Properties button in the usual manner. Figure 36.27 illustrates a sample Floppy Properties dialog for the floppy. The Properties dialog details the resources, their current values, and the bus on which they are located.

FIGURE 36.27.

Floppy Properties dialog.

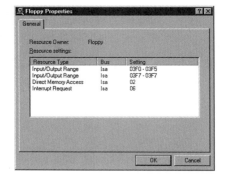

Services

The Services tab lists the currently loaded services and their status (see Figure 36.28).

FIGURE 36.28.

The Services tab.

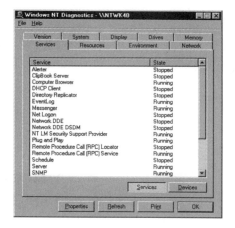

You can also view the currently attached devices to the system by selecting the Devices button at the base of the tab. Figure 36.29 illustrates an example of the list of loaded devices.

To get a greater insight into a service or device, you can view its associated properties through the Properties dialog. Figure 36.30 is an example of the DHCP Client Properties dialog.

The first tab, General, details the path to the service's associated executable, its status on startup, the account under which it runs, its error severity, and group. The General tab also includes service flags that the selected service supports. The second tab, Dependencies (see Figure 36.31), details the services on which the current service is dependent. The properties for a device are as those given for services.

FIGURE 36.29.
*Devices on the
Services tab.*

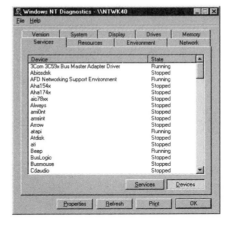

FIGURE 36.30.
*DHCP Client
Properties dialog.*

FIGURE 36.31.
The Dependencies tab.

Additional Functionality

The Refresh button located at the base of the Windows NT Diagnostics window forces the
system to refresh the details currently displayed in the window.

The Print button allows you to generate reports from the information displayed by NT Diagnostics. When you select the Print button, you activate the Create Report dialog (see Figure 36.32).

FIGURE 36.32.

The Create Report dialog.

The Create Report dialog allows you to generate a report on all the tabs of NT Diagnostics or just the current one. You can also define the level of detail of the report and send the report to the Clipboard, a printer, or a file. When saving the report to a file, it is saved in text format. You can choose the name and location of the file through the Save As dialog. The following is an example of a summary report of the Version tab:

```
Microsoft Diagnostics Report For \\NTWK40
- - - - - - - - - - - - - - - - - - - - - - - - - - - - - - - - - - - - - - - - - - - - - - - - - - - - - -
OS Version Report
- - - - - - - - - - - - - - - - - - - - - - - - - - - - - - - - - - - - - - - - - - - - - - - - - - - - - -
Microsoft (R) Windows NT (TM) Workstation
Version 4.0 (Build 1381) x86 Uniprocessor Free
Registered Owner: Mike Sheehy, World Merchandise Exchange (WOMEX) LTD.
Product Number: 50036-040-0097694-79057
- - - - - - - - - - - - - - - - - - - - - - - - - - - - - - - - - - - - - - - - - - - - - - - - - - - - - -
```

The Save Report and Print Report entries on the File menu at the top of the NT Diagnostics window invokes the same dialog as in Figure 36.32. The Destination is defined to File or Default Printer as appropriate. The Print Setup option allows you to configure a printer for printing the reports.

The Select Computer option on the File menu allows you to choose another computer against which you can run the NT Diagnostics. You can select another server or workstation from the Select Computer dialog (see Figure 36.33).

FIGURE 36.33.
*Running NT
Diagnostics against
another computer.*

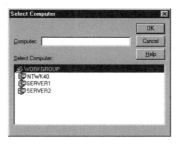

The Run option on the File menu allows you to run any of the NT administrative tools by selecting them from the predefined list of tools (see Figure 36.34). Additionally, you can run any other application or program by entering it in the Open text box or by using the Browse button.

FIGURE 36.34.
The Run dialog.

The About option from the Help menu displays the About Diagnostics window, which displays details similar to the Version tab plus the memory available to NT (see Figure 36.35).

FIGURE 36.35.
*The About Diagnostics
window.*

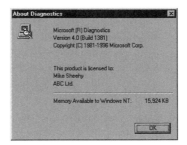

Summary

In this chapter, you looked at the Windows NT Diagnostics tool. This tool is useful when troubleshooting your system. NT Diagnostics is divided into nine tabs covering Resources, Version, Memory, Services, System, Display, Drives, Network, and Environment. You can generate reports on the information contained in NT Diagnostics, which is useful when sending information to support technicians for review.

Troubleshooting NT Workstation

by Mike Sheehy

IN THIS CHAPTER

CHAPTER 37

Not everything goes according to plan, and this can be especially true when it comes to computers. This chapter will identify some of the problems with NT Workstation 4 and will also include suggested solutions. Problem resolution is as much about using proper troubleshooting methods as it is about possessing good technical ability. Without a clear plan of action and good diagnostic skills, you are already at a disadvantage. Fortunately, you can cultivate good diagnostic skills and prepare a clear plan of action in advance.

When trying to solve a problem, always eliminate the obvious first. Time after time, people rush in and tear open the chassis to look inside a computer when the problem can be something as simple as an unplugged socket to a computer monitor. Such simple tests can save you time and effort. Slow down, step back, and define the problem as you see it before you do anything. Microsoft's Knowledge Base or Technet infobases can be great sources of assistance. In addition to these are a myriad of newsgroups and usergroups on the Internet who are always willing to share information and problems. When you gain more experience with NT, more and more problems will be solved intuitively.

My System Will Not Start Properly

If your system will not start properly due to corrupted system files or boot sector, you can invoke the Last Known Good Menu (LKGM). The LKGM is a snapshot of the system that you can apply to your workstation. To learn how to create the LKGM, see the next section. How do you invoke the LKGM? When your system boots and you have selected which operating system to load, the following message appears: `Press spacebar NOW to invoke Hardware Profile/Last Known Good Menu`. Press the spacebar as instructed. The next screen you are presented with will give you the choice of exiting the repair or proceeding. Press L to select the Last Known good configuration. In the next screen, choose the saved configuration and press Enter. The system will attempt to invoke the stored configuration and boot into NT.

My System Will Not Even Boot

If your system is seriously corrupted, it might not be able to boot from its hard drive. If this is the case, you have to boot from boot disks and choose to repair the system using an emergency repair disk (ERD). During installation, NT will prompt you to create an ERD. If you choose yes to creating an ERD during installation, NT will take a snapshot of the system as it currently exists and save it to a floppy. If you have not created a set of NT boot floppies, I suggest you do so. To create a set of boot floppies, you can use the `winnt` or `winnt32` executables that are found on the NT Workstation distribution media. You have to apply an `/ox` option when using `winnt32`. To start these executables, use the Run option on the Start menu (see Figure 37.1).

Figure 37.1.

Creating NT boot disks.

If you encounter problems later, you can apply the ERD and return the system to a previous stable state. The ERD can repair system files and your boot sector if they are damaged. Remember to update your ERD regularly; this should always be done after system configuration changes. To take a system snapshot or create an ERD, follow these steps:

1. Activate the Run option from the Start menu and enter `rdisk` (see Figure 37.2).
2. Click OK to activate the Repair Disk Utility dialog.

Figure 37.2.

Activate the Repair Disk Utility from the Run dialog.

3. You are now presented with the Repair Disk Utility dialog. Click on the Update Repair Info button to copy a snapshot of the system to your hard disk (see Figure 37.3).

Figure 37.3.

The Repair Disk Utility dialog.

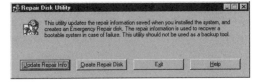

4. To create an ERD and copy a snapshot to it, click on the Create Repair Disk button.
5. Another dialog appears, informing you that it will overwrite the current snapshot with a new one. Click Yes to continue (see Figure 37.4).

Figure 37.4.

Overwrite previous snapshot?

37

TROUBLESHOOTING NT WORKSTATION

6. A dialog now appears, asking whether you want to create an ERD that will contain a copy of the repair information just captured. Click Yes to proceed with the creation of an ERD (see Figure 37.5).

FIGURE 37.5.

Create an ERD?

7. You are now prompted to insert a floppy disk into the floppy drive. This floppy will be formatted by NT, and the repair information will be copied to it. Click on Yes to proceed (see Figure 37.6).

FIGURE 37.6.

Enter floppy for formatting.

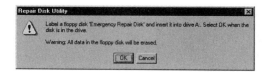

Once the floppy is formatted and the repair data is copied, you are returned to the main Repair Disk Utility dialog. Click Exit to leave the utility.

Windows NT Was Unable to Start the Network

The most common problem encountered during network installation is a misconfigured or incorrectly detected network interface card (NIC). If the network card is improperly configured or not seated properly into its slot, or the wrong card is specified, you receive an error message stating that Windows NT was unable to start the network.

From this point, you are given the option of going back and reconfiguring network settings or canceling network installation. If you choose to cancel network installation, networking components are removed, and you are informed that you can install Windows NT Networking at a later time. If you choose to go back and reconfigure network settings, return to the settings that you think are incorrect, reconfigure them, and try to continue. You might also ensure that the card is correctly seated in its expansion slot.

The DHCP Client Was Unable to Obtain an IP Address

Typically, this indicates a physical network connectivity problem. Figure 37.7 shows a sample dialog reporting the workstation's failure to secure an IP address from a DHCP server. First, verify that there is a DHCP server on your network and that it has IP addresses available for allocation. Verify the TCP/IP settings and network card configuration.

> **NOTE**
>
> Dynamic Host Configuration Protocol (DHCP) is a service whereby a server can dynamically allocate an IP address to a requesting DHCP client.

FIGURE 37.7.
Unable to locate the DHCP server.

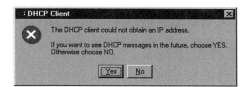

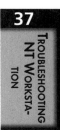

Once you have confirmed that a DHCP server does exist on your network, you must now confirm that it is reachable. From the command prompt, use the ping utility to confirm that the server is reachable. If ping fails to reach the DHCP server, use the tracert utility to determine where the breakdown in communication occurs. For more on the ping and tracert utilities, see Chapter 26, "Windows NT Networking Protocols." If it appears that your workstation is the point of failure, recheck your system settings and the physical connectivity points to your network.

I Am Unable to Contact the Domain Controller

If a domain controller for your domain could not be contacted or the domain controller for this domain could not be located, it can indicate a physical connectivity problem with the network or a problem with the current configuration. Usually, these problems arise when you are logging on to the network, attempting authentication with the network, or trying to join a domain. Verify that the domain controller for your domain is up and functioning properly, that it is reachable, and that the workstation and domain controller are using compatible protocols. Again, you can use ping and tracert if you are a member of a TCP/IP network. These two utilities should always be used to confirm connectivity to a TCP/IP network and should always be used after you are satisfied with your physical connections.

The following is a general troubleshooting list that can be applied to most networking problems:

- Has the network ever worked?
- What, if anything, has recently changed on the system? This will solve most problems. Determine what has changed on the system that might be preventing it from operating properly.

- Is the physical connection to the network functioning properly? If you are using a twisted-pair network card (10Base-T), is the link light on the card lit and is there activity on the card? (Always check things such as making sure a cable is plugged into the network card before you get your protocol analyzer out; simple things are easy to forget and can be time-consuming if overlooked.)

- Is the domain controller for the domain up and available?

- Are the workstation and the domain controller using compatible protocols and are they configured properly?

The RAS Connection Automatically Disconnects After 20 Minutes

RAS is configured to disconnect after 20 minutes, by default. To disable this feature, execute the following steps:

1. Open the Registry Editor from the Run option on the Start menu (see Figure 37.8).

FIGURE 37.8.

Start the Registry Editor, regedt32.

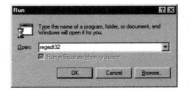

2. Select the HKEY_LOCAL_MACHINE window.

3. Select the key `System\CurrentControlSet\Services\RemoteAccess\Parameters`.

4. Select the value Autodisconnect (see Figure 37.9).

FIGURE 37.9.

Select the Autodisconnect value.

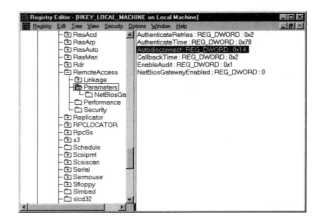

5. Select DWORD from the Edit menu.

6. The DWORD Editor dialog box appears as in Figure 37.10. Type 0 in the Data field.

FIGURE 37.10.

The DWORD Editor dialog.

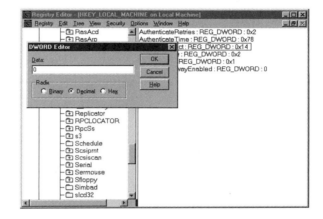

7. Click OK to return to the main Registry dialog.

8. Close regedt32 and reboot to allow the changes in the Registry to take effect.

NT Will Not Detect My Modem

When installing a modem into an NT workstation, you can either choose to let NT detect the modem itself or you can manually select it from a list. If NT fails to pick up your modem, select it manually from a list of modems. Make sure that you have the right manufacturer and model before you do so (see Figure 37.11).

FIGURE 37.11.

Manually install the modem.

Summary

In this chapter, you explored a few classic troubleshooting problems that are encountered with NT Workstation. Remember: Technical know-how is only half the battle when resolving problems. A calm, planned approach to problem resolution is equally important.

VII
PART

IN THIS PART

Appendixes

Glossary

by Mike Sheehy

Access Control List (ACL)   A list of permit and deny conditions to a resource.

ActiveX   An Internet version of Microsoft's Component Object Model (COM).

Administrator   The account used to administer NT computers, domains, and workgroups.

Applet   A Windows NT dynamic link library (DLL).

AppleTalk protocol   A protocol that allows Apple computers to use resources shared from an NT system.

Auditing   The capability to record events and user actions while they are logged on to an NT computer of Domain.

Authentication   Validation of a user through a username/password combination.

Backup domain controller (BDC)   An NT server that holds a copy of the security database within an NT domain and can authenticate users locally.

Binding   The process of establishing communication between network protocols and a network interface card.

Boot partition   A volume that contains the Windows NT operating system and its support files.

bps (bits per second)   A measurement of the speed with which a device can transfer data.

Browser Service   An NT service that displays a list of currently running NT systems, domains, workgroups, file and print shares, and other shared resources on a network.

Cache   A store of information containing the most recent or most frequently accessed data.

Client Service for NetWare (CSNW)   A service that allows NT connectivity to NetWare resources.

Common Object Model (COM)   A standard that defines interfaces between objects to enable seemless integration of objects between applications.

CSLIP (Compressed SLIP)   *See SLIP*

Default gateway   A router or computer that possesses routing capabilities and can direct traffic to its intended destination within or without the local network.

Device driver   A piece of software that allows a piece of hardware to communicate with NT.

Dial-Up Networking (DUN)   The client version of Remote Access Service, allowing the client to connect to a network remotely over a phone line.

Domain   A collection of NT systems defined to share a single security database.

Domain Name Service (DNS)   A service that has the capability of resolving an IP address, given an IP name, or vice versa.

Dynamic data exchange (DDE)   The capability to exchange data between two or more applications.

Dynamic Host Configuration Protocol (DHCP)   An NT service that allows a client to lease an IP address from an IP pool that is maintained by a DHCP server.

Dynamic link library (DLL)   A file that contains routines and functions that are loaded when needed.

Encryption   The process of protecting data by changing its contents so that it is decipherable only with a special key.

File replication   The capability to replicate files and directories between two or more NT machines.

File sharing   The capability to share files and directories over the network.

File Transfer Protocol (FTP)   A protocol to transfer files between remote machines.

Group   A collection of users. Permissions granted at group level are inherited by its members.

Guest   A built-in account that is used by casual users connecting to the NT network.

Hardware Compatibility List (HCL)   A list of devices supported by Windows NT.

Host   A device on a TCP/IP network identified by an IP address.

Hypertext Markup Language (HTML)   A language used to create hypertext documents used for publishing on the World Wide Web.

Hypertext Transfer Protocol (HTTP)   An IP protocol used to transfer HTML data from a Web site to a user's desktop browser.

Integrated Services Digital Network (ISDN)   A digital communication service that has found popularity in providing WAN connectivity.

Internet   A network made up of a number of public networks.

Internet Service Provider (ISP)   Used to provide access to the Internet as a service.

Internetwork Packet Exchange/Sequenced Packet Exchange (IPX/SPX)   A transport protocol used in a Novell NetWare network.

Interprocess communication (IPC)   The capability of two or more processes to communicate, independent of whether they reside on the same machine.

Interrupt Request (IRQ)   A hardware signal used by a device to gain the attention of the processor.

Intranets   A private version of the Internet found primarily within corporations and businesses.

A

GLOSSARY

IP address   A unique 4-octet number separated by a dot, used to identify nodes on an IP network.

Java   A programming language developed by Sun Microsystems, designed for use in applet and agent applications.

LMHOSTS file   Used to resolve NetBIOS names to IP addresses.

Local Area Network (LAN)   A collection of interconnected computers dispersed over a relatively small area, usually within a building.

Local Security Authority (LSA)   The main component within the NT security model. It is used to generate access tokens, maintain the system security and audit policies, and log audit alerts.

Media Access Control (MAC)   The network layer that deals with network access and collision detection.

Modem   An electronic device that converts binary data to analog tones and voltages that are suitable for transmission over standard dial-up or leased-line telephone lines.

MS-CHAP   Microsoft implementation of Challenge Handshake Authentication Protocol, used to secure an encrypted connection between a RAS server and client.

Multi-homed   A machine that has more than one Network interface card attached to separate physical networks.

Network Basic Input/Output System (NetBIOS)   An IBM-developed standard software interface to a network adapter.

Network Basic Input/Output System Extended User Interface (NetBEUI)   A non-routable broadcast LAN protocol (an extension of NetBIOS).

Network Interface Card (NIC)   An expansion card used to connect a computer to a network.

Novell Directory Service (NDS)   Novell's method of distributing resource information to LAN clients.

Novell NetWare   A network operating system that is implemented by Novell and utilizes the IPX/SPX protocol.

NTFS   A file system specifically designed for NT.

OLE   A Microsoft implementation of data transfer and sharing between applications.

Packet Assemblers/Disassemblers (PAD)   A connectivity device to an X.25 network.

Paging file   A file used to store data temporarily swapped out from RAM.

Password Authentication Protocol (PAP)   An authentication protocol that uses clear text passwords.

Ping   A command-line utility used to verify connectivity within an IP network.

Plug-and-Play   An operating system's capability of identifying and configuring newly added hardware.

Point to Point Protocol (PPP)   A standard framing and authentication protocol that is used within Microsoft's RAS.

Point To Point Tunneling Protocol (PPTP)   The capability to tunnel network protocols within a PPP connection. This can be used to create secure virtual private networks (VPNs).

Port   A location used to pass data in and out of a computing device.

Portable Operating System Interface (POSIX)   A standard that defines a set of operating-system services.

Primary Domain Controllers (PDC)   The NT server within an NT domain that authenticated users and maintains the security account database.

Process   An executable program, a set of virtual memory addresses, and one or more threads. When a program runs, it is called a process.

Process Identifier (PID)   A unique number assigned to a running process.

Protocol   A set of rules and conventions used to transfer information over a network.

Proxy   A machine that accepts incoming calls and validates them against an access list. A proxy operates at a service level.

Registry   A database containing systems configuration information stored in a hierarchical fashion.

Remote Access Service (RAS)   An NT service that allows remote users to connect to an NT network via a telephone connection.

Remote Procedure Call   Interprocess communication between processes residing on different machines.

Router   A piece of equipment that links networks. Routers find the best paths to destinations on the network and direct traffic via these best paths.

Routing Information Protocol (RIP)   The exchange of routing information between routers to build up a knowledge of the network. This information allows routers to decide on a best path.

Security Account Manager (SAM)   A database containing account information, such as passwords, account names, and policies.

Security ID (SID)   A unique identifier to identify a user to a security system.

Services   A process designed to execute specific system functions. Because services are RPC-based, they can be invoked remotely.

A

GLOSSARY

Simple Mail Transfer Protocol (SMTP)   A TCP/IP suite of protocols that covers the transfer of electronic mail.

Simple Network Management Protocol   A protocol used to monitor that state of a host on a TCP/IP network. Hosts can be monitored remotely via SNMP.

SLIP (Serial Line Internet Protocol)   An old communication standard. It is still incorporated within RAS to ensure interoperability with third-party remote access software.

Small Computer System Interface (SCSI)   A standard high-speed parallel interface for connecting computers to peripheral devices such as hard drives and printers.

Subnetmask   A 32-bit value that divides an IP address into a network ID and host ID.

TCP/IP   A suite of networking protocols that provide connectivity across interconnected networks.

Uniform Resource Locator (URL)   A pointer to a unique resource on the Internet.

Universal Naming Convention (UNC) name   The full name of a shared resource on an NT network—for example, \\servername\sharename.

Uninterruptible Power Supply (UPS)   A battery-operated source of power that automatically supports your computer if your main electricity supply fails.

User Accounts   A way of associating attributes to a user when logged into an NT domain or computer. These attributes include username, password, group membership, and so forth.

User Datagram Protocol (UDP)   A complementing protocol to TCP that offers a connectionless datagram service that does not guarantee delivery or sequencing.

User Manager   An NT tool used to maintain users, groups, and security policies within NT.

User Rights   A set of actions users can execute within an NT computer or domain.

Virtual Memory   A space on your hard drive used to hold data swapped out of memory temporarily.

Virtual Private Network (VPN)   The capability to connect private LANs via a public network such as the Internet.

Wide Area Network (WAN)   A network connected over a large global area.

Windows Internet Naming Service (WINS)   Microsoft's name resolution service for NetBIOS names.

Workgroup   A collection of computers grouped together for viewing purposes. Computers within a workgroup all have their own separate SAM databases.

WWW (World Wide Web)   An information service in the Internet whose content contains hypertext, graphics, and multimedia.

X.25   A packet-switching network.

Well-Known Service Ports

by Mike Sheehy

APPENDIX B

A *port* allows multiple connections to a computer. You can think of it as a subdivision of an IP address. Certain functions are tied to ports, so you need to communicate with a particular function or service via a particular port. A number of "well-known" ports have been reserved for various functions. This appendix lists these well-known ports and their associated functions.

Table B.1 lists both the UDP and TCP port assignments for well-known ports. This table is an excerpt from the Request for Comment (RFC) 1340.

Table B.1. Port assignments for well-known ports.

Keyword	Decimal	Description
0/tcp	Reserved	
0/udp	Reserved	
tcpmux	1/tcp	TCP Port Service Multiplexer
tcpmux	1/udp	TCP Port Service Multiplexer
compressnet	2/tcp	Management Utility
compressnet	2/udp	Management Utility
compressnet	3/tcp	Compression Process
compressnet	3/udp	Compression Process
	4/tcp	Unassigned
	4/udp	Unassigned
rje	5/tcp	Remote Job Entry
rje	5/udp	Remote Job Entry
	6/tcp	Unassigned
	6/udp	Unassigned
echo	7/tcp	Echo
echo	7/udp	Echo
	8/tcp	Unassigned
	8/udp	Unassigned
discard	9/tcp	Discard
discard	9/udp	Discard
	10/tcp	Unassigned
systat	11/tcp	Active Users
systat	11/udp	Active Users
	12/tcp	Unassigned
	12/udp	Unassigned

Keyword	Decimal	Description
daytime	13/tcp	Daytime
daytime	13/udp	Daytime
	14/tcp	Unassigned
	14/udp	Unassigned
	15/tcp	Unassigned [was netstat]
	15/udp	Unassigned
	16/tcp	Unassigned
	16/udp	Unassigned
qotd	17/tcp	Quote of the Day
qotd	17/udp	Quote of the Day
msp	18/tcp	Message Send Protocol
msp	18/udp	Message Send Protocol
chargen	19/tcp	Character Generator
chargen	19/udp	Character Generator
ftp-data	20/tcp	File Transfer [Default Data]
ftp-data	20/udp	File Transfer [Default Data]
ftp	21/tcp	File Transfer [Control]
ftp	21/udp	File Transfer [Control]
	22/tcp	Unassigned
	22/udp	Unassigned
telnet	23/tcp	Telnet
telnet	23/udp	Telnet
	24/tcp	Any private mail system
	24/udp	Any private mail system
smtp	25/tcp	Simple Mail Transfer
smtp	25/udp	Simple Mail Transfer
	26/tcp	Unassigned
	26/udp	Unassigned
nsw-fe	27/tcp	NSW User System FE
nsw-fe	27/udp	NSW User System FE
	28/tcp	Unassigned
	28/udp	Unassigned

B

WELL-KNOWN
SERVICE PORTS

continues

Table B.1. continued

Keyword	Decimal	Description
msg-icp	29/tcp	MSG ICP
msg-icp	29/udp	MSG ICP
	30/tcp	Unassigned
	30/udp	Unassigned
msg-auth	31/tcp	MSG Authentication
msg-auth	31/udp	MSG Authentication
	32/tcp	Unassigned
	32/udp	Unassigned
dsp	33/tcp	Display Support Protocol
dsp	33/udp	Display Support Protocol
	34/tcp	Unassigned
	34/udp	Unassigned
	35/tcp	Any private printer server
	35/udp	Any private printer server
	36/tcp	Unassigned
	36/udp	Unassigned
time	37/tcp	Time
time	37/udp	Time
	38/tcp	Unassigned
	38/udp	Unassigned
rlp	39/tcp	Resource Location Protocol
rlp	39/udp	Resource Location Protocol
	40/tcp	Unassigned
	40/udp	Unassigned
graphics	41/tcp	Graphics
graphics	41/udp	Graphics
nameserver	42/tcp	Host Name Server
nameserver	42/udp	Host Name Server
nicname	43/tcp	Who Is
nicname	43/udp	Who Is
mpm-flags	44/tcp	MPM FLAGS Protocol
mpm-flags	44/udp	MPM FLAGS Protocol

Keyword	Decimal	Description
mpm	45/tcp	Message Processing Module [recv]
mpm	45/udp	Message Processing Module [recv]
mpm-snd	46/tcp	MPM [default send]
mpm-snd	46/udp	MPM [default send]
ni-ftp	47/tcp	NI FTP
ni-ftp	47/udp	NI FTP
	48/tcp	Unassigned
	48/udp	Unassigned
login	49/tcp	Login Host Protocol
login	49/udp	Login Host Protocol
re-mail-ck	50/tcp	Remote Mail Checking Protocol
re-mail-ck	50/udp	Remote Mail Checking Protocol
la-maint	51/tcp	IMP Logical Address Maintenance
la-maint	51/udp	IMP Logical Address Maintenance
xns-time	52/tcp	XNS Time Protocol
xns-time	52/udp	XNS Time Protocol
domain	53/tcp	Domain Name Server
domain	53/udp	Domain Name Server
xns-ch	54/tcp	XNS Clearinghouse
xns-ch	54/udp	XNS Clearinghouse
isi-gl	55/tcp	ISI Graphics Language
isi-gl	55/udp	ISI Graphics Language
xns-auth	56/tcp	XNS Authentication
xns-auth	56/udp	XNS Authentication
	57/tcp	Any private terminal access
	57/udp	Any private terminal access
xns-mail	58/tcp	XNS Mail
xns-mail	58/udp	XNS Mail
	59/tcp	Any private file service
	59/udp	Any private file service
	60/tcp	Unassigned
	60/udp	Unassigned

B

WELL-KNOWN
SERVICE PORTS

continues

Table B.1. continued

Keyword	Decimal	Description
ni-mail	61/tcp	NI MAIL
ni-mail	61/udp	NI MAIL
acas	62/tcp	ACA Services
acas	62/udp	ACA Services
via-ftp	63/tcp	VIA Systems - FTP
via-ftp	63/udp	VIA Systems - FTP
covia	64/tcp	Communications Integrator (CI)
covia	64/udp	Communications Integrator (CI)
tacacs-ds	65/tcp	TACACS-Database Service
tacacs-ds	65/udp	TACACS-Database Service
sql*net	66/tcp	Oracle SQL*NET
sql*net	66/udp	Oracle SQL*NET
bootps	67/tcp	Bootstrap Protocol Server
bootps	67/udp	Bootstrap Protocol Server
bootpc	68/tcp	Bootstrap Protocol Client
bootpc	68/udp	Bootstrap Protocol Client
tftp	69/tcp	Trivial File Transfer
tftp	69/tcp	Trivial File Transfer
gopher	70/udp	Gopher
gopher	70/udp	Gopher
netrjs-1	71/tcp	Remote Job Service
netrjs-1	71/udp	Remote Job Service
netrjs-2	72/tcp	Remote Job Service
netrjs-2	72/udp	Remote Job Service
netrjs-3	73/tcp	Remote Job Service
netrjs-3	73/udp	Remote Job Service
netrjs-4	74/tcp	Remote Job Service
netrjs-4	74/udp	Remote Job Service
	75/tcp	Any private dial-out service
	75/udp	Any private dial-out service
	76/tcp	Unassigned
	76/udp	Unassigned

Keyword	*Decimal*	*Description*
	77/tcp	Any private RJE service
	77/udp	Any private RJE service
vettcp	78/tcp	vettcp
vettcp	78/udp	vettcp
finger	79/tcp	Finger
finger	79/udp	Finger
www	80/tcp	World Wide Web HTTP
www	80/udp	World Wide Web HTTP
hosts2-ns	81/tcp	HOSTS2 Name Server
hosts2-ns	81/udp	HOSTS2 Name Server
xfer	82/tcp	XFER Utility
xfer	82/udp	XFER Utility
mit-ml-dev	83/tcp	MIT ML Device
mit-ml-dev	83/udp	MIT ML Device
ctf	84/tcp	Common Trace Facility
ctf	84/udp	Common Trace Facility
mit-ml-dev	85/tcp	MIT ML Device
mit-ml-dev	85/udp	MIT ML Device
mfcobol	86/tcp	Micro Focus Cobol
mfcobol	86/udp	Micro Focus Cobol
	87/tcp	Any private terminal link
	87/udp	Any private terminal link
kerberos	88/tcp	Kerberos
kerberos	88/udp	Kerberos
su-mit-tg	89/tcp	SU/MIT Telnet Gateway
su-mit-tg	89/udp	SU/MIT Telnet Gateway
dnsix	90/tcp	DNSIX Securit Attribute Token Map
dnsix	90/udp	DNSIX Securit Attribute Token Map
mit-dov	91/tcp	MIT Dover Spooler
mit-dov	91/udp	MIT Dover Spooler
npp	92/tcp	Network Printing Protocol
npp	92/udp	Network Printing Protocol

B

WELL-KNOWN
SERVICE PORTS

continues

Table B.1. continued

Keyword	Decimal	Description
dcp	93/tcp	Device Control Protocol
dcp	93/udp	Device Control Protocol
objcall	94/tcp	Tivoli Object Dispatcher
objcall	94/udp	Tivoli Object Dispatcher
supdup	95/tcp	SUPDUP
supdup	95/udp	SUPDUP
dixie	96/tcp	DIXIE Protocol Specification
dixie	96/udp	DIXIE Protocol Specification
swift-rvf	97/tcp	Swift Remote Virtual File Protocol
swift-rvf	97/udp	Swift Remote Virtual File Protocol
tacnews	98/tcp	TAC News
tacnews	98/udp	TAC News
metagram	99/tcp	Metagram Relay
metagram	99/udp	Metagram Relay
newacct	100/tcp	[unauthorized use]
hostname	101/tcp	NIC Host Name Server
hostname	101/udp	NIC Host Name Server
iso-tsap	102/tcp	ISO-TSAP
iso-tsap	102/udp	ISO-TSAP
gppitnp	103/tcp	Genesis Point-to-Point Trans Net
gppitnp	103/udp	Genesis Point-to-Point Trans Net
acr-nema	104/tcp	ACR-NEMA Digital Imag. & Comm. 300
acr-nema	104/udp	ACR-NEMA Digital Imag. & Comm. 300
csnet-ns	105/tcp	Mailbox Name Nameserver
csnet-ns	105/udp	Mailbox Name Nameserver
3com-tsmux	106/tcp	3COM-TSMUX
3com-tsmux	106/udp	3COM-TSMUX
rtelnet	107/tcp	Remote Telnet Service
rtelnet	107/udp	Remote Telnet Service
snagas	108/tcp	SNA Gateway Access Server
snagas	108/udp	SNA Gateway Access Server

Keyword	Decimal	Description
pop2	109/tcp	Post Office Protocol, Version 2
pop2	109/udp	Post Office Protocol, Version 2
pop3	110/tcp	Post Office Protocol, Version 3
pop3	110/udp	Post Office Protocol, Version 3
sunrpc	111/tcp	SUN Remote Procedure Call
sunrpc	111/udp	SUN Remote Procedure Call
mcidas	112/tcp	McIDAS Data Transmission Protocol
mcidas	112/udp	McIDAS Data Transmission Protocol
auth	113/tcp	Authentication Service
auth	113/udp	Authentication Service
audionews	114/tcp	Audio News Multicast
audionews	114/udp	Audio News Multicast
sftp	115/tcp	Simple File Transfer Protocol
sftp	115/udp	Simple File Transfer Protocol
ansanotify	116/tcp	ANSA REX Notify
ansanotify	116/udp	ANSA REX Notify
uucp-path	117/tcp	UUCP Path Service
uucp-path	117/udp	UUCP Path Service
sqlserv	118/tcp	SQL Services
sqlserv	118/udp	SQL Services
nntp	119/tcp	Network News Transfer Protocol
nntp	119/udp	Network News Transfer Protocol
cfdptkt	120/tcp	CFDPTKT
cfdptkt	120/udp	CFDPTKT
erpc	121/tcp	Encore Expedited Remote Pro. Call
erpc	121/udp	Encore Expedited Remote Pro. Call
smakynet	122/tcp	SMAKYNET
smakynet	122/udp	SMAKYNET
ntp	123/tcp	Network Time Protocol
ntp	123/udp	Network Time Protocol
ansatrader	124/tcp	ANSA REX Trader
ansatrader	124/udp	ANSA REX Trader

B

**WELL-KNOWN
SERVICE PORTS**

continues

Table B.1. continued

Keyword	Decimal	Description
locus-map	125/tcp	Locus PC-Interface Net Map Server
locus-map	125/udp	Locus PC-Interface Net Map Server
unitary	126/tcp	Unisys Unitary Login
unitary	126/udp	Unisys Unitary Login
locus-con	127/tcp	Locus PC-Interface Conn Server
locus-con	127/udp	Locus PC-Interface Conn Server
gss-xlicen	128/tcp	GSS X License Verification
gss-xlicen	128/udp	GSS X License Verification
pwdgen	129/tcp	Password Generator Protocol
pwdgen	129/udp	Password Generator Protocol
cisco-fna	130/tcp	cisco FNATIVE
cisco-fna	130/udp	cisco FNATIVE
cisco-tna	131/tcp	cisco TNATIVE
cisco-tna	131/udp	cisco TNATIVE
cisco-sys	132/tcp	cisco SYSMAINT
cisco-sys	132/udp	cisco SYSMAINT
statsrv	133/tcp	Statistics Service
statsrv	133/udp	Statistics Service
ingres-net	134/tcp	INGRES-NET Service
ingres-net	134/udp	INGRES-NET Service
loc-srv	135/tcp	Location Service
loc-srv	135/udp	Location Service
profile	136/tcp	PROFILE Naming System
profile	136/udp	PROFILE Naming System
netbios-ns	137/tcp	NETBIOS Name Service
netbios-ns	137/udp	NETBIOS Name Service
netbios-dgm	138/tcp	NETBIOS Datagram Service
netbios-dgm	138/udp	NETBIOS Datagram Service
netbios-ssn	139/tcp	NETBIOS Session Service
netbios-ssn	139/udp	NETBIOS Session Service
emfis-data	140/tcp	EMFIS Data Service
emfis-data	140/udp	EMFIS Data Service
emfis-cntl	141/tcp	EMFIS Control Service

Keyword	Decimal	Description
emfis-cntl	141/udp	EMFIS Control Service
bl-idm	142/tcp	Britton-Lee IDM
bl-idm	142/udp	Britton-Lee IDM
imap2	143/tcp	Interim Mail Access Protocol v2
imap2	143/udp	Interim Mail Access Protocol v2
news	144/tcp	NewS
news	144/udp	NewS
uaac	145/tcp	UAAC Protocol
uaac	145/udp	UAAC Protocol
iso-tp0	146/tcp	ISO-TP0
iso-tp0	146/udp	ISO-TP0
iso-ip	147/tcp	ISO-IP
iso-ip	147/udp	ISO-IP
cronus	148/tcp	CRONUS-SUPPORT
cronus	148/udp	CRONUS-SUPPORT
aed-512	149/tcp	AED 512 Emulation Service
aed-512	149/udp	AED 512 Emulation Service
sql-net	150/tcp	SQL-NET
sql-net	150/udp	SQL-NET
hems	151/tcp	HEMS
hems	151/udp	HEMS
bftp	152/tcp	Background File Transfer Program
bftp	152/udp	Background File Transfer Program
sgmp	153/tcp	SGMP
sgmp	153/udp	SGMP
netsc-prod	154/tcp	NETSC
netsc-prod	154/udp	NETSC
netsc-dev	155/tcp	NETSC
netsc-dev	155/udp	NETSC
sqlsrv	156/tcp	SQL Service
sqlsrv	156/udp	SQL Service
knet-cmp	157/tcp	KNET/VM Command/Message

B

WELL-KNOWN
SERVICE PORTS

continues

Table B.1. continued

Keyword	Decimal	Description
knet-cmp	157/udp	KNET/VM Command/Message
pcmail-srv	158/tcp	PCMail Server
pcmail-srv	158/udp	PCMail Server
nss-routing	159/tcp	NSS-Routing
nss-routing	159/udp	NSS-Routing
sgmp-traps	160/tcp	SGMP-TRAPS
sgmp-traps	160/udp	SGMP-TRAPS
snmp	161/tcp	SNMP
snmp	161/udp	SNMP
snmptrap	162/tcp	SNMPTRAP
snmptrap	162/udp	SNMPTRAP
cmip-man	163/tcp	CMIP/TCP Manager
cmip-man	163/udp	CMIP/TCP Manager
cmip-agent	164/tcp	CMIP/TCP Agent
smip-agent	164/udp	CMIP/TCP Agent
xns-courier	165/tcp	Xerox
xns-courier	165/udp	Xerox
s-net	166/tcp	Sirius Systems
s-net	166/udp	Sirius Systems
namp	167/tcp	NAMP
namp	167/udp	NAMP
rsvd	168/tcp	RSVD
rsvd	168/udp	RSVD
send	169/tcp	SEND
send	169/udp	SEND
print-srv	170/tcp	Network PostScript
print-srv	170/udp	Network PostScript
multiplex	171/tcp	Network Innovations Multiplex
multiplex	171/udp	Network Innovations Multiplex
cl/1	172/tcp	Network Innovations CL/1
cl/1	172/udp	Network Innovations CL/1
xyplex-mux	173/tcp	Xyplex

Keyword	Decimal	Description
xyplex-mux	173/udp	Xyplex
mailq	174/tcp	MAILQ
mailq	174/udp	MAILQ
vmnet	175/tcp	VMNET
vmnet	175/udp	VMNET
genrad-mux	176/tcp	GENRAD-MUX
genrad-mux	176/udp	GENRAD-MUX
xdmcp	177/tcp	X Display Manager Control Protocol
xdmcp	177/udp	X Display Manager Control Protocol
nextstep	178/tcp	NextStep Window Server
NextStep	178/udp	NextStep Window Server
bgp	179/tcp	Border Gateway Protocol
bgp	179/udp	Border Gateway Protocol
ris	180/tcp	Intergraph
ris	180/udp	Intergraph
unify	181/tcp	Unify
unify	181/udp	Unify
audit	182/tcp	Unisys Audit SITP
audit	182/udp	Unisys Audit SITP
ocbinder	183/tcp	OCBinder
ocbinder	183/udp	OCBinder
ocserver	184/tcp	OCServer
ocserver	184/udp	OCServer
remote-kis	185/tcp	Remote-KIS
remote-kis	185/udp	Remote-KIS
kis	186/tcp	KIS Protocol
kis	186/udp	KIS Protocol
aci	187/tcp	Application Communication Interface
aci	187/udp	Application Communication Interface
mumps	188/tcp	Plus Five's MUMPS
mumps	188/udp	Plus Five's MUMPS
qft	189/tcp	Queued File Transport

B

WELL-KNOWN
SERVICE PORTS

continues

Table B.1. continued

Keyword	Decimal	Description
qft	189/udp	Queued File Transport
gacp	190/tcp	Gateway Access Control Protocol
cacp	190/udp	Gateway Access Control Protocol
prospero	191/tcp	Prospero
prospero	191/udp	Prospero
osu-nms	192/tcp	OSU Network Monitoring System
osu-nms	192/udp	OSU Network Monitoring System
srmp	193/tcp	Spider Remote Monitoring Protocol
srmp	193/udp	Spider Remote Monitoring Protocol
irc	194/tcp	Internet Relay Chat Protocol
irc	194/udp	Internet Relay Chat Protocol
dn6-nlm-aud	195/tcp	DNSIX Network Level Module Audit
dn6-nlm-aud	195/udp	DNSIX Network Level Module Audit
dn6-smm-red	196/tcp	DNSIX Session Mgt Module Audit
dn6-smm-red	196/udp	DNSIX Session Mgt Module Audit
dls	197/tcp	Directory Location Service
dls	197/udp	Directory Location Service
dls-mon	198/tcp	Directory Location Service Monitor
dls-mon	198/udp	Directory Location Service Monitor
smux	199/tcp	SMUX
smux	199/udp	SMUX
src	200/tcp	IBM System Resource Controller
src	200/udp	IBM System Resource Controller
at-rtmp	201/tcp	AppleTalk Routing Maintenance
at-rtmp	201/udp	AppleTalk Routing Maintenance
at-nbp	202/tcp	AppleTalk Name Binding
at-nbp	202/udp	AppleTalk Name Binding
at-3	203/tcp	AppleTalk Unused
at-3	203/udp	AppleTalk Unused
at-echo	204/tcp	AppleTalk Echo
at-echo	204/udp	AppleTalk Echo
at-5	205/tcp	AppleTalk Unused

Keyword	Decimal	Description
at-5	205/udp	AppleTalk Unused
at-zis	206/tcp	AppleTalk Zone Information
at-zis	206/udp	AppleTalk Zone Information
at-7	207/tcp	AppleTalk Unused
at-7	207/udp	AppleTalk Unused
at-8	208/tcp	AppleTalk Unused
at-8	208/udp	AppleTalk Unused
tam	209/tcp	Trivial Authenticated Mail Protocol
tam	209/udp	Trivial Authenticated Mail Protocol
z39.50	210/tcp	ANSI Z39.50
z39.50	210/udp	ANSI Z39.50
914c/g	211/tcp	Texas Instruments 914C/G Terminal
914c/g	211/udp	Texas Instruments 914C/G Terminal
anet	212/tcp	ATEXSSTR
anet	212/udp	ATEXSSTR
ipx	213/tcp	IPX
ipx	213/udp	IPX
vmpwscs	214/tcp	VM PWSCS
vmpwscs	214/udp	VM PWSCS
softpc	215/tcp	Insignia Solutions
softpc	215/udp	Insignia Solutions
atls	216/tcp	Access Technology License Server
atls	216/udp	Access Technology License Server
dbase	217/tcp	dBASE UNIX
dbase	217/udp	dBASE UNIX
mpp	218/tcp	Netix Message Posting Protocol
mpp	218/udp	Netix Message Posting Protocol
uarps	219/tcp	Unisys ARPs
uarps	219/udp	Unisys ARPs
imap3	220/tcp	Interactive Mail Access Protocol v3
imap3	220/udp	Interactive Mail Access Protocol v3
fln-spx	221/tcp	Berkeley rlogind with SPX auth

B

**WELL-KNOWN
SERVICE PORTS**

continues

Table B.1. continued

Keyword	Decimal	Description
fln-spx	221/udp	Berkeley rlogind with SPX auth
fsh-spx	222/tcp	Berkeley rshd with SPX auth
fsh-spx	222/udp	Berkeley rshd with SPX auth
cdc	223/tcp	Certificate Distribution Center
cdc	223/udp	Certificate Distribution Center
	224–241	Reserved
sur-meas	243/tcp	Survey Measurement
sur-meas	243/udp	Survey Measurement
link	245/tcp	LINK
link	245/udp	LINK
dsp3270	246/tcp	Display Systems Protocol
dsp3270	246/udp	Display Systems Protocol
	247-255	Reserved
pawserv	345/tcp	Perf Analysis Workbench
pawserv	345/udp	Perf Analysis Workbench
zserv	346/tcp	Zebra Server
zserv	346/udp	Zebra Server
fatserv	347/tcp	Fatmen Server
fatserv	347/udp	Fatmen Server
clearcase	371/tcp	Clearcase
clearcase	371/udp	Clearcase
ulistserv	372/tcp	UNIX Listserv
ulistserv	372/udp	UNIX Listserv
legent-1	373/tcp	Legent Corporation
legent-1	373/udp	Legent Corporation
legent-2	374/tcp	Legent Corporation
legent-2	374/udp	Legent Corporation
exec	512/tcp	Remote process execution; authentication performed using passwords and UNIX loppgin names
biff	512/udp	Used by mail system to notify users of new mail received; currently receives messages only from processes on the same machine

Keyword	Decimal	Description
login	513/tcp	Remote login a la Telnet; automatic authentication performed based on privileged port numbers and distributed databases that identify "authentication domains"
who	513/udp	Maintains databases showing who is logged in to machines on a local network and the load average of the machine
cmd	514/tcp	Like exec, but automatic authentication is performed as for a login server
syslog	514/udp	
printer	515/tcp	spooler; alias=spooler (The print server LPD service will listen on tcp port 515 for incoming connections.)
printer	515/udp	spooler
talk	517/tcp	Like tenex link, but across machine; unfortunately, doesn't use a link protocol (This is actually just a rendezvous port from which a TCP connection is established.)
talk	517/udp	Like tenex link, but across machine; unfortunately, doesn't use a link protocol (This is actually just a rendezvous port from which a TCP connection is established.)
ntalk	518/tcp	
ntalk	518/udp	
utime	519/tcp	unixtime
utime	519/udp	unixtime
efs	520/tcp	Extended filename server
router	520/udp	Local routing process (onsite); uses variant of Xerox NS routing information protocol
timed	525/tcp	timeserver
timed	525/udp	timeserver
tempo	526/tcp	newdate
tempo	526/udp	newdate

B

**WELL-KNOWN
SERVICE PORTS**

continues

Table B.1. continued

Keyword	Decimal	Description
courier	530/tcp	rpc
courier	530/udp	rpc
conference	531/tcp	chat
conference	531/udp	chat
netnews	532/tcp	readnews
netnews	532/udp	readnews
netwall	533/tcp	For emergency broadcasts
netwall	533/udp	For emergency broadcasts
uucp	540/tcp	uucpd
uucp	540/udp	uucpd
klogin	543/tcp	
klogin	543/udp	
kshell	544/tcp	krcmd
kshell	544/udp	krcmd
new-rwho	550/tcp	new-who
new-rwho	550/udp	new-who
dsf	555/tcp	
dsf	555/udp	
remotefs	556/tcp	rfs server
remotefs	556/udp	rfs server
rmonitor	560/tcp	rmonitord
rmonitor	560/udp	rmonitord
monitor	561/tcp	
monitor	561/udp	
chshell	562/tcp	chcmd
chshell	562/udp	chcmd
9pfs	564/tcp	plan 9 file service
9pfs	564/udp	plan 9 file service
whoami	565/tcp	whoami
whoami	565/udp	whoami
meter	570/tcp	demon
meter	570/udp	demon

Keyword	Decimal	Description
meter	571/tcp	udemon
meter	571/udp	udemon
ipcserver	600/tcp	Sun IPC Server
ipcserver	600/udp	Sun IPC Server
nqs	607/tcp	nqs
nqs	607/udp	nqs
mdqs	666/tcp	
mdqs	666/udp	
elcsd	704/tcp	errlog copy/server daemon
elcsd	704/udp	errlog copy/server daemon
netcp	740/tcp	NETscout Control Protocol
netcp	740/udp	NETscout Control Protocol
netgw	741/tcp	ntGW
netgw	741/udp	netGW
netrcs	742/tcp	Network-based Rev. Cont. Sys.
netrcs	742/udp	Network-based Rev. Cont. Sys.
flexlm	744/tcp	Flexible License Manager
flexlm	744/udp	Flexible License Manager
fujitsu-dev	747/tcp	Fujitsu Device Control
fujitsu-dev	747/udp	Fujitsu Device Control
ris-cm	748/tcp	Russell Info Sci Calendar Manager
ris-cm	748/udp	Russell Info Sci Calendar Manager
kerberos-adm	749/tcp	Kerberos administration
kerberos-adm	749/udp	Kerberos administration
rfile	750/tcp	
loadav	750/udp	
pump	751/tcp	
pump	751/udp	
qrh	752/tcp	
qrh	752/udp	
rrh	753/tcp	
rrh	753/udp	

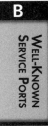

continues

Table B.1. continued

Keyword	Decimal	Description
tell	754/tcp	send
tell	754/udp	send
nlogin	758/tcp	
nlogin	758/udp	
con	759/tcp	
con	759/udp	
ns	760/tcp	
ns	760/udp	
rxe	761/tcp	
rxe	761/udp	
quotad	762/tcp	
quotad	762/udp	
cycleserv	763/tcp	
cycleserv	763/udp	
omserv	764/tcp	
omserv	764/udp	
webster	765/tcp	
webster	765/udp	
phonebook	767/tcp	phone
phonebook	767/udp	phone
vid	769/tcp	
vid	769/udp	
cadlock	770/tcp	
cadlock	770/udp	
rtip	771/tcp	
rtip	771/udp	
cycleserv2	772/tcp	
cycleserv2	772/udp	
submit	773/tcp	
notify	773/udp	
rpasswd	774/tcp	

Keyword	Decimal	Description
acmaint_dbd	774/udp	
entomb	775/tcp	
acmaint_transd	775/udp	
wpages	776/tcp	
wpages	776/udp	
wpgs	780/tcp	
wpgs	780/udp	
hp-collector	781/tcp	hp performance data collector
hp-collector	781/udp	hp performance data collector
hp-managed-node	782/tcp	hp performance data managed node
hp-managed-node	782/udp	hp performance data managed node
hp-alarm-mgr	783/tcp	hp performance data alarm manager
hp-alarm-mgr	783/udp	hp performance data alarm manager
mdbs_daemon	800/tcp	
mdbs_daemon	800/udp	
device	801/tcp	
device	801/udp	
xtreelic	996/tcp	XTREE License Server
xtreelic	996/udp	XTREE License Server
maitrd	997/tcp	
maitrd	997/udp	
busboy	998/tcp	
puparp	998/udp	
garcon	999/tcp	
applix	999/udp	Applix ac
puprouter	999/tcp	
puprouter	999/udp	
cadlock	1000/tcp	
ock	1000/udp	

Service Pack Review

by Joshua Allen

IN THIS APPENDIX

APPENDIX C

Modern operating systems are constantly evolving, continually adapting to volatile market conditions. There is a very good chance that the version of Windows NT that you have installed on your machines is already out of date, leaving you vulnerable to freshly discovered security problems and denying you the benefits of some of the newest functionality. This appendix will show you how to make sure that your Windows NT 4 workstations are always properly loaded with the most up-to-date components.

Microsoft addresses updates to Windows NT in a number of ways. The most basic update mechanisms are patches known as *service packs*. Service packs are patches that you can obtain for free from Microsoft to incrementally patch older installs of Windows NT Workstation and Server to fix various bugs and add new features. Keep in mind that these updates are meant to fix bugs and add features to your current version of Windows NT; to upgrade between major versions (such as NT 3.51 to NT 4) you need to buy an actual upgrade. Service packs usually combine a large number of fixes and are released at longer intervals (every few months to a year). Service Pack 3 is the latest service pack for Windows NT Workstation 4.

> **NOTE**
>
> Current to this writing, Service Pack 3 is the latest service pack for Windows NT Workstation 4. Service Pack 3 has been well tested by Microsoft and includes a large number of changes, so it will probably remain current for some time. You should check `ftp://ftp.microsoft.com/bussys/winnt/winnt-public/fixes/usa/nt40`, though, to make sure that there are no more recent service packs before proceeding. Much of this appendix will focus on Service Pack 3 specifically, but the advice here applies to any future service packs and hotfixes as well.

For fixes that users might want to apply immediately, Microsoft releases *hotfixes*, which normally apply to only one specific bug or problem and must be installed individually by you. These hotfixes are meant to address specific problems you might be having right now that must be repaired sooner than the next service pack release.

Finally, the newest operating system features that have been developed since the last service pack, or that were not included in the service pack, can often be downloaded in released or preview version from Microsoft's site. Personal Fax for Windows is an example of one non–service-pack component that you might want to add to your Windows NT 4 installations.

Downloading and Installing Service Pack 3

At a minimum, you should always have installed the most recent service pack to your system. As of this writing, this means Service Pack 3 for Windows NT 4 Workstation or Server. Working with service packs can be frustrating, so follow these steps carefully to minimize your hassles when downloading Service Pack 3:

1. Try to get the service pack on CD-ROM. The CD-ROM version of Service Pack 3 includes some features that does not, including IIS 3.0 and Microsoft NetShow. If you have a subscription to Microsoft Technet, the CD-ROM is included with your mailing. If you participate in the Microsoft Select program, as well, you will have a CD-ROM version of the most recent service pack. Otherwise, you can call 800-370-8758 to order the service pack CD-ROM from Microsoft (there is a $20 charge, purportedly to cover media cost).

> **NOTE**
>
> Many Windows NT security functions rely on encryption technology. Make sure to get the service pack that has the highest strength encryption that you are permitted to use. If you are in a North American country, this means 128-bit encryption. If you are anywhere else, this means 40-bit encryption, which is basically useless. The U.S. government forbids the export of any encryption technology greater than 40 bits to any countries outside of North America. What this means to you is that those countries eventually get strong encryption anyway, but you have to jump through ridiculous hoops to get 128-bit encryption for your own use even if you are a U.S. citizen. The Service Pack 3 that comes with Technet, for example, supports only 40-bit encryption. If you install this atop your existing installation, you will ruin much of your protection. If you get your service pack CD-ROM from your Microsoft Select CDs, make sure to use the one with a red label (U.S. version). The other Select CDs support only 40-bit encryption. If you are ordering the CD-ROM by calling 800-370-8758, you need to claim to be a U.S. citizen to get the 128-bit version.
>
> This applies equally to the download version. The service pack updates that you download from the Microsoft FTP site will support only 40-bit encryption. If you point your Web browser to http://206.204.65.109/cgi-bin/ntitar.pl, however, after answering a few questions, you will be permitted to download the 128-bit version of the service pack.
>
> Finally, once you have obtained the 128-bit version, be careful not to accidentally have a copy in your bag when you travel overseas, and do not leave a copy available for download from your servers. Although foreign terrorists will probably not be interested in your service pack (because they already have a copy), the government does prosecute such violations and you might end up in federal prison.

2. If you cannot obtain the service pack on CD-ROM, you can download it for free from Microsoft's site. The crippled, 40-bit version is available from ftp://ftp.microsoft.com/bussys/winnt/winnt-public/fixes/usa/nt40/ussp3/i386/nt4sp3_i.exe. The version for Digital's Alpha chip is in the ussp3 directory under alpha/nt4sp3_a.exe. Notice that there is no longer a PowerPC version; PowerPC support by Windows NT is being abandoned in the same way that MIPS support was abandoned. Go to http://206.204.65.109/cgi-bin/ntitar.pl if you need the 128-bit version.

Follow these steps when installing the service pack:

1. The service pack can be installed directly from the source CD-ROM or the downloaded file, but I do not recommend this. If you are using the CD-ROM, just copy the contents of the i386 directory into a subdirectory on your hard drive (c:\ussp3 is a good choice). If you have downloaded the service pack, copy the .exe file (for example, nt4sp3_i.exe) into c:\ussp3 and then execute it with the /x option from your Run menu (type `c:\ussp3\nt4sp3_1 /x` at the Start menu | Run option).

TIP

It makes sense to keep a copy of the service pack available on your hard drive. Many of the times you'll need to use a service pack involving situations where the network or CD-ROM drive might not be available. If you have never had the experience of struggling to get access to the service pack to help repair a damaged machine, keeping a copy of the latest service pack on your hard drive might just keep your record spotless. Any time you add or remove new components (such as a new network adapter or service) to Windows NT, files are copied back from the original install source, often reversing certain changes that were added by the service packs. To be safe, you should always reinstall the service pack after making changes to Windows NT. In addition, any setup disks that you generate from your Windows NT CD-ROM will have to be modified by adding a file from your service pack source. If you ever need to uninstall the service pack, too, you can simply execute update.exe from your hard drive.

---

2. Once you have a good copy of the appropriate service pack expanded to your hard drive, simply install it by typing `c:\ussp3\update.exe` into the Start menu | Run box.

3. When you are installing, answer Yes to the question that asks whether you would like to create an uninstall directory. Service Pack 3 is remarkably stable, as far as service pack updates are concerned, but when service packs go bad, they generally cause a considerable mess, so you will want to have the uninstall enabled.

4. If you are running a prerelease version of Internet Explorer 4 on your workstation, you need to uninstall it before running the Service Pack 3 update. If you try to run update.exe before uninstalling IE4, the service pack install will just pop up a nice message telling you to uninstall IE4 and then abort. As soon as you are done installing Service Pack 3, though, you can reinstall IE4 with no problems.

5. Finally, after you have installed the service pack, you need to update any setup disk sets that you have lying around. If you ever need to use the emergency repair disk utility that is part of the setup disk set, you will have to use a setup disk set that has been modified for Service Pack 3. It is better to modify these disks now than to try to copy the necessary patch from your hard drive when your machine is in a state of needing emergency repair. Perform this update by copying the file setupdd.sys from your c:\ussp3 directory to setup disk #2 of any setup disk sets that you have.

6. You are done! Just reboot your machine. You should see that the blue start-up screen has added the text (Service Pack 3) to the end of the OS description line.

Continue reading if you would like to find out more about some of the changes that were included in Service Pack 3, or skip forward to find out how to install some important post–Service-Pack-3 updates.

Important Security Fixes in SP3

Many of the changes included with any service pack are built to address information security issues. In some cases, these changes correct operating system errors that have caused vulnerabilities, but in other cases, the changes update the system to compensate for advances in security cracking technologies. Service Pack 3 includes changes of both kinds.

New Concept for Guest Access

Installation of Service Pack 3 introduces some changes to the user and group concepts covered in Chapter 28, "Users and Groups on NT." After installing the service pack, you will notice that there is a new Global Group, Authenticated Users, that you can use when assigning permissions to resources on your workstation. Basically, the Authenticated Users group is a refinement of the Everyone group. Service Pack 3 includes a new account, the NULL session or Anonymous user, which is a member of the Everyone group but is not a member of Authenticated Users. Previous to Service Pack 3, it was possible for machines outside of the domain to attach to the domain and list all users of the domain, without ever having to authenticate to the domain. This is not necessarily a hole in the operating system, but it could give a hacker a head start at cracking your network. Service Pack 3 now allows Registry access and account database access only to the Authenticated Users group. You can still assign permissions for various resources to the Everyone group if you like—SP3 just gives you more control by allowing you to use the Authenticated Users group if you want to avoid giving permissions to anonymous users.

Upgraded CIFS (SMB)

The protocol upon which file sharing for Windows NT and Windows 95 are based is known as Common Internet File Sharing (CIFS). This protocol, also called SMB, has been used with no serious modifications since the days of Microsoft Lanman and Windows for Workgroups 3.11. Support for CIFS is now available for other operating systems, such as OS/2 and UNIX. Standard CIFS is vulnerable to some sophisticated attacks, however, including the man-in-the-middle attack and the session hijacking attack. With the man-in-the-middle attack, a malicious entity could insert itself between two machines that want to establish communications and impersonate each end of the connection to the machines. Both machines would think that they were connected to one another, when in fact, all communications would be proxied by the middleman. The man in the middle could then view any data or insert spurious data into the data stream. The hijacking attack is similar to the man-in-the-middle attack, with the middleman simply taking over the communications channel after the initial authentication has already transpired. Service Pack 3 introduces some changes to the CIFS protocol that make it a more viable option in light of today's security realities. Initial authentication is negotiated in a manner that prevents a middleman from impersonating either machine, and all transmitted data includes a digital signature that is impossible for a middleman to forge, effectively blocking a hijacker. This security scheme is nearly identical to the way that Secure Sockets Layer (SSL) protects connections between your Web server and Web browser. For more information about CIFS, see `http://www.microsoft.com/intdev/cifs`.

> **NOTE**
>
> If you are using any non-Microsoft CIFS products, such as SAMBA for UNIX (a free package that allows you to mount NT to UNIX and UNIX to NT), your connections will fail after installing Service Pack 3 on your NT machines. This is because these packages have not yet been modified to support the new CIFS. If you need to connect to these servers, you can disable some of the new CIFS security by adding a value named `EnablePlainText Password` of type `DWORD` and value 1 to the `HKEY_LOCAL_MACHINE\System\CurrentControl Set\Services\Rdr\Parameters` subkey of the Registry. You need to restart your machine after doing this. For more information about working with the Registry, see Chapter 11, "The NT Registry." For more information about SAMBA, point your Web browser to `http: //lake.canberra.edu.au/pub/samba/`.

Strong Encryption of Accounts Database

User account and password information for Windows NT is stored in an area of the Registry known as the Security Accounts Manager (SAM). Previous to Service Pack 3, the data stored in this Registry location was weakly encrypted, because Windows NT relies on the fact that the area is readable only by administrators. Recently, however, some easily obtainable tools have been released that allow administrators (and potentially, malicious users) to raid and crack the SAM. A free program called PWDump (`ftp://samba.anu.edu.au/pub/samba/pwdump`) will dump and partially decrypt the SAM, and another free program called NTCrack (`http://www.secnet.com/ntinfo/ntcrack.html`) will brute-force scan the output of PWDump to discover user and administrator passwords. Strong encryption of the accounts database is only part of the solution to this wide availability of cracking tools, though. For more extensive protection, you should enable the password filtering feature of Service Pack 3, as described next.

Password Filtering

Brute-force cracking programs, such as NTCrack, rely partially on the fact that many users choose passwords that are easy to guess. Many users select permutations of their names, children's names, computer names, or birth dates as their passwords. Forcing your users to select passwords that are difficult to guess will make the job of a brute-force password scanner considerably more difficult. Even before Service Pack 3, Windows NT included the capability to reject or accept passwords based on uniqueness. If you wanted to use this feature, though, you had to create or obtain a special DLL to install as a password filter. With Service Pack 3, Microsoft includes a password filtering DLL, passfilt.dll, that you can enable on your machines. Just copy passfilt.dll into your system32 directory and then create a Registry key `HKEY_LOCAL_MACHINE\SYSTEM\CurrentControlSet\Control\Lsa\Notification Packages` of type `REG_MULTI_SZ` and set the value to `Passfilt.dll`. This change should be made on any domain controllers in your domain. Now, whenever a user changes her password, the system Local Security Authority (LSA) notifies passfilt.dll, and passfilt.dll makes sure that the new password contains uppercase and lowercase characters, contains special characters, and is not a permutation of the user's name.

New Features in Service Pack 3

In addition to IIS 3.0 and ASP, described in Chapter 28, Service Pack 3 includes some new features that might interest you.

ODBC 3.0

Service Pack 3 includes a major revision to the Open Database Connectivity (ODBC) layer, version 3.0. ODBC is used by database programs to access SQL databases without having to use vendor-specific instructions. ODBC 3.0 has tons of new features that allow developers to write applications that will have significantly better performance than ODBC 2.0 applications. For example, ODBC 3.0 includes a number of new features that allow developers to use a database's bookmarking features to quickly return to various locations in a table or recordset. Another ODBC 3.0 feature that you'll appreciate is the ability to store ODBC connection information in a settings file that you can copy to other machines; this saves you the hassle of ODBC.INI and Registry modifications that you previously had to endure to install ODBC connection information. A full list of the new features in ODBC 3.0 can be viewed at `http://www.microsoft.com/odbc/features/default.htm`. Because most of the new ODBC 3.0 capabilities will make programmers' lives easier, you can expect that programmers will be using these features right away in new developments. This means that you'll want to have Service Pack 3 installed on all of your machines in order to take advantage of the added performance. And, although Microsoft recommends that developers attempt to make their programs backward-compatible to use ODBC 2.0 functionality if 3.0 drivers are not available, you can bet that many vendors won't bother heeding this advice but instead will write programs that run *only* on ODBC 3.0 machines.

> **NOTE**
>
> ODBC 3.0, carrying on the tradition of the previous versions of ODBC, allows users to turn on ODBC tracing to a log file. This permits any user of a system to capture the full SQL of all calls made to the database engine. If any of your systems use authentication that is based on passwords stored within a table in the database, this tracing feature could pose a potential problem. If you can think of any situations where you would not want your users to be able to view the SQL statements of your code, you should check out `http://www.microsoft.com/ODBC/download/DMDownload.htm` for information on how to protect against tracing.

CryptoAPI

CryptoAPI is a new Application Programming Interface that programmers can use to include support for a number of popular encryption techniques in their programs. CryptoAPI includes everything that you need to write and run programs using digital signatures, certificates, public key encryption, and basic encryption. Because CryptoAPI isolates programmers from the encryption implementation routines, programmers can write applications that are secured with very strong encryption without having to worry about how to write the routines correctly or efficiently. This means that you will see most new security-aware applications for NT taking advantage of this API. In particular, new electronic commerce and electronic data interchange (EDI) programs for NT will probably require CryptoAPI. For information about using CryptoAPI, see `http://www.microsoft.com/intdev/security/capi/toc.htm`.

Additional Important Patches

Though you can rely on service packs to provide most of your current needs, you should periodically check the Windows NT home page at `http://www.microsoft.com/ntworkstation` and particularly the Windows NT hotfixes at `ftp://ftp.microsoft.com/bussys/winnt/winnt-public/fixes/usa/nt40/hotfixes-postSP3/` for new updates that you might need. You can download an add-on for Windows NT Workstation that ties faxing capabilities into Microsoft Exchange and Outlook from `http://www.microsoft.com/ntworkstation/fax.htm`. New hotfixes are constantly being added to Microsoft's FTP server. Some current ones that might interest you follow.

The file java-fix/javafixi.exe repairs a bug in the Internet Explorer Java applet display routines that was made evident by the installation of Service Pack 3. After installing Service Pack 3, Internet Explorer will fail to properly run Java applets if your display settings have specified 32-bit (True Color) color. You can fix the IE bug by downloading javafixi.exe (or javafixa.exe for Alpha processors) and double-clicking it.

> **NOTE**
>
> Notice that this bug in IE was not revealed until the stricter display control routines of Service Pack 3 were installed. Quite conceivably, there are other programs that you may use that could have used the same erroneous color management techniques that Internet Explorer used. These programs, too, could be broken by Service Pack 3 but, unfortunately, might not have hotfixes available. This should underscore to you the necessity of keeping the service pack uninstall feature available, as described earlier.

The file oob-fix/oobfix_i.exe will patch a problem through which a malicious user could crash your workstation by sending out-of-band data to your machine. Scripts to crash machines in this manner are publicly available. This problem was supposed to have been remedied by a hotfix released prior to Service Pack 3, and then was intended to have been fixed in Service Pack 3. This time, the patch seems to have worked. Install it by double-clicking oobfix_i.exe.

> **NOTE**
>
> When looking through the hotfixes, you should install only the ones you feel you really need. Hotfixes are not regression-tested as thoroughly as the service packs are, and they can sometimes break things that might be more important than the original problem that the hotfix is to patch.

One last hotfix that you might want to apply to your system is a patch that corrects performance problems in Active Server Pages (ASP). This patch is located in asp-fix/aspfix.exe. This one you need to install by first double-clicking aspfix.exe (a self-extracting executable) and then copying the extracted file asp.dll over the top of asp.dll in your winnt\system32\inetsrv\asp directory. Before you copy the new DLL, you'll have to shut down the WWW service, as described in Chapter 28. When you have finished, you can restart the WWW service.

Notice that the installation procedure for the ASP hotfix was quite different from the installation procedure for the other hotfixes mentioned here. When browsing through the hotfix directories, you should always look for a readme file of some sort before attempting to apply the patch. The readme file will tell what special steps you might need to take to apply the patch. Additionally, if a hotfix is meant to address any particular knowledge-base–reported bugs, copies of the relevant knowledge-base articles will be stored in the hotfix directory with the patch. Reading these knowledge-base articles might help you determine whether that particular hotfix is one that you need to install.

NT Command Reference

by Paul Cassel

IN THIS APPENDIX

Starting the Command-Line Interface

You can start the command-line interface for Windows NT Server by clicking Start | Run and then entering CMD (case-insensitive) in the Run dialog box. CMD is the Windows NT command processor similar in function to COMMAND.COM used in DOS and Windows 95. To make a shortcut for the CLI on your desktop, start the Windows Explorer, locate the file CMD.EXE in \[NT Location]\System32 and right-click it. Drag it to the desktop and release the right mouse button, choosing the Make Shortcut option when offered. Windows NT will, by default, place the MS-DOS icon for this shortcut. As with any shortcuts, you can change the icon or the title to one of your choosing.

Creating a shortcut gives you an easy way to modify the appearance of your command-line interface. Figure D.1 shows the Options tab in the Properties sheet for such a shortcut. You can also reach the command-line interface by clicking Start | Programs | MS-DOS Prompt.

The Buffers option button shown in Figure D.1 is where you can set how many commands the interface stores—similar to DOS's Doskey command. It has nothing to do with the Buffers statement used in CONFIG.SYS for DOS or Windows.

FIGURE D.1.

The Properties sheet for the CLI shortcut has many options, including the capability to run the interface in a window or in a full screen.

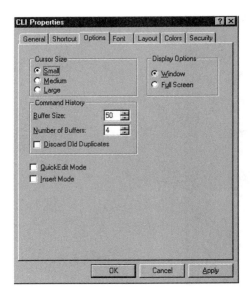

Note that this tab gives you the choice of running your CLI either in a window or in a full screen. The Colors tab is where you can set a color and font set for your interface. There's nothing stopping you from creating several shortcuts for the CLI, each with its own set of properties.

If you've used other command-line interfaces, such as those in MS-DOS or UNIX, starting the CLI will put you in a comfortable place, as shown in Figure D.2.

D

Figure D.2.

MS-DOS users will be at home with the command-line interface.

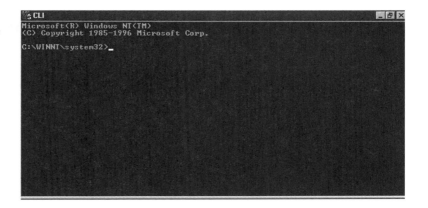

From here, entering commands is as simple as entering the command followed by its parameters, or switches, and pressing the Enter key.

Getting Help on Commands

Most commands respond to the `Command /?` convention used in Microsoft's other operating systems. Alternatively, you can see a list of some commands by entering `Help` after launching the CLI. The Help command, shown in Figure D.3, will bring up only a summary sheet for the most commonly used commands. If you want to see a complete listing of the commands along with some help text, choose Start | Help and select Windows NT Commands from the Contents tab.

Figure D.3.

The Help command at the CLI will bring up a short summary of the most often used commands.

```
For more information on a specific command, type HELP command-name.
ASSOC      Displays or modifies file extension associations
AT         Schedules commands and programs to run on a computer.
ATTRIB     Displays or changes file attributes.
BREAK      Sets or clears extended CTRL+C checking.
CACLS      Displays or modifies access control lists (ACLs) of files.
CALL       Calls one batch program from another.
CD         Displays the name of or changes the current directory.
CHCP       Displays or sets the active code page number.
CHDIR      Displays the name of or changes the current directory.
CHKDSK     Checks a disk and displays a status report.
CLS        Clears the screen.
CMD        Starts a new instance of the Windows NT command interpreter.
COLOR      Sets the default console foreground and background colors.
COMP       Compares the contents of two files or sets of files.
COMPACT    Displays or alters the compression of files on NTFS partitions.
CONVERT    Converts FAT volumes to NTFS.  You cannot convert the
           current drive.
COPY       Copies one or more files to another location.
DATE       Displays or sets the date.
DEL        Deletes one or more files.
DIR        Displays a list of files and subdirectories in a directory.
DISKCOMP   Compares the contents of two floppy disks.
--- MORE ---
```

The help system supplied by Microsoft isn't as complete as the written documentation provided in some of the company's older operating systems. Especially missing are usage examples for some of the trickier commands that can yield unexpected results or a lot of frustration. So with that in mind, on to the commands.

The Commands, Their Syntax, and Usage Examples

The following section lists the most often used commands exclusive to the CLI. They are classified by use. Some of these commands can and should be used within the file CONFIG.NT or AUTOEXEC.NT—both located in \[Windows NT]\System32. These files, similar to the DOS and Windows CONFIG.SYS and AUTOEXEC.BAT respectively, control some environmental variables for command sessions within Windows NT Server. You can alter the contents of these files using any text editor such as EDIT or Notepad.

Many of the following commands will be familiar to those who've used DOS or Windows in the past. The reason for their inclusion is their unfamiliarity to those coming to Windows NT Server from other operating systems such as UNIX, VMS, or MVS.

Unless noted, all commands and parameters are case-insensitive.

File and Disk Commands

Append: Allows programs to open data files in remote directories as if they were in the current directory. Syntax:

```
append [;] [[drive:]path[;...]] [/x:{on ¦ off}][/path:{
on ¦ off}] [/e]
```

/x tells the operating system to first search the current directory and then to extend its search to other specified directories; /e stores the append path in the environment.

Usage examples:

```
Append /x /e
```

```
Append c:\newpath
```

These two commands will instruct the application to first search the current directory for data and then c:\newpath. The \e switch tells the operating system to store the newpath information in the environment.

Assoc: Associates a file extension with an application. This command will also display and delete associations. Syntax:

```
Assoc [.ext[=[application]]]
```

Usage examples:

To show file extensions and their associations, enter

```
Assoc
```

To delete an association, enter

`Assoc .ext =`

where the `.ext` is the three-letter extension.

To add an association, enter

`Assoc .ext =application`

where the `.ext` is the three-letter extension and `application` is the name of the application.

Attrib: Sets certain attribute bits for a file. Syntax:

`Attrib [+r¦-r] [+a¦-a] [+s¦-s] [+h¦-h] [path\file] /s`

The parameters `r`, `a`, `s`, and `h` represent the bits for read-only, archive, system, and hidden, respectively. The `/s` switch tells the operating system to process similarly all files in downstream subdirectories.

Usage example:

`Attrib -r -h \mypath\myfile`

will remove the read-only and hidden attributes from `myfile` located in `mypath`.

CD and **Chdir**: Change the working directory. These commands are interchangeable in all ways. Syntax:

`CD or Chdir [\] path`

Usage examples:

`CD \`

Changes to the root directory.

`CD..`

Moves up one entry in the tree.

`CD \mypath`

Changes the working directory to `mypath`.

Chkdsk: Checks a disk and a file for errors. Similar to `Chkdsk` in DOS or Windows. Note: Later versions of DOS and Windows have a similar utility, `Scandisk`. This utility is not part of Windows NT Server. Syntax:

`Chkdsk [path] [/f] [/v] [/r]`

where

`/f` tries to fix the problem(s) found.

/v verbose mode. Echoes filenames to the screen.

/r tries to recover lost information from bad sectors. Chkdsk must have exclusive access to the volume for this switch.

Usage example:

Chkdsk c:\ /v /f

Checks the volume c: in verbose mode and tries to fix problems encountered.

Comp: Compares the contents of two files or two sets of files. Syntax:

Comp [files1] [files2] [/d] [/a] [/l] [/n=number] [/c]

where

files1 and files2 are the file sets for comparison.

/d yields a decimal display.

/a yields an alpha display.

/l shows the line numbers for differences rather than offset.

/n forces the line-by-line comparison for n lines even in different length files.

/c removes case sensitivity.

Usage example:

Comp \path1*myfiles* \path2*myfiles* /l

Will compare the files in \path1*myfiles* with those in \path2*myfiles* and show the line numbers of any discrepancies.

Compact: Applies, removes, or displays file compaction for NTFS systems. Compact can use standard wildcards. Syntax:

Compact [/c] [/u] [/s] [/i] [/f] [/a] [/q] filename(s)

where

/c compacts the file(s).

/u removes compaction from file(s).

/s processes subdirectories.

/i ignores errors.

/f forces compaction on files, even those already compressed.

/a forces compaction of system and hidden files. These are usually omitted from compaction.

/q quiet mode (little echoed to screen).

Usage examples:

```
Compact
```

Shows the compaction state of the current directory. Figure D.4 shows this command run without parameters.

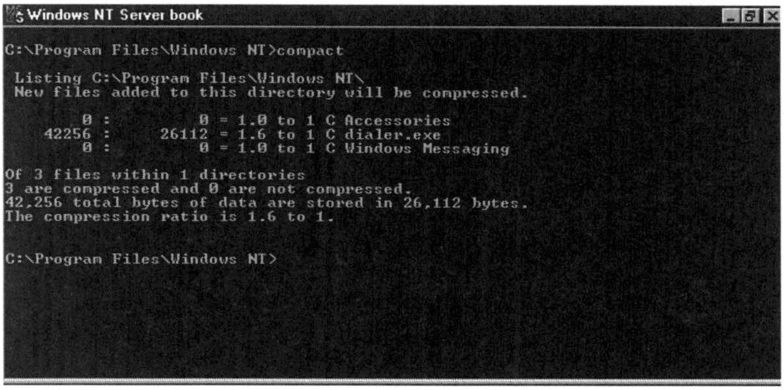

FIGURE D.4.

The Compact *command run without parameters will show the state of the compression of the current directory.*

```
Compact g:\bitmaps /s
```

Will compact the bitmaps directory and all its subdirectories on the g: drive.

Convert: Alters FAT volumes to NTFS ones. When run, Convert will need to absolutely control (lock) the disk volume slated for conversion. If it cannot, it will offer to do the conversion on next bootup. Syntax:

```
Convert [volume:] /fs:ntfs [/v] [/nametable:myfile]
```

where

volume is the volume (drive) to be converted.

/fs:ntfs means to convert to the file system NTFS. This is an obvious switch now. Microsoft might have some future plans for more types of switches.

/v signifies verbose mode.

/nametable:myfile creates a name table using the filename you specify. Use this if you encounter conversion problems due to having bizarre FAT filenames.

Usage example:

```
Convert d: /fs:ntfs /v
```

Will convert drive d: from FAT to NTFS echoing messages to the console.

Copy: Copies files from one addressable device to another. Copy can use standard wildcards. Short syntax:

```
Copy [source][destination] /a /b /v /z /n
```

where

`[source]` is the location of the files to be copied.

`[destination]` is the target location of the files.

`/a` copies ASCII files that have a `^z` character as their end of file marker.

`/b` copies binary files which can include the `^z` character as part of their data.

`/v` attempts to verify the copy operation.

`/z` copies across networks.

`/n` forces the 8.3 DOS file-naming convention.

Usage example:

```
Copy c:\myfile a:\yourfile /v
```

Copies *myfile* in the root of c: to the root of a: giving it the name, *yourfile,* and then attempts to verify the write.

Del and **Erase**: Two commands doing exactly the same thing. These commands delete the directory entries for a file or files. They can accept the usual wildcards. Syntax:

```
Del (or erase) myfile
```

Usage example:

```
Del myfile
```

Deletes the file *myfile* from the current directory.

Dir: Gives a directory listing for the current or specified directory. Syntax:

```
Dir [path][filename] [/p] [/w] [/d] [/a: (attributes) /o: (sortorder)
➥ [/t: (time) [/s] [/b] [/l  [/x] [/n]
```

where

`/p` pauses the display.

`/w` shows a wide display without details.

`/d` sorted wide display (in columns).

`/a:` shows files having attributes hidden, system, directory, archive, or read-only by using the first letter of their attribute with the switch. Also accepts the - for the inverse of the attribute.

D

/o: sort order, name, extension, date, size, grouped by directory first by using the first letter of the order with the switch.

/t: time field using the following first letters of the field, creation, access (last), written to (last).

/s shows or searches subdirectories also.

/b bare display without headers or footers.

/l lowercase unsorted.

/x shows 8.3 filenames also.

/n long listing with filenames on right.

Usage examples:

```
Dir
```

A listing of the current directory.

```
Dir /s /x
```

A listing of the current directory, its subdirectories, and the 8.3 filenames for the files shown.

```
Dir /a:h
```

A listing of the hidden files.

Diskcomp: compares the contents of two disks. Syntax:

```
Diskcomp [driveA] [driveB]
```

where driveA and driveB are two disk drives. You can use one floppy disk drive with Diskcomp by specifying the same drive on both parameters.

Usage example:

```
Diskcomp a: a:
```

Will compare a disk in drive a: and then prompt you for the next disk to insert.

Diskcopy: Duplicates disks. Syntax:

```
Diskcopy [driveA] [driveB] /v
```

where

/v tries to verify writes

Usage example:

```
Diskcopy a: a:
```

Will copy the disk in drive a: and then prompt you for a target disk to use for a duplicate.

> **NOTE**
>
> You will need to use a disk that is formatted the same as the one to be copied. `Diskcopy` requires identically formatted disks or it aborts the copy process.

Expand: Expands cabinet (`.cab`) files or compressed files (`.ex_`) by non-destructive extraction. Cabinet files are files Microsoft uses to distribute many of its programs and operating systems. Compressed files with the `.ex_` suffix are also widely used. Common expanders, such as those that work for `.zip` or `.arc` files, won't work with `.cab` files or `.ex_` files. Syntax:

```
Expand [-r] cabfile [target]
```

where

`-r` renames the file.

Usage example:

```
Expand cab1.cab
```

Will expand the contents of the `cab1.cab` file to the current directory.

or if you have an `.ex_` file,

```
Expand f:\user32.ex_ c:\winnt\system32\user32.exe
```

will expand the contents of the `user32.ex_` file to the `user32.exe` file located in the `c:\winnt\system32\` directory.

FC: Compares two individual files for discrepancies. Syntax:

```
Fc [/a] [/b] [/c] [/l] [/lbx] [/n] [/t] [/u] [/w] [file1] [file2]
```

where

`/a` abbreviated display of discrepancies.

`/b` binary compare (ASCII is the default for files not having a binary extension).

`/c` case-insensitive.

`/l` ASCII compare for files having a binary extension (such as `.exe`).

`/lbx` buffer size (the x part) for how many discrepancies `Fc` should tolerate before exiting.

`/n` shows line numbers during ASCII compare.

`/t` skips expanding tabs to spaces.

`/u` unicode compare.

`/w` skips consecutive whitespaces.

Usage example:

```
Fc myfile1 myfile2 /b
```

Compares and reports differences in the files *myfile1* and *myfile2* using a binary compare.

Files: Used like DOS and Windows to tell how many files a session can have open at the same time. Use in CONFIG.NT.

Usage example:

```
Files = 99
```

Findstr: This is a superior version of the older Find command, also included in Windows NT Server. Syntax of the most often used switches:

```
Findstr [/b] [/e] [/l] [/c:mystring] [/r] [/s] [/i] [/x] [/v] [/n] [/m]
```

where

/b finds pattern at start of line.

/e finds pattern at end of line.

/l uses literal find pattern.

/c:*mystring* is the string to search for.

/r (default) searches for non-literal strings.

/s also searches subdirectories.

/i is insensitive for case.

/x exact matching lines only.

/v opposite of /x—shows non-matching lines only.

/n prints line numbers.

/m shows matching files only.

Usage examples:

```
Findstr "A string"myfile.txt
```

Finds the string, "A" and string "string" in the file *myfile*.txt.

```
Findstr /c:"A String"myfile.txt /i
```

Finds the string "A String" (case-insensitive) in the file *myfile*.txt.

Format: Formats disks. Usage is the same as DOS or Windows with extensions noted below. Syntax for extensions:

```
Format drive1: [/fs:file system choice] [/a:unitsize]
```

where

/fs is FAT or NTFS.

/a is unit size for NTFS volumes.

Usage example:

```
Format e:/fs:ntfs /a:1024
```

Format drive e: as NTFS with a unit (similar to old cluster size in practice) size of 1,024 bytes.

MD and **Mkdir**: Usage is the same as in DOS or Windows.

Move: Usage is the same as Copy in default mode but deletes source file.

Print: The print spooler from DOS and Windows. Usage is the same.

Usage example:

```
Print myfile
```

Prints a file to the default printer.

RD and **Remdir**: Identical expressions of the same command. Usage is the same as in DOS or Windows. This removes or deletes empty directories. Syntax:

```
RD (or Remdir) [/s]
```

where

/s means delete subdirectories also.

Usage example:

```
RD mydirectory
```

Removes the directory from the directory listing.

Ren and **Rename**: Renames files and directories. Usage is the same as later DOS and Windows.

Usage example:

```
Ren mine yours
```

Renames the directory (or file) mine as yours.

Xcopy: This is similar to the DOS or Windows XCOPY utility. It is an extended version of the internal COPY command. The chief differences are its intelligence and its capability to copy directory structures intact. Syntax of the basic command along with its more commonly used switches:

```
Xcopy source [target] [/c] [/v] [/q] [/f] [/l] [/d:] [/u] [/s] [/e] [/t] [/r]
➡ [/h] [/n] [/exclude:myfile.txt]
```

where

/c copies despite apparent errors.

/v attempts verification of copy.

/q quiet mode (suppresses messages).

/f Displays full source and destination file names while copying.

/l lists filenames during copying process.

/d: with date after colon, copies only files with dates on or after specified date.

/u copies only files from source that already exist on target (update).

/s copies subdirectories. If used with the /e copies empty directories.

/t copies the directory structure (tree), not the files. It will include empty directories if used with the /e switch.

/r copies over read-only files.

/h copies files with the system or hidden attribute bits set.

/n copies using the 8.3 naming convention.

/exclude:*myfile*.txt excludes files listed in the text file *myfile* from being copied.

Usage examples:

```
Xcopy c:\mypath d: /s
```

Copies the files in c:*mypath* and its subdirectories to an identical directory structure on d:.

```
Xcopy r:\mypath\my long file a: /n
```

Copies a file with a long filename to the a: drive and excludes the long filename, instead using the 8.3 naming convention.

The Net Commands

Many of the Windows NT Server CLI network commands start with the word Net followed by the command itself. These commands, where practicable, can be run from batch files. When run from either batch files or interactively, these commands will accept the /y and /n switches for a Yes or No response to the command's query without user intervention. The /y and /n switches are especially useful for batch file operations.

Keep in mind that Net commands have their analogs in the graphical user interface (GUI). Many administrators prefer to use the CLI version of a command because they are usually faster than navigating through the Start menu system or even locating the shortcut icon located in a handy program group on the desktop. What you choose is up to you. In some cases, the CLI method for running a command is superior to the GUI because you can call it from batch files, optionally running them using the AT command.

Following are the most commonly used Net commands along with the most often used switches, their syntax, and usage examples.

NBTStat: Displays the status of a network running NetBIOS over TCP/IP. Note that following UNIX standards (the origin of TCP/IP), the switches below are case-sensitive and use a dash (-) not a slash (/). Syntax:

```
NBTStat [-a namedcomputer] [-A IP] [-R] [-r] [-S] [-s]
```

where

-a is the computer's name, such as tirilee (see Figure D.5).

-A is the IP, such as 100.101.100.100 (see Figure D.6).

FIGURE D.5.

The -a *switch for* NBTStat *uses the computer's name for parameter input.*

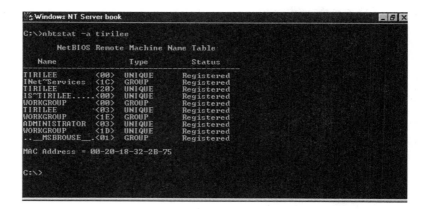

-R reloads the LMHosts file.

-r lists WINS name resolution. Requires WINS configuration to use.

-S attempts to list all clients and servers by IP.

-s same as -S but attempts to list all by computer name using the LMHosts file.

Usage example:

```
NBTStat -A 100.101.100.100
```

Shows status for a computer with the IP 100.101.100.100.

FIGURE D.6.

The -A *switch for* NBTStat *gives the same information as the* -a *switch, but takes the IP address as an input parameter.*

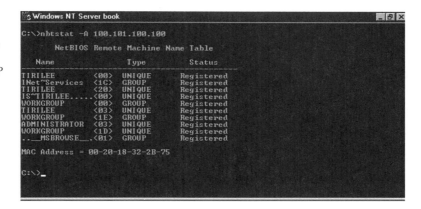

```
C:\>nbtstat -A 100.101.100.100

        NetBIOS Remote Machine Name Table

    Name               Type        Status
   TIRILEE       <00>  UNIQUE      Registered
   INet~Services <1C>  GROUP       Registered
   TIRILEE       <20>  UNIQUE      Registered
   IS~TIRILEE....<00>  UNIQUE      Registered
   WORKGROUP     <00>  GROUP       Registered
   TIRILEE       <03>  UNIQUE      Registered
   WORKGROUP     <1E>  GROUP       Registered
   ADMINISTRATOR <03>  UNIQUE      Registered
   WORKGROUP     <1D>  UNIQUE      Registered
   ..__MSBROWSE__.<01> GROUP       Registered

   MAC Address = 00-20-18-32-2B-75


C:\>_
```

Net Accounts: A CLI version of the utility available in the GUI User Manager. Most administrators prefer the GUI version for administering accounts, but use the CLI version for a quick look at account status because it's faster when lending interactive support over, say, the telephone. This command is also useful for forcing user logoff. Syntax for the most often used parameters:

```
Net Accounts [/forcelogoff:{timetologoff}]
```

where

`/forcelogoff` takes the *timetologoff* and forces the user(s) off at that time.

When run without parameters, Net Accounts shows the current settings for user profiles. Note: You must start this service before the command will work. You can start this service either through the Services GUI in Control Panel or the CLI Net Start.

Usage example:

```
Net Accounts
```

Shows the status of the user profile in effect.

Net Config: Shows a list of devices you can configure and allows modification of these devices. This command controls either the server or workstation side of Windows NT. Syntax of the most commonly used parameters:

```
Net Config server [/autodisconnect:time] [/hidden:]
```

or

```
Net Config workstation [/charcount:] [/chartime:] [/charwait:]
```

where

`/autodisconnect:time` is the time in minutes to automatically disconnect from an inactive client.

/hidden: is used with yes or no to hide the server from the list of servers. Does not affect permissions of the server.

/charcount: in bytes, the buffer NT has for a communications device or port.

/chartime: in milliseconds. Same as /charcount, but in milliseconds.

/charwait: time in seconds NT will wait on a communications device.

Usage example:

```
Net Config Server /hidden:yes
```

Run from the console, this hides the server from the list of available servers without affecting the permissions of the server.

Net Continue, Pause, Start, Stop: Continues, pauses, starts, and stops services, respectively. This is the CLI version of the Services applet available in Control Panel. Syntax:

```
Net [continue] [pause] [start] [stop] service
```

where

service is the service you want to continue, pause, start, or stop.

Usage examples:

```
Net stop alerter
```

Stops the alerter service.

```
Net start alerter
```

Starts the alerter service.

Net File: Displays a list of shared files and any file locks. Syntax:

```
Net File [/close]
```

where

/close will close a file, releasing any file locks.

Run without parameters, Net File will list open shared files.

Usage example:

```
Net File
```

Displays a list of open files.

Net Helpmsg: Displays help on an error message number. Syntax:

```
Net Helpmsg messagenumber
```

Usage example:

```
Net Helpmsg 2000
```

Tells you that error number 2000 means you have an invalid pixel format.

Net Print: Displays or manipulates a list of pending print jobs in queue. Similar to the Printers GUI applet in Control Panel; however, much faster if you have a CLI window open. Syntax most commonly used:

```
Net Print \\computername\printername [/delete] [/hold] [/release][/pause]
```

where

\\computername is the name of the computer hosting the shared printer.

\printername is the name the printer is shared under.

/delete purges print jobs.

/hold pauses print jobs.

/release restarts paused print jobs.

Usage example:

```
Net Print \\tirilee\rainbow
```

Shows a list of pending print jobs for the printer rainbow hosted on the server tirilee.

Net Session: When entered from the local console, gives information about computers located on the server. Syntax:

```
Net Session \\anycomputername /delete
```

where

/delete ends the session with \\anycomputername.

Note: Net Session given without parameters gives information about the local computer.

Usage example:

```
Net Session \\barbara /delete
```

Ends the session connection with the computer named barbara.

NetStat: Shows statistics for connections on a TCP/IP network only. This command requires the TCP/IP protocol to be installed and running. Note that like NBTStat, this command uses the UNIX-like dash (-) rather than the more common slash (/), and the parameters aren't case-sensitive. Syntax:

```
NetStat [-a] [-e] [-n] [-s] [-p] [-r] [time]
```

where

-a displays listening ports.

-e displays Ethernet statistics.

-n provides a numeric display of ports rather than the default names.

-s displays per protocol. Can be combined with -e for comprehensive information.

-p is used with a protocol (such as TCP) to display only that protocol.

-r displays routing information.

[time] is the time in seconds to update the display. If omitted, it displays the instantaneous information.

Net Statistics: Displays statistics for the local computer. Syntax:

```
Net Statistics [server] [workstation]
```

Usage example:

```
Net Statistics server
```

Displays relevant statistics.

Net Time: Determines and can synchronize computer clocks. Syntax:

```
Net Time \\anycomputername /set /domain
```

where

/set sets the time on the local computer to that of the queried one.

/domain sets the time to a domain.

Usage examples:

```
Net Time \\tirilee
```

Displays the time on the computer named tirilee.

```
Net Time \\tirilee /set
```

Sets the time on the local machine to the same time as tirilee.

Note: Administrators often use this command within batch files triggered by the AT command to synchronize the clocks of all computers on a network or domain.

Net Use: Allows or disallows the use of a shared resource. This command also displays status information for shared resources. Syntax of the more often used parameters:

```
Net Use  [\\computername\sharename] [password or *][/persistent:]
```

where

*computername**sharename* is the computer and the share name of the device to use.

password or *, where password is the actual password for the shared device. If you use the *
(asterisk) in the place of the password, Windows NT will prompt the user for the password.

/persistent:, when used with yes or no, will control whether the use persists from session to
session.

Note: When used without parameters, Net Use will display shared resources on the local computer.

Usage example:

```
Net Use \\tirilee\lily
```

Uses the shared resource lily on the computer tirilee.

The TCP/IP Commands

Windows NT Server comes with several utilities commonly used in TCP/IP networks. Given
the new visual tools for Internetworking, few people use these CLI commands anymore, but in
some cases they work well enough that they will be worthwhile tools for inclusion in your
toolbox. The following are three of the most commonly used TCP/IP commands. You must
have TCP/IP installed to have these commands, and the protocol must be functioning for them
to work.

Ftp: A utility to transfer files (usually a binary file), using the file transfer protocol, to or from
a computer running the Ftp daemon. As is common with the TCP/IP origin utility, Ftp uses
the dash (-) rather than the slash (/) for switches. Note that the usual

```
ftp /?
```

for help will not work with Ftp because the Ftp utility will interpret the /? as a computer name
and deliver an error message. Syntax for the most often used switches:

```
ftp [-i] [-d] [-g] [-s:myfile.txt] [daemoncomputer]
```

where

-i stops interactive mode, which prompts you in cases of multiple file transfers.

-d enables debug mode (echoing all messages).

-g disables wildcard use on local files (globbing in Ftp talk).

-s: used with a text file to script a series of Ftp commands. A batch file substitute.

Usage example:

```
ftp -d mack.rt66.com
```

Connects to a remote host running the daemon. When running the Ftp utility, your prompt will indicate this to avoid the problem of trying to execute commands remotely when you think you're local only. After you connect to the site, you navigate similarly to when you're on a local computer using the command command, Dir, CD, and even MD or RD if you have permissions. When you find the file you want to transfer, use the Get command to transfer the file from the host to you or use Put to transfer the file from you to the host. Windows NT Help system has a complete listing of the 14 online Ftp commands.

When you install the TCP/IP protocol on Windows NT Server, you also get a shorthand version of Ftp called Tftp. This is less flexible, but also easier to use.

Note: Ftp (even Tftp) isn't one of those utilities that most people enjoy using interactively. There are several visual utilities, at least one of which is freeware, FTP-32 Client For Windows, copyright John A. Junod, that make Ftp a joy. You can find these utilities at all the usual online sources.

NOTE

Some of the more predominant sources of freeware and shareware on the Internet are

```
http://www.windows95.com
http://www.stroud.com
http://www.winntmag.com
http://www.shareware.com
```

Ipconfig: Displays information about IPs, adapters, and Dynamic Host Configuration Protocol (DHCP). It's especially useful for the latter purposes. Syntax:

```
Ipconfig [/all OR /renew [adapter] OR /release [adapter]]
```

where

/all shows a complete listing.

/renew renews DHCP information for a specified adapter.

/release releases or disables DHCP for a local computer.

Usage example:

```
Ipconfig /all
```

Displays complete information about a local computer. Note: When run without parameters, Ipconfig displays a short information screen.

Ping: A very useful command that's unfamiliar to those new to TCP/IP. Ping tries to echo a signal from a remote computer. This tests whether the remote computer (Internet or intranet) is responding. As with other utilities stemming from TCP/IP, `Ping` takes the dash (`-`) switch rather than the slash (`/`). Like `Ftp` and `Telnet`, `Ping /?` won't work because `Ping` will interpret the `/?` as a computer name. Syntax for the most commonly used switches:

```
ping [-t] [-n #] [-r #] [-w time] computers to ping
```

`-t` pings until told to stop with a `^c`.

`-n #` pings # times.

`-r #` echoes the route up to # times. # can be from 1 to 9.

`-w time` milliseconds to time out.

`computers to ping` are the IPs or the names of the computers to `ping`.

Usage examples:

```
Ping -n 2 192.100.221.000
```

Pings the computer with an IP of `192.100.221.000` twice.

```
Ping tirilee.techtryx.com
```

Pings the computer named `tirilee.techtryx.com` once.

`Telnet`: This utility isn't included in the online help system. Instead, Windows NT Server treats it like its own program, complete with an included help system. It allows you to become a remote console on a host computer. What you can do with such a remote console depends on your permissions. As with `Ftp` and `Ping`, `Telnet /?` won't work. Syntax:

```
Telnet computer or IP
```

where

`computer or IP` is the computer name or the IP for the computer you want to be connected to. Figure D.7 shows the start of a `Telnet` session.

Commands to Control the CLI

The following are the most often used commands to control the CLI environment.

`Exit`: Exits or quits a `CMD` instance. This command takes no parameters. It works identically to the `Exit` command from DOS or Windows.

`Path`: Same usage as in DOS or Windows. Can be used in `AUTOEXEC.NT`.

Usage example:

```
Path = newpath;%path%
```

Appends the path, `newpath`, to the existing path.

FIGURE D.7.

Starting a Telnet
*session requires logon
just as if you were
operating from the
local console.*

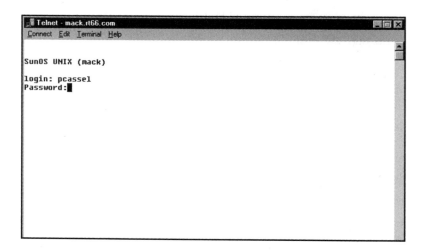

Popd and **Pushd**: Similar in usage to identically named utilities in DOS and Windows. The names come from programmers' use of the LIFO stack where program items are pushed (stored) then popped (returned). The concept comes from a stack of spring loaded dishes in a cafeteria. Pushd stores a path, Popd restores the path.

Usage example:

Pushd *mypath*

Stores the path *mypath*. Now change directories and do some action.

Popd

Restores you to your former *mypath*.

Prompt: Alters the CLI prompt. Syntax of some of the more often used switches (of many):

Prompt [$t] [$d] [$g] [$p] [text]

where

$t is the time.

$d is the date.

$g is the greater-than sign (>).

$p is the path (default).

text is the text you want to display.

Usage examples:

Prompt $t $p

Shows the system time and then the path as a command-line prompt.

```
Prompt
```

Returns to the default prompt.

Subst: Substitutes an addressable device letter for a path. Similar to the `Subst` in later DOS or Windows. Syntax:

```
Subst [Drive1] [path] /d
```

where

`/d` deletes the substituted drive.

Usage examples:

```
Subst g: c:\mypath\mypath1
```

Substitutes a "false" drive g: for the path `c:\mypath\mypath1`. When you enter g: on the command line or look for it in Explorer, the files contained will be those in `c:\mypath\mypath1`.

```
Subst g: /d
```

Eliminates the substitution.

Note: Use caution with the following commands on a `Subst`- created drive:

Diskcomp, Format, Chkdsk, Restore, Label, Recover.

Title: Changes the title of the CLI window. Syntax:

```
Title text
```

where

`text` is the text you want to show in the CLI window.

Usage example:

```
Title Windows NT Rules
```

Displays the text `Windows NT Rules` as a title for the CLI window. Figure D.8 shows the results of entering this command.

Batch Files

Windows NT Server can use batch files just like DOS or Windows. A batch file is a text file containing a series of commands that execute in order unless the program control is altered by a `GOTO` command. Batch files under Windows NT Server can take the command line replaceable parameters `%1` through `%9`. The following are the most often used commands used in batch files, along with a concise usage example.

FIGURE D.8.

The Title *command alters the title of the CLI window.*

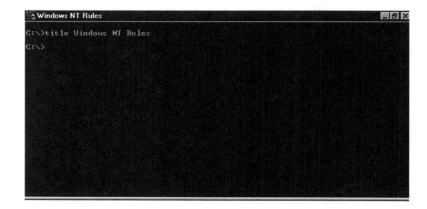

Call: Calls another batch file. Then after execution, returns control to the calling batch file.

```
Call mynew.cmd
```

Calls the batch file mynew.cmd from within another batch file and then returns control to the calling file.

Echo: Echoes a line to the screen. By default, all batch file commands are echoed to the screen.

```
Echo off
```

Ends echoing of batch file commands to the screen.

```
Echo my line
```

Echoes my line to the screen after the Echo off command.

For: Applies a command to a set of files in a list. Uses the replaceable parameter %f to avoid confusion with the %1 through %9 used as replaceable parameters in batch file command lines.

```
For %f in (*.~mp) do del %f
```

Deletes files having the ~mp extension.

Goto: Branches to a label in a batch file. A label in a batch file is a line ending in a colon (:).

```
If exist r:\myfile goto quit
...
...
quit:
```

Will jump to the line below the last line shown if the file, *myfile*, at the root of drive r: exists.

If: Tests a condition. If used with the Not switch, tests for the inverse of a condition. Often used with the Goto command to change program flow within the batch file.

```
If not exist myfile Goto quit
```

Tests for the existence of the file, *myfile*, and if it doesn't exist, branches to the batch file label `quit`.

Rem: Remark. Tells the batch file not to process this line.

```
Rem Now test for existence of file and branch if it doesn't exist
```

This line isn't evaluated, displayed, or executed by the batch file. Its only use is to inform. Note: If you want to display a line or lines, use the `Echo` command.

Setlocal and **Endlocal**: Must be used in combination with each `Setlocal` having an `Endlocal`. Environmental settings run after `Setlocal` will expire upon the `Endlocal` statement.

```
...
Setlocal
(set some environment variable here)
Endlocal
(environmental variable set above expires)
```

Shift: Rotates the replaceable parameters in a batch file. Given the following command line:

```
Mybatch file1 file2
```

the `Shift` command will replace the variable `file1` with the variable `file2` when encountered by the batch file processor. So with that command line in mind, the batch file

```
...
Goto FirstRun
Shift:
Shift
FirstRun:
Copy %1 a: goto shift
...
```

will jump to the label `FirstRun:`, copy `file1`, jump to the label `Shift:`, and copy `file2`.

Symbols Used in the CLI

Following are some symbols used to control the CLI. Some of these symbols will be familiar to DOS, Windows, or UNIX users. Window NT Server expands on the older DOS and Windows symbol set. Symbols don't have parameters. Each is shown with a short explanation and a usage example.

<: Redirects input to a program or utility.

```
Sort < myoutput.out
```

Sorts the file *myoutput*.out using the `Sort` utility.

>>: Appends output. Also **1>>**.

```
Dir c:\*.* >> mylist.txt
```

Adds the output of `Dir c:\*.*` to the end of the file *mylist*`.txt`.

>: Redirects output. Also **1>**.

`Dir c:\*.* > prn`

Directs the output of `Dir c:\*.*` to the default printer.

¦: Piping. Pipes the output of a command to another program, often the `More` utility.

`Type myfile.txt ¦ More`

Pipes the output of `Type myfile.txt More`, which will pause the display at each screen.

¦¦: A non-strict Or symbol. Used in batch files. Will execute the command to the left of the ¦¦ only, unless there is an error executing it. In that case, it will also execute the command to the right of ¦¦.

`Error.exe ¦¦ Good.exe`

Will try to execute `Error.exe`. Upon finding an error, it will execute `Good.exe`. If `Error.exe` doesn't error, `Good.exe` will be ignored.

2>>: Redirection of error display. Useful for making log files.

`Mycommand 2>> error.log`

Will redirect the error output of `Mycommand` to the file `error.log`.

,: (comma) Separates command-line parameters. Also use **;** (semicolon) for the same purposes.

`Mycommand 1,2`

Will feed the parameters 1 and 2 sequentially to `Mycommand`.

^: literal. Accepts the next symbol as a literal.

`Mycommand ^>`

Passes the > character as a literal parameter rather than a command-line symbol to `Mycommand`.

&: Used to separate commands on a command line.

`Dir c: & Dir d:`

Will execute first `Dir c:` and then `Dir d:`.

&&: The And symbol twice. Will execute the command to the left only if the command to the right succeeds.

`Dir c: && Dir d:`

Will execute `Dir c:` only if `Dir d:` completes successfully.

(): Groups commands together.

```
Command1 (Command2 && Command3)
```

Will execute `Command1` first, then `Command2`, and `Command3` only if `Command2` succeeds.

The AT Command

The `AT` command is so useful and so frequently used that it deserves its own section. In a nutshell, the `AT` command will execute a command or run a batch file at a given time of day. You need to have administrator rights to run `AT`. Also, Windows NT Server will not start the `AT` service by default. You must start it using the `Net Start` command or by using the Service applet in Control Panel. Because `AT` can start batch files, its use is only limited by imagination. The syntax for `AT` is

```
AT [\\anyconnectedcomputer] time [/interactive] [/every:] [/next:]
➥ command [[id] [/delete [/yes]]
```

where

`\\anyconnectedcomputer` is a computer where the command is to run.

`time` is the time to run the command or batch file.

`/interactive` means to run the called command or batch file interactively (involving human responses).

`/every:` runs on specified days of the week (`M,T,W,Th,F,S,Su`) or days of the month (`1-31`). If the parameter after `/every:` is omitted, `AT` will assume the current day.

`/next:` runs on the next day or date. If the parameter after `/next:` is omitted, `AT` will assume you mean the next occurrence of the current day of the week.

`command` is the command or batch file you want `AT` to run.

`id` is a job ID assigned sequentially by `AT`.

`/delete` removes the specified job ID from the queue. If no ID is specified, `AT` will remove all pending jobs from the local computer.

`/yes` runs the command or batch file, supplying a yes to all system queries rather than allowing the system to prompt for a yes or no.

Usage examples:

```
AT \\tirilee 18:00 /every:Th,S archive.exe
```

Runs the command `archive.exe` every Thursday and Saturday at 6:00 p.m. on the computer named `tirilee`. As with all Windows NT commands, you don't need the extension `.exe` as part of the command-line argument.

```
AT
```

Displays pending job information and job IDs.

```
AT 23:59 Net Time \\tirilee /set
```

Synchronizes the local system time with the computer `tirilee` at 11:59 p.m. today.

```
AT \\tirilee
```

Displays a list of jobs slated to run on the computer named `tirilee`.

```
AT 18:00 /every:1,10,20,30 back.cmd
```

Runs the batch file `back.cmd` every 1st, 10th, 20th, and 30th day of the month at 6:00 p.m. As with all Windows NT commands, you don't need the extension `.cmd` as part of the command-line argument.

```
AT 18:00 /next: back.cmd
```

Runs `back.cmd` at 6:00 p.m. on the next occurrence of day of the week in which the command was entered.

Note: Windows NT Server stores all AT sequences in the Registry. To preserve your AT settings, create a Registry backup or a new emergency rescue disk (ERD) or both after setting up a series of AT commands.

Obsolete Commands

The following is a list of commands and utilities that have been part of DOS or Windows but aren't included in Windows NT Server.

Deleted Commands

These commands aren't part of Windows NT Server. There are some alternatives to these commands shown when applicable:

Assign, Choice, CTTY, Defrag (use third-party utilities), Deltree (use RD /s), Dosshell, Drvspace (replaced by Compact), Fasthelp (use Help), Fdisk (use the Disk Administrator), Join (NTFS makes this pointless), Interlnk, Intersrv, Keyb (Keyboard.sys is no more), Mirror (use NTBackup and an ERD), MSAV (use third-party anti-virus programs), MSBackup (use NTBackup), MSD (use Windows NT Diagnostics), Nlsfunc, Numlock, Power (Windows NT Server 4 doesn't support APM), Ramdisk (and the earlier Vdisk), Scandisk, Smartdrv (NT Server does its own caching), Sys (NT system will not fit on a floppy), Undelete (use third-party utilities or the Recycle Bin), Unformat.

The following utilities and routines aren't in Windows NT Server due to its inability to support multiple DOS configurations: Include, Menucolor, Menudefault, Menuitem, Submenu.

The following commands aren't applicable to Windows NT Server due to its memory management, as opposed to DOS or Windows: Memmaker, EMM386, MSCDEX (real mode drivers don't work under any Windows NT).

Rump Commands

The following commands will not generate an error in Windows NT Server but aren't a part of it either. Their inclusion is apparently to provide backward compatibility with old batch files: Break, Buffers, Driveparm, Lastdrive, Share, Verify.

Strange Stuff Still in Windows NT Server

The following commands and utilities are holdovers from DOS or Windows, but still function under Windows NT Server. Their actual value is questionable, however. Country, Command (use CMD), Debug (watch out), Edlin (old soldiers never die in Windowsland), Exe2bin, FCBS, Graphics, Mem (can be useful in rare instances), Setver.

Summary

The foregoing are the most commonly used commands for the command-line interface (CLI) of Windows NT Server. The rare commands, including those used in command line OS/2 and retained in Windows NT Server for compatibility, have been passed over to allow for sufficient room for the ones used more often.

This is a case of one size not fitting all, however. If your situation uses OS/2 character-based applications or the old IPX protocol still found in NetWare, there are commands included in Windows NT Server that haven't been mentioned here. Instead, this appendix concentrates on commands an NT Server administrator will use most often with or without the TCP/IP layer.

The final part of the appendix discusses commands either deleted or made obsolete in the migration from DOS or Windows to Windows NT. Some of these commands remain unchanged in function, but have lost their purpose as Windows NT takes over from previous Microsoft operating systems.

I

INDEX

Symbols

MACMILLAN COMPUTER PUBLISHING USA
A VIACOM COMPANY

Technical

Support:

If you need assistance with the information in this book or with a CD/Disk accompanying the book, please access the Knowledge Base on our Web site at **http://www.superlibrary.com/general/support**. Our most Frequently Asked Questions are answered there. If you do not find the answer to your questions on our Web site, you may contact Macmillan Technical Support **(317) 581-3833** or e-mail us at **support@mcp.com**.

What's on the Disc

The companion CD-ROM contains an assortment of third-party tools and product demos. The disc is designed to be utilized using a newly created program group and the Windows Explorer. Using the icons in the program group, you can view information concerning products and companies and install programs with a single click of the mouse.

Windows 95/NT Installation Instructions

To create the Program Group for this book, follow these steps:

1. Insert the CD-ROM disc into your CD-ROM drive.
2. With Windows NT installed on your computer and the AutoPlay feature enabled, a Program Group for this book is automatically created when you insert the disc into your CD-ROM drive. Follow the directions provided in the installation program.
3. If AutopPlay is not enabled, using Windows Explorer, choose Setup.exe from the root level of the CD-ROM to create the Program Group for this book.
4. Double-click on the Browse the CD-ROM icon in the newly created Program Group to access the installation programs of the software or reference material included on this CD-ROM.

To review the latest information about this CD-ROM, double-click on the icon About this CD-ROM.

> **NOTE**
>
> For best results, set your monitor to display between 256 and 64,000 colors. A screen resolution of 640×480 pixels is also recommended. If necessary, adjust your monitor settings before using the CD-ROM.

Technical Support

If you need assistance with the information in this book or with the CD-ROM accompanying this book, please access the Knowledge Base on our Web site at

http://www.superlibrary.com/general/support

Our most Frequently Asked Questions are answered there. If you do not find the answer to your questions on our Web site, you may contact Macmillan Technical Support at 317-581-3833 or e-mail us at support@mcp.com.